D0734696

The Empowerment Approach
to Social Work Practice

Building the Beloved Community

The Empowerment Approach
to Social Work Practice

Building the Beloved Community
Second Edition

Judith A. B. Lee

COLUMBIA UNIVERSITY PRESS   NEW YORK

Columbia University Press
Publishers Since 1893
New York, Chichester, West Sussex

Copyright © 2001 Columbia University Press
All rights reserved

Library of Congress Cataloging-in-Publication Data

Lee, Judith A. B.
The empowerment approach to social work practice /
Judith A. B. Lee. —2d ed.
p. cm.
Includes bibliographical references and index.
ISBN 0-231-11548-2 (cloth: alk. paper)
I. Title
HV91 .L355 2000
361.3'2—dc21
00-059655

Casebound editions of Columbia University Press
books are printed on permanent and durable acid-free
paper.
Printed in the United States of America

c 10 9 8 7 6 5 4 3 2 1

SIMMONS COLLEGE LIBRARY
SSW COLLECTION

This is dedicated to the dear ones
whose acts of love and courage have
nurtured and empowered me
and to those who will carry it on

To my precious
beloved community

and
to the memory of Carel B. Germain, MS, DSW,
dear friend, mentor, and inspiration
and
to the dearest everloving spirits of
Ella Adelaide Shotwell Robinson Weinmann, my grandma
Anne Marie Weinmann Beach, my mother
who always encouraged and believed in me
Warren Jay Robinson and Jack Lewis Weinmann, my uncles
and to the
Ngut Gue and Howa Nang Lee family
and to my beloved
Aunt Edith M. Dougherty and Uncle Julian C. Robinson
who were always there for me

and especially
to Judith A. Beaumont
the wind beneath my wings, always

and
to the next generation of social workers and educators
especially Gail Bourdon, SSJ, MSW, Ph.D.
and
Robin Woods-Barrant, M.Div., MSW

and to the children
who are writing the future where there will not be any more
people called clients, only children of God.

In justice shall you be established far from the fear of oppression where
destruction cannot come near you.

—Isaiah 54:14, *New American Bible*

For People of Difference

Brothers, sisters
of difference,
people of color,
people of poverty,
gay and straight,
black, white, Asian, Hispanic,
Jew, Christian, Muslim,
or whoever you are,
hitherto invisible ones,
stand together and
affirm yourselves,
in your difference,
and in your unity.
Do not accept for
one more minute
the insidious forces
that hold you back
by act, word, or tone.
Forge a chain and
break the chains,
you do not stand alone.
And to you beyond the walls,
in mental hospitals,
in prison stalls,
in chairs of steel,
in hospice beds,
in boxes made of cardboard,
or numbed by substances that
eat away at brain and heart,
for you who bear the stigma
of difference
and the judgments of all,
join together, make it start!
Do not go silently;
do not withdraw;
do not say "yes sir"
even once more.

Trust what you think
and what you know and feel.
Cry, shout, scream,
find your anger,
dare to dream,
find your strength locked
arm in arm.
Do not go gently or in shame.
You have a legacy of hope,
of courage more than pain.

JUDITH A. B. LEE

Adapted from the seventh stanza of a poem entitled "A Plea for Unity," read at the Tenth Annual Symposium of the Association for the Advancement of Social Work with Groups, Baltimore, 1988.

Contents

Preface

This book offers a direct practice approach to social work practice undergirded by knowledge that can empower practitioners, students, and other helping professionals who work with people who are poor, living with oppression, and seeking liberation (openly or in the secret places of the heart). People called "clients" or "consumers of services" may also use it to empower themselves. The style of the book is consistent with the empowerment approach. In this approach the worker is a fellow human being who struggles with issues of daily life, developing vision, raising consciousness, taking action, and engaging in praxis (action, reflection on the action, return to action, and reflection) in order to develop critical perspective and challenge the indirect (internalized) and external power blocks that keep us oppressed. It is addressed to members of the oppressor group and the oppressed, for both must be transformed to win a local and global beloved community characterized by the ethic of love, care, power, and justice for all. Whenever possible and appropriate, the worker in this approach shares her own experiences with oppression and stigma in order to make bridges and coinvestigate reality with those who seek help. Hence I write at times in the first person and share both personal and professional experiences in these pages. Though it was not easy to blend the personal/political with the formalized style of most scholarly books, and though it opens my life to all who read it, it is an important modeling of the approach.

The purpose and the process of human liberation necessitate each human being saying her own word. This authentic word is equally important for the helper and the helped in dialogic encounter (Freire 1973a). Hence we write as we speak and as we attempt to live, in authentic communication. We are known even as we seek to know. This may cause some discomfort or self-consciousness at first, but it helps tremendously in subjectifying (as opposed to objectifying) the client-worker relationship. In this way a potentially paternalistic relationship can become enlivening and transforming. In the best sense it is then a corrective relationship—one that presents the opportunity to develop empowerment in the context of genuine caring and mutual searching for that which disempowers. The names of several people called clients and others are therefore proudly acknowledged in the text. Their stories are written in the first person whenever possible, excerpting exact quotes from oral or written communication (so that the client's word does not get lost in the worker's words). Those who were directly known by the author and who would accept it were paid for their contributions to this book. Some clients are introduced in the introduction of the book and the early chapters, and they appear again in the chapters on empowerment work with individuals and families, special populations, groups, and communities working on personal and political issues. Hence we see the different ways in which people may become empowered. The names of actual social workers are acknowledged, and some also appear in the text. The credit for the work goes to those who did it and who continue to work on the front lines where the blows are the hardest.

The new and the old, a translation of critical understanding into clinical and political work, and tried and true social work principles and methodology are blended to create the empowerment approach. The book is written so that it can be used solely in direct practice courses or in conjunction with courses in human behavior, social welfare policy, human oppression, and practice methods courses in a unified curriculum. It can also be read as a scholarly work or by consumers in pursuit of empowerment. It is complex yet simple, broad, and deep. It is therefore not possible to digest it in one gulp. I am reminded of the novelist Chaim Potok's words:

> I say it to myself today when I stand before a new class . . . or am about to start a new book. . . . All beginnings are hard, for I touch the raw nerves of faith, the beginnings of things. Often students are shaken. I say to them what was said to me: "Be patient. You are learning a new way of understanding." And sometimes I add what I have learned on

my own: Especially a beginning you make by yourself. That's the hardest beginning of all. (1975:9)

This approach is the beginning of a new way to practice social work. You, the reader/practitioner/consumer, will refine and develop it as you make it your own. You will find the "kinks" and experience the difficulties and the power of it. As you do, you will write your own word. I hope this is a start in your empowerment journey or an interesting turn in the road.

Acknowledgments

The power comes from God and I am thankful. I am indebted to those who have gone before me and paved the way. Your work and your lives are quoted in these pages and etched in my heart. My arms are linked with and strengthened by leaders in social work throughout the ages and up until today. I am especially grateful to Rev. Melvin G. and Virginia Maniti Williams, Grace Thorpe-Brathwaite, Evelyn Thorpe, Violetta Bowman and Rev. David P. and Eleanor Ver Nooy, Jean Cornella Bauer, Dr. Danielle Nisivoccia, Dr. Robert Kavesh, Dr. Gail Bourdon, SSJ, Dr. Maxine Lynn, Dr. Felix A. and Ginger Delerme, Dr. Joseph and Pearl Cudjoe, Jill Bergner, Sr. Jo Wear and Sr. Marie McBride, Jean P. Low, Ruth P. Low, Martha Williams, Sook and John Liebert, Dr. Kasumi Hirayama, Dra. Daysi Mejia, Ella Harris, John and Carol Ramey, Theresa L. Held, Edna M. Davis, and Rose Gutman for being courageous role models of love, activism, wisdom, empowerment, and builders of the beloved community.

I acknowledge the excellence of the doctoral faculty of the Wurzweiler School of Social Work of Yeshiva University, New York City, in their challenging preparation of thinkers and scholarly practitioners. And I particularly thank colleagues and friends Alex Gitterman, Catherine P. Papell, Ruth R. Middleman, Gisela Konopka, Helen Northen, Ruby Pernell, Aaron Beckerman, Sylvia Aron, Toby Berman-Rossi, Ruth R. Martin, James Garland, Dr. Lorrie Greenhouse Gardella, Joseph Lassner, Margot Breton, Norma C. Lang, Betty Lewis, Carol R. Swenson, and Mary Bricker-Jenkins for their strong encouragement, helpful dialogue, and friendship. William Schwartz and his wife, Ruth, and Hy Weiner, first mentors, provided a firm foundation and shoulders to stand on; their work lives in these pages, though their careers were all too short.

I deeply miss and continue to be grateful to Carel B. Germain, dear friend and mentor. I would not have attempted the original work without her confidence. I especially thank Professor Barbara J. Ballard, Ph.D. in American studies, for reading and discussing the sections on African American history. She and Dr. William D. Wallace, M.D., Ph.D., are my wonderful sister and brother for life. I also thank my cousins who are sisters to me, Jacqueline L. Marion and Lillian Ebner and their families, and my remaining uncle, Uncle John McGarry, and his wife, Aunt Millie, and my dear cousin Bobby Robinson and his wife, Barbara, who assure me that our family is looking down on us and that family is forever.

I acknowledge and thank the people who lived the empowerment stories I wrote about. Their lives shine forth. Some wanted to name themselves and own their empowerment openly: Laura Rubin, Stacey Miles, Vanessa Mason, Christy King, Alice De Cordova, and Roy C. Talbot. You have been my best teachers. I also thank my church families at St. Michael's Parish in Hartford, Connecticut, especially Fr. Al Jaenicke, and at St. Peter Claver AFCAAM in Fort Myers, Florida, especially Sr. Elaine Robbins and the children, for inspiration and the challenge to walk the walk.

I admire and appreciate the social workers who shared their practice with me. Jean Anmuth opened the world of New York's homeless women to me. In the practice examples the worker is often disguised because of confidentiality, but the following people have contributed substantive practice: Mary Bricker-Jenkins of Temple University and KWRU, Stella Odie-Ali, Lieutenant Colonel Christine King, Sharmin Prince and Sr. Jacinta Sukhraj of Guyana, South America, Sr. Helen Owens of Adelaide, Australia, Nuala Lordan and Mary Wilson of Cork, Ireland, Marshall Rubin of Tucson, Arizona and Madelyne S. Bailey, Dr. Gail Bourdon, SSJ, Mary Beth Hammond-Cullina, Jessy Faubert, Lisa Galipo, Jean Konon, Evelyn Thorpe, Jennifer Ligner, Melanie Harrington, Margaret Hoefling, James O'Connor, Carol Sherman, Robin Taylor, and Marlene (Marty) Howard. I am appreciative of your work and grateful. Some of the examples are from my own practice. I extend my appreciation to the Connecticut Coalition to End Homelessness for initially challenging me to conceptualize and teach this approach and the Guyana Association of Professional Social

Workers (GAPSW), especially Lt. Colonel Christine King, Sybil Patterson, Patrice LeFleur, Venus Wayne, Patricia Gray, and Waveney Allen, Aaron Blackman who is also an inspiring poet, and Lecturer Stella Odie-Ali of the University of Guyana, Department of Social Work, and all the UG social work faculty and students for the opportunity for true cross-cultural fertilization of ideas and lives.My deepest thanks and love are to my partner in life and work, Judy Beaumont and to our chosen family of beloved and assorted people and pets, especially the loving and loyal Beau, Rafie, and gentlesweet Bartholomew Boots, who died suddenly this summer and lives in our hearts. Judy and I worked together with the Successful Women's Group, although the interventions are ascribed to one worker. She was my bridge to the women, my inspiration in activism and faith, my collaborator in the work in Guyana, Connecticut, and Fort Myers and my unfailing support in all I do and for the best of what I am.

My gratitude to the students, friends and colleagues at the University of Connecticut School of Social Work who supported me and rooted for this book. Special thanks to Cheryl Brown and Sandy Visco, and to Lenore Benefield for sharing her enthusiasm and able assistance in the final preparations of this manuscript. Special acknowledgment to the skillful readers of the manuscript: Meredith Hanson, Sue Henry, and Gretchen Cotrell. And to Susan Pensak, senior manuscript editor, and John L. Michel, executive editor of Columbia University Press, thank you for your confidence, help, kindness, patience, excellence, and support!

The Empowerment Approach to Social Work Practice

Building the Beloved Community

1 Dreaming Justice and the Beloved Community in the Twenty-First Century

You are the social workers of the new millennium, living and practicing in the early moments of the twenty-first century. Only one in fifty generations have experienced the turning of a millennium, a time when hopes are high that everything can be made new. It is in this spirit of hope that this revision of the empowerment approach to social work practice is offered. Read revision as "re-vision" to see again, as for the first time. Building the "beloved community" is both the process and the hoped for outcome of individual and political empowerment. It is where we are going and how we will get there. It is the essence of Dr. Martin Luther King Jr.'s dream: a caring community where race and class is transcended and social and economic justice is the rule and not the exception. It is also the dream of this empowerment approach to social work practice. The approach deepens and expands in this second edition to include further elaboration of how-to (empowerment-oriented skills with systems of all sizes) and why (a contemporary look at poverty, oppression, and dehumanization), enriched by stronger clinical, community, research, multicultural, and global perspectives on empowerment practice and the celebration of differences.

Bell hooks, world-renowned postmodern black feminist writer, clarifies that the conditions of King's dream must include affirming, not forgetting, our differences.

Many still long

> to live in a society where beloved community can be formed—where loving ties of care and knowing bind us together in our differences. We cannot surrender that longing. . . . We need such bonding not because we cling to utopian fantasies but because we have struggled all our lives to create this community. . . . The small circles of love we have managed to form in our individual lives represent a concrete realistic reminder that beloved community is not a dream, that it already exists for those of us who have done the work of educating ourselves for critical consciousness. (1995:263–264)

Hooks emphasizes that to build this community we must "de-colonize" our minds through a process of unlearning ingrained and often unconscious attitudes of superiority or the internalization of the dehumanizing views of powerful others. This consciousness-raising process would transform our minds and our habits of being.

Honkala, Bricker-Jenkins, and Baptist (1999), leaders of the Kensington Welfare Rights Union and its network of allies, the Temple University Underground Railroad (URR; chapter 13), speak of what divides people who have an activist's commitment to social and economic justice. "We believe that the dynamics of racism, sexism, and even heterosexism eroded organizing efforts in these and other struggles of poor women, but the riptide that carried them away had to do with class. . . . The barrier was class" (1999:2).

We have been carefully taught not to recognize class privilege and condescension, white privilege or male privilege. It becomes, therefore, "an invisible weightless knapsack of special provisions, assurances . . . passports, visas . . . and blank checks" (McIntosh 1998:95). McIntosh elaborates on these privileges, adding that religion and geographical location (and, I would add, heterosexual orientation) are also privileging factors that are intricately intertwined. We cannot build the beloved community without relinquishing these privileges through self-awareness and a critical education process (hooks 1995; McIntosh 1998; Swenson 1998). Moreover, in social work practice we must go farther than personal or professional self-awareness to developing practice approaches and conceptualizations that will help bring about the beloved community with and on behalf of our clients.

Carol Swenson, a leading social work educator and practitioner, notes the ultimate importance of community practice as context for the clinical social worker (1994, 1998). She sees the role of clinical community practitioner as essential to the core of the social work mission. The hallmark of the beloved community is social justice. The clear and ultimate mission of the social work profession is to promote and enhance social and economic justice (Swenson 1998).

The beloved communities that I have built in my personal and professional worlds are the sustaining force in my life. They span all arbitrary divides. They include people once called clients, now called cobuilders of the beloved community. Caring, power, and hope are essential to individuals (social workers and clients) in building this community. Small groups are the building blocks of community. They are, or can be, the circles of love and action hooks describes. Positive attachment, an outgrowth of experiencing caring, is a pre- or co-condition of empowerment and community building. Groups can also challenge us to individual growth and social change. Knowledge about groups and the skills of working with groups toward the ends of building the beloved community will be strengthened in this revision of the approach (chapters 11 and 12).

One way to revision life on the planet, the lives of the people we serve, and social work practice for a new century is to incorporate the words of poets, and other artists, and insights from a variety of disciplines into our understanding. Creative artists are often visionaries simplifying the complex into what can be known. This book will continue to include the words of poets and plain people along with traditional social work research and sources of data that illuminate empowerment practice. In chapter 2 I more clearly establish the links between life model, narrative, and constructivist approaches to practice, Paulo Freire's critical education, and the empowerment approach (Germain and Gitterman 1996; Dean 1993; Carpenter 1996; Freire 1998).

When our clients tell their stories "from the heart," they are revealing their unique selves and the struggles of their communities. This revision of empowerment practice will continue to emphasize the importance of the story in the process of personal and political/community transformation. But telling the story is not enough. Action does not automatically follow. We need theory and conceptualizations that unite action to authenticity to bring personal, communal, and societal change forth from the labor pains and catharsis of the true story. The role of clinician-activist is valued to help clients tell their stories and act (Walz and Groze 1991; Swenson 1998). The story told is about the business of everyday life, present and past, in the context of experiencing poverty, discrimination, and other forms of human oppression. Assisting clients to challenge obstacles and actualize potentialities, to affirm life, build community, and work to change structural arrangements and toxic environments is the aim of the empowerment approach. In this approach we are challenged to talk the talk and walk the walk of transformation together.

We can make concepts and ways to approach life and social work practice new as we define and name them for ourselves with greater clarity, in contemporary terms and meanings. Walt Whitman, known for breaking new ground in poetry, viewed language as power to break through time, space, and matter to "vivify" (a neologism meaning to bring to life) the persons, places, and things of his world, making them available to his readers. This book seeks to vivify the world of social work practice with people who are poor and experience stigma and external and internalized oppression.

The words we use about practice and the people we practice with make a difference (Lee 1980; Rappaport, Smith, and Hess 1988). An approach that helps people to empower themselves and, ultimately, their communities, one that is both personally/clinically and politically/community oriented utilizes words to guide the worker in the direction of certain kinds of activities. The word *empowerment* itself and the empowerment approach developed here conveys a language of helping "that is steeped in symbols that communicate the powerful force for change contained within ourselves, our significant others and our communities" (Rappaport, Smith, and Hess 1988:16). The words *caring, power, hope,* and *community* further define this approach and convey both meaning and energy for a different kind of practice. However, we note Whitman's caution:

> What do you think words are? Do you think words are positive and original things in themselves?—No. . . . Words are a result—they are the progeny of what has been or is in vogue. . . . A perfect writer would make words sing, dance . . . or do anything . . . . Likely there are other words wanted. When the time comes for them to represent anything the words will surely follow. (Pearce 1966)

Spoto (1999) notes that all words are metaphors, "sounds, lines on a page, 'meanings' and referents—everything is metaphor, which is the closest we can get to the reality." Empowerment, then, is a metaphoric concept that conveys the hope of the fullness of life for all people. The words "raising critical consciousness, praxis and critical education" (Freire 1973a, 1990, 1998) are processes that lead to empowerment within this empowerment approach. As they are not everyday usage in social work they will need further explication and illustration. This edition will include elaboration of Freire's ideas and their translation into practice skill in chapters 2, 3, 9, 11, and 12. Other words to describe the approach will always be wanted and will evolve as does the profession in relation to human needs and as you find words to describe your contemporary practice.

Empowerment practice is an idea whose time has come. There are, for example, almost six hundred articles written internationally on the subject of empowerment in social work practice (Miley, January 21, 1999, personal communication). Miley and DuBois (1998) have developed a comprehensive annotated bibliography of 131 recent articles or books on empowerment. Many agree that the concept of empowerment remains vital to the contemporary scene.

The empowerment of minority groups and individuals living on the margins of society is an incremental process, not an absolute outcome. Moreover, the empowerment of minority groups can frequently be reduced to token representation of individuals who are acceptable to the dominant group. Despite later twentieth-century progress in civil and human rights, and the dismantling of "entitlements" in some contemporary social welfare systems, the dawning of the millennium has not ushered in a post-empowerment era for the majority of people who are poor, of color, or of difference (Breton 1998). Instead, this era is marked by continued poverty, discrimination, and violence. On average, 60 percent of all American adults will experience at least one year of poverty during their lifetimes and more than one out of every five American children lives in poverty (Rank and Hirschl 1999; Sherman 1997). The socioeconomic and political climate in the United States at the turn of the twenty-first century produced particularly disdainful and tragic hate crimes against members of minority groups. The brutal murders of Matthew Shepard, a gay youth who was tortured and left to die in Wyoming in 1997, a young gay army private in 1999, the dragging to his death of James Byrd Jr., an African American man, in Jasper, Texas in 1998, the torching of the Macedonia Baptist Church in Bloomville, South Carolina in 1995 by the KKK, the killing of a Filipino postal worker and the shooting of children in a Jewish day care center by Buford Furman in the summer of 1999, and a number of other church and synagogue burnings by neo-Nazi groups and senseless shootings of high school peers by youthful members of militia style groups in 1999 are cases in point. Minority groups continue to be scapegoats for those who hate. While legal victories in these heinous cases may bode well for a brighter future, their very existence signifies the need for empowerment-oriented social welfare and social work practice.

The successes of empowered individuals and communities, such as Emelda West a seventy-three-year-old African American grandmother who led a successful fight to stop a giant Tokyo-based chemical plant from erecting a life-threatening power plant in her nearly polluted rural Louisiana community, speak to the transforming effects of individual and community empowerment (*Life*, January 1999). Similarly, the Poor People's Summit, led by indigenous groups and social work activist and educator Mary Bricker-Jenkins and the other examples of community empowerment described in chapter 13 of this book provide clear examples of social workers' abilities in helping people to empower themselves and others like them. The role of the social worker is to aid people in empowering themselves where this is possible. As African American poet laureate Maya Angelou clarifies: "I don't ask . . . anyone to win my freedom/or fight my battles better than I can." Yet she adds that she longs for and believes in "every man's responsibility to man" (Angelou 1981:46).

Whether in vogue or not, a product of history or a new formulation (or both), the words we use about practice, such as *empowerment*, have the power of guiding thought and defining the territory (Rappaport, Smith, and Hess 1988; Lee 1980). The territory defined by the empowerment approach is personal/political—intensely personal and unavoidably political. Strong clinical knowledge and skills are needed to practice with the most vulnerable, stigmatized, and economically disadvantaged groups and communities. Armando Morales's concept of the "generalist-specialist" who can competently deliver high quality clinical services yet facilitate social action and social change is still the ideal social worker of the empowerment approach (1977:391). The role descriptions of the clinical activist, the clinical community practitioner, and the clinical social justice practitioner also capture the social worker's role in the empowerment approach (Walz and Groze 1991; Swenson 1998).

This book is relevant to generalist, advanced generalist, and integrated practice curricula as well as to specialized advanced year methods preparation. The concept of clinical community practice is relevant as the practitioner seeks to attend to private and public troubles with simultaneous concern and interventions. The case of Shandra Loyal, which was a centerpiece study of empowerment-oriented practice, is continued in this edition. The update on events in her life underscores the need for empowerment-oriented social work interventions with clinical knowledge and skills. The charge of the worker is to deliver quality clinical services while attending to the needs for development and change in the communities and societies where clients live. What is conceptualized here is knowledge and skill to address the troubles and strengths in the lives of everyday poor and working people and other vulnerable groups and communities and the policies and structures that keep poverty and discrimination firmly in place.

One of the inventors of modernist poetry, Ezra Pound, writing in the early years of the twentieth century, plumbed the depths of ancient knowledge in many nations, making it available to everyday people. In canto 53 he sings about the eighteenth-century Chinese emperor Tching Tang, who faced years of drought and a suffering people. "Tching prayed on the mountain / and wrote MAKE IT NEW on his bathtub, / Day by day make it new, / cut the underbrush, / pile the logs, / keep it growing . . . (adding) Consider their sweats, the people's, / If you wd / sit calm on the throne" (1957:147).

How we long to make all things new. We long to make social work practice vital and growing in the service of social transformation. We long for the beloved community in our global neighborhood. In this era of global economy and global interdependence, social work practice approaches must be relevant wherever injustice is in force. The empowerment approach has been developed from the realities of social work practice in many nations. This edition will expand on the international relevance of the approach and include a chapter (14) on international practice. The greater the unmet need, the more we hope for a miracle, a cure-all. Empowerment practice, as direct practice, is of necessity an incremental process. The energy of all social workers with people called clients or community members is needed to usher in the reign of justice bit by bit and day by day.

As a founding mother of empowerment practice in social work, Bertha C. Reynolds, noted, we are all neighbors with common concerns. Social workers are neighbors who have specialized expertise that can help in the process of transforming people and systems (Reynolds 1964 and chapter 4). The words of poet Wallace Stevens (1967) provide a reality check on our dreams: "I cannot bring a world quite round / although I patch it as I can." Whether we carefully weave patches that can hold or design new cloth, the alternative to community responsibility and action is to tacitly accept the

ravages of poverty and turn ourselves to a kind of "value neutral," anti-
septically safe social work practice that "fits" with the requirements of powerful funding sources operating ultimately on the profit motive. Empowerment
practice is driven by social work values and ethics, the rich though complex
heritage and mandates of the profession, and the needs of the poor and others
living, in the vivid words of the celebrated poet Langston Hughes (Rampersad 1994), in a festering or explosive "dream deferred." Social work empowerment practice can bring new life to the dream and to its realization.

The Voices of Children: A Metaphor from My Practice

It was in late spring of 1997. A seventy-four-year-old widow, Mrs. Pam
Ciano, Italian-American great-grandmother, contacted me. She was "at her
wits end" caring for her thirteen-year-old great-granddaughter Nicole. Several months ago she assumed care of Niki when her daughter, Rita, went to
family court and relinquished custody, telling the judge to take Niki before
she killed her. Niki, who looked more like sixteen, could not be kept in at
night, she was stealing and, some said, prostituting. The straw that broke
Rita's back was Niki's involvement of her younger brothers, Tony, age eight,
and Joe, age six, in her activities. Joe had special needs and demanded all
of Rita's attention. They were all sneaking out at night now.

The three were vulnerable children born to a cocaine- and alcohol-
addicted mother, Kim, Rita's daughter, who had been in and out of their
lives repeatedly over the years. When Niki was six she lived with Kim and
Kim's boyfriend, both heavily addicted. Niki was taught to steal sweets from
the supermarket to satisfy Kim's cravings. The children were homeless with
Kim when Joe was born. Rita was awarded custody and Kim was incarcerated
on multiple charges. They were again homeless with Rita a few years later
when her own alcohol use and substandard housing precipitated flight to a
shelter. Finally all was stabilized, and they have been in good housing for
four years. Rita is fearful of losing her housing as she gets cut off of Aid to
Dependent Children next month when her "time is up." She doesn't know
how she will work full-time and care for Tony and Joe with their special
needs. Kim was now in prison for the tenth time on drug-related charges.
Niki's father, whom she met at age eleven, was also in jail on drug charges.
Niki and Joe were born addicted and hyperactive, and Joe was later diag-

nosed and treated for ADHD. Niki is now scheduled for a special education class. Rita says this is several years too late.

Mrs. Ciano could not hold on any longer. Her rescue attempt had failed in her eyes. Niki had run away and was now living on the streets. Mrs. Ciano wanted help to let go, but, she said, it "went against every grain of her being." She was the strong one and had always held her family together. She didn't know what went wrong with Rita or Kim or Niki. The rest of the family is doing so well, living in the suburbs, keeping good jobs, but they want nothing to do with "Rita's family." Besides, everyone works three jobs. Mrs. Ciano lives in her own home with her older and also widowed sister, Zia Rosa, age seventy-seven. Her four children all want her to come and live with them in the suburbs, but she and Rosa want to keep their own home and stay as long as possible in the community where they grew up and raised their children. Pam also wants to stay near Rita to help out. Mrs. Ciano said, "I want to help but I'm sick myself, and can't take care of nobody anymore. I get only $428 a month from social security and Niki is robbing from me. The family court told the child welfare to help, but they didn't even answer my calls. Could you please help me? Could you help Niki?" she asked. "Yes, we will work on this together," I answered.

But, even with all of my experience I was overwhelmed. So much pain and so few resources, so much trouble and so many strengths. There are no fast or easy answers here. As in many inner-city neighborhoods, including this one and the one I grew up in, the last stronghold of the family is the grandmother. The Cianos live in a once strong, now shrinking Italian-American working- and lower-middle-class enclave in Hartford, Connecticut. It is on the border of a poor and working-class Hispanic community now riddled with street gangs and drug trade. But, sometimes, even matriarchs have to let the awesome responsibility go.

The Ciano "case" would involve intensive work with everyone named above and intervention with many formal and informal systems. This service, offered free through Mrs. Ciano's church, would be time consuming and difficult. Imagine how many managed care social workers it would take to follow up, if the family met insurance guidelines (which they did not) and if they would regularly attend office visits (which was unlikely). This is work best done in the community with home visits and case collaborations that include the entire "nuclear" and extended family, close friends (*amici*), the church, the schools, and the child welfare system. Moreover, it illuminates community problems and not only one family's troubles. There are many young teens on the streets like Niki, many grandmothers in this great-grandmother's shoes, and no fast solutions. Empowering clinical and community intervention can't be accomplished in forty-five-minute hours once a week. Yet these are typical contemporary cases that social workers respond to regularly. They are not easy. There is usually drug/alcohol involvement somewhere in the story. They do not often have storybook endings. This family's story as told by each member is one of struggling for health (mental and physical), attachment, stability, and resources—for life itself. When life is sustained there is "success." Sometimes the work goes beyond survival to personal and community empowerment—and thereby we are all strengthened.

The process continues. It is summer. We are in the car driving to the women's prison. Niki's strongest wish was to visit with her mother. She hadn't seen her in over a year. The privilege of the visit has been earned through her compliance with the plans we arrived at with her great-grandmother. Rita has sent Tony and Joe along too and they are bouncing around in the back seat. Niki is happy to see them. She has also brought Jes, her best friend whose mom has been helping Mrs. Ciano with Niki's care. Trips to the countryside are a treat, even if the destination is a prison, especially if it is where your mother lives. The children are laughing and the siblings are swapping funny stories about when they lived together. But there are stories Niki will not tell today. This child has been forcibly held down and raped in the interim, though her story is one of consensual sex with an adult man. She cannot control her impulses to court danger and men in the evenings. She knows she will not be remaining with Mrs. Ciano and that she has to go to court next month—both family court and criminal court (on a felony). I know her alternatives are not good. I have concluded that resources for children like Niki, who are poor and suffer from complex neurological, behavioral, and attachment disorders and have run out of family energy and alternatives are almost nonexistent. Placement possibilities hold little promise that therapeutic containment and attachment with a caring adult will be available.

Yet today she is happy. I do not mind that the radio is blaring on the rock station. Then a beautiful thing happens. The children begin to sing sweetly in unison: "I know a place that offers shelter / a city of justice / a city of love, a city of peace for every one of us. . . . Children are drowning in their tears. . . . We need a place where we can go . . . City of justice, city of love." I wipe away sudden silent tears and turn down the radio. I ask them to tell me about "Gotham City" by R. Kelly (1997), the theme song of the *Batman* movie. They sing it again. We sing it together several times. Even Joe understands the meaning. Niki says she's going to move there, and Joe asks if he can go too. I ask where they think it is. Tony thinks it is in New York. But Niki says, "It ain't nowhere, I guess." Joe says, "Uh, uh, she's wrong. It's where the jail and Mommy is." They all laugh. I say, gently, we gotta try to make that city happen for them right where they live. "Word" (meaning yes), Niki says, and they are onto the next song. I think of the beloved community.

Contemporary Trends

The practice described above illuminates many private troubles and public issues that remain in full force in the twenty-first century. I will examine the "public" or policy side of the equation here and discuss the "private" or direct practice side, including the empowerment-oriented strategies and skills used in the Ciano case, in chapters 3, 5, 7, and 8. Empowerment practice must ultimately address both interrelated sides. As William Schwartz, writing in the spirit of C. Wright Mills, notes, "A private trouble is simply a specific example of a public issue, and . . . a public issue is made up of many private troubles" (1969, cited in Berman-Rossi 1994). He suggests that the job of the social worker is to mediate between clients and systems in both public and private spheres. There are many public issues in the Ciano case: child and family poverty and poor services, the struggles of women who are being cut off AFDC cash benefits, family, neighborhood, and community breakdown, the lure of the streets and the drug culture for inner-city youth who want to cash in quickly on the media-induced dream of wealth and the easy life, the plight of the "street child," the challenges of grandparents in inner-city communities, the marginal economic status of elders living solely on Social Security benefits, homelessness, the resilience of children, and the possibility of neighborhood-based and community-oriented social services, and, finally, the dream of the beloved community. I will elaborate on the trend of increasing child and family poverty here, as it illuminates the need for an approach to social work and social welfare that empowers people to work for social and economic justice.

Child and Family Poverty

Nearly one-fourth (24.6 percent) of American children under age six live in poverty. This figure has gone up 3 percent since 1983. Sixteen states exceed the national norm, with the highest rates (40 percent or above), in Louisiana, West Virginia, and the nation's capital (44 percent). Connecticut, California, Texas, and New York have risen steeply since 1983 (*News-Press*, July 10, 1998:5; NCCP 1998). In 1996 more than one in every five children, 14.5 million children, lived in poverty in the United States. Nearly half of poor children live below one-half of the poverty threshold of $16,400 for a family of four (43 percent as compared to 28 percent in 1978). Poverty measures currently in use, however, were developed in the 1960s, and they are, for many reasons, inadequate to reflect the complexities of today's poverty. Recommendations for a revised poverty measure were proposed in 1995 by the National Research Council (NRC) of the National Academy of Sciences. However, the revised NRC measures that would show a greater depth of poverty among children, including those from two-parent working poor families, have not yet been adopted (Betson and Michael 1997).

Poor children are getting poorer (Sherman 1997:7). This trend is even more dramatic when we look at African American and Hispanic children. Poor children do not reflect a random cross-section of all children because poverty is unequally shared (Corcoran and Chaudry 1997). In 1992 the poverty rates for African American children (46 percent) and Latino children (40 percent) were 2.5 to 3 times the rate for white children (16 percent) (Corcoran and Chaudry 1997). In 1990 the poverty rate for African American children under three was 52 percent, 42 percent for Hispanic children, 21 percent for other ethnic minority children, and 15 percent for white children under three (NCCP 1997). Children born poor run the risk of long-term poverty. Over one-third of African American children experience long spells of poverty that last seven to ten years during childhood (NCCP 1997). Although white children constituted 60 percent of all children who were poor in 1992, almost 90 percent of the long-term poor children were African American (Corcoran and Chaudry 1997).

Education, race, and age as well as single-parent family structures are predictors of poverty among children. The inequality of earnings among workers has increased over the past thirty years, resulting in higher poverty rates, particularly among younger people with relatively low levels of education (Lewit, Terman, and Behrman 1997). However, race relates to inequality of earnings. For example, 1989 data shows that African American and Latino men were more likely to be earnings poor than white men with the same completed schooling. This includes male college graduates who were poor. Race-based differences in earnings and race-based housing segregation must be addressed if effective antipoverty policies are to be developed (Corcoran and Chaudry 1997). Gender-based differences in earnings are also important to note and to address. Women continue to earn less than their male counterparts (ranging from sixty-three cents to eighty-seven cents on the dollar, which reflects regional and other differences) and mother-only families run a high risk of poverty (Corcoran and Chaudry 1997; IWPR 1998).

Poor children have higher incidents of infant death, low birth weights, and inadequate prenatal care. They have a greater chance of repeating a grade or being expelled from school. They are one-third less likely to attend college and one-half as likely to graduate from college. They have less access to all material resources and less access to community resources such as good schools, safe neighborhoods, and adequate governmental services than do children raised in families with adequate incomes. Clearly, life chances and options are diminished by poverty (Sherman 1997:3; Corcoran and Chaudry 1997:41).

An International Perspective on Child Poverty

The United States is doing poorly in child poverty rates compared to eighteen other industrialized nations, according to the Luxembourg Income Study conducted in Europe, Scandinavia, Canada, Australia, and Israel over the past decade by Rainwater and Smeeding (1996). Of the nations studied, the United States ranks seventeenth. Child poverty rates mirror real income deficit and low and falling social expenditure rates for children. In contrast, high-income children are better off than their counterparts in every nation studied and the gap between U.S. rich and poor children is the greatest. The United States has the greatest income disparity of any modern democratic nation. The median wage of working men has fallen steadily over the last twenty years, resulting in proportionately more children living in poverty in the United States than in any other industrialized nation (Schorr 1997:xvi, xvii).

Internationally, poverty is also clearly related to families headed by single mothers. As noted above, in the United States women still do not earn equal pay for equal work (IWPR-Institute for Women's Policy Research, October 1998). In this global economy similar socioeconomic forces influence all the countries studied. Divorce, out-of-wedlock births, and single-parent families in which the mother must work are on the rise in all of the countries studied. What distinguishes the United States from the other nations studied is the more generous transfer and tax policies of the other nations (Plotnick 1997). The effects on children of recent demographic trends are social policy concerns in all the countries (Rainwater and Smeeding 1996). However, in the United States there is a policy retreat instead of an attack on the problems such social forces produce. This retreat, often framed in the guise of reform, will be discussed in chapter 4 along with other contemporary trends that establish the mandate of the empowerment approach.

Global Perspectives on Social Work and Social Problems

There are remarkable similarities in socioeconomic themes in highly industrialized nations and there is the potential of learning from each other (Rainwater and Smeeding 1996). Similarly, there is much to be learned from developing countries that face comparable problems with fewer resources (Midgley 1997). Dealing with social underdevelopment in practice and policy areas like homelessness and the plight of street children in economically advantaged as well as economically disadvantaged countries are cases in point (Lee, Odie-Ali, and Botsko 2000; Lee and Odie-Ali 2000). The U.S. Council on Social Work Education recognizes global interdependence and expects curricula to include international content. It is important to promote a bidirectional flow of knowledge from South to North as well as in the usual reverse direction. To that end, chapter 12 will center around social work practice outside the United States in both fully industrialized and less industrialized countries, with practice in Guyana, South America, including the author's collaborative relationship with Guyanese social work educators and practitioners on issues of the empowerment of women and children and homelessness, as a central focus.

In the practice metaphor of the Ciano family both homelessness and children living on the streets were noted. Empowerment-oriented social work with homeless men, women, and children was a focus of the practice material in the first edition of this book. While the focus will be expanded to include other disenfranchised groups, with a greater emphasis on children, the original materials continue to be relevant to today's practice and will remain in this edition. Homelessness, including the growing presence of street children, is a global phenomenon. A 1987 United Nations study estimated that one billion people live under conditions of inadequate shelter or are literally homeless (Glasser 1994). Heads of nations and official delegates at the United Nations Conference on Human Settlements (Habitat II) held in Istanbul, Turkey in 1996 endorsed the universal goals of ensuring adequate shelter for all and making human settlements safer, healthier, and more liveable, equitable, sustainable, and productive in an urbanizing world. The strategies for achieving this included forging new partnerships for action at the international level and preserving human diversity and the richness of cultures (UNDP n.d.; Lee and Odie-Ali 2000). There continues to be high rates of homelessness in industrialized countries where homelessness need not exist at all (Blau 1992; Glasser 1994; Alston 1999; Lee 1999a; Lee, Odie-Ali, and Botsko 2000; Lee and Odie-Ali 2000). However, the majority of homeless people live in developing countries affected by high rates of population growth, urbanization, and underemployment. Rural-urban migration, chronic alcoholism and the increasing availability of street drugs, other substance abuse and mental disorders, the lack of affordable housing and the deinstitutionalization of the mentally ill are factors commonly associated with homelessness worldwide (Glasser 1994; and Lee, Odie-Ali, and Botsko 2000) Midgley (1991) sees homelessness as a way of life for billions of the world's people.

The Habitat Agenda (UNDP n.d.) places street children as a priority on their agenda action. A 1980s UNICEF Report estimates that there were over thirty million children living on the street in urban centers worldwide, although they are particularly difficult to count. Family breakdown, the gap between rich and poor, and inner-city community disintegration are global problems precipitating homelessness (Agnelli 1986; chapter 14 in this volume). Inner-city violence and victimization and neighborhoods as war zones are also global problems affecting children (Nisivoccia and Lynn 1999). At thirteen, Niki was fast on her way to becoming a victimized street child, although earlier victimizations while homeless with her addicted mother may have laid the foundation for her current proclivity for street life. Niki faced homelessness twice before this in her young life. The fastest growing population of homeless people in the United States and elsewhere is women and children (Boxhill 1990; Nunez 1994; Lee 1999a).

Continuing on Dreams

The Dreams of Children

Niki, Jess, Tony, and Joe dreamed of a city of justice and love. In the stories presented below Sara dreams of helping homeless children and Sudeka dreams of going to a place where she could "be someone." She longed to be a poet.

Sara is a nine-year-old African American girl who lived in a shelter for homeless women and children with her mother and seven-year-old sister. For Dr. Martin Luther King Jr.'s birthday the children at Sara's school were asked to complete Dr. King's famous words, "I have a dream." Sara brought this "home":

> I have a dream. my dream is to be a foster moht Becuse I wold like to help homelest Kids. So they wold no be eating from the dumpstes and wold not be dricking drty water.becuz thay will be sick and hunge. and I don't like ttat. And one day I had 9 foster kids and thay was happy and I was to. AND THAT WAS MY DREAM!

The teacher corrected the spelling and returned it to the child. That night her mother abandoned her at the shelter. She would have a foster mother again.

Poverty is misery. Sudeka, a fifteen-year-old girl living in a poor community asks (excerpted):

> . . . *What we see?*
> *Misery*
> *Falling like rain.*
> *(Thomas 1978)*

Since the first printing of this book in 1994 little has changed for the Sudekas and Saras and Niki's and Joe's America except that the ranks of poor children are fuller, as noted earlier in this chapter. But something has changed for this social worker and social work teacher, who has known too many children of poverty in her three and a half decades of social work practice. It is the congealing of an approach to social work practice that stands side by side with people who are poor, who are of color, who are women, or who are different to confront the obstacles imposed by class and race and difference. It is an approach that joins with people to help them find the strengths they need internally, interpersonally, and politically to live rather than merely survive and to have an impact on oppressive systems on behalf of themselves and others. Sudeka's story (Thomas 1978) is presented along with the story of Niki and her family to introduce the clinical and political dimensions of this "empowerment approach" to social work practice.

Sudeka is a bright fifteen-year-old African American girl from a working poor family. Her mother, a proud woman, cleans bathrooms in hotels. Her brother, Les, a veteran, is an addict. She has a twenty-three-year-old boyfriend, Jamal, a Jamaican. Sudeka's sister, Deena, returns to leave her four-year-old child, Bunky, and seek work elsewhere. Sudeka's one bright hope is school. She is asked to leave school to work with her mother to help support the family and save for an operation for Bunky. She doesn't want to leave school but sees it as her obligation.

The journalist deftly weaves entries from Sudeka's journal into her story. Jamal gave Sudeka books and introduced her to Bob Marley's music. She began to build herself a black history library and struggled to discover her heritage. She loved reading, poetry, and writing in her diary. The time came for her to leave her beloved school. On January 3 she writes: "I won't, won't, won't do it. Sudeka don't cry now. I'm in the black hurt now." She then vows to write correct English and "to write smart things here, like dreams and aspirations." She tells of her wish to go to Jamaica and the conflict she feels between family need and joining her mother in cleaning hotel toilets: "Man, my dreams get dead. . . . Mama all smell of bleach. Next its me all smell of bleach." Then the resignation: "Tomorrow I am going to work. . . . Cross yourself, kneel down deep. Bad luck is me." On January 21 she reflects:

Frederick Douglass say don't live in meekness and humility. What this mean? . . . Let your discontent grow upon you. Let it open your eyes. . . . The master is the white man. The white man got the power. Frederick Douglass say loosen your bonds by thinking and then slip away. . . . He live in those times when slaves was around. Jamal say just like today. If kindness was the rule how do they forget us? No man should be judged by his skin. No man should sit and stare at his hongry childrens. No boys should rob and hit their mamas. Girls shouldn't get crying. . . . America she sit like a queen little fingers folded in her lap but the revolution, it come and no time for peace. I warn the American people by all that is just and honorable, to beware! (Thomas 1978:27)

Sudeka then decided to leave home to find Trenchtown (Jamaica), which symbolized hope and liberation. She left a goodbye letter saying she had to leave "to be someone." Three days later she called her mother from the airport. She didn't have the airfare. Her hope dwindles and she is despondent. "Write make your fingers write no head just dead empty where i be . . . don't wait in vain for me." And Wednesday, February 8, "I can't lift my head to write so that's why I'm leaving you. I used to think."

Thomas writes: "On Friday February 10, in New Jersey, Sudeka Linda Harrison took 15 Valiums and slashed her wrists with a broken bottle. She was found dead in a hall closet" (1978:1). This tragic story exemplifies all the levels of human suffering social workers must address. On one level it is the story of racism and abject poverty and its ultimate toll on human life. On another level it is a story of inadequate resource systems that make no provision for poor children and families. It is a story of a young woman's justified and silent rage and of the strengths and struggles of family life in poverty. The policy, program, services, and basic socioeconomic changes needed to change the facts of this story are still dramatically absent. It is a story of an adolescent girl's crisis and exceptional life transitions, including her struggle to affirm her identity. But her dream is out of reach. With the reality of demeaning work and the loss of school and of her hope of going to "a better place" where dreams can be actualized, her self-esteem falls so low that suicide is clinically predictable (Mack and Hickler 1981). Drugs combine with this loss and extraordinary fall in self-esteem to herald tragedy.

To help Sudeka and her family the social worker needs to stand by them on all fronts. She must work with this family and others like them for the program and policy changes that can deliver adequate resources for all families. Equally important, she must be clinically astute to issues of depression, adolescent development, drug use, and ethnically sensitive practice; otherwise Sudeka is lost, although some larger battles may eventually be won.

My social work practice and teaching became a search for how to hold on to the individual and still wage the battle for socioeconomic justice, to be both clinical and political, for to lose one or the other is too great a cost. Sudeka and her family waited in vain for the love of a compassionate America. Something else was needed: their personal and political empowerment. This book is about helping all Saras and Sudekas and Nikis and Tonys and their families attain that empowerment. The dream of this writer is to provide a social work translation of political consciousness into a fine-tuned ("clinical") understanding of people in the everyday struggles of life and to show how individuals struggling together can make changes for themselves and others.

A Contrast: Empowered Women Naming Themselves

As a contrast to Sara and Sudeka, who experienced no empowerment intervention, an excerpt from a middle-phase meeting of an empowerment group composed of five African American women, ages twenty-one to thirty-four, who were "graduates" of a shelter for homeless women and children is presented.

"We've been meeting for a long time," said Tracey, the president of the group, "we've got to have a name." "Who are we?" asked Vesalie. "We are successful women," said Tracey. "Yeah," said Latoya, "the Successful Women's Group." "No," said Vesalie, "we can't call ourselves that." "Why?" asked Shandra. Vesalie strongly replied, "It implies too much power, that we are powerful." The worker asked if they felt powerful. Vesalie said, "Yes, we are more powerful now—we got good jobs, we're good mothers, we help others who are homeless, we are meeting our goals, but we haven't gotten there yet." The worker asked, "When you get there, then you have power?" Tracey replied, "But that's just it—we need that power to get there, and we're on our way. Let's convey that we *are* powerful women, we *are* successful women; let's take that name and make it ours. We deserve to walk with that name!" The others strongly agreed. Vesalie thoughtfully accepted this and the name *Successful Women* was enthusiastically adopted.

Names mean a great deal. The worker's questions here are critical consciousness-raising questions, a skill to be discussed later in the book. This naming effort illuminates important processes and questions and goes to the central question in this work: What is empowerment? Power attainment, or empowerment, is both process and outcome. Developing power can be frightening, but it is not presumptuous, nor is it contradictory to caring and mutual support. Empowering practice necessitates a focus on love and power and hope.

The journey from being "homeless women" to being "successful women" is a 360-degree turn. It evolves from a process of conscientization (consciousness-raising, chapter 2) and critical thinking in which the personal and political levels of being members of an oppressed group are examined and challenged. Empowerment comes about as systems as well as people are changed by people's actions. The Successful Women's Group and its members will be discussed in chapters 11 and 12. Updates on the lives of Tracey and Shandra will be provided in chapters 8 and 9.

One Last Dream

It was 1960, the year of my high school graduation. We lived in the Bedford-Stuyvesant area of Brooklyn, New York, in a small wood frame house heated by a coal stove in the kitchen. We were the remaining white family in the heart of a strong, black working-class and poor community others called a ghetto. The church was the heart of this community. It was attuned to the civil rights movement and taught a gospel of God's love and "social gospel," including nonviolent resistance. Our two young pastors, David P. Ver Nooy and Melvin G. Williams, a host of church elders, a church youth group leader, Grace Thorpe Brathwaite, my peers, and a few exceptional high school teachers like Theresa L. Held and Rose Langleben challenged me to think critically. They were my role models, along with my family.

I grew up in a close extended family, many of whom lived on our street until 1951, when, with many tears, the last and favorite aunt, Edie, left for Long Island. My grandmother, Ella, was a matriarch in our family, in the church, and in our neighborhood. At eighty-two she was as beloved and loving as she had been for the fifty-odd years she ministered and acted as midwife on St. Mark's Avenue. Nana often said, "If our house could talk, what stories it would tell! The births, the deaths, the tears, and laughter." Young and old, neighbors and extended family still came to her, and we in turn received from them. When family came we gathered in a circle and everyone (including children) had a turn to contribute to the conversation. There was often laughter and singing. The family circle was the first group I knew. Our "nuclear" family—my mother and I, my two uncles, and my grandmother—"got by," like everyone else on the block. My mother, Anne, a beautiful, artistic, and intellectually gifted woman, was the only one of our family who completed high school, and at a college preparatory level. Mother worked intermittently as an executive secretary. She was hospitalized in a psychiatric facility for several months when I was four. A lifelong struggle with schizophrenia without the intervention of the mental health system followed. Periods of health and illness occurred sporadically. This struggle began two years after my father survived World War II and failed to return to her. My Uncle Jack, a decorated World War II hero and a post office supervisor, was now a late-stage alcoholic estranged from his wife and daughter. And my quiet, gentle Uncle Warren was on service-connected psychiatric and physical disability from World War II. We survived on his small pension. We could not afford even a city college. Some members of the extended family argued that I should work full-time. My mother and grandmother disagreed and dreamed for me. My friends dreamed too. Pastor Mel Williams challenged members of our youth group to "do something with our lives."

Bobby asked, "So what are you all going to do? I'm going into the army, I'm going to get my college education while Uncle Sam pays the bills. I'm not living in those roach trap projects forever." "Me either," said Willy, "but I'll probably be dead before I become a doctor." "Willy, I'm sick of you saying that," Barbara Jean (Bubba) said. "It's all you ever say: 'Physician, heal thyself!' " " We all broke into laughter as Willy acted out a faith healing in which Bubba's mouth was healed. "Seriously now," said Bobby, "what you gonna do, Judy?" I said I'd try to go to college. Bubba said, "I'm going to work now and go to college at night, but I'll be a writer some day and write about all of us." "Not about me," said Kiki, "there's nothing to say." Bobby said, "But ain't you going into the Coast Guard, Kiki?" "Sure," said Kiki, "but that's not much." Mary chided Kiki, "You have to believe in yourself. I'm going to be an artist." Mark said, "I'm going away to college and I'll be a football hero." He threw a fake pass to Kevin. Kevin laughed, "They'll never expect a Chinese boy to do that!" "Right," said Mark. "What are you going to do, Kev?" Kev shrugged, "I really don't know." "And don't care either," laughed Willy. "You just want to get next to Linda." Everyone laughed and everyone dreamed.

———

On a cold winter's afternoon a few months later I asked my grandmother, who was trying to nap under some blankets and overcoats,

"Nana, what do you dream about?" "I dream," she said, "that you will become something, maybe a nurse, a missionary nurse. And that you will walk always with your hand in God's hand." I responded, "But for yourself, Nana. What do you want for yourself? Maybe I can get it for you now." "Oh," she replied, "that in heaven I will have a pretty little house, like an English cottage, all surrounded with flowers . . . a house with good heat!" "But now, Nana," I pressed. "Now," she laughed, "I want you to get me your coat and let me nap!"

I dreamed that I could get Nana that house where she wouldn't need to huddle under coats to keep warm and that no one would have to wait for heaven to get the simple things they need to live. I dreamed my friends' dreams would all come true. As for Nana's dreams for me, two out of three ain't bad! God didn't let go; I worked nights and summers at PAL youth programs and went to college. I studied after midnight and slept through morning classes, but I did not become a nurse!

The close-knit group of friends is still there for each other. Pastor Mel Williams is now, tragically, a victim of Alzheimer's disease. And yet, from his congregate living facility for Alzheimer's patients, he is able to reach out his arms in love to his family and friends and fellow sufferers whose names no longer make a difference. The essence of Mel—his love—is still there, almost miraculously. The courage of Mel and his devoted wife, Virginia, is a lesson in the power of love. The flock reaches out to visit with and offer support to them across the miles.

Some of us dreamed bigger than others and some of us got further than we ever dared to dream. Of the eight young people (seven of color) who dreamed that day, five attained master's degrees, three got their doctorates, and one obtained an M.D. There are five educators, including a high school principal, three university professors, and the dean of a medical school, an American Studies historian, a social worker, an engineer, and a colonel in the army. There were other members of the group and countless accomplishments, though not without struggle. Many are parents. Three of us are gay, though I did not know that about myself until many years later. The two young men knew then and couldn't say it, even to each other. One member of the group stayed in the community and struggles with unemployment and alcoholism. One, a leader among us, left and then returned. He died from complications of AIDS in 1992. It was a profound loss. He loved others but he never learned to love himself. His world did not accept gay men. Did God still care? he agonized. Racism, sexism, poverty, classism, heterosexism, and combinations of these evils: Which is the worst to live or die with? Across the United States this empowered group grasps hands, united against the oppression any one of us experiences. Out of such love books are written and lives are empowered.

A Firm Foundation

Life and practice have taught me that *both* personal and political levels of change must be addressed in an approach to social work practice with oppressed groups. To quote Carla, a young woman describing abuses in a New York City shelter, "These are the fruits of oppression." I agreed they are (Lee 1987). Practice with people who are pushed to the edge of this society necessitates a validation of that experience and a dual focus on people's potentials and political/structural change. It requires reaching across boundaries. As bell hooks writes,

> Radical postmodernism calls attention to those shared sensibilities which cross the boundaries of class, gender, race, etc., that could be fertile ground for the construction of empathyùties that would promote recognition of common commitments and serve as a base for solidarity and coalition. (1990:26)

We need a side-by-side stance. We *are* all in this together.

The Book

This book advances an empowerment approach to direct social work practice. It makes connections between inadequate social policies and programs, personal vulnerabilities, and the need for a fair start in obtaining vital internal and external resources. Its aim is to help the social worker develop knowledge to help people to empower themselves in the personal, interpersonal, and political levels of life. It focuses specifically on practice with oppressed groups based on an understanding of past and contemporary history and social policy issues. Utilizing empowerment theory as a unifying framework, it develops an empowerment approach that is integrative, holistic, and pertinent to the needs of stigmatized and vulnerable populations while being applicable to other client groups.

This approach adapts an ecological perspective to empowerment practice (Germain 1979, 1991; Germain and Gitterman 1980). This perspective helps us see the interdependence and connection of all living and nonliving systems. Within the ecological perspective the professional task is seen as "maintaining a dual simultaneous concern for people and environments" and "releasing the potentialities of people and environments" (Germain 1979). Potentialities are the "power bases" that exist in all of us and that develop when there is a "goodness of fit" between people and environments. By definition, poor people and other oppressed groups seldom have this "fit," because discriminatory social and economic forces create a noxious environment that stifles human potential. To change this unfavorable equation, people must join together to examine the forces of oppression; they must name, face, and challenge them as they have been internalized and encountered in the external power structures that exist at close range, mid range, and wide range in our society. The greatest human power to tap is the power of collectivity: "Two [people] can resist an attack that would defeat one [person] alone. A rope made of three cords is hard to break" (Ecclesiastes 4:12). Collectivity and the three strands of personal, interpersonal, and political empowerment make a strong rope. Weaving the rope is the work of empowerment practice. The revisions and additions to this book, including new chapters on skill (3), community practice (13), and international social work practice (14), all add texture and strength to the rope of empowerment, a lifeline for vulnerable and oppressed populations.

Communications Technology: A Source of Power

Access to knowledge is power. The information revolution marked by the greater availability of computer technology to all sectors of society offers a new tool to social workers and their clients. Social workers and the people they help can develop computer literacy in order to keep up with knowledge that is beneficial to groups struggling for equity and to advance in the job market. Courses in computer skills are available in many universities, community colleges, and continuing education programs. Most communities also offer such programs in adult education programs, through the local public library, and in community centers where costs are minimal. As social workers become knowledgeable we can help our clients to gain access to technology to enrich their lives and self-empowerment efforts. Concerned parents groups can advocate for appropriate computer education, software and internet access in schools and community centers, even when owning a personal computer is not possible. We can help residents of poor communities learn to utilize public libraries as places to gain access to the knowledge they need through computers as well as books. Through the use of interactive software and internet access to the world wide web, social workers and clients are able to obtain state of the art knowledge quickly and easily.

Whether it is for basic adult literacy training or conflict resolution skills for children or specialized knowledge on community organizing, environmental problems, child development, mental or physical illness, or the history of oppressed groups, the world opens through the use of computer technology. Corrections programs for adults and youth, for example, have begun to employ distance education and interactive software to help those who gave up on education gain a fresh start. In addition to the usual cultural, educational, and recreational activities of settlement house type community centers, computer technology is used to engage youth and adults in a quest for knowledge. For example, a newly developed community center in a low-income African American, Latino, and white ethnic area in Southwest Florida planned a computer room as a central area in its new facility. Major area businesses donated up-to-date computer terminals and software; programs and technical assistance were obtained from the local university, other area schools, and volunteers. Computer literacy was taught in summer day camp and educational and culturally appropriate games engaged children who have great difficulty in traditional learning modes. They then felt comfortable in using interactive software in their tutorial programs during the school year. A transitonal living facility for homeless women and children utilized a similar strategy in engaging the women in a self-tutoring program to learn basic computer skills. The mothers and children also learned through playing computer games together. The women said that they felt prepared when they then enrolled in a training program mandated by a state work readiness program. Social workers can help make computer technology available to members of disenfranchised groups.

Contemporary social workers will want to use the internet to research topics such as poverty, women, children, cultural knowledge, and legislative issues among others. For example, three websites were used in researching data for this chapter: www.iwpr.org/ Release 98.htm (from Hartmann's Institute for Women's Policy Research), www.childrensdefense.org (Children's Defense Fund), and www.undp.org/un/habitat/agenda (from the United Nations' data base). Some schools of social work and leading social work educators have developed websites. For example, Richard Estes at the University of Pennsylvania has developed PRAXIS, a website where students can learn how to access and obtain information on international social work issues. For beginners he gives basic instructions as to how to use a search engine and browser to navigate a web site (Estes 1999). The Kensington Welfare Rights Union has established an award-winning website (www.libertynet.org). Social workers can enrich their practice and research through utilizing the world wide web for information in all areas of practice. A special section of the references for this book will guide the reader to many helpful sites.

Multifocal Vision

Empowerment practice is aimed at joining with people called clients to help them gain access to power in themselves, in and with each other, and in the social, economic, and political environment. Multiple perspectives are used to develop an empowerment practice framework. Multifocalvision consists of a *historic perspective*: learning a group's history of oppression, including related social policy (chapter 4), an *ecological* view, including a stress-coping paradigm and other concepts related to coping—ego psychological and cognitive behavioral concepts (chapter 5), a *critical* perspective, an *ethclass* and a *feminist* perspective, a *multicultural* perspective (chapter 6), and a *global* perspective (chapter 14). The additional *multicultural and global* foci are new to this edition. The concept of multifocal lenses leaves the possibility of adding other foci as theory and practice evolves. If the reader can imagine a pair of glasses with multiple lenses ground in (not bifocal or trifocal, but multifocal lenses), that is the view of the world and of practice that illuminates this approach. Since there is a good deal of overlap in these perspectives, it will not take long to get used to these new lenses. The broad-based ecological view is an overarching concept explaining person/environment transactions. The different emphases provided by adding the other six lenses help us to see closely and at several distances and sharpen the views we need to practice this approach. We may also need to add other foci as theory and practice evolves. Ultimately, these are political lenses.

A Conceptual Framework

In addition to the multifocal theoretical perspective, this empowerment approach is based on values, principles, and skills that will be integrated into an overall conceptual framework introduced in chapter 2 and utilized throughout this book. Helping processes—including consciousness-raising and dialogue as method between individuals, in small groups, and in the wider community—will be highlighted in chapters 7 through 14. A broad knowledge and skill base will be elaborated with full illustrations from practice.

The group/collectivity—in particular, the "empowerment group" discussed in chapter 11—is seen as the heart of empowerment practice. The uniqueness of this book will be the synthesis and integration of an empowerment approach to practice with poor and oppressed people on the personal, collective, and political levels of being and of social work practice.

Keeping Hope Alive

Lisbeth Schorr, renowned social analyst, has written a well-researched and very hopeful book entitled *Common Purpose* in which she describes several excellent demonstration programs that work to turn the poverty of individuals and communities into economic, personal, and communal empowerment. She notes, quoting the poet Edna St. Vincent Millay, "Wisdom enough to leech us of our ill / Is daily spun; but there exists no loom / To weave it into fabric" (1998:xxvii). Empowered social workers, clients, and community members are the weavers. Schorr weaves the elements of successful programs together to produce guidelines for what works. Her main argument is that we already know what works. There are numerous examples of innovative and effective programs throughout the United States (Biegel and Blum 1999; Nunez 1994; Devaney, Ellwood, and Love 1997; Schorr 1998). Argeriou and McCarty took a similar approach in presenting nine community demonstration grants that worked in treating alcoholism and drug abuse among homeless men and women (1990). Effective programs to end homelessness are well documented (Lee 1999a; Nunez 1994). The literature of the helping professions is full of such success stories. The evidence is compelling, but the problem is the commitment of public and private resources to take these programs to scale. For such resources to be released it will take the joining together of all concerned citizens with the common purposes of establishing policies and programs that work and restoring trust in our ability to defeat poverty and related ills, particularly those inflicted on children. By joining together in one voice, one that goes beyond traditional political divisions, we can turn the most challenged neighborhoods into communities of hope. This is the work of empowered people supported by the beloved community. Empowered social workers and those they work with (usually called clients) can lead in responding to this call to action. Schorr says:

> Together we can be sustained by the conviction that we have the resources-material, intellectual and spiritual-to assure that every American family can expect its children to grow up with hope in their hearts and a realistic expectation that they will participate in the American Dream. (1998:385)

I believe that this dream is a universal dream for those of every land who dare to dream. Though material resources are not equal, and such equality is central to the dream of a beloved global community, empowered people in many nations will realize the dream of a better life for children. Empowerment-oriented social workers are uniquely suited to help people every where make such dreams reality. We continue now in our weaving of the empowerment approach to social work practice.

These lines, adapted from the last stanza of a poem I wrote for colleagues attending the Tenth Annual Symposium of the Association for the Advance-

ment of Social Work with Groups (Baltimore, Maryland, 1988), succinctly
contain the message of this book:

> *Brother, sister*
> *social workers,*
> *take our hands,*
> *say the people*
> *called clients.*
> *Understand this:*
> *You provide*
> *one shoulder more,*
> *one special guide*
> *with different tasks.*
> *We need your skill,*
> *your strength,*
> *your will,*
> *but you need us to*
> *get there still.*
> *You cannot lead,*
> *you cannot steer,*
> *but come aboard,*
> *and we'll get there!*
> *Brothers, sisters,*
> *take my hand,*
> *it is against that*
> *night we stand.*

—From "A Plea For Unity"

2 The Empowerment Approach: A Conceptual Framework

People who must deal with exceptional life tasks because they belong to oppressed groups may be lost, as Sudeka was, or they may, in varying degrees, develop the power to live their lives fully and contribute to the life of the community. They may succumb to a sense of hopelessness and powerlessness, or gain a sense of potency and actual power to influence, with others, the conditions of daily living. They may gain relative mastery over their affairs or remain constantly reacting. They may develop resilience, ego strengths, assertiveness, self-healing, mutual-aid networks, activism, and other coping devices. Groups and communities may gain relative control of their destiny or may stagnate and dissolve. A sense of actual and perceived power in determining the course of one's life and community is *empowerment* (Simon 1990). Social workers must promote and support individual and group strengths and potencies and, with clients, go beyond to include fortifying communities and making an impact on political systems. All social work should be empowering (Germain 1990). But what is empowering social work practice? This chapter seeks to explore the answer to that question by further defining the empowerment approach to social work practice. Precise definitions can direct our thinking and practicing (Hayakawa 1962; Lee 1991).

The empowerment approach is an integrated method of social work practice driven by the unified personal:political construct and a commitment to the unleashing of human potentialities toward the end of building the beloved community, where justice is the rule. It is therefore a *clinical* and *community-oriented* approach encompassing holistic work with individuals, families, small groups, communities, and political systems. It is clinical in the sense that Swenson defines clinical social work as broad-based and tailored to individuals' unique personalities and needs (1997). It is clinical because casualties of poverty, marginalization, physical and emotional violence, and oppression may become the "walking wounded." The economically poor need and deserve the same range and quality of services, including therapeutic services, as their well-off counterparts. The biopsychosocial needs of vulnerable and at risk people need attention and healing that does not blame the victim even as the society that inflicts such wounds to human worth must seek healing. The healing, however, does not come from an expert's hands but from the collaboration of people with peers and helpers in a self-healing and self-empowering process. It is community oriented because living, growing, empowered people can not adapt to dead communities. They change them or leave them in the process of active adaptation (Germain 1991). This approach embodies the classic group work goals of individual growth toward social ends promoted by positive group attachments (Pernell 1986). We are one with the context of our lives. Foreground (people) and background (context) are one picture. Empowerment is the process and outcome whereby communities are enlivened. The power of obtaining resources (material and internal), knowledge, and know-how builds individual lives and the beloved community.

The empowerment approach is technically neither a formal theory nor a model of practice except in the sense Turner uses *theory* to denote a variety of conceptually coherent social work approaches and frameworks for practice (1996). A theory is a system of thought and a set of related hypotheses that have been empirically tested. Theories can explain and predict phenomena. Models help us to understand what is, what is possible, and how to achieve the possible (Turner 1996). Theories and models are both predictive and prescriptive. They make the statement "If you do this, this will happen." The more comprehensive and complex a phenomena is, the less likely it is to be quantifiable and "testable." The person:environment territory of the social worker is a case in point. Most if not all theoretical or conceptual approaches to social work practice fall short of attaining formal theory status. Turner delineates eight pragmatic criteria to determine practice theory in social work. All of the twenty-seven approaches he includes in his *Interlocking Theoretical Approaches*, including the empowerment approach presented here, meet most of the criteria to varying degrees. Approaches are perspectives on practice—ways of thinking about and doing practice. An approach is a flexible and open system that accommodates the user's unique style, judgment, and use of self. It is based on (and must make clear) the professional purpose, values, ideology, concepts, knowledge, and methods it selects as its purview. These are, in a sense, a "package deal" that shape practice. The practitioner must know what the whole approach or package is, not just one appealing aspect of it, and attempt to put it into practice. This chapter presents the conceptual framework of the empowerment approach. We begin with definitions.

Some have suggested that *liberation* more accurately describes processes and objectives that challenge oppression. They suggest that *empowerment* connotes only a psychological and personal sense of well-being, that it is a depoliticized word, acceptable to "people changers" but not to those who seek institutional change. They argue that *empowerment* means only a "transformation that takes place inside of us, not a transformation of the conditions of our oppression" (Mann 1987:111). Liberation is seen as the opposite of oppression and is defined as the "process of reclaiming our role as creators of culture" (Pence 1987:25). There is some validity in this view. However, by defining our terms to include political processes, objectives, and transformations along with personal and interpersonal power, we restore *empowerment* to its original meaning. Liberation is a social movement that, by definition, is greater than the domain of any one profession (Germain 1990). Social work *can* assist people who are oppressed in empowering themselves personally, interpersonally, and politically to work toward liberation and actualization of their potentialities.

Personal and political power are inextricably intertwined. Solomon identifies direct and indirect blocks to power for African American people. Members of all negatively valued groups may resonate with the concepts. Indirect power blocks represent internalized negative valuations (of the oppressor) that are "incorporated into the developmental experiences of the individual as mediated by significant others." Such power blocks occur when, in the words of W. E. B. DuBois, written in 1903, one "looks at one's self through the eyes of others, measuring one's soul by the tape of a world that looks on in contempt and pity" (1964:45). Direct power blocks "are applied directly by some agent of society's major social institutions," Solomon notes. Other negatively valued groups—"the handicapped, women, gay men and lesbian women—have also begun to push for reduction of their powerlessness" (1976:21).

Powerlessness, or the lack of individuals' empowerment, is based on several factors including economic insecurity, absence of experience in the political arena, absence of access to information, lack of training in critical and abstract thought, physical and emotional stress, learned helplessness, and the aspects of a person's emotional or intellectual makeup that prevent them from actualizing possibilities that do exist (Cox 1989). The actual and perceived ability to use available resources (if and when they are available) contributes to a sense of power that is directly connected to self-esteem (Parsons 1989). Society "blames the victim" for power deficits even as power is withheld and abused by dominant groups (Ryan 1971). Victim blaming can be subtle. For example, labels such as *codependent, enabler, masochistic,* or *love addict* obliterate the issue of power in abusive male/female relationships and contribute to the woman's self-blame and internalization of oppression. Such labels focus on the personal change of the oppressed with little attention to the oppressor or the socioeconomic/political realities that maintain oppression (Mann 1987).

Empowerment Defined

Empowerment "deals with a particular kind of block to problem solving: that imposed by the external society by virtue of a stigmatized collective identity" (Solomon 1976:21). Although the general population may also experience powerlessness at this time of constant societal change, our focus here is on members of stigmatized groups. Webster's definition (eighth edition) of the word *empower*—"to give power or authority to; to give ability to, enable, permit"—implies that power can be given to another. This is very rarely the case. Staples sees empowerment as the process of gaining power, developing power, taking or seizing power, or facilitating or enabling power (Parsons 1991). Simon stresses that "empowerment is a reflexive activity, a process capable of being initiated and sustained only by (those) who seek power or self-determination. Others can only aid and abet in this empowerment process" (1990:32). The empowerment process resides in the person, not the helper.

Solomon defines *empowerment* as

a process whereby the social worker engages in a set of activities with the client . . . that aim to reduce the powerlessness that has been created by negative valuations based on membership in a stigmatized group. It involves identification of the power blocks that contribute to the problem as well as the development and implementation of specific strategies aimed at either the reduction of the effects from indirect power blocks or the reduction of the operations of direct power blocks. (1976:19)

It is this definition that is used in this book.

Empowerment Concepts

There are three interlocking dimensions of empowerment: 1) the development of a more positive and potent sense of self, 2) the construction of knowledge and capacity for a more critical comprehension of the web of social and political realities of one's environment, and 3) the cultivation of resources and strategies, or more functional competence, for attainment of personal and collective goals. As we break down and operationalize the concept of empowerment, empowerment can become the keystone of social work (Beck 1983). It is also, as Simon notes, "a series of attacks on subordination of every description—psychic, physical, cultural, legal, political, economic, and technological" (1990:28).

Empowerment practice seeks to create community with clients in order to challenge with them the contradictions faced as vulnerable, hurt, or oppressed persons in the midst of an affluent and powerful society. Practitioners must develop effective interventions to deal with individual pain by taking social forces into account. Mancoske and Hunzeker define empowerment practice as "using interventions which enable those with whom we interact to be more in control of the interactions in exchanges" (1989:14, 15).

Critical consciousness and knowledge of structural inequities and oppression are power. Transformation occurs as people are empowered through consciousness-raising to see alternatives. Transformation is a vision of social change as well as a process and outcome of throwing off oppression in one's life and in the life of the community. It requires restlessness and anger at injustice and the dehumanization of poverty, negative valuations, and the culture of personal greed (Mancoske and Hunzeker 1989).

Freire's Pedagogy of Hope, Caring, Thinking, and Acting

The words *critical consciousness* are borrowed from the works of Paulo Freire, a world-renowned Brazilian education scholar who wrote and developed *The Pedagogy of the Oppressed* (1973a). Freire's aim in teaching literacy to impoverished adult learners is that they should be able not only to name the word but also the world. Learning to read and write is necessary in order to think, read, and write about the world they live in and their place in it as makers of culture. As they see themselves as culture makers they see class status not as fate but as maintaining the economic-political-ideological context in which they live. They become literate, politically speaking (Freire 1998). In the same way, as clients who are impoverished economically and through carrying stigmatized statuses develop their awareness of self and the world they move beyond a focus on solving immediate problems to political understanding and activity that serves more than the self. Attaining a measure of self-advancement, they are able to move on to the advancement of the community.

It is not surprising that Freire began his career teaching aides in a school of social work (Freire 1990). In a 1988 speech to the International Federation of Social Workers he defines social work as "inherently educational-pedagogical" and social workers as "co-makers of the dream of justice and transformation of individuals and their society" (1990:5). Freire notes that we must examine the culture and class biases that shape us and then learn to ask critical questions to promote the client's thinking about societal reality and their place in it. Curiosity about the way things are is natural to social workers. Yet promoting curiosity beyond the psychological or interpersonal level in our clients is less natural, as we like to promote answers more than questions and psychological growth more than holistic growth that includes political understanding and action (Freire 1998). *Consciousness-raising* is cognitive activity prompted by questioning with the hoped for outcome of a new awareness of self in relation to all society. For Freire, however, neither the act of sharing personal experiences nor the awareness itself is the end product. The product of *critical awareness, or conscientization*, is action. Reflection must be followed by actions, both personal and political. That is the nature of *praxis*, the process by which we reflect, act, then reflect again in a spiraling manner. However, the view of the person in the empowerment approach is not simply that of "doer" (Turner 1996). The view of the person in this approach is thinker, feeler, and doer in a nondichotomized fashion. Freire, like John Dewey, is very clear that thinking and feeling (cognition and emotion) can not be separated. He asserts that we must literally dare to teach/practice social work, without separating thinking from doing. His is a pedagogy of hope, caring, questioning, and thinking—all leading to acting with the whole being (Freire 1997, 1998).

> We must dare, in the full sense of the word, to speak love without the fear of being called . . . antiscientific. We must dare to say scientifically . . . that we study, we learn, we teach, we know with our entire body. We do all of these things with feeling, with emotion, with wishes, with fear, with doubts, with passion, and also with critical reasoning . . . never with the last only. (1998:3)

A love of the whole person, a love of justice, a hope of changing conditions that are unjust and a willingness and ability to act are necessary in a Freirian approach to empowerment practice in social work.

Empowerment practice requires critical thinking as it addresses individual, familial, and organizational resource problems (multiple dimensions of poverty), problems of asymmetrical exchange relationships, problems of powerlessness and inhibiting or hindering power structures or constraining power structures, and problems related to arbitrary social criteria or values. Staub-Bernasconi defines *powerlessness* as low social attractiveness due to poor resources (material resources and knowledge). To help empower we must first learn to speak openly about power with clients and then engage in examination of power bases stemming from personal resources (psycho-biosocial strength and socioeconomic power), articulation power, symbolic power, positional power, or authority, and formal and informal organizational power. Unfair social stratification and unfair distribution of goods constitute the most difficult question facing most societies. Globally, critical education and advocacy for guaranteed basic incomes are imperative. International social work can help link different groups and cultures together to claim a fair share of power resources and resist domination (Staub-Bernasconi 1992).

The "radical pedagogy" of Freire (1973a, 1998) is an underpinning of empowerment practice in social work (Lee 1989b; Mancoske and Hunzeker 1989; Gutiérrez 1990; Breton 1989; Parsons 1989; Freire 1990). Freire's notion of the dialogical process is particularly relevant: "Every human being is capable of looking critically at his world in a dialogical encounter with others. . . . In this process . . . each man wins back his own right to say his own word, to name the world" (1973a:11–13). Critical education method as it applies to empowerment-oriented social work will be discussed in chapters 3 and 12.

The Central Importance of the Group

Freire's methods are group- and community-oriented methods of dialogue that promote critical thinking and action. Mann (1987) demonstrates how abused women can develop raised consciousness through the use of critical questions. Breton (1991) describes consciousness-raising as an objective in a drop-in center for homeless women in Toronto. Lee (1991) discusses empowerment strategies with groups of formerly homeless women. Liberation theology, with its use of critical thinking in small groups in base communities, is also pertinent to social work thinking (Breton 1989; Mancoske and Hunzeker 1989; Germain 1990; Lewis 1991). Freire defines *conscientization* as "learning to perceive social, political and economic contradictions and to take action against the oppressive elements of reality" (1973a:20). Critical consciousness-raising and dialogue are the key methods in empowerment practice. Going beyond the sharing of experiences and catharsis, these methods help people to think, see, talk, and act for themselves, which are Freire's ultimate objectives (1973b).

Gutiérrez cites consciousness-raising as goal, process, and outcome in empowerment work (1989a, 1989b, 1990). She writes, "It is not sufficient to focus only on developing a sense of personal power or developing skills or working toward social change. These three elements combined are the goal of empowerment in social work practice" (1989a). Gutiérrez sees developing critical consciousness, reducing self-blame, assuming personal responsibility for change, and enhancing self-efficacy as critical to empowerment (1989a). She sees group work as critical to empowerment practice based on her research on the effective use of groups with Latino college students and women of color (1989b, 1990; Gutiérrez, Parsons, and Cox 1998). Members of ethnic identity and consciousness-raising groups were significantly more likely to pursue political involvement than those who were in control groups (1989b).

Parsons (1989) also emphasizes the central importance of the group to empowerment practice. She defines empowerment as an outcome and process that comes initially through validation of peers and a perception of commonality. She notes that Schwartz's conceptualization of the mediating function of the worker (Schwartz 1994) is useful for envisioning empowerment practice with groups as mutual aid, support, and collective action help people gain resolution of problems with systems that seem intractable.

Groups may focus on consciousness-raising, help to individuals, social action, social support, and development of skills and competence in order to help members facing oppression gain equality and justice (Garvin 1987). Parsons, a group worker, identifies three kinds of empowerment: a developmental process that begins with individual growth and may culminate in larger social change, a psychological state marked by heightened feelings of self-esteem, efficacy, and control, and liberation, resulting from a social movement that begins with education and politicization of powerless people and later involves a collective attempt on the part of the powerless to gain power and change those structures that remain oppressive (1989).

Kindred Systems of Thought and Useful Grafts

While it is beyond the scope of this book to explore comparative theories in depth, it is useful for the reader to be able to locate the empowerment approach in relation to other contemporary approaches to social work practice. While some kindred approaches or systems of thought are obvious connections others may need amplification. It is important to note that some of the approaches that are compatible are relevant only on certain variables of empowerment while others are comparable more holistically. Approaches that may be omitted here as compatible may also have certain aspects that are useful to employ with clients so *kindred* implies some philosophical compatability beyond the borrowing of skills. *Feminist theory* for social work is such a kindred spirit (Bricker-Jenkins and Hooyman 1986; Bricker-Jenkins, Hooyman, and Gottlieb 1991; Bricker-Jenkins 2000; Valentich 1996).

The techniques of behavioral theories such as positive reinforcement or systematic desensitization in the case of a phobia (as illustrated in the case of Lorna in chapters 5 and 10) may be helpful in practice with certain clients, although behavioral theory itself, with its problem focus in the person as learner and lack of focus on societal change, is not a particular fit with empowerment theory.

First, we note that the empowerment approach encompasses a *biopsychosocial* understanding of the wholeness of the person and the person-situation gestalt and accepts the *psychodynamic* premise that while the past, including early relationships to parents, can not be changed, it may influence present problems and is sometimes therefore relevant reflection in the helping process. Similarly, an understanding of *ego functioning* is valuable in assessing and intervening in the facilitation of *adaptation* and *coping*, especially in stressful and oppressive environments. Ego assessment is discussed in chapter 5. Aspects of the psychosocial, psychodynamic, and ego-oriented approaches to practice are helpful in developing clinical understanding and interventions. Hollis's classification of treatment interventions and Goldstein's work on ego assessment are discussed in chapters 3 and 5 (Woods and Hollis 1990; Goldstein 1995). Northen's approach to *Clinical Social Work*, which includes group work, also includes many compatible ideas and applications (1995). However, some of the underlying premises of psychodynamic and ego-oriented approaches are deterministic and not compatible with current understanding of infant development (Germain 1991; Stern 1985), nor, despite the inclusion of indirect practice (environmental) techniques, do they have an equal focus on societal change. Saleebey's *strengths perspective* is a kindred thought system (1997).

Germain's *ecological perspective* is a foundation of the empowerment approach and will be discussed later in this chapter and also in chapter 5. The *life model* approach of Germain and Gitterman (1980, 1995), which grows out of the ecological perspective and its *stress-coping paradigm*, is the clinical/direct practice theory that most closely relates to the empowerment approach. Its "dual simultaneous concern" with the people:environment construct and commitment to the alleviation of social pollution and oppression make it a forerunner and allied approach to empowerment practice. When I teach both approaches, I point out the differences that a multifocal perspective and an emphasis on oppressed and marginalized groups and the addition of critical education to the repertoire of helping processes and desired outcomes makes. I incorporate the categories of life transitions/developmental/status and role/and crisis, interpersonal relationships, and environment as foci of assessment and intervention in chapters 5, 8, and 9. All people negotiate the tasks of living in these interrelated areas, and they remain useful in prioritizing helping to enable people to gain power and mastery in daily life. The attention of the life model to systems of all sizes (individuals, families, groups, and communities) and the use of all modalities of helping also make it a kindred approach. Mancoske and Hunzeker see the life model as a "praxis model which joins the contradictions between the levels of systems in which direct services are carried out" and empowerment as a goal that gives direction to the life model (1989:33, 34).

Of the newer thought systems imported into social work practice, *constructivism* and *narrative therapy* have potential for use with the empowerment approach. Constructivist ideas are popular in contemporary philosophy and literary criticism and in reconceptualizing cognition, learning, and behavior. Essentially, personal constructs of meaning are how individuals construe the world. What is important in constructivism is the meaning the client gives to phenomena (Dean 1993; Carpenter 1996). The premise that "nothing is universally and intrinsically true—there are only different interpretations of reality" is the opposite of locating reality entirely in the social and economic environment (Carpenter 1996; Burghardt 1996). Neither "radical constructivism" or "radical social work" thinking based on primarily materialistic or Marxian theory (Galper 1980; Burghardt 1996), which are either/or formulations, are viewpoints of this empowerment approach. However, both together capture aspects of "reality" for oppressed groups. Unequal resource distribution and discrimination exist whether individuals think so or not and individuals make unique meanings of these and other phenomena that have impact on their lives for better or for worse. There is a type of constructivist thinking that is more compatible with empowerment practice: *critical constructivism*. In this thought system individuals are co-creators and co-constructors of personal realities along *with* their physical and social environments. While societal change is not equally emphasized, inequities are recognized as existing externally. The basic premise is that we know the objective external world through the filter of our own perceptions, cognitions, affects, and belief systems (Carpenter 1996). Critical constructivism has much to say about internalized oppression or the indirect power blocks identified by Solomon (1976).

The application of *cognitive theory* in excising false perceptions and beliefs based on "faulty filters" clouded by internalized oppression is discussed in chapter 5 (Berlin 1983; Carpenter 1996; Lantz 1996). Cognitive methods "directed toward helping the client identify challenges, and change thinking patterns that result in dysfunctional forms of emotion, behavior and problem solving" (Lantz 1996) are very useful in working on issues of internalized oppression (chapter 5). The case of Shandra (chapters 8 and 9) includes vignettes in which her internalized views of her intelligence and abilities are deconstructed and a positive view of self reconstructed with the help of cognitive techniques that examine false beliefs and constructivist and narrative methods of deconstruction and rewriting the story. Narrative therapy is the method most closely aligned with critical constructivism (Dean 1993; Kelley 1996). Based on constructivist principles, the aim is to help the client tell the story that reveals her view of the presenting problem and her understandings, meanings, and beliefs. The social worker is concerned with the client's individuality and her right to be who she is as a unique person. The worker also conveys that the client is highly valued and respected by the practitioner (Carpenter 1996; Kelley 1996). The emphasis on uniqueness is especially important as there is a dangerous tendency to generalize about members of stigmatized and oppressed groups. The value on individuality is central to empowerment practice. It helps the worker to hear nuances and uniqueness in each person's story. In narrative therapy the helping role is collaborative and mutuality is valued, another level of compatibility to empowerment practice. The client is helped to tell/"write" his story through a series of questions asked from a not knowing point of view that helps the client construct, deconstruct, then reconstruct the story with a more positive ending to the client. The limitations of narrative theory are that it is value neutral on issues of oppression and the need for external/ societal change. If the client has no words for the experience of oppression and its effects, the story and its rewriting would not include this dimension, although the dimension of marginalization may be central to the client's life.

Sennett (1998), who is interested in the relationship of capitalism and the effects of this postindustrial era on people's lives, ponders how we construct a life narrative in the context of a world based on the expediency of the market—that is, when corporations "downsize" and people move frequently to work where skills are needed and jobs develop. Jobs used to be a source of security, identity, and attachment; workers stayed for lifetimes in them. Now jobs are transient and workplace attachments are corroding.

Even for top management executives there are no promises for the future. Sennett met with groups of dismissed IBM executives and called attention to the dilemma of organizing their life narratives. He emphasizes the need for workers to take control of their lives and their narratives. When they are able to do this, "now the story can flow: it has a solid center, 'me,' and a well made plot, 'what I should have done was take my life into my own hands.' The defining moment occurs when the programmers switch from passive victimhood to a more active condition" (Sennett 1998:132). This moment can be likened to empowerment, but we must note that lower-level workers will have less resources to do this and thereby empower themselves without joining with other workers in active collectivity and union. Hence the narratives of the poor and working poor present even more of a challenge.

There are also thought systems and approaches that have no particular clinical practice focus that are highly compatible with the empowerment approach. The close kinship of *feminist theory* to empowerment practice was noted in chapter 1 and will be further explored in chapters 6 and 13. Schwartz's *interactionist approach* with the worker as mediator of the tie, sometimes almost severed, between people and the systems they depend on for life has been introduced in chapter 1 (Schwartz 1994; and Shulman 1996; Parsons 1989). This mediating function is an integral part of the empowerment approach, and the skills of helping that flow from the interactionist appproach will be discussed in chapter 3. Other comprehensive and integrated approaches that call for intervention aimed at people and their problematic environments are also compatible, for example, the *structural approach* of Middleman and Goldberg (1974) and Goldberg Wood and Middleman (1989), the *integrated approach* of Parsons, Hernandez, and Jorgensen (1994), and all the variations on empowerment practice in social work. Similarly, practice approaches related to working with people of color, lesbian women and gay men, and people with disabilities like Lum (2000), Devore and Schlesinger (1999), Hopps, Pinderhughes, and Shankar (1995), Hopps and Pinderhughes (1999), Gutiérrez (1990), Woodman (1992), Anastas and Appleby (1998), Van Wormer, Wells, and Boes (2000), Renz-Beaulaurier (1996), and others inform empowerment practice.

Since groups are the heart of empowerment practice, theory related to group development and working with groups is essential to our understanding. Classics like Hartford 1971, Northen 1988, Garvin 1981, 1987, Schwartz and Zalba 1971, Papell and Rothman 1980a, 1980b, Lang 1986, Pernell 1986, and others blend with more recent thinking—Toseland and Rivas 1998, Brown 1991, Glassman and Kates 1990, and others—to form a solid underpinning to the empowerment group approach.

Theory related to community organizing, wider systems, and political interventions such as Richan 1991, Baptist, Bricker-Jenkins, and Dillon 1999, Minkler 1998, Tropman, Erlich, and Rothman 1995, Rothman, Erlich, and Tropman 1995, Rivera and Erlich 1992, Devore 1992, Brager, Specht, and Torczyner 1987, Netting, Kettner, and McMurtry 1998, Alinsky 1969, 1972, and others is essential knowledge in developing the beloved community. Intervention on the community and political level will be discussed in chapter 13.

At this point we have introduced the empowerment approach, defined our concepts, and discussed theories and approaches that are compatible with it. We now turn to the conceptual framework of the approach itself. The total overarching framework that defines the component parts and the territory of this unique approach to social work practice—intensely personal and intensely political—is important to envision and understand.

The Conceptual Framework

The conceptual framework presented here integrates *personal, interpersonal,* and *political* empowerment into a *unified* approach. It rests on *professional purpose,* a *value base,* a *knowledge base/theoretical foundation, practice principles,* and *method*—roles, processes, and skills.

Professional Purpose

The profession of social work itself is a critical source of sanction for social work practice. When members of the profession met under NASW auspices in a now historic conceptual frameworks conference in 1976, Minahan and Pincus stressed the rights of people to self-determination, dignity, and access to resources (1977). In the same conference Cooper (1977) described social work as a dissenting profession that serves as a professional mechanism for societal change. Social work has also been an acquiescing profession, tolerating and depending on a "social welfare system that does exactly the opposite of what it professes to do for the ill, the poor, the disadvantaged and the oppressed" (Souflee 1977:919). This professional dilemma must be resolved. "The mission of social work is not bound to the specifics of method, but to changing individuals, institutions and policies" (Dean 1977:373). Morales emphasized that poor people and poor communities are in need of multiskilled practitioners who "would have both the breadth and depth of knowledge and the skills to perform competent clinical work as well as to intervene via social action in larger community systems" (1977:391).

A second conceptual framework conference, held in 1981, further refined the earlier ideas and continued to maintain the dual focus on people and environments (Brieland 1987). This dual emphasis has been the domain of social work throughout its history, although it has been enacted in serial, not simultaneous, fashion. Bartlett (1958) and Gordon (1962) advanced the transactional and unitary nature of the people/environment concept. The "dual simultaneous concern" for people and environments as the professional purpose of social work is most strongly articulated in the ecological perspective and the writings of Germain (1979).

Theory for practice must include strategies related to the political, economic, and social bases of the disempowerment of groups that are vulnerable because of color, age, ethnicity, gender, disablement, and sexual preference (Germain 1991).

The dual focus allows for attention to indirect power blocks and to the more obvious direct power blocks. A unitary conception of person:environment prevents us from blaming the victim, on the one hand, and naïveté about the panacea of environmental change, on the other. It leads toward developing helping "technologies" (strategies, methods, knowledge, and skills) that are both clinical and political. It necessitates "both and" conceptualizations of practice (Van Den Bergh and Cooper 1986; Bricker-Jenkins and Hooyman 1986). People can and must take themselves and their environments in hand to attain empowerment. To envision social change that comes about without the full efforts of oppressed people is to envision a Machiavellian utopia. To envision oppressed people making this effort without changing themselves—to refuse oppression, to actualize potentialities, and to struggle actively to obtain resources—is to negate the effects of oppression in the lives of the oppressed.

Professional sanction also comes from our professional organization, the National Association of Social Workers, and the Council on Social Work Education—the body that defines and promotes standards and content for social work education. Both NASW and CSWE definitions rely on a person:environment frame of reference (Germain 1991). In July 1992 the CSWE adopted curriculum policy statements for master's degree and baccalaureate degree programs in social work education that include the following: programs of social work education must present theoretical and practice content about patterns, dynamics, consequences of discrimination, economic deprivation, and oppression. The curriculum must provide content about people of color, women, and gay and lesbian persons. Such content must emphasize the impact of discrimination and oppression upon these groups. Each program must include content about populations at risk that are particularly relevant to its mission. In addition to those mandated above, such groups include, but are not limited to, those distinguished by age, ethnicity, culture, class, religion, and physical or mental ability.

The concepts of social justice and appreciating human diversity are a strong feature of the most recent curriculum policy statement of the council.

Similarly, the value base of the profession, stated so well in the NASW code of ethics, is a consensual agreement representing the commitments of this profession:

> The social worker should *act* to prevent and eliminate discrimination on the basis of race, color, sex, sexual orientation, age, religion, natural origin, marital status, political belief, mental or physical handicap, or any other preference. . . . The social worker should *act* to ensure that all persons have access to the resources, services and opportunities that they require. The social worker should *act* to expand choice and opportunity for all persons, with special regard for disadvantaged or oppressed groups or persons. (*Encyclopedia of Social Work* 1987:951)

The verb *to act* is highlighted by this author. Our code of ethics gives us a way to assign priorities to the overwhelming needs that social work addresses. It also tells us to *act* concretely on our beliefs to change the status quo—with *special regard to oppressed persons*. Such actions also need to be taken *with* oppressed persons who know best what their realities are. The *professional purpose* of this empowerment approach is summarized as follows:

> Based on a dual simultaneous concern for people and environments: to assist people who experience poverty and oppression in their efforts to empower themselves to enhance their adaptive potentials and to work toward changing environmental and structural arrangements that are oppressive.

In the "case" of Sudeka presented in the introduction, enacting this purpose would mean clinical/political assessment of Sudeka and her family and interventions to deal with the stressors imposed by poverty and Bunky's need for an operation that precipitated the request for Sudeka to leave school and work. Her interpersonal conflict (with Mama and Jamal), her struggle for a positive proactive identity as a young African American woman, her lowering self-esteem and deep depression, and her possible use of drugs would be the clinical foci of our attention. The environmental change focus would be to assess and intervene in the power imbalance and noxious social and systemic influences that set off the events: in the direct power blocks in the nearby systems of school, welfare, Medicaid, SSI, veteran's benefits, and whatever else might be needed to meet basic needs in unjust local, state, and federal policies. The family and community are key structures that mediate against the effects of oppression and enable people to cope. They must be strengthened so that people can enact wider changes. Joining with and involving powerful others in these efforts may also be needed (Middleman and Goldberg 1974; Goldberg Wood and Middleman 1989). Societal pollutions, such as racism and classism, can be addressed by such joint efforts at local and wider levels (Germain 1990). The following chart illustrates the transactional view of political and personal change and the unity of professional purpose in an empowering social work approach.

The Value Base

Values and ideology are an inherent part of any practice approach or theoretical base (Morales and Sheafor 1983; Levy 1976).

> What social workers do is based on values—that is, on what social workers regard as preferably done. How it is done is also based on values—preferences concerning the ways of doing what is done. . . . Preferences—or values—have to be clear, however, if they are to serve as a reliable basis for action. (Levy 1976:14)

Levy is concerned with the obligatory in professional social work practice. We are obliged to act to prevent and change oppressive conditions, even as we serve all people (Morales and Sheafor 1983). Levy notes that "ethics is values in operation" (1976:14). The NASW code of ethics operationalizes the value base of the profession. Each social work approach must conform to the code of ethics, although each may also rest on additional values. An

FIGURE 2.1
A Transactional View of Political and Personal Change:
The Unity of Professional Purpose and Tasks in the Empowerment Approach

ENVIRONMENTS

PEOPLE

Social pollutions;
policies and programs;
institutional and
socioeconomic
structures
    ← Social Worker →

Individuals, families
communities and small
groups

Process: Social worker
assists and mediates to
help environments
respond to personal and
political activity,
coalitions and collective
action: change is
incremental and uneven
but ongoing

**MEDIATING
STRUCTURES**

Family
Culture
Subculture—small and
larger groups,
empowerment groups
Social agencies
Community

Process: Social worker
assists and mediates to
help people talk and
work together to
actualize potentialities
by supporting each
other in challenging
indirect and direct
power blocks; raising
consciousness regarding
their oppression and
taking individual and
collective action which
is then reflected upon in
praxis and continued

Goal: Socioeconomic
justice; reduction of
institutional power
blocks and social
pollutions; changed
socioeconomic
structures and
institutions to make
them empowering
structures

s   w

Process: Social worker
assists and mediates to
reduce stress and
strengthen these
structures

s   w

Goal: Strong mediating
structures to help people
actualize potentialities
and challenge unjust
socioeconomic
structures

Goal: To develop
strengths and options
and rename, recreate
and reconstruct their
realities: empowerment

Social | Worker

s   w

COLLECTIVE ACTION

s   w

Social and political action

Process: Social worker assists and mediates to help people
reconstruct reality and participate in the collective change
process, create building blocks for developing effective
political actions and movements

Goals: changes in oppressive, unjust structures that remove
direct blocks to empowerment and allow all people access
to resources, opportunities and options. To make an
optimum fit between all people and environments through
political empowerment

ethic of our profession is that social work should serve all people impartially (Levy 1976). Yet most approaches that serve "all people" neglect to pay adequate attention to those who are poor, of color, and otherwise oppressed (Lum 2000). This empowerment approach fills that gap by placing a priority on practice with people who face issues of oppression. Does a particular approach that specializes in certain populations (e.g., oppressed people) violate the ethic of impartiality? Levy notes, "The principle of impartiality implies that the social worker is ready to take on any and all comers who may need his service and talents no matter how pessimistic the prognosis or ordinary the attempt" (1976:123). The principle of impartiality entreats us to reach out to those clients who face bias and discrimination. Poor people, women, minorities of color, lesbian women and gay men come to a variety of agencies, where they may meet with worker or institutional bias as well as a lack of knowledge regarding who they are and what special issues they may bring. Attempts at equanimity minimize these central aspects of people's lives that necessitate exceptional coping tasks and extraordinary coping abilities. To be truly impartial and able to serve "any and all comers," the social worker must have special knowledge and skill in working with these at-risk populations. We must hope that knowledge and information about clients who face oppression, in addition to ethical injunctions and caring, will enable all social workers to serve all clients.

Color, class, gender, stigma, or difference "blindness" is not useful to clients (Lum 1986). Empowerment means that people (both workers and clients) draw strength from working through the meaning of these different statuses in their lives. This enables them to be who they are—persons with a rich heritage to draw on. It also means enacting our ethical obligation to work together toward changing the oppressive conditions with special regard for oppressed groups. The value base that underpins this empowerment approach follows:

> Preference for social work activities that give priority to work with oppressed and stigmatized groups: to strengthening individual adaptive potentials *and* making environmental/structural change through individual and collective action; preference for holistic transactionally oriented helping concepts that include knowledge about oppressed groups; preference for social policies that create a society where equality of opportunity and access to resources exists.

Knowledge Base: Theoretical Foundations and Multifocal Vision

The empowerment approach assists people who experience oppression in empowering themselves on three interrelated levels: the personal, the interpersonal, and the political. There is generic knowledge that helps us know about all levels and there is knowledge that is particular to each level.

Developing "multifocal vision" will enable the practitioner to envision the whole, yet intervene in the particular configuration of needs each oppressed person may have. The seven foci of this approach are:

1. A *historical view* of oppression, including the history of social policy related to oppressed groups.
2. An *ecological view*, which encompasses knowledge of individual adaptive potentialities, including a stress-coping paradigm (Germain 1979, 1984, 1991), ways of conceptualizing how people cope that come from a knowledge of ego functioning in the face of stigma, social learning, and cognitive behavioral learning (Germain 1991; Goldstein 1995; Berlin 1983), and knowledge about power, the abuse and withholding of power, and structural inequities and socioeconomic pollutions.
3. An *ethclass perspective* (Gordon 1978), which sharpens our knowledge about the realities of racism and classism and their interplay, including the particulars of class structure and the effects of poverty on human beings as well as the adaptive mechanisms that people of color have developed to deal with victimization (West 1993), marginality, and oppression (Devore and Schlesinger 1996; Lum 2000; Logan 1990; Freeman 1990).
4. A *cultural/multicultural perspective* (Green 1999) that attends to the norms and nuances and expectations of the client's ethnic background. It is a mistake to to see all whites as American, without the heritage of other countries of origin, or all blacks as African American, when many are of Afro-Caribbean (and each Caribbean country has its own unique culture) or other heritages as well. Similarly, one must attend to which Asian country or Latin country a person has roots in. This is true for all groups, and especially important as we help stigmatized groups retain and celebrate heritage. Ultimately, this appreciation of cultural diversity is a *multicultural perspective*.

5. A *feminist perspective*, which highlights the particular oppression of women but also conceptualizes phenomena in a different voice, seeks out the unity of such concepts as "the personal is political," and envisions power itself in limitless terms (Bricker-Jenkins and Hooyman 1986; Van Den Bergh and Cooper 1986).

6. A *global* perspective that focuses the worker on global interdependence and acknowledges social and economic injustice to be a worldwide problem. The concept of social exclusion is essential in developing a global perspective. Initially a French, and European concept, the concept has been tested in a range of non-European, "global South" countries and found to be universal in describing the marginalization of groups who are denied access to employment or have restricted job opportunities, exclusion from credit, consumer cultures, education, transportation, housing, welfare, and other social services. Social exclusion also describes disadvantage experienced because of difference caused by race, ethnicity, sexual orientation, age or disability, and discrimination against a person considered deviant including immigrants or members of ethnic or racial minorities. Exclusion may also occur because of a lack of participation in political processes. Such exclusion implies powerlessness and injustice. Ultimately, social exclusion is a global phenomena emanating from poverty that includes a variety of situations characterized by powerlessness and stigmatization (Elliot and Mayadas 1999).

7. A *critical perspective* is needed to critique all forms of oppression and develop strategies that link individual and social change (Longres 1995; Freire 1973a, b).

Radical social work thinking makes an important contribution to an empowerment approach. Radical social work sees the individual-versus-society split as a false dichotomy and advocates dealing with the connections between private troubles and the structural sources of trouble whenever possible (Mullaly and Keating 1991). This book subscribes to no single view but agrees that fundamental obstacles to human well-being include capitalism, patriarchy, and racism and that the general solution is an egalitarian society based on nonsexist, nonracist, nonhomophobic, and socialist principles. Disagreement exists mainly on how the solution should be achieved (Mullaly and Keating 1991:72).

Levels of Empowerment

The Personal Level

Dealing with the oppressions of class, color, or difference necessitates exceptional coping abilities. The onslaught of negative valuations can affect self-concept and sense of self-worth, though these are mediated by strong familial and community structures. Individual vulnerabilities and the direct obstacles posed by institutional racism and classism block opportunity structures, limit life choices, and pose threats to the development of competence, self-direction, and self-esteem. Person:environment transactions in the presence of oppression can never achieve a "goodness of fit." Oppression must be relieved. But people must also strengthen themselves to enhance potentialities, refuse oppression, and join with others in working toward its elimination. People's unique life experiences may combine with the internalization of oppression to block personal empowerment or to actualize it. Hence knowledge of adaptive capacities and of how people cope with particular oppressions is essential. This includes knowledge of how oppressed people with particular mental or physical challenges empower themselves. Lum stresses that people who have experienced oppression since early childhood must understand the meaning of events. He suggests that persons of color cope with oppression by thinking about who they are and the reality of a racist society, but they must also experience power by rising up and changing [the] situational predicament (2000). Further, the consumer and the social worker can act together to correct discrimination. Lum encourages practice that explores the themes of oppression, powerlessness, exploitation, acculturation, and stereotyping on all levels.

The Interpersonal Level

The structures that mediate against personal damage caused by oppression and the tremendous force of direct power blocks are strong family, group, and community structures and biculturality, the ability to live in two cultures: the nurturing culture of one's own group and the wider culture that oppresses even as it offers some opportunities for actualization (Chestang 1979; Logan 1990; Freeman 1990). It is therefore important to know how families, groups, and communities develop strengths to deal with oppression.

Power is defined in interpersonal terms as the ability to influence others to attain desired resources and goals. This ability begins with early attachments, which set the stage for the ongoing lifelong development of relatedness (James 1994). Those securely attached to loved ones and community are bolstered against the forces of oppression. The primary group, whether natural or formed, is a vehicle for enhancing relatedness and motivating, directing, and accomplishing change objectives (Lee 1987, 1990, 1991). Collective action depends on the affiliation of persons in groups (large or small) who come together to plan and take action toward change goals. Both consciousness-raising and critical education take place most effectively in groups. As consciousness about oppression is heightened, collective action is inevitable (Freire 1973a; Pence 1987). It is therefore natural and imperative that people empower themselves through group connection and collective action. Knowledge of how groups of all sizes form, develop, and achieve these tasks is therefore centrally important to an empowerment approach. The particular nature of the empowerment group is base knowledge in this approach.

The Political Level

Empowered people with knowledge about oppression and change processes can come together in small and large groups and take action as communities. Ultimately, oppression is a political problem that requires political solutions. Workers and clients alike must develop the knowledge and skills needed to affect political processes. Building coalitions and joining with others who have raised consciousness about issues of oppression multiplies political power around specific issues (Richan 1991; Staples 1984). Achieving a heightened level of political awareness, motivation, and ability completes the empowerment process. Through collectivity people draw the strength they need to empower themselves and attain actualized, unique personhood and social responsibility (beyond egocentricity to group, community, and social centricity: "If I am empowered, my people will be empowered, all people will be empowered").

In the Ciano case introduced in chapter 1, empowerment practice was directed at all three levels. Mrs. Ciano, a seventy-four-year-old great-grandmother, suffered a good deal of pain because of family problems. She had taken on the care of her thirteen-year-old great-granddaughter, Nicole, who could not control her behaviors and was "living on the street," with all of the sexual and physical exploitation that status implies. Her family was in turmoil and her own health and well-being were failing. Systems that were supposed to help were not helping. The child welfare agency involved protectively "passed the buck" to the family court, which passed it back to the child welfare agency to locate placement, yet nothing was happening. Mrs. Ciano was increasingly anxious and depressed at what she perceived to be her failure to keep her family safe and well and her difficulties in negotiating the systems involved. She blamed herself for everything that was going wrong and her sense of guilt was overwhelming. Niki was in great pain and needed a loving but structured approach that no one in her immediate or extended family could give. Placement options were poor, revealing major gaps in the service delivery system. It is obvious that interventions were needed with Mrs. Ciano, Niki, and other family members as individuals (personal level), with the family as a whole, including other community members who were trying to help (interpersonal level), and with the overburdened systems and workers who simply put this crisis situation "on hold" and ignored the cry for help (the wider systems and political level). The actual interventions will be discussed in chapters 3, 8, and 9.

Knowledge Base and Theoretical Foundations

The knowledge base and theoretical foundations include:

theory and concepts that encompass knowledge about person/environment transactions in situations of oppression, including structural change. This includes knowledge to develop "multifocal vision"; the history of oppression; ecological, ethclass, cultural, feminist, and critical theory perspectives, including knowledge of class structure and its effects; knowledge of individual adaptive potentialities, unique personhood, and the ways people cope—ego functioning, social and cognitive behavioral learning, and problem solving in the face of oppression; empowerment group, mutual aid, family and community group processes and dynamics; and larger systems, political and structural change processes so that we may assist people in empowering themselves on the personal, interpersonal, and socioeconomic political levels.

This knowledge base attends to issues of gender, ethnicity, and class—to the effects of racism, sexism, and poverty on adaptive potentials and on opportunity structures. It recognizes that being poor, a person of color, a woman, or a person of stigmatized difference are not peripheral statuses in people's lives. They are central to who people are and as such they relate directly to self-direction, self-esteem, and the empowerment that leads to social action and social change. Social workers are only one resource people may use in empowering themselves on these three levels. We are not responsible for the process of empowerment in a client's life, only for our potential contribution to it. Social work has a special go-between, or mediating, role between client and community and between people and systems that oppress (Reynolds 1934; Schwartz 1974a). Our need for knowledge and skill will be limited by our particular function as social workers. Teachers, community leaders, political leaders, community members, self-help organizations, religious organizations, and others must also take their place in assisting oppressed people toward full empowerment. Our unique role has the potential to help activate all empowering systems in a person's life.

The final constructs of the empowerment approach are the principles, roles, processes, and skills or the method of the approach. Chapter 3 defines and illustrates the skills and method of the approach.

What follows is a summary of the conceptual framework for the empowerment approach.

FIGURE 2.2

A Conceptual Framework:
The Empowerment Approach to Social Work Practice

Professional Purpose: Based on a dual simultaneous concern for people and environments: to assist people who experience poverty and oppression in their efforts to empower themselves to enhance their adaptive potentials and to work toward changing environmental and structural arrangements that are oppressive.

The Value Base: Preference for working with people who are poor, oppressed and stigmatized to strengthen individual adaptive potentials and promote environmental/structural change through individual and collective action; preference for holistic and tranactionally oriented concepts and knowledge about oppressed groups; preference for social policies and programs which create a just society where equality of opportunity and access to resources exists.

Knowledge Base and Theoretical Foundations: Theory and concepts about person: environment transactions in situations of oppression. This includes "multifocal vision": the history of oppression; ecological, ethclass, cultural, feminist, global, and critical theory perspectives; Knowledge about individual adaptive potentialities, unique personhood, and the ways people cope- ego functioning, social and cognitive behavioral learning and problem solving in the face of oppression; empowering individual, family, group and community helping processes; and larger systems and structural change processes in order that we may assist people in empowering themselves on the personal, interpersonal and political levels.

Method—Principles, Processes and Skills: The empowerment method rests on empowerment values and purposes and the eight principles that undergird the approach. The method may be used in the one to one, group or community relational systems. It depends on a collaborative relationship that encompasses mutuality, reciprocity, shared power and shared human struggle; the use of empowerment groups to identify and work on direct and indirect power blocks towards the ends of personal, interpersonal and political power; and collective activity which reflects a raised consciousness regarding oppression. The method uses specific skills in operationalizing the practice principles to address and promote action on all levels of living.

3   Empowerment Method: The How-To

> How-to-do-it is the bread and butter of the lawyer, the doctor, the engineer—and the social worker. Without it, they fail to differentiate themselves from the knowledgeable . . . layman. . . . The professional distinguishes himself not by his wisdom . . . but by his ability to perform . . . to help a person in trouble.
> —William Schwartz

> Caminante, no hay camino, se trace el camino al andar.
> [Traveler, there is no road. The road is made as one walks].
> —Antonio Machado

Applying the Empowerment Approach to Practice

How does the worker use the values, purposes, and theoretical foundations/knowledge base of the empowerment approach in actual practice? This chapter addresses the how-to of the empowerment approach, utilizing examples from practice. It is introductory to the specifics of practice how-to, as there are examples and explanations of skillful empowerment practice with systems of all sizes throughout the book, particularly in chapters 7–14.

Skill is "knowledge in action" (Phillips 1957; Henry 1992). Yet, one must also know how to do what needs to be done (Schwartz 1994). Knowledge in social work practice comes from accumulated professional knowledge, including empirically tested variables and practice wisdom, the knowledge base of a preferred theory or approach, knowledge about particular modalities, and knowledge about the people served and their environments. Henry notes that "a worker's wisdom developed through practice is a valid source of knowledge" (1992:vi). Applying such wisdom to practice is both art and skill (Schwartz 1994). The professional purpose, values, and principles of a social work approach are also forms of knowledge that strongly influence what we do in practice.

Since the empowerment approach incorporates aspects of Freire's criti-cal education conceptualization, it is important to note Freire's distrust of method (1973a, b, 1990, 1998). Freire cautions that North Americans seem to have an obsession with method and mechanistic techniques that may do injustice to the richness and complexity of his ideas and the unique and creative ways in which those ideas can be translated by various cultures and professions. Freire pleas, "Please tell your fellow American educators not to import me. Ask them to re-create and rewrite my ideas" (1998). His ideas can not be reduced to a "mere set of techniques associated with learning reading and writing"; they are about the fullness of being and political literacy as much as they are about the literate use of language (1998). To an extent Freire's method is antimethod. His aim is to help people become owners and makers of their own cultures. The critical ques-tions What? Why? To what end? For whom? Against whom? By whom? In favor of whom? and In favor of what? provoke learners to consider the "substantiveness of things," their reasons for being, their purpose, and the way things are done so that the disenfranchised may learn to read the world and take their rightful places in it. This can never be accomplished by rote adherence to a way of working with people. Neither can empowerment through social work intervention be promoted by technique. While dia-logue is the essence of empowerment method, the dialogic method loses its power if it is reduced to "a form of psychologically focussed group psychotherapy. The sharing of experiences must always be understood within a social praxis that entails both reflection and political action" (Ma-cedo and Araújo Freire, cited in Freire 1998:xiv, xv). As noted in the pref-ace to *Teachers as Cultural Workers*, "No pre-bought videotapes or work-shops can instantly empower teachers . . . one must become 'Freirian' by rigorous scholarship and a commitment to social justice" (1998:xxii). The varied threads of an empowerment approach to social work practice are woven together here, including the skills that may be used to help people empower themselves. We will describe processes but steer away from simple formulas or exact prescriptions that may minimize both the how-to and the outcomes of empowerment. We will rewrite Freire with as much faithful-ness as social work can muster in the translation of his method of critical education into social work processes and goals. Freire's method will be discussed and utilized here and throughout this book. We are mindful of the caution "Traveler, there is no road. The road is made as one walks" (Machado, cited in Freire 1998:xviii). Learners will learn best how to make interventions that help people empower themselves as they work with people themselves.

Middleman and Goldberg Wood (1990) note that skill may be attributed to the purposeful use of self, the qualities of what the "good" practitioner needs to be, a collection of behaviors derived from the analysis of the tasks at hand, or what the good practitioner needs to do, and, behaviors derived from the transactional context in which the worker and client exist or what the good practitioner needs to construct out of the emergent situation. Here is the perspective of a client, Lorna Rabinowitz, now sixty-two years old, who is an empowered woman and indigenous leader in a residential program for people with mental disabilities. I met Lorna when she resided in a New York shelter for homeless women where I provided individual and group service and consultation (Lee 1990, 1986, 1996). We have maintained our dialogue via mail and visits throughout the years. I continue to learn from her strength and her wisdom. We will learn from Lorna again in chapters 5, 9 and 10 of this book. Lorna says:

> Being a dedicated social worker can be very rewarding. The reward comes not from money but from helping people who are in need. However, these days, due to the large amount of paper work, the quality of services are low. Social workers spend a lot of time with chart work and little time with clients. Listening, understanding, and caring play an important part in helping, also not being judgmental. I know what I can and can't do. Allowing me to make my own decisions and have input in my treatment plan is important to me. Although I am open for suggestions, the final decisions are mine. Being informed about the services that are available for clients can also help a lot. Social workers can't help everyone, but they can be there when needed. Clients need a person who they can talk to without being looked down on. Giving me support works for me when I do well or not. Social workers sometimes prefer high functioning clients. This is not fair. All clients deserve an equal chance to get to their next steps in life.

Like Lorna, Middleman and Goldberg Wood define skills more as what workers do than what they are. While workers may have degrees of skill competency, Middleman and Goldberg Wood are more interested in whether the worker can utilize the indicated behavior in an appropriate context or not. They are interested in two levels of skill: inner skills, skills of perception and cognition, and interactional skills, the skills of working directly with clients. Regarding inner skills, multifocal vision supplies a perspective through which empowerment-oriented workers view people and their environments/contexts and hence how they think about all practice and intervention, including the use of strategies, techniques, and skills. Specificity is needed in order to learn what helpful attitudes and behaviors are and how to apply them in appropriate contexts. This chapter will be specific about skills utilized in empowerment practice. However, it is important to note that the why of the work is intricately connected to the how-to of the work. The why is derived from values and the practice principles of a given approach. As Middleman and Goldberg Wood note, "The effort here is to specify behavior through which social workers . . . can apply the principles of their practice orientation in response to the demands of people needing help with various problems and to the broader social imperatives for a just society" (1990:11). Thus we turn first to the principles of the empowerment approach.

Principles of the Empowerment Approach

Principles determine the structure of an approach and contain constraints ("shoulds") that prescribe the limits of choice of action open to the worker. The worker then uses principles creatively and skillfully in enacting the approach (Lewis 1972). There are empowerment principles, roles, processes, and skills that are generic to all social work practice and others that are specific to the relational system with which the worker is dealing: the one-to-one, family, small group, community, and program, policy, and political levels.

Principles that undergird an empowerment approach to social work practice are drawn from many sources, basic social work principles, a range of social work theories, practice itself, and civil rights, women's liberation, South American liberation theology, and critical education movements, including the work of Paulo Freire and others. These principles can guide us in thinking about situations of oppression, in making relationships, and in using empowering helping processes such as the development of critical thinking, praxis, and raised consciousness.

1. All oppression is destructive of life and should be challenged by social workers and clients. A parochial view of oppression that negates the experiences of other groups leads to divisiveness, fragmentation, and loss of power. We do not need to choose among oppressions but to share our expertise and unite against them.

2. The social worker should maintain holistic vision in situations of oppression. The development of multifocal vision is needed to maintain a holistic view. We should be able to see both the forest and the trees, the wider scene and the individual picture—and attend to both with our clients.

3. People empower themselves: social workers should assist. Beyond the principle of self-determination (Biestek 1957; Lee and Nisivoccia 1989), the principle of self-empowerment emphasizes the client's rights and responsibility in the process of human empowerment.

4. People who share common ground need each other to attain empowerment. This principle focuses on the power of collectivity in the empowerment process and the worker's role in assisting people through groups.

5. Social workers should establish a mutual and reciprocal relationship with clients. We need to value the unique personhood of each actor and the ways in which people help each other so that two whole persons of dignity and worth stand together against adversity and oppression.

6. Social workers should encourage the client to say her own word. People who are oppressed have learned to think and talk in the language of the oppressor. The client may need to work on re-naming and re-creating her own reality. The worker should observe rules of equity and symmetry in communicating; this frees the client to find her own voice.

7. The worker should maintain a focus on the person as victor and not victim. Clients do not choose to be oppressed, but only they can throw off internalized oppression or challenge the oppression forced upon them. To throw off the role of victim, the client should be helped to obtain the resources needed and take action.

8. Social workers should maintain a social change focus. Whereas principle 7 is directed toward the client's primary role in personal

and political change, principle 8 is directed to the role of both client and worker in working toward structural change, human transformation, justice, and liberation. While holding on to the client's struggles, the worker should connect clients to wider issues of oppression and take joint action toward social change.

Empowered people acting together are a force yet unreckoned with by those who maintain a status quo based on greed and exploitation. The social worker should support strong means of making nonviolent change, ranging from demonstrations to acts of resistance and civil disobedience, if these are needed. Neither inaction nor violence is an option for persons in a profession that upholds the value of human life. Strong actions that could have major consequences may be taken along with clients. Once information that raises consciousness is shared, decisions for political participation and action are up to the client. Some clients may understandably be too preoccupied with personal suffering to develop this level of critical understanding. In that case it is enough to work toward alleviating the suffering. As with Biestek's formulation on self-determination (1957), the worker's role is to open the doors and windows to let the air, light, and sunshine in. No one can breathe or see for another.

These eight principles all speak to having eyes to see and ears to hear the human situation that we enter in the role of social worker. It is no longer enough to listen with the third ear of understanding and discernment regarding the solitary individual. It is necessary to have a stance regarding oppression and the person who is oppressed. These principles are not written in stone, so they can be changed and developed by the wisdom of those who use them.

In discussing these eight principles, helping roles, processes, and skills were implied. We will now highlight them.

Empowering Roles

The roles of a *partner, collaborator, co-teacher, coinvestigator, dialogist, critical question poser, bridge builder, guide, ally and power equalizer, cobuilder, coactivist,* and *coworker* are needed to enact the principles of an empowerment approach to social work practice (Freire 1973a, b; Germain and Gitterman 1995). The prefix *co-* is used to indicate that these are roles

FIGURE 3.1
Principles of Empowerment Practice

The

lenses

through

which

we

view

social

work

practice

with

people

who

are

poor

and

members

of

oppressed

groups

Multifocal Vision:

1. A historical view of oppression including the history of social policy related to oppressed groups.

2. An ecological view encompassing knowledge of individual adaptive potentialities and ways people cope, and of power structures and their inequalities.

3. An ethclass perspective: realities of class structure, racism, ethnocentrism and classism as well as heterosexism.

4. A cultural perspective: valuing the different ways people structure their behavior, cognitions, beliefs, values, norms, rhythms and patterns of life and construct a world view. Culture is a broader perspective than ethnicity as it may apply to people on the basis of power, age, gender, sexual orientation, religion, region, and other divides among people. An empowering multicultural perspective mandates that each group should be accorded respect and dignity.

5. A feminist perspective: the oppression of women, the different voice, the personal is political. Power may be infinite.

6. A global perspective: knowledge that goes beyond local boundaries is needed for problem solving in this era of global interdependence and worldwide violations of human rights. A global perspective moves us beyond ego and ethnocentrism to cross-cultural competence in empowerment work and building the beloved community.

7. A critical perspective: the critique and conscious awareness of all of the above.

1. All oppression is destructive of life and should be challenged by social workers and clients.

2. The social worker should maintain holistic vision in situations of oppression.

3. People empower themselves: social workers should assist.

4. People who share common ground need each other to attain empowerment.

5. Social workers should establish a reciprocal relationship with clients.

6. Social workers should encourage the client to say her own word.

7. The social worker should maintain a focus on the person a victor not victim.

8. Social workers should maintain a social change focus.

clients share, with each partner bringing her own expertise and perspective to the processes of empowerment. These roles are additional to those of *mediator, advocate, resource broker, clinician, mobilizer, organizer, innovator, coach, facilitator,* and *enabler* that are used in direct social work practice (Germain 1984). We are partners against oppression, but in this dance leading and following may be fluid and interchangeable. The concept of co-teaching implies that clients and workers teach each other what they know about the presenting problem and about the oppression(s) faced.

Señora Luz: Co-Teacher and Activist

The following example illustrates several of the roles noted above and the skills used to enact the roles (bracketed). Workers' interventions are italicized. Skills are neutral tools that can be used within the bounds of many theories, while some roles belong to specific approaches. These skills were used to enact the principles and roles of empowerment-oriented practice. The principles illustrated are principles 1, 3, 4, 5, 6, and 8. Essentially, the worker acts as dialogist and ally to help Señora Luz strategize on an issue of community empowerment. Señora Luz is a sixty-eight-year-old Mexican-American community activist in a mixed ethnic lower-income community in southwest Florida. In this practice excerpt she is consulting with a social worker/program administrator in a community center about how to develop support for a community issue effecting elders.

"Did you know that the Town Council is meeting now, in these two weeks, to decide important issues for us?" asked Señora Luz. *I said I was not aware, but this was important.* [Offering validation and recognizing the client as co-teacher and coinvestigator], Señora Luz responded, "We don't usually go to these meetings and we don't vote enough." *I agreed.* [Validation]. She said this time she will make sure we rally around candidates that can help us, and that we vote. All seniors have the power of the vote and it is free. *I said that's a great idea, perhaps we could get a poll set up here* [Validation and enacting the role of cobuilder]. She was very excited about that as many seniors live near here and are not afraid to come here. She continued, "Transportation was on the agenda last night and I went with five other seniors and we raised the issues. We learned that there is a bill on the floor that could help us." She elaborated. *I said she was right to seize this moment with the council for these issues. Our people are often overlooked. I thanked her for informing me of the issue and the urgency. How could I help?* [Offering more validation of critical understanding and strategies and making an offer to help on her own terms. This enacts the roles of dialogist, critical educator, coworker, and coactivist]. Señora Luz replied, "We need to reach out to the whole community, not just Latinos, and we need to organize a campaign to write letters and make calls and send a petition. Also we could all go on next Thursday when this will be on the agenda before the vote." *I said those were excellent strategies. I gave her the names of Leon Pitt and Mary Perkins, who were leaders in the African American and Jamaican communities here. I said I could make the copier and a computer available to them and help with any technical assistance necessary.* [Validation of her strategies, giving information, acting as an ally and resource broker]. She asked for use of the telephones and *I agreed.* She then asked if they could have the big room for next Tuesday to hold a rally. *I said I would arrange it* [Making resources available, resource broker]. She asked me to be there and *I said I would and that I could call other administrators in the community* [Offer of help—ally and power equalizer]. She eagerly agreed. *I then asked Señora Luz if she thought the elder community leaders might be interested in forming a seniors club here at the center.* She said it would be a good idea to bring the elders together. She asked if a lunch program might be included and *I said I loved the idea and would look into it and get back to her.* She thought we really could pull this off and maybe it would be the start of a seniors group too. [I recognize indigenous leadership and suggest we build collectivity if she agrees—beginning a preparation stage for group work and community organizing, enacting roles of cobuilder, ally, bridge builder, innovator, and organizer].

———

In this example the worker and community leader collaborate on strategies to support action and build community. Roles and skills work hand in hand to achieve empowerment as a process and goal. The group work skill of recognizing and building upon indigenous leadership is central here (Pernell 1986). Señora Luz, as a community leader, is at the committed phase of self-empowerment and she seeks to help others in this process, going beyond her own needs to work toward community empowerment. Hence the dialogue to raise critical consciousness need not be lengthy. Yet it is important that she knows where the worker stands on the factors that make for the neglect of a community and that she and the worker are allies, helping each other, in the empowerment process.

Empowering Processes

In the empowerment approach empowering processes include Freire's critical education methods (1973a, b, 1998) as well as a blending of more traditional social work processes, roles, and skills. The essence of empowerment process and method is as follows. We are in a dialogue in which the client is helped to "say her own word" about her experiences of internalized and external oppression as we investigate oppressive conditions together. Each partner may pose questions that promote reflection, action, and the development of a critical consciousness. The worker learns what questions to pose from the client. The worker must build bridges to the client's unique experience and can guide the processes of consciousness-raising and praxis: action, reflection, and action repeated until change and raised consciousness occur. We are an ally, on the client's side, against suffering and oppression, and one whose aim is to strengthen capabilities. When we mediate or intervene with or for the client, we also add our strength to equalize the power differential the client faces in dealing with oppressive formal systems. We discover and build ego strengths, problem-solving skills, and strategies for change together. We develop strategies for additional coping tasks like those faced by people suffering from mental illness, substance abuse, or other biopsychosocial problems. We work together for change and take action together as is needed. Ultimately, the client will assume these roles for herself and with others in similar situations. The worker is then no longer needed except as another human being who can stand side by side in common struggle.

The *central processes* of this approach are developing individual potentialities and critical consciousness in the context of relationship through consciousness raising and praxis, strengthening individual capabilities, and problem-solving skills, building group, collectivity, and community, and taking action to change oppressive conditions. Skills and processes that undergird these central processes will be noted and illustrated here.

The Helping Relationship

Basic to all social work processes and outcomes is the process of building relationships. Relationships form the bridge on which all work takes place. Certain skills are needed in order to build relationships, especially when clients or group members have experienced discrimination and oppression. The worker needs to use multifocal vision (described in chapter 2) in order to see the client's realities and to convey understanding of the client's experiences. The skill Middleman and Goldberg Wood call "engaging in the medium of the other" is extremely useful in this regard (1991:49). This is a nonverbal or verbal method that increases the comfort of the other person. Essentially it is joining the client in an activity of interest by doing with or even talking about the activity the other person is engaged in. When the medium expresses an ethclass or cultural reality this "joining in" or "showing interest in" enables the worker to bridge a communication gap with a relationship-building skill. The worker may also propose a medium that is congenial to the client if there is discomfort, for example in an office setting. This might be to take a walk, to view a relevant exhibit at a museum, and so on.

The skills of relationship building are verbally and nonverbally conveying accurate and reciprocal levels of empathy on a frequent basis (Hepworth and Larsen 1986): sharing workers' feelings, clarifying workers' purpose and role, and reaching for feedback. Negotiating a mutually agreed upon contract is a process necessitating a set of skills in itself: it also enhances relationship building. The process of mutual contracting includes partializing clients' concerns and supporting clients in taboo areas (such as the experience of oppression). It might also include the skills of making empowerment an explicit part of the contract. Shulman (1992) divides these skills into two categories: the skills of helping clients to manage their feelings and of helping clients to manage their problems. Both sets of skills correlate to clients' positive feelings about the working relationship and positive outcomes. These skills that are critical in the beginning phase of work, and include relationship building and contracting, are also important in the ongoing and end phases of the work. They are particularly suited as well to issues of trust, and the charged content emerges while reflecting on experiences of oppression.

Henry's particular interest is knowledge about groups and how that influences worker's actions. She notes that a worker knows what to do in reference to four interacting variables: the stages of group development, the contract form in effect, the role and location of the worker, and the program media (activities) utilized (Henry 1992). The worker in the empowerment approach is located in a side-by-side stance and has a reciprocal and facilitating, often variable, role in the helping process. The worker moves, as quickly as the group is able to develop, to a more peripheral, almost consultative role so the group can empower itself to do the work it set out to do. The contract form moves from a reciprocal to a mutual and then interdependent one during the life of the group. The interacting variables noted by Henry can also relate to the helping process with systems of all sizes, with slight modification of the first and fourth variables. Worker's actions relate to whether we are at the beginning, middle, or end stages of the helping process and to what we are doing with the client.

Workers' Tasks and Phases of Work

Schwartz (1994; Shulman 1992) discusses the tasks of the worker in the helping process as related to where the worker and client are in the process. His attention to tuning-in/preliminary empathy and contracting is one of the earliest and clearest descriptions of worker's skills in beginnings in the literature. In tuning-in the worker prepares to enter the life process of his client using prior knowledge and empathy (knowledge and affect). She attempts to walk in her clients shoes. Freire calls this phase of entry "gathering thematics." In his approach the worker is a participant observer listening to the words people use about their lives in order to find the "generative themes" of the work—everyday themes that are vested with feeling and meaning, including political/structural realities. These themes may also be unearthed in "culture circles," a gathering of representative community members, including those who could be clients, to explore community themes. These are akin to "focus groups," but may be used for tuning-in based on actual experience of the community. In chapter 11 the worker uses Friere's methods to tune-in to the group of "alumnae" of a homeless women's shelter introduced in chapter 1. Whether these steps

are taken or tuning-in is done more traditionally, the worker uses his multifocal vision to tune-in to the history of the client's experiences as a member of an oppressed or marginalized group, to culture and ethclass variables,
to gender, and to the client's place in his society as well as to what the
worker's differences or similarities on those and other variables may represent in the client's life. The worker must also anticipate that the client
is completely unique and be prepared for the ways in which this person
does not fit into any preconceptions. Middleman and Goldberg Wood
(1990) speak of the skills of "looking with planned emptiness" (leaving a
space for not knowing), "looking at the old as if new," "jigsaw puzzling,"
and "looking from diverse angles," including looking with a zoom lens
(close-up to the person) or a wide-angle lens (seeing the whole picture) as
ways to see the novel, the unique, and the unplanned for expression or
event. We must also tune-in to the dynamics of offering services when the
client reaches out for them (when they are voluntary), when they must be
proffered, and when they are mandated or involuntary services, particularly
since people must choose to empower themselves and that empowerment
can not be mandated or legislated. Germain and Gitterman (1995) delin-
eate the workers' skills in these different circumstances. Taken together, all
the skills noted here may assist clients in making a good start in empowerment-oriented helping processes, essential in tuning-in before and during
encounters with clients.

Mrs. Ciano and Niki: Tuning-In

In my work with Mrs. Ciano and Niki (introduced in chapter 1) I
thought there would be some level of comfort as they have seen me as a
part of their church community where others have been helped. Mrs. C.
sought the service through the church, a shared belief system in a normative setting. Niki, however, was not a voluntary client. She may experience all adults in her life as coercive and disapproving. They may not
have known the services a social worker has to offer, but, as members of
the the Italian-American working-class/lower-middle-class and/or poor community, they might have distinct ideas about my use of authority and my
ethnic difference. I would need to understand the Italian-American experience, especially in Hartford. We are all female, and this may increase
comfort, but I am a generation younger than Mrs. C. and two generations

older than Niki. Youth culture constantly changes. The materialism of to-day's youth disturbs me, especially when drug culture and other types of hustling are the only way a child like Niki could wear expensive designer clothes and heavy gold chains (Anderson 1990). Can I suspend my judg-ments on the value of such materialism long enough to hear the pain of this child and her peers? How would I now relate to a thirteen-year-old girl who wants to "hang in the streets"? How have her early experiences influ-enced her present behaviors? Is she feeling frightened and out of control? This child seems attached to no one. And it is no wonder, she has lived on the promises of a mother who spent most of Niki's thirteen years in jail, her grandmother seems not to even like her (and I need to find out when this powerful anger began), and her great-grandmother has tried to make up for all of it. But is that ever possible? Is Niki secure in anyone's love?

I know the pain of seeing a beloved child one has raised sucked into the strong undertow of life on the streets. Yet I only had this child in a fostering arrangement for a few years of his life. How much more it must hurt and anger and promote guilt and the "what ifs" when it is a lifelong blood tie. Maybe offering her a group of parenting grandparents facing similar issues might soften this blow. I know that "losing the children to the streets" is a recurring community theme. Can I use my experiences as a bridge, yet see this very unique situation as theirs alone? Can I build the bridges?

The Skills of Contracting for Empowerment

The essential skill in beginnings is to discover what help is desired and make a clear uncomplicated offer of service so people can determine if they are in the right place, lower anxiety and ambivalence, and begin to approach the work. The process and goal of empowerment may be dis-cussed explicitly at this point or it may be negotiated later in the process. The worker and client then negotiate together on what this helping en-counter is all about, what the client wants, what their respective roles and tasks are, and what they can expect of each other (Schwartz 1994; Henry 1992; Germain and Gitterman 1995). Getting-to-know-you and ice-break-ing activities may be helpful in prompting an approach to the work and in building trust (Henry 1992). These activities may include an introduction to issues of empowerment.

Contracting with Niki

(The reader is referred to chapters 1 and 2 for work descriptions of the work with Niki and her great-grandmother, Mrs. Ciano).

This is our first time to talk as Niki appeared only briefly at the end of the first family meeting. *I chose a relaxed outdoor spot in a picnic area of a nearby park for our first meeting. I brought some snacks and arts and crafts supplies, including glitter markers and a simple key chain project.* [Proposing a medium congenial to the other—the park and activities]. Niki was dropped off by a church staff member. She reluctantly came over to see what I was doing. Tall and dark, she was dressed in a tight orange mini-dress and heels. A study in contrasts, she carried a Winnie-the-Pooh knapsack with a little Pooh Bear sticking out. *I smiled at her and asked if she remembered me from the family meeting* [Establishing who I am]. She nodded yes and asked to see a marker. *I gave her the markers and paper and said she could use everything she saw here* [Offering the activities]. She inspected the supplies and smiled, choosing several markers to draw her name. *I complimented her on her art work and asked her whole name* [Sustainment and getting to know her]. She wrote it, adding, "Silk," surrounded by stars. *I asked if that was her street name* [Establishing I knew something about youth culture]. She said, "Word up" (yes). *I drew my name and wrote "social worker" after it; I asked if she understood what that was* [Working in her medium; introducing my role and clarifying, making sure she knew what I could help with]. She said, "Yes, you help people—like getting me the summer job." *I said yes, and by talking about what's happening with her and how she felt about what was happening.* She said nothing was happening. *I said she knows that I have been talking with her Grandma R. and her Nona P., so I knew things were happening.* She laughed and said she's in trouble because she wants to be on her own. *I asked what it was like on her own* [Exploring]. She said she had fun and described a weekend trip to Bridgeport where she went to a party. She said everyone thought she was eighteen. *I looked at her incredulously* [Getting real, gentle confrontation]. She replied, "Well, they didn't care that I'm sixteen." *I looked again* [not buying it], and she said, "OK, fourteen." *I said, "Try thirteen, and without permission* [Starting contracting on a problem area]. She laughed and said,

"Caught." *I nodded yes, smiling, and asked if she understood why her Nona asked me to help* [Exploring to establish a contract offer and to promote reflection on the situation]. She picked up the key chain project and asked me to show her how to do it. *I did* [Working at her pace and in her medium]. As she worked she said, slowly, "Because my Nona can't keep me any more." *I said that was true and that I would like to help her and Mrs. C. get along until we can find her a good place to live. I added, that she is going through many changes and I would like to go through them with her and help her with them* [The contract offer]. *I asked what she thought* [Asking for feedback and reciprocity on purpose]. She shrugged and said Mrs. C. was mad at her because she goes out at night but she can handle it. *I asked what she could handle* [Getting the specifics, exploring]. She said the night. *I said we were concerned about her getting hurt and getting AIDS or other diseases* [Naming the taboo, contracting further]. She said she didn't do needles. *I asked what she did do* [Exploring for drug abuse] and she laughed and said, "Weed." *I asked how much* [exploring], and she said she didn't really use it. *I said I wasn't so sure about that* [Not buying it but not pushing it for now]. She laughed again. *I asked if she knew how else people got AIDS* [Exploring in a taboo area]. She said no. *I said through having sex* [Giving information; opening a taboo area]. She laughed again and said then she would never get it. *I looked at her incredulously* [Not buying it]. She gave me her key chain to straighten out and *I did, complimenting her work* [Sustainment; Working at her pace and in her medium]. And she said, "Well, maybe once, a long time ago." *I said nights and streets and sex can go together* [Continuing to explore]. She looked at me like I was crazy. I said, *"I may be old but I'm not dumb"* [Using humor to stay in the taboo area]. She laughed and said she liked men. *I asked, "And . . . ?"* [Exploring]. She said, "And I don't do the nasty." *I said we could talk about it when she was ready* [Allowing for her pace]. She said OK and opened the snacks.

As she ate she started drawing a house. As she drew she said she has a rash in a bad place and it hurts too, so she couldn't have sex even if she wanted to. *I said I'm sorry she was hurting. It was important to see the doctor. I asked if I could tell Mrs. Ciano so she could take her* [Direct influence and suggesting a way to work]. She said, "She knows already. That's another thing she's mad at." They already went to the doctor and she got a shot—I could ask her Nona about it. *I said I would.* Niki drew herself, her two brothers, and a man and woman in the house. *I asked her to tell me about the picture* [Asking for her story]. She said it was her mother and father and brothers. She added that her mother just had a baby in the prison but the baby's father has it so she's not drawing the baby. She said the man in the picture was her father. *I asked her to tell me about her father and when she last saw him* [Exploring]. She said he was Irish and German but she didn't know his family. He worked construction sometimes. She saw him about six months ago before he went back to jail. She visited when his wife had a baby. She noted his wife was very nice to her. She is Puerto Rican, so now she has three Puerto Rican half-siblings, since Joe and Tony had Puerto Rican fathers too. She wrote "My Home" on the picture. *I said it was a very nice picture* [Sustaining]. She said yeah, but she'll have to wait 'til they get out to make it come true. *I asked if she thought it could come true* [Reality testing]. She said yes, but added in a low voice that she hadn't seen her mother in a long time. *I said, gently, that's hard. You miss her?* [Empathy and checking out the feeling]. She nodded. *I asked if she would like to see her* [Exploring]. She said yes enthusiastically. *I said if she could follow her Nona's rules for three weeks I would arrange to take her for a visit at the prison. I elaborated on which rules* [Contracting and developing a behavioral plan]. She said she could do it. *I said it wouldn't be easy and we would meet and talk every week at this same time and I would help her. I wanted to be in her corner as she faced some hard times* [Offering my support and contracting]. She agreed, showing me how nice her key chain turned out. *I said it was beautiful* [Sustaining]. She asked if she could take another one home to do. *I said yes, if you bring it back so I can see it* [Making a small gift and showing interest]. She smiled and agreed, running to show the arriving staff member her project.

The contracting process here shows a range of interventions, some of which are related to beginning with a child. Although Niki is a thirteen year old with the problems of one much older, she is also a child whose attention and ability to talk abstractly is limited by her age and level of educational attainment. The use of a nonauthoritarian setting and arts and crafts materials and snacks helped engage her and make talking easier (Lieberman 1979). The worker took a risk that "kid stuff" would further alienate this streetwise child, but it actually did what it was intended to do—establish a nonthreatening and interesting atmosphere for work. It also made it

OK to be a child. Similarly, the worker did not buy evasions or minimize Niki's life-threatening behaviors. While she accepted the child with her negative behaviors, she also avoided the trap of siding against the great-grandmother by noting that they talked, she was informed, and they would proceed by including Mrs. Ciano in the plans. She was aware of the multiple social stressors in Niki's life (Canino and Spurlock 1994). She opened and stayed with taboo areas and made her role and offer of service clear. The contract pertained to immediate behavioral goals as well as longer-term goals regarding placement. She found Niki's stake in establishing a behavioral contract—the reward of seeing her mother. And she offered to help Niki get that important reward, not just set her up for failure. Niki experienced her as an ally establishing the beginnings of trust in the helping process.

Relating Skills to the Phases of Empowerment Development

Parsons, Jorgenson, and Hernandez (1994) note that there are phases in the self-empowerment process that include entry with a problem, advancement of critical awareness, incorporation of critical comprehension into the self in a way that effects daily living, and commitment to a continuous use of empowerment skills and abilities in living and in helping others to do the same. In the example below Mrs. Ciano is in the process of advancing her critical awareness. Citing Torre (1985), Parsons, Jorgensen and Hernandez note that phases of empowerment involve positive perceptions of personal worth, efficacy, and internal locus of control as well as validation of one's perceptions and the ability to think critically and influence systems of all sizes. Workers' actions need to be related to where the client is in the process of developing critical awareness. Four components of empowerment practice are offered as organizing principles for practice strategies and use of skills: power-shared relationships, competency-based assessment, collectivity for mutual aid, and education for critical thinking with the accompanying knowledge and skills for finding resources and taking action. These components locate the role of the worker as power sharer, mutual aid facilitator, and critical educator. Hence teaching, training, and education with systems of all sizes and the use of groups, community organizing, and other large system strategies, such as legislative lobbying and campaigning, are appropriate strategies for empowerment practice. Each strategy requires a set of skills, for example, such skills as giving/sharing information, dealing with feelings and conflict, and promoting critical consciousness.

A *Dialogical Encounter*

This is an example of a leader using a critical education approach in a dialogical encounter in a base community in South America (Brown 1984). It is Freirian in question-posing method and based in liberation theology. The method here is applicable for work with groups and communities in social work. It is also a subtle example of power sharing. The group itself exemplifies an advanced phase of critical consciousness.

First the leader asks the group's reflections on the date, September 12. One person responds that it is the date of Allende's murder in Chile. Another reflects that Allende is like Martin Luther King Jr. The leader *asks why.* A person responds, "Because both were concerned with oppressed peoples." The leader *reaches for other associations to the date.* A member responds that it is the feast of the Holy Name of Mary. The leader *reaches for connections among the three names associated with the day* [Skills of critical question posing]. A member responds that there would only be a connection if Mary were also concerned with oppressed peoples. The leader *reads* a lesser-known section of the Magnificat— Mary's Song. "God has scattered the proud in the imagination of their hearts, put down the mighty from their thrones, and exalted those of low degree; has filled the hungry with good things, and the rich has sent empty away" (Luke, chapter 2). A member responds that Mary in the "holy pictures" doesn't look like a person who would talk that way. The leader *asks for their reflections on the picture they are holding up* [Using a code]. One responds, "In the picture she is standing on a crescent moon, wearing a crown, rings on her fingers, and a robe embroidered with gold." The leader *asks if the picture has betrayed the Mary of the song.* Group members suggest that her position on the moon is incorrect, as she would not have left all her friends, and that she would not be wearing a crown or golden rings and garments. The leader *asks what the Mary of the song would look like* [Another critical question related to the picture and reading as codes]. Members respond that she would be standing in the dirt and dust where we stand. She would wear an old hat so she didn't faint from the heat and she would be wearing old clothes like they are. One woman concludes, though she says it is "awful to say, Mary would look just like me!" The leader responds, "No, *I don't think it is awful to say that. I think the Mary you have described is more like the Mary of the Bible than the Mary we hear about in the cathedral or see in the holy pictures*" [Validating their work].

A member responds, "I think she'd be more at home here in the slum with us than in the cathedral or the General's Mansion. . . . She says God would fill the hungry with good things." *The leader responds, "Now, let's see, how could we begin to help God bring those things to pass?"* (Brown 1984:85–88). [In the final intervention the leader moves the group from reflection to thoughts of action.]

Working on the Personal and Political Level

The above example illustrated many things, including the skillful use of codes and critical questioning (Freire 1973a, b, 1998). This is another example of using a code (chapter 1 and Freire 1973a, b) with an individual client, Mrs. Ciano, whose story is introduced in chapter 1. We can see in this example that Mrs. Ciano has a good level of critical awareness, and here we work on advancing this awareness by decoding the living drama of the streets. This strategy was used midway in the work, after many systems negotiations were made together. As noted in chapter 1 and 2, Mrs. Ciano continued to berate herself and drown in guilt. The point here was to broaden the problem definition and externalize the problem:

On this day I suggested Mrs. Ciano meet me a few blocks away from the church and walk with me to where we would meet. *As we walked I asked Mrs. Ciano what she saw* [Suggesting a living code]. She replied, some nice houses, some dilapidated eyesores, some old friends, and some people that looked like addicts, scary and ugly. She told me stories of how beautiful the neighborhood used to be. *I said it was sad* [Conveying empathy]. *I asked her what she thought made the difference* [Promoting reflective consideration and critical reflection]. She said the drug trade was the problem. There is a residential program for addicts nearby. As we reached it she commented on the "ruined lives," adding tearfully that Niki's mother Kim went there once. *I said Kim's life is a very sad one* [Empathizing]. Mrs. Ciano wiped her eyes *and I held her arm as we walked. I asked what she thought kept the drug trade so alive here.* She thought a while and looked me in the eye and replied, "Greed." *I asked her to explain* [Promoting critical reflection]. She said the addicts were greedy for the drug, the pushers were greedy for their cut, the ones who owned the business were greedy for power, and so were the people who put drugs here in the first place. I said, "Wow, I think you are right" [Validation]. "Who do you think put them here?" She broke eye contact and said, "Rich people." *I asked why they put the drugs here* [Another critical question], and she replied, "Cause we are stupid enough to buy them." *I said rich folks buy them too, lots of them* [Challenging internalized oppression]. She said "Yeah, but sometimes I think poor kids don't count to anyone. They don't have a chance. This is no longer a land of opportunity if you are poor." *I said I think she has something there—but why?* [Validation and posing a critical question]. She said so they can keep all the money and power and have servants like maids and waiters and garbage men. She added that she used to clean rich people's houses and elaborated. *I said she had just beautifully described why Niki's problems are bigger than her or her family* [Critical education; Direct influence]. She looked at me puzzled, then laughed and said, "Yeah, you're right—they are part of the whole scene where the pushers pimp the young girls to grow their business. *I agreed and shared my own experience with our foster child and "the undertow"* [Appropriate self-disclosure]. Mrs. Ciano said it was an undertow into a cesspool and began to share her own anger at the "drug people," speaking with much feeling and animation. *I added, as hard as they try, that she, and every parent and grandparent around here are up against some very strong forces. They did not cause the problem of kids turning to the streets and sometimes they can't stop it* [Validation; Information; Sharing a liberating point of view; Direct influence]. She thoughtfully agreed and added, "I oughta stop beating up on myself, huh?" *I said, "Exactly," and we both laughed* [Validation of her work].

The skills utilized are italicized and explained in brackets. The use of the street scene as a code to be deciphered and the use of critical questions and brief self-disclosure successfully broadened and deepened the work and minimized self-blame so problem solving could continue on a personal and political level.

There was a group of people from the church who, along with the priest and staff, and members of other churches and community organizations, were doing a nightly "walk and shout" on drugs, exposing the "crack houses" and saying the community did not want them here. Mrs. C. said she was old but not too old to go and stand with them now that she understood how her own life was turned upside down by the drug trade. Here we also see a more politicized Mrs. C. who moves beyond her problem to the community issue.

Contracting for Empowerment with a Group

This is a group in a shelter for homeless women and children. Such groups are open-ended but may have a nucleus of women who have been in them for several weeks. Therefore, it is sometimes difficult to determine which stage of development such a group is in. It is necessary to make a contract offer on both levels of empowerment in each meeting when new members are present. There are eight women present for this meeting (four African American women, three Puerto Rican women, and one Italian-American woman. They range in age from nineteen to forty-six. Three are new today.) The coworkers are a Franco-American woman experienced in working with groups who recorded the meeting and an African American woman learning the empowerment group process.

I began by welcoming the three people who are new to the group today and asked them to tell a little about themselves and why they're here [Bringing new members aboard; Asking for their stories]. As each one shared, the others echoed their stories. *I said, "Everyone here has had a difficult time before coming here"* [Empathizing]. *"This group is an opportunity to talk about the things they have experienced and the problems they face that make finding housing difficult. Some of the problems are personal, like the ones with relationships you have already described or trouble with drug and alcohol abuse for yourself or someone close to you*" [Pointing out the common ground; Offering handles to get the work started; Developing the contract]. Daria said, "That's me!" And Maritza said, "Me too. I just got out of a drug program and have nowhere to go." *I said it was coura- geous to share that. It is a hard struggle, and one we will work on together here* [Contracting; Offering encouragement on sharing personal strug- gles]. *My coworker said, "Drugs are oppressive"* [Making a political state- ment; Critical education]. Daria said, "They made me a slave." Maritza said, "And they made me a fool!"

Janine said, "My mother married a guy who drinks. He gets so nasty and makes a play for me. That's why I left. But what I'm upset about is that they lost my application for a Section 8 certificate and I have to start all over again." Mary said, "No, you don't. You should contact the su- pervisor; I bet they'll find it." Others echoed this advice. *I said, "The systems they have to deal with are often inefficient and cause frustration"* [Empathizing; Educating regarding system's abuse]. *"Helping each other to deal with these systems is an important part of our work too"* [Contract- ing; Lending a vision]. *"But sometimes this kind of treatment represents bigger things that go on in our society, like racism and sexism or discrim- ination, which can also influence how you feel about yourselves"* [Devel- oping the wider/political level of the work]. They were nodding and Ma- tilda said, "You feel like you're no good." *I said, "This is the time to talk about and question such things and get an understanding of what's going on. You're up against big barriers to your success"* [Suggesting a critical approach; Defining the struggle]. Janine said, "*Barrier* is a good word for it. I think the secretary I spoke to is prejudiced against blacks. I think I'll go in person so she can at least see me. Maybe I'll offer to help her look for it." After the laughter, *my coworker said that going in person was a good idea—to make yourself known as a person, not a black voice on the phone. She shared an experience from her own life in which a personal appearance made a difference. She then told a story of a storekeeper's rudeness to all his black customers. She said it took her a while, but even- tually she stood her ground and this stopped his behavior* [Disclosing her own experiences with oppression and how she handled it]. Mary said, "It's hard to stand your ground. That was brave." *I said, "It is, and these are good examples of handling oppression"* [Clarifying, Naming].

Mary asked what oppression meant, if it was like depression. *I said, "Oppression, discrimination, or disadvantage because of race or sex or being poor can certainly cause depression or deep sadness." I asked what oppression was to them* [Defining and asking them to define]. Matilda said, "Oppression is living in one room with four kids, and no heat or hot water. That happened to me, and I got so depressed someone had to rescue me and pull me out of that building. I thank God for that person and for this shelter." Janine said, "It is oppression to be disregarded." *I asked, "Lost in the shuffle?"* [Clarifying; Reaching for feeling]. Janine said, "Exactly, like a piece of useless paper." Daria then began to cry and say that that was how she felt. Everyone drew close to her. *My coworker said, "Substandard living conditions are oppressive"* [Defining; Critical education]. Mary said, "I get so mad I want to hit the landlord with my fist and make him do right by us." Janine said, "Or slap him with a big fine, take him to court! We pay the rent; we should get the services!" Everyone agreed. *I said, "Now you're talking!"* [Validating the feelings and beginning to Define and encourage action].

Clearly, the connection between oppression and depression discovered by group members is a valid one. Hence the contracting process included both oppression and depression (the political and the clinical). In the middle phase interventions are also made on the personal (clinical) and political levels of work.

A Later Stage Group in a Transitional Living Program for Homeless Women

The social worker is R., an African American woman in her mid-thirties who is also the program director. The group consists of eight women. Four African American women in their twenties, three Puerto Rican women ranging in age from twenty to forty-three, and Kate, a white woman of Irish-American background in her mid-forties. She has been in the program two months. The other members of the group have been in the group for several months. The *critical question* posed is, "What power blocks contributed to your homelessness?" Kate's openness brings the group into a *taboo area* that they have avoided.

Kate said, "My husband had all the power. Do you know, this is the first time in my life I've ever been free and on my own? I got married when I was twenty years old. I stayed married to my first husband twelve years and three kids later until he left me for a younger woman. Then I met my present husband—that jerk—a month after I was divorced, so I got into another relationship and had another child right away. . . . Twelve years of his rule. This is the first time that I've ever had to do anything for myself. I didn't have to pay for the car (she begins to sob) or the rent. He hasn't given me any money since we broke up and it's been so hard." Nilsa gave her some tissues and was crying with her. *I said, "It's OK to cry. It's hard to be on your own when you're used to someone doing everything for you"* [Empathizing and generalizing the theme]. "How could I have been so stupid to fall for this guy? You know, I read an article about recognizing the signs of a batterer. He lost his mind and practically killed me. The signs were all there."

The worker asked, "Would you like to tell us what some of those signs were, Kate?" [Opportunity for work; Asking her to share information]. "Well, he began to not want me around my family and I used to just think that it was because he loved me so much that he wanted to spend time with me. When I met him he seemed to be the nicest guy, because he always brought things for me and the kids. Now I see it was all about control. I used to have to have sex with him every damn day and every damn night. It wasn't love; it was control, just like the article said. If I resisted he would threaten me. That's when I knew he was sick. Just the thought of it—I hated it." (She began to sob again.) *I was watching the expressions on Maria's face.* Her eyes lit up and widened when Kate mentioned being made to perform sexually. *Our eyes met* [Scanning the group]. Maria began shaking her head in agreement. "I know what you mean. My husband, he started trying to control me. He became very jealous, he made me quit my job, and he tried to keep me to himself all the time. When he started hitting me, that's when I said that I wasn't going to continue to let it happen. He'd always say I'm sorry and he would do better for a little while, but then in about a week he would start up again." Debby said, "That's how men are. They can look at any women they want to but they don't want you to look at anyone. My kids' father know that I don't like a man who drink and do drugs. He used to do that and want to fight me. He hit me too. But he doesn't do that anymore because I won't take it." Sandy sits up and dives right in. "Yes, I don't take anything from a man because they try to own you and control you. I work and can get anything I want for me and my kids." Kate said, "I sometimes say to God, 'Why did you let this happen to me?' but I believe that everything happens for a reason. If I hadn't had this experience I wouldn't have ever felt good about myself again. Now I know he was the sick one." The women reflected on how they were made to feel crazy when they tried to leave the abusive partner. Maria said she knew leaving him was the smartest thing she ever did. At the end of the meeting *I said, "I would like to thank all of you for sharing your hurts and some healing with each other and for Kate sharing the information about battering with us. Several of you began to recognize the signs and grow in awareness."* They nodded. *Then I said, "You did some good work here tonight"* [Encouragement and crediting the work].

This group is in the *maintenance or work phase of group development* (Henry 1992). We note that the women are highly supportive of one another and that the flow of communication is more member to member than member to worker. The worker is located in a more peripheral position. She enters to deepen and facilitate the work, but she is not center stage. The members have developed a mutual aid system through which they help each other. The worker uses empathic and exploratory/reflective skills to help the women tell their stories with the attendant feelings. She also promotes consciousness-raising and critical awareness through having the women share knowledge on batterers and how to leave abusive situations.

Incorporating Clinical and Political Skills in Empowerment Intervention

As we reflect on the examples of work with Mrs. Ciano and the women's groups, we see the worker using both clinical and political skills. For clarity here we separate the two types of skills, but we bear in mind that they can work hand in hand.

When working with clients (individuals and families) Hollis found that helping procedures could be placed in six very useful metacategories: sustainment, direct influence, exploration, description, and ventilation, person/

situation reflection, pattern dynamic reflection, and developmental reflection (Hollis and Woods 1981). These categories were used in describing the
beginnings with Niki in the example given above and in most of the other
examples as well. Empathic, or sustaining, skills are necessary to support the
client in doing difficult work and to build and maintain trust. They have
been found to be the most effective of the helping skills (Woods and Hollis
1990; Shulman 1996). They are used throughout the work in most approaches to social work practice, including this one. Feelings and cognition
are relevant in all six areas, but the latter three of Hollis's procedures focus
on cognitive and problem-solving skills. Direct influence is used sparingly
in the helping process, just as seasoning is used carefully in preparing a good
meal. Too much of it can disempower. This is also true in implementing a
critical education approach as education is primarily direct influence unless
people are helped to discover truths for themselves. This typology is useful
in working across relational systems, as it also can apply to work with groups
and communities regarding the content level of the work.

The skills of sustainment are empathic and feeling oriented, including
reaching out, acceptance, and encouragement. For example, the worker
gently asking Niki if she misses her mother is also conveying empathy and
sustaining. The skills of direct influence include direct advice, less direct
advice, teaching, coaching, or persuading. Suggesting a reward system for
Niki's obedience of her great-grandmother's house rules and saying that a
visit to the doctor is important are examples of direct influence. The skills
of exploration include posing questions that follow the client's thoughts and
feelings or that elicit them in order to help a client "get it off his chest"
(ventilate) or describe and clarify the facts of the situation. Asking Niki if
she wants to see her mother or when she last saw her father are exploratory
questions. With exploratory and reflective questions we begin to engage a
client's cognition in problem-solving processes.

Sustaining skills are basic throughout all work with clients. The skills that
promote the client's thinking are especially important in empowerment processes. The reflective skills do this to a degree. When Niki is asked if she
understands why she is seeing the social worker, the worker is beginning to
promote Niki's reflection on the person-situation gestalt. However, Hollis's
use of reflective thinking leads more to focusing on the person than to changing unjust wider conditions, although Hollis notes that her procedures work
with the environment as well. In an empowerment approach the worker
promotes reflection, thinking, and problem solving on person/environment

transactions, including the client's role in them and the experience of oppression. Along with the client's self-defined problem focus, oppressive conditions and proposed solutions are the content of the reflective procedures. The reader is invited to review the preceding examples of practice with the Hollis classification and its connection to empowerment in mind. You will find that the same intervention can be understood using a variety of intervention categories. Thus, for example, most of the interventions with Mrs. Ciano and the women in the transitional living facility can be seen as both clinical and political. The use of consciousness-raising and critical education skills with Mrs. Ciano, in the example where Mrs. Ciano and the worker take a walk together, can also be viewed from a clinical point of view. The questions asked were also used to promote ventilation, or the expression of pent-up feelings, and to promote reflective consideration of the person:environment situation. The empathy and validation given was sustaining. The advice given to Mrs. Ciano of externalizing the blame to the drug culture was a form of direct influence utilized to bolster self-esteem and reduce self-blame. Both personal and political benefits can come from the same intervention.

Processes and Skills to Promote Coping and Adaptation/Social Change

People must attain certain attributes in order to cope and adapt. In turn, the environment must provide correspondingly favorable conditions to facilitate adaptation, including changing the environment. The attributes achieved by good enough person:environment transactions are motivation, which corresponds to the incentives and rewards provided by the environment, problem-solving skills, which corresponds to the strengths and efficacy of society's socializing institutions (including the family and schools), maintenance of psychic comfort (including managing feelings) and a favorable level of self-esteem, which corresponds to the kind and degree of emotional and other support in the environment, and self-direction, which corresponds to the provision of information, choices, adequate time, and space (Germain 1984, 1991; White 1974; Mechanic 1974). It is also helpful to understand the clusters of behaviors that make up some of our coping skills. In some frameworks these are called ego functions (Goldstein 1995). The development and exercise of these and other ego functions also correspond to environmental nutrients or insults and deprivations. Some important ego functions are competence, reality testing, impulse control, the management of affect/feelings, particularly sadness, anger, and anxiety, and judgment. These and other ego functions and how to assess them are discussed in chapter 5 and applied in chapters 8 and 9. The work with Niki included encouraging and developing competence in the areas of arts and crafts and the development of beginning work skills in her summer job, strengthening her judgment and impulse control through talking things out, clarifying limits, establishing structures, and behavioral rewards, and helping her to express instead of act out her feelings. The social worker may be helpful in strengthening the client's coping and in obtaining the corresponding provisions of society to sustain the client's life (Germain 1984:125–163.)

Empowering Skills to Bolster Motivation: Keeping Hope Alive

Skills particular to the empowerment approach that help bolster a client's motivation must encompass and extend beyond skills used in ordinary situations. First, motivation can only be sustained if basic needs for housing, food, clothing, and support (financial and emotional) are met. As these needs are met—through mutual skills of gaining resources and opportunities and attending to presenting problems—the worker can keep hope alive by acknowledging and discussing external causes of oppressive conditions as they are reflected in the presenting problems. This is the essence of the work with Mrs. Ciano described above. With Niki, the location and provision of resources including an appropriate placement was essential to providing motivation for behaviors that would be life giving instead of destructive of the child's life. Similarly, battered women must have a safety plan in order to sustain life and maintain hope. Encouraging the client's own words about the problems and her life and accepting the client's problem definition also provide motivation. We see this in the examples of May and Shandra in chapter 7 as well as in the work with the Ciano family. The worker can also reach for and convey understanding of feelings of difference, isolation, and alienation and being misunderstood as well as her experiences of discrimination at the hands of systems needed to sustain life and growth. The case of Shandra in chapters 8 and 9 illustrate this well. As the worker partializes the stressful demands into workable segments with the client, she also encourages the client to share how she has dealt before with similar problems.

The skill of having the client name and own her strengths also provides motivation to continue. Hope of changing the oppressive systems must also be offered through the worker's skills, which lend a vision of how these systems might be changed, and by beginning to enlist the client's energy in this thinking. The worker might also use skills of appropriate self-disclosure around dealing with oppressive conditions to build bridges to the client's experiences and to offer further hope of change. When the African American worker shares her own experiences with a bigoted storekeeper with members of the women's shelter group described earlier in this chapter, their understanding of her courage sparks their own. As in the case of Mrs. Ciano, the worker also uses skills of systems' negotiation with the client so that the client gains expertise in this area. The worker could also work directly with agencies to increase their responsiveness to client needs.

Empowering Skills to Maintain Psychic Comfort and Self-Esteem

In helping the client to maintain psychic comfort, manage feelings, and attain an optimal level of self-esteem, the worker has the additional tasks of externalizing the sources of oppression in order to reduce self-blame and foster pride in the client's oppressed group membership. Here she has the role of co-teacher and critical educator as she helps the client identify and own his group's achievements and heighten his subcultural awareness and appreciation. Once again the worker uses skills of conveying understanding of the experiences of oppression and focuses the client outward on unjust structures in order to reduce self-blame. These skills are illustrated well in the examples of working with groups and individuals noted above and in the cases of Tyrone in chapter 8 and Shandra Loyal in chapters 8 and 9.

The worker uses family and group skills to help members share and validate each other's experiences with oppression. As members discover they share a common experience, self-deprecatory feelings may diminish. Here also the worker co-teaches about the oppressed group's achievements against the odds, which builds communal and self-esteem. In the work with Shandra Loyal and her family and in examples of work with Brenda Gary and the group of African American and Hispanic women with mental illness illustrated in chapters 9, 10, 11, and 13 we see strategies of pride building and raising communal self-esteem. Conveying hope and strategizing for systems' appreciation of the members' culture is another skill to be used. Giving information that helps clients gain familiarity with how systems work and how to gain access to resources also diminishes fear and adds to feelings of competence. The worker helps to mobilize natural helping networks and structures. Simultaneously, the worker must address systemic inequities that promote the clients' discomforts and anxiety.

Empowering Skills to Enhance Problem Solving and Promote Self-Direction

The skills of problem solving are especially important in an empowerment approach. Ultimately, the aim is to help people to think and act differently not only in solving personal problems but in dealing with the ever connected problems of oppression on personal and political levels. Berlin (1983) suggests a nine-step problem-solving process that moves from awareness of the problem to taking action. (See chapters 5 and 9 with the example of Shandra's problem solving). Germain (1984) adds the dimensions of teaching the skills needed for achieving the solutions, providing group experiences for such learning, providing advice and information as needed, supplying opportunities for trying out new skills, and using role rehearsals, modeling, and anticipatory coping activity for skill acquisition. She also emphasizes working with the environment to offer the options and services needed.

Particular Skills Needed to Problem Solve in an Empowerment Approach

Incorporating Freire's Critical Education Method

The skills needed to problem solve in an empowerment approach include consciousness-raising, praxis, and critical education. Skills of maintaining equality in the problem-solving process are critical. This includes observing the rules of symmetry and parity in communication. The worker who is overly directive and lectures or filibusters or interprets frequently in the process is not providing the conditions necessary for empowerment.

Consciousness-raising is a process of developing a heightened awareness and knowledge base about situations of oppression. As with all skills and processes discussed here, it may be done on one-to-one, family, group, or community levels. "Critical consciousness is a way of thinking and seeing reality by the oppressed acquired through learning about the nature of oppression and the oppressor which leads to new ways of thinking and seeing the social order" (Mancoske and Hunzeker 1989:19). This is a tall order. The worker may begin with a focus on the client's personal pain and broaden the work to include reflection on oppression that is essential to both problem solving and to attaining a raised consciousness. The cases of Mrs. Ciano and Niki, noted in chapters 1, 2, 5, 6, 7, and 8, and Shandra as well as several of the group examples illustrate these strategies. The four attributes (motivation, psychic comfort, problem solving, and self-direction) are interdependent and must be sustained throughout the helping process. A raised consciousness provides motivation, but motivation and psychic comfort are necessary to raise consciousness because ultimately it means change in thinking and doing. Change is often feared, not welcomed. To view the world differently may be initially both a frightening and a freeing experience. The worker's skill of working with feelings will include hearing, validating, and helping clients to express the pain, anger, and sadness that come with consciously realizing that they have been oppressed and victimized socially and economically. Using books, dialogue, art, music, poetry, and other ways of reaching people's level of conscious awareness can be both helpful and painful. A facilitator who worked with a group of battered women reflects on Mary Daly's description of the painful unbinding of women's feet in China in the 1920s:

> It was so painful that they could peel only a few layers of binding off at a time. . . . While reading [Janeway's book] I could unbind only a little of my mind at a time because it was so painful. . . . Sometimes women actually stop attending group because the awareness they are gaining is too painful. They have to wait until something else has happened in their lives before they come back. Now when I facilitate a women's group I've become aware of how gentle with each other we must be in unbinding our minds. (Pence 1987:20)

The skills of gently sharing information in the co-teaching role are critical here as well. Knowledge is power. To be kept from knowledge is oppression. We have already spoken of fostering pride through sharing cultural achievements. Work with the foster children's group illustrated in chapter 7 is a good example of fostering appreciation of cultural differences.

The skills of cognitive restructuring (Berlin 1983) are needed to raise consciousness about being oppressed. The worker helps clients to identify thinking patterns, revise false beliefs, devise more adaptive ways of dealing with internalized and external oppression, and talk and think in a more healthy way about herself, her group, and her situation. The worker then encourages the client to rename and re-create her own reality using her own words. The work with Shandra Loyal in chapter 8 illustrates problem-solving work well.

The worker's skills of guiding in the process of praxis are extremely important. As noted, praxis (action, reflection, and return to action) involves sometimes painful unpeelings of awareness and feeling that takes place over time. A worker's feeling-oriented skills, particularly of naming and staying with the client's feelings, are essential to this process. The ability to promote competence and action is also critical. The example of the empowerment group of mentally ill women in chapter 11 is a particularly good example of guiding praxis. This is also a good time for the worker to share her own struggles in challenging such obstacles, which, after all, do not yield easily, as in the example noted earlier (Pence 1987).

The skills of critical education are central to the empowerment process. This includes the skill of posing critical questions that help people think about the oppressive situation in new ways. This is combined with the skills of information giving noted earlier. For example, in one agency staff group I shared a newspaper article entitled "Steep Pay Difference Found for Educated Whites, Blacks" (*Hartford Courant*, September 20, 1991:C6). I asked the group members, all women (three black and four white, ranging in education levels from high school through graduate school) who were workers and administrators in programs for homeless women, to reflect on why the following quote was so: "Black men 25 and older with four years or more of college on average earned $31,380 in 1989. White men of equal education earned $41,090." The room was full of energy as they answered the question by recounting experiences of racism and discrimination. The article discussed other economic inequities between blacks and whites. This made for excellent dialogue between black and white group members. Sandwiched in the article were also these two lines regarding those with high school education only: "black men earned $20,280; white men $26,510; black women, $16,440; and white women, $16,910." I posed the question,

"What do you see here?" The common ground of gender oppression was easily located, and our common experiences were shared and exposed. The next question to be explored was, "Why are black women at the bottom of the economic ladder?"

Critical Education Method

Freire's method of critical education (Freire 1973a, b; Mancoske and Hunzeker 1989; Pence 1987) is an important set of processes and skills social workers can learn and utilize. These steps are best illustrated with the Successful Women's Group in chapters 1 and 10. The process has five steps that are taken with a team of representative persons. First, a survey is conducted. The team listens to what is on people's minds, assessing what people talk about and what emotions are linked to. This work must include emotionally cathected concerns. These concerns then become the basis for the proposed group's study. Second, a theme is chosen and problems are posed in question form. Themes broaden the base of an issue. For example, a theme in Pence's battered women's groups was, "What is the effect of abusive behavior on women?" (Pence 1987). Third, the problem is analyzed from three perspectives: the personal, the institutional, and the cultural. Questions are asked about each perspective. Fourth, a code is developed. A code is chosen when a theme generates work on all three levels. It is a teaching tool to focus group discussion, such as the newspaper article or the books by Daly and Janeway noted earlier. It may also be a picture, a role play, a story, a song, a chart, or an exercise. The code is a powerful way of focusing a group's attention on a generative theme. Finally, options for action are generated on all three levels. When actions are taken, a process of praxis, described earlier, is used to consolidate and deepen the work of developing critical understanding and a vision of social change.

Ultimately, work that promotes motivation, problem solving, and psychic comfort contributes to a client's self-direction and empowerment. All the processes and skills noted previously are used toward this process and end as well.

For example, the use of "codes" in the empowerment approach to help the client "say her own word" and promote critical thinking (Freire 1973a, b discussed below and throughout this volume) is similar to using program media in some ways and can be used with systems of all sizes, as can other "nonverbal" types of doing together. In the beginning of the empowerment process the use of codes may help the group members get to know each other and also define the empowerment-oriented work to be accomplished; later in the group's life, codes may explore emotionally charged and taboo personal/political themes. Workers may take walks with clients reflecting on the surroundings (as with Mrs. Ciano) and use art, writing, drama, or other media to engage in the medium of or congenial to the client, thereby enhancing comfort with the helping process as with Niki in this chapter (Middleman and Goldberg Wood 1990).

An International Example: A Women's Group in Guyana, South America

The initial codes used with a group of community women preparing to help battered women in Guyana, South America were to artistically portray their chosen names and to trace each other's hands, pondering how hands can express caring and hurt (Lee 1999; chapter 11). Guyana is a multicultural Caribbean nation located on the northern coast of South America. In this group of rural community leaders there were seven Afro-Guyanese women, six Indo-Guyanese women, and two white Canadian nationals. Beyond effective ice breaking in a cross-cultural setting, this offered a chance to reflect on how men's hands and women's hands are experienced and how patriarchy is revealed in the names we carry. All beginnings carry a sense of awkwardness and anxiety along with anticipation. The following example shows how a worker uses codes (familiar experiences that will be analyzed for their personal, cultural, and societal/political meaning) to break the ice and start the personal/political work.

After we began and I elicited their expectations of this group, *I suggest that we all "sign in" on a large piece of paper with colored pens as artistically or as simply as they like. I say that we all have the power to name ourselves in addition to the names we have been given by birth or marriage, confirmation or other religious rite. I ask them to write the name they would like to be called here and the name that best tells who they are* [Proposing to use names as a code related to empowerment]. *When this was finished, I held it up and said it was a "work of art" that had many meanings. I said that these meanings are a code and we can decode them. I added the meanings could be personal or cultural or even political* [Explaining critical thinking; Explaining critical process]. *I asked each to tell her name or names to the group and to say something about the meaning of the name.* After several said their names were their married names or their husband's last name, one woman identified herself as "Teacher Pokoo," a combination of a role and status she values and a nickname given in early childhood due to her precocity. *I shared the meaning of the initials A.B. I write in the middle of my name, explaining these "were for my middle name and my 'maiden name,' but they are also my mother's initials—for 'Anne Beach.' I use them so I can carry my mother's name, as she raised me and I honor her." I shared an anecdote about my father, too* [Appropriate self-disclosure]. The women responded with stories about their own mothers and grandmothers and wonderment that one could identify oneself with a mother's name. *Then I asked why is it women present themselves by their husband's and father's names* [This was a critical question to help them look at the meaning of patriarchy and thereby establish a context for physical abuse, and it worked]. Gene, who spelled her name G-e-n-e, said, "My parents gave me a man's name, but I affirm it. I like to tell people how I spell my name so they can realize a woman can have any name. Men don't own names." "Nor do they own women," Shirley replied. Wendy said all countries she knew were patriarchal. One woman then told the story of an abusive husband (Lee 1999).

The skills used here are put in italics. They include ice breaking, using and explaining a code, appropriate self-disclosure, and posing a critical question. To be appropriate, self-disclosure should be brief and related to the client's focus, not the workers own needs in telling the story. When used properly it opens the work and equalizes the power differential. This is particularly helpful in a multicultural and international context when the worker is of a group that once represented the oppressor. (Empowerment-oriented international work will be discussed throughout the book and specifically in chapter 14).

Skills to Promote Social Change

Beyond the gains to the self, empowering work also helps empower communities. Group- and community-centered skills are essential. Much of the preceding work is done most effectively in small groups, which then may build coalitions with other groups and forces in the community to effect social change. As we have illustrated in this chapter and in chapters 11 and 12, empowerment group skills include making a clear, mutual contract that bridges the personal and the political and includes a social change focus (Lee 1991), establishing the common ground and common cause among members, challenging the obstacles to the group's work, lending a vision, and reaching for each member's maximum participation in the process. These are a variation on Schwartz's skills and tasks of the group worker (1974b, 1994). The worker will also skillfully pose critical questions and develop codes to focus the group's work, as discussed earlier (Freire 1973a, b). Community skills include coalition building and the skills of task-oriented action. Here one wants to help members choose initial tasks at which they can achieve success. Wider political skills include lobbying and testifying at legislative hearings as well as organizing meetings, protests, and resistance activities (see chapter 13). These are skills for workers and clients to develop together. All the preceding processes and skills will be discussed and illustrated in the practice chapters of this book (chapters 7–14).

The conceptual framework of this empowerment approach is concluded with the formulation of the empowerment methodology.

The Empowerment Method: Principles, Roles, Processes, and Skills

The method, roles, processes and skills rest on empowerment values, purposes, and the eight principles that undergird this approach. The method may be used in one-to-one, group, or community relational systems. It depends on a collaborative relationship that encompasses mutuality, reciprocity, shared power, and shared human struggle, the use of empowerment groups to identify and work on direct and indirect power blocks toward the ends of personal, interpersonal, and political efficacy, and collective activity that reflects a raised consciousness regarding oppression. The method uses specific skills in operationalizing the practice principles to address and promote action regarding indirect and direct power blocks on all three levels of living.

We turn now to developing the knowledge base necessary for multifocal vision.

4 Establishing Multifocal Vision: The History of Oppression

The past matters, more than we realize. We walk on its ground
and if we don't know the soil we're lost.
— William Carlos Williams

The first step in establishing multifocal vision is to bring the history of a group's oppression into sharp focus. The documentation of this history is also the foundation of empowerment practice. The need for empowerment practice is rooted in the historic and contemporary treatment of people who are poor and oppressed, especially women, African Americans, and all people of color, who continue to make up a disproportionate number of poor people. Knowing this history enables us to tune in to the experience of oppression and to raise consciousness with our clients. American history and social policy heritage reflect conflicting ideologies and ambivalence about people who are poor and different from the dominant group.

Empowerment practice places the responsibilities and possibilities of enlightened knowledge and action on all of us. We are all members of this society and responsible for and to each other as well as ourselves, yet some of us reap its benefits more than others. A collectivist "social membership perspective" is what is needed for human survival (Reynolds 1951; Falck 1988). In an empowerment approach the analysis of history, policy, and social change is conceived to be a joint effort of *all* affected. This implies an exchange of knowledge and resources. We can learn best what changes need to be made from those who suffer most from the inequities and shortcomings in the ever diminishing American welfare state. Except for a few golden moments in social work history, we have participated in deciding what we think is good for other people. However benevolent and well motivated this may be, it is not empowering.

Social workers may feel as powerless to make an impact as those who use their services on the destructive, complex social/political/economic forces of our times. This feeling of shared impotence could drive us back into a narrow polarization of practice that is apolitical, intensely personal, and easily open to scientific measurement and validation (as in the 1870s).

I will present an examination of American history and social policy that provides a compelling argument for the necessity of an empowerment approach to social work practice and a challenge to the profession as it considers issues of professional survival and the temptation to abandon poor and oppressed people in the context of serious economic constraints. As social workers, we must develop a historic and longitudinal view of oppression to develop critical understanding in ourselves and in our clients.

A society, like a human chain, is only as strong as its weakest link. A women-and-children-last philosophy is basically un-American. Yet it happens here. In addition to being bought and sold, seen as property, disenfranchised, and denied civil rights, women and African Americans, like other minorities of color and low-status working people, were not adequately covered by the progressive social insurance policies of the New Deal, which favored white male urban workers in long-standing "covered employment" situations (Hamilton and Hamilton 1986; Jansson 1993; Morales 1986; and Abramovitz 1989a).

People who are working poor and poor are disadvantaged by the unequal distribution of rights and life-sustaining and life-enhancing opportunity structures. They continue to struggle disproportionately with the least desirable jobs and occupational statuses of this society (Jones 1985). They may also internalize it as their fault that they are in such a position (Ryan 1971; Solomon 1976; Morales 1986).

Germain stresses that

> disempowerment and [social and technological] pollution are major stressors that afflict the entire population, including the oppressors. But the burden is heaviest on vulnerable, disenfranchised and excluded groups. They form the conditions of life—the context—in which the development and functioning of members of those groups take place. They threaten health and social well-being, and they impose enormous adaptive burdens . . . over the life course. (1991:24)

The ideals of the Declaration of Independence concerning the inalienable rights of all people to life, liberty, and the pursuit of happiness will not be realized in our society until its social policies equalize rights and opportunities (Gil 1981). Practice informed by history and policy understanding must be part of an empowerment approach that stands side by side with poor people in the struggle for justice.

The Colonial Period: Unjust Treatment of Poor and Wage-Earning People

Social welfare in the Colonial period (approximately 1607–1800) was marked by the transfer to America of English institutions and concepts. Extraordinary differences in wealth and landholdings existed in Colonial America as it does in the United States today (Jansson 1993). The early colonists were primarily concerned with survival. Mutual aid was the earliest form of social obligation utilized (Lee and Swenson 1986). This sometimes included Native Americans who protected the settlers and also became converts (Pumphrey and Pumphrey 1961). This approach of extending social obligation and compassion with strings attached marked the earliest form of ambivalence toward those in need. The settlement of territory that was not theirs exemplified settlers' ethnocentrism/racism. Ultimately, Native Americans were exploited, deceived, massacred, and objectified (Jansson 1993).

As society became more complex, reliance on the English poor laws of 1601 took precedence over laws of mutual aid. The underlying principles of Elizabethan poor laws have remained essentially unchanged in the twentieth century. Poor laws had humane and social-control intent. Each parish classified those in need and provided appropriate kinds of relief for each category of persons: apprenticeship for children, work for the able-bodied, almshouses for the incapacitated and "the impotent," financing through taxation with the provision to share excessive burdens with other parishes, and legally enforced family responsibility. Those "able to work" who resisted were considered the undeserving poor, punished, and sometimes indentured. Widows and children, the disabled, and the elderly were gradually considered deserving.

Because of the need for labor, the indenture system accounted for one-third to one-half of all immigrants to North America until the American Revolution (Abramovitz 1989a). Another one-fifth of the population was made up of slaves (Jansson 1993). Thus a large portion of the population was bound in servitude. Poor laws also safeguarded a labor supply. The need for women's reproductive and productive labor led to an increase in slavery and the recruitment and selling of "wives," indentured female servants, and white female "slaves" to the colonies. This "provision" of women was also used to control the impulse of social protest (Abramovitz 1989a). The importation of African slaves was used to ease class conflict between former indentured servants and the landlord gentry (Morgan 1972).

Landless wage earners were seen as an "underclass" in colonial American society. Although the "able-bodied poor" were forced to work with punitive measures, their labor was not valued. Wage earners represented a moral and political threat. Social protest and slave uprisings were especially feared. In fact, the needs of wage earners were not recognized as legitimate until well into the twentieth century. The working person's vulnerabilities to poverty were disregarded and the myth of "equal opportunity for all" persists until the present time. It was not expected that workers would exist in any numbers at all in the projected agrarian utopian society of the colonists. In varying degrees, wage earners, along with women, African slaves, and Native Americans were seen as nonpersons (Jansson 1993).

Women

During the eighteenth century women's labor was needed. The patriarchal family was at the center of the colonial social order. The role of a woman was to marry, have a family, and be submissive to her husband and at the same time be economically productive at manufacturing goods for use and trade. Women's work was acceptable as long as the husband agreed and it was close to home. White married women were not given equal rights or granted full social participation, but within these boundaries their roles were valued. All single persons had to live within an established patriarchal household, and single women were shunned as "disagreeable old virgins unable to catch a man" (Abramovitz 1989a).

Voting was not yet even a dream. Married women could not sign contracts or own property. Children were the legal property of the husband (Jansson 1988). Female indentured servants were not seen as respectable women but as "units of labor." They were forbidden to marry and were sometimes sexually exploited, and all their worth was reckoned by their productivity to the master's family. If a white servant became pregnant, her term of indenture might be extended. Husbands to be could purchase the remainder of a woman's term of indenture (Abramovitz 1989a). Women who were servants (poor women) were treated as objects. Although widows were accorded rights and respect, all other women in need were seen as the undeserving and immoral poor.

African Americans

The first Africans (twenty in all) to arrive in America traveled on a Dutch ship to Jamestown in 1619, a year before the *Mayflower*. The exact nature of their status is unclear (Jordon 1974). It is likely that they were sold as indentured servants and that they began the history of free blacks in America. But most Africans arrived as slaves (Abramovitz 1989a; Jordon 1974).

White indentured servants were a major source of labor in the colonies, but they presented a political problem because they sometimes agitated against oppressive working conditions. As the English economy improved, the harsh working conditions of the colonies became well known. It became impossible to recruit indentured servants, particularly to the tobacco crops of Virginia and the Carolinas. To meet this need many black slaves were imported. Slaves were kept for life and were an ongoing source of labor with no legal or property rights. Slaves who resisted the inhuman working conditions of the tobacco fields were labeled lazy and indolent (Jansson 1993).

Those Africans who survived the voyage to America brought a rich West African culture and a multitude of languages, skills, and crafts to the New World. The trip was deliberately brutal, as an indoctrination process to slavery. The first ships contained only a few women, but over time their numbers grew to about one-third. They were completely vulnerable to white men aboard. Many plantation owners continued to torture, terrorize, and brutalize their slaves into submission. Rape of slaves became institutionalized (Davis 1981). Once the slave trade was abolished in 1808, African women were used as breeders as well as laborers. Slavery became a key factor to American industry and European commerce (Abramovitz 1989a).

In the seventeenth century slavery was codified into law. Indentured servants and blacks had often worked side by side in the fields under their common masters in the early colonies. They intermarried and sometimes rebelled together against harsh treatment. The new laws gave white indentured servants more rights than blacks and threatened to punish any alliances between them. This consolidated white support for slavery (Jansson 1993). In 1790 the Congress enacted legislation that restricted citizenship to Caucasians (Jansson 1993). Classist, sexist, and racist attitudes dominated the thinking of the new nation's colonial elite.

The Nineteenth Century: Social Welfare and Social Work

Before the nineteenth century few specialized institutions existed. Almshouses/workhouses were "catchalls" set up to serve the poor, the mentally ill, and the physically incapacitated. Prisons were short-term holding places, as punishment was swift—fine, whipping, or execution. Problematic strangers were sent out of town. Children attended schools irregularly. Families and communities coped informally with social and personal issues. But, by the middle of the nineteenth century, institutions dealing with crime, poverty, disease, mental illness, blindness, deafness, and the ignorant proliferated, so that state boards of charities were created to coordinate their efforts. The goals of social intervention were to produce good and able workers. Schools were the only institution that became destigmatized by middle-class usage (Katz 1989a). The term *dangerous classes* was popularized by Charles Loring Brace, founder of the Children's Aid Society, an organization that sent children west to rescue them from their indolent parents. By the 1880s settlement houses and youth-serving agencies such as the YMCA were formed to meet the diverse needs of immigrant populations. Private philanthropy also proliferated. By the mid-1870s Charity Organization Societies were set up to organize private charities and promote "scientific" investigation and rehabilitation of the poor.

In the first half of the nineteenth century few were concerned with the barbarous working conditions in the new industries of New England, the circumscription of free blacks, the suffering of slaves, the plight of tenant farmers on the harsh frontier, the invasion and destruction of Native Americans, or massive land accumulation by speculators and railroads in the West. Americans were preoccupied with personal and national economic issues. Issues of socioeconomic inequality were masked by the scope and mythology of the American frontier. Small landowners were the dominant social group. A social and political elite of clergy, businessmen, and landowners dominated local politics and commanded deference. Extraordinary differentials in wealth existed. Six major recessions hit New York City from 1819 to 1893, and working people were hit the hardest, repeatedly causing a sharp rise in the use of crowded, unsavory almshouses and soup kitchens. In the 1850s in New England 1 percent of the population held 50 percent of the wealth. (It is striking to note that during the 1980s 1 percent of the population owned 60 percent of the wealth [CBS, *World News Report* 3/5/92]. Today's "alms-houses" are shelters for "the homeless" [Katz 1989b].)

The Gilded Age: Civil War to the End of the Nineteenth Century

The period from the Civil War to the end of the nineteenth century, which was a gilded one only for the wealthy, marked an acceleration of industrialization and capitalism. With the help of the railroad and cheap labor supplied by internal migration and immigration, it was a period of prosperity for industrial capitalists. The growth of cities came at the expense of devastating social and economic problems. There were two classes, the laboring and the entrepreneurial. Factory laborers were transient and often exploited. Some policy victories regulated working hours and conditions for women and children. Corporations and financiers came into power after the Civil War. There were few strong unions to balance this control by business as unions were suppressed. It was at this time that social Darwinism became a prevailing social philosophy (Jansson 1988).

The Civil War was prompted by competition for economic and political expansion on the frontier, regionalism, nationalism, and the desire on the part of abolitionists and free blacks to end slavery. The writings of abolition-ists and especially the slave narratives provide rare and shocking glimpses into the devastations of slavery and the perseverance of the slave. The best-known slave narrative was written by Frederick Douglass (1968 [1845]). Douglass was a brilliant man who taught himself and many others to read and write. He led and lived through an insurrection and fled to the North. The publishing of his book spurred his career as a militant uncompromising leader. Douglass describes his travail: "Scarce a week passed without his whipping me. . . . We worked fully up to the point of endurance. Long before day we were up . . . we were often less than five minutes taking our meals. . . . Midnight often caught us in the field binding blades" (1968: 72–73).

The war and postwar political issues distracted attention from the pre-existing social problems. To the North the war brought prosperity, and to the South, impoverishment. Industrialization and massive immigration of both whites and blacks transformed poverty from a local to a national problem and accentuated the contrast between the conditions of the rich and the poor (Bremner 1967).

Freed Persons

With regard to the growing number of blacks freed after the Civil War, Jansson observes: "A strong moral case can be made that decision makers tragically erred by not helping these destitute people, for example, by providing free land on the American Frontier" (1988:4). This shortsightedness combined with racism and the vested political and economic interests of the powerful have had far-reaching consequences for the oppression of African Americans. Most Southern lands given blacks by the Freedmen's Bureau were taken away by President Andrew Johnson after the war. The passage of the Fourteenth Amendment in 1868 rescinded the Dredd Scott decision of 1857, which declared that blacks were not persons and not entitled to constitutional protection. The passage of the Fifteenth Amendment (1870) guaranteed the vote to all males, but poll taxes and literacy tests were used to disenfranchise blacks, and Jim Crow laws lasting into the mid-twentieth century were used to deprive blacks of basic civil rights (Franklin and Moss 1988).

Antebellum African American communities were extremely poor. The wealthiest 10 percent of the black population owned 70 percent of the total black wealth. Blacks were politically disenfranchised and were frequently the victims of riots and mob actions. In Philadelphia, for example, African Americans had created strong communities with schools, churches, and beneficial societies. However, they could not prosper in the face of overwhelming obstacles.

Nineteenth-Century Women

The industrial era marked a change in women's economically productive role in the home. Some single working-class women worked in factories until the immigrant labor supply no longer permitted this, but married women of all classes had a more singular role thrust upon them. Women's new sacred place was in the home. They were excluded from economic productivity and motherhood was glorified. The idea of female selflessness intensified in industrial America. Legal rights continued to be accorded only to men. A New York divorce judge noted in 1837 that "marriage for women approximated slavery for the blacks" (Abramovitz 1989a:118).

On the other hand, abolitionism and the Civil War also precipitated the entrance of wealthy women into politics in a daring way. Female abolitionists like Harriette Beecher Stowe and the Grimké sisters defied the widespread custom of not speaking to mixed audiences or signing public petitions, despite congressional legislation in 1834 that disallowed petitions signed by women. They also began to apply the logic of emancipation to themselves. The first convention devoted to women's suffrage and other rights was held in 1848 in Seneca Falls, New York. The convenors issued a Declaration of Sentiments to protest property laws to allow married women to inherit their husbands' property and to keep earned wages as well as to advocate for liberalized divorce laws and universal suffrage. When the Fourteenth and Fifteenth Amendments did not apply to women, these women became disillusioned (Jansson 1988, 1993).

To justify the "Family Wage" (a higher pay scale for male heads of family) the working-class press regularly extolled the virtues of woman's place in the home. Women supplemented family income by taking in boarders or doing piecework. Working-class men of all groups kept their women home as long as it was possible to survive economically. As many as one-fourth of the wives of foreign-born men may have worked in factories, as did native-born white women without male breadwinners. Working women lived marginally and were not seen as respectable. Black women were excluded from factory employment in Northern cities until World War I and were not employed in significant numbers until World War II (Harley 1978). Black women were confined primarily to domestic work. There was some union activity among white working women in the 1820s through the 1840s. Free black washerwomen in Mississippi organized for collective action in 1866. Female workers and paupers in America eventually became visible. Their new visibility contributed to punitive reforms in the earlier poor laws (Abramovitz 1989a). For whites and blacks (despite limited employment opportunities) poverty was seen as a willful violation of the work ethic and a threat to the family ethic. Almshouses/poorhouses and mental hospitals were seen as curative for white female paupers and immigrant women, and jails were used for indigent blacks. Most Americans believed in no government intervention and no "special compensation" for specific groups, such as the violently displaced Native Americans and Hispanics of the Southwest and, most notably, freed slaves.

The Profession of Social Work: Some Stones to Build On

The profession of social work has a "checkered past" as it relates to people who are poor and oppressed. The roots of modern social work can be directly traced to two late-nineteenth-century movements, the Charity Organization Society (COS) and the settlement house movement. Two popularly defined eloquent spokespersons of these movements were Mary Richmond and Jane Addams. Both movements had their roots in England and flourished here from the 1870s through the turn of the century. Casework, community organization, and social research can be traced to the COS movement and group work is traced to the settlement house movement (Woodroofe 1966). As we look at the beginnings of the COS and its popularly defined "representative," Mary Richmond, a leader from the working class, we see germs of relatively broad social and holistic thinking moving forward even as the earlier view of the "undeserving poor" held on. Mary Richmond, for example, was against mothers' pensions, whereas she actively campaigned with the Pennsylvania legislature for child labor and housing legislation (Woodroofe 1966).

As the COS movement took hold by the end of the nineteenth century, knowledge in the social sciences proliferated and differentiated, and with it a growing emphasis on scientific method, theory, and research. Social work began to grope its way to a clearly defined and ordered methodology. At the same time, social work in America began to develop a consciousness of itself as a social force. In many social agencies there was a strong interest in social action in addition to ministering to the needs of poor families (Beck 1959).

Although charity agents were not radical, in the long run their work, including collecting statistics, helped undermine many cherished opinions regarding the "causes and cures" of poverty (Pumphrey and Pumphrey 1961; Bremner 1967). However, the emphasis in science on fact gathering and method also led to a "scientism" (almost a worship of scientific method) that obscured the realities of oppression for decades (Germain 1974). The COS represented one incremental step forward and one foot in the past.

The "age of anxiety" that characterized the United States after World War I welcomed psychiatry as a panacea. This culminated in a psychiatric deluge from which the profession hardly emerged (Woodroofe 1966). By the Milford Conference of 1929 the preference for a psychoanalytically oriented psychological underpinning began to displace Mary Richmond's more integrated approach, labeled "overly social." It was in this context that Porter Lee, in his presidential address to the National Conference on Social Welfare (NCSW), expressed concern that casework had become preoccupied with method at the unfortunate expense of social reform, or "social cause." In Lee's view both cause and function (method) are valuable and essential for social welfare (Germain and Gitterman 1980). The tension between cause and function is ongoing and must be recognized for what it continues to be, an inevitable dialectic that will persist as long as socioeconomic injustice prevails. Leaders in the emerging COS and the settlement house movement engaged in sharp debate on these issues. By 1910 there were over four hundred settlements in the United States. Jane Addams's Hull House in Chicago was the most famous of these (Katz 1986).

The Progressive Era and Beyond: Jane Addams—Collectivity, Community, and Reform

Jane Addams's life was a testimony to the merger of cause and function. Addams had a particular talent for dealing with "baffling complexity" and seeing things whole. The establishment of Hull House in Chicago in 1889 with Ellen Gates Starr as well as her leadership in domestic reform movements gained her a national reputation among major political and social theorists by 1900 (Pottick 1989). At Hull House she advanced a group-oriented reciprocal approach to sharing the struggles of working and poor people. Her international work on behalf of women and peace made her the first of two Americans and the first woman (the prize was shared) to win the Nobel Peace Prize in 1931.

It is important to note that great and special women are the predecessors of an empowerment approach. These women did not have the right to vote, to live alone or unmarried without scandal, to attend universities of their choice, or to enter the professions freely as they made giant steps in building the profession of social work. Through Jane Addams the social work profession inherits the settlement movement and group work method, roots in the international and national women's movement, the labor movement, and the peace movement, a passion for social equality, social justice, and social reform, a respect for difference and the richness of diverse cultures, and a sense of world consciousness and responsibility (Addams 1922, 1930). At Hull House outstanding and ordinary women and men gave their lives to living and working side by side with oppressed groups so that "reciprocity and a fair share of resources might flow between the classes" (Addams 1961 [1910]).

The settlement utilized a collective approach from two vantage points: 1) the collective living experience of the settlers who nurtured and supported each other in the work and 2) the experience of settlers and neighbors in dialogue and discussion working on common current issues.

Parkes notes that "social work heritage is the story of women who challenged social norms personally and politically, whose relationships with women supported them in their drive for social reforms and who were anything but lonely spinsters" (1981:2). Addams said such women are "strong, resistant and active" (1930:198). Jane Addams's life and work were one. She drew strength from "enduring friendships" (her words) with the women of Hull House and especially from her particular relationship with Mary Rozet Smith, with whom she shared a life, a room, a house in Maine, travels to colleagues abroad, and Hull House for forty years (Addams 1961 [1910], 1930). Addams's consciousness was raised and she was eager to raise consciousness with her neighbors on issues of economics, bread and labor, politics, women's issues, and all aspects of life.

She provided astute analysis of the international suffragist movement and why women finally got the vote. She spoke directly to issues of women's power:

> Some of us feel that women in politics thus far have been too conventional, too afraid to differ with men, too ill at ease to trust their own judgements, too skeptical of the wisdom of the humble to incorporate the needs of simple women into the ordering of public life.
> . . . [It] is much easier to dovetail into the political scheme of men than to release the innate concerns of women, which might be equivalent to a revolutionary force. I am at times inclined to agree with

Chesterton when he wrote: "The real danger of feminine politics is too much of a masculine policy." (Addams 1930:110)

Jane Addams believed firmly in the impact women could have on the world in issues of peace and war. Her pacifism as well as her affirmation of women's strengths had the effect of silencing her work until the 1930s. In 1914 Addams, president of the Woman's Peace Party, organized women to address issues of "Peace and Bread in Time of War." She saw peace and the meeting of basic human needs as inseparable (Addams 1922). Remarkably, this major peace movement was begun "early in the Fall of 1914, when a small group of social workers held meetings at the Henry Street Settlement in New York" (Addams 1922). From these meetings the Women's International League for Peace and Freedom developed, with Jane Addams at its head. Global concern and local action are building blocks for an empowerment approach.

United with African American Women to Fight the "Gravest Situation in American Life"

Addams was always dedicated to racial justice established in dialogue with the African American community. Blacks were forced to develop their own helping institutions because of rigid segregation laws (Solomon 1976). Robenia and Lawrence Gary have documented the social welfare leadership of fifty-six women. Noting that the "Black church, mutual aid and fraternal organizations were the major social welfare institutions of the Black community," they emphasize that black women played important roles in these organizations. Some black women's clubs worked cooperatively with white women. Three were named, including Jane Addams. "White and Black women worked together to find jobs and decent homes for Black immigrants, open playgrounds for Black children, break down the color barriers in employment, improve health and protect Black domestics from exploitation of employment agencies" (Gary and Gary 1975:11).

By the turn of the century African Americans were included in a separate and unequal service system. COS, for example, served almost entirely white families. An exception was the COS in Memphis, which operated a "Negro auxiliary" (Solomon 1976).

Most settlement houses were segregated, as were the communities they served, and blacks entering white communities were usually met with violence and were sometimes killed (Berman-Rossi and Miller 1992; Katz 1986). Hull House served large numbers of Mexican-Americans, despite the neighborhood sentiment against serving people of color. It is not clear whether it helped any African Americans directly, as the black community was located on the South Side of Chicago until the 1930s and Hull House was on the West Side (Addams 1961 [1910], 1930; Lemann 1991).

The black women's club movement was instrumental in promoting social reform. "There have always been black women activists—some known . . . and thousands upon thousands unknown—who had shared awareness of how their sexual identity combined with their racial identity to make their whole life situation and the focus of their political struggles unique" (Combahee River Collective 1982).

The activism of black women has not been properly credited in the social work profession. But African American women founded such local black organizations as neighborhood improvement clubs, women's clubs, houses for the aged, and children's homes. The women's clubs offered services similar to settlement house programs (Gary and Gary 1975).

African American Women Who Led in Social Reform

Leading black social reformers during the Progressive era were Janie Porter-Barrett, Sarah A. Collins-Fernandis, Mary Eliza Church Terrell, and Ida Bell Wells-Barnett. Janie Porter Barrett was a social welfare leader who founded the first settlement house in Virginia, the Locust Street Social Settlement. She also helped organize the Virginia State Federation of Colored Women's Clubs. Sarah A. Collins Fernandis was the founder of the first black social settlement in the United States in the District of Columbia and of a second settlement in Rhode Island. She also organized the Women's Cooperative Civic League, which worked for improved sanitation and health conditions in black neighborhoods. Mary Eliza Church Terrell was a leading social reformer and a participant in the international women's movement. She is best known for her professional lecture tours and writings on race relations and women's rights.

In 1904 she represented black women at the International League for Peace and Freedom in Zurich under the presidency of Jane Addams. A lifelong social activist, Terrell was also involved in the organizing meetings of the NAACP, belonged to the National American Women's Suffrage Association, and demonstrated actively against segregation until the time of her death (Peebles-Wilkins 1987:942).

Scholarship continues to illuminate the role of African American women in the development of the profession. Echols and Martin (1989) focus on the history of African American leadership in integrated and segregated settlement houses in Connecticut during the early and middle years of the twentieth century. They document the versatility of African American women, like Joyce B. Yerwood, M.D., who had to wear many hats in service to their communities and to several professions.

Perhaps the most famous, versatile, and radical of the African American social reformers was Ida B. Wells-Barnett (civil rights spokeswoman and civic organizer), a courageous journalist born to slave parents in Holly Springs, Mississippi, in 1862. Her journalism career began in 1892, and she was co-owner of the Memphis *Free Speech and Headlight* until its offices were destroyed by a mob. After that she continued to write and lecture here and abroad about the plight of blacks in the South, particularly the lynching of black men. Her activity in the women's club movement led to the organization of a Negro women's club in Chicago. She also founded the Negro Fellowship League, which maintained a settlement house. She participated in the founding of the NAACP and established the Alpha Suffrage Club of Chicago, the first black women's organization of its kind. Wells-Barnett's *A Red Record* (1895) includes autobiographical material and data on lynching (Peebles-Wilkins 1987). She and Jane Addams were known to work together on pressing issues of the day (Holt 1982).

It is extremely important that we write the accomplishments of black social welfare leaders into our history, as they empowered not only black people but also the profession of social work. Social work is not middle- and upper-class white history. There are countless people of color and others whose names never appeared in a *Who's Who* because they were poor and working-class people who simply and eloquently served their communities. Yet, for the most part, social work history has "whited out" and "classed out" this contribution (Berman-Rossi and Miller 1992).

Prominent black intellectuals who were major social welfare leaders, such as W. E. B. Du Bois and E. Franklin Frazier, had a profound impact on the profession of social work. W. E. B. Du Bois (founder of the NAACP) was the head of the Department of Sociology at Atlanta University from 1932 to

1944, a towering antidiscrimination leader, and a prolific writer. *The Souls of Black Folk* (1903) and *Black Reconstruction in America* (1964), the latter presenting an excellent analysis of blacks and political power, are among his best-known works (Rudwick 1982). Du Bois also published *The Philadelphia Negro* (1899), the first in-depth study of a black community in the United States (Rudwick 1982). The teaching and work of W. E. B. Du Bois are acknowledged influences in the work of Bertha Reynolds (1964). He was also a contemporary of Jane Addams and a dynamic speaker at Hull House gatherings (Addams 1961 [1910]).

E. Franklin Frazier was an internationally acclaimed research sociologist and writer with a specialty in black families. He became the director of the Atlanta University School of Social Work in 1922. He was director of social work programs and the Department of Sociology at Howard University from 1934 until 1959. Beatriz Lasalle, a Puerto Rican social welfare leader, is another unsung heroine of this period. She is the recognized pioneer in institutionalizing social work practice in Puerto Rico (Longres 1987).

"The Gravest Situation": Racism and Economic Discrimination

One of the important areas of dialogue at Hull House was race relations. Addams recognized the role of economics in racial oppression. She describes a 1929 investigation that analyzes black women in industry from studies made in fifteen states. As today, their earnings were found to be below those of most white women. (It does not speak of white men.)

Addams writes, "Because we are no longer stirred . . . to remove fetters, to prevent cruelty . . . we have allowed ourselves to become indifferent to *the gravest situation* in American life" (1930:401; emphasis added).

In drawing attention to "the gravest situation," Jane Addams was a lonely herald and prophet within the social work profession. Jane Addams's leadership and intellectual activism in the social reform issues of her day, including those relating to the vote of women and unfair labor practices, is well known. She saw the alliance of settlement houses with labor unions as natural and "obvious" (Addams 1930). One sees an early consciousness-raising method in her description of residents and neighbors debating on such matters as the Stockyard Strike as they grapple with the "close connection of their own difficulties with national and even international movements" (1930:168).

Reform, Not Revolution

The reform efforts of the Progressive era represented a diverse agenda, including prohibition, prostitution, immigration, child and woman's labor, unsafe working conditions, food and drug laws, banking laws, the regulation of politicians' activities, and obtainment of unemployment insurance. Democracy was perceived to be under fire by industrial capitalism's "jungle law" competitiveness and its effects in the stark poverty seen in the aftermath of two depressions. It could be restored by a spirit of reform and cooperation.

The theories of Karl Marx (1818–1883) also had a strong effect on Progressive era thinkers. Marx was not only the founder of modern theories of socialism but also the organizer of the International Working Men's Association in 1864. He devoted his later years to the completion of *Das Kapital*. He saw economic factors as determinants of all history and emphasized that the state should therefore own all tools of production. This theory was directly opposed to the philosophy of laissez-faire and rugged individualism. Many of the social reformers in the United States took their stand somewhere between these two extremes. They were still wrongly branded as communists (Cohen 1958).

Sixty percent of the American labor force was born abroad. This immigrant status put them at a distinct disadvantage in finding the power together to organize against injustice (Jansson 1988). Although unions picked up members, they were relatively weak. Each successive group was pitted against the next. By 1890 immigration reached a new high of 5.25 million. Most immigrants from 1880 until 1900 were from eastern Europe, the largest number being Jews fleeing the pogroms of czarist Russia. Many were artisans and merchants. By 1920 there were 4 million Jews settled mostly in the large cities of the East. They developed an elaborate parallel social service structure, as they were shut out of mainstream services (Cohen 1958). Besides the abominable living conditions and meager wages that all immigrants endured, they faced not only ethnocentrism but anti-Semitism. The Immigration Act of 1924 was primarily intended to reduce southern and eastern European immigration and was anti-Semitic and racist in intent. Sadly, many reformers saw the uneven restriction of immigration as desirable.

The nonpartisan position of most reformers had not given them a political base. When Theodore Roosevelt moved toward a reformist position in 1912, such leading reformers as Jane Addams backed him in the hope that one of the two then conservative parties would represent a more liberal view. This did not happen, nor did the hope of establishing a Progressive party by 1916. It would take the catastrophic depression of 1929 to galvanize workers, the poor, and minorities behind social reforms (Jansson 1988; Katz 1986).

Women and Progressivism

Although the settlement movement provided the opportunity for women to join together in a cause, industrial expansion opened new jobs for many middle-class women as nurses, teachers, and clerical workers and increased the demand for women in domestic and factory jobs. Few of these jobs were open to black women, who occupied domestic service jobs, except for some who were midwives and teachers and a smaller number who were college educated. Protective labor laws can be seen as beneficial in some aspects and as regulatory of women's lives and choices in other aspects. The labor force was protected from an influx of women in "male jobs," and most women were kept "in their place." Both white and black organizations arose to provide services and support for working women. Working women, such as Mary Kenney, who lived at Hull House, also organized on their own behalf, particularly in the garment industry. In 1912 thousands of women textile workers, in what became known as the Bread and Roses Strike, walked out of the mills in Lawrence, Massachusetts. Women met with societal ridicule and male opposition as they attempted to organize (Abramovitz 1989a).

Mothers' pensions were a result of a movement that swept the country between 1911 and 1919, when it became apparent that women's wages could not support them and their children if the husband died or left them. When they applied for poor relief, they had to enter a poor house and give up their children. This destruction of families ran counter to progressivism. Meager mothers' pensions permitted women to stay home with their children (Jansson 1988); they also kept women out of the workforce and living at a subsistence level. Few day nurseries existed, and fewer still accepted black children, whose access to public kindergartens was also blocked. By and large, those who qualified for mothers' pensions were both widowed and white (Abramovitz 1989a).

The issue of women's suffrage became the central reform issue of the woman's movement by 1890, although, ironically, many women perceived the issue to be tangential to their economic and social needs. More progress was made after 1905 because feminist leaders developed organizing skills and because suffrage seemed less radical in the context of a reform era. Twelve states had granted women the vote by 1916. The Nineteenth Amendment to the Constitution was finally enacted in 1920. Males objected to placing eminent women on commissions or in administrative positions, even in the emerging social work profession (Jansson 1988).

Racism in the Progressive Era: Progress for Whom?

With notable exceptions, such as Jane Addams, the leaders of the reform movement saw no contradiction between social reform and racism. Civil rights gains of freed persons were nullified when the South regained power in the post-Reconstruction era. Most blacks lived in the rural South as tenant farmers. In the wake of World War I and the Great Migration, increasing numbers moved to Southern (and Northern) cities, where they were unemployed or had unskilled jobs in a segregated society held together by Jim Crow laws, police, courts, and white racism (Franklin and Moss 1988). A key to understanding the twentieth century is to realize the enormous effect the great migration from farm to city had on socioeconomic structures (Lemann 1991).

Northern blacks also experienced great hardships. The steady migration to cities, where jobs in meat packing and steel that paid better than wages in the South made for marginal living conditions. African American neighborhoods had poor housing and no health or other formal services (Katz 1986). African Americans experienced keen discrimination in the job markets as they were barred from unions, used as scabs, and dealt with violently when they competed with whites for unskilled jobs. Both Theodore Roosevelt and Woodrow Wilson took no actions against Jim Crow legislation. Wilson, raised a Southerner, openly supported segregated restrooms in federal buildings and condoned lynching in the South. His policies were so detestable that many blacks continued to vote Republican (Jansson 1988). The landmark *Plessy* v. *Ferguson* (1896) decision that mandated "separate but equal" facilities was upheld by the Supreme Court seven times. In 1954 Thurgood Marshall and a group of NAACP lawyers established that separate could not be equal. The 1896 decision was overturned under Chief Justice Earl Warren's Supreme Court leadership. Until then, legal segregation had been the law of the land.

Racism was also perpetuated against Hispanics. Mexican immigrants to the Southwest were brutalized by American growers. The Immigration Act of 1917 imposed a literacy test and a head tax, but when legal immigration decreased undocumented workers increased and subjected even more to racism and cruelty (Jansson 1988). In July 1898 the United States invaded Puerto Rico and took over the island in the name of saving the Puerto Ricans from Spain in the context of the Spanish-American War. In the Foraker Act of 1900 a civil government was provided, and the United States governed Puerto Rico. Puerto Rican citizens had only "commonwealth status" in the United States and lost control of their own land. In 1899 peasants owned 93 percent of their farms and had a three-crop economy: coffee, tobacco, and sugar. The United States turned it into a one-crop (sugar) economy dependent on the price in the market, which was controlled by a few absentee corporations. This exploitation began our relationship with Puerto Rican citizens, who migrated here of necessity after industrial "development" of the island began in 1942 (Morales 1986).

Asian immigrants, who were wooed to California in large numbers to work on the railroads and in mines from 1880 until 1920, also faced non-person treatment and brutal discrimination and poverty. Backbreaking labor and menial service were the lot of the Chinese immigrant. Getting into the country legally was almost impossible. Maxine Hong-Kingston writes:

Arriving in San Francisco Bay, the legal father was detained for an indefinite time at the Immigration Station on Angel Island. . . . In a wooden house, a white demon [crudely] physically examined him. . . . [He was ushered into a crowded dormitory]. These must be the hundred China Men who could enter America, he thought. . . . Every day at intervals men were called out one by one . . . [The endless questioning contained endless traps.] The demons did not treat people of any other race the way they did the Chinese. . . . At last, they said, "You may enter the United States of America." (1980:53)

Racism was consistently their lot. From 1868, with the driving out of 440,000 miners of Chinese ancestry as a result of the Burlingame Treaty, through the Chinese Exclusion Acts of the 1880s and 1890s (extended in 1904 indefinitely), and various Supreme Court decisions relating to the Immigration Act of 1924, immigration was forcibly limited for Asians. The only exception to these oppressive and racially motivated laws was that a Supreme

Court victory was won in 1898 stating that a person born in the United States to Chinese parents is an American. It was not until 1946 (and the War Bride Act) that Chinese wives and children could immigrate. The immigration laws were not made more equitable until the late 1960s and 1970s (Hong-Kingston 1980). Chinese elders who could not marry present problems of isolation and poverty in old age that bring them to the attention of social agencies today (Lum 2000).

Policy in the Progressive Era on Balance

The tenacity and breadth of concern of the reformers were remarkable. Many worked from the 1890s until the nation turned to conservatism during and after World War I. Progressives dramatically expanded social obligation to include a host of regulations that had a direct salutary effect on the lives of poor and working people. Yet regulations hardly constituted formal assaults on poverty, low wages, or limited and means-tested government programs for people who were poor (Jansson 1993). Perhaps most important to note, as we consider an empowerment perspective, poor people had not spoken widely for themselves, nor had they joined with the reformers or others to develop an agenda for more far-reaching reforms. It would take the Great Depression to begin to achieve the realignment Progressives envisioned.

From the New Deal to the New Right: Still Trickling Down, Still Poor

In the 1920s a "trickle-down" economic philosophy was the dominant ethos. It was believed then (as in the Reagan-Bush era) that economic assistance to the rich and stimulation of industry would bring jobs to poor and working-class Americans. New tax laws reduced taxes on individuals and corporations, but Progressive era reforms were not monitored. The few government programs operating were short-lived demonstration programs. Strikes were violently suppressed and companies seduced workers by giving out stock and starting their own unions. Although the trickle-down philosophy held no benefit for the poor before 1929, it may have been one of the complex forces leading to the Great Depression (Jansson 1988).

The America moving into the Great Depression was an industrial and urban society dependent mostly on cash wages for support. By 1932 unemployment reached 34 percent of the nonagricultural workforce and national income dropped 43 percent. By the mid-1930s the lifetime savings of millions of people were gone and countless aged people lived in destitution and dependency. This set the stage for the Social Security Act of 1935 (McSteen 1989).

President Roosevelt was strongly in favor of work as opposed to cash relief. In 1935 he created the WPA and established old-age and unemployment insurance and federal subsidies for a variety of public health and welfare projects affecting mothers, dependent and neglected children, the handicapped, and the blind (the worthy poor). Support for social insurance was attacked as often from the left as from the right, forcing the passing of a Social Security Act of modest proposals. It contained no provisions for insurance against sickness, for the unemployed after the covered period, or for a host of other categories of people needing relief. Yet the Social Security Act is the major milestone in the history of American social reform. It brought an expansion of public welfare activities and made many eligible for assistance, opened the way for national policy on public welfare, and was declared constitutional. A minimum-wage and maximum-hour law was adopted on the same day as the constitutionality of the Social Security Act was upheld—May 24, 1937 (Bremner 1967).

No Deal for Children, Women, African Americans, and Others of Color

It is important to note what the Social Security Act did not do and for whom. Earlier reformers have suggested that the task of making fundamental improvements in the income and living conditions of the masses might be beyond the ability of capitalism (Bremner 1961). However, the inclusion of Aid to Familes with Dependent Children (AFDC) in the Social Security Act was an important step, although uneven local administration often rendered it inadequate (Bremner 1989).

The WPA provided jobs for many poor people and began to make an impact on poverty, but it, along with many emergency measures, terminated after the election of 1936. The new insurance plans for aged and unem-

ployed workers covered only certain classes of workers in preferred occupations. Low-wage workers (e.g., those in agriculture, domestic service, and
nonprofit charitable and educational organizations) were excluded. This severely limited benefits to women and people of color. Although social workers on the Advisory Committee on Public Employment and Relief strongly
opposed categorical assistance and called for federal authority over state relief
programs, Congress narrowed those eligible within categories. State control
was promoted by Southern congressmen, who maintained wording that was
discriminatory to blacks. After World War II only the categorical assistance
programs for the old, the blind, and the orphaned remained.

To help families survive, married women entered the workforce in increasing numbers before the Depression and until the end of World War II.
After the war the debate about "woman's place" was accompanied by the
expulsion of women from the labor force. Organized labor (e.g., the AFL)
refused to hire married women with working husbands. The railroads fired
all married women, and other companies means-tested wives with husbands
earning more than $50 a month. Seventy-seven percent of all school systems
refused to hire wives as teachers, and 63 percent dismissed women teachers
who married. From 1932 until 1937 Section 213 of the Federal Economy
Act had prohibited more than one member of the same family from working
in civil service. This of course also limited class mobility, thus maintaining
the needed unskilled labor force while enforcing women's economic dependence on men (Abramovitz 1989a).

Hamilton and Hamilton add a critical dimension in emphasizing that
"race . . . has always been fused with class in the political struggle to obtain
equitable policies to alleviate poverty" (1986:287). They observe that two-
thirds of the black labor force was not covered by the Social Security Act.
Others say that up to 90 percent were not covered (Jansson 1988). The
NAACP and National Urban League fought hard for the coverage of these
workers. In 1941, as a result of pressure and the threat of a national march
from A. Philip Randolph, leader of the Brotherhood of Sleeping Car Porters
and Maids, President Roosevelt issued Executive Order 8802, which prohibited discrimination in the defense industries. Blacks were still the last to
be hired and the first to be fired. Demand for labor during World War II
opened new opportunities and union memberships that were restricted after
the war. In 1946 the NAACP and National Urban League were in favor of
a "Right-to-a-Job Act," but the bill enacted was highly compromised. The

black organizations of the 1930s and 1940s strongly favored "jobs, not alms" (Hamilton and Hamilton 1986; Franklin and Moss 1988).

Although all Asians continued to experience violent discrimination, the most horrendous U.S. policy during this period was the evacuation of 110,000 persons of Japanese ancestry to relocation camps at the beginning of World War II. Equally shocking is that no Americans protested the evacuation policy (Kitano 1987; Jansson 1988).

Native Americans had suffered repeated massacres and extermination, the last being at Wounded Knee, South Dakota, in 1870. The Dawes Act of 1922 marked the end of the extermination period and the introduction of assimilation and loss of tribal property. In the 1950s the Bureau of Indian Affairs began the termination of federal status and U.S. government responsibility in many areas. The widespread termination was stopped when tribal governments rallied in opposition. However, P.L. 280, enacted in 1953, relinquished federal responsibility for direct financial resources and social services in a number of states while providing for state jurisdiction over matters of dependence and that resulted in the removal of Indian children from their families. This was not reversed until the Indian Child Welfare act of 1978. Native American organizations, such as the National Congress of American Indians, founded in 1944, came into being to secure the rights, self-determination, and well-being of American Indians and Alaska natives. Yet massive unemployment, serious health problems, and early deaths continue in American Indian communities (Blanchard 1987).

Many Puerto Ricans fought in World War II, and the island itself has been used for military purposes. In 1941 a garrison was maintained in San Juan, intensifying the problems of a newly industrialized society. The Puerto Rican Development Corporation was established in 1942 (Operation Bootstrap), yet relatively few jobs were created. This led to higher per capita income for Puerto Ricans, but the wealth of the island remained in the hands of a chosen few. Indeed, light-skinned Puerto Ricans were hired over darker ones, perpetuating the racism of the United States in the island. After World War II and the new anti-immigration laws, industries began to woo Puerto Ricans to the Northeast to provide a source of cheap labor. Puerto Ricans emigrated to New York to find themselves in competition with all those already at the bottom rung of the ladder (Morales 1986).

The New Deal vastly expanded the role of the federal government; it modified but did not make structural changes in income redistribution or welfare's role in the regulation of the labor market or the preservation of the

social order (Katz 1986). It was, at its best, an insurance-based annuity for
those who had a stable attachment to the labor force (Heclo 1986).

Bertha Capen Reynolds: A Radical "Psychiatric Caseworker" Who Stood Between Client and Community

Where was the profession of social work in the years preceding and following the Great Depression? There was an intense focus on systematically
developing the methodology of the profession, and between the 1930s and
the 1960s few social workers made connections between major socioeconomic events and social work. Bertha C. Reynolds (1885–1978) was an
exception. She was influenced by her teaching experience with Dr. W. E. B.
Du Bois at Atlanta University in 1910. She graduated in 1918 from Smith
College School of Social Work and was associate director from 1925 until
1938. She combined the day's psychoanalytically oriented casework practice
with a progressive, democratic socialist, and collective action view of society
to develop an unparalleled depth and integrated perspective on social work
practice. Reynolds said:

> Could I possibly have guessed in the burgeoning 1920s that well-
> adjusted individuals were not to be the salvation of our world? Adjusted
> to what? took on sinister meaning in the 1930s when the economic
> substratum of our life turned up in a mighty earthquake, grotesque
> examples of an underworld of human misery which we had thought
> only incidental to a well-ordered civilization. Now we began to wonder
> if there was something wrong with what we called civilization itself.
> (1964:312)

In 1953 Reynolds, banned from social work conferences for her "un-
closeted" Marxist views, gave a paper entitled "Fear In Our Culture" at the
Cleveland Council of Arts, Sciences, and Professions that decried Mc-
Carthyism and challenged us to become empowered people:

> The whole purpose of these witch hunts that violate our most precious
> American democratic tradition can be defeated if plain people like
> ourselves, workers, and intellectuals, know of certainty one fact and
> act upon it. We do not need to acquiesce in the production of a way

of life which is adjusted to continuous war, which glorifies violence and denies the use of intelligence and cooperation. . . . Clear-eyed men and women have been all too few. We need an aroused whole people speaking out in their labor unions, churches, lodges wherever they are, for peace. We need to forget all unessential differences in our common danger . . . we must let nothing keep us apart. This choice is before us. What kind of country will we have? What kind of people will we be, as we live in this most critical time of all history? . . . The point is to get to work with others, where we are and now. (1953:73)

Using her experience in the United Seamen's Service as a springboard, Reynolds launched social work on a critical journey into the meaning of belonging and human connection. She, like Jane Addams, believed that "social work had its taproot in what people did for themselves and for each other" (1963:236). She championed a vision of people working together to shape the forces that "move toward the welfare of people . . . and fight against the forces which bring death and destruction" (1951:175). She saw social work as leading to "more social approaches to solving problems" where clients "take part in a real effort of the plain people to see that their social services are truly social and really serve" (1951:174). This is critical to the empowerment approach, which assumes that social work has a mandate and interest in working with the "plain people," to be "ever and always a go-between profession" (Reynolds 1964:17). Reynolds sees social work as a "mediating function." Politically, her vision includes the highest ideals of democracy—full citizen participation and equity in the distribution of resources more common to socialism. The vision places social workers in the arena where people work and live. It offers "penetrating social appraisal" into how people cope in order to "meet their reality or change it" (1951:131).

Reynolds also takes social workers to task, and we sadly see that what was true more than thirty-five years ago is even more true today:

Social work . . . has tried to deny incurable poverty, illness and social maladjustment, first by assuming that the solution lies in the treatment of unconscious conflict within the person, instead of in society itself. Then, in self-protection, social agencies have moved away from contact with cases in which poverty, illness and friction were too obviously beyond the reach of a change in the client's feelings. (1951:130)

Reynolds noted that this was our tendency as early as the Lawrence Woolen Mills strike (1912):

> In that distressed city there were soup kitchens to be kept going; shelter had to be found for the homeless. . . . In all this, were social workers contributing their skills and resources as they would have done in a flood or fire disaster? We have no such record. But the work was done . . . by the strikers themselves. (1963:26)

Reynolds emphasizes: "Our practice is in the world of social living, whether we like it or not, and whether or not our theories correspond with it" (1951:ix). Social work is not a matter of the "haves" giving to the "have-nots"; instead it involves being neighbors in a common struggle.

Reynolds concluded that helpers need to find interdependence with the helped so that helping systems and processes do not hurt or destroy people. This should include the following:

- Basic forms of full employment and social insurance that provide a decent income base for all people (1951).
- A basic sense of social membership/belonging in society and basic rights for all oppressed groups. Reynolds was quite clear that there was considerable underlying discrimination as to who was a preferred client and that there is a public and moral obligation to all members of society (1951, 1963).
- A notion of reciprocity and recognition of the capacity to repay in some form at some time. This speaks to a belief in the value of the client to society (1951).
- A concept of professional help that allows for common humanity and "minimal" professional distance and authenticity of the workers (1963).
- The ability to approach a client on his or her own terms without requiring that our standards for change and growth be met (1951).
- A recognition of the groups to which a person belongs and an ability to use this in practice, including actual intervention in these groups to supplement natural helping systems that have become weakened (1951).

Reynolds urged social work's cooperation with existing progressive forces as she reflects on social work's inability to change socioeconomic forces single-handedly: "It was not we, a handful of social workers, against a sea of human misery. It was humanity itself building dikes, and we were helping in our own peculiarly useful way" (1963:183). Empowered people themselves are the builders. We are fellow workers and neighbors with special expertise in the struggle for social living and social justice.

The Return of "Good Times" — for Some

After World War II a period of relative prosperity began that lasted through the 1950s. It was an era of economic growth, rising expectations, and the pursuit of security. Benefits were added to the welfare state incrementally, but those who would fill its programmatic gaps or give it a more egalitarian base were at a stalemate with conservative forces. Truman, in his Fair Deal proposals, attempted to establish national health insurance, "full employment" mandates, more consistent national standards, and the extension of social security programs. These all failed, except for the Federal Housing Act of 1949, which created public housing and cleared slums (because of middle-class support that resulted from the postwar housing shortage) and the 1950 extension of Social Security benefits to small, self-employed businessmen, war widows, and domestic servants. Conservative forces and vested interest groups, such as the American Medical Association, succeeded in stopping such important proposed advances as national health insurance (Critchlow and Hawley 1989).

The Eisenhower years were marked by a belief in the ability of the private sector to provide for all and the passage of one important piece of policy legislation — the addition of disability insurance provisions to the Social Security Act. By 1960 disability insurance coverage had been expanded to all age groups. While "Ike" had his eye on resolving international crises, the bureaucrats who engineered and continued to believe in the Social Security Act worked to consolidate some of the gains of the New Deal (Berkowitz and McQuaid 1989).

Civil Rights: Human Rights

In terms of civil rights for people different from dominant Americans, the 1940s and early 1950s were not "good times." Truman's proposed federal civil rights legislation was defeated. African Americans and other people of color returned from the war to face segregation and discrimination in every area of life. Truman had desegregated the armed forces, but this had little impact on civilian life (Jansson 1988).

Between the early 1940s, when the mechanical cotton picker went into mass production, and the late 1960s, more than five million African Americans migrated from the rural South to big cities. They had hoped to find the "Promised Land" of economic opportunity and social justice. Instead they were forced to live in segregated ghettos and met with discrimination and violence (Lemann 1991). Yet the mid-1950s marked a turning point in the history of oppressed people in the United States. The civil rights movement began under the leadership of Dr. Martin Luther King Jr. The courage of Rosa Parks, an African American woman who was arrested for refusing to give up her seat to a white man on a bus in Montgomery, Alabama, acted as a catalyst to the Montgomery bus boycott. Dr. King, in analyzing the boycott, said that the intimidation, force, and violence of the authorities served to unify the black community. The arrest of Rosa Parks, the harassment of motorists, the arrest of King on a false charge, the bombing of King's home, and the arrest of eighty-nine persons (twenty-four ministers) for the nonviolent protest engendered support for the boycott throughout the nation (Ansbro 1982). This boycott and the other 1950s and 1960s civil rights actions of African Americans on their own behalf in coalition with others was a major moment of empowerment in American history.

The 1954 landmark decision of the U.S. Supreme Court in *Brown* v. *The Board of Education of Topeka* marked the first legal victory of African Americans since the Emancipation Proclamation. The NAACP also secured the U.S. Supreme Court decision that desegregated the buses in Montgomery and ended the need for the boycott. The place of litigation in the Civil Rights Movement cannot be underestimated.

Despite these victories in the civil rights struggle, many forms of discrimination were commonly practiced. Women were consigned to low-paying jobs and rarely given day-care assistance. Many pink- and blue-collar workers lacked health insurance. Mentally ill and developmentally disabled people faced unjustified and long-term admissions to institutions, for very few community programs existed. Gay people faced outright hatred and discrimination: bylaws outlawing their private sexual activity, mental health professionals who defined homosexuality as a form of mental illness rather than as a different sexual orientation, and discrimination in housing and em-

ployment. Many gay persons were involuntarily committed to mental institutions to be "cured," and many were fired from the federal civil service,
the State Department, and the armed forces. Public discrimination existed
toward most minority groups in the 1950s—political radicals, feminists, gays,
religious and racial/ethnic minorities included (Jansson 1988). This climate
of repression against the backdrop of the civil rights movement and the
Democratic victory of John Kennedy in 1960 set the stage for a new era of
rights and reform.

The 1960s: "We Shall Overcome"/"The Times They Are a-Changin' "

The 1960s was a decade of optimism and accomplishment for oppressed
groups and their allies. However, policies lagged behind program innovations, which were a long-term strategy with short-term reversible gains.
People-changing solutions, such as job training and education, were advanced to solve structural problems. Yet poor people felt something good
was beginning to happen.

Then the optimism caused by mass involvement in civil rights victories
and a heightened national consciousness regarding poverty and racism was
shattered with the assassinations of John and Robert Kennedy and Martin
Luther King Jr. African Americans and poor Americans gave these leaders
honored places in their hearts and in their homes, often placing their pictures on the wall next to a picture of Christ. Their murders were cause for
national mourning and disillusionment. For many, the assassination of Malcolm X (or El-Hajj Malik El Shabazz) in 1965 added a fourth outrage to
this decade of dashed hopes, mourning, and disillusion. Malcolm X attacked
the cancer of racism with a strategy of self-affirmation, economic self-help,
and self-defense for African American people. His earlier attacks on white
racists and avid support of separatism put him outside the acceptance of the
majority of whites or blacks. It is ironic that his later movement toward
embracing classic Islam and unity with all oppressed people, a stance that
brought his ideas close to King's, and to being heard more widely also
brought him death (Malcolm X 1965). A vacuum was created that reactionary forces would fill.

The reforms of this era deserve to be carefully examined to determine
what was gained and what opportunities were missed. The successful Mont-

gomery bus boycott initiated a long sequence of actions that successively challenged segregation in interstate transportation, lunch counters, train stations, public swimming pools, public schools, and colleges. Voter registration drives and protests against literacy tests and poll taxes won voting power rights in the South. As these were bloody victories, the whole nation was sensitized to issues of racism, poverty, and inequity.

President Kennedy proposed his own civil rights legislation in 1963 that prohibited job and voter registration discrimination. The policy gains for poor people during the Kennedy administration included the Manpower Development and Training Act of 1962, the nation's first major job training program, major increases in the minimum wage, partly due to the pressure of unions, the Area Redevelopment Agency in 1961, the Community Mental Health Centers Act of 1963, which funded a national network of outpatient centers, and a "services strategy" for AFDC. Each of these gains also represented opportunity lost, since training did not guarantee jobs, the vulnerable mentally ill needed more than therapy to survive, and adequate income alone could lift people out of poverty. These measures did not change the picture of poverty substantially, leaving them open to reactionary criticism. Yet Kennedy shattered the conservative complacency of the 1950s and established a policy agenda for his successor. Civil rights legislation, the War on Poverty, food stamps, Medicare, federal aid to public schools, and tax reforms were enacted by Lyndon B. Johnson soon after Kennedy was assassinated (Jansson 1988).

Many of the gains of Johnson's War on Poverty were long-reaching, others created only the illusion of relieving poverty. Progressive bills were defeated and attacked by both the right and the left. Funds were diverted to job creation or training programs and some health services. The direct participation of poor people was worrisome to many.

The War on Poverty was effective in liberalizing social security, welfare, and veterans benefits and in increasing expenditures in these areas. The growth of AFDC doubled and the middle class became concerned. Now the ethic was that (poor) women should work. The WIN program was one answer to this sentiment, though jobs were not created. The number of persons classified as poor from 1959 until 1968 decreased by 36 percent. Johnson's greatest accomplishments were establishing Medicare, Medicaid, and food stamps and further extending Social Security, though these transfers were not the primary focus of the War on Poverty. The focus of federal health care, however, remained on the elderly (Medicare) and not on those receiving public assistance (Critchlow and Hawley 1989). A multiplicity of forces brought some success during this period. Given the American history of treatment of the poor and minorities of color, we may ask how the War on Poverty did as well as it did rather than why it failed.

In 1964 the Council of Economic Advisers concluded that income transfers of $11 billion would eliminate poverty. But they concluded that this would leave the "roots of poverty" untouched. They saw employment for the poor and job training as far better (Critchlow and Hawley 1989:219). They continued to believe that poverty is temporary and will disappear with a good economy and that the work ethic would solve all problems. Hence they determined that poor people should change themselves but that poverty would remain unchanged.

The war in Vietnam required tremendous resources. Martin Luther King Jr. warned, "The pursuit of widened war has narrowed domestic welfare programs, making the poor, white and black, bear the heaviest burdens at the front and home" (Ansbro 1982:258). In his 1967 essay "Where Do We Go from Here: Chaos or Community?" King challenged the separatist pulls of the times and called for a change of the slogan "Black Power" to "Power for Poor People." For this he was criticized on all sides. His global vision and his antiwar stance were consistent with his a priori assumption of nonviolence as the means of active resistance against oppression. His leadership of the Poor People's Movement gained momentum. Coretta Scott King noted, "He spoke out sharply for all the poor in all their hues, for he knew if color made them different, misery and oppression made them the same" (Ansbro 1982:36). This could hardly be tolerated. Poor people of all racial and ethnic groups were beginning to join together and break the stereotypes of political passivity and quiescence (Critchlow and Hawley 1989). They marched and formed tent cities on the White House lawn. They became vocal, visible, and empowered. King's antipoverty and anticlass leadership was powerful. On April 4, 1968, Dr. Martin Luther King Jr. was assassinated in Memphis as he organized a Poor People's March for antipoverty legislation and worked to line up support for a sanitation workers' strike in Tennessee. With his death many diverse voices were silenced.

The civil rights gains of blacks had created a climate in which other minority groups demanded policy changes. The feminist movement flourished. Congress enacted an Equal Pay Act in 1963 and included gender discrimination in Title VII of the Civil Rights Act of 1964. The National Organization of Women (NOW) and other groups pushed for an equal rights amendment to the Constitution. After the Stonewall Riot in 1969, when gay men resisted brutal harassment by the police at a gay bar in Greenwich Village, the gay community was strengthened. Local and national gay civil rights organizations formed. Farm workers under Cesar Chavez and the United Farm Workers obtained landmark legislation in California to guarantee collective bargaining rights. The American Indian movement took over the Bureau of Indian Affairs building in Washington, D.C., in 1972 and at Wounded Knee in 1973 in a symbolic gesture of strength (Blanchard 1987). However, a renewed fear of difference and change, combined with economic insecurity for majority Americans and the depletion of resources during the Vietnam War, hastened the end of the War on Poverty and reform era.

Turning Back Time: The Divide-and-Conquer Strategy

Although many thought that the New Deal and the Great Society formed a divide of a minimal institutionalized welfare state that would never dare be crossed, the conservative Republicans began the contest of ideology in 1964 with Goldwater's candidacy, which represented an attempt to turn back the clock to the pre–New Deal mentality of antigovernmentalism (Annunziata 1989).

The momentum of the War on Poverty created bipartisan support for a continuation of reform legislation in Congress that lasted through the 1970s, despite three conservative presidents. Spending increased markedly in Nixon's first term, and his second term marked a deliberate use of destructive rhetoric to split and polarize Americans against reformers, activists, and the newfound strength of oppressed groups. His identification of mainstream working- and middle-class whites as the "silent majority of law-abiding citizens" implied that minority groups were too vocal and not law-abiding. Surely, the reasoning went, the "unsilent minority" is the problem, not the economy. Yet major welfare state gains were made in the midst of this divisive rhetoric: Social Security Insurance (SSI) for older and disabled Americans, revisions in the food stamp program, the consolidation of the social services in Title XX to the Social Security Act, health legislation programs such as the Occupational Safety and Health Administration (OSHA) and the Community Education and Training Administration (CETA), the Community Block Grant Development Program, and a Child Abuse Protection Act. The expansion of cash and in-kind programs reduced poverty in the 1970s more than in any other era. Under bipartisan pressure, Nixon proposed two welfare reforms that were not enacted—the Family Assistance Program (FAP) and national health insurance (Jansson 1993).

The defeat of the Family Assistance Program was a missed opportunity. This act called for a minimum income floor, help for the working poor, and workfare. Because it included the working poor, it was a leap toward treating poverty as a permanent basic social policy responsibility of the federal government. Such groups as the National Welfare Rights Organization (NWRO) were outraged that the proposed floor was ridiculously low. But the NWRO failed to see the opportunity to establish a precedent for government responsibility toward the working poor (Hamilton and Hamilton 1986). Similar criticism is leveled at the missed opportunity to enact a national health insurance act that would have paved the way for greater reform.

The failure to enact President Jimmy Carter's "comprehensive welfare reform bill" was another missed opportunity. Carter had supported the Humphrey and Hawkins Full Employment and Balanced Growth Act, which might have been the equivalent of a strong right-to-a-job act. However, it was a diluted and meaningless version of this act that was enacted in 1978 (Jansson 1988; Hamilton and Hamilton 1986). The failure to enact Carter's "National Agenda for the Eighties" was another lost opportunity.

Carter's "President's Commission for a National Agenda for the Eighties" report, completed in December 1980, exposed the extent of poverty and its effects on women and blacks. It recommended that Congress legislate a minimum security income for all Americans related to the poverty level, from two-thirds to three-fourths of that amount with a relatively low tax on earnings. The program would have replaced AFDC, food stamps, and general assistance programs, providing permanent effective reform. The working poor would have been aided and welfare benefits raised to an adequate level. Recommendations were made regarding provisions for comprehensive national health insurance, disease prevention, and care for the elderly. The needs of children were also addressed. The recommendations of this report were intended to "reduce the outstanding inequities that are inconsistent with the broader goals of social justice for America in the Eighties" (Colby 1989).

However, by 1978 Carter, in a desperate effort to lower double-digit inflation, had effected massive cuts in social programs and a substantial increase in military spending that launched a conservative assault on social spending under Ronald Reagan (Jansson 1988).

Reagan/Bush and Back to the Future

Enter Ronald Reagan, the most conservative president since before the New Deal, with promises of huge tax cuts to restore a time of plenty and "law and order." Seeing himself as a "New Federalist," Reagan hoped to return to the values of the 1770s. Reagan approached income security with these major goals: (1) to reduce short-term growth in spending, (2) to turn over greater responsibility for welfare assistance to the states, and (3) to promote "self-sufficiency" through work and asset accumulation and lessen dependence on public benefits (Storey 1989).

Reagan's unprecedented increases in military spending necessitated severe domestic spending cuts. He took all the social spending cuts from programs that gave services and resources to poor persons. In the 1984 budget nearly 60 percent of the cuts occurred specifically in low-income assistance programs. The in-kind programs—food, housing, and fuel subsidies—were hit hardest. These in-kind programs had gone the furthest to reduce poverty in previous decades and continue to have the best potential for reducing it unless high employment rates can be achieved (Danziger and Weinberg 1986). Reagan's block grants all involved significant spending cuts (Doolittle 1987).

Under Reagan's schema all were to share in growing prosperity by a "trickle-down" effect or through voluntarism and charity (Morris 1989). History has established that very little of the gross national product actually trickles down to people who are poor.

Reagan's rhetoric failed to match reality. When the Reagan administration announced its Program for Economic Recovery in February 1981, it established "preservation of the social safety net" as the first of nine criteria to be used in revising Carter's budget. What this meant was that those programs with a powerful constituency would be exempted, at least temporarily, from the cuts. There was no national income floor. The food stamp program was treated most harshly (Storey 1989). The safety net was full of gaping holes. The working poor fell to the bottom. Cuts affecting the middle class took their toll in college student benefit phase-outs, the administrative review of disability claims, limitations on unemployment benefits, and cuts in federal subsidies for school meals (Storey 1989). From 1979 to 1987 the poorest fifth of our citizens, more than 40 million, had their standard of living decline by 9 percent, while the living standard of the top fifth increased by 19 percent (Gitterman 1991:6). This situation resulted from social welfare cutbacks and increases in social security taxes, decreases in corporate and capital gains taxes, and inelasticity in real estate taxes (Morris 1989).

The dramatic nationwide increase in homelessness is one tragic trend related to "Reaganomics." Under Reagan, low-cost housing support dropped more than 75 percent (Ehrlich 1988). Homeless families (mostly mothers and children) became the fastest-growing segment of the homeless population (Connell 1987). Most working-class people are only two or three paychecks away from poverty and homelessness. Additionally, the "underclass"—the poorest of the urban poor—had tripled from .75 million in 1970 to 2.5 million by 1980 (Alter, Bradford, and Springer 1988). Unemployment and underemployment remained an increasingly grave concern as the nation experienced ongoing "deep recession." Working-class families were devastated by structural unemployment in steel, automobile, and other industries. Cities faced the loss of jobs to industries moving to rural or foreign locations and minority unemployment rates were several times that of whites (Silverman, Simon, and Woodrow 1991:711).

Reagan's conservative counterrevolution substantially reduced domestic spending, massively increased military spending, and drastically reduced the policy roles of the federal government. Tax reforms penalized the working poor and drastically reduced the tax rates of affluent Americans. Affirmative action policies were attacked by the president, the Justice Department, and the director of the Civil Rights Commission. Reagan achieved only a part of his conservative agenda, but his administration demonstrated the fragility of the welfare state (Hopps 1987).

Women and People of Color

No matter how poverty is measured, women and people of color suffer most. "The major factors in reductions in poverty that have occurred in the past 15 years have been increases in cash and in-kind transfers." However, 22.46 percent of all post-transfer poor households are headed by black women with children under age six, making them the group most vulnerable

to poverty. Post-transfer poverty rates in 1982 for blacks, Hispanics, and female household heads remained above the official rates for whites in 1966,
when in-kind transfers had little impact (Danziger 1987).

"Children living in mother-only families were more than five times more
likely to be poor than were those living in two-parent families: 38% compared with 7%" (Corcoran and Chandry 1997:41). The feminization of poverty is not a new phenomenon; women's impoverishment dates back to Colonial America (Abramovitz 1989a). Poverty has always been a woman's
issue.

Similarly, it has always been an issue for people of color. Hopps (1987)
states that although the programs cut during these years affected a larger
number of white recipients, the impact was felt more severely by people of
color, who have a disproportionate dependence on these programs. Like-
wise, cutbacks in the federal (and state) workforces had a greater impact on
minorities of color because this employment was a major route to the middle
class. Hard data on median incomes also show the disparity in the earnings
of black, white, and Hispanic families. The median income for white families was $21,900, whereas it was $12,670 for black families and $14,270 for
Hispanic families, according to the 1980 census (Hopps 1987). It was
$15,418 in American Indian households (Blanchard 1987). Rural Black pop-
ulations have the highest poverty rate despite the fact that the rural poor
have a higher rate of living in working two-parent families (Dudenhefer
1993).

Children of all races are the largest group of impoverished persons in the
United States. Children of color are disproportionately poor. (The reader is
directed to chapter 1 and McAdoo 1987; Corcoran and Chaudry 1997). It
is astounding to think that almost half of all black children are raised in
poverty. It is equally astonishing to note that 75 percent of all the black
students in public schools are concentrated in approximately 2 percent of
the nation's school districts, which are segregated, and in urban areas (Mc-
Adoo 1987). When we look at the employment picture, facts are equally
disturbing. Although the black middle class has grown since 1960, the black-
white salary gap is widening. In 1987 blacks' median weekly salary was 78.6
percent that of white salary for the same period (Kantrowitz and Springer
1988). In 1930 the proportion of adult black men who were employed was
80 percent and in 1984 it was only 56 percent. At the end of 1984 the
unemployment rate of black male teenagers (sixteen to eighteen years old)
was 44 percent. Educational achievement did not seem to help. In 1984 the

unemployment rate of black youths who completed high school (38 percent) was higher than that of white school dropouts. McAdoo concludes, "Race is still a powerful determinant of who does not get employed" (1987). Hispanics are just behind blacks in overall poverty rates, yet they are the fastest-growing population in America. Hispanics may someday replace blacks as the largest minority group in America, and they are at high risk of remaining poor (Estrada 1987). Morales's work substantiates this. In New York City, for example, Puerto Ricans run ahead of blacks in the poverty indicators, such as income and being on welfare, and behind blacks in job training and having good jobs. "Relative to other communities, Puerto Ricans have moved backwards" (Morales 1986). The absence of bilingual education contributes to this problem. Estrada concludes, despite gains in education and employment, "The descriptive portrait [of the 1980s] is not different than that of the 1970s, when Hispanics had the lowest level of educational attainment and the highest rate of unemployment" (1987). In the twenty-first century, these groups represent the majority of our children and our future.

Bush and the Continuation of Reagan's Principles

George Bush's presidency translated, as forecasted, into "four more years" of Ronald Reagan. President Bush's term was marked by economic disaster and a "brief" but costly war effort in the Persian Gulf (January–March 1991) that followed Reagan's emphasis on military might to a tee, "vindicated" Reagan's massive military spending, and improved Bush's media image. His precipitous rise in popularity masked deep trouble on the domestic front as the nation plunged deeper into recession (the most severe since the Great Depression), and the working poor and poor continued to sustain the brunt of his ongoing massive cutbacks. Bush's "Thousand Points of Light" program emphasized the virtues of voluntarism and absolution of the federal government's social obligation. Bush's fiscal year 1992 proposed budget was a rerun of the 1991 budget proposed to terminate 238 domestic discretionary programs that served working poor and poor people. Bush's tax proposals regressively favored the wealthy.

Although defense spending was automatically limited by the 1991 budget law, the 1992 budget included substantial increases for the Strategic Defense Initiative (Star Wars) and for the B-2 stealth bomber. The expenses for the

Persian Gulf War were also exempt from limitations, and there was evidence that the Pentagon charged even routine defense costs to Operation Desert Storm, thus making room under the budget cap for more and more defense spending. Perhaps most ominously, new civil rights legislation was threatened by Bush's presidential veto.

Congress tempered some of these proposals, as did the so-called end of the cold war, which changed some military priorities. The economy fared worse under Bush in growth of domestic product, jobs, disposable income, industrial production, and hourly wage than under any president since the Great Depression (*New York Times*, November 4 1992:B13). The fears that conservatives in power, still representing the affluent, would turn against the welfare state were well founded.

The Economy Falters: Twelve Years of Conservative Republican Rule Is Ended

In the November 1992 election the American people voted for change. Democratic insurgent Bill Clinton, the governor of Arkansas, won the presidency by a decisive margin. He held on to traditional Democratic voters, carrying more than three-fourths of the black vote, more than one-half of the Catholic vote, and an overwhelming majority of Jewish votes. He courted and won the votes of Southern Democrats (Hamilton and Hamilton 1997). The blue-collar Democrat and middle-class suburbanite coalition that carried Bush in 1988 splintered because of concern about the economy. Clinton also carried women (about 50 percent), more than half the first-time voters, as well as seven out of ten gay people. Voters indicated that jobs and the economy were their top priorities. The "family values" argument of the Republican campaign that denounced nontraditional family forms alienated more voters than it attracted (*New York Times*, November 4, 1992). Ron Brown, the chairman of the Democratic National Committee, said that it was a watershed election for America. "The case for change . . . resonated so much that it broke down traditional political lines. It's a new day" (Toner 1992:A1). Illinois elected its first African American senator, Carol Moseley Braun of Chicago. There were more women (six), blacks, Hispanics, and other minorities of color in the Congress than ever before (*New York Times* 1992:A1). This was also true of the Cabinet.

The Clinton Years

The politically empowered used the democratic process and brought change. Clinton began with challenging Republican social policies—including those affecting women, families, and gay people in the military—with a heavy focus on the economy (Friedman 1992:A1, A18). Positive changes in policies affecting the poor and working poor do not come overnight. They do not come at all if empowered voters become complacent. Empowered people need to hold the president and the Congress to the fire, otherwise positive change will not come, despite partisan change or the political rhetoric of campaigns. The people must direct any president in what is needed and desired for social justice.

The accountability of government is a worldwide concern. Guyanese social worker and poet Aaron Blackman puts it this way in his poem entitled "The Presidents":

> This I expect of all Presidents
> Respecting and loving the nation's residents
> Fighting to stop further dissent
> The use of arms they must resent . . .
> The poor and needy they should assist. . . .
> Nutrition and education they must give priority
> To stop the world's growing insanity
> Listen they must to the workers. . . .
> This I expect of all Presidents
> To limit the borrowing of big bankers' money
> Yet yielding to the cries of many
> In this world of plenty. (1997)

The jury is still out on the Clinton presidency. The years of economic expansion, low inflation, and a soaring stock market meant greater prosperity for those who already had a foothold in economic security. But this prosperity did not filter down to the almost 37 million (15 percent) poor and working poor Americans who live below the poverty line. Children's Defense Fund statistics indicate that in 1998 top CEOs earned 185 times as much as the average worker while the nation's poorest fifth of families lost $587 each in purchasing power and the richest 5 percent added $29,533 (Jones 1999). Clinton's economic Empowerment-Enterprise Zones improved the quality of life in several poor communities, but they were not widespread. The most disappointing aspect of the Clinton years was his signing of the so-called welfare reform legislation in 1996 (Hamilton and Hamilton 1997). This demonstrated to millions of poor citizens that they have no friend in the White House. They must instead develop their own leaders and act in their own best interests.

Welfare "Reform" and Other Policy Retreats

On August 22, 1996, during an election year, President Clinton signed a welfare bill introduced by the Republican-led legislature that drastically changed the public assistance system that provided a gossamer safety net for poor individuals and families for sixty years (Hamilton and Hamilton 1997; Seccombe 1999). This bill was heralded by the right as necessary reform, but by many well-known Democrats concerned for the poor it was seen as "mean," " lowdown," a "moment of shame" in the nation's history. Some felt it was the beginning of dismantling the Social Security system. Poor children were seen as the greatest potential losers with the new legislation (Hamilton and Hamilton 1997; Jones 1999). Clinton signed a third version of the bill as he thought the first two versions were too punitive (Seccombe 1999). Yet the bill remained a harsh one.

It is difficult to judge the effects of sweeping social policy changes like welfare repeal. Senator Patrick Moynihan called the 1996 repeal of the federal welfare guarantee changing Aid to Dependent Families (AFDC) to Temporary Assistance to Needy Families (TANF) the largest gamble in the twentieth century. State governments charged with monitoring barely have the capacity to assess these changes. The Urban Institute predicts 2.6 million additional Americans falling into poverty, but results are not yet in. The short time limits and work requirements without the availability of appropriate jobs are the most difficult and dangerous aspects of this bill. While almost ten million AFDC families were removed from the roles in 1997, it is not yet clear how many of them continue to live in poverty (Schorr 1997). A newly released report by the National Conference of State Legislatures revealed that 40–60 percent of those who leave welfare obtain jobs, but often at below poverty level wages (13,330 a year for a family of three in 1997). Many say they were better off on welfare. About one-fifth of the families returned to welfare within a few months. Among those who left welfare for work in September 1996, only 16 percent earned above poverty wages. Lack of child-care and transportation were most frequently cited as major reasons for not being able to keep a job. Clearly, getting off welfare is not equal to getting out of poverty (CDF 1998). People cycle on and off work, make less than $7 an hour, and have minimal or no health or other work-related benefits (Jones 1999). While welfare reform held out a promise of employment, the jobs are marginal-type jobs and there is little support to help parents prepare for, find, or keep a good job. (See, for example, the case of Shandra in chapter 9.) Welfare has been repealed, but reform has not yet happened. Training for and availability of good jobs may make the difference (Hamilton and Hamilton 1997; Rainwater and Smeeding 1996; and Schorr 1997). But a solid jobs initiative is costly and no recent president has endorsed such a strategy (Schorr 1997:179).

Indeed the "welfare problem" is better conceptualized as a "work problem" (Seccombe 1999). Hamilton and Hamilton argue that the most disadvantaged of Americans are not wanted or needed in the regular labor market, as structural unemployment works to put a cap on inflation. There are not enough real wage (or full-wage) jobs available for all those able and willing to work, and "there is no intention in the market economy for this to be otherwise" (1997:267). Civil rights organizations have been calling for real jobs/full employment for all for over sixty years. This call thus far remains unheeded as the divisions in American society become increasingly ominous (Hamilton and Hamilton 1997). Notes Schorr, "The phony welfare reform of 1996, could, ironically, open the door to real welfare reform if jobs and supportive strategies are endorsed by policy makers and the public" (1997:196).

Jansson (1993) documents the need for an expanded welfare state. He points out that single parents (and working two parent families) need supportive services and access to predictable job markets in order to get and hold a job and care for families.

There is little public support for child care subsidies for working parents or some form of child or family allowance, or even a $750 per child tax credit across the board that could be helpful to working poor families. Child allowances and guaranteed child support mitigate against child poverty in many of the other nations studied by Rainwater and Smeeding (1996). Food stamps and earned income tax credits do work in the United States and could also be used in other countries, but these are presently politically insecure forms of aid (NCCP 1996). For example, the National Center for

Policy Analysis reports that critics of the government bring up mismanagement of entitlements such as food stamps as a major justification for dismantling such benefits. Citing the *Investor's Business Daily*, February 19, 1999, they note: "Critics contend that the problem will only be solved when government agencies get less money, or better still, when unnecessary programs are eliminated altogether" (NCPA 1999). This regressive mentality endangers the lives of children and other poor individuals and is exactly why "entitlements" are "politically insecure forms of aid."

Corporate Welfare

In contrast to locating the problem of the public debt in programs for the poor such as food stamps or Aid to Dependent Children, a recent series in *Time* (November 1998 issues) underscores the tremendous cost of corporate welfare. Tax breaks and government subsidies to large corporations far outweigh the cost of entitlements and subsidies to impoverished individuals. Further, many corporate subsidies do not achieve the ends to which they were applied. Depressed areas stay depressed and the working poor get poorer, although the company may thrive. In the case of one giant agribusiness that specializes in pork and poultry processing, worker's wages are so low only transients and migrant workers are attracted to jobs. This corporation also has subsidiary companies in several developing countries where costs are low and labor is exploited. Environmental waste problems produced by their factories add to the costs of corporate welfare, as does the costs of education and social services for the working poor perpetuated by the company and homelessness, increased crime, dwindling property values, and deteriorating communities. Meanwhile, over the seven years of subsidy, the company holdings of the CEO soared to 425 million dollars and the public was left holding the bag (Barlett and Steele 1998). Until public consciousness is raised, the real welfare culprits will continue to exploit the American economy and poor workers and unemployed mothers will continue to be blamed for the public debt.

The Global Economy and Interdependence

The cycle of production involving large U.S. companies and the exploitation of workers here and in developing countries has been well illustrated in the example given above. Between 1970 and 1995 international trade as a percentage of domestic economy rose from 10 to 24 percent, with a resultant weakening of the position of organized labor in the United States, particularly when companies threaten to move. The new trade is not resource dependent, which offers worker's some leverage, but relys on technology and the increasing interchangeability of labor, which weakens both labor and social provision (Blau 1998). What is less clear is the affect on the global and local economies of rising and falling overseas markets. In December 1998 dramatic falls in the Asian market led to the layoff of forty-eight thousand employees of Seattle's Boeing Industries (*CBS Evening News* 12/2/98). The federation of European States in economic alliance and the Eurodollar will also have a yet unknown impact on the U.S. and other markets (*Participant*, November 1998). While some see globalization of the economy as a different kind of capitalism, others see it as an expansion of a system that ensures the poverty of the masses (Blau 1998). In either view, global economic interdependence means that our lives are tied together in a new way. Our common stakes as citizens of the world become palpable and real. Ramanathan (1999) suggests that economically powerful countries need to forge a new relationship with less powerful countries that shifts from the old ideas of "aid" to the new idea of mutual empowerment and gain through exchange and cooperation.

Empowerment: The Ability to Run the Race

In 1989 Morris suggested a modest agenda for "palatable" government responsibility that consisted of four parts: agreeing to agree among advocates for any governmental responsibility, selecting work and income, plus a national health system as the basic core, redesigning social programs before expansion, and creating institutional capacity for analysis, research, and development (1989).

Must we, as Morris suggests, agree to agree? Or can we, together with people who are poor, help form a dialectic that will come to a solution perhaps not seen here? What is desperately needed is a "fair start" (Heclo 1986).

Although "taking the poor away from view," getting antipoverty policies in "through the back door" (Heclo 1986), and soft-pedaling legislation may engineer some gains for poor people and people of color, they do nothing

to empower them. Poor and working people, women, and people of color
have acted for themselves throughout history. They joined together in mass
action during several depressions and recessions of American history to demonstrate. Unions of working people have successfully used strikes and walk-
outs. Economic boycotts have been used successfully. Sometimes people
who suffer the most from injustice have had to disrupt business as usual to
be heard; sometimes they have rioted and resorted to violence. Most often
they have acted politically and demonstrated peacefully and nonviolently.
During the 1960s and the 1992 presidential election they demonstrated that
they could mobilize to vote when they percieved choices to be made. Despite images of poor people as apathetic (Heclo 1986), there has been ample
evidence that the mythological "passive poor" can certainly act in their own
interests and in the interest of justice (Piven and Cloward 1977; Katz 1989b;
Baptist, Bricker-Jenkins, and Dillon 1998 and chapter 13 in this book).
Empowerment-oriented social workers with more radical perspectives can
also act (Jansson 1993).

The people whose journey we share in this book are anything but passive.
Their ancestors have valiantly fought the centuries of oppression documented in these pages. They are strong people empowering themselves. We
turn now to other aspects of multifocal vision needed for an empowerment
approach to social work.

We ain't where we aughta be.
We ain't where we gonna be.
But, thank God! We ain't where we were!
(Traditional gospel song)

5   Establishing Multifocal Vision:
The Ecological Perspective and Coping

Establishing an ecological perspective and understanding how people cope are essential to both the personal and political levels of empowerment. An ecological view provides an integrative framework for social work practice. The science of ecology studies relations between living organisms and their environments. Ecology provides an appropriate metaphor for taking a holistic view of people and environments as a unit in which neither can be fully understood except in the context of its relationship to the other. That relationship is characterized by continuous reciprocal exchanges, or transactions, in which people and environments influence, shape, and sometimes change each other (Germain 1991:16).

In the case of Sudeka and her family, social work intervention that challenges the circular transactions between the Harrison family and the non-nutritive, oppressive environment could help to make life with dignity a reality. The life model approach to social work that flows out of the ecological perspective can be life-giving (Germain and Gitterman 1980; Germain and Gitterman in press). The ecological view is an evolutionary, adaptive point of view that leads to a philosophical conception of human beings as continually growing, changing, and learning. It rejects all deterministic points of view, whether they be psychic, environmental (including some forms of learning theory), genetic, or economic, as overly simplistic (Germain 1991). People are born with a "bundle of potentialities" and the capacity for many "life scripts" that may be released or stunted by the qualities of our environments (Dobzhansky 1976). Freedom and equal opportunities to realize potentialities can also be released by political means (Germain 1991).

Several sets of ecological concepts flow from this perspective: adaptedness and adaptation, stress and coping, withholding of power as oppression or prejudicial discrimination and abuse of power as social and technological pollution, and human relatedness, competence, self-direction, and self-esteem/self-concept (identity). These concepts are transactional and do *not* refer to personal or environmental concepts alone (Germain 1991).

Adaptation is the central *action-oriented* concept of an ecological framework. It is *not* to be confused with the notion of adjustment, which connotes passive accommodation. Sudeka and her family cannot adjust to a lack of economic resources, systemic neglect, and inaccessibility. They must not accept grueling poverty and slave wages for hard work as their lot in life. They must make adaptations that help change this situation as well as their own circumstances and viewpoints. Little or no "goodness of fit" is possible between their needs, rights, capacities, and aspirations and the qualities of their environment (Germain 1991). Whenever there is substance abuse, as with Les and ultimately Sudeka, it is not adaptive, and it must *stop* for life to continue—this is a biopsychosocial level of change. Medical and social programs must be available to make this change possible. Concerned family members (significant others) and communities must be part of the solution. Some communities are focusing on drug abuse prevention and eradication as a number one priority. These are adaptive responses.

On the personal level consciousness must be raised to view the situation differently. Sudeka began to view her situation as a by-product of racism, but she did not yet understand why "Mama all smell of bleach" when she died. Consciousness-raising that renames reality restores hope and provides options for further adaptive actions. Passive avoidance is only adaptive when one is in control of the decision-making process and not controlled by either internal or environmental forces (Germain 1991). Sudeka and her family were not in control. They were "controlled by." This is the nature of oppression and exploitation that people themselves must change as they name, rename, and challenge oppressive realities. The Harrisons adjusted as best they could, but they did not attempt to adapt by changing the environment that stifled life. And it won.

The *life stressors* and *subjective stress* that Sudeka experienced were extraordinary. Life stress can be a challenge ("to write, to have dreams and aspirations," "to learn") but it "can also . . . arouse negative and often disabling feelings, such as anxiety, guilt, rage, helplessness, despair, and lowered self-esteem" (Germain 1991:19). This is exactly what happened to Sudeka. She needed help to broaden her repertoire to deal with the flood of feelings and harsh realities. Most of all, Sudeka needed the environment to provide hope and sources of motivation (incentives, rewards, resources, and options) for continuing to live and grow.

Coping responses are the special adaptations we make when we are experiencing stressful demands. Adaptations occur all the time, sometimes "on automatic pilot," outside of our full consciousness. Coping necessitates *active problem solving* (what needs to be done to reduce, eliminate, or manage the stressor) and *regulating the negative feelings* aroused by the stressor. These are interdependent functions. Progress in managing feelings and restoring self-esteem frees the person to work more effectively on problem solving (Germain 1991; Lee and Park 1978, 1983).

The stressors of poverty and discrimination are continual, and they necessitate creative coping responses. Language and humor are also helpful defenses in situations of oppression that enable survival (Draper 1979; Lee 1991). At fifteen Sudeka had not developed either her defensive mechanisms or her problem-solving skills.

> What seems to take place in successful coping with severe stressors is a partial blocking out of negative feelings, and even enough blocking out of the situation's reality, so that hope is maintained and some problem solving can begin. As problem solving proceeds, self-esteem is elevated, hope is strengthened, and the defenses that were needed at the outset begin to relax. Thus reality perception clears bit by bit, the negative feelings are regulated, and problem solving continues in an upward spiral. (Germain 1991:22)

Sudeka might have turned to drugs to block out negative feelings. She needed to find more adaptive and life-giving ways of relieving both the feelings and the realities of her situation. Sharing the terrible sadness and anger would have been a positive way of dealing with the immobilizing despair she felt. Taking action would then relieve the situation.

African American psychiatrists Grier and Cobbs speak of a sorrow particularly relevant to Sudeka:

A life is an eternity and all throughout that eternity a black child has breathed the air of cruelty. . . . Black people have shown a genius for surviving under the most deadly circumstances. They have survived because of their close attention to reality. . . . The psychological devices used to survive are reminiscent of the years of slavery, and it is not coincidence . . . [the same danger is faced]. . . . The overriding experience of the black American has been grief and sorrow. . . . If the depth of this sorrow is felt, we can then consider what can be made of this emotion. As grief lifts and the sufferer moves toward health, the hatred he has turned on himself is redirected toward his tormentors. . . . When the mourner lashes out in anger, it is a relief, for he has returned to health. (1969:175)

This brings us to Germain's second set of ecological concepts: *power* (withheld and abused), *oppression*, and *pollution*. "These concepts derive from the concept of dominance in the science of ecology. They denote person/environment relations that are unequivocally negative. They impair human growth . . . and are destructive of physical and social environments" (1991:24). In 1969, in an era of inner-city violence and riots, Grier and Cobbs saw the powerful expression of accumulated black rage as the inevitable outcome of oppression. We stand today at the edge of another precipice. In chapter 1 I discuss the prevalence of hate crimes at the turn of the century. In chapter 4 Hamilton and Hamilton (1997) argue the case for the existence of structural unemployment and its fruits in the inner city. Black youth and black men have both been spoken of as "endangered species" (Gibbs 1984; Strickland 1990). West (1993) sees the "accumulated black rage" of our day as a critical issue. Some estimate that nearly one-fifth of black males die of homicide and one-fifth goes to jail instead of college. Black youth lead the nation in suicides (West 1993). The loss of hope and meaning caused by oppression leads to a threat of nihilism that destroys culture as a coping mechanism (West 1993). *Collective action* is a means of coping with oppressive life stressors. It is also a means of dealing with *social pollutions:* the prejudicial discrimination or disempowerment of vulnerable groups related to the abuse and withholding of power from these groups (Germain 1991). It is a way to address this power discrepancy.

The positive person/environment relationships that occur across the life course of individuals are *human relatedness, competence, self-direction,* and *self-esteem.* These attributes depend on the environment and are relatively free of cultural bias. They are independent concepts and equally important, but relatedness appears first and remains central (Germain 1991).

Relatedness refers to the capacity of the human being at birth to form attachments to other human beings and to the quality of the attachments. Stern's infant research (1985) enlightens us on the active stimulus- and relationship-seeking nature of the human infant. Stern's findings shed strong doubt on earlier assumptions about infant relatedness, such as "normal infantile autism," "passivity," "merger," and "symbiosis" (Mahler, Pine, and Bergman 1975). *Attachment theory* (Bowlby 1969, 1973, 1991; Germain 1991; James 1994; Parkes, Stevenson-Hine, and Marris 1991) provides us with a basis for understanding human development. People bond for human connection and protection. Throughout the life course "intimate attachments to other human beings are the hub around which a person's life revolves" (Bowlby 1980). It begins with a primary or preferred attachment — "a reciprocal, enduring, emotional and physical affiliation between a child and a caregiver" who may be a biological parent or relative or a foster or adoptive parent or another more mature figure in the child's world. Major disturbances or trauma such as abandonment, separation, loss, neglect, violence, and physical and sexual abuse may try or break attachments and damage the person's ability to form them. Children and adults who have suffered an attachment disorder as a result of acute or chronic disruption or trauma in primary attachments may have a range of developmental difficulties including trouble with relationships, self-esteem and identity, trust, loyalty, moral/conscience/spiritual development, cognitive processing, affect management, and self-confidence (James 1994). Attachment disorders manifest symptoms before age five. While many people are resilient and are not "irreversibly damaged" by early imperfect, disrupted, or even traumatic caretaking or later difficult life experiences, intervention may be needed to restore attachment abilities and a range of functioning. The provision of positive caretakers and attachment figures and trustworthy relationships are important interventions for children. Human relatedness is restorative and essential for functioning throughout the life course. Social work practice with individuals, families, and groups may enhance and help restore relatedness (Lee and Park 1978; Lee 1981, 1986, 1990). Niki Ciano (the thirteen year old whose case discussion begins in chapter 1) suffered an attachment disorder due to repeated and chronic attachment disruptions, exposure to violence and neglect, and, perhaps, physical and sexual abuse. Her self-destructive behaviors included chronic running away, stealing, courting danger, and sexual relationships with adult men who sexually and physically abused her. As family members were no longer able to provide care, the essential intervention was the provision of a therapeutic foster home or specialized group home or long-term residential treatment center where she would have the opportunity to experience trust of worthy caregiver(s) who could love and be there for her and establish limits and structures to grow by. Without this chance, sadly, the juvenile then adult criminal justice systems would be the next stops for this out-of-control child whose biological mother had already spent over one-third of her life in jail. Niki's history and treatment intervention will be discussed in chapter 8.

Competence is an innate capacity for effectiveness or mastery that depends on the environment (White 1959; Germain 1991). Effort and success breed more success (White 1974). Competence is essential throughout the life course and may be promoted through social work practice (Maluccio 1981). Children may develop a sense of inferiority when, through discrimination and prejudice, they are not permitted to develop success in learning and doing (Erikson 1969). Children who are successful in meeting the demands of their environments accumulate a sense of competence as well as actual competence (Lee 1986). Social and physical environments may provide for the development of competence or stifle and inhibit it (Germain 1991). Niki had talent in art and was able to learn academically. Yet her disruptive behaviors in school coupled with her inner sense of disorganization and chaos and later her truancy meant that little actual competence in mastering academics was established.

Self-direction goes beyond the concept of ego autonomy to include the social structure. In ego psychology autonomy refers to the person's ability to maintain some degree of freedom from the demands of internal forces and the demands and pressures of the environment. However, self-direction also connotes social responsibility and recognizes that disempowered persons occupy positions that block access to options, choices, resources, and opportunities (Germain 1991). Both the personal power of self-direction and political power are needed to obtain access to options. Niki was at the service of her wants/desires. Lacking an internal guide, she could not control either her feelings or her actions. Hence while developing a pseudo-autonomy she became dependent on others who controlled her toward their own ends. Mrs. Ciano needed access to options and services that were scarce—

placement options for young teenage girls. Instead, she faced bureaucratic runaround and frustration while the child continued in life-threatening activities. The worker functioned as a power equalizer in this instance.

Self-esteem refers to positive feelings about oneself acquired through experiences of relatedness, competence, and self-direction across the life course. It begins in infancy with the incorporation of the caretakers's perceptions and is potentially renewed (or harmed) in every other important relationship (Mead 1934; Germain 1991). The *self-concept/identity* thereby developed continues to develop over the life course. The ethnic minority child is nurtured in her own family and community and faces (at the least) prejudicial attitudes and discrimination in the wider community.

Research data are divided on the question of whether the experience of *stigma* and *oppression* ipso facto lowers self-esteem. We can generalize that the negative labels and representations of the dominant society toward minorities may at some point be internalized and lead toward lower self-esteem. The work of Allport (1958), Goffman (1959, 1963), Adam (1978), the Clarks (1939), and Grier and Cobbs (1969) and recent research replicating the Clark study by Powell-Hopson and McNichol (Goleman 1987) substantiate this. However, other research disputes this (Hraba and Grant 1970). These authors and others (Chestang 1988) show that self-esteem that can withstand assault can be drawn from family, community, and opportunities to do well. Obviously, more research is needed. Yet there is agreement on how to respond to oppression. "Dominated people ought to . . . develop and draw strength from their own institutions" (Longres 1990:441). Family, community, and culture may serve as *mediating structures* between oppression and empowerment. In Niki's case as in Sudeka's the family and other institutions needed to be supported and strengthened to meet their children's needs and act as mediating structures.

The efficacy of *cultural solutions* and of *physical* and *social environments* is critical in the empowerment process. "Environments and culture become internalized in the person's self-concept" (Germain 1991). Sudeka was torn between three cultures: the dominant oppressive culture, the African American culture, and the Jamaican/Rastafarian subculture. The protective black culture became riddled by a level of internal conflict difficult for a sensitive, bright teen to sustain. Well aware of the social pollution of racism and poverty, she was surrounded by a deteriorated physical environment and a family in crisis. It is no wonder that Sudeka's self-esteem was shattered. It is more amazing that so many in her situation succeed in spite of such conditions.

Communities as well as individuals and families seek to attain relatedness, self-direction, competence, and self-esteem/positive identity. Communities with these attributes help produce people with these attributes (Germain 1991; chapter 9).

The Family

In an ecological view the family is the most intimate and influential environment in which human development takes place. Families transact regularly and are structurally arranged (organized) in a variety of ways to ensure survival. Family content and processes are influenced by the context of oppression (Germain 1991). The family and its context are the "unit of attention" in an ecological view, whether or not all are present with the worker. Niki's and Sudeka's struggles are their families' struggles. Our vision must include Niki *and* her great-grandmother, her grandmother, her mother and father and her siblings, aunts, uncles and cousins, and close friends of the family (*amici*), Sudeka *and* her mother, brother, sister, nephew, and boyfriend. They can be a buffer in a harsh world, or they can be the source of additional conflict as they face cruel socioeconomic realities.

When Mama "cries and say the family thing" (Thomas 1978), she is attempting to pull her family together. Sudeka feels family *is* important. Yet her obligations run counter to an adolescent's needs for learning and self-direction. This is a family crisis. Deena's return affects all family members. Family forms have changed and adapted to meet modern demands (Germain 1991). People have families of origin that have biological ties, although nonkin "aunts and uncles" and others psychoculturally close may be included, as is often the case in African American and other ethnic families (Logan 1990) and families of choice, which may include legal marriage, opposite-sex or same-sex couples, with or without children, extended kin, friends, siblings, people living in a group setting, and so on. The African American family will be discussed in chapter 6.

As human systems go, the family is—on a continuum of open and closed systems—an open system in varying degrees. It is a unique system with structures, norms, recognizable role formations, patterns of behavior, communication patterns, and ways of relating to the larger society. It is greater than the sum of its parts (Scherz 1974). Families attain some level of dynamic balance or relative equilibrium. When this is disturbed—often because of external events or the addition (such as Bunky's arrival), loss, or demoralization of family members (experienced by Les and Sudeka)—the family enters a crisis state. Quick intervention is needed on the cognitive, affective, and task levels (including attaining basic resources) in order to restore the family to at least a precrisis level of functioning (Golan 1978; Hartman and Laird 1983). Family assessment will be included in chapter 7, and community functioning will be discussed in chapter 13.

How People Cope: Additional Concepts from Ego Psychology and Cognitive Behavioral Theory

The attributes of *relatedness, competence, self-direction, and self-esteem/ identity* (discussed earlier in this chapter) form a basis for human being and growing. Like the "ego functions" about to be described, they depend on a good enough environment for development. We have noted that people cope by managing feelings and problem solving when environments provide a basic level of resources. The ways in which people do this can be broken down into specific behaviors. In a psychodynamic frame of reference these behaviors are called *ego functions* (Freud 1936; Goldstein 1984).

The *ego* is a metaphorical structure defined by Freud (1961) to describe the "executive" part of the person that mediates in both the outer and internal environments between drives and "wants" (the id) and "shoulds" (the conscience, or superego). Ego spheres and *ego functions* are simply names given to *observable clusters of human coping behaviors* (Germain 1991). Although one may question Freud's metaphors and psychosexual theory, conceptualizing ego functions provides understanding about *how* people cope. Goldstein notes that the "conception of what constitutes normal ego development . . . is a complex matter. The concept of effective coping requires redefinition if it is to encompass and respect difference rather than view such difference in pathological terms" (1984:20). In our discussion of ego functions we use a multifocal view that keeps culture and oppression in mind and defines ego functioning/behaviors transactionally/ecologically and through feminist, ethclass, and critical lenses.

A sense of power is essential to self-esteem and survival. A mentally healthy person must be able to perceive herself as at least minimally powerful (capable of influencing the environment), and this sense of power must be based upon the actual experience and exercise of power (Ryan 1971). Personal empowerment begins at birth, as we develop interpersonal influence, and continues throughout life with successful transactions, including political ones. Perhaps it is a "mega-ego function."

The ego/behavioral repertoire grows by learning, maturation, and identification. Basic ego-strengthening interventions consist of an empathic and reflective (ego-supportive) approach in the context of a caring relationship (Goldstein 1984; Hollis and Woods 1981). In times of crisis anyone may need this assistance. Assessment must be made to see if people might also profit from insight-oriented or "ego-modifying" work, which also includes anxiety and confrontation (Goldstein 1995). Rather than speaking of ego impairment, deficit, or developmental arrest, we must learn to describe and evaluate a person's specific ego functions/behaviors (chapter 5).

Ego Functions

Ego functions are interrelated and may be categorized in many different ways (Bellak, Hurwich, and Gediman 1973; Green 1972; Goldstein 1995; Germain 1991). Here special considerations for persons experiencing oppression are factored in.

1. *Somatic perception.* Are sight, hearing, sensory apparatus, and muscles and bone structure for speech and movement unimpaired? Are medical care and basic resources for growth and development adequate?

2. *Basic intellectual capacities.* Are these in the wide range of normal, using ethclass-sensitive appraisal devices? Have learning opportunities been adequate? Can the child read and perform on grade level? (Or is the whole school behind on reading scores?) Has the person been in a "special education class"? What does this "catchall" mean for this person? Is he mildly mentally retarded (developmentally delayed), learning disabled, hyperactive, "emotionally disturbed"? Does he have ADD or ADHD? Emotional and environmental factors can influence intellectual functioning. For example, physical or sexual abuse, substance abuse, physical illness and medication, nutrition, brain dysfunction, and poor learning opportunities can affect memory and concentration. Niki read on a fourth-grade reading level in the seventh grade for many reasons that would need to be assessed in order to intervene appropriately to promote learning mastery and competence.

3. *Affectivity.* This involves patterns of emotional responsiveness as observed by others—kind, range, and appropriateness of affect. When the situation calls for it, does the person laugh, cry, mourn, show anger, smile, and so on. These of course are culturally relative concepts and must be appraised within cultural norms (Lum 2000; Green 1999). Flat affect over time, however, is of concern in most cultures and subcultures. We must understand the expression of feelings even when it is not open and nonverbal. Behaviors convey feelings quite clearly in children and teens.

4. *Reality testing.* This function is concerned with the ability to distinguish between actuality and fantasy. Its major components are distinction between inner and outer stimuli, accuracy of perception of external events, and accuracy of inner-reality testing. In early childhood we may believe that wishes and fantasies control events (magical thinking). Beyond that, this belief is maladaptive. Defenses (e.g., projection [attributing our own unconscious thoughts to others] or denial [negating or nonacceptance of reality]) may hamper reality testing when used over an extended period of time. When reality testing is severely "off," there is a bizarre quality to it. Niki actually did not connect danger to a speeding car ride out of state, or to being tied up by an adult man during sex. In another example, there was a strikingly beautiful pregnant African American woman who resided in a New York City shelter. She had the delusion that she was Nefertiti, queen of the Nile. She also believed that her baby would be born at home with the palace doctor attending to her. When the time came for delivery, she violently resisted police and ambulance attendants who took her to the hospital.

The biochemical reasons for such schizophrenic thought processes are not well understood, but the schizophrenias are classified as a group of brain diseases in which the individual may undergo both structural and functional neurological changes. There is as yet no effective medical cure, although some psychotropic medications control delusions (Longres 1990; chapter 9). People cannot, therefore, be talked out of their delusions, although one can help the person function by stepping inside of the thought system. One might say, for example, that we recognize that this very important mother to be must receive special treatment and that the palace doctor will meet her at the hospital. It is usually of no avail to say, "You're not a queen and you have to go to the hospital." A frequent delusion of very poor people with paranoid schizophrenia is that they are royalty or rich persons in disguise. This can be a harmless break with reality that enables them to survive psychologically under grueling conditions. However, when one older woman informed the Social Security Administration that she no longer needed their help because she had "come into her inheritance" and the checks stopped, leaving her with no income, it was a matter for intervention. When she had the elevator repaired in her senior citizen's residence by calling as the owner of the residence (which she believed she was) and "authorizing immediate repair" of a system that had inconvenienced and endangered the lives of her peers for two weeks, it was a matter of joy for her peers, although the building management was less than pleased. These gross distortions of reality are easier to pick up on than equally problematic but less bizarre ones.

Reality testing is of even greater complexity, however, when we factor in poverty and membership in an oppressed group. Except for severe distortions of reality, we need to ask the following questions: Whose reality is it? A lack of cultural understanding may produce a misassessment in this area. Grier and Cobbs, for example, have pointed out that black people have survived because of extraordinarily good reality testing vis-à-vis white people (1969). If minority clients do not trust dominant group members or workers readily, it is probably good reality testing. We must be able to distinguish "adaptive wariness" from paranoia (Grier and Cobbs 1969).

Do we really understand what the client is communicating? Communication styles are different among classes and ethnic groups. Have we really understood a client's viewpoint and meaning? Have we asked where we might falter in understanding? In an empowerment approach we must ask if the client has named her own reality accurately. This is related to consciousness-raising in instances of self-blame, self-hatred, and familial and community blaming. Does the client consciously think about and reframe realities that are oppressive?

5. *Judgment.* In appraising reality people also decide what courses of action are appropriate in certain circumstances. They anticipate consequences of intended behavior and plan for minimal negative consequences. The range of options available influences judgment. Good judgment relates to an accurate perception of reality and to good cognitive functioning. Niki's judgement was, therefore, impaired. It is important in problem solving. It also takes place in an ethclass context in which judgment is validated or questioned. To evaluate judgment it is important to understand the context and what the person is trying to achieve by his actions (Goldstein 1995). A worker may risk getting fired if it is for a cause he believes in, for example.

We must be aware of our own value judgments and identifications with the client that may distort our view of the client's behavior.

6. *Regulation of impulses.* From the time we are born we begin to learn that we cannot always have what we want when we want it. It therefore becomes necessary to regulate our impulses and expression of feelings. Children who have not experienced good enough caretaking may lack this ability, as Niki did. In situations of organic impairment, including moderate to mild mental retardation, both judgment and impulse control are affected. It takes extra learning to compensate for this problem.

Impulse control is a critical problem in instances of substance abuse. In the range of life situations violence and suicide can be the most tragic result of impulsive action. In suicide the impulse to die wins out. Developing a full range of coping capacities and ego strengths may mitigate against suicides such as Sudeka's, but societal change is a corequisite for hope.

We all face occasions when controlling impulse or affect is *not* appropriate as well. Particularly in instances of oppression, it is important to allow our feelings of anger, sadness, anxiety, joy, or frustration to fuel action. We must act on moral impulses when it is important to do so. For example, there is a national gay/lesbian group called Act Up that is made up of a wide range of persons from all strata of society. Their purpose is to be disruptive in the cause of their human rights. There are also groups of physically and mentally handicapped persons who share this type of purpose. This is the aim of peace activists on behalf of all of us. Creativity too demands spontaneity and the ability to act on impulse and feeling.

7. *Motility.* This category includes the patterns of activity manifested through behavior. The adequacy, appropriateness, and range of the kind and amount of activity (or inactivity) with which the individual meets life situations are evaluated here (Green 1972). The brain/mental disease of manic depression manifests excessive motility in its manic phase and little motility in the depressive phase. One woman suffering from manic depression paced and talked incessantly, driving residents and staff in a small shelter to frustration. It took weeks for medication to stabilize her activity level. The phobias, including agoraphobia, involve restricted motility. Substance abusers also manifest a variety of typical motility patterns. Although these diseases have complex biochemical components, the extremes of motility are always

of concern. What we assess in this category is the freedom from internal and/or external pressures to take appropriate action.

The situation of Lorna (Lee 1986, 1990; chapter 3) illustrates how motility must be seen in transactional terms. A middle-aged, observant Jewish woman with otherwise good ego functioning, Lorna was agoraphobic and experienced panic attacks at leaving the New York shelter. These attacks began after her parents died and continued when she was a live-in caretaker for an elderly woman in the same tenement where muggings of the vulnerable were frequent. When the older woman was placed in a nursing home, Lorna was homeless. The shelter was located in a frightening, drug-infested neighborhood. Lorna regained a higher degree of motility through a relationally based behavioral approach and environmental change. (Lorna will be discussed in chapter 9.) To be active, people need a relatively safe and adequate environment, skills in negotiating it, and resources and reasons (incentives) to venture forth. Self-direction, a wider concept that we discussed earlier, is impossible without motility. Many poor inner-city dwellers, especially the elderly, become relatively immobile for reasons that begin in the environment. "Doing, not just viewing" is essential in human growth (Perlman 1986).

8. *Competence/mastery.* This is an inborn, active striving toward interaction with the environment leading to experiencing actual and perceived effectiveness (Goldstein 1984). We have discussed this very important function as an achievement of good enough person/environment fit earlier in this chapter.

9. *Synthetic/integrative function.* This is the capacity of the ego to organize mental processes into a coherent form, including the integration of sometimes discrepant or contradictory attitudes, values, affects, behaviors, and role expectations—the capacity to unite, bind, integrate, and create (Goldstein 1995). Living biculturally in two or more different worlds as members of cultural minorities of color or sexual orientation makes greater demands on this complex function (Chestang 1976; Lum 2000; Moses and Hawkins 1982; Van Wormer, Wells and Boes 2000).

10. *Human relatedness.* This is the degree and kind of attachment and relatedness to others. As noted earlier, this is the *most important* achievement of a goodness of fit between people and environments (Germain 1991). Human life depends upon human relatedness throughout the life course.

The facilitation of human connections and attachments, especially for those who have lost such vital ties, is essential in an empowerment approach. With Lorna, restoring ties with friends, making new friends, and reestablishing ties with her religious community were essential. The small, intimate group goes far in helping restore attachments and relatedness (Lee 1990). With Niki restoring attachment was essential to her well-being.

11. *Defensive functioning.* Defenses, like coping mechanisms, are efforts to deal with an external or internal stressor and the negative feelings it arouses. Defenses represent passive avoidance of an unwanted condition and are largely on the unconscious level, whereas coping is active and largely conscious and preconscious. Defenses are based on past methods of dealing with threat, and they may not always be helpful in present threats (Germain 1991). (For a listing of the traditionally defined mechanisms of defense see Freud 1936; Bellak, Hurvich, and Gediman 1973; and Goldstein 1995.)

Other Behavioral and Cognitive Behavioral Ideas About Coping

The clusters of behaviors discussed earlier are both cognitive and affective, and they are (except for the traditionally defined defenses) all dependent on environmental transactions. To that extent they overlap with behaviorist and cognitive behavioral concepts that are also useful to our understanding of coping and adaptation.

Behavioral methods run the gamut from traditional behavior analysis approaches popularized by B. F. Skinner to cognitive behavioral approaches. The traditional behavioral approach has been criticized as being linear and simplistic. It does, however, have the virtue of partializing some kinds of complex problems into measurable units. This works well, for example, in helping people recognize the antecedents of drug use behavior and with Lorna's agoraphobia, discussed earlier. In the cognitive-affective approach, behavior is assumed to consist of affective, cognitive, and overt behaviors (Gambrill 1987). Traditional behavior modification emphasizes the changing of "environmental contingencies" or "antecedents" (meaning proximal environments like the crowded buses Lorna learned to negotiate) and provides incentives for new behaviors. Newer cognitive behavioral approaches may include proximal and distal (wider environmental) antecedents (Gambrill 1987; Berlin 1983). In helping Lorna, systematic desensitization procedures were useful. This includes relaxation techniques, a scale of subjective anxiety, the development of an anxiety hierarchy, including the presentation of scenes either in imagination or in vivo as this is tolerated, and actual deconditioning and relearning (Schwartz 1983). In time Lorna mastered several of her fears of going outside to a specific place, of riding buses, and of entering specific stores. She began by going outside at a time of day when very few people were on the street and increased this until she could handle some level of crowded conditions. At the same time, she needed to move to a secure and dependable environment in a relatively safe neighborhood. When this was done she made progress using ego-supportive help, new attachments, and behavioral methods. She took important steps in strengthening motility, relatedness, self-direction, competence, and self-esteem. The concepts from two psychologies easily interrelate. Informed eclecticism works well with the empowerment approach. Berlin proposed a cognitive learning approach, but she did not think of it as able to stand alone as a treatment modality (Werner 1986).

Behavioral methods share the view that people are doing the best they can under current circumstances. This is a nonpathologized and non-victim-blaming stance. This approach does not, however, provide any technology for changing oppressive environments beyond the proximal level of change for which there are clearly prescribed techniques (Gambrill 1987; Schwartz 1983). Traditional behavioral interventions focus on behaviors not in the repertoire that need to be learned (Lorna's travel), behaviors in the repertoire that need to increase in frequency (going into stores), behaviors that occur in wrong situations and that need to be used in right situations, behaviors in the repertoire that need to be reduced or eliminated (Lorna's anxiety and immobility), and maintenance of the treatment effects (Schwartz 1983). In Niki's case she was rewarded for learning to obey house rules and not rewarded for sassy or rude words spoken to Mrs. Ciano. When her behaviors were self-destructive, the withdrawal of privileges and grounding with surveillance were imposed. In the short run these strategies had some effect.

A cognitive behavioral approach gets back inside human beings, where more traditional behaviorists are uncomfortable (Werner 1986). Cognitive behaviorists believe that "unless the client changes the way he perceives or interprets the experience, unless he changes his way of thinking, these gains will not last; therefore it is necessary to intervene in the area of cognition" (Schwartz 1983:217).

Cognitive approaches involve *cognitive restructuring, coping skills,* and *problem-solving skills*—all of which can be learned. *Cognitive restructuring* consists of identifying thinking patterns, revising false beliefs, and learning more adaptive ways of dealing with realities. Beck speaks of examining and unraveling misperceptions, and Meichenbaum works with people who are schizophrenic, helping them to "talk healthier" (Schwartz 1983). Cognitive restructuring relates directly to the central skill of the empowerment approach: consciousness-raising that postulates oppressed people have internalized false beliefs about themselvesthat need to be restructured to reduce self- and community blame, raise self- and community esteem, and take positive action. The use of cognitive restructuring in consciousness-raising paves the way for accurate reality testing and action for oppressed people. One group of physically challenged social work students founded an activist group called CAN—Creative Access Network. Not only did its members act to gain access in the school library and other areas, but they formed a powerful group. When the civil rights movement adopted the slogans "Power to the people," "Black is beautiful," and "I'm black and I'm proud," this was a type of "healthier talk" that could be internalized and contribute to communal cognitive restructuring. Helen Reddy's song "I Am Woman" helped to do this for women.

Cognitive approaches see an individual's thinking as the seat of all difficulties and see intervention as talking about or being guided into direct experiences that will alter distorted thinking (Werner 1986). Great importance is placed on imagery, or mentally picturing safe times and places, and healthy responses and images (Werner 1986). Freire's use of symbols (e.g., art and music) as more powerful than words is also an example of the use of imagery in the conscientization process (1973b).

Coping skills in this framework are strategies that help the individual deal with problem situations. This may also involve cognitive restructuring, relaxation, modeling, social skill training/visualization, rehearsal, and other behavioral procedures. According to Bandura's theory of self-efficacy, which is part of a *social learning approach*, a person must have feelings that he *can* cope with; then he can act on them. The person must also feel there will be consequences, that the behavior will make a difference. Persons must have efficacy expectations and outcome expectations (Schwartz 1983). *Actual* success must accompany perceived ability, and the environment must be conducive to providing opportunities for efficacy (Berlin 1983; Germain 1979, 1991). Coping is a "transactional process; a reaction to and shaper of environmental demands. . . . Unfortunately, but not accidentally, persons who are exposed to more hardships (for example, persons who are poor, uneducated, and women) tend to be less likely to have the means to fend off attendant stresses" (Berlin 1983:1097).

Positive self-attitudes and expectancies and access to social resources affect how people avoid, attenuate, or exacerbate the impact of problems. Information exchange is at the heart of person/environment transactions. As people become aware of the possibility of alternative perspectives about themselves and the world, they can change thought systems and response repertoires to gradually divest themselves of internalized social imperatives and exert more effective influence on their environments (Berlin 1983). Hence cognitive work is extremely helpful in both the personal and political levels of empowerment.

Problem-solving concepts were introduced in social work literature in 1957 by Helen Perlman, although the general concept can be traced back to the earliest foundations of social work. Many approaches use the problem-solving concept in a central way. It is an important component of an ecological view and the stress-coping paradigm (Germain 1991), of crisis intervention, and of task-oriented and brief-intervention approaches (Golan 1978). Ego psychological concepts also subsume cognitive functioning.

Berlin (1983) delineates nine overlapping steps in the problem-solving process:

1. *awareness* of cues.
2. *expectations* about alternative courses of action—the expected ability to exert control over one's destiny. The client is helped to differentiate between externally imposed necessities and those that are self-perpetuated and subjective. This is analogous to awareness of direct and indirect obstacles to empowerment.
3. *problem definition*, which relies on verbalization regarding behaviors, cognitions, emotions, and situations. This also relates to the empowerment principles of reducing self-blame and accepting responsibility for changing what can be changed (Gutiérrez 1990).
4. *formulate and implement solution alternatives*, which makes the client a causal agent.
5. *analyze options and decide on behavioral strategies*. This helps change the locus of internality from a belief in "fate" or external forces to the person and the resources available (Parsons 1989).

6. *affective strategies* must also be used to help "dissipate the power of emotions" by helping people experience, identify, and accept feelings. However, in an empowerment approach one wants to concentrate rather than "dissipate" the powerful emotion of outrage at oppression, as the feelings are important and lead to actions.

7. *social environmental strategies*—to influence social factors. Berlin challenges the cognitive behavioral notion of social circumstances as "fixed": "Understanding society's shared delusions allows one, for the first time, to refuse to participate in them" (1983:1110). This is analogous to consciousness-raising.

8. *analyze progress and modify the plan.*

9. *maintain change*—to reduce problems, to learn the process (to transfer the learning), and to cope with setbacks, since they are, like problems, inevitable. These steps apply well to an empowerment approach, as is illustrated in the case of Shandra presented in chapters 7 and 8.

Coping with Stigma: Social Learning and Labeling

Stigma is socially defined, and stigmatizing consists of applying negative labels that influence our perceptions of people (Moses 1978; Anderson 1988). Self-concept, identity formation, and self-esteem are influenced by social labeling. Robbins, Chatterjee, and Canda (1998) provide a helpful and comprehensive review of social learning theory for the social worker. Goffman categorizes three types of identity: *social identity* (the way society defines a person, and this is usually negative for those bearing stigma), *personal identity* (comprised of identity pegs that differentiate an individual from all others—the outstanding social and biographical facts), and *ego identity* (the felt, subjective sense of one's own situation, continuity and character resulting from social experiences, and the fashioning of one's self from social and personal realities; 1963). Social identity is often assumed without any personal knowledge of an individual.

A "stigma is an attribute that is deeply discrediting . . . a special kind of relationship between attitude and stereotype" (Goffman 1963:3). There are three types of stigma: various physical deformities, "blemishes of character" (e.g., a mental disorder, imprisonment, addictions, homosexuality, unemployment, suicide attempts, and radical political behavior), and the tribal

stigma of race, nation, and religion (Goffman 1963:4). Sudeka's family bore
the stigma of race, poverty, addiction, and eventually of suicide. When
stigma is visible, it is discredited by dominant society. When it is not visible,
it is discreditable (Goffman 1963). Therefore people tend to cover discreditable attributes and try to pass as "normal." Passing is a way of coping, but
it is often dysfunctional. In Sudeka's family it may have been the covering
of their poverty and Les's addiction that led to increased familial and socioeconomic stress. The "in group" or the group of fellow sufferers (e.g., AA
and other self-help groups) can be a support against the stress of bearing
stigma. Yet self-help groups often do not organize to fight for their human
rights in their cautiousness about being identified with the group. "Wise"
others may also be helpful to the stigmatized—that is, people who do not
share the stigma but whose "special situation has made them intimately privy
to the secret life of the stigmatized individual and sympathetic with it, and
who find themselves accorded a measure of acceptance, a measure of courtesy membership in the clan" (Goffman 1963:28).

A social worker may be given the status of "wise." Often "wise," trusted
others must share the stigma "secondhand"—a "courtesy stigma" (Goffman
1963). The "righteous gentiles" during the Holocaust in Nazi Germany fit
in this category. Dr. George Getzel of the Hunter College School of Social
Work has used the term *righteous gentiles* to describe the alliance of straight
and non-HIV + people in the fight against AIDS, particularly within the gay
community. Through his tireless ministering and advocacy, he has become
a "righteous gentile" and "wise" helper. The "wise" may doubt their acceptance into the group and may not always have the full support of the group
(Goffman 1963).

The healthiest way to cope with stigma and oppression is through a process of positive identity formation bolstered by a supportive in group in which
the stigma is seen for what it is (society's view) and thereby robbed of its
poison.

Gay Men and Lesbians: An Example of Dealing
with Stigmatized Identity

One of the coping behaviors of stigmatized groups is to rename and
redefine reality. During the 1960s, African Americans reclaimed the name
black and defined it as beautiful, strong, and good. They also affirmed Af-

rican heritage with the term *Afro-American* (now *African American*). During the 1970s the people who had been called "homosexual" by clinicians and others (for whom the word was synonymous with pathology and deviance) chose the in group word *gay* and *gay man* and *lesbian woman* as affirmative descriptions of being. People with mental and physical difference are also naming themselves as differently abled, or mentally or physically challenged, or simply as persons with disabilities, rather than as disabled, thus taking the power of the name away from the oppressor. This coping mechanism can be considered communal cognitive restructuring.

For gay men and lesbian women managing an identity socially labeled as deviant requires some major decisions. In the vernacular of the gay community, should I "stay in the closet" and pass, or "come out" (of the closet)? The decision is not made "once and for all," for each day brings new possibilities of oppression, but "coming out" is a turning point in positive identity formation and affirmation. Passing is done by everyone some of the time. Its rewards are great (socially and economically), and its stresses are many. But when people who are gay lead life "in the closet," it can take a high toll in ego integration, positive identity, and self-esteem. To understand this toll one must "imagine life as a lie. A lie that must be carefully protected and nurtured every day" (Sancier 1984:3). Passing "requires a great deal of management—e.g., vigilance, resourcefulness, stamina, sustained motivation, pre-planning, sharpness, wit, knowledge, making explanations and avoidance of situations" (Moses 1978).

The "coming out" or identity formation and affirmation process is a nonlinear, multifaceted process that has identifiable aspects (Lee 1992a; Van Woermer, Wells, and Boes 2000). Many have called these aspects stages (Cass 1979), but they may occur simultaneously for some and in a variety of orders for others. They may take several months to several decades. No value judgment is involved in being in earlier or later stages. Peer support is invaluable, for environmental conditions and responses are critical in influencing this process (Lee 1991; Appleby and Anastas 1998).

Most authors agree on the phases or components of the process. First is "coming out to oneself" or "emerging." Frequently people express a feeling of "being different." They may go through a lengthy period of denial and may feel dissonance between themselves and the world. When they are able to say, "I am gay" to themselves, they may also go through a grieving process as they fear (and often experience) the loss of acceptance by loved ones and the loss of heterosexual privilege and a socially accepted identity. Unlike

Kubler-Ross's (1969) final stage of grieving—the identity acceptance stage—it is not one that is void of feeling, as in the death of a loved one, but full of joy, peace, and affirmation.

A second "phase" is "coming out sexually and emotionally" in a relationship. For some people this may precede the cognitive level of "coming out to oneself." This is cause for joy and affirmation as well as for ambivalence and turmoil. As people accept themselves and are in a love relationship, they may often want to "shout it from the highest mountain" and "tell the world." Most people know, however, that this will bring recriminations. They have to choose carefully whom they will trust with this knowledge. Some people practice writing letters "coming out" to their parents and loved ones that may not be sent. If they do disclose, they will meet acceptance from some and painful rejection from others. This *relational level of "coming out"* and not "living a lie" with friends and family is a most important level of living comfortably in the world. When one partner is more "out" than the other, it promotes great stress in couples' relationships. Finding a sense of community with gay and nongay people provides an important buffer.

Coming out publicly usually happens when most people in the individual's life know about the self-identity of being gay. People are now more comfortable sharing who they are beyond the level of close friends in a range of circumstances. *Coming out politically* is a part of this phase for many who choose to act legislatively, by means of protest or lobbying, or to speak publicly to educate or attain the rights of gay human beings. At this stage those with a mature "world concern" may also identify and work for justice for all oppressed groups. The personal is political on many levels—this is empowerment. Although this phase may sometimes follow the next and final phase, it may also help lead to it. The phase of *identity integration*, or the establishment of a stable gay identity, involves a synthesis of gayness into an overall sense of identity, a full self-acceptance and self-definition, and a reintegration of being gay with all other aspects of one's life. It is one more identity peg, but it should not overshadow all the unique aspects of a person's being. There is an externalization of feelings of oppression, and being gay is one part of a full life. These identity formation processes are used by many other stigmatized groups as they deal with the power of societally projected stigma (labeling) and seek to rise above it. One student who had a physical deformity hidden by clothing wrote passionately in her human behavior class journal about her own painful "coming out" process:

For a very long time I told practically no one about my hidden disability. Since this disability is invisible when I have clothing on, I could "pass" easily in the colder months. I dreaded the arrival of many summers and skipped going to the beach. The passing affected the quality of my life. As stated by Goffman, I found I wanted to protect others from having to be sensitive and tactful. "Coming out" meant for me coming to grips with my surgery and body image. In time I was able to share the truth with those I trusted. Even ten years later there are those who know and those who don't. I have often asked myself when do you know someone well enough to tell them. . . . I guess that in a way I have come out in my journal.

Dealing with stigma necessitates exceptional coping, problem-solving skills, cognitive restructuring, and strengths in ego functioning, particularly in maintaining self-esteem/identity and in exercising judgment. Stigma is in the eye of the merciless beholder (reflected in the environment). Stigmatizing is a virulent form of oppression. An ecological view challenges us to work together to make environments significantly less noxious and positively nutritive to all people and to fight against the multiple forces that maintain oppression. In her poem "Urged to Deny the Secrets," Blanche Weisen-Cook (1986:1) concludes, "We are taught to be fearful of ourselves and contemptuous of others. . . . This is not an accident."

6 Multifocal Vision: Developing Ethclass, Feminist, Cultural, and Critical Perspectives—One Clear Lens, Many Foci

This chapter will continue to develop our multifocal vision by adding ethclass, cultural, and feminist foci to examine issues of adaptation, power, and oppression. Questioning the realities of oppressive situations as seen through these lenses with a worldwide global perspective will assist us in cultivating a critical perspective on power and oppression. Using multifocal lenses will enable us to see both the breadth and depth of a person's environment transactions—both the forest and the trees. This is necessary in assessment and intervention with systems of all sizes.

The Ethclass Perspective

The term *ethclass* was coined by Gordon (1978) to refer to the social participation and identity of persons who are confined in their own class and ethnic group because of oppression. In a recent empowerment workshop I posed the challenge of creating a visual image to describe "oppression." One older West Indian-American woman, well experienced in life's struggles and victories, proposed the image of the maze. She said that oppression was being locked into the smallest box of the large, almost infinite maze of opportunities with no way out. This apt metaphor illuminates the ethclass definition—confined to their own social class and ethnic group. Although some people may escape the bonds of class when opportunity is presented, the obstacles imposed by ethclass membership, especially for poor people of color, are tremendous. Ethclass-sensitive practice must know the realities of being "locked in" and marginalized by oppression. More broadly, it means paying particular attention to the interplay of ethnic and social class influences in working with persons of any group. We turn first to examining the meaning of social class membership in a society stratified by class.

The Open Injuries of Class

Being poor is both like and unlike being a minority of color, of sexual orientation, or of any other stigmatized status. It is a universally discredited status that carries with it all the rejection and discrimination of any other minority group. Yet it is not a status that one wants or must accept as part of one's identity. It is an economically caused status that must and can be changed. Poverty takes its toll on poor individuals in life-threatening ways: on health, infant, and adult mortality, mental health, coping resources and abilities, and often the positive outcomes of relatedness, competence, self-direction, and self-esteem (Gitterman 1991). Unfair social stratification and unfair distribution of goods constitute the most difficult questions in world society, and their remedies depend on the empowerment and coalescing of oppressed groups (Staub-Bernasconi 1992).

Women and minorities of color are disproportionately affected by unemployment, which institutionalizes poverty. Poor children learn early in life that they have limited control over their lives, that things happen and are done to them (Parsons 1989; Gitterman 1991). All poor people face sharply increased health hazards. The cancer survival rate of poor people is 10–15 percent below that of those living above the poverty line, with blacks having higher rates of virtually all cancers than whites, significantly higher rates of hypertension and lung cancer, and twice the level of infant mortality. Additionally, domestic violence, child abuse, and violent crime, although universal societal phenomena, are often associated with economic stress (Pelton 1978). Poor communities are prime targets for drug pushing and saturation by cigarette and alcohol advertising. The high rate of suicide among black inner-city males coincides with joblessness and economic despair (Devore and Schlesinger 1981). Gitterman counts the poor first among "vulnerable populations at highest risk" (1991).

Social stratification, or the class system, in this society has been described as a ladder consisting of a series of rungs or "prestige rankings." The amount of money earned and the level of education completed, the prestige of their occupation and the prestige conferred by their community place people on the ladder. When income, education, jobs, and community status are low, people are on the bottom rungs of the ladder: those on the highest rungs constitute the upper class, and those at the midpoint are the middle class (Longres 1995). The usually conceptualized *six-level class structure* (from upper-upper to lower-lower) is no longer enough. There is also an *underclass*, which receives no money or status from work or education and whose members often are, for several generations, dependent on public assistance and seem to live more or less permanently in poverty (Longres 1995; Wilson 1987; Sawhill 1988; Prosser 1991; Anderson 1990). They cannot get up to the bottom rung of the ladder and have no stake in the current political system (Reischauer et al. 1987). The "underclass" defies even Marxian analysis, which is related to roles in the workplace. Owners form the upper class, white-collar workers are usually middle class, and blue-collar workers may range from lower middle class or working class to lower-lower class (Longres 1990). Marx looked for conflict among these roles and called it class conflict. The "underclass" is not competing in the workplace, though it may provide a large supply of unskilled labor. Their competition for goods may take place largely outside of the workplace because of the free market economy's inability to create enough jobs (Reischauer et al. 1987). What happens next is unpredictable because the system offers so few rewards. The lack of an opportunity structure for poor African American youth, the high unemployment among young men, the massive invasion and lure of drugs and drug money, and the impact of these forces on the family and community may combine to create an underclass youth culture that values appearance, clothing, and "cool" more than education or finding a way up the ladder through work (Souljah 1999). (The latter are values of the black working class.) The effects of intergenerational poverty and oppression seem the hardest to overcome (Anderson 1990).

Understanding the sociology of liberation, which includes the sociology of class stratification and the sociology of movements, is critical for the practitioner concerned with empowerment (Estes 1991). Social class position is correlated with many variables of human behavior, particularly *life chances* and *life conditions*. The higher up one is on the "class ladder," the greater life chances one has and the better life conditions will be. Longres presents five social classes: 1) the *upper class*, whose members have very high income and a great deal of wealth going back generations—they have decision-making power over the economy and over civic affairs and attended elite schools; 2) the *upper middle class*, whose members have high incomes but not necessarily a lot of family wealth; they own property and have a good deal of savings. They are professionals and managers just below the top, approach occupations as a career, and are generally college educated; 3) the *lower middle class*, whose members have modest incomes and savings. This group includes small business people, those in less prestigious professions (e.g., many social workers and teachers), and clerical or sales workers. Many do not have college educations; 4) *the working class*, whose members have low incomes and minimal savings and work in skilled and semiskilled jobs. Many are high school graduates. They live adequately but on a narrow margin; 5) the *lower class*, whose members have an income at the poverty level even when they work. They are unskilled laborers, have the lowest-paying jobs, and suffer much unemployment. Few are high school graduates, and they bear the burden of stigma. They are often looked down upon by others in society (Longres 1990). The poor face double jeopardy—not only are their life chances low and life conditions barely minimal, but they are despised. The *underclass* is not explained by the "culture of poverty" my-thology or solely by institutional racism. The term is sometimes used pejor-atively, and hence it is disputed (Devore and Schlesinger 1999). Used pre-cisely, it is a socioeconomic classification, although, through a parallel, drug-related "underworld" system, some persons, at least temporarily, are well above the poverty level (Souljah 1999; Wilson 1987; Anderson 1990). Underclass communities do have social processes that help to perpetuate the underclass, but they also have strengths to combat this fierce cycle and stigmatization. We must differentiate and individualize when such labels are used about individuals or communities (Moore 1985). It is also important to note that earnings, where ethnicity intersects with class, are affected de-spite the attainment of education. Devore and Schlesinger (1999) show that whites and some Asian groups have the highest earnings, according to the 1996 census, while black and Hispanic groups rank lowest on median earnings.

Whatever label is given (usually by those who are not of that class), the experience of poverty or near poverty is indisputably and universally de-meaning. Gisela Konopka—internationally acclaimed social worker, edu-cator, writer, activist, and humanitarian—wrote:

My parents were young and poor and struggling. They had this little grocery store which I hated all my life. It made us "a living," but it ate out my father's soul because he had to be subservient to rich clients from the neighborhood. . . . I tried never to meet one of my schoolmates. If you grow up in a class society you may not feel poverty, but you feel the horrible sting of being someone "inferior," and I hated it, fought it, resented it. It continues through all my life. (1988:2)

As a child I thought that grocery store owners were rich until I met Louie and Bertha. They (like Konopka) were Holocaust survivors who owned a small store on the edge of my neighborhood. They gave my family credit and made my lunch sandwich with care during my last year of high school. When I worked nights to pay the grocery bill, I did it for them as well, but soon I stopped taking lunch. It was hard to hold your head up high when your eyes met the stares of creditors. Working-class and poor people share "worlds of pain," often driven by difficulties in "paying the bills" (Rubin 1976).

Poverty and Self-Esteem

Josetta is a seventeen-year-old African American girl in Joyce Ladner's study of young women coming of age in a poor black St. Louis community. She describes herself as having "strong perseverance." Despite institutional racism, the young women in the study had positive views about being black, though most wanted to change their neighborhood (Ladner 1972). Consider Josetta's feelings about being poor: "I know girls at school who have their own telephones in their bedrooms. I like to go to school to watch the fashions. Some of the girls wear real fine clothes. . . . I don't like for them to come home with me because I don't want them to see how we live . . . poor and all" (Ladner 1972:96).

And consider this autobiographical anecdote of poverty written in 1929:

I felt very shy and humble in that school. In the front seat on the outside row sat a little girl. Her skin was white, her hair was thick and nearly white, and her dresses, shoes and stockings were always white. . . . But for all her perfection, victory was mine that year. . . . When all other children failed to answer a question the teacher would turn with confidence to the seat of honor! . . . with the word—

"Marie?"

With eyes that never left her face I arose and answered. The whole
schoolroom watched and listened, waiting for a mistake. I, for all my
faded dresses and stringy ugly hair, who had never seen a toothbrush
or a bathtub, who had never slept between sheets or in a nightgown,
stood with my hands glued to my sides and replied without one falter
or one mistake! And the little white girl whose father was a doctor had
to listen! (Smedley 1976:47)

One might conclude that the experiences and feelings attending poverty
are universal, regardless of historical context or cohort. The author, Agnes
Smedley, was raised in rural poverty and eventually was appointed ambas-
sador to China (1928–1941).

Poverty is like a destructive and virulent disease process that strikes all
races. Few resources go into research to stop its spread as it eats out the
minds and hearts of almost 37 million Americans. The force of poverty is
inextricably connected to and compounded by institutional racism. Poverty
is born of oppression and creates its own oppression.

Developing an Ethclass Perspective

Class membership, or "being poor," may occupy a central position in the
life of an individual, family, or community. Ethnicity is also central in our
lives.

Ethnicity describes a sense of commonality transmitted over generations by family and reinforced by the surrounding community. . . . It
involves conscious and unconscious processes that fulfill a deep psychological need for identity and historical authenticity. Ethnicity patterns our thinking, feeling and behavior. . . . It plays a major role in
determining what we eat, how we work, how we relax, how we celebrate holidays and rituals, and how we feel about life, death, and illness. (McGoldrick, Pearce, and Giordano 1982:4)

Pinderhughes (1984) amply demonstrates the connections between class,
race, gender, ethnicity, and power. She advances a model for developing
self-awareness and empathy in social work with minority groups that gives
helping professionals an opportunity to grapple with their own biases. Biases
are debilitating on both sides of the power equation. Practitioners must be

aware of and deal with the need to exercise power over others. This frees in the helper a tolerance for difference and the ability to empathize through accurately perceiving others. This is an important part of all good clinical work, but it is critical in an empowerment approach.

When class transacts with race, the picture is one of greater complexity and double indemnity regarding power differentials. The class system in the United States is reinforced and maintained by the caste system of race (Pinderhughes 1984). Pinderhughes notes, "The sheer fact of class affiliation has enormous power over a child's life. . . . There is a point where a family's psychology and psychopathology engage with social and economic life [the ghetto child will experience narcissistic despair], whereas for a child of wealth, narcissistic entitlement is the likely possibility" (Pinderhughes 1979:315).

The lack of power experienced by people who are poor reinforces their need for a strong ethnic identity and their tendency to relate to other ethnic groups in terms of the perceived power of that group (Pinderhughes 1979). Although people of a particular minority group may occupy different social classes, coping with survival and the reality of racism are forces that can bond people of color together (Lum 2000).

Devore and Schlesinger (1999) advance a set of assumptions and principles relevant to ethnic sensitive practice (paraphrased):

1. Knowing the history of a minority group's oppression and the experience of migration. Learning individual and collective history.
2. The present is most important.
3. Familiarity with ethnic perceptions of environmental conditions that shape the scope of the problem and the solutions.
4. Attunement to ethnic reality and institutional structures (places of worship, schools, and so on) that may be a source of strength, cohesion, and identity or of strain, discordance, or intergenerational strife.
5. Paying simultaneous attention to micro and macro issues and intervention on individual and systemic levels of change.
6. Familiarity with the client's ethnic community.
7. Gathering information on ethnic background, social class, and issues of racism or prejudice is important.
8. Nonconscious phenomena affect functioning. The music, sounds and smells, and textures of our homes and precious experiences

may be not quite articulated or within awareness, but they are important nevertheless.

Culture and Ethnicity

It is important to differentiate between the interrelated concepts of *culture* and *ethnicity* to explain why a *cultural perspective* has been added to multifocal vision. *Culture* defines the different ways human groups structure their behavior, their worldview, and the rhythms and patterns of life (Devore and Schlesinger 1999). It is the evolving beliefs, values, and norms governing social interaction (Longres 1995). *Culture* is a broader term than *ethnicity* in that it may apply to people on the basis of power, age, gender, sexual orientation, accent, religion, education, region, and other divides among people. We may say, for example, youth culture, hip hop culture, gay culture, Jewish culture, Catholic culture, Southern culture, New York culture, and so on. There are cultural features of any defined or distinctive communities (Green 1999). These features are important to in order learn to promote empowerment and cultural heritage and pride. Culture is also a shared "cognitive map" that contains people's categories of meaning. The concept of *minority group* applies not to culture, or to numbers, but to a power differential in access to resources or social and economic disability (Green 1999). Culture is also accumulated wisdom about survival transmitted over time from generation to generation (Segall, Dasen, Berry, and Poortinga 1990). *Multiculturalism* is the perspective that where many groups exist each should be accorded respect and dignity. Multigroup societies should promote and accommodate, value and appreciate human diversity (Longres 1995). Both cultural and multicultural perspectives are needed to help people empower themselves.

Cultural competence is needed to develop a cultural perspective. Cultural competence is a systematically learned and tested awareness of the values and behaviors of a specific community and an ability to carry out professional activities consistent with that awareness (Green 1999:87). The practice of cultural competence consists of an awareness of self-limitations: an interest in cultural differences, systematic learning, the utilization of cultural resources, and an engagement with diversity. It starts with an ability to immerse oneself in another culture even when one may be in the minority (Green 1999). Cultural competence is a tool to be used both locally and globally.

Ethnicity basically speaks to a sense of participation in a distinctive community based on common ancestry and identity including perceived similarities of culture, language, or physical type. Its core elements are kinship, affinity, comfort zone and affiliation, food and other preferences and intimate sharings and beliefs, personal, family, and group preferences, and values and ideology (Longres 1995; Green 1999; Devore and Schlesinger 1999).

Lum (1986, 2000) developed a process-stage approach to working with ethnic minority clients. He emphasizes the *joint* formulation of goals, contract agreement, and matching of *intervention levels and strategies* on the micro, meso, and macro levels of intervention. He also suggests concepts for *interventive strategies*: liberation, empowerment, parity, maintenance of culture, and unique personhood. *Liberation* is the experience of release or freedom from oppressive barriers and control. As a result of growth and decision making, the oppressive circumstance will be resisted and not dominate the client, alternative options will be generated, and environmental change (e.g., new political leadership) will provide opportunity for liberation. *Empowerment* is the ability to experience power in the sense of rising up and changing one's situational predicament. Lum's emphasis is on access to resources and rights as empowering. *Parity* relates to a sense of equality, or having the same power, value, and rank as another. Its focal theme is fairness and entitlement to rights. *Maintenance of culture* is a strategy that maintains the importance of the ideas, customs, networks, skills, arts, and language of a people instead of insisting on acculturation and loss of culture. *Unique personhood* is an interventional strategy that seeks to transcend stereotypes. Client and worker must *work together* to produce acts that they hope will result in the creation of a new system, including clinical and community dimensions (Lum 1986, 2000). Knowledge is needed to transcend and be liberated from stereotypes.

Ethnic understanding is important, as each new child is a "new recruit to ethnic realities and culturally passed on modes of adaptation" (Devore and Schlesinger 1999). These realities include discrimination and racism (Moore-Hines and Boyd-Franklin 1982). In the face of such realities, what are the cultural modes of adaptation and coping that have ensured survival? The African American family presented here is a case in point. But the practitioner must consider the influence of ethnicity with all clients. People are not black or white, Asian or Hispanic; they come from distinct cultures. Our ethnic and religious pasts give us ways to handle oppression and skills for coping. The reader is referred to Longres's description of family life in

African American, Native American, Latino, and Asian American families
and in poverty class and gay and lesbian families as well (1995).

The African American Family

There is a wide variety in the forms and structures of the African
American family. African American families may be nuclear, extended, or
augmented (including nonrelatives). Using these categories, Billingsley defined twelve types of families (1968). Yet researchers are able to generalize
certain coping strengths common to African American families regardless
of family form. Until the 1970s most writers defined black family life in
pathological terms. Hill's 1972 research on the strengths of black families
began to turn the tide to an appreciation of strengths. Hill and other
"revisionist historians"

> affirmed a black family kinship system that was strong, intact, resilient
> and adaptive in both rural and urban environments from slavery until
> a few years before the Great Depression, when all families—especially
> black families—were devastated by the economy. Contemporary stud-
> ies on black family kinship patterns continue to describe viable func-
> tional systems. (Logan 1990:74)

The strengths of African American families include a set of core values
and behaviors centered around a sense of peoplehood, pride in blackness,
and psychic security. This is provided by strong kinship bonds, flexibility,
and fluidity of family roles and high values placed on religion, education,
and work. There are also values on collectivity, sharing, affiliation, obedience to authority, belief in spirituality, and a respect for the elderly and the
past (Hill 1972; Pinderhughes 1982a, b; Moore-Hines and Boyd-Franklin
1982; Freeman 1990). This sense of peoplehood includes the African concept of "survival of the tribe," which includes every member of the tribe as
family in "oneness of being" with all ancestors and future generations in a
spirit of unity (Germain 1991).

The fluidity of roles, including the inclusion of nonrelatives as kin, was
adopted to deal with the barriers imposed by the system of slavery. Relatives
other than parents participate in child rearing, providing buffers against
mothers in the workforce, single parenting, divorce, or separation and multiplicity of supports. Role sharing is a coping device well suited to the com-

plexity of modern family pressures. Providing supports for the educational attainments of even unrelated children is often seen as a task of generativity of older African American family members. This may include both mentoring and sharing resources. Beyond role sharing, research shows that poor black and Puerto Rican families are fluid in taking in and raising children of relatives and providing a high level of love and nurturance because of the value placed on children and the web of social relationships. The fastest-growing black family form consists of three generations residing in a single household—a mother, one or more adolescent daughters, and the daughters' children. This facilitates the sharing of resources and support (Longres 1995).

The adoption of a *dual perspective*, or *biculturalism* (the ability to function in the dominant society *and* in the black culture), enabled black families to cope and function successfully. This is contrasted with attempts at complete assimilation or exclusive immersion in black culture. The dual perspective is another strength of most black families that leaves them open to the resources of both cultures (Freeman 1990). Logan suggests several helpful tools for assessing and helping black families. One is to place the concept of functioning on a continuum instead of seeing it as an absolute. Family functioning on several variables related to nurturance falls along a continuum, and, regardless of class, individual black families range from highly stable and functional to highly unstable and dysfunctional. The latter is often in response to severe external forces, such as high unemployment (Logan 1990). Sudeka's family crisis was precipitated by the addition of four-year-old Bunky. Mama could no longer earn enough at her two jobs to meet family needs, including Bunky's need for an operation; Sudeka had to become a wage earner at fifteen. Despite the strengths of black families, the stressors on them are severe.

Female-Headed Families

There are many myths about nuclear families that are cherished by the American public. The mythology of father/breadwinner and mother/homemaker creates bias against all other family forms. By 1987 40 percent of all mothers of young children worked. Now most children have both parents working outside the home. In 1987 78.3 percent of white families were two-parent families and 41.5 percent of black families were two-parent families (Germain 1991). This is contrasted with the 1960s, when 78 percent of black families were two-parent families. The dramatic decline in black two-parent families can be accounted for by a variety of harsh socioeconomic factors—high unemployment rates, increasing divorce and separation rates, a high rate of unmarried parenthood, and the early death rates of black men (Logan 1990).

Single-parent female-headed families constitute a growing structure among black families, largely because of teenage parenting, although teenage pregnancy has been increasing in white families and decreasing in black families (Logan 1990). In 1991 17 percent of white children lived with a mother only, whereas 27 percent of Hispanic children and 54 percent of black children lived with a mother only (Longres 1995). Research on single-parent families has focused on poor families and rarely relied on the participants' description or interpretation of their experience, adding to the negative stereotypes (Logan 1990; Germain 1991). Women raising families alone have limited earning power and fewer economic options than men, across the board. Additionally, some 60 to 80 percent of all fathers, regardless of professional status, fail to comply with support orders, which are woefully inadequate to begin with (Germain 1991).

Stereotypes about the inadequacies of women in general and black people in particular add fuel to the myths about the dysfunctional nature of single-mother families. A 1987 NASW study of 307 single mothers concluded that "practitioners 'should recognize and appreciate the strengths and resources of single parent families and help them build on their strengths rather than on weakness and isolation" (Germain 1991:98–99).

This is consistent with the self-reports cited by Logan: "What is viewed as 'pathology' by researchers becomes a strength when children and families are allowed to speak for themselves. The 'matriarch' becomes a strong, secure force against a hostile world, and a 'broken home' becomes a network of best friends, neighbors, uncles and aunts" (1990:77). Yet female-headed single-parent families are more at risk because of the lack of adequate family policy and severe economic hardships.

The Feminist Perspective

Radical sociologist C. Wright Mills posed the question "What is the structure of this particular society as a whole?" The structure of American society is one of inequality between women and men. Women make up over 40 percent of the workforce but earn from sixty-three to eighty-seven cents (depending on the region of the country, with the Deep South being on the low end of the continuum) for every dollar earned by men, and, combining housework, they work longer hours than men employed full-time. Although women own only 1 percent of the world's property, in some societies they exercise more control of production and reproduction than in the United States (IWPR 1998; Anderson 1988).

Feminist approaches to social work grew out of women's experiences with oppression and reflections on them in the process of shared consciousness-raising and action. They are not for women only (Bricker-Jenkins and Hooyman 1986). Like all oppressed groups, women must ultimately liberate themselves from internalized and external sources of oppression. Pro-feminist men are important as colleagues and allies in this struggle. The myths of feminists as "man haters" or "separatists" have served to alienate some women and men from struggling with the principles of feminist social work practice that have universal application. The consistent position in this book is one of unity in struggle.

Smith examines the myths that have divided issues of racism, poverty, and feminism for black women. She asserts, "Black feminism . . . has finally given us tools to comprehend that it is not something we have done that has heaped this psychic violence and material abuse on us, but the fact that because of who we are, we are multiply oppressed" (1986:55). Hooks (1990) has also connected gender, race, and oppression as a postmodern tragedy capable of uniting those with common concerns.

It may be possible to "go it alone" in combating ethclass and gender inequities, but addressing the issues together will make for the greatest change as those with ascribed power recognize its corrosive effects on their own lives and develop empathy. For example, Tolman and colleagues (1986) have developed useful principles for developing a pro-feminist commitment among men in social work. These include developing a historical, contextual understanding of women's experience, being responsible for themselves and other men, redefining masculinity, accepting women's scrutiny without making women responsible, supporting the efforts of women without interfering, struggling against racism and classism, homophobia, and heterosexism, and working against male violence in all its forms.

The principles and "unity stance" of this book relate strongly to feminist principles (Van Den Bergh and Cooper 1986; Bricker-Jenkins and Hooyman 1986; Sands and Nuccio 1992):

1. Eliminating false dichotomies and artificial separations by viewing reality in a holistic, integrated, interdependent, and ecological fashion.
2. Reconceptualizing power as infinite, widely distributed, facilitative, and for action rather than for domination.
3. Valuing process equally with product.
4. Realizing the validity of naming and renaming one's own experience.
5. Understanding that the personal is political.
6. Ending patriarchy—the recognition of a need for a fundamentally transformed, nonexploitative social order, however dim its features may appear or however unachievable it may seem.
7. Working for empowerment. The feminist worldview of connectedness makes each of us responsible for the well-being of the whole. Empowerment takes place as we make common cause with each other and as we withdraw our silent assent to oppressive conditions and actively value and promote human liberation.
8. Promoting solidarity by affirming diversity as a source of strength and as a potentially powerful organizing tool. The importance of difference is stressed in postmodern feminist theory.
9. Validating the nonrational. Although not negating the value of rationality, analytical skills, order, and efficiency, feminism restores long excluded dimensions: spirituality, multidimensional thinking, feeling, intuition, and synthesis. Subjectivity is stressed as important in postmodern thinking.
10. Raising consciousness and praxis. Through these processes empowerment and achieving liberation of all people may be attained. The process of deconstruction or making the silent voices of a text heard is a later concept related to these processes.

It is also important to learn the history of feminism among women of color and how it may differ and be similar to feminism among dominant group women. Johnetta Cole (1998) notes that we are both bound by our similarities and divided by our differences. The patriarchal oppression of women knows no boundaries, yet we cannot conclude that the oppression of all women is identical. We must investigate each group's and each woman's unique history and response. As privilege can exist along with oppression, women can oppress each other within groups and across groups even as they can be oppressed by men. The renowned African American female social critic bell hooks notes, in an essay on revolutionary feminism (1995), that postmodern feminism is not antimale, but is anti-oppression. While not minimizing the major impact of male domination, the "new" feminism stresses the ways people oppress each other. While some point to the ways in which women of color have not been included in feminist history and also subordinate gender discrimination to racial discrimination (Lum 2000), hooks has always maintained that eradicating sexism and eradicating racism must be done simultaneously. We do not have to choose between oppressions but acknowledge the interlocking nature of systems of domination and work to end them as women, and men, of many races working together. She notes that the value of "revolutionary interdependence must be shared if we are to reclaim a vision of feminist sisterhood that proudly acknowledges feminist commitment to anti-racist struggle" (1995:106–107).

Power between the worker and client must continually approach equality in feminist direct practice. In indirect services decision making and input to planning and policy should be collegial, with flexible arrangements and peer accountability. Overall the social work practitioner is seen as an activist role model who facilitates social change (Van Den Bergh and Cooper 1986). The empowerment of social workers, most of whom are women, is essential to empowerment practice. Feminist visions for social work are inclusive of all practitioners and populations and are highly compatible with empowerment principles (Van Den Bergh 1995).

A Global Perspective

It is not enough to develop ethclass, cultural, and gender sensitivity in one's own locality. Issues of oppression go far beyond one's local boundaries. All cultures face the millennium with problems and solutions that work. Some of these problems are universal, like poverty, the changing nature of the family, the continued oppression of women and children, the plight of the aged, and the struggle for basic human rights and dignity, which includes the issue of social exclusion of less powerful groups. A global perspective on theory and theory development, and oppression and human empowerment and interventions that challenge oppression are essential in this age of economic and social interdependence. Comparative analysis and cross-national research with a scope that goes beyond local boundaries can develop our repertoire of helping interventions. An example of comparative research on street children in Guyana, South America is presented in chapter 14. Expanding our intellectual and knowledge base horizons to include international themes also moves us from egocentric and ethnocentric positions and tunnel vision in our local and international cross-cultural work. Learning the cross-cultural meanings of key concepts sheds light on the fuller meaning of a construct. For example, the definitions of intellect and social maturity differ by culture. We can learn from differences when we do not see them as deficits. In the Ivory Coast in Africa, for example, intelligence (*n'glouèlê*) is seen as social and technological; cognition is in a subordinate position. The intelligent child is obliging, honest, responsible, polite, and respectful. She (or he) has "know-how" in valued activities. She can retell a story with precision (has verbal memory) and can speak in a socially appropriate way. She is willing to help spontaneously. Adults must know how to use proverbs, develop wisdom, and act like an adult. Memory for "school learning"—observation, attention, and fact learning—are valued, but so is manual dexterity including handwriting and drawing. The concept is: "The hands are intelligent." Culturally different values also prompt different behaviors. Studies show that children in industrialized societies value individual competition but do not pull their weight in group projects. Children in rural, less industrialized societies strive for excellence as a group and value and enact cooperation. (Segall, Dasen, Berry, and Poortinga 1990). As the well-known psychologist Leonard Doob of Yale University says:

> Look beyond that self of yours and way beyond your own history and the history of your society. You may be unable to jump out of your own shell, but (you can) at least peer outside of it. . . . Whoever and wherever we are, we are human, and we possess similar strivings from birth to death." (Segall, Dasen, Berry, and Poortinga 1990)

And we also present important differences to value and learn from. There will be examples of social work practice and policies from a variety of countries throughout the book and in chapter 14.

Developing a Critical Perspective on Power and Oppression

Power is the "exercise of interpersonal influence and the performance of valued social roles" (Solomon 1976). *Powerlessness* among minority groups is a consequence of the *abuse of power* by the dominant group, as in the case of racism and discrimination, and the *withdrawal of power in the form of resources* (Germain 1991). Powerlessness accompanies the experience of minorities of color in America, although anyone who is valued negatively and "haunted by severe limitations of their self-determination and an inevitable sense of dependency" is also powerless (Solomon 1976).

Powerlessness is perpetuated by the *inadequacy of social solutions* in the lives of individuals and communities. Powerlessness is the "inability to manage emotions, skills, knowledge, and/or material resources in a way that effective performance of valued social roles will lead to personal gratification" (Solomon 1976:16). It is low social attractiveness due to having poor resources (Staub-Bernasconi 1992). Personal resources and interpersonal and technical skills can be used to perform effectively in valued social roles. Indirect power blocks may also limit the development of interpersonal and technical skills and the performance of valued social roles. Hence power must be restored on many levels to break the chain of events that make people powerless (Solomon 1976).

People may have the personal resources required to develop the needed skills but not be permitted to do so by direct power blocks. Direct power blocks must be dealt with by contending directly with power sources through political activity. Empowerment strategies are therefore aimed at the reduction of the effects from *indirect power blocks* and the reduction of the operations of *direct power blocks*. In groups and communities powerlessness is the inability to use resources to achieve collective goals. *Collective action* may obtain power, reduce power failure, and address the absence of power. Not all poor or minority group members are powerless, and those who have power can best help their cohorts to attain power.

Power was a primary issue in the civil rights movement of the 1960s. The massive nonviolent marches and protests led by Dr. Martin Luther King Jr. and others demonstrated the power in numbers of black Americans, poor and working people, and their allies (Carson 1998; Garrow 1987). Riots in many urban areas also made the statement "We won't take it [second-class citizenship] anymore." The concept of black power became synonymous with such riots and fell into disuse. It included Frederick Douglass's notion of power:

Those who profess to favor freedom yet depreciate agitation are men who want crops without plowing up the ground. . . . Power concedes nothing without demand. It never did and it never will. . . . The limits of tyrants are prescribed by the endurance of those whom they oppress. (Carmichael and Hamilton 1967).

The effort was to develop the group solidarity, bases, and political constituencies needed to attain bargaining power in a pluralistic society. The visibility of individual African Americans is not the same as black power because the "power must be that of a community and emanate from there" (Carmichael and Hamilton 1967:46).

There are many explanations for powerlessness. From the viewpoint of *liberation theology* powerlessness is caused by poverty, which is a scandalous condition inimical to human dignity and contrary to the will of God. When poverty is described biblically, it is in the context of God's indignation. The Hebrew prophets condemn every form of keeping the poor in poverty or of creating new poor people. Throughout both the Jewish and Christian scriptures, as well as in the Muslim Quran and the laws of other religions, oppression by the rich is condemned. The Hebrew concepts of *tzedakah* (righteousness, justice, and charitable aid) and *chesed* (loving-kindness) (Linzer 1978; Levine 1990) are especially relevant to an empowerment approach. Levine (1990) makes the case for a Jewish imperative to social action, and Breton (1989) and Evans (1992) make connections between oppression, empowerment, and Christian liberation theology. In scriptural views "powerful people" turn their backs on religious laws that limit greed. Poverty is seen as an expression of the sin of the oppressor, a negation of love. To eliminate it through participating with oppressed people in their liberation (and hence empowerment) is to be in union with humankind and with God (Gutiérrez 1973; Tamez 1982).

Although socioeconomic explanations on the causes of powerlessness and poverty run the gamut, Marxists and other socialists offer a particularly cogent explanation. Longres (1990) sees Marx's ideas as in keeping with contemporary humanistic psychology, which sees the self-actualizing and creative potential in humankind. Marx saw human beings as rational creatures concerned with collective self-interest. Capitalism, he believed, dehumanizes people and is socially destructive. Marx proposed that because people created capitalism, they reified it and internalized its values (e.g., "looking out for Number One"). Capitalism consists of the relationships between owners and managers and the workers in businesses and industries that form the basis for social class position. Marx believed that capitalism was exploitative and produced alienation. Workers should have profits equal to owners' profits, since they contribute as much as owners. Marx saw workers as alienated from the means of production, from the product, from others, and from the self. This leads to people thinking of themselves as objects that can be packaged, sold, and bought.

For Marx scientific socialism was the answer to the ills of capitalism. He hoped for a system of socioeconomic justice based on "from each according to his ability, to each according to his needs." He believed that capitalists could not be expected to give up their power and control freely and that conflict was therefore inevitable. This is a "zero-sum" power formulation. Power is a scarce commodity owned only by the rich and powerful. It will not be given away, so struggle must occur. Engels and other Marxists, however (e.g., Bertha C. Reynolds), believed in nonviolent conflict to bring about change. Melvin Seaman redefines Marx's concept of alienation as powerlessness, which also shares aspects of social isolation and self-estrangement (Longres 1990). The major cause of human ills and powerlessness in working people is seen as economic injustice, which must be addressed directly by those who are oppressed. Other views propose that *both* the oppressed and the oppressor must address these inequities.

Another view of power comes from *feminist thinking*. Women have been rendered powerless from severe socioeconomic oppression in patriarchal settings (Abramovitz 1989a). Yet many feminists have a different view of power than the zero-sum formulation. Power is seen as an infinite resource that can be released as people learn, grow, are creative, and take collective action. Power is a "market concept" in patriarchal understanding. It is presumed to be a finite resource that must be appropriated and wielded. The feminist definition stresses that power is derived from the ability to realize potential and accomplish aspirations and values. Power is limitless, rooted in energy, strength, and communication. Most important, it is collective and inclusive, not individualistic and exclusive (Bricker-Jenkins and Hooyman 1986).

The Latin root of the word *power* is *posse*, meaning "to be able" (to act, to cause or prevent change), but the concept is associated with the need to prove one's worth through self-assertion, which frequently rests in one's desire to exert power over others. Women and people who are working poor or poor have frequently been the victims of those needing to assert their powers. Power often comes from having access to resources needed by others by virtue of personal resources or institutional connection (Weick 1982).

Social workers, as agents of societal institutions, may also (sometimes un-wittingly) use power coercively to disempower those seeking resources. Women have always lacked economic and political power, and like other oppressed groups they have been enlisted in their own enslavement. Social workers who view themselves as experts need to be careful to encourage women as the experts on their own lives so that powerlessness is not re-inforced in the professional relationship (Weick 1982).

Power in a patriarchal society is most often exercised through the use of exploitation and force, manipulation and competition. The notion is that to have power is to control, limit, and possibly destroy the power of others (Weick 1982). This comes from a conception of power in which dominance and "mastery over" are seen as normal and desirable.

The acceptance of this definition of power (force, manipulation, com-petition) means the acceptance of others' definitions as the bases for change (Weick 1982). Other types of power, defined *humanistically*, are nutrient power (for the other) and integrative power (with the other). In this view power is needed to grow but not to limit the development of others. Human cooperation, sharing, and collective action then become the essential ingre-dients of power. As oppressed people experience power, they become history makers, not victims of history. The full participation of women and other oppressed groups in social systems and institutions—including the political decision-making process—is essential in attaining power (Weil 1986).

Kenneth Boulding defines and categorizes power socioeconomically. Power is, broadly, a *potential for change*; more narrowly, it is the *ability to get what is wanted* individually or collectively. It is characterized also by the *range of options, decisions,* and *possible futures*. Force is only one aspect of power, and it is linked to the concept of domination. The roles and statuses we occupy relate to the kind of power we exercise. Conflict arises when the power of one is reduced and the power of another is increased, usually over boundary issues. A very small group of people has most of the power, and a large group of relatively indigent workers is mostly powerless, with about 25 percent of the human race living in extreme, life-destroying poverty (1990).

From the point of view of it consequences, there are three different kinds of power: *destructive, productive,* and *integrative. Destructive power* is the power to destroy things. The future of the human race rests on its ability to abandon the means of destroying the planet. "*Productive power* is found in the fertilized egg, in the blueprint, in the idea, in tools and machines that make things, in the activities of human brains and muscles" (Boulding 1990:25).

Integrative power is the aspect of productive power that involves the capacity to build organizations to create families and groups, to inspire loyalty, to bind people together, to develop legitimacy. It can also create enemies and alienate people, so it can be destructive as well as productive (Boulding 1990:24). Collective action for social change contains all these elements. It is fueled by love, loyalty, and strong ties as much as by outrage at injustice.

Boulding also discusses *economic power*: "*Economic power* is what the rich have a lot of and the poor, very little of. It has a good deal to do with the distribution of property. . . . Its core is the productive and exchange power systems . . . [and] a good deal of threat" (1990:30).

The empowerment of people who are poor must include productive power (the skills and opportunities to be an integral and valuable part of the workforce) and exchange power (resources to bargain with and economic stability). Systems based primarily on integrative power are free to all and can be strong power bases—the family, churches, religious and charitable organizations, nongovernmental organizations, activist and reformist organizations, and so on. This *social power* is the capacity to make people identify with some organization to which they give loyalty. One of the definitions of *power* in the *Oxford Dictionary* is "a large number; a multitude; a host of persons." *Energy* is a very important condition of both destructive and constructive power. *Knowledge, know-how, information*, and the *capacity for communication* underlie all forms of power (Boulding 1990). Staub-Bernasconi (1992) describes five types of power: *resource power* (including personal strength and socioeconomic power), *articulation power, symbolic power, personal power/authority*, and *organizational power* (formal and informal). These sources of power can be developed to gain empowerment.

Organizations and Power

Institutional racism, sexism, and classism are expressed through organizational structures, which must therefore be objects as well as vehicles of change efforts (Brager and Holloway 1978; Setleis 1974). The social worker's mediation function is a "hedge against the complexity" of organizations (Schwartz 1974b). Within organizations power is linked to authority. Authority is the right to require action of others. It goes with a particular role or status. Power must be given. A worker must permit his behavior to be affected. Patti and Resnick discuss five sources of power for organizational actors: *coercive power* (the ability to reward and punish), *referent power* (the ability of a person or group to attract others, to serve as a role model for identification [liking and respect go with this type of power]), *expert power* (the possession of knowledge, information, or skills in a valued area), *legitimate power* (the capacity to evoke authority officially vested by the agency), and *value power* (the ability to articulate values to which people are drawn) (Patti and Resnick 1975). Coercive and legitimate power both share aspects of threat power, although they may also be destructive or integrative. Referent, expert, and value power form part of integrative and social power. Competence is the keystone of power in the professional environment (Wax 1971).

Workers in organizations have access to many types of power. It is the "social capital" they may trade with (exchange) in order to make changes in the services (*technology*), staff attitudes and knowledge (*people*), or even *structures* of the agency. This kind of *bottom-up change* effort is imperative in empowerment practice (Brager and Holloway 1978). Workers are closest to hearing and seeing how agency services empower or disempower clients. They may act with clients for desired changes or on behalf of clients within their own agency structures or in negotiations with other organizational structures.

The Critical Perspective

A *critical perspective* goes beyond the observation and description of social conditions and transactions. It develops a critical and analytical view in order to identify and solve. This entails questioning all forms of oppression and assisting in the development of alternative social forms. Knowledge is used to develop ideals of a good society, which are then operationalized into doable tasks. In envisioning change we cannot shy away from conflict, though neither do we court it. Saul Alinsky, the famous organizer and writer, said that conflict is the "essential core of a free and open society. If one were to project the democratic way of life in the form of musical score, its major theme would be the harmony of dissonance" (1972:62).

In critical thinking we need to be careful of all deterministic thinking. Paulo Freire said that "rightists" predetermine the present and "leftists" predetermine the future, and in doing so neither understands the essence of critical thinking. "Radicalization, nourished by a critical spirit, is always creative . . . and . . . liberates" (1973a:21). He defines a radical as someone "not afraid to confront, to listen, to see the world unveiled. He is not afraid to meet the people or to enter into dialogue with them. He does not consider himself . . . the liberator of the oppressed; but he does commit himself, within history, to fight on their side" (1973a:24).

By these definitions many people who care passionately and act with those who are oppressed are *radicals*. Jane Addams used the word about herself and settlement workers. But it is not necessary for people who enact these values to label themselves in any particular way. Alinsky points out, for example, that adherence to any particular "truth" of ideology may make a person rigid, inflexible, and unable to deal with an ever changing society. "Curiosity becomes compulsive. . . . [The organizer's] most frequent word is 'why'? (Some say the question mark is an inverted plow, breaking up the hard soil of old beliefs and preparing for the new growth)" (Alinsky 1972:11).

Critical consciousness always submits causality to analysis, "naive consciousness considers itself superior to facts, in control of facts, and thus free to understand them as it pleases. . . . Magic consciousness is characterized by fatalism, which leads men to fold their arms resigned to the impossibility of resisting the power of facts" (Freire 1973b:44).

Learning to question "reality" is the essence of a critical perspective. Questioning must be coupled with action and with the belief that "if people have the power to act, in the long run they will, most of the time reach the right decisions. The alternative would be rule by the elite—either a dictatorship or some form of political aristocracy" (Alinsky 1972:11). This commitment to democracy is the essence of personal and political empowerment. Longres notes it does little good for a worker to declare that a client is a "victim of social injustice" when only a major revolution could change that per se. "Critical theory can only be of use by trying to develop strategies in the here and now which link individual and social change" (1990:15). This is the thrust of this empowerment approach to social work practice.

A *critical perspective is a process of inquiry* brought about through dialogue in which the worker and client develop a critical perspective and methodology together. It cannot be a "jug and mug" approach where clients/students are seen as empty containers to be filled by knowledgeable workers/teachers. Poor teaching and poor social work have "telling" in common. We know it is incorrect, but inwardly we believe that we can tell people what is good for them and that they will do it.

> Knowledge emerges only through invention and reinvention; through the restless, impatient, continuing, hopeful inquiry. . . . Projecting absolute ignorance onto others, a characteristic of the ideology of oppression, negates education and knowledge as a process of inquiry. (Freire 1973a:57)

The process of inquiry is characterized by *praxis*—action, reflection, and action—not merely reflection. It therefore assumes doing together as well as talking together as part of the method of dialogue. The teacher and student (worker and client) are partners in the effort to engage in critical and authentic thinking and the quest for mutual humanization (Freire 1973a).

Developing a critical consciousness is not leading people to a predetermined conclusion about their reality. It is acting and reflecting with people in relation to that reality with skills that promote inquiry regarding oppression. Both reflection and action are comfortable territory for social workers, but in a critical perspective they are inseparable. This is less likely to happen in an office where the worker cannot be part of the action. The critical inquiry involves posing the problems of people in relation to their environment. We are teacher/students with student/teachers. We are coinvestigators of reality. Through empowerment oppressed people must become thinkers as well as doers to achieve transformation and freedom from oppression (Freire 1973a).

Social workers have a long-standing mandate regarding persons and environments. But we have new ground to cover in developing multifocal vision, which enables us to see the realities of oppression and to stand side by side with clients as coinvestigators and scholarly peers. This equal partnership will be addressed in the remainder of this book.

7 Making Beginnings in Individual and Family Empowerment: Processes and Practice Skills

> The process by which the client reconstructs his experience is not one the worker creates; he simply enters, and leaves. . . . He is an incident in the life of his client. Thus the worker should ask himself: what kind of incident will I represent. . . . How do I enter the process, do what I have to do, and then leave?
> —William Schwartz

People who face oppression have lifelong struggles with discrimination, exploitation, powerlessness, acculturation, and stereotyping (Lum 2000). Some seem to transcend these experiences and work to transform the oppressive environment; others experience self- and communal depreciation. Yet each oppressed person has both aspects to her character, the transcendent and the depreciated, and both call for social work response. "The transcendent differentiates itself from the depreciated by this central trait: the depreciated will sell its soul to survive; the transcendent will give its life to be" (Chestang 1972:10). Empowerment work promotes transcendence and may make the difference between a person who simply works out a solution to a problem and one whose life is empowered by the process.

According to Schwartz's formulation, the client's life is like a train directed on its journey by the client. The worker gets on, does her work, and gets off. The client may not come to the worker to seek help with issues of oppression per se. He may feel a present hurt more sharply and may or may not have consciously considered the place of oppression in the problem definition. The worker's role is to open the door to this level of consideration, but not to push the client to enter.

In response to Schwartz's central question—"What kind of an incident will I represent?"—the worker should represent an empowering incident, one that can help the client seek transcendence, a full and empowered life. How does the worker enter? What does she do? How does she leave? This chapter focuses on empowering beginnings and the early phases of the work, including preparation, engagement, assessment and contracting processes, and attendant skills. Assessment is discussed in chapter 8 as a more formal process. However, informal assessment permeates all phases of work.

The Phases of the Empowering Helping Process:
An Overview

We enter to offer social work assistance at a point where it is needed in the midst of a lifelong process of empowerment. We do not begin the process, nor do we contribute the final word. People do not "become empowered" instantaneously. The job will not be finished when we leave. The process may or may not involve conscious awareness. The social worker's job is to enter the client's experience, join forces with the client, and begin to assess blocks to power. Worker and client will focus first on blocks related to the presenting problem and, in time, locate the internalized blocks as well, including managing feelings of fear, anger, or despair and hopelessness. Raising consciousness together, they will agree upon what obstacles are to be moved, strategize and work toward their removal, and leave. The worker may also move with the client from the personal to the political, from case to cause.

Time is a medium of the helping process that can, when properly used, enable people to apply their energy to solving the problems at hand and raise critical consciousness. Brief treatment contracts, from six to twelve meetings, possibly renegotiable, can energize and focus the work (Budman and Gurman 1988). Long-term work is often indicated when people face complex and interconnected problems and when their natural helping networks are weak. However, the duration of a helping relationship should be dictated by the nature and complexity of the problem, the client's needs and sense of how long it will take to problem solve, and the mutual assessment. Under most managed care guidelines used by agencies for insurance and reimbursement purposes, time is determined by the insurance company and not by the worker and client. Hence, complex problems are overly simplified to fit in managed care guidelines. Depending on what kind of insurance the client has, contracts may or may not be renewable. Clients who do not carry any insurance may not be seen at most managed care agencies. Many homeless people carry no entitlements or insurance. Also, undocumented immigrants are not covered by insurance. The most vulnerable groups and, often the working poor, may be denied services because they are not fully covered by insurance. Social work organizations act as watchdogs on managed care and urge accountability mechanisms (Currents 1999). Additionally, under managed care, DSM IV categories must be used, whether or not they fit. It is usually necessary to assign the more severe Axis I and II categories to get service approved. While managed care agencies may provide efficient and effective services for clients whose needs are able to fit in a very brief treatment structure, it is doubtful that they can provide the outreach, ongoing support, flexibility, and time needed to serve poor, oppressed, and socially excluded clients. Corcoran and Vandiver (1996) note that "every stick has two ends." The reader is referred to their book to consider the pros and cons of managed care for the most vulnerable populations.

Beginnings, middles, and endings are time phases with distinct characteristics and corresponding necessary processes and tasks for the worker (Smalley 1967; Germain and Gitterman 1996). In beginnings workers need to make the agency's service structure, purposes, processes, and mutual tasks of the worker and client known. This includes the purpose and processes of empowerment. A mutual agreement or contract is then made that orders the priority of the work. Assessment proceeds concurrently, and it informs the work. As the client and worker build a relationship, in the pursuit of working on the client's concerns, beginnings can be an energized and exciting time. Middles, however, may lose energy if clients and workers conspire in unhelpful ways. Clients must take responsibility for the work (be the *causal agents*), and workers need to help them do that. When workers take over clients' tasks and act as experts on the client's life, the work lacks energy and affect and is an illusory process. Critical skills and tasks for the worker in the middle phase include the ability to detect if work is going on, to contribute facts and vision, and to challenge obstacles to the work (Schwartz 1974). Endings are a time of potential sadness, as saying goodbye is difficult and can reawaken the remembrance of other partings. But this is also an energized time of owning the gains and "graduating" to managing again on one's own as a more empowered person.

There are various ways to categorize the phases of the helping process. See, for example, Hepworth and Larsen (1986), Woods and Hollis (1990), and Pincus and Minahan (1973). Schwartz (1974 defines a preparatory tuning-in phase, a beginning phase, a work phase, and a transitions and ending phase. Shulman (1992) elaborates on the skills of these phases, and Germain and Gitterman (1980, 1996) divide the initial phase into worker preparation (cognitive and affective); entry, including exploration, problem definition, and contracting; they continue with an ongoing period; and ending, or termination.

Lum (2000) delineates five phases and the worker-client practice issues: a contact phase, when a relationship is developed and information about the client and his world is gathered, a problem identification phase, an assessment phase, an intervention phase, and a termination phase. During problem identification and definition, Lum suggests the client and worker should look together at themes of oppression, powerlessness, exploitation, acculturation, and stereotyping as they play themselves out in the client's life. This identification is made at the macro level of complex organizations, the meso level of local communities and organizations, and the micro level of individual, family, and small-group life. He suggests brainstorming and listing problems at all these levels using a chart form (2000). During the contact and problem identification phases, Lum recommends an ethnographic approach where the worker is the inquirer and learner and the client is the teacher and clarifier.

The phases in our empowerment work with individuals, families, small groups, and communities are

- preparing to enter the client's world,
- entering and joining forces,
- mutual assessment, problem definition, and contracting,
- working on the problems,
- leaving and evaluation.

Preparing to Enter the Client's World

In "tuning-in" Schwartz says that the "worker readies himself to receive cues that are minimal, subtle, devious, and hard to detect except by a very sensitive and discerning instrument" (1974a:13). The worker in this process uses prior knowledge to anticipate these cues; she is, in effect, tuned to the client's frequency. Schwartz also calls this a kind of preliminary empathy (1974b). Germain and Gitterman (1980, 1996) divide the tuning-in process into cognitive and affective preparation. Cognitive preparation includes an "examination of the data so far at hand . . . and tentative evaluation of their potential impact on the client's situation and on the initial encounter"

(1980:35). The data include any available records and a review of knowledge about the age, ethnicity, gender, and social class of the client and any special case features. The worker then tries to view the client's life situation through the client's eyes with anticipatory empathy. Schwartz (1974b) describes this as "getting into the client's shoes." Empathy is accomplished through a process of identification, incorporation (What might it be like to be this person?), reverberation, and detachment, or stepping back to view the situation objectively (Germain and Gitterman 1996). See chapter 3 for an example of tuning-in in the case of Niki and Mrs. Ciano.

To *tune-in* to the client's frequency, the worker must first tune in to herself, particularly regarding issues of class, race, gender, sexual orientation, and other dimensions of oppressive difference. Garcia and Swenson (1992) describe a process by which members of a social work faculty wrote in a journal about their own experiences with white racism and then shared their writing with paired partners. Such consciousness-raising dialogue can take place among faculty members, students, supervisors, workers, and clients. Pinderhughes (1984) discusses having structured dialogues on race, including making self-statements on one's own awareness of ethnicity, race, class, and power differentials. Such statements can help a worker realize when there are bridges to cross. Lum (2000) adds two important dimensions to the process of developing preliminary empathy. First, the agency itself should go through a self-study and tuning-in process to develop a service delivery system particular to the needs of minority clients. New workers should be offered training in ethclass-sensitive practice. When this is unavailable, workers must gather this information for themselves. Second, tuning in must include firsthand knowledge of this particular minority community, of relationship protocols, and of styles of communication. This may be attained through visiting the community with a worker who is comfortable there (Lum 2000).

A member of an oppressed group may make a cautious or apparently indifferent entry into the helping process. This may be seen as resistance. Resistance is a transactional concept, and the worker's responses to such caution may create actual resistance (Germain and Gitterman 1996). The client has a legacy of oppression to consider as he looks into the worker's eyes. Will this be one more oppressive experience? Is there any possibility of trust? Will this "helping" person stereotype me or see my uniqueness? Will he see me in totality—a person who endures depreciation, responds with strength, and strives to transcendence—or only see one side of me? Will she be fair? What does she know about what I live with? The minority client may overcome resistance by finding out about the worker, evaluating the worker's inner character, and, in the best scenarios, bestowing a sense of kinship. The worker should be open to a new level of personal sharing, come across as a real person, and demonstrate caring and empathy (Lum 2000).

With careful preparation the worker is ready to create, build, and cross the bridge of relationship from her world to the client's world. Each new client is deserving of this time spent in tuning-in, and so is each worker! Once the worker cultivates this "habit of preparation," of tuning-in to each new situation, there is a part of it that goes on "automatic pilot." This time spent in tuning-in is invaluable to keep the worker sensitive to nuances in each new encounter.

Entering the Client's World and Joining Forces

With *cognitive and affective preparation* the worker is ready to meet the client. The following process excerpt shows a young first-year MSW student (of middle-class, suburban WASP background) meeting with an inner-city African American client, Keisha, age nineteen. The setting is a program for young mothers located in a wealthy section of midtown Manhattan. The worker reflects:

At first, Keisha came across as pretty tough, and I thought she's going to be a tough nut to crack, but the veneer was so thin. Once we started talking we immediately clicked and liked each other. Keisha shared that she had to move because of the condition of her building. She asked if I could help her find new housing for herself and her two toddlers. I offered to make a home visit to see what she is going through. She said she would come meet me and show me the way. But I was almost sorry I said I'd go. I've never been to the Bronx, and I was very anxious about my safety. It's easy to make bridges in my mind. It's hard to really cross that bridge into another world. My supervisor suggested that I drive and that I also take our parent aide, Mrs. Nyles, an older African American woman who lives in the Bronx. I was still anxious when I got home. So I asked my husband to drive up there with me so I could look over my home visit. It was as bad as I imagined (she gives details), but my having seen it relieved some of my tension.

The idea of a "previsit" paid off in practice that was attuned to where the client was and not to the worker's own anxiety.

Crossing the Bridge: The Worker's Reflection Continues.

Keisha, Mrs. Nyles, and I met to drive uptown. Keisha explained her children were sick and we began by discussing them. As we rode, Keisha observed, "It gets dirtier and dirtier as we go uptown." I responded, "Yes, it's like going from one world to another. How does it feel coming all the way down to midtown every day?" Keisha said, "It's white people's territory. You have to get used to them staring at you, wondering why you're there." I said I could understand a little. "Coming up here I feel like a stranger and an outsider, but I have you with me."

The sharing of "outsiderness" draws the two young women closer. The worker may not fully understand the bridges Keisha crosses everyday, but she is trying, and her own sharing helps build the relational bridges where understanding can take place. Keisha tried to help her understand.

Keisha said, "But it's more than not fitting in. You have to learn how to talk to white people too." I asked, "What do you mean?" "Well," said Keisha, "if I'm uptown I say, 'You asshole; you're full of shit.' But if you talk to white people, you say [in a high-pitched voice], 'You are quite naive, and I don't wish to associate with you anymore!' I practically drove over the Willis Avenue Bridge I was laughing so hard. We all were! The laughter came to an abrupt halt as we got to her building. As we entered the door the stench of urine was overwhelming. Keisha pointed out the notice on the wall that said the electricity was turned off, as the landlord had not paid the bill. She shook her head slowly and asked, "Do white people have to live this way?" I said, "Some do, but racism makes it this way for so many black people; it's unfair." She said, "You got that right. I want to get out of here so bad." "I'll help you," I said as we climbed the stairs.

The worker entered the client's world and joined forces. Her response about the injustice of racism might have allayed some of Keisha's fears about the worker's naïveté. Keisha enjoyed being "the guide" and appreciated the worker's sincerity. The worker's ability to laugh and her openness drew them closer. It also opened the door for contracting on the experience of oppression. The worker's willingness to see the client's world in person deepened her understanding of the client's struggle and strengths and their working relationship.

Beginnings: Mutual Exploration, Mutual Assessment, Problem Definition, and Contracting

In actual practice the processes of the beginning phase of work are interdependent and not in "lockstep" progression. We might reverse the order or shift the processes around for as we work with people who are oppressed we seek to have them tell their own stories, complete with affect and their own perceptions. We cannot therefore artificially propose an order that loses the client. In her work with Keisha the worker records, "Keisha and I have made such a good start. This is our first formal session in my office. She came to the door so enthusiastically, but her enthusiasm soon faded as we had to do the agency intake form. We couldn't even talk because of all the questions to be answered. I think we both resented it."

A more experienced worker might have been able to ask questions without detracting from the work and also have known when to abandon questions and share the client's concerns. But such forms can be an impediment.

The worker's task is to join with the client as problems are explored and to offer hope and vision. Initial interviews are a time for bridge making, starting to form a bond, and determining what will be worked on together. Intake-type questions can be assaultive and extract from people at a point of vulnerability.

Asking for the Client's Story

Exploration must not be an excavation into every corner of the client's life. It should proceed according to the principles of *salience and relevance* to the problem at hand (Germain and Gitterman 1996). Since problems are transactional, both the client's troubles and the resources of the environment are the focus of exploration. Exploration consists of asking questions that reach for facts and feelings and offering sustainment in the process. Assessment, problem definition, and a mutual contract are achieved through sensitive exploration.

It is important to start with asking for the client's own story. There is a gospel hymn that says, "I'm gonna put on my robes, tell the story how I made it over—When I get home!" Telling the story of faith, courage, strength, struggle, and perseverance against the odds need not be saved for eternity. In fact, the story (the client narrative) must be told as a source of strength for the self and the community (Germain 1990, 1991; Dean 1993). The story may also be deconstructed and reconstructed with an empowering ending (Carpenter 1996). Oral history is also a powerful therapeutic and research-oriented tool in working with black clients (Martin 1989).

Whether the service is *sought* or *proffered* (as in many medical, educational, and other host settings) or *imposed* (as in authoritative agencies), the client has a story to tell (Germain and Gitterman 1996). The worker may recognize the less than voluntary circumstances of the latter two categories, make clear what help is available, and suggest that getting to know the client and having her decide what she wants to work on are essential. Then meetings can be empowering, not just two (or more) people sitting together in a room with one attempting to "pull teeth" and the other appropriately defending by shutting her mouth. The worker is not passive during the client's unfolding narrative. The skills of active listening are important (i.e., following and tracking the story), and it is important to respond with empathy, verbally and nonverbally, to seek clarification of important points, to explore them more deeply, and to convey actively the message "I hear you, I'm interested in the details, and we can work on this together."

Clients who are poor often have to "tell their stories" in order to be given resources. The stories given for this purpose are often empty—devoid of feeling, energy, and subjective meaning. It is as if the client says, "Oh, she wants me to play that tape again." To avoid this and to engage a real person in an energized helping process, one might guarantee from the start that help will be given. The empowering helping encounter is not a means test. We have to start with new rules of the game.

Telling the Story

The following encounter takes place in an inner-city shelter for homeless women and children. May is a twenty-six-year-old African American woman with two little girls: Taisha, three, and Julie, one. She is eight months pregnant with her third child. She has lived in motels for over four months. She has been in this shelter for three weeks. The worker was asked to see her because "she is cooperative, but comes across as hard and doesn't talk." The worker records the initial meeting (the worker's skills are italicized and bracketed):

May was sitting on the couch in the living room fixing Julie's hair. I sat in the chair to the corner of the couch so we could have *eye contact and introduced myself as a social worker who* "helped out" here working with some of the women to make sure they got housing. I knew from the service coordinator that she had been without housing of her own for five to six months. That must be so hard on her and the children. I wondered if we could talk, so I could help her get what she wants. [Positioning; Asking indirectly for the story; Telling my role and offering the service.] She said we could. It feels like forever, but she's used to waiting. I asked her daughters' names and said they were beautiful children. She smiled warmly but briefly and told me. *I observed that little Julie had spent half of her life without a home.* [Offering empathy.] Her eyes filled up and she said, "It's longer than that; it's almost her whole life. I don't want that to happen to my new baby." [Shares her pain.] I said, "No; it must not happen." [Offering hope.]

I asked, *"Can you tell me what happened?"* [Asking directly for her story.] She said that almost one and a half years ago the children's father started using drugs heavily. *I said, "Uh, oh," ominously.* [Empathizing.] She said, "Right!" Before that he had a job and they were managing. When it started they lost their apartment and they moved into his mother's house. *I asked how that was.* His mother is nice and they got along for about six months. Then he began to beat her. She was pregnant with Julie and afraid of losing the baby. His mother tried to stop him, but she couldn't. *I said that was horrible.* She said it was. She looked into my eyes and the tears streamed down her face. *I reached over and took her hand in mine. I said, "No woman deserves that, and you were pregnant too."* [This was empathic but also the beginning of consciousness-raising work.] She said, "Yes, and he had never been like that before." *I said it was awful and asked, "Then what happened?"* [Worker empathized, then asked for more facts.] She said that once he pushed a chest of drawers at her but instead Taisha was pinned under it. Somehow the child was OK.

I said it was a miracle. She nodded, and added, "She screamed so much the neighbors came in and called the police, but he ran off." She did get an order of protection, but he was just gone. Period. She hadn't seen him since, until nine months ago, when he came back saying he was clean and begging her forgiveness. She patted her stomach, and *I nodded*. [Conveying understanding.]

I asked where he was now. [Determining her safety.] She said she told him to get out of her life when he started drugging again. She left the area. She hasn't seen him for about seven months. *I said that she acted wisely to get away and asked if she pressed charges.* [Affirming her strength in acting.] She said she hadn't. She couldn't do that to his mother. *I asked if he knew where she was now.* She said he didn't, and no one in his family did either. [Worker determines safety and lets it go for now.] She moved here and went from relative to relative, then to motels. I said, *"May, you have been through so much."* [Continuing to empathize.] She dried her tears and straightened up and said she had, but she never talks about it. *I asked, "Why not?"* [Asking her to reflect.] She said, "I GUESS NO-BODY'S EVER REALLY ASKED." *I thanked her for telling me and asked if we could talk again tomorrow about the same time.* She easily agreed. She stood up as I did and *we hugged*. [The telling of this very personal and pent-up story moved me deeply.] The girls joined in the hug. *I put my hand on the baby in the womb and said, "The baby won't be homeless; we will work together if you agree."* [Conveying caring and joining with her hope to have a home before the baby was born; offering again to help.] She looked at me like I was crazy and said, "Sure, I do."

Discussion

In making this beginning with May, the worker used her empathy verbally and nonverbally. The empathic connection made it possible to ask the questions that would help her tell her story. The skills of exploration or asking questions in the beginning phase of work are used to elicit facts and feelings about the problem as the client sees it. She responded intuitively to the sense of aloneness and hurt May conveyed. The connection was made with empathy and with a clear offer of hope. Her purpose was explained clearly— to help May get the housing she needed. This was also the contract offer that she would later expand upon. The roles were touched upon: We would work together." May readily agreed and experienced "feeling better" because her story was shared with another human being.

Preparatory Work

What may seem to be an instantaneous bridge between a young black woman and an older white woman also needs explanation. Before meeting with individual clients, the worker visited the small shelter for several weeks, building relationships with administration, staff, and clients. She accompanied groups on summer trips, played with children, and was informal and easy, sharing whatever was asked about who she was and doing whatever was needed. Her relationships with trusted staff members were a bridge to the women. The worker was given the "pass" of a trusted or "wise" outsider. (See chapter 6.) All the literature on white workers and black clients stresses that race must be made discussable early on and that obstacles must be confronted directly (Lum 2000; Devore and Schlesinger 1999; Solomon 1986). When the worker began with May, she was already standing on a bridge. If this hadn't been the case, she would have needed to reach for the obstacles she only listened for here. If she perceived a "wall," to begin dialogue on their difference and start the work she might have asked, "Maybe you wonder if this white lady knows what you're talking about and what you have to deal with?"

Mutual Role Definition

The worker offered May the opening contract of "working together to find housing." In subsequent meetings the roles were spelled out. First, the worker determined what actions May had taken on her own. Then they decided together what each of them would do. She had applied for a Section 8 subsidy (not available) and was on two lists for public housing. She had not called about the lists' progress. After dealing with her feelings of hopelessness ("What's the good of calling anyhow?"), she agreed to call and find out. She was fifth on one list and eightieth on another. The shelter director mediated regarding the shorter list, and May moved up to second on the list. Within two weeks of her baby's birth she was in her own apartment in public housing. She then joined the newly formed "alumnae" empowerment group, where she continued in her resolve not to see her abuser again.

Problem Definition and the Contracting Process

Problem definition is the process of defining what problems will be the centerpiece of the work. *Contracting* is the process by which the client and worker agree upon what the work is, what is to be done, and who is to do it. The two processes are invariably related. See chapter 3 for an example of contracting with thirteen-year-old Niki, whose story began in chapter 1.

Problem definition relies on the client's ability to tell the story, including a description of the situations that are causing discomfort and the attendant behaviors, cognitions, and emotions (Berlin 1983). Clients may feel problems acutely or chronically, specifically or vaguely. The worker listens to the client's story and gives it back to her in a more organized, less punishing way. The work in this phase is to come to a common conceptualization of the problems and to transform the amorphous into workable components. Consciousness-raising may also broaden the problem definition. See chapter 3 for problem definition work with Niki's great-grandmother, Mrs. Ciano.

In May's situation the problem definition began with homelessness and expanded to include feelings of sadness and hopelessness, the need for prenatal care, financial concerns, physical abuse from a male partner, and racial and class bias in dealing with basic life support systems. May's safety was not an imminent issue. Yet, she needed to share the events and think about them to raise her own consciousness about tolerating such life-threatening abuse and to use anticipatory planning should he reappear. She needed to focus her energies to deal with the responses of institutional racism and gender and class bias that she received in seeking housing as a single African American mother. Her reflection on this also raised her consciousness, externalized oppression, and reduced self-blame.

The *contracting process* consists of worker tasks and client tasks. The client offers the problems that she wants to work on and works at prioritizing and clarifying her concerns. The worker makes an uncomplicated statement about what he thinks the work is. The client's stake and the worker's stake (related to agency purpose and resources) can then be reconciled. The worker must describe her own part in the proceeding as clearly as possible (Schwartz 1974b). Clients often expect workers to "solve problems for" them and thereby relinquish their own power. Workers need to refuse this impossible omnipotent role and help the client keep the power in his own hands (Goroff 1981). The worker needs to reach for feedback on the emerging agreement. The contract may be renegotiated frequently as the situation changes and as mutual assessment develops. It is usually not a formally written legalistic document, but an oral agreement between client and worker. If it is written, it helps if the client supplies the wording and if it is open to change.

The process of contracting must include agreeing on the nature of the problem/need in transactional terms, agreeing on realistic goals, and determining next steps to reduce stress and enhance internal and external coping resources. The units of attention in ecological field must be carefully determined, although they may shift over time (Germain and Gitterman 1996).

Empowerment Content

Empowerment needs to become a part of the problem definition and contracting process. The timing of this is crucial. In some instances this can be done right from the start, in others (as with May) it is a matter of re-negotiating the contract as pressing needs are met. In all instances it is best if the empowerment process and hoped-for outcome are discussed explicitly, so that the client can choose to empower himself.

The worker's role in the empowerment process is important to define from the beginning. Clients are often wise about what workers actually do, as shown in the next example.

This is a middle-aged, Anglo-Saxon, second-year social work student's first visit to the home of Mrs. G., a forty-year-old immigrant from a rural village in Portugal. The setting is a public school that offers support to mainstreaming special education children and their families. When Mrs. G.'s younger daughter reached the third grade, she was placed in a special education class. The school saw Mrs. G. as "slow" and "unresponsive." Maria was "mainstreamed" in the sixth grade. The new worker planned a home visit when Mrs. G. did not respond to her letters requesting an introductory meeting. (Mrs. G. had no telephone.) In the first part of the interview the worker and Mrs. G. were alone and Mrs. G. haltingly (because of language difficulty) but readily unburdened her concerns in response to the worker's warmth and empathy. Then Gerry, a bright fourteen-year-old who acts as the executive leader in the family, and Maria returned home from school. Although Maria related easily, Gerry put the worker on the spot. (The contracting skills are in italics.)

Maria entered, eager to find out who I was. I introduced myself as the new social worker from her "mainstreaming program." I asked how the "regular" sixth grade was. She said it was OK, except for two boys who called her names, teasing her about big feet and being fat. I said that name calling can really make kids feel bad—that I remembered being teased about my name, Madelyne Strauss—and kids calling me Stradilyne Mouse sometimes. I said it used to hurt my feelings and made me mad too. I wondered how she felt. She said, "I punch them. That's why I have to stay after school. I also have to stay after school because I can't read good." Gerry came in, took one look at me, and started singing. Maria said, "This is our new social worker." Gerry flopped down in a chair and stared at me. I introduced myself. She continued staring and said, "WHAT KIND OF A SOCIAL WORKER ARE YOU? ARE YOU THE KIND THAT THINKS THEY CAN FIX THINGS AT SCHOOL OR HOME, OR ARE YOU THE KIND THAT TRIES TO FIX US?" *I laughed and said that it sounded as if she had a lot of experience with social workers. I said that it would be pretty nervy for me to walk in and think I could fix anything or even decide what needed to be fixed. I said, "I don't even know you guys yet!"* They all laughed, including Mrs. G. *I said that I was hoping that they could tell me what kind of things we could try to work on together.* Gerry said, "One at school, four at home and three miscellaneous." I asked her if more things seemed to be problems at home for her. She replied, "The biggest problem to work on is Maria's school problems. She can't read, and she doesn't care." Maria was looking down at her hands during this. *I said that reading problems could be embarrassing and asked if Maria could tell us about her problems.*

An Empowering Contracting Process

The young client's question was courageous and highly perceptive. There are social workers who come in with a "fix it" or "fix you" attitude. Both attitudes rob clients of their power. The worker's reply puts the clients in the driver's seat as causal agents in their own lives. She skillfully invites their perceptions of the work. When Gerry is clear on her number one priority, the worker misses the message. But Gerry clarifies this. The worker's empathic reply to Maria restored the power of telling her own story to her. The work continued, and Maria said that she was having trouble with her reading teacher.

Mrs. G. said that she would like to go talk to the teacher, but she doesn't "talk good." *I asked Maria and Mrs. G. if they would like me to go with Mrs. G. to talk to the teacher!* Mrs. G. said, "Oh, yes." But Maria said that she didn't want the "dummy with no brains" to go with me. Mrs. G.'s face fell. *I said that names like that can hurt mothers too.* Mrs. G. nodded and said that her own sister would not visit because of the way the girls spoke to her. *I asked if Maria felt embarrassed* about her mother's English. She said she did. *I said that too was hard. I related my own experience in another country. . . . I said that I was really impressed with Mrs. G.'s English and how many things she had learned to take care of.* Gerry said her mother wants to go to the teacher, and Maria agreed she could go. I replied, "*I really think that's great. Her mother really has a lot of bravery for trying so hard.*" Gerry said, "You know, we have to learn how to get along better with our mother, but she has to learn how to get along with us too. The old country ways are not right here." Mrs. G. said she would try to learn about the new ways. *I offered to help her in this and added that getting along was a two-way street, as Gerry said, and we could all work on this together.* It was agreed.

The worker shares her own experiences, which normalizes Mrs. G.'s experiences and draws the worker and client closer together. The offer to "go together" allows Mrs. G. to assume the control of her family, a control that Gerry has assumed. The mediation between Mrs. G and Maria helps them to hear each other's pain. Children are more respectful of elders in most ethnic cultures, and their disrespect left Mrs. G. shunned by her own family. A strong beginning contract is made with the family as a whole, and no one member is singled out any longer as "the problem."

Contracting for Content on Dealing with Oppression

In the examples we have given so far clients who experienced oppression by virtue of poverty, race, language difference, developmental disabilities, and age have asked for help with the problems of everyday living. They have not conceptualized their problems as relating to oppression. Yet in each example, as we explored the client's reality, issues of oppression were quite clear. It was up to the worker to name the oppression as oppression and check out the client's perception of it and whether the client wanted to work on these issues.

In the following example a worker *makes multiple oppression an explicit part of the contract.* This takes place in the sixth session between an Irish-American worker in her late thirties and an African American woman in her late twenties who was referred to a mental health agency for depression. The client, Alma P., left her job after making a job-related disability claim that the employer is disputing in court. She is angry, depressed, and unwilling to accept the employer's decision. She has always worked and been the "most responsible one" in her family. It is difficult for her to accept welfare until she can work again. The loss of the job, of the status of worker, and of her related sense of self has precipitated problems in her relationship with her family and a "close friend."

Alma easily discussed her need for legal counsel and was helped with this and given information on OSHA, the government agency regulating conditions in the workplace. Her job was not unionized, so no other mediating structures were available. Once sure that the worker was interested in her rights as a worker, she went on to describe the interpersonal problems she was having. The worker then *risked reaching for a hidden and taboo area of difference—the client's sexual orientation—discussed oppression openly, and offered to include oppression in the contract.* (These skills are put in italics.)

After Alma described an argument she had with her friend, I said it seemed like this friend did not understand what the job situation had been like for her. She said, "Well, my . . . uh . . . friend should understand. . . . Uh . . . my friend . . . works there too!" *I asked directly if her friend was a man or a woman.* With a sigh, she said, "A woman." *I asked her friend's name so we could use it in our conversation.* She said, "Tamara.

She's thirty-five years old and we've been together for two years." She added, "It's true we're lovers, but I've had men in the past too." She began to discuss a relationship with a man she had in adolescence. *I asked her if she felt I had a preference about who she was with.* She said, "I don't care if you do!" *I said, "Good for you, Alma, but I don't have preferences for you."* She laughed, and *I said that it was difficult to be a lesbian in a homophobic society and it took courage to share it with me.* She asked what homophobia was and *I explained.* She said, "I sure have experienced their looks and attitudes, but I never knew it had a name besides hate." *I said hate was sometimes a good name for it—and fear.* She said, "I'm sick of hate and fear. At work I say I'm Spanish and Indian because I know they see black people as stupid." *I said, "Living with racism and sexism and homophobia is three too many oppressions to live with!"* She agreed. *I asked if it would be a good idea to talk about these oppressions, as they can contribute to depression too.* Alma agreed. She talked about her relationship with Tamara and how she feels pressured by her to "come out" to her family, but she is not ready. *I said that that was a big pressure and we agreed to work on this next time.*

On occasion clients seek directly to explore issues of oppression. The worker needs to be prepared to move quickly, based on his own knowledge of oppression and the client's unique experience. In the following excerpt the client, a twenty-seven-year-old graduate student in American studies, defines his problems as related to oppression at the onset of his work with an older, white, Jewish male social worker in an agency that serves many of the university's students. (The contracting process is italicized. Empathic, exploratory, and "joining processes" that help cement the contract are also italicized.) The worker writes:

Tyrone is a tall, handsome African American man who wears wire rim glasses and a cap made of Kente cloth. (*I admired his cap*, and he told me about the beautiful cloth from Africa.) *When I asked what motivated him to come to the agency for help,* he responded that he needed professional counseling to help him heal from the societal wrongs he had survived. I have never had anyone focus on oppression before. I wondered to myself if I, a white, middle-class man, could understand enough to help him. I kept that in mind. *I asked if he could tell me about his specific struggles with racism.* He spoke of being one of the few African Americans in most of his classes and of a pressure to do better than the other students. *I said that must be very difficult and asked how he was doing.* He said OK, but that he needed to do better. He said he was lonely in New York, as he came from a small black college. He said that he was a "political person" who understands that poor black people suffer so rich white millionaires can retain their power. *I nodded and said, "Ultimately, it comes out that way."* He then told me of his activity in several progressive organizations and of a study trip to Nigeria. He also let me know of his activity in antiapartheid rallies against the university because of its investments in South Africa. He said he was thinking of transferring to another university next semester because of this. *I asked if that decision was something he'd like to work on here.* He said it was; he thought it was politically right but would be disruptive of his plans. *I said that that was a tough decision, that apartheid was an evil that shouldn't be supported by universities.*

I asked if he could tell me more about his background. He said that his family was poor. They all relied on him now to help them out. He missed them and liked calling home. But every time he did, he got depressed because everyone's problems were described and he was not in a position to help. *I said that was a difficult position to be in.* He then added that he had made a relationship here with a white woman, a fellow grad student who was also an activist. This was the first interracial relationship he had had. He had never wanted such a relationship, but it had happened. It was going so well and then she ended it a month ago because she couldn't take the pressure from her family. His family didn't like the idea but were open to it. He said that it wasn't fair; racism had now cost him another high price. *I agreed that it wasn't fair and was also sad and suggested maybe we could talk about this.* He said angrily that it was infuriating, not sad. Then added, "Yes, it hurts." He then looked at me and said, "Do you feel able to work with me as a black man?" I said, *"Yes, but I recognize that we are from different cultures and that I am white."* He interrupted and asked if I was Jewish. *I said I was,* and he said, "Well, I guess you know something about oppression. Jews have always faced oppression." *I said, "Yes, we have, but you would have to help me know your experiences. I think it is easier in this society with white skin."* He said, "You know it!" He added that he found our talk helpful and that he thought he could work with me if I could work with him. We shook hands warmly, agreeing to give it a try.

The worker, although experienced, was not prepared for a beginning that included explicit work on issues related to oppression. Nevertheless, he rallied and used himself in an authentic way. His ability to share his empathy was consistent. His willingness to name racism as the "societal wrong" Tyrone had to deal with opened the work. His ability to share political points of view about class structure and apartheid also helped him connect to Tyrone, who was then able to share personal pain about family pressures and the loss of his girlfriend. He trusted the worker with this private and taboo issue. When Tyrone opened this issue of race, the worker used the word *white* about himself and answered a personal question about his own ethnicity and experience of oppression that formed a common bond. He also again recognized racism as oppression. Tyrone then gave him the present of his beginning trust and of his willingness to return to work on the several issues they had agreed upon. A contract was made that explicitly included racism because of the client's raised consciousness and the worker's empathic skill and willingness to look at himself and be more open than he might otherwise be.

Beginnings are a critical time for relationship building, the heart of the matter in helping others to empower themselves (Perlman 1979). The feeling of being understood creates a possibility of genuine sharing with a virtual stranger. The worker utilizes the beginning phase to convey a caring attitude and understanding of the client's pain; establishes rapport through adjusting her or himself to the client's style, language, and pace and, by the use of verbal and nonverbal responses while listening and exploring the presenting problem with the client, educates about the helping process itself and offers information relevant to immediate needs; establishes a mutual agreement/contract of what to work on and how to do it; and motivates clients to be committed to their transformation (Fox 1993). Essentially this sets a pace for the communication and caring that launches middle-phase empowerment work.

8   Assessment for Empowerment: Content and Process

In all the preceding examples from the beginning phase of work the worker was forming a mental assessment of the client/environment transactions that made for discomfort and pain in the client's life. An assessment is a gathering and weighing of the objective and subjective facts (and perceptions) of the situation by the worker and the client. This involves making inferences, checking them out with the client, and responding to inferences. The weighing process is used to sort out what is happening and to determine what is prominent, amenable to, and in need of immediate attention. Assessment is a "habit of mind" present from moment to moment as the worker tunes-in to what the client is saying and monitors her own responses. Assessment also occurs during and at the end of each session and, more formally, at particular points in the helping process, where thoughts are pulled together and discussed with the client (Germain and Gitterman 1996). This mutual "taking stock" can keep the helping endeavor on track and avoid worker takeover of client responsibility. The helping process itself is also assessed: Where are we in our work together, how is it going, what is left to do?

Germain and Gitterman (1996) suggest that assessment is needed in three interrelated spheres of living and that interventions should be differentially matched to what is needed: *life transitions*, including normative, developmental, and crisis events and changing status and role concerns, *interpersonal relations*, and *environmental negotiations*. The *physical and social environment* must be assessed for its *nutritive* and *toxic* qualities. Different kinds of skills are needed in helping clients to empower themselves in these spheres of living.

To make empowering interventions we also need to assess *the manifestations of oppression*, including discrimination, disempowerment, *powerlessness or powershortages, inequality*, conflict caused by acculturation and *loss of cultural solutions*, and the presence of *stereotyping and bias in the client's life* (Lum 1986). We also assess the private troubles/public issues continuum and where we might move from "case to cause" (Schwartz 1974a). *Ethnic-oriented assessment* includes a balance between objective external factors and subjective, internal reactions. *Ethnic beliefs and family solidarity, communal support networks, and other cultural assets* may be intervening variables in adaptation. Lum (2000) suggests looking at newcomer syndromes, including basic survival issues, psychosomatic syndromes, identity issues of second and third generations, major mental illness, and elder issues as areas of assessment.

In the assessment process equal attention must be given to the client and the environment. Community strengths and problems related to the client's difficulties must be assessed along with individual and familial strengths and problems. Netting, Kettner, and McMurtry (1998) note that trying to understand a community is a major job. They recommend a systematic community assessment regarding the needs of the target population. In Niki's case we need to understand the resources available for early adolescents who can not be sustained in their own homes. We need to learn the counter-culture forces that such teens may gravitate toward and why other community structures are not working well enough to promote positive growth. We need to assess:

1. The demographics of the target population group.
2. The health and mental health resources available.
3. The welfare resources: services available, especially family and child treatment agencies and child welfare agencies, access and admissions procedures, and waiting lists.
4. Educational resources: offerings, access and admissions policies, and special services available.
5. Housing resources: public and private, conditions, and availability.
6. Recreational facilities, public and private, youth serving facilities.
7. Additional resources: social agencies, courts, and advocacy services (Netting, Kettner, and McMurtry 1998:150).

8. We also need to use a schema of conceptualizing community to determine community characteristics and structures, recognize formal and covert mechanisms of oppression, and analyze power structures and resource availability (see, for example, Netting, Kettner, and McMurtry 1998:156–158).

With regard to the individual client, we are looking for the biopsychosocial picture, including health and mental health factors. We need to assess the energy that the client has to work with and how the client is managing multiple stressors.

In assessing children, it is important to be aware of new knowledge about the relationships between the brain and behavior. Neurobiological research has changed our understanding of etiology and made a repertoire of biopsychosocial interventions possible so that children with learning and/or emotional difficulties have increased opportunities to lead productive and full lives. It is important to assess such biological factors as genetic predispositions, neurobiological functioning, diet, allergies, immune responses, endocrine functioning, and atypical early development in what appear to be emotional problems (Quinn 1997). Since Niki was born with withdrawal symptoms due to her mother's drug abuse during the in utero period, her early development, and her behaviors in school needed careful monitoring. One should not assume "purely" psychosocial or biological or environmental causes but should make a holistic assessment. Crises, a variety of problems in daily life, and physical or sexual abuse may also precipitate behavioral and emotional responses. Similarly, in assessing elderly persons, it is important to rule out pseudo senility and the use of medications or the presence of illnesses (including depression) and severe stressors (including poverty, malnutrition, or elder abuse) before concluding that organic mental disorders exist. We must refer older persons for thorough medical work-ups when symptoms of disorientation or forgetting appear (Lee 1981, 1989a; APA 1994; Kaplan, Sadock, and Grebb 1998). With elders and children, especially, *family context* and *environmental stressors* must be thoroughly assessed. We cannot help empower people dependent on families unless families themselves are empowered.

Assessing a Family

When we assess family life and coping abilities, we need to use our multifocal vision to analyze six levels of family life:

1. *Content.* What events are causing stress? What concerns them? Are they first-order (natural, developmental) or second-order (sudden, unexpected, disturbing) events? Is this family bicultural? What is the family worldview and what is the family mythology that may affect the presenting problems? What cultural solutions and external resources are available to meet the needs? What part does oppression play in the family's life?

2. *Family processes.* Types and patterns of communication, both verbal and nonverbal; patterns of alliances and relationship, nature of human relatedness within the family attachments, room for growth, dependence, independence, interdependence; the handling of feelings: intergenerational culture conflict; degree of biculturality; the regulation of closeness and distance; the (metaphysical) boundaries between the family and outsiders (Where do they fall on a continuum?); patterns of conflict and resolution, the normative system; values and their transmission.

3. *Family structures.* The family form (its strengths and weaknesses, the hierarchy); the division of labor (arrangements of statuses and roles for carrying out tasks needed for maintenance, nurture, socialization, and growth; gender roles, biases, and constraints; and the patterns of authority and decision making. Is this an under- or overorganized family? Does its organization meet its needs?

4. *Family history.* Relevant dates, significant events, changes, and traditions, family mythology; and the history of oppression and related coping skills.

5. *A focus on the separate parts.* The individual development, health, strengths, and difficulties of ego functioning, and ways of coping of each family member (Germain 1991; Scherz 1974; Hartman and Laird 1983; Lum 1986; Logan 1990).

6. *The environmental context.* The physical and social environment the family lives in, including manifestations of oppression in the environment.

In assessing the Ciano family, the worker recognized Mrs. Ciano's role as the matriarch in a large and predominantly well-functioning Italian-American family. Mrs. Ciano helped the worker assess the extended family's ability to absorb Niki, and, after speaking with her aunts, uncles, and cousins, we both concluded that, sadly, no one was able to do more than remain in close contact with Niki. An adult cousin agreed to visit her regularly. Rita and Kim, Niki's grandmother and mother, were the only family members who had not made it economically because, in part, of substance abuse issues. Mrs. Ciano was worried most about Niki but was also concerned for them. As Rita faced the loss of benefits because of welfare "reform," the worker helped her investigate and consider her options. One option was to become a kinship foster parent for her two remaining grandchildren. This would also afford her additional support for the special needs presented by six-year-old Joe. Reconciliation with Niki was suggested, but rejected by both of them. Reconciliation between Kim and the family was broached and cautiously began. Kim would be out of jail later in the same year. She expected to live with Rita, but Rita disagreed and communicated this to Kim. Although Mrs. Ciano was not able to care for Niki, she retained her position of respect in her family and helped arrange Niki's care. Family energies were turned to supporting Niki in her new placement.

Ego Assessment

An assessment of the client's coping behaviors, including ego functioning, is helpful in determining what strengths the client has and what aspects of functioning need to be developed to problem solve and deal with oppression. In chapter 5 we described and discussed the clusters of behaviors called "ego functions" that enable people to deal with inner and outer realities. We should not generalize about "ego strengths" or "ego weakness"; rather we should "weigh" each function based on our work with the client, using examples of behavior as evidence, on a continuum of 0 to 4:

0: The ability to exercise the function is completely lacking.
1: The function can be exercised erratically with consistent full support from others.
2: The function can be exercised only as long as constant full support is available.
3: The function can be adequately exercised, but occasional support from others is needed.
4: The function can be adequately and consistently exercised independently of support or pressure from others.

Scores on the individual ego functions will range between 3 and 4 when ego functioning is mature and a high degree of integration is achieved be-

tween functions (Green 1972). Lower scores indicate more serious problems. Consistently low scores may indicate mental disorders, illness, or other
organically based problems, including substance abuse, physical illness, developmental disabilities (e.g., mental retardation or traumatic brain injury).
Low scores may well indicate a problem with environmental resources as
well.

An Ego Assessment of Niki

We began our assessment of thirteen-year-old Niki, including an ego
assessment appraising some of her coping behaviors, in chapter 3. It is
important to note that ego assessments of children are very tentative as
the ego is growing as the child grows. Developing rapidly through learning
and identification, the child's ego is fluid and malleable. Hence interventions can make lasting changes and hope for genuine growth is possible.
Yet Niki was out of control and her support system was vanishing. It was
important to get some hold on how she dealt with the demands of growing up under difficult, now crisis, circumstances. (Niki's story is told thus
far in chapters 1, 3, and 5).

After many observations of Niki, we noted that Niki, who had serious
behavioral difficulties, also suffered from an attachment disorder related to
trauma, abandonment, and inconsistency throughout her childhood (APA
1994; James 1994; Rapoport and Ismond 1996). She had minimal or no
attachments to her grandmother and great-grandmother (Nona), and she
had an idealized image of her mother, who repeatedly left her. Mrs. Ciano
and Rita note that Niki would "go home with anybody" as a toddler and
preschooler. However, at age two, when she was hospitalized for Hepatitis
B for several weeks, her response was one of constant crying, almost mourning, which Mrs. Ciano experienced as "heart-wrenching." Niki attached
herself to all of her mother's friends and boyfriends and was not upset when
placed back with her mother at age five or replaced with her grandmother
at age six. For several months she had lived in the halls of the housing project
while her pregnant mother was addicted to alcohol and cocaine. Her family
traces her problems to this time but do not know exactly what she endured.
They noted that she was stealing from stores and "flirting with grown men"
by age eight. Niki developed problems in relatedness and a minimal internalization of "right and wrong" (moral development). Although she said she

loved her little brothers, she frequently led them into dangerous activities. While she was talented in art and could do many things competently, her academic achievements were three years behind grade level. Her actual competence and mastery levels were uneven and in need of further assessment. Niki's reality-testing and judgment were very poor and her self-destructive behaviors (including running away and sexual promiscuity with adult men) were life threatening.

While Mrs. Ciano owned a restaurant with her husband several years before, owned her own home, and was a pillar of the community, Niki's environment included a deteriorating inner-city neighborhood and a drug-driven youth culture. Families tried hard to keep their children from "the streets," but Mrs. Ciano told the worker that the "undertow" was too strong and was "sucking in" many children. At the same time, Niki was unable to regulate her impulses and tended to show little appropriate affect, though she was clearly angry when thwarted. Her great-grandmother found her sexual behaviors, along with her lying, stealing, and "sassy" behaviors, intolerable. Niki showed neither remorse nor sadness when her grandmother, then her great-grandmother, said they could no longer care for her. Nor was there any sadness at meeting or parting from a visit with her incarcerated mother. Niki seemed to dull herself to feeling, relying on feelings of excitement to fill the void. In addition to concern regarding Niki's attachment abilities, a sexual abuse history is possible. While no one, including Niki, reported any early sexual abuse, one wondered if this might indeed have happened while she was homeless and living from hand to mouth with her drug-addicted mother for several months at ages five to six. The reader is referred to Finkelhor (1979, 1987) and James (1994).

It is extremely important to note and work with Niki's strengths. While most of Niki's ego functioning (except her areas of competence) could be rated at level 2, as she needed constant support and structure to function adequately, Niki was resourceful, able to communicate with peers and adults, able to care for her own needs on an age-appropriate level, and able to utilize structure when motivated. She also reached out for help in her own way, finding herself a substitute family among family friends until placement could be made. She was able to use public transportation well and travel to family and to her summer job on her own. The following is the worker's DSM IV thinking, used for referral for the psychiatric consultaion and later for the family court judge, who ordered a therapeutically oriented placement.

DSM IV and Narrative Assessment of Niki

On the basis of the worker's assessment of Niki's current situation and behaviors, including her ego functioning, her earlier history, summarized above, as well as her family and community support systems, the following assessment was made. Niki's behaviors are reckless, life threatening, and out of control. Mrs. Ciano and her daughter are no longer able to provide Niki with the kind of structure and care that she needs in order to contain her behaviors and grow. They are aging, worn out, ill, and have all they can do to manage the care of her younger siblings. Mrs. Ciano and the worker have assessed extended family resources and found no one able to take Niki on at this time, although the network is mobilized to visit Niki and "stick with her" during her placement. Niki's problems are both behavioral and emotional. Niki has apparently never formed adequate attachments to a mothering figure. She has no internalized sense of "right and wrong." Niki has experienced neglect and homelessness at three points in her life while her mother pursued her addiction to drugs and alcohol. She did not attach to her caretaking grandmother who also had problems with alcohol. At seventy-four, her great-grandmother does not feel up to the task of raising Niki, who has run away, stayed out over night, and was verbally abusive when caught. Niki's attachments have been indiscriminate and now include men who have sexually and physically abused her. She is open to placement and almost relieved to have the option as she understands her family members are unable to keep her.

Axis I—313.89—Reactive Attachment Disorder of Infancy or Early Childhood, Disinhibited Type.

312.8 Conduct Disorder, Childhood Onset Type
She met criteria A1,11,12,13,14 and criteria B. These criteria reflect current behavior for at least 6 months, out of control, risky and reckless.

Rule out 314.xx and 314.9-ADD and ADHD when school resumes and records are available. Also rule out 995.5, early sexual victimization.

Axis II—799.9—Deferred due to Niki's age and unstable living situation.

Axis III—Possible Sexually Transmitted Disease—Deferred pending complete medical.

Axis IV—Lack of Permanent Caretaker at Present

Parent-child relational problems
Serious school problems
Axis V- GAF- Hard to be accurate with children but symptoms are
serious.

Based on the above assessment, Niki is in need of immediate placement
with a structured therapeutic focus. Given the available resources, the options include a strong therapeutic foster home where "tough love" and attachment is available, a group home of a similar description, or a residential
treatment facility. She will also continue to work with an individual therapist
and be placed in a girls' counseling group. It is critical that family ties are
maintained during the placement period. Once school records are available,
psychiatric consultation will be used to determine the presence of a learning
disorder, ADD or ADHD. If a learning disorder is present, she will be evaluated for medication. She seems bright enough to succeed at school. Art
classes are also recommended to enhance her level of competence and self-
esteem.

It is important for social workers to be able to use ego evaluation and
other tools to help in assessment. While it is important not to "label" in-
advisably or without a sound basis, or to use labels to pathologize or dismiss
people, social workers need to empower themselves with knowledge about
functioning, including behaviors, that, taken together constitute mental conditions or disorders in both children and adults. A "strengths" approach does
not imply ignorance of clinical conditions but finding a way to capitalize
on the strengths present in all of us. If labels tell what is in a package with
good accuracy, we are no longer in the dark about seriously troubled behaviors or the environment that continually transacts with them. But we
must remember the label is not the package! DSM IV has five axes of assessment. It does have a "social" axis (Axis 4), but as this is not first but fourth
in consideration it is important for social workers to use such a schema as
only one part of an overall assessment process.

Social workers today are expected to learn and use the DSM IV (APA
1994). This taxonomy is best used in consultation with qualified psychiatrists. Social workers are not educated or ethically able to diagnose medical
conditions and should not be primary diagnosticians. They may, however,
share relevant observations that seem to add up in certain troubling directions. Kutchins and Kirk (1987) caution that organic conditions must be

assessed by medical persons, for a mistake by a nonmedical practitioner could cost a person his life. A worker suspecting a serious mental disorder should offer the client help in referral and act as a bridge to appropriate clinical and psychiatric consultation. Many clients are suspicious and distrustful of mental health professionals and the worker needs to take care in the referral process. Such services must be ethnically and culturally sensitive. Mrs. Ciano was searching for explanations of Niki's troubles, and for ways to help her, and apprehensively but willingly sought clinical consultation to help Niki. The worker's faith in a nearby mental health agency that served children acted as a bridge for Mrs. Ciano and, ultimately, for Niki. After her placement in a therapeutic foster home, Niki was referred to a female social work therapist at this agency who also offered her support to Mrs. Ciano. A grandparents group was available, but Mrs. Ciano preferred the individual contact with Niki's therapist and this worker, who continued seeing them until a therapeutic foster home placement was underway. Mrs. Ciano was also comfortable with the consulting psychiatrist, Dr. Garcia, who concurred with the worker's assessment and helped in the recommendation of a structured therapeutic environment. The therapeutic foster home was a second choice for all involved because of Niki's running away and life-threatening behaviors, but the only residential setting that could be helpful had long waiting lists. The positive in the foster home was another chance for Niki to attach to a caring and consistent mother substitute. Niki made a strong start at this in her new home.

There is an International Classification of Disease (ICD) that facilitates communication about functioning across national boundaries. Those who value a global perspective note that the U.S.'s adherence to a nationally accepted taxonomy (DSM IV) works against international understanding and cooperation. ICD is acceptable to most hospitals and third-party providers in the United States. Karls and Wandrei (1991, 1992), under NASW auspices, devised a social work assessment tool that puts stressors and coping abilities in a "Person in Environment" (P.I.E.) framework. It does not call for conclusions on biochemical/organic factors, although it takes them into account when they have been appropriately diagnosed. A universally used assessment tool would be very helpful. However, particular practice approaches also necessitate particular assessment tools.

The following outline pulls together the areas of assessment for empowerment practice.

Assessment for Empowerment: Content and Process

The categories presented are interrelated and not mutually exclusive, though emphasis in each is different. The client and worker should dialogue in these categories, provide facts (objective and subjective), and weigh or assess the situation together. If worker and client see facts differently, the different views should be noted. If the client is a whole family, give information on each member and utilize the concepts relevant to family assessment discussed earlier in this chapter.

1. *Basic information*. Name and very brief "thumbnail" description of client; relational status (e.g., single, part of a couple [do not make a heterosexist assumption], living or not living together; parent; caretaking child or other special status); socioeconomic class, including job or source of income; religion; ethnic/racial/cultural background; pertinent outstanding health or mental health issues, including substance abuse; and a very brief description of the presenting problem.

2. *Life transitions*. Current developmental issues, including where the client is in the life course by virtue of age and role; normative and exceptional changes occurring at the present time; status and role issues, stigmatized statuses; immediate crisis events. If the client is a child or adolescent, a developmental history is needed. A history pertinent to the presenting problem may also be stated (e.g., the loss of a parent in childhood or a difficult divorce that has a bearing on the current situation). But this section should not track a historical view of all life's transitions.

3. *Health and mental health*. Describe the client's physical appearance. Elaborate on current, past, or ongoing problems that affect daily life. This would include acute or chronic physical illness; physical or mental challenges; organic, biochemical, and neurological problems, such as developmental disabilities (specify); major mental illnesses (specify); substance abuse (specify—includes alcohol and all other drugs and history of disease and recovery process); and other serious emotional problems, such as anxiety disorders or depressive reactions and situational disorders. For all physical or mental illnesses note when and where diagnosed, history of hospitalization, and current and past medications. Note also any cultural ways in which illness or stress has been handled using clergy, spiritualists, natural healing networks, and so on.

Include an assessment of ego functioning that takes into account trans-actions with oppressive environments. Each ego function should be assessed. (See chapter 3 and this chapter.) Briefly include the client's incentives for motivation, state of psychic equilibrium, and problem-solving patterns.

4. *Interpersonal patterns.* Patterns of relationships and communication with significant others and support networks. Be specific: Who are the family members and supportive people in the client's life? Assess the nature of these relationships. A genogram and ecomap are helpful visual tools (Hartman and Laird 1983). Meet with significant others whenever possible. Note strengths and problems. Mutual reflection on the client's relationship to the worker would be included here.

5. *The environment: physical and socioeconomic.* Describe the physical environment—the community, neighborhood, housing unit, and home at-mosphere. It is also helpful to describe the client's work environment. Does the environment offer adequate resources and supports? Describe the qual-ities and responsiveness of the environment. Are there linkage problems or excessive, inadequate, adequate, or nutritive or noxious stimuli? (This in-cludes overcrowding, drug availability, and related violence and crime, and so on.)

6. *Manifestations of oppression.* What manifestation of oppression is the client experiencing? These may be in areas of basic survival (e.g., housing, food, clothing, health care, jobs, income); of discrimination or other direct blocks to attaining wants and needed resources; and of internalized oppres-sion (indirect power blocks—lack of confidence, knowledge, or skills to ne-gotiate the hostile environment; self-hatred; or low self-esteem). Or they may be relational, as in cases of physical or sexual abuse, wife battering, or sexual harassment. What inequalities in power does the client experience as a result of oppression?

7. *Areas of powerlessness or inadequate power.* What knowledge, skill, attitudes, awareness, or resources does the client feel are lacking? These power deficits can be on the personal, interpersonal (collective), and politi-cal levels.

8. *Focus on the strengths.* Looking back over the seven areas of assess-ment, describe the client's strengths. What ways of coping have worked well? What ego strengths are present? How has the client coped with exceptional tasks? What cultural solutions have been helpful? What interpersonal re-sources can the client draw upon? What are the strengths of the client's

community? What opportunities does the environment offer? What responsibility does the client take in order to refuse oppression and attain the needed power? What raised consciousness does the client have regarding oppression? What steps has the client taken to challenge oppression in her life? How has the client demonstrated potential for and acted to attain empowerment? Is the client interested in raising her consciousness?

9. *The weighing/assessing process.* The final step in mutual assessment is for the worker and client to look at the objective and subjective facts collected over time in these eight broad categories and weigh them. On balance, what is the nature of the problems at hand? Given this assessment, where do we begin? What is the work before us, and who will do what? These last questions make for a more formal renegotiation of the contract.

10. *The working agreement and next steps in intervention.* The contracting process discussed earlier in this chapter comes full circle here in greater depth and formality. Having this more formal assessment and contract completes the beginning phase of the work. It may take just a few or several sessions to develop an accurate assessment and related contract. Work may take a broader or deeper direction once understanding is based on this mutual assessment process.

We will present the case of Shandra Loyal in the assessment, contracting, working, and ending phases. Chapter 9 will include a second edition update on Shandra's situation. Some parallels to the situation of Sudeka, discussed in the introduction and elsewhere in this book, are striking. It is hoped that empowering interventions will make a difference in the outcomes.

An Assessment of Shandra Loyal

Basic Information

Shandra Loyal is a twenty-two-year-old African American woman who is in a verbally and physically abusive relationship with Thomas, age twenty-three, the father of her two-year-old daughter, Tomika. Shandra and Thomas do not live together, though Thomas stays often and provides child care and some material support. Her brother, Ron, age fifteen, also stays often. Thomas is not a high school graduate and is not legitimately employed. He deals drugs but says he does not use them. Shandra has a general diploma from a vocational high school. She has been employed as a dietary assistant in a large nursing home for five years. After a brief pregnancy leave without pay, she returned to work to be reduced to part-time employee status. It is difficult to make ends meet. Shandra is part of an extended family headed by her grandmother. Shandra was raised by her parents and has three younger siblings. They moved to her grandmother's home after a divorce related to both parents' substance abuse when Shandra was seventeen. Shandra suffers from severe migraine headaches and occasional fainting.

The Presenting Problem: Depression and First Psychiatric Hospitalization

Shandra has been known to the agency, a three-tier program for homeless and formerly homeless women that includes a mental health component, since two weeks before Tomika's birth. Shandra lived in the shelter two months before attaining subsidized housing. Before this she had slept on the floor of her grandmother's home. During her time in the shelter she worked on attaining housing, medical follow-ups of her high-risk pregnancy, and the pressures of her family. She connected easily to the social worker and felt comfortable in sharing many concerns. However, she did not disclose the severe beating by Thomas that precipitated her shelter stay. He was incarcerated for assault and parole violation. Shandra regularly attended a long-term follow-up "alumnae empowerment group." She was an active, well-liked, though often quiet group member. Once again, she did not disclose that she had been beaten by Thomas, who remained in jail. Several months after this group ended she contacted the group's social worker from a local psychiatric hospital, where she was hospitalized for "breaking down, crying at work." She described her problem as "depression." The precipitating factors she described were that Thomas was about to be released from prison, her migraine headaches were unbearable, and she couldn't get things done or make ends meet. She minimized the impact of Thomas's release from prison, though the worker saw this as serious.

Life Transitions: Developmental, Status, Role, and Crisis Issues

The nearing release of Thomas provided a crisis that precipitated in her "breakdown at work" and hospitalization. The psychiatric hospitalization was itself a crisis event, as her self-esteem fell dramatically. Developmentally,

Shandra is a young adult struggling with issues of love and work, parenting, and self-direction. She says that she "lost love" for Thomas because of his violence. Yet she "wants Tomika to know him." She has hopes and dreams of higher education and a career, but the realities of motherhood, work at a low-paying job, and her family roles have put these dreams "on hold." Shandra was raised by her parents, who were both substance abusers. In her teens her parents divorced and her mother's drug use increased. Shandra helped her mother manage the family. When the family moved to the grandmother's home, there was more extended family support and additional responsibilities. Shandra has a realistic and yet caring attitude toward her mother. She expresses mild anger at her father, who was strict and verbally and physically abusive.

Tomika is an active, bright, and normally developing two-year-old. Her speech development is normal. There were no delivery or birth complications, and Tomika reached all her first- and second-year developmental milestones appropriately.

Health and Mental Health

Shandra is a pretty, short, dark-skinned young woman who pays particular attention to her appearance. She wants to lose the extra weight she put on during her pregnancy. Shandra's migraine headaches are very painful and a chronic health problem. She has had medical work-ups and consultation, but only over-the-counter pain and sleep relief was prescribed. Although there have been new breakthroughs in medical understanding of migraines (they may be triggered by stress but are not "psychosomatic"), new medication was not prescribed for Shandra. On occasion, right before a headache, Shandra has fainted. Medical work-ups to date show no cause for this. Shandra also had a very difficult pregnancy, and a lengthy but uncomplicated delivery. During and after pregnancy her migraines worsened. Shandra does not use drugs or alcohol, having "seen enough of it."

Shandra's entry into the mental health system was the result of "uncontrolled crying" at work. When she arrived at the emergency room she responded that "life was not worth living" and was admitted as suicidal. She was put on antidepressant medications and released within two weeks. Her "follow-up" was to be a monthly medicine check. She was given Prozac, at best a controversial drug. She finished the medication and said that she felt no better on or off of it. The agency was able to offer her weekly follow-ups through the mental health unit. (It is important to note that Shandra's mother recently told her that she too was hospitalized for depression when Shandra was small. It is not clear if this preceded or followed her drug abuse, but clarification of this is important regarding genetic predisposition for depression.)

An ego assessment of Shandra using Green's scale (described earlier in this chapter) is as follows: Shandra's intellectual capacities are good, as are her sight and hearing, placing her autonomous functioning in the top range. Shandra's abilities in human relatedness are also good, in the 3 range. She has positive relationships with all family members and friends, and she extends caring to Thomas. She relates easily and well to social workers and has made a close friend in the empowerment group. She genuinely cares and trusts and does not use others as objects to meet her needs, nor is she overly dependent, but she does allow herself to be misused and abused by others. This includes tolerating the physical abuse by Thomas (which she says is "past history") and not being able to say no when demands from family members are too high. This probably relates to a problem in self-esteem, which is in the 2 range. When family members are angry at her and withdraw their love and approval, she feels less good about herself. When they are supportive, her self-affirmation is higher. Tomika is now two and willful; Shandra finds this difficult to handle. She says sometimes she just wants to hit her; instead she speaks sharply, gets her to nap, and "takes a rest." Family members are critical when they see harshness toward Tomika.

To the extent that her self-esteem is tied to the approval of those who inappropriately (at times) use her, both her relatedness and sense of self suffer. But this must also be understood culturally and not as a failure to form a separate sense of self. Her identity is tied to her family. The African American value is collectivity over individuality. Shandra is a member of an extended African American family where there is much financial need. She is better off than most family members. Her resources are seen as their resources, and she also receives in return. She pays her grandmother for child care services. She takes care of her brother, Ron, age fifteen, but he presents a male presence in an unsafe neighborhood. His drug activity compromises her safety, however. This cultural norm of reciprocity must be weighed as one assesses difficulties, strengths, and conflicts.

Shandra's judgment is also in the 2 to 3 range. It is often accurate, but with regard to the probability that Thomas will attempt violence against her again (there have been two events of domestic violence that warranted lengthy imprisonments) her judgment is poor. She believes that "it won't happen again." She uses denial regarding the effects of drug use and involvement on both Thomas and Ron. "It's not that bad," she said. She says her mother is now in recovery. Her family loyalty clouds her vision of those she cares about. Shandra's own impulse control seems quite good, in the 3 to 4 range. She is substance free. She makes plans, delays immediate gratification for her long-term goals, and sticks with necessary situations (like her job) that are difficult. The one exception to this is in spending "what she doesn't have" on credit to dress Tomika stylishly. Placing this value on expensive clothing for children is also a part of her peer culture (Anderson 1990).

Shandra's sense of competence and actual competence are in a different range. Actually, she is very competent at work, at mothering, and in other areas, such as hairdressing and cooking for others and in managing everyday affairs on her own. She perceives herself as not very competent. "I might can do it, but I'm not sure—I don't think so" is a statement she often makes. On balance this put her competence/mastery in the 2 to 3 range. Shandra's reality testing is good, in the 3 to 4 range, except for family members. Her thought processes are unimpaired in some areas and impaired in others because of her depression. She is not delusional or hallucinatory. She is logical, except with regard to family members. But she does strongly express that she is not sure whether life is worth the effort. She has had thoughts of taking an overdose of sleeping pills. Since depressive thinking is quite serious, her otherwise good thought processes are closer to a 2. Her motility is impaired by her depression and her headaches. She puts off grocery shopping until she has nothing. This presents a crisis of getting out of the house, getting a ride and a babysitter, and so on. She is often exhausted and finds she needs to sleep a great deal.

Interpersonal Relationships

Shandra's life is full of interpersonal relationships that are both positive and stressful. The most important ones are with her daughter, Tomika, her grandmother, her mother, her younger brother, Ron, and Thomas. Other family members and friends are also important in her life. There is a system of reciprocal relationships. The extended family system appears somewhat closed to outsiders. Her family was upset that she reached out to the agency for help. She is clearly not to "tell the family business."

Part of the problem Shandra has in relationships has to do with her style of communication. She is quiet and waits to be drawn out. When she is asked and carefully listened to, she has a great deal to say. She enjoys sharing her thoughts and feelings, but she does not have the self-esteem needed to venture them spontaneously. Therefore in the presence of others who are more vocal or self-absorbed she may not even state her own words. This is true with family, friends, or members of the empowerment group. On one level, she needs to be more assertive. But to do that, she needs to feel her self-worth more strongly and learn to think about and value herself in different ways. She has stated that her family and Thomas often depress her with their problems. She, in turn, has not shared her problems with them, because she feels "they can't really help."

Communication is important to work on. Family-oriented work may produce solutions other than relying on Shandra as primary caretaker for her brother and as the provider for relatives who use her resources, run up her bills, and move in and out of her house. Most important, Shandra needs to think out her relationship with Thomas, come to grips with being beaten, and learn to keep herself safe from harm. This involves making difficult decisions about his part in her life.

Environment

Shandra lives in a two-bedroom subsidized apartment in an adequately maintained eight-unit apartment house on a fairly safe, well-lighted block in a working-class and poor minority neighborhood. Some of the buildings on surrounding blocks are known for drug dealing. Shandra's grandmother's one-family house, where her mother and several family members live, is within walking distance. Thomas's mother's home is a little further away. There are no large supermarkets in the area, and shopping requires a car. She takes the city bus to work. Shandra likes her apartment and has taken care in furnishing and maintaining it. She feels it is "too small" (since her brother and at times other family members join her), but the subsidized rent goes with the building, which has only two-bedroom units. She cannot afford market rate housing.

Shandra likes her work as a dietary aide. Recently, she has found the pace too hectic, the supervisor too critical, and the hours too few to live on. There is no room for advancement and only empty promises of reinstatement to full-time status. Her job is located in a racially mixed area. She has suffered racial discrimination on the job. Neighborhood day-care centers are over-crowded.

Manifestations of Oppression

Shandra has not received adequate health care. Although she was seen often at the local hospital for her migraines and fainting spells, she has not received a "state-of-the-art" work-up. It must be clarified whether this hospital does not have the new technology or whether her insurance coverage is too minimal to cover it. Advil and, recently, sleeping medication have been prescribed for her migraines. This is ineffective. Helping her attain adequate medical diagnosis and care is a first-order priority. Similarly, she is not receiving adequate mental health follow-up. She is in need of more than a "once-a-month medication check." The mental health resources in her community are very poor.

Market rate housing in nearby areas is far beyond what she can afford. Her job required vocational high school preparation, but the pay is barely above minimum wage. She experiences racism and discrimination on the job. Her work on this problem will be discussed in chapter 6. As noted, she has internalized a negative view of her abilities and doubts that she can go to school or learn another line of work. Even if she and her worker could help motivate family members for drug treatment, the services within the community are woefully inadequate. The most threatening manifestation of oppression in her life is from Thomas. He has put her life in jeopardy on two major occasions.

Areas of Powerlessness or Power Shortages

Shandra's lack of knowledge about what good medical care is, what she is entitled to, and where resources are have hampered her in assuming control of her own medical care. She also needs help to negotiate complex, overburdened medical systems. On the interpersonal level her relationship with Thomas has been a life-threatening one and one in which she feels powerless. Until her consciousness is raised about this, she will be in jeopardy. This is a priority issue. Her denial and family loyalty values must also be taken into account here. Her family caretaker role is a stressful one in which she feels another degree of powerlessness. She also needs further education and training to develop more marketable career skills. Her experiences as a battered woman are power issues, as are the state of health and mental health services, job opportunities, and affordable housing shortages in her community.

Focusing on the Strengths

Shandra is a bright young woman who has many strengths that have enabled her to cope with an overload of stressors, oppression, and person/ environment difficulties. She has a good level of relatedness that enables her to utilize available supports. She is a caring mother to Tomika, who is a thriving toddler. She receives support from and provides support to many family members and close friends. She reaches out for help, as is shown in her utilization of the agency's services. A particular strength of Shandra's is her perseverance. She completed a high school course in vocational preparation, has held a job for five years, and has established good credit in her two years of maintaining her own apartment. She has been competent at her job and in learning the mothering role. Although she is surrounded by a drug culture that is shared by her peers and her family, she has remained substance free. Her perceptions of reality are accurate. She has begun to develop consciousness on issues of race, age, power differentials, gender, and class. These areas are to be strengthened. Shandra has enjoyed participating in her group's political activities. She is seeking to reconnect to a church and to mental health and medical services. Her motivation to change her situation and attain empowerment on all levels is high. She must learn to include her personal worth, safety, and equality and her own psychic comfort in her empowerment.

Weighing the Facts and Making an Assessment Statement

Shandra Loyal is a twenty-two-year-old African American working mother who experienced her first depressive episode five months ago. It is not clear whether this is situational depression or the start of a major depressive illness. Her migraine headaches and occasional fainting spells are long-standing problems that have not received adequate diagnosis or treatment. Her strengths are remarkable, as summarized earlier. She minimizes family drug involvement and continues to have a relationship with Thomas, who has beaten her severely. Strong family reciprocity and loyalty notwithstanding, the caretaking role weighs heavily on her. Her experiences of discrimination and powerlessness further corrode an ebbing level of self-esteem, and low wages and a dead-end job limit her life options. Intensive intervention should alleviate stress, promote her strengths, challenge oppressive obstacles, and create new options. This should significantly alleviate depression if it is situational. Further mental health follow-up is needed, particularly if the depression does not lift as the situation improves.

Although Shandra faces significant multiple stressors, assessment indicates that she has sufficient strengths to change relationships and situations in which she lacks power and parity and to pursue life, her own health, and full empowerment.

The Working Agreement and Intervention Strategies

Shandra and the worker have prioritized the following steps to "get things better."

1. Regarding immediate survival needs: on a short-term basis (one to three months), until other ways are found, the agency will provide regular transportation for shopping for food, paying bills, and keeping appointments so that daily life is manageable. She will use the agency's "special funds" to pay outstanding bills, buy groceries, and get caught up this month. She will begin to think about leaving her stressful and low-paying part-time work situation. This might mean working toward getting another job in time or accepting state aid as she pursues further education and training.

2. Her mental and physical health are an interrelated priority. The worker will help her obtain a full medical and psychiatric work-up and appropriate diagnosis and treatment.

3. Shandra will look at her relationship with Thomas in order to assure her physical safety. She is open to raising her consciousness and working on what she needs to do. The worker will be using the "power and control wheel" (Pence 1987) to help Shandra identify the levels of abuse she suffers and educate around the batterer's inability to "self-reform" without help. The worker is willing to offer help to Thomas. Shandra's physical safety is a

first-order priority issue in the worker's mind. Although Shandra now knows where to turn for safety and help, she has not been willing to stop Thomas from visiting Tomika in her home or to refuse the "strings attached" to the material help he sometimes gives. She has agreed to think about this situation.

Shandra has suggested that Thomas get treatment and is willing for the worker to meet with him. Thomas needs to be known and assessed, and the nature of their current relationship needs to be explored to decide how to proceed with individual and group work for each and whether any conjoint work should be attempted and at what point.

4. Shandra is willing to look at her family relationships in order to build on the positive and supportive aspects and identify and work on the stressful aspects. The worker honors extended family loyalty as an African American value that Shandra holds very strongly. In addition, her caretaking may be a role she learned in her substance-abusing nuclear family, and this will also be explored. Maintenance of cultural values will be stressed, and the importance of Shandra's own mental and physical health will be prioritized. The openness of the family system to outside intervention will be assessed.

5. Shandra has identified inadequate power in the personal and interpersonal area, identified defects in the community's resources, and named internalized power blocks. She sees herself as being too quiet and not sharing her feelings and thoughts, not saying her own word and believing she is "not good enough," believing it is "all her fault," and believing that she "can't do anything." She wants to work on saying her own word to herself and others. She understands the concept of cognitive restructuring of false beliefs, and she is willing to look at her beliefs along with experiences of racial and gender discrimination. She has identified two or three different educational/career roads she might take and wants to identify those she wants most and the resources that are available. She has, on her own, researched information on a college preparatory course. With all she has to deal with, it is noteworthy that she does not feel this course as a burden, but as an opportunity. She will again join one of the agency's empowerment groups, where all levels of empowerment are explored. She will think about attending a local battered women's group.

6. She has identified that she feels less adequate as a mother as Tomika grows older. She would like to work on parenting issues and will work on obtaining good day-care resources for Tomika.

Shandra and the worker have identified and prioritized the concerns that Shandra wants to work on. The work will be shown in chapter 9. Accurate assessment and clear beginnings that include an explicit focus on issues of oppression and empowerment set the stage for working together with the client toward her empowerment.

9 Working on Problems Together: The Empowerment of Individuals and Families

This chapter focuses on the "work phase" of the empowering helping process with a variety of clients who live with oppression. The case of Shandra Loyal, a twenty-two-year-old African American woman discussed in chapter 8, will be updated for this second edition and continued through the ending phase, with commentary on the worker's interventions.

Work begins as soon as worker and client meet. Pressing concerns may be handled before formal assessment and contracting take place. However, the mutually determined goals emerging from these processes launch us *into the work phase*, when *the client must take responsibility* for empowerment work. The social worker has particular roles and tasks in the empowerment process. But the client must think about the situation, invest the work with feeling, name the oppression, work toward finding or creating options, decide on the best course for herself, and act on it.

The worker assists in these processes, giving empathic support and expertise about particular problems and systems. She shares her awareness of the threat that external and internalized oppression pose as the client tries to surmount obstacles to gaining the resources, skills, and power to change the situation. The work of promoting reflective consideration and raising the consciousness of the problematic person/environment transactions is enriched by the worker's ability to pose critical questions and share in a process of praxis (action/reflection/action) about the place of oppression in the midst of everyday problems in living. There are truths that set people free that can be discovered in the process of problem solving. The worker also asks "coping questions," which are designed to underscore the client's abilities in imagining solutions to difficult life tasks. When people can discover their own personal and communal strengths and can locate problems in the socio-economic structure of American society, they are paradoxically free to take responsibility for making liberating changes. Self-esteem, identity, and action for social change grow out of this process. Chapters 1, 2, and 3 in this book elaborate on the empowerment method we illustrate here. The following examples of practice with clients in the work phase will illustrate a variety of worker's and client's tasks in this process of empowerment. Attention will also be given to the ending or transitional phase of work, where the gains of the total helping process can be solidified. It is through working together, ending the work, and going on alone (wherever possible) that empowerment takes root and grows.

Shandra Loyal: Taking Control of Her Life

In chapter 8 we completed a "formal assessment," developed a working agreement (contract), and made a beginning with Shandra, who had been briefly hospitalized for a "depressive episode" while undergoing a great deal of stress. Now we will reflect on excerpts from the working phase of the empowering process. New information will necessitate a revision of the original assessment and the role of clinical knowledge in empowerment practice will be illuminated.

Meeting Basic Survival Needs   Since Shandra perceived everyday life as stressful, helping strategies began with *stress reduction*. The worker acts as partner, collaborator, guide, power equalizer, coworker, question poser, mediator, advocate, resource broker, coach, or enabler, as the work dictates. The worker helped Shandra obtain information and resources for paying bills because her phone and lights were about to be shut off. She also provided transportation for paying the bills and grocery shopping. In this excerpt from practice Shandra shares that she has spent a "bad night," unable to sleep and thinking about all of her troubles, which left her exhausted and depressed the next day.

The worker asked, "What happened yesterday that made you so upset?" Shandra replied, "It wasn't anything big. I needed some groceries and I called my family and no one wanted to do it. I felt bad about asking. I got upset and started to cry and think about everything else that was wrong from there." The worker replied that she could understand Shandra felt let down and powerless to get what she needed and that that added to her depression. Shandra said that was it. The worker suggested, "We have to get you feeling powerful again, able to find a way to do for yourself, but since grocery shopping is such a problem, we can go today and do it together until we find that way." Shandra was visibly relieved and appreciative. The worker asked what other kinds of things posed a problem for her? Shandra said she'd like to explore WIC, Medicaid for Tomika, food stamps, and a bus pass. "It's hard to get to those places, and I'm afraid to go by myself—they'll just say no anyway." The worker replied that it was a great idea to explore those entitlements and offered to accompany her. Shandra said, "I know I *can* do it myself, but I need the help and support."

This empathic approach and "going with" helped Shandra to mobilize, take action, and raise hope. Breton notes, "Do not be afraid to do for and with people before you ask them to do for themselves" (1985:17). The "fear" of making the client dependent can represent the worker's rationalization for not getting involved. Doing with or for is a level of demonstrating competence, and it models effective interaction with the environment that helps lead to client empowerment (Breton 1985).

The worker and Shandra then identified what tasks Shandra could do on her own. She was able to make appointments and discuss income guidelines and eligibility on the phone. The worker rehearsed with her what she wanted to say about these entitlements. As Shandra felt so overwhelmed the worker helped Shandra go through her papers and organize them for the meetings. Shandra did speak for herself, but the worker remained at her side. She mediated and acted as power equalizer only in one situation, when an uninformed worker attempted to give them the "brush-off." Together they were able to negotiate complex systems and attain basic resources. This kind of work continued on an as-needed basis as Shandra became increasingly able to do it herself. At twenty-two, these are skills to be learned, and the skills and knowledge gained in this learning are a form of power.

Shandra's physical health was a top priority. Her headaches and dizziness frightened her and caused her to lose time at work, putting her job in jeopardy. They also heightened her depression. The worker was able to coordinate her health care, including psychiatric care, and set up a complete medical work-up. With proper medical attention and medication she began to feel much better physically.

By responding quickly and in tangible ways to the client's need for help and eliciting, responding to, and partializing global concerns into small, manageable pieces, the worker helped Shandra sustain her motivation, maintain psychic and physical comfort, manage overwhelmingly depressive feelings, and engage in problem-solving behaviors. Thinking about her situation was a luxury Shandra had not had. Rather, she was used to reacting to constant demands and bottling up her feelings until she felt nothing but being overwhelmed and depressed. In the following example the worker helps Shandra reflect on problematic interpersonal transactions with family members.

Saying Her Own Word and Feeling Her Own Feelings: In the Family Context   As an African American and a woman, Shandra faced two central tasks: to do her part in meeting the needs of close and extended kin and to maintain relationships as part of the collective (Pinderhughes 1982b; Gilligan 1982; Logan 1990; Germain 1991). The needs of the self can be lost in both perspectives. Reflection is needed to include those needs, particularly when this omission increases stress and feelings of powerlessness and depression. People who are depressed need to experience their own feelings and to articulate what they want and need. Shandra blunted her feelings until they were dull. She stilled her voice until it was silent, yet she had much to say. Shandra's experiences with a physically abusive stepfather, her wish to disappear in explosive family situations brought about by substance-abusing parents, and her treatment at Thomas's hands as well as her status as a younger grandchild of the family matriarch "kept her in her place." Yet she must find and assert her voice to gain the parity she deserves as a woman, head of household, and human being. This newfound voice must be heard at home, in the workplace and in the community for Shandra to be empowered.

Shandra said, "My sister just called me and told me that my cousin and her baby will be coming to live here for awhile because of a fight with her husband." She is holding her head and not looking at the worker. *The worker asked how she felt about that.* [Reaching for feelings in pursuit of a task.] Shandra said, "It is OK *if* she stays a few days, but she can't stay more than that. She's not on the lease and I could lose the apartment." *The worker affirmed that she was right about that.* Shandra said,

"I want to help her, but it can't be forever." *The worker affirmed this thinking and asked Shandra to put the problem into words.* [Asking the client to define the problems and to use her own words.] Shandra replied, "I don't want to hurt her feelings, and I don't know how to draw the line with my sister, mother, and grandmother. They just tell me to do it, I don't have much say." *The worker said, "You're in a really tough spot."* [Empathizing.] *"You have a strong and caring family, and you want to do your part, but you would get in trouble if you broke your lease, and that's scary."* [Recognizing cultural values and the problem.] Shandra added, "I need the peace and quiet to get my own head together. I'm afraid I can't handle this." *The worker affirmed that Shandra had now defined the problem very well and asked what steps she needed to take to handle this problem.* [Affirming/validating and asking for her thinking.] Shandra said, "Maybe I could tell my cousin about the shelter. You could help her get in?" *The worker said those were good ideas and she would do that* [assuring her help]. *But what about talking to your family? Perhaps we could rehearse what you might say?"* Shandra and the worker then role-played various scenarios with family members, including the cousin herself. [Guiding in rehearsal and role-play.]

Soon after, her cousin and her toddler arrived. Within a half-hour the toddler tore down Shandra's curtains and hit Tomika in the face. Shandra held her head and patiently intervened. The cousin said that she would think about shelters but not today, as she was too upset. Shandra was able to empathize genuinely with her cousin's plight and firmly but gently let her know that she could only stay three days, as the building inspector would be coming and she'd have to leave. The cousin agreed. Shandra then left with the worker. Once outside she thanked the worker for helping her find a way out of that. *The worker credited Shandra with the work.* Shandra added, "Doubling up with her would have put me back in the hospital for sure. I'm glad I could think it out and say what I had on my mind."

In this example the client was able to say her own word to herself and others, and exert her power as head of her own household in a difficult interpersonal situation.

Another example involved the matter of family members running up her telephone bill to hundreds of dollars. Using this kind of a problem-solving process, she was able to set limits on the use of the phone without alienating her relatives. It is important that Shandra could feel and express a portion of what she felt *and* take action to change the situation. When this work is multiplied in numerous situations, the client not only is saying her own word but is learning a problem-solving process (Berlin 1983; Germain 1984). The worker can then reflect on the process itself and on how able the client is to use it. All these new skills are transferable to other situations involving interpersonal power (Berlin 1983).

The worker also kept the client in the driver's seat: it is her life, her culture, her family, and her problem. She used a "transactional process" in which client and worker share expertise in the problem-solving process. Shandra thereby assumed control of her own life within family parameters. With Thomas it was much more difficult.

Dealing with Oppression at Home: "I Will Not Be Beaten Again"   When Shandra first disclosed that Thomas had beaten her and was imprisoned for assault, her affect was flat and her tone matter-of-fact. Her tears were reserved for the shame of having to enter a psychiatric facility, for this was a new pain. Old pain was treated like an everyday occurrence and defended against with layers of protective devices that enabled her to live through the physical and verbal abuse sustained during her earlier years, and the past and current violent surrounding of a drug culture. She had insulated her feelings in so many ways that his imminent return from jail was the last thing on her conscious mind. Since her best defense had been suppression of feelings and her silence and smile, her uncontrollable crying frightened her.

When the worker asked what she was crying about, the answers were as new to Shandra as they were to the worker. Although the answers were many, as detailed in the assessment (see chapter 8), the sharing of her beating was told and felt as if it had happened to someone else. She said quietly, "I won't be beaten again." The worker empathized; then she asked what would make it different this time. Shandra, crying, admitted she did not know. The ego functions of reality testing and judgment needed strengthening through knowledge and reflection. She needed help to feel her pain and to think things out clearly. The worker provided understanding and education on the facts of recurrence and measures she could take to assure safety, including legal orders, orders of protection, how to reach a safe space, and referral to a battered women's group (Pence 1987). Shandra had used the legal orders previously and knew how to reach help. She did not feel up to attending the group. She felt she could not stop Thomas from visiting Tomika or get the orders again unless he became violent. Might that be too late? She did not think so.

With Shandra's numbness to her own needs and attachment to Thomas, the work proceeded slowly and carefully. As many battering spouses do, Thomas cried and threatened suicide if she did not take him back. She gave in. She also said that she did not want to be alone and that he had some good points. She asked him to see a counselor, and he refused, convincing her that prison had "reformed him." There was a period of calm. She asked him to stop dealing drugs and get a regular job. He refused. He then asked her to marry him. She very much wanted to marry "in the church," but she admitted she was frightened. As she put his offer off, he became increasingly jealous and aggressive toward her and others. He was also involved in another incident of drug-related violence. This was an entry point for some intense reflection. It took several months and near crisis events for Shandra to work on how she might assure that her promise to herself—that she would not be beaten again—could be kept. Workers cannot expect a linear and easily solved progression as women struggle with attachments and victimization. As Shandra began to feel her feelings, develop a wider support network, and find her voice in a range of areas, she began to deal with this complex and life-threatening issue. Wish as she might, the worker could not hurry this readiness, but she waited for the opportune moment. The following excerpts will show the tools and skills the worker used to help Shandra, now ready, to raise consciousness and take action.

First, the worker listened to Shandra's descriptions of Thomas's aggression and shared Shandra's pain, naming the feelings of anger and betrayal as Shandra expressed her feelings. Then she affirmed Shandra's perceptions of not being safe and asked Shandra to think out her options. Shandra decided to call the police and ask Thomas for her apartment key back with the police present. She did this and Thomas angrily returned the key.

In the next interview the worker supported Shandra's action and re-hearsed what might happen if Thomas came to the door. Shandra again decided she would call the police. Then the worker suggested that she and Shandra look at the "Power and Control Wheel" together (Pence 1987), which shows levels and types of physical and sexual violence. Shandra did this with much interest, identifying that her stepfather also used many of the tactics described with her mother and herself. This was an excellent code to stimulate Shandra's thoughts, feelings, and action (see chapters 3 and 11 on using codes).

The wheel is divided into eight pie-shaped sections, each describing ways in which men may assert power and control over women. Shandra wrote her own response to each of the eight categories; later her responses were the substance of the work. Under "Using Coercion" she wrote, "He threatened to kill me and pushed me around when I was pregnant. I felt safer when he was in jail." Under "Using Intimidation" she wrote, "He makes me afraid by mean looks and threatens to trash my apartment to get me evicted — like punching holes in the walls. And his friends also fear him." Under "Emotional Abuse" she wrote, "He says I'm a big baby. He does things to irritate me and makes everything a joke. He doesn't care about my feelings. He doesn't care about me. He says I'm fat and humiliates me in front of others." Under "Using Male Privilege" she wrote, "He won't let me talk to any male friends. He possesses me — acts like my stepfather." Under "Using Isolation" she added, "He uses jealousy to justify anything he does to keep me away from others." Under "Economic Abuse" she noted, "I pay all the bills; he has a free ride"; and under "Using the Children" she wrote, "He uses Tomika to get to see me." The worker records:

After the work on the chart *I picked up on the part where she said she felt safer when Thomas was in jail.* [Focusing on her safety.] She described how on one occasion Thomas tried to shoot two people but missed them and hit two other people instead, one in the head and one in the neck. *I noted how serious an incident that was and that he could have murdered people.* [Affirming her perceptions, putting it into words.] She described how he pushed her several times when she was four months pregnant and threatened to kill her. That's when she called the police and they arrested him for parole violation and threatening assault. She said that he's like that again but that she hasn't let herself see it until now. *I affirmed her ability to see it now.* [Strengthening her reality testing; Encouraging the lowering of her defenses.] She said it makes her angry that he checks up on her and tells her who she can talk to, what to do, and how to do it. *I agreed that it must make her angry.* [Recognizing her feelings.] She went on to describe how his friends fear his anger. *I said it seemed like she had reason to fear him, noting his friends fear him, he has shot people in the past and he has "pushed her around" when she was pregnant and threatened to kill her.* [Summarizing what she has said and seen; Reinforcing her new vision.] She said she knows other people are worse off, that some people end up with broken bones . . . but if she does not do anything to change things now she could experience much worse things than what she has. *I seriously agreed, adding she is such a good person and I would not want to see anything like that happen to her or Tomika.* [Conveying empathy and reinforcing her judgment.] She paused and agreed, stating that that is why she need to make a change now. *I said that Thomas presents a threat of physical danger and that he possesses physical power, which she does not have.* She agreed. *I added that using the police is a way of changing that power balance. I said she should not have to live with that fear in her own home.* [Empathizing; Naming her feelings.] She agreed, noting he is not even on the lease. She described how he came to live there by taking care of Tomika and then he just stayed all the time. *We discussed child care arrangements.* [Focusing on a problem area.] She stated she would no longer have Thomas babysit for her in the apartment. She added that her grandmother is going to babysit for her. We ended with her saying that she felt more in control of her own life now.

When Shandra was ready, the worker skillfully helped her reflect on her oppression, safety, and actions using a "code" as a means to open the work in an area that has been covered over and hidden. The power and control wheel helped Shandra write and say her own word, examine her own feelings, and plan further actions. The work also focused on her attachment to Thomas, which was now weaker and easier to break, but still painful. This work opened the door for Shandra to share other areas of oppression in her life.

Dealing with Oppression in the Workplace   Shandra shared that she was unhappy on her job. The worker asked her to tell the story.

Shandra said, "Well, it's the way we are treated. There is a lot of the black/white thing. *The worker asked if she experienced prejudice from the staff or the patients.* [Clarifying; Naming the oppression.] She said, "The staff mostly. Like the other day I was trying to read this chart for dietary notes

and this RN comes in and snatches the chart out of my hand." "*Wow.
How did that make you feel?*" *asked the worker.* [Empathizing; reaching
for feelings.] "I got mad! So I asked her if she could let me do my job.
And she got mad and said I probably couldn't even read the chart. I know
that was racist. I was upset." *The worker validated, "You have a right to
be!"* How did you handle it? "Well, I wanted to tell her off, but instead I
left and wrote a formal complaint." "*Good for you!*" "Yes, but what good
was it? To this day they have not done anything about the complaint."
*The worker said, "Did you feel you were not being heard even though you
followed all of the procedures?"* [Using accurate empathy; Reaching for
her work.] "Yes, and it started getting me down. I don't want to work this
job forever . I want to move up, and then everything wrong started to get
to me and I cried, like I got on a roll downhill." *The worker said that was
a very good way to think about what happened. Maybe she could teach
herself to take one thing at a time. The racist remark was enough to think
about, and what she might do next about that, and then what to do about
the job itself—but when you think about everything at once you get overwhelmed and can't do anything!* [Teaching problem solving.] Shandra
said, "That's just what she does." They then focused back on the event
and its meaning and possible methods of recourse.

———

On one level this was a *consciousness-raising* discussion. Validation in
naming such events for what they are is freeing, as is recognizing the disappointment that dealing with the system can bring. Wider reflection on
Shandra's experiences of racism and systemic responses may also have been
helpful here. Although consciousness raising may be easier in a group setting, it can occur between any two people as experience is shared and explored. It was helpful to have Shandra express her feelings and words and
have them understood. *Learning to interrupt her "snowballing" thought pattern* herself also combined with these other skills to relieve her depression
(Berlin 1983). Owning her own good coping skills also helped her to see
she could handle it. She learned new thinking patterns that affirmed her
perceptions and actions. Self-blame was reduced as the locus of problems
of oppression was externalized. She perceived and handled an offensive
event accurately and well. This is a moment of affirmation and reflection.
As they engage in this *process of praxis* the client is freed to focus on further

action. (A follow-up to her formal complaint.) These practice moments build empowerment and are liberating.

Developing a Critical Consciousness: Cognitive Restructuring   False beliefs are playbacks of tapes that we have internalized from agents of society's institutions and significant others throughout our lives. To change false beliefs people need to identify thinking patterns, receive and reflect on counterbalancing information, and revise the beliefs (Schwartz 1983; Berlin 1983). Revision means taking different actions and further reflection in a process of praxis. As false beliefs are revised, people think and talk healthier, devise more adaptive ways of dealing with oppression, and rename and re-create their own reality (Bricker-Jenkins and Hooyman 1986; Van Den Bergh and Cooper 1986).

To identify false beliefs with Shandra the worker pulled together several of the themes and events they worked on and asked Shandra what these examples said about the way she saw herself. Reflecting on and analyzing these events, Shandra identified that she held several false beliefs: that she is not "good enough," that her problems are her fault, that she "can't do anything right," that she could control Thomas's violence, and that her family's drug use and Thomas's dealing were "not so bad." To revise the first four beliefs necessitated a level of political awareness, and the fifth also called for education. All these beliefs involved feelings to be dealt with. Coming to grips with the need for parity and above all safety in the relationship with Thomas was part of this work. Her beliefs about not being "good enough" extended to the pursuit of further education or job training. She thought, for example, "I know I can do hair, but I don't think I can go to college, so I had better take cosmetology." *Posing a critical question*, the worker asked where the belief came from that she was "not good enough" for college.

She said that in junior high school her grades were good, so she thought she'd go to an academic high school. But her stepfather and mother told her to take a trade instead. She initiated an appointment with the guidance counselor, who told her she was not "college material" and recommended a vocational high.

This thinking is then analyzed.

"You had good grades. Why did they say that?" the worker asked. [Posing a critical question.] Shandra said when she had the work-study program,

her parents just wanted her money for their drugs. *Wow how did you feel?* "Sad. . . ." *"And a little mad too?"* [Reaching for feelings.] Shandra smiled, "Yeah. I tried to spend my pay before I got home, or they'd take it. I was mad." *"And what about school?"* Shandra thought and said, "Well, it was funny; only the black kids seemed to go to vocational school, no white kids went." *The worker asked what Shandra made of that?* [Asking for her work.] "Racism?" she asked, "You're asking me?" The worker replied, *"What do you think?"* Shandra said, "The white kids were always in the smart classes. Now, some of us must be smart too. I think I might be smart, but they kept it a secret. It's like the teachers thought all of us were the same and dumb!" *The worker reflected that that was institutional racism and that Shandra began to believe that of herself.* Shandra said, "Well, I still think I might be able to go to college." *The worker encouraged her to "go for it,"* and they talked about the *specific next steps* in pursuing it. Another corollary step was to *identify how much energy it was taking to struggle against messages that she was not good enough as a young black woman.* After analyzing her examples she concluded, "No wonder I have headaches and am tired."

In the examples, Shandra was encouraged to say her own word, to name, rename, and revise her false beliefs, and to take action to challenge them. The work was then generalized to her ongoing battles in a racist society and Shandra began to revise the belief that her problems were all her own doing. As Shandra identified this, a significant feeder source for her depression was lessened. Her energy began to go into action.

Realizing the Dream   It is essential to help clients who face multiple oppressions to act to challenge the "isms" that limit their options and to create the options that help make dreams become reality. Shandra's next task was to research her options. She did this thoroughly and with enthusiasm. She considered her choices and decided that she could do hair to make additional money while she pursued an associate's degree, which would open more doors. She began a college preparatory course at a local community college. She also completed a 530-hour certified training program in direct care paraprofessional work at the community college. While she could not find work with this certification, her perceived and actual competence and life satisfaction increased significantly, and she gained more control in her life.

Continuing to Dream   Five years have passed since Shandra started her preparation for community college with optimism and self-confidence. As noted in chapter 4, the world has changed since 1993 and Shandra's life has changed with it. The most noteworthy change for poor families came on August 22, 1996, when President Clinton signed a bill repealing the Federal Welfare guarantee of assistance to poor families by changing AFDC (Aid to Families with Dependent Children) to TANF (Temporary Assistance to Needy Families).

Under TANF thousands of mothers attending college in New York City, for example, were forced to leave school and give up their dreams of a brighter future (*Currents* 1999).

The tremendous stress produced by income insecurity as she tried to work, go to school, and raise Tomika has taken a toll on Shandra's health and sense of well-being.

Help with Making a Major Life Transition   Shandra moved out of the inner-city to a nearby suburb in the winter of 1994. She used her Section 8 subsidy to get an attractive two-bedroom apartment in a safe area near a school and playground for Tomika, who would start school in the fall. She was delighted with her move and noted how much courage it took to leave her family and friendship networks and strike out on her own. Yet she was lonely and felt apprehensive at being one of the few African American families in this area. A second year social work student from the agency's mental health unit provided ongoing support as Shandra made this major life transition. Together they *researched the community's resources.* Shandra was quite adept at registering Tomika for school and finding her a pediatrician, but she was discouraged because she could not find a dentist in the area who would take Medicaid.

Slowly, she broached the subject of feeling different and isolated in a mostly white more affluent area. She told the worker, "They are not used to people on AFDC or African Americans around here. I feel I have to go back to the city for everything—dentists, hair supplies, even church!" Shandra elaborated, concluding she also missed home. The worker said *it was very hard to go it alone in a strange place. She asked Shandra if she felt isolated.* [Empathizing and asking for elaboration.] She replied that she did, and, she added, "worse than that I experience more discrimination here than in the city." She gave examples of stares and rude treatment in a beauty supply shop and a bank. The worker was surprised, and responded that she *was unaware there were so many ignorant and prejudiced people in this town.* [Naming the taboo of racism.] Shandra replied, "If you were black you would have to know." The worker agreed, and said it made her angry. [Validating the experience and reaching for feelings.] Shandra replied, "It makes me sad, and angry too, but this is still a better place for us to be."

By helping Shandra deal with an amazing degree of newness and manage complex experiences and feelings while doing it the worker and Shandra became allies. Shandra remained challenged, not defeated, by the new experience. The most helpful resources they located together was a *town outreach worker* and *a group for women who had experienced spouse abuse.* From there Shandra found new friends and was also strengthened in her resolve not to return to Thomas even as a "friend." Child-care payments were arranged through the courts although they were sporadic. He sent messages that he would give more if he could see her, but she held her ground. Her geographic distance also helped her in this regard. The worker for the battered women's group referred Shandra to *a self-help group of women of color who had recently moved to this community.* Shandra was enthusiastic about this group and became a regular member. Her support network grew, and she found out where to shop and where integrated churches were. She began to enjoy her new community as her anxiety relaxed. She also made beginnings at the community hospital for medical and mental health follow-up. After Tomika entered school, Shandra completed a nail specialist course that enabled her to work part time in a beauty shop. The following semester, she entered community college.

Although she began supportive therapy with a social worker at the clinic in March, she also chose to continue working with the student social worker until May on a biweekly basis. She was not quite ready to let go of the agency that had helped for six years. Although she grew to like her new therapist at the clinic and soon felt she had things "under control," she continued to desire connection to the agency. The student helped her to let go of having a regular agency worker with the knowledge that she could still keep in touch with the other workers and administrators she knew at the agency on a "touching base" and/or crisis basis. This open door policy is practiced at this agency, based in part on feminist principles, as the relationships made are usually real and strong ones in the lives of women who have lost many attachments before and during the period of their homelessness. Shandra continued "touching base" but settled well into her new life. This was a very exciting time for her—one of accomplishment and hope.

Shandra sent me her reflections on empowerment during this period of time (Lee, Group Members, and Martin 1997):

The Successful Women's Group was a great source of support and empowerment for me. It was a way to reach out to other women like myself with similar issues. It gave me the confidence to join other women's groups. The group empowered me to cope with my issues. Getting acquainted with other group members was inspiring and encouraging to me. The best thing about the group was the "coming together" and having that support system we needed. Moreover, being able to express what was on my mind and not have others be so judgmental.

Being a Black, African American, in the United States is somewhat oppressing because I feel limited in obtaining employment, education and public services. I feel some sense of prejudice in the community or work force. Talking about racism and being oppressed helps me deal with others and their differences. Being able to understand the issues helps me relate more.

The racial differences of my workers helped me feel more secure with white people. Some may have felt inferior with whites as a result of believing prejudice. Another issue is trusting white people. Black women, especially young black women, may have a hard time opening up to white people because they may feel intimidated. They learned from their parents not to trust white people or tell family business. Sometimes not trusting is with good reason. Once I trusted a white male social worker at a Clinic and he told my abusive step father what I said. I didn't think I could ever trust one again. But the group with you and Judy B. provided a different experience of white people as I learned I could trust you and that some white people can be trusted, not all are prejudiced.

I would like to see more people of "difference" work with an empowerment group so the women involved can learn about various backgrounds and experiences of others. . . . All minorities should learn about each other's cultures so they can be united against oppression. Lack of knowledge makes people quick to buy stereotypes and to judge people. We should not be afraid of each other. We face common issues.

Recently, my College Professor took the class on a trip to the Schomberg Center in Harlem, in New York City. I learned a lot of things you would never find in a history book. One exhibit showed how our ancestors came over on boats and how they were chained together, suffering from many diseases. I learned we were inventors, craftsmen, politicians and so much more. I was so touched that I started to cry. The man giving the tour told me he cried too when he first saw this, and that his tour guide had cried too, as had many taking the tour. It's good to be able to share these feelings with those who share a common bond and to teach our children our history.

I am presently in a Women of Color support group. Although I feel more could be done in the group, it's a way for me to get support and relief from stress. Being able to share and give to others as well as receive makes for a stronger me. This is a poem for my sisters:

Strive for the Best

You should insist on the best,
Because you deserve the best.
If we want the best, then
We can have the best.
You have to believe in the best
In order to receive the best.
So always remember now,
Don't settle for less!"

The Next Year   Shandra continued to work toward "getting the best" for herself and Tomika. She completed her first semester at community college and began a difficult legal assistants course of study. She held a part time "work-study" job at the college and continued to receive AFDC benefits for Tomika. During this time she intensified a relationship with a somewhat older friend of the family. Her therapist at the clinic was transferred and she decided not to begin with someone else, as she felt positive about her life. Several months later she was in touch with me as her boyfriend had become verbally abusive. She was able to break up with him after only a few sessions and she resumed her studies with success. We agreed she would return to the clinic and resume her therapy as she realized she had another "close call" with physical abuse and continued to experience periodic depression.

Shandra then shared concerns for her mother, Selina, who was over two years in recovery. Selina was being evicted from her home because of the drug-related behaviors of Shandra's younger siblings. In response to outreach, and Shandra's concern, Selina also entered the shelter and maintained and strengthened her recovery from drugs. Over time Selina became a leader among the women at the shelter and genuinely supportive of Shandra and Tomika, a bright, trusting, and happy child, according to her teachers. Eventually, Selina moved into the transitional facility and then on to permanent housing. She was hired by the agency and promoted to a highly responsible position. Both she and Shandra were relieved that Selina was again able to be an effective head of the family.

Toward the end of her second semester, Shandra began to experience mood changes. She now sometimes felt "up" and wanted to go out and shop or party, dressing more loudly than before. She was also "into eating" and experiencing a weight gain. Her trouble in paying the bills increased and she was unable to sleep. Suddenly the mood would change and she was "down in the dumps" again. She was now on antidepressants and monitored at the mental health clinic. I discussed and educated about the possibility of bipolar illness based on the symptoms. Shandra followed up with requesting a psychiatric evaluation. Then she was sexually assaulted by an acquaintance. This was a major trauma for her. We were called in, at her request, by a crisis team member. With much support, she got through the experience but sank deeper into depression. She took incompletes in her courses and slowly got her life back together. By the summer she was functioning well again.

In September of 1996 she learned that she would have eighteen months to find and hold a job and then her welfare benefits would be discontinued — "ready or not," as she said. This peaked her anxiety and depression again. Tomika's father was not able to pay regular child care. Tomika had also begun to overeat and needed special foods, clothes, and medical follow-up. Shandra wanted to continue her studies at the college. She had worked hard over the summer to make up her incompletes. College studies were unacceptable to the welfare department and she was forced to work. She continued her studies and found a night clerk (6–11 P.M.) position at a nearby motel. She paid a close friend to babysit for Tomika. She did well and was promoted, but her schedule was grueling and the job isolated her and sometimes frightened her. Of equal importance, it was only a part-time job and no full-time hours were available. She became physically ill with hypertension and dropped out of college. This further depressed her. She maintained the job but grew to hate it. Her employment counselor helped her find another part-time job in a department store. She got full hours only during the holidays. Her mood swings worsened. She was cut off of AFDC in March of 1998 and continued her half-time job.

Shandra panicked at having to raise her child and make ends meet on a half-time salary. She entered an "up" phase with her moods and began to stay awake around the clock. I encouraged her to increase her visits to her therapist. In May 1998 she was diagnosed with bipolar illness and medicated accordingly. She now saw a psychiatrist regularly and related well to him. She continued working at the department store. She did not get enough to live on. By September she began hearing voices. She was placed on Trilafon, an antipsychotic drug. Her depression increased. In October she induced a stupor with an overdose of over-the-counter medication. Fearing hospitalization, she told no one. It was not until three weeks later that she told this to her doctor and social work therapist. She was then placed in a partial hospitalization program. She had to terminate this program prematurely as her insurance only covered part of the time. Continuing therapy and battling her demons, she continued working but changed her employment to a third part-time job at an insurance company. She held this about a year, passing all of the internal examinations. She was terminated when she did not pass the state licensing test, failing by only two points. After trying so hard, this devastated her. She stopped looking for work and went off her medications for three months. Although depressed, she did not need hospitalization. She turned to family and faith and slowly got her motivation back. At the time of this writing she is living on sporadic child support and the possibility of a full-time job that she found for herself. State employment counselors have not come up with even one full-time lead for her. She is anxious and writes, "I haven't given up yet. I ran out of medicine last month but will find a way to pay for it soon. I am continuing at the clinic. Tomika is doing much better. I think I may join a NAMI chapter here to teach others about this illness. I thank God for having a healthy and loving child. She can go out for Teams now and is excited about that. I trust God and know I will find a job somehow. But it's not supposed to be this way and I wonder why it is."

Shandra is a woman of courage and strengths. Empowerment is a daily process, not an absolute. While the onset of her bipolar illness was not a surprise, it was a major change necessitating exceptional coping. People with bipolar illness often go off medications as they feel normal, then the illness suddenly returns (Kaplan and Sadock 1998; APA 1994; and Berger and Berger 1991). She also has another stigmatized status to carry. She once said to me, "Isn't being a black woman without a good job enough to deal with?" Indeed, it is, and one wishes life was fair. She is dealing now with the "unfairness" of having a biochemical brain disorder manifesting arbitrarily and triggered by stress and the major challenge of caring for herself and a nine year old without employment and few real options. Indeed, there will be times when she can not work at all. It may be that SSDI will be necessary if her illness manifests continually and strongly. It is ironic that "getting off welfare rolls" may help to precipitate getting on disability rolls. Yet Shandra will not lose the essence of who she is nor the empowerment and inner liberation she has attained. As the interventions in Shandra's case show, the empowerment-oriented social worker must be clinical. She must also work with clients and organizations that support families and children, including welfare rights organizations, to have a minimal guaranteed income as a human right.

Working with Strengths

It is important for workers to assess and work with the different strengths, weaknesses, and vulnerabilities of clients. Where there is less biochemical damage, the worker and client may move more quickly. With Tracey, a twenty-five-year-old African American woman who also came through the shelter, the road to empowerment was quicker, for she had no biochemical disorders. Her problems were situational and her strengths were more available to mobilize. She is now thirty-one, and we will update her situation here.

Tracey is a bright, thoughtful, and assertive young woman who entered the shelter at the age of twenty-one with her two children, Chia (one year old) and Larry Jr. (a newborn infant). She saw herself as one who "tried to do everything right, and it still came out wrong!" She married after graduating from high school and moved west when her husband, Larry, joined the military. Their first year of marriage necessitated the compromises of any new relationship. The couple was delighted with the birth of Chia, and it helped with the loneliness they felt so far from home. However, Larry began to gamble and run up large amounts on his credit card. They were no longer able to manage financially, and he did not come home after work. Eventually, Tracey offered him an ultimatum. When he was unable to stop gambling, Tracey left him and returned home, carrying his second child. Unable to afford market rate housing, she lived with her mother in a crowded project apartment and entered the shelter just after Larry Jr. was born.

Tracey was angry at having no alternatives after "doing it all by the book." She made strong relationships with the shelter staff and was open to sharing and analyzing her situation and exploring options. In her association with a worker who had a high degree of political consciousness and used many critical questions, Tracey concluded that it was not her fault, for she did what she was taught to do. She concluded that women need to learn to take care of themselves financially and emotionally. Furthermore, she identified that for African Americans a high school diploma opened few doors. She had attended only segregated inner-city schools and felt that her education was inferior. She was highly interested in a local school desegregation lawsuit, *Sheff* v. *O'Neill.* She was well aware of pay differentials and limited job opportunities. She felt she needed further job training. She reflected that the military was a way out of poverty but that her life with her husband on a military base had been even more segregated than in her northeastern city. She experienced racism and loneliness in a very forceful way.

During her shelter stay of six weeks, Tracey successfully completed a training program at an insurance company. She advanced to a supervisory position. She held a second job and was active in her church. She lived in a well-kept housing project where she was an officer in the tenants' council. She was chosen by her peers as the president of the alumnae empowerment group (Successful Women) and is a close friend and mentor to Shandra. She researched treatment approaches to gambling addictions and shared these with her husband, letting him know that if he received treatment she would "try again." She made a life of her own. She says her philosophy is "Nothing comes free; you have to get it for yourself. But when you get it, give some back." She contributes fully to her community and educates groups on issues of homelessness. She describes herself as a different person after working on her own empowerment. Tracey won an employee recognition award for "Achievement Against the Odds." Her work on the job and in the community was described as "excellent and outstanding on behalf of herself and others." She was also on the agency's board of directors.

Tracey continues with the strengths and high level of empowerment she demonstrated earlier. She has maintained and been promoted in her job, lasting through several "downsizings." She has now been employed there over ten years and is eligible for a pension if there are further layoffs, a constant worry. She still works a second job as well. She weathered the storm of a reunion with her husband, only to find that his infidelity was more than she could bear. After a painful legal divorce, she was able to pick up the pieces without losing ground. She set her sights on home ownership and battled endless bureaucracy until she obtained a mortgage and her own home. She also became a foster mother for her addicted niece's ten-year-old daughter. When Tracey and her three children moved in to their own home, she described it as "the happiest day of my life, yet I know I paid my dues to get it." She added, "I still see Shandra. I don't understand her illness very well, but I will always be there for her." These two friends couldn't be more different, yet each is empowered in her own way and both continue to work for justice and look beyond their own lives to community interests.

Working-Class Blues

Marriage is difficult under the best of circumstances. The American divorce rate has been close to 50 percent. Domestic violence, a problem in every stratum of society, plays a part in more situations than we will ever know. It knows no color or caste. Yet the economic stressors faced by working-class and poor families in this economy heighten feelings of frustration and rage that are displaced onto women and children by men who see their roles as primary wage earners eroding and disappearing. In addition to racial oppression, economic stressors were severe in Shandra's situation, and violence and mental illness took root in the rich soil of poverty. Thomas's unemployment was chronic and rooted in institutional racism. He turned to drug dealing as an alternate means of support, although it led to his incarceration, violent behavior, and loss of Shandra.

In the following case of a white working-class family, economic factors are also at play.

Lisa, a waitress (age thirty, Irish-American), and Greg, a factory worker (age twenty-nine, Polish-American), have been married two years. This is the second marriage for Lisa. The couple has regained custody of Lisa's two children, John (age six) and Kevin (age eight). Lisa's ex-husband, Jeff, has had custody of the children since their divorce four years ago, when Lisa had a psychiatric hospitalization for a "major depressive episode." Eighteen months prior to her hospitalization Jeff (Irish-American) was laid off of his job in the shipyard. For the first time in his life he drank to excess and beat her. Her earnings as a waitress supported the family after his unemployment ran out. He beat her more frequently. After her hospitalization he left her for another woman. The judge, nonetheless, awarded Jeff full custody of the children. Three months ago he beat John so severely that the child was hospitalized. Lisa, remarried and stabilized on medication, then regained custody of the boys, who present serious behavioral problems.

In addition, Lisa and Greg are facing severe economic problems. They had been living far beyond their means and recently filed for bankruptcy. The children returned home in the midst of this process. Lisa sought help at a family agency, since the boys were belligerent and hostile. Greg was reluctant to be firm with them. He wondered if he could handle this marriage. The focus of the work was on the marital stress and on parenting and child therapy.

Interestingly, it was not until the author reviewed the case in consultation that economic stress was seen as a significant problem. The worker was concerned that the middle phase of the work had "bogged down" and lacked energy. The worker and supervisor (upper-middle-class women) had "benignly" overlooked class factors. No focus was placed on discussing or ameliorating the effects of low-status or low-paying jobs. Greg wanted Lisa to have "all the fine things" neither had had growing up. This included life in a middle-class neighborhood and a state-of-the-art stereo, TV and VCR equipment, expensive clothing, and expensive car. All these things were now being repossessed, and they had to move "backward" to a less desirable area. Greg had always wanted to fix air conditioners and refrigerators (a skilled trade) but had never pursued anything except factory work. He said, "I figured that was all I was good for, dropping out of high school and all. My father worked in a factory too." Lisa was interested in computer training but "never had the time or money" to look into it.

As economic problems and "getting ahead" were added to the work, the couple became hopeful, and the lagging middle-phase work became energized in a new way. Their very real problems in survival had not been taken as seriously as their intrapsychic and interpersonal problems. McSettin and Bramel (1981) point out that professionals carry class bias into their work with working-class clients. Males in a higher social class are seen more favorably by the helping professional, whereas the opposite is true for females. In this case Greg was ignored except for his ability to be firmer with the children—yet he was now supporting this family and taking a husband's and father's share of responsibility. When the work shifted to include how they might get better jobs, he was immensely interested. The worker helped them find resources, options, and schools. Greg was able to attend a technical institute and was graduated and licensed in his new trade. He obtained a higher-paying, more secure job. Lisa began computer training. This did not detract from their parenting roles, but made them more secure as wage earners, as parents, and as persons who valued their own worth. Class discrimination and consciousness-raising on issues of class would have been well worth exploring for both clients and worker. Greg made many statements about the "system keeping the poor man down" that would give an empowering worker ample opportunity to open discussion.

In terms of work on marital and parenting issues there were four strategies. The focus was on helping Greg and Lisa to develop their own effective ways of dealing with the problems, on modifying inappropriate behaviors and thinking out situations, on using positive reinforcement (Schwartz 1983; Berlin 1983), and on helping each family member communicate about thoughts and feelings. This included psychoeducation, open discussion of Lisa's psychiatric condition, and play therapy for the children. The children were victims of violence and abandonment and of being shifted from parent to parent. They felt much and said little directly. Feelings were not spoken of in either Lisa or Greg's family of origin. Learning to share thoughts and feelings was good for the marriage and for parent/child communication. The following excerpt shows the use of these skills as the couple works on sharing feelings and setting consistent limits for the children:

The couple discussed how hard the kids' backtalking was for them, especially when Kevin said, "I hate you. I want to go back to Dad." *The worker asked how that made each of them feel.* Lisa said, "Guilty for ever losing them." *The worker said,"That's a hard burden to bear. Was it your fault you got sick?"* She thought and said, "No, I know it was biochemical and I was under a lot of stress." Greg said that it makes him angry because they are disrespectful to Lisa. She smiled at him. *The worker noted that Greg was supportive to Lisa and asked, "How do you feel about him saying it to you, Greg?"* Greg said, "Angry because I try hard to be good to them. I never hit them and . . . it makes me feel outside . . . like I don't belong." *The worker said, "That was a lonely place to be . . . outside wanting in."* Lisa said, "Greg, you *are* in, especially in my heart," and he beamed.

After feelings were "on the table," the work on what to do about the backtalking proceeded. *The worker suggested that they set up a behavioral contract around the backtalking.* "First, we'd come up with a reward. Then if the children can go a half-day they'll get a special treat, and we could extend the time and kind of rewards. What do you think?" Both parents agreed it was a good idea. Lisa said she had tried something like that once before on her own and it was working, but they failed to do it consistently. She added, "I tried something of my own this week too with Kevin. When he does it, I say, 'Are you talking back or are you angry about something?' Once he told me what he was angry about and I promised him I wouldn't do that again. It worked." *The worker credited this as a great idea.* Lisa said, "I figured if I feel better talking about feelings, he might too. Greg said, "Maybe we should talk about all we've been through. We never talk about it." *The worker affirmed* that that was an excellent idea when they felt the time was right. Lisa then got the behavioral chart she used before and we all discussed it. Greg suggested that they bring poster board to the next meeting and make the chart really nice—important. Lisa liked that idea and added that the boys should name their own rewards. The worker credited them for fine work, and they continued to plan the family meeting.

Traditional behavioral methods are particularly effective when people need immediate results (Schwartz 1983). Balanced by sharing real feelings, this effort began to turn the situation around in this family. The worker was careful to let them "run with the ball" after she put it into play. She might also have asked them from the start how they wanted to deal with the problem. The "expert role" of the professional is far too comfortable to working-class clients. Asking "coping questions" and helping them discuss what they did effectively before she proposed an answer would have been even more helpful. It is empowering to have the clients find their own expertise, as the worker did later in the interview. Ending with Lisa and Greg helped them consolidate the gains they made in improving their job situations and in their marital and parenting relationships. They felt pleased and empowered to resume full control of their lives.

Key Tasks at Endings

Dealing with Feelings and Consolidating the Gains

Endings are potentially the most empowering phase of work as people move on to lead their lives unaided. Endings may carry feelings related to dying and loss if the relationship has been a strong one. The literature on helping clients to make endings and transitions is replete with concepts to describe this process that are borrowed from Kübler-Ross (1969), who pioneered in thinking about helping people to die: denial, anger, bargaining, and resignation or acceptance. Social work writers have used similar concepts. The worker uses different skills if the client is in the "denial phase," is "indirectly or directly expressing anger toward the worker," is in the "mourning period," or is "trying ending on for size." Workers need to help clients "systematically add up the experience," "identifying major learnings" and areas of future work that will continue after the ending (Shulman 1992). Endings bring tasks of "mourning for the lost person" and of establishing a new equilibrium. The feelings attendant to endings are common, whether the ending is of a single person or of a group. The worker's tasks are to help the clients evaluate the experience, cope with their feelings, maintain beneficial changes, utilize the skills, attitudes, and knowledge gained through the experience, and seek out and use new services, if needed. With groups the worker must also work to reduce the cohesion that has been built, and ending ceremonies may be particularly meaningful (Garvin 1987).

Although the stages of separation differ in quality and degree from experiences of death, they are analogous: denial, negative feelings, sadness, and release. Yet, "not every client will go through every stage. Some may not experience any stage except release!" (Germain and Gitterman 1980:261). Ending rituals, such as the exchange of small gifts or pictures, are appropriate in empowerment work. Clients often like to "give back" in this way, and the acceptance of the gift symbolizes the reciprocity of the relationship. Workers and clients need time to prepare to end the experience.

Just as workers learned to take time for tuning-in, they must make time in each session to bring it to a close and to prepare well ahead with the client for the ending of the empowering relationship itself. Wherever possible, endings should be planned ahead with the client. Some clients may just drop out of the process. Some organizational structures and realities may mitigate against planning. Workers may leave the job before the client feels ready to end the process. It is hopeful that there will be time to "own the gains" and to help the client to recall how loss and separation have been managed in the past to·prepare for continued coping. It is important to note that what we may call a "transition" because the client is going on to a new worker is still an ending with the worker.

The "graduation" effect and celebration of the gains are important. A worker may overestimate the meaning of the relationship to the client (Shulman 1992; Germain and Gitterman 1980) and may underestimate what the client has done for herself (Maluccio 1979). The social work literature on endings has two important themes: dealing with the feelings, whatever they may be, and pulling together and naming the gains made so that they can be maintained and empowerment can continue.

Reunification with a Community

Lum (1986) adds another dimension in working with people of color. He sees the "destination" of the work and the termination process as a reunification and identification of people with the ethnic community network that can nurture and support them.

It is hoped that attaining raised consciousness has been an empowering part of the work for the client. Instead of emphasizing separation and loss from a worker, a professional helping person, Lum sees ending as a positive way back into "peoplehood," community life, and communal hopes. He also sees "recital" or "review" and "playback" of the growth process, so that the new song is truly the client's own composition. Termination connotes completion, in the sense of goal accomplishment. Touching base after formal endings may also be helpful, as is having "an open-door policy."

Identifying Power Gains

Ending an empowering helping relationship must attend to the principles of ending we have noted here. Furthermore, we must look at what specific kinds of power the client has attained. Even as the end is contained in the beginning, the beginning is contained in the end. It was agreed upon to identify power shortages, deficits, and blocks in the areas of personal, interpersonal, and political power. Have they been identified and challenged or changed? Has there been an increase in economic power, including a variety of resources? Has there been an increase in knowledge or skill based on new information and opportunities? Has the client grown in relatedness, competence, self-direction, and self-esteem? Have external power blocks been challenged, circumvented, or removed? Have false beliefs that include the internalization of stereotypes been revised? Have feelings been managed better? Has consciousness been raised in areas of oppression? Has a pride in the ethnic or other community of difference been raised? Has the person joined with others in an effort to fight against oppressive policies or programs or to attain needed resources? Is transformation or liberation taking place? The work may not be finished as the formal helping relationship ends, but is it solidly in progress? Can the client go on alone? What empowerment work remains to be done? In what areas can the person describe her own empowerment (actual and perceived)?

Some Comments on Evaluating Empowerment Practice

Quantitative evaluation of practice, research, and scientific methodology is "in vogue" in social work, although there is somewhat of a shift in paradigm toward more naturalistic and qualitative methodology (Tyson 1995; Pieper 1994; Bein and Allen 1999). Many members of oppressed groups are at best skeptical of the usefulness of research.. Geneticists have "used science" to stereotype and oppress African American women and other groups. Solomon (1976) cautions that research must employ ethnosensitive knowledge and techniques. Ethnosensitive research practice must choose things central to the cultural experience to measure. Measuring peripheral things may show changes but not capture the spirit of change, which reflects the values of empowerment practice. Central issues for practice or research are the impact of oppression, strengths of ethnic perspectives, and ethnic language styles, identity concerns in being a "minority" (Mancoske and Hunzeker 1989), and unique ethclass coping strategies.

There are also concerns related to research methodology and gender. There has been a debate in the literature as to whether empirical, behaviorally oriented, and quantitative research is "male model" thinking (Davis

1985). Such research values "hard data" and empirical "evidence." Even these concepts are in male modes and value laden. Davis has a preference for qualitative research, which is less valued in the current academic scene. Many researchers see the two forms of research—quantitative and qualitative—as of equal value (Maluccio 1979; Goldstein 1991; Heineman-Pieper and Tyson 1999). However, studies of the types of research published in social work journals would shed serious doubt on this, as quantitative studies are overwhelmingly dominant. Like African Americans, poor people, women, and gays and lesbians have been exploited in quantitative research literature. "Science" has been used against oppressed groups. It has been reified while the wisdom of data drawn from practice, a form of participant observation, and self-reflection as a form of evaluation have been minimized (Goldstein 1991; Heineman-Pieper and Tyson 1999; Schon 1995).

Research is a tool that can be used by and for oppressed groups (Abu-Samah 1996). Recently, research on oppressed groups has been helpful in building knowledge about diversity and strengths (Appleby and Anastas 1998; Logan, Freeman, and McRoy 1990; Martin 1987, 1989, 1995). Research also documents the risks of poverty for all Americans and the double jeopardy faced by African Americans (Rank and Hirschl 1999). It is also important in maintaining accountability to clients (Bloom and Fischer 1997). It is empowering for clients to evaluate a service. However, there are serious limitations in using research methodology, particularly quantitative methodology, to capture the central themes and essence of empowerment practice. Individual change per se is not the major interest in empowerment practice, but changes in power relations are the unit to be researched (Mancoske and Hunzecker 1989). Single-system studies (also called single-case studies) and time studies are good ways to measure individual growth. They can be used to show, for example, whether people are developing a raised consciousness and whether they are acting differently.

However, this may not measure power relations. Power relations are extremely hard to quantify. It is also difficult to measure group or community empowerment. That does not mean we cannot obtain a little of "the truth." But we may run the risk of capturing tiny increments of change that are minutely examined while the sweeping whole is ignored (Harrington 1965).

The danger is also that we overvalue that which is not complex and easily measurable (Ivanoff, Blythe, and Briar 1987). Oversimplification of issues of oppression must be avoided. Given this caveat, single-system designs, goal attainment scaling, standard measures, measures of group structures and

processes, and measures for evaluating environmental changes all have potential in judging the effectiveness of empowerment practice (Reid and
Smith 1989; Babbie 1989). Ethnographic studies, life histories, and oral
history can optimally capture cultural strengths (Goldstein 1991; Martin
1987). Respondents may also be empowered as research collaborators
(Mischler 1986). Surveys to determine needs and social indicators to assess
needs are also tools clients can use themselves. Client self-observation and
client observation of change impact on systems may be particularly empowering (Reid and Smith 1989). The success of research methods depends on
the skill of operationalizing variables related to the process and outcomes of
empowerment. This skill, which involves categorizing experiences, needs to
be developed before successful research on the effectiveness of an empowerment approach can be undertaken. This means starting with a qualitative
approach.

Although not all researchers agree (Padgett 1998a, b), methods of qualitative research, including using grounded theory, are ideologically compatible and well suited for developing conceptual categories related to many
forms of direct practice (Bein and Allen 1999; Tyson 1995; Heineman-
Pieper and Tyson 1999; Sherman and Reid 1994), including empowerment
practice (Goldstein 1991; Chenitz and Swanson 1986) In a beginning effort
this author used process recordings of empowerment groups written by workers in an "empowerment workshop" to generate conceptual categories related both to clients' lives and to how workers' learn (Lee 1991). The reader
is also referred to the "Patwah" example in chapter 13 and to chapter 14
(Lee, Odie-Ali, and Botsko 2000; and Lee and Odie-Ali 2000) for examples
of how both quantitative and qualitative research may empower individuals,
groups, and communities with an international perspective. Oral history
research is particularly effective in reclaiming the story of oppression in the
lives of clients whose voices have been silenced, such as the African American elderly (Martin 1989, 1995). The empowerment approach looks forward to the development and utilization of research methods that are useful
to clients (individuals, families, groups, and communities) in empowering
themselves. This includes the evaluation of the empowerment approach
itself. Partnership with such research endeavors will add additional strength
to the approach.

In this chapter we have shown a variety of empowerment principles and
skills that may be utilized in the middle and ending phases of the helping
process with a range of individuals and families. In chapters 8 and 9 we have

traced one case, that of Shandra Loyal, from the beginning to its ending. Endings with groups will be illustrated and discussed in chapter 12. Issues in the evaluation and research of empowerment practice have been raised. There is specialized knowledge about social work practice with particular vulnerable groups that is also necessary for empowerment work. We turn now to selected populations.

10 Empowering Special Populations

This chapter will look at empowerment work with people who are mentally ill and their families, with substance abusers, with gay people, and with persons with AIDS. This certainly does not cover all special populations, for there are many vulnerable groups in American society (Gitterman 1991). It does conceptualize empowerment strategies with those who have multiple oppressions, including persons of color, women and elders, those facing issues of mental retardation, death, and physical disability, and children coping with a parent's AIDS.

Empowerment of People with Mental Illness

In chapters 7, 8, and 9 we have discussed the depressive episodes of Shandra and Lisa. It is not clear, despite Lisa's DSM IV diagnosis, whether her first hospitalization was situational and reactive to severe life stressors or whether it indicated the onset of a major depressive disorders. This is usually determined in retrospect when recurrence does not appear (Elmer-Dewitt 1992; APA 1994). It is clear as discussed in chapter 9 that Shandra is coping with a bipolar disorder. It is also clear that for these women empowerment strategies lowered depression and increased coping, self-esteem, and assuming control over their own lives.

All human beings encounter some mental and emotional obstacles in the course of living. Some theorists see mental illness as simply a matter of degree or mythology caused by labeling (Szasz 1970; Zastrow 1992). But the suffering of the mentally ill goes beyond their stigma. New breakthroughs in brain research identify distinct biochemical disorders that cause great suffering but may be improved dramatically or at least be managed with appropriate medication (Wallis and Willwerth 1992; Austrian 1995; APA 1994; Kaplan and Sadock 1997). Assessment strategies include a full psychiatric and medical work-up, behavioral observations, ego assessments, basic mental status exams, and other diagnostic devices. Workers must be able roughly to assess undiagnosed mental illness so that a psychiatric evaluation is obtained. A basic text in psychopathology is essential in learning about mental illnesses (e.g., Kaplan, Sadock, and Grebb 1998; Austrian 1995). But all diagnostic determinations must be made with psychiatric consultation. It is unethical for social workers to "diagnose" mental illness or any other illness. Kutchins and Kirk (1987) discuss a situation in which a brain tumor caused psychosislike symptoms. This went undiagnosed as a social worker overstepped professional boundaries and acted as a medical diagnostician.

Biochemical brain disorders ("mental illnesses") pose a particular set of obstacles because the state of the art in psychiatric medicine, although more optimistic because of remarkable progress in brain research, still precludes cure (Wallis and Willwerth 1992; Kaplan, Sadock, and Grebb 1998). Stabilizing medications all have debilitating side effects. Among the newer drugs in the treatment of schizophrenia are Clozapine (Clozaril) and Risperidone (Risperdal). Significant improvement was shown in more than half of the twenty thousand American patients who were given Clozapine. One in ten of these experienced a dramatic reawakening to life and a restoration of thought processes. However, the drug and medical supervision costs are so high that most state and federal facilities treat few persons with it and many private insurance companies won't pay for it. Clozapine also has serious side effects—including drooling, drowsiness, possible seizures, and most seriously, a lethal blood cell deficiency—which affect a small percentage of those who take it (Wallis and Willwerth 1992; Austrian 1995). Risperdal is equally or more effective and has fewer side effects. It works faster and affects both positive and negative symptoms (Austrian 1995). However, it too is expensive and not available to all. The cost of drugs and, additionally, the related blood work is both a national and a global issue. In speaking with the doctors and staff in Guyana, South America, for example, I learned that the only antipsychotic drug available in the major mental hospital in Guyana is chloropromazine (Thorazine), discovered in 1952, and even that is not available in full supply. Thorazine was also used for nonpsychotic illnesses as it was often the only drug available. United Nations standards on health uphold every human being's right to proper health care, but there is no doubt that wealthy individuals and countries have access that poor people here in the U.S. and worldwide do not have. This is a human rights advocacy issue.

Lithium is given for bipolar (manic depressive) illness, including the depressive form of the illness. It is in many ways the least noxious and most stabilizing of psychotropic medications, particularly when other family members have had successful treatment with it (Kaplan, Sadock, and Grebb 1985). Depakote and Tegretol are also used in mood disorders. All three require intensive blood monitoring (Austrian 1995). Lisa was stabilized on lithium, though she experienced kidney and bladder control symptoms. Drugs, such as Prozac, used in the treatment of clinical or major depression are effective in seven out of ten cases, although major depression returns for most patients (Elmer-Dewitt 1992). Prozac is also associated with increased violence and agitation in some people. Other psychotropic drugs, particularly those most frequently used in the schizophrenias to control delusions or hallucinations, have a variety of serious side effects (e.g., tardive dyskinesia, a result of long-term use of Prolixin, Haldol, and Thorazine, which affects some clients with stiffness of muscles and involuntary movements of the face and/or extremities). Eighty percent of patients on Thorazine suffer with dulled emotions, foot tapping, restlessness, and tardive dyskinesia (Wallis and Willwerth 1992). Delusions and voices are controlled, but patients are left listless and indifferent. It is hopeful that continued research will produce effective and affordable psychotropic medications. Such research is a highly political issue.

Living with mental illness requires coping with exceptional problems: altered thought processes and emotions, psychiatric treatment and medicine management, often inadequate and understaffed service systems, symptom and rehospitalization management, a sense of well-being at some points and disorganized or symptomatic behavior at others. Other major tasks are accepting the illness while challenging the stigma society places on the mentally ill (this may include political action and educating others), managing daily life, and finding meaning in life.

The following examples describe empowerment during the work phase with three persons who had mental disorders ranging from a severe anxiety disorder to chronic paranoid schizophrenia. All three women were also formerly homeless. Only one, Brenda Gary, had prior psychiatric treatment for schizophrenia before becoming homeless. Schizophrenia has been described as a "one-way ticket to the bottom of the socioeconomic ladder," that is, an estimated one-third of America's homeless and a disproportionate number of prisoners are afflicted (Wallis and Willwerth 1992).

Lorna Rabinowitz entered a shelter for homeless women at age forty-five after a series of tragic events. *Mary O'Shea* never entered a shelter but lived on the street for five years with her dog, Bob. *Brenda Gary* lived on the streets and in several shelters until she had a firm connection to mental health services. Their stories are stories of empowerment. We begin with Mary O'Shea, for she represents the strengths of one with untreated chronic schizophrenia.

When persons do not accept mental health services, it is possible to reach a level of partial empowerment. Such persons may have periods in which the illness is not active and find levels of enjoyment and accomplishment in life. Untreated, the torment of the delusions or hallucinations of paranoid schizophrenia precludes consistently being able to manage one's daily life or to have an impact on socioeconomic and political conditions. People with schizophrenia experience alterations of the senses, severe difficulty in sorting out and synthesizing stimuli, and difficulty in responding appropriately, delusions and hallucinations (auditory and/or visual), an altered sense of self, and unpredictable changes in emotions and behavior (Kaplan, Sadock, and Grebb 1998; Bowker and Davis 1988). Untreated, the illness seems to appear, retreat, and reappear unpredictably. It is difficult for persons with schizophrenia to feel in control of their lives. Good support systems are particularly important. Mary and others like her function well enough to survive until the illness causes the loss of support systems, ranging from relationships to the basics of income and housing. Even then they are able to use intellect and ingenuity to survive and sometimes enjoy life.

Mary

Mary O'Shea is a gentle, fifty-five-year-old woman who loves animals and is kind to her fellow human beings. She is an avid reader. When she is not working at collecting and redeeming cans to survive, she sits in the park with Bob and reads. Like many schizophrenics, Mary says very little about her early years. An only child, she left home in her late teens and worked as a secretary for most of her life. She lived alone with her beloved pets and had little contact with family members. In her mid-forties she lost her job and found it difficult to find work because the "bosses preferred the young and pretty girls." Work is very important to her, as is self-determination and control of her life. The onset of her mental illness is not clear. She may have struggled with it from young adulthood, since the age of onset for schizophrenia is usually between fifteen and twenty-five for males and twenty-five and thirty-five in women (Wallis and Willwerth 1992; Matorin 1991). Or it may have appeared after her midlife job loss and subsequent eviction from her apartment.

Mary accepted general assistance for two years before her eviction. The requirement for her to work at "workfare" jobs proved too difficult. She was not recertified, because she could not report to a work site. Once on the street, much of her income went to feeding Bob. One of her delusions was that food was contaminated with radiation. This delusion may have helped her tolerate having little food and no place to cook it. She slept anywhere "kind people" looked the other way, in basements, abandoned houses, stairwells, and city parks. She is so small that her frail body could hardly be seen under a pile of blankets. Bob was as loving to her as he was vicious to anyone who endangered her. With keen intellect, Mary used newspaper coupons to shop and swap with others. She accepted canned food from food banks and never used soup kitchens or shelters because they would not let Bob in. She showered in a church rectory on occasion. Every few weeks she would go to a buffet-style restaurant, eat a hot meal, and bring Bob a napkin full of food. She bought clothing for herself and Bob at a local thrift store. She bought paperbacks at a used bookstore and traded them when she was finished. Her shopping cart contained all she owned and still had room for a day's collection of cans.

When the outreach worker from the shelter's mental health program met her, Mary was feeding squirrels in the park. The worker used their shared love of animals as a bridge. Slowly they developed a relationship. Reciprocity was very important to Mary. She accepted some money, clothing, and books but shared what she received with other homeless people and directed others to the worker. She did not use alcohol or drugs. When Mary felt well physically and emotionally, she thoroughly enjoyed her days in the park with Bob. Her concern for all living beings moved all those who came in contact with her. She initially declined the worker's offer to help her "get back inside," saying she did not want to deal with the public welfare system again. Mary "disappeared" when she felt sick, but the worker searched for her.

Finally, she reappeared and let the worker know that she wanted housing, but only because "my last illness and the winter almost killed me, and I was all alone. Who would take care of Bob?"

Mary located a subsidized apartment complex for people with physical and mental disabilities. The worker was able to get her placed on the top of the list because of her homelessness. Within a month she moved in. Now the obstacle of public assistance loomed. Two workers helped her negotiate all the systems, and again she had to face workfare. She very much needed SSI but would not go to a psychiatrist for certification. She did agree, however, to go to a medical doctor who reached out to her. He brought his little boy and made conversation about children and animals. Mary was severely malnourished, weighed only eighty-five pounds, had a lump in her breast, and had emphysema. She obtained SSDI for medical reasons. She was profoundly grateful for all the help and began to manage well in her own apartment. Now she had more control over her life, and her basic needs were met. For a month she continued her relationship with her worker and enjoyed her life.

Suddenly, however, her visual hallucinations returned with a vengeance. She saw and felt "charges of radiation" everywhere in her apartment. This may have been precipitated by pain or by the doctor's referral for a mammogram, which she refused. A fixed delusion about SSDI as an FBI system that was chasing her and robbing her of a secret inheritance returned. She began sleeping on her back porch "to avoid the radiation inside" and refused her checks. She saw the worker and told her this was happening. The worker intervened with the landlord, who allowed her to sleep on the porch in the good weather but said she had to cash the checks and pay the very small rental fee. Mary did this and held on to her home, sleeping indoors in the winter. It is critically important to note such strengths even as illness persists (Bowker and Davis 1988; Libassi 1988).

Perhaps afraid of involuntary hospitalization, Mary incorporated the worker and agency into her delusional scheme and refused all contact. No mention was made of hospitalization after she refused to see the psychiatrist, but the issue was certainly a struggle in the worker's mind. For better or worse, this difficult ethical dilemma was resolved in favor of Mary's self-determination so that she would not flee her new housing. In another, similar, case Betty, age fifty-three, whose daily coping skills were not as good as Mary's, was hospitalized involuntarily. Betty wore about ten layers of "protective" clothing year round and her voices told her to wear only one shoe in even the bitterest winter. She also seemed unable to control her bowel movements. While hospitalized she received a complete medical and a prolapsed uterus and rectum were corrected. By the time she left the hospital she was well stabilized on her medications and described herself, gratefully, as a changed person. Betty, a college graduate, was able to obtain and keep an apartment and also volunteered as a reader for the blind and as agency receptionist for over two years. Although Betty later had trouble staying on her medication, she responded to her workers and is still in her apartment. Involuntary hospitalization literally saved Betty's life. It is always a difficult call to make.

Mary lived life on her own terms until she passed away. She had her home, her porch, her income, her books, Bob, and some sunny days in the park to enjoy for about four years, but she avoided all outreach during this time. We mourned for her and Bob, who was loyal until the end, and for all the women and men like her who live too long on the streets before "coming in." We also extended support to the helpers who tried to reach her and felt they failed. This level of outreach work is very difficult and it is tragic to lose such special people.

We turn now to two situations where fuller empowerment was possible as social work help and services of the mental health system were accepted and used.

Lorna

Lorna Rabinowitz, cited in chapters 3 and 5, an observant Jewish woman, entered a shelter at age forty-five after a series of tragic life events. These included the successive deaths of close family members and major surgery for a benign tumor. This tumor was discovered at the same time the elderly woman she lived with entered a nursing home, leaving Lorna homeless and with no means of support. Although never treated in the mental health system, Lorna had a severe panic disorder and was agoraphobic. She had not been outside of her inner-city apartment for eight years. A friend helped Lorna enter a shelter for homeless women. Lorna was initially terrified of the place and the other residents. Yet she responded easily to the social worker. As she felt safe in the shelter she participated in individual and group services. She resumed her caretaking role with several of the more vulnerable residents and coped by engaging in activity. "Productivity" (her word), caring for others, and observation of the Torah (religious law) are Lorna's compelling desires.

Observing that several of the women in the shelter had lost all family ties, the worker formed a small mutual aid group to provide a source for new relationships and caring and an opportunity to work on common concerns. Lorna was the hub of this group (Lee 1994a, 1990). As the four group members worked and lived together for nine months, positive sentiments and attachments grew and primary group ties were formed. The renegotiated contract went beyond mutual aid and included "being like family for each other." In a work phase meeting of the "primary group" these poignant sentiments were expressed:

Lorna said, "When I was well, I was a sister. I cooked and babysat for them. Now I bring them shame and I'm not a sister anymore." Carla responded, "Yes, I have parents and six brothers and sisters, but I'm alone."

Donna said, "My parents are dead but I have thirteen brothers and sisters, and I'm alone." Nina, who is mildly retarded and has cerebral palsy, said slowly, "I've always been alone and different. But now at least I have you." She smiled shyly, adding, "I know I have somebody in the world." Lorna said, "We have each other." All agreed.

Many mutual aid groups do not attain this level of intimacy. But small groups that have frequent interaction over long periods of time have this additional potential that the worker can promote. It is significant to note that Nina and Donna joined Lorna in the mental health transitional living facility and they continued to "be there" for each other. Tragically, two years later Nina was diagnosed with full-blown AIDS and sent to a government hospital to die. Lorna overcame her fear of travel and visited Nina as a family member until she died a year later. Nina's story is painful and tragic, but she had Lorna's support until the end.

In the group and in individual work Lorna worked hard to identify the obstacles she faced, including the false beliefs she held about herself as a poor person and single woman. It was easy for Lorna to identify her fears of going outside. It was harder for her to discuss the successive losses that caused an underlying depression. This work would have to come once she was in a more stable environment. She and the worker agreed that it was a priority to mobilize her so she could leave the shelter. First, Lorna was helped to credit the major accomplishment of adapting to shelter life. Lorna had overcome a fear more basic than going out—her fear of people. She discovered that she liked people and that she had very good relational skills. Then, using a traditional behavioral desensitization approach (Schwartz 1983; Zastrow 1992), Lorna identified a hierarchy of fears in going outside and what would help her venture forth (see chapter 5). She asked to go outside with her small group. She crossed the street and looked at the building. With wonderful Jewish wit she observed, "Why did I ask this? Such a building!" but she laughed and said, "I didn't even know where I was; now that I know, I'll definitely stay inside!" In a series of accompanied small journeys she began to regain mobility. She was able to ride the bus with the worker to attend a mock seder across town. This effort maintained cultural identity while it shored up her confidence that she could travel if accompanied. She noted, "Here I was afraid of people and even of my own shadow. I never knew anyone but elderly Jews. Now I see everyone has to struggle, and I'm not worse or better; I struggle too." She needed to learn to credit her own considerable efforts. As she did so, she began to grow in self-esteem, self-confidence, and competence. Lorna chose to go to a transitional living facility so that she could get the help she needed. The facility is a large-single-room occupancy situation with communal meals and a nearby day workshop and therapists. Lorna does not trust drugs and continues to refuse antianxiety medication. Lorna was soon able to walk to her workshop unaccompanied. In time she learned to take the bus to her therapist. The facility is located in a relatively safe downtown business area. Going shopping in neighborhood stores was a major obstacle for her that she has overcome slowly. She now enjoys shopping on her own in the smaller stores. The therapist continued to provide a supportive relationship and behavioral methods. Psychoeducational approaches (Zipple and Spaniol 1987) were also used so that Lorna could understand her illness and educate others. She did this by leading group meetings with other residents.

Lorna is mobile in the neighborhood but still does not leave the community unaccompanied. Her agoraphobia has not been cured, but it has been managed. She makes the most out of a situation others would find too restrictive. It is her preference to remain in this facility, although several other options were offered. In part she stays because she has mastered her fears and is afraid to start over again elsewhere. In part she stays because the facility has become home for her, and a place where she can enact the role of caretaker and help others empower themselves. It is her work. She has reached an unofficial paraprofessional staff level even though she is not paid. Optimally, she would be regarded as live-in staff, for that is the role she plays, and would be paid accordingly.

The Political Level of Empowerment

For a long time Lorna believed she was a failure since she did not hold a "real (salaried) job." Reflection on the value of the work she did in the facility and the positive feedback and service awards she receives helped her to conclude she was productive.

"I learned not to measure it in money. The rich get rich and the poor get poorer. The not for profit gets the profit. That's the way it is. People with mental problems will always be poor unless they were born rich. So it's what you do that counts, not what they pay you." She realized that her labor was exploited, but, she concluded, "I use them as much as they use me. I want to stay here. It is my choice."

Although we may wish another choice for Lorna, her productivity and political understanding and activity are unquestionable. The following are some of her keen observations from letters to the worker:

On "The System": Mental health is a business like any other, only the residents are the products. We have very little to say about the program even though we have meetings every week. I am on the Food Program Committee, meeting with staff to get better food. . . . They just closed two buildings of apartment living because of substandard conditions. If money was put into upkeep instead of managers' pockets, all of this could have been avoided. . . . One good change is that all the programs will now have psychiatric nurses in residence. . . . On the negative side again, the staff is occupied with paperwork and not with dealing with us on a one-to-one basis. . . . All they are interested in is to bill Medicaid and to shortchange us in what we need. I help fellow residents to speak up for what they need. They are paying customers through Medicaid!. . . .

My work in the Food Program lets me advocate for what residents want and need. Food is very important to all of us. . . . I have even gotten

Kosher, vegetarian and health food as options—that took a lot of organizing people to speak for themselves. . . . I finally had a mock Seder last
year. We don't get everything we negotiate for, but we are heard, and that
is what we want.

These excerpts show astute analysis and an important level of empowerment for residents in a mental health program—saying their own word and
being heard. The Food Program Committee and the following innovations
were Lorna's own ideas.

I now have two boutiques where residents buy donated goods for a small
fee. I supervise the residents who run each boutique. What a word,
supervise! I prefer to say *work with*, like a coworker. They trust me and
do their best. My fears were getting in the way, but I got these programs
started anyway.

Lorna also describes her work to organize residents to participate in a
community event, the street fair. Her raised consciousness began with individual and group work while in the shelter and continued in her ongoing
communications with the worker. Once she attained a level of critical understanding and self-esteem, Lorna continued to grow on her own:

Being a part of the community is very important to most of us with mental
problems. To participate in the street fair, we collect donations to sell all
year. The money we make is used to buy holiday gifts for each resident.
When people ask who we are, we educate them on mental illness. We
show people that we do a nice job even though we live in a building for
the mentally ill.

   Now I am on the Community Advisory Board. When I go to meetings
I dress up like a professional. At first I was afraid, but now I do speak up.
During the renovation of the facility I let the Board know what the residents are going through. It was the residents who had to put up with a
lot, not the higher-ups, and I will keep reminding them about it, in case
they forget. The Board is interested more in the business end, not the

service and the residents. I am the one who mentions the needs of the residents. Recently I suggested that the former residents who now live alone should be invited back for Thanksgiving dinner and other celebrations. People are thankful for this and for the boutique where they can get nice inexpensive clothes. It shows we care enough about them to see that their basic needs are met. We are people first and people with disorders second!

Lorna's level of self-acceptance and raised consciousness is shown in the way she uses and takes the power out of the stigmatizing words *mentally ill* and *people with mental problems and disorders*. In doing so she also liberates herself and the other residents. Her life empowers other lives.

Brenda

Brenda Gary, a thirty-nine-year-old African American woman with multiple physical problems and chronic paranoid schizophrenia, experienced periods of intermittent homelessness for five years. Unlike Mary O'Shea, Brenda was open to help and aware of her need for support. Her delusions persisted, although she took her medication and utilized mental health services. Leaving her children with relatives, she moved cyclically from the streets to the hospital to several shelters. Then she entered the shelter's new residential support program, which set her up in her own apartment and offered daily support services, regular meetings with a social worker, an outside therapist, case manager, and psychiatrist, and weekly empowerment group meetings. She was able to thrive with this level of support and to have her children visit regularly. She received follow-up for her medical conditions. She has made a friend in the program and enjoys participation in all program activities. On occasion she becomes mildly delusional, but she has not needed hospitalization for the five years she has been in the program. For the first time since the onset of her illness in her late twenties, Brenda experiences inner peace. She has structures she can depend on. Brenda's appearance is marred by skin eruptions that are aggravated by the psychotropic medication she must take, but she radiates a quiet joy that shines through and engages others. She is not spontaneous, but when she is called on to state her opinions or feelings she reveals her good intellect. Recently, Brenda volunteered to testify at public hearings on proposed state cutbacks of mental health programs. She had gone to the legislature with her empowerment group on other occasions but never felt able to speak. She surveyed group members and composed a statement that she read at the hearings. This is an excerpt:

We need our programs to keep us aware of life's possibilities. No matter what you want to be, it's possible. These programs kept me on track and looking forward to life. If the state cuts these programs, the state also cuts the good that they do. . . . We have a women's group every week. We talk about what goes on in our lives—the problems we experience and solutions to them by getting feedback from other group members. . . . These programs are essential. . . . Please maintain these programs for the many people that need them.

Brenda's legislative testimony was powerful. The press sought her out. The group's reflection on her testimony can be found in chapter 13. Brenda is empowered at all levels. Although she has to manage life with mental illness, she now does so as a person of worth who knows she has a positive impact on her environment. People with mental disabilities and mental illness, like those with physical disabilities, can act to attain their share of resources and services and to change public opinion that labels them as powerless and ineffectual. But, to facilitate this, the worker must see beyond illness to whole persons who manage exceptional tasks daily and can attain empowerment. The worker and client must identify abilities and capitalize on them. This philosophy of "ableism" helps assure respectful mutual relationships and helps people define themselves as victors and not victims. Ultimately, this leads to empowerment.

Empowering Families of the Mentally Challenged

Families of people who are mentally ill often blame themselves for the illness of the stricken member. Before the biochemical nature of mental illness was understood, professionals perpetuated mother and family blaming (Hatfield and Lefley 1987). Families need support in facing the extraordinary coping tasks related to their mentally challenged or profoundly mentally ill member. Often persons with mental illness are unaware of the nature of their difficulties; they may deny problems and refuse help. When the person with mental illness finally enters the system, it may be after verbal or physical abuse is directed toward family members. Stigma and the fear of exposure to the mental health system often keep families from seeking help for their afflicted member or for themselves. This is particularly so in poor communities. Family loyalty and distrust of hospitals and outsiders may influence families to attempt care at home when it is no longer feasible, causing great strain and tears in the family fabric. It is important to welcome such families into the mental health system and enlist them as allies on behalf of their member and others who are mentally ill in their communities. A warm, individualized approach that educates about mental illness, destigmatizes the member's problems, discusses new findings in brain research that offer hope while being realistic is helpful, as is giving information about resources, rights, and self-help groups.

An Elderly Mother Faces the Illness of Her Son

Mrs. Leticia Smyth is a seventy-six-year-old African American retired widow who has five adult children. Miss Lettie, as she is respectfully called, is an elder in her church. She sought help from a church-connected social worker when she could no longer tolerate the situation with her oldest son, Sam. However, it took quite a while before she disclosed her well-kept secret. The worker, a middle-aged white woman, recognized that Miss Lettie would tell her story when trust was established. Miss Lettie said she had "some things that weighed heavy on her heart," but she could not pursue this further in early contacts. Part of establishing trust included the worker's disclosure of stories about her own family members who had "troubles" too. She moved at Miss Lettie's pace, sharing in a life review process that included moving stories of Miss Lettie's roots in the South and oppression. Material needs were subtly disclosed and met. Miss Lettie was well able to discover resources for herself and only needed help when systems proved intractable. She always spoke for herself, but she "appreciated the information and the encouragement."

As the relationship between Miss Lettie and the worker deepened, Miss Lettie made these observations:

"Here I am, an old black woman from Mississippi, the great-granddaughter of a slave, and here you are a white woman sitting here being my true friend, and we talking as equals, telling true things. We would have never met if God didn't arrange it, and I would have never known that this could happen." The worker replied, "Miss Lettie, you are a gift from God for me too. Your life teaches me about courage, strength, and perseverance."

A week later Miss Lettie said, "The time has come that I must tell you something." The worker encouraged her, saying she knew something was troubling her heart. Miss Lettie said, "Elder abuse is true. It is happening to me. I have never told no one, not even my other children, for it is a shame for a son to hit his mother. You have never met Sam because he stays away most of the time, and I could never put words on it before, but I must now." She told what happened tearfully as the worker sat with her arm around her sharing her pain and expressing outrage that this could happen to Miss Lettie.

She went on with Sam's story. He had returned from California a few months ago. He is an intelligent man with a degree from a prestigious university. Since the war in Vietnam he "hasn't been the same" and constantly traveled, trying new endeavors wherever he went. She heard from him infrequently and assumed he was all right. But when he returned home, he was "very strange." As he punched the wall and yelled loudly at someone Miss Lettie could not see, she felt he would "get it out of his system and get over it." But recently he hit her and she "knew he must be crazy." When it was about to happen the second time, she called the police and "sure enough, they put him in a psychiatric hospital." Miss Lettie told this as if his behavior (destroying the home and hitting her) and his illness were the greatest shame in the world. The worker assured her that she did the right thing in protecting herself and getting help for Sam. The worker explained:

Sam had a mental illness which in some ways was like all other illnesses, like diabetes or high blood pressure, for example. There's no shame when the chemical balances in your body go off, and affect the brain's good functioning. Her son, Sam, was a smart man, but he just got sick and needed medical help. [Giving empowering information; Psycho-education.] Miss Lettie responded that she felt guilty that he went homeless and lived in cardboard boxes in California. She was frightened that he heard voices that told him to kill her. She felt he must hate her for something. She thought she "caused it" because she sent him to a Catholic school when he was a little boy.

The worker [Reaching for her explanation] *asked her to tell how this might cause it.* Miss Lettie said that Sam was the only black boy in his class. He loved the school and did well, although some of the children excluded him from play and called him racial names. Sam always wanted to be just like the other boys. He often asked why his hair wasn't straight like the white boys' hair! She said, "I told him he was and would always be a black boy—his hair was just screwed in—but his brain was as good as anyone's, so he should learn all he could. After that all he did was study. He didn't live, just studied. I think I should have sent him to the public school because maybe the pressure made him sick." The worker said, *"It is hard for mothers to know everything—you wanted the best for him. It is hard for children to deal with racism, but you cannot take the blame for racism. Sam's illness was not caused because of this particular experience of oppression. There is no doubt that lifelong experience with racism adds to pressures that may trigger illness. But mental illness is in the body, in our biochemical makeup and is not caused by isolated external events."* [Empathizing; Giving empowering information; Psycho-education.] Miss Lettie reflected that he had been much better since he received medication and he had even thanked her for getting him help.

─────────

The worker and Miss Lettie planned for the worker to follow up with the hospital and to meet Sam in person. A shy and well-spoken man, Sam connected easily with the worker and was open to a supervised apartment program and vocational screening with the mental health agency. Sam was relieved that his illness could be treated. Miss Lettie was relieved at having someone to share her secret burden with and especially relieved that Sam was getting help.

People often have explanations for illness (Germain 1984). It is helpful to elicit these and help the client look at them, whether they are personally or culturally fashioned. Miss Lettie accepted new information on brain chemistry and mental illness and felt relieved and empowered.

Culturally Sensitive Work with an Elder

Knowledge of the client's cultural belief systems is critical. Mr. Hom, an eighty-year-old Chinese man, had much difficulty with the death of his wife to a lengthy and painful cancer. They had done everything together for fifty-five years, including running a small business. Their children were assimilated and did not embrace much of the Chinese ways. They had friends, but the closest ones were no longer in San Francisco. Mr. Hom felt isolated and alone. Mr. Hom requested cremation. He constantly sat near the green jade jar containing his wife's ashes that he had placed in his living room. He often spoke to it and included it in conversation with visitors. Although he could speak adequate English, he now spoke only in Cantonese. His children missed much of the subtlety of this dialogue, as they spoke little. He ate little and began to be highly forgetful and to neglect his appearance. His children were gravely concerned. A Chinese social worker from a nearby senior citizen's center was called upon and began to visit regularly. The worker was fluent in Mr. Hom's dialect. Mr. Hom said he felt guilty for not honoring Mrs. Hom's wishes about burial, but he wanted her with him always. The worker was able to enter into Mr. Hom's grief with him and support his feelings that his wife's spirit was with him (Lum 2000). Understanding the Chinese value of filial piety and its importance to elder parents (Ho 1994), he arranged culturally appropriate ways for the adult children to pay more attention to Mr. Hom and to pay respect to their mother. Mr. Hom was invited to live with one son, but he wanted to remain in his own home. Chinese Meals on Wheels from the center were supplied. A medical work-up was arranged, and it was found that Mr. Hom had suffered a series of minor strokes that affected his memory. Another son was able to live with Mr. Hom for several months. As Mr. Hom's grief became more manageable he again related well to his family. Eventually, he went to the center and shared meals with other elders. This culturally sensitive intervention averted further morbid grief and mental breakdown (Lindemann 1965). It was empowering in restoring cultural solutions to the family.

Elsie Riley: Mother and Advocate for the Mentally and Physically Challenged

Mrs. Riley is a seventy-three-year-old widow living on a small pension. She is the mother of three adult children, one of whom, Phil, age fifty, is mildly to moderately mentally retarded, physically ill and wheelchair bound, and in need of lifelong residential services. Although she managed her candy store for many years as her husband did skilled assembly work, Mrs. Riley's identity and sense of purpose was built around her caretaking roles. A working-class woman, she never dreamed that her love for her son would make her an activist.

While Phil was in the state institution for the retarded, Mrs. Riley learned that she had to "fight the system" for him to be given basic care and be sent to the crafts classes he loved. Phil is an easygoing, loving person with amazing resilience and will to live. He works well in a sheltered workshop and enjoys many activities.

When Phil was finally placed in a group home in a nearby community, Mrs. Riley was greatly relieved. Now the whole family could visit often. But as soon as the group home opened, a cross was burned on the lawn. Mrs. Riley was angered and amazed at this bigotry. Next there was an attempt to burn the house down. Mrs. Riley felt strongly that they should hold their ground and not yield to this pressure. She volunteered to speak to community groups. She spoke eloquently about Phil and his peers. She noted, "Here I was, just like them. Phil and those like him are good and special people, but they couldn't see it until I spoke up." These efforts were effective and the home remained. More group homes were needed. This time Mrs. Riley contacted a state senator who had been a customer at her candy store. She asked the senator for his support of group homes for the mentally and physically challenged like her son. She invited him to a community meeting on the new homes. He came and lent his support, commending her for her activism. The community accepted two other homes.

On another occasion, Mrs. Riley contacted a local assemblyman because the town had no recreational facilities for the physically challenged and no buses to take them to a program in an adjoining town. Once again she was effective and the town got the bus service it needed. She inspired other mothers to join her in her efforts. They pledged to support the assemblyman at election time in exchange for his support of their issues. This activism is a complete metamorphosis for Mrs. Riley, who had been taught "to leave the politics up to the men." She has concluded, "If you don't open up your mouth, you don't get nothing." Mrs. Riley is an empowered woman. The role of the social worker in this instance is simply to listen and respond and to help clarify and define issues with Mrs. Riley and other parent advocates.

Substance Abuse and Empowerment

Empowerment cannot be attained by active substance abusers, although we can help motivate entry into treatment and recovery. Until recovery has begun, power over the addiction is what is needed. This is obtained through treatment and regular participation in self-help networks like AA or NA (Narcotics Anonymous; Royce and Scratchley 1996). Since most active substance abusers fervently deny any problems, the worker needs to observe functioning carefully and to take a detailed drug and alcohol history when substance abuse is suspected (Raskin and Daley 1991).

Many groups are at high risk for alcoholism. As women have become more "visible" in American society, their drug and alcohol problems have been recognized as comparable to those of men (Hanson 1991). However, women are more heavily stigmatized by alcohol use. Feelings of powerlessness often contribute to women's alcoholism. An empowerment approach promotes hope and control over life's difficulties. Black women are more likely to be nondrinkers than white women, but they are more likely to have cirrhosis and other health problems caused by drinking (National Council on Alcoholism and Drug Dependence 1990; Brisbane and Womble 1985). Women have success rates in recovery that equal or surpass those of men (Hanson 1991; Wright, Kail, and Creecy 1990). Culturally sensitive services for women of color who are substance abusers are rare. Many treatment programs will not accept pregnant alcohol and drug-dependent women (National Council on Alcoholism and Drug Dependence 1990; Wright, Kail, and Creecy 1990). Although substance abuse is unlikely to be the primary presenting problem of clients who use social work agencies, many do suffer from it. The knowing worker needs to have open eyes and a strong knowledge of alcoholism and other types of drug abuse.

Although it is not clear which comes first—substance abuse or homelessness—the high incidence of substance abuse among the homeless is a particularly tragic fact (Blau 1992). For a long while it was considered "politically incorrect" to discuss this issue, which has led to inappropriate services and programs that enable addiction rather than help toward recovery (Hanrahan 1991). In addition to poor people and women, African American, Puerto Rican, Mexican-American, Native American, Irish-American, and French-Canadian (Franco-American) ethnic groups are at high risk for alcoholism and other drug abuse because of predispositions to alcoholism and severe economic and social stressors (Gordon 1994; Wright, Kail, and Creecy 1990; Burman and Allen-Meares 1991; Brisbane and Wells 1989; Graham 1990; Hanson 1991; Herd 1989; Lawson and Lawson 1989; McGoldrick 1982; and Langelier 1982). The rate of alcoholism in Puerto Rico is four times that of non-Puerto Ricans on the mainland, and the consumption of large quantities of alcohol is considered more acceptable in

Puerto Rico. Alcoholism is a significant problem for mainland Puerto Ricans, who also may experience cultural conflict about how it is viewed (Solomon 1992). Cultural sensitivity and knowledge is essential in the assessment and empowerment of chemically dependent individuals (Gordon 1994).

There are many contributing factors to drug and alcohol addiction, ranging from biological and physiological predispositions to severe environmental and interpersonal stress to social learning and behavioral habits (Hanson 1991; Bratter and Forrest 1985; Vaillant 1983). All aspects of etiology must be addressed, particularly when working with oppressed groups. However, the biological disease process of substance abuse and addiction cannot be minimized. There is ample evidence that drug addiction in general and alcohol addiction in particular is caused by some combination of preexisting physiological deficiency, inheritable genetic traits, and/or metabolic changes resulting from drug use (Hanson 1991:67, 76; Bratter and Forrest 1985; Vaillant 1983).

The definition of alcoholism by the American Society of Addiction Medicine and the National Council on Alcoholism and Drug Dependence (1990) is as follows:

> Alcoholism is a primary, chronic disease with genetic psychosocial and environmental factors influencing its development and manifestations. The disease is often progressive and fatal. It is characterized by continuous periodic impaired control over drinking, preoccupation with the drug alcohol, use of alcohol despite adverse consequences, and distortions in thinking, most notably denial.

This is consistent with later definitions by the National Council on Alcoholism (NCADD/ASAM 1992). When alcoholism is obvious but denied, the worker can use "evidence" from daily living to deduct with the client: problems in job performance, interpersonal conflicts or loss of relationships, trouble with the law, fighting, physical problems like ulcers or liver problems, forgetting, headaches, and erratic behavior. And so on. Taken together these add up to hard data (Hanson 1991; Raskin and Daley 1991).

The worker can also conduct an "intervention" by bringing together the clients significant others who tell the client how her alcoholism has been affecting their lives.

Dorothy: A "Little Problem"

Working with Dorothy, age thirty-seven, an African American substitute teacher who held a responsible position in her inner-city church, was particularly difficult as Dorothy denied her cocaine and alcohol abuse and refused to consider treatment. Tuning-in and intervention sensitive to Afrocentric values on family and spirituality helped Dorothy to challenge her addiction (Gordon 1994).

Dorothy's oldest child, Leah, was in prison for two years for dealing drugs and her elderly parents were helping raise Dorothy's seven-year-old son, Toye. Dorothy said that trying to keep Leah out of jail got her hooked. Dorothy thought if she was more of a "girlfriend" she could talk Leah out of dealing. Instead she herself started taking the drugs. She said that inside she thought Leah would see that it hurt her mother and stop dealing drugs. Instead Leah was incarcerated and Dorothy developed a "little problem." The problem had cost her first a full-time job and then her substitute teaching job because of lateness and erratic behavior. Soon, her pastor and fellow church members asked her to step down from her job at the church. She spent a lot of time in expressing anger at everyone. Yet concern for Toye and her parents did prompt her to seek counseling. As long as the worker talked about Dorothy's family, she participated fully. When it came to helping her acknowledge the advanced stage of her addictions, she retreated to denial and minimizing.

When Dorothy's parents were frightened after Dorothy's drug apparatus started a fire in their home, they threatened to put her and Toye out. They actually could never have done this, but this did motivate Dorothy to agree to an intervention involving significant others. The worker assembled her parents, a church friend who offered to be her Twelve-Step sponsor if she could acknowledge her need for help, her pastor, and Dorothy. Dorothy first debated, then was silent as each one spoke of how her substance abuse affected them. She then began to cry softly, saying she was sorry she had hurt everyone. The worker suggested that all hold hands in a circle of caring. Dorothy stood between her parents. She said she loved them and thanked them for all they were doing to help her. She felt loved and not judged, and "you're all right, she added, I am addicted to cocaine and when I can't get it I drink sherry. I do need help. I can't stop any more. Everyone drew close and hugged her. Her mother, who is very dear to her, asked if she would go into a program and get the help she needed. She said she would. She did follow-up with entry into a three-month residential program outside of the inner city. When she was released, she began a day program and attended Twelve-Step meetings daily for several months. She resumed her church job. She did slip, but this time she did not use denial. She began her recovery again and continues to live and struggle with addiction "one day at a time."

The most important behavioral change that influences recovery from addiction is total abstinence. Learning how to drink moderately through behavioral interventions has had some minor success for some alcoholics but these successes occurred in studies performed on middle- to upper-class white males (Vaillant 1983). With the life stressors related to poverty and oppression, abstinence, inpatient and outpatient treatment, residential facilities, and Twelve-Step group memberships seem most effective. There have been promising recent breakthroughs in the treatment of alcoholism with Naltrexone, a drug used successfully in heroin addiction. This drug, which inhibits the experience of feeling high, however, is highly experimental. In addition, any drug use is frowned upon by Twelve-Step programs. Twelve-Step programs subscribe to the biological/disease nature of addictions and promote and facilitate abstinence thorough mutual support. The "faith in a higher power" element of Twelve-Step programs increases the effectiveness with groups for whom religious faith is important, such as African Americans and others (Wright, Kail, and Creecy 1990). Cocaine or crack cocaine addicts in recovery often become alcoholics because they minimize or are unaware of the serious nature of alcohol addiction (Weiss and Mirin 1987; Brisbane 1989). The dangers of marijuana use are also minimized by African American youths (MacGowan 1990). Recent studies have shown that marijuana is addictive and biochemically destructive (Royce and Scratchley 1996). A multiple substance abuse educational approach must be taken when working with working-class or poor addicts who accept alcohol or marijuana as "safe."

The disease of alcoholism progresses more quickly in women and African Americans, and the latter tend to seek treatment earlier, perhaps because of earlier physical and neurological symptoms (Herd 1989; Brisbane and Womble 1985; National Council on Alcoholism and Drug Dependence 1990). Outpatient treatment is recommended for early-stage substance abusers. But hospitalization and residential programs are needed for persons who, for example, abuse alcohol for two or more years and have failed at other attempts to stop as well as for those whose health or life roles are impaired (Hanson 1991; Wright, Kail, and Creecy 1990).

According to Wright, Kail, and Creecy, experts on alcohol and blacks conclude that alcohol abuse is the number one health and social problem in the black community (1990:203). Alcohol use is part of life in the black community and is an all too convenient way to alleviate some of the feelings associated with racism, discrimination, and oppression. Laws concerning the sale of alcohol are often poorly enforced in poor black communities. Janine Lee (1994) points out that communities must be helped to deal with alcoholism and other drug addictions as a community problem using a community empowerment model. Alcohol has been used politically as a tool of oppression since slavery. Heavy drinking on holidays, on weekends, and at special events is still a pattern among African Americans who have substance abuse problems. Although marijuana is the drug of choice of black inner-city youths, alcohol also has a profound effect on homicide, suicide, and crime among young black males (MacGowan 1990). Alcohol and drug abuse are both the cause and result of numerous problems, including poverty, unemployment, crime, and family breakdown (Wright, Kail, and Creecy 1990:218). This is also the case with domestic violence across the board (Pence 1987). Alcohol has been used in similar ways to exploit and control Native Americans throughout history.

The connection of substance abuse to past and present slavery is an effective use of consciousness-raising that helps in the recovery of black substance abusers. Strategies that promote racial, gender, and cultural awareness and pride are also particularly effective (MacGowan 1990; Wright, Kail, and Creecy 1990; Burman and Allen-Meares 1991; Gordon 1994). This is also a useful strategy with Native Americans, Hispanics, gay men, and lesbian women (Atteneave 1982; Graham 1990; Blume 1985; Soriano 1994; Burgos-Ocasio 2000; Kominars 1989).

The National Lesbian and Gay Health Foundation noted that the rate of substance abuse in the lesbian and gay community is nearly triple that in mainstream society. When the gay individual enters recovery, he or she must face feelings of "not being OK, of being alien in their own communities, schools, churches and homes" (Kominars 1989; Graham 1990:4). Alcohol and drugs are used to numb feelings related to stigma, discrimination, and oppression (Lawson and Lawson 1989). Recovery processes for members of oppressed groups must include raising consciousness to deal more adequately with internalized and externally caused oppression. This must take place in one-to-one work on recovery as well as in treatment and self-help groups such as AA or NA (Kominars 1989). As recovery continues and individuals take responsibility for their lives and challenge oppression, they are ready to begin an empowerment process. Empowerment is an ultimate goal of recovery in the treatment of members of oppressed groups.

An ecological perspective that involves family and other systems, such as the church, is also central in achieving empowerment in recovery. The client in recovery is given the responsibility for his or her own empowerment, but all helping systems (including the family) can collaborate to help bring this about (Wright, Kail, and Creecy 1990). Women may need to look at the ways in which they relinquish power and be encouraged to take control over their own lives (Burman and Allen-Meares 1991). Health issues related to substance abuse, maternal and infant health issues, infants born addicted to alcohol or drugs, and, most poignantly, the sharp upswing of AIDS in the African American and Latino communities related to IV drug use also make substance abuse a life-and-death issue, particularly for increasing numbers of women and children infected with the HIV virus (Soriano 1994; Getzel 1991; Stuntzner-Gibson 1991).

Working with Substance Abusers: A Difficult Road

The road to recovery is often rocky and never linear. Slips and setbacks are expected, especially in early recovery. Many individuals make several unsuccessful tries before maintaining a more steady course. Many who complete programs and have a period of successful recovery become lax in attending Twelve-Step programs and counseling and think they can go it alone. In addition, vast numbers of substance abusers deny the problem until it is too late, despite the outreach of professionals and significant others.

Luke: A Gay Multisubstance Abuser in Early Recovery

Luke Amato is a twenty-eight-year-old Italian- and French-Canadian American gay man attending an outpatient drug treatment center. He has used and dealt cocaine and methamphetamine since late adolescence and began recovery again two months ago, when he returned to his parents' home. He was also alcoholic and in denial. He was depressed, described paranoid symptoms, and was unemployed. As depression and paranoia are later-stage manifestations of cocaine use, it was difficult to tell the difference between what was situational or related to mental illness and what was the aftermath of lengthy drug abuse (Royce and Scratchley 1996; Weiss and Mirin 1987; Abadinsky 1989). As he attained recovery, he remained depressed. The worker, an African American man in his late thirties, focused with Luke on managing each day without drugs and asked him to tell his story. Luke conveyed the following:

"I am gay and I have been lonely all of my life. That's no excuse for drug abuse, but it is a fact I deal with. I've been through counseling enough times to know not to make excuses for my drug abuse so what is there to say?" *The worker replied that he would not hear what Luke is saying as an excuse but just as the story of what he struggles with in life.* [The worker avoided the party line in drug treatment, "confronting excuses," and reached for Luke's story.] Luke laughed and said, "I don't know what's worse, being a junkie or being gay, for both you get treated like dirt, like you're worth nothing. Soon you begin to believe it and nothing matters." The worker said, "*Society has some harsh views of both; it's true. How is being gay for you?*" [He opened the taboo area.] Luke said, "Harsh isn't the word. Let me tell you." *The worker said that he wanted to hear.* Luke responded to the encouragement: "I have known I was gay since I was a child. When I was sixteen I was an honor student at a Catholic boys high school and there were dances with the girls' school. I just couldn't go, so I told my parents I was gay. They said they always suspected it. My mother cried every time she looked at me. She began to drink too much. I think her father, a big French-Canadian logger, drank too. I think alcohol problems are genetic possibly. *The worker nodded and said there could be a genetic predisposition.* My father refused to talk about my gayness, he continued. They tried to accept me, but they treated me like a freak. I left home after I graduated from high school and worked my way through college. My family didn't even come to my graduation." The worker said, "*Those were depressing events.*" [Empathizing with feelings.] Luke continued, "I finally found some gay people, but they did the bar scene, so I did too—and the man I liked did cocaine, so I got started. I was in the in group. I think it gave me the courage to have my first gay relationship. I continued using while I worked until it finally got me. I got fired and started dealing."

The worker said, "The loneliness sounds very hard." [Staying with the feeling.] Luke agreed and said, "And the rejection. There's two kinds:

outright and subtle. I prefer outright. It's easier." *The worker said, "None of it is easy. Did the rejection have to do with homophobia?"* Luke said, "Of course" [Validating; Elaborating.] "Or is that paranoid?" The worker said it sounded very real [Validating feelings; Normalizing.] Luke said, "You're damned if you come out and you're damned if you don't." The worker replied, *"It is hard to face stigma and stereotyping. I too face it as black man everyday"* [Sharing his own experience of oppression.] Luke said, "Yes, you can't hide, and neither can I." *The worker answered that Luke carried a lot of pain and asked how it was to talk about it.* [Continuing to ask for his work.] Luke replied, "I've had a lot of counseling but I never talked about how hard being gay was for me." *The worker asked, "Why not?"* Luke said, "Other counselors never helped me like you did today. . . . You understood." *The worker said, "You have had a very hard time and staying clean is hard." They agreed Luke needed to stay clean and to find different ways to handle his hurt"* [Focusing on the addiction.]

The worker's focus on Luke's experiences with homophobia opens the painful feelings Luke has sought unsuccessfully to numb. Talking on this level brings a new kind of relief and a new experience—that of being understood. These aspects of his depression and paranoia certainly have a basis in reality. This does not negate the possibilities of biochemically caused depressions or brain damage, or withdrawal reaction to the drugs (Weiss and Mirin 1987), or the possible onset of schizophrenia (Matorin 1991). Luke needs first to work on staying clean "one day at a time." Part of that effort is learning to deal with painful events and feelings such as those caused by homophobia without drugs (Saulnier 1997; Kominars 1989). Cain (1991) points out that "coming out" is no magic solution to managing a stigmatized identity, for disclosure comes with its own set of problems, as Luke noted so well. Some of the reasons for coming out include therapeutic disclosure (disclosure to feel better), relationship-building disclosure, problem solving, preventive disclosure, and political disclosure. Some disclosures are spontaneous. People also conceal gayness at times when "pay-off" will be low or not worth it, or in deference to others' feelings—particularly those of elderly loved ones (an unselfish act). Self-acceptance and self-integration are benefits of self-disclosure, but contextual reasoning is also important (Cain 1991). The experience of sharing these struggles with someone objective and empathic will be a new one for many.

As the work progressed, Luke also discussed his fear of AIDS. He indicated that he drank heavily when he thought he might enter a sexual relationship. The worker recognized that it was a frightening situation and asked him to look at that behavior rationally. Luke said he knew that drinking did nothing to prevent AIDS and could cloud his judgment. He knew about "safe sex" but thought he would die anyway, so that it did not matter. He said he could handle liquor because he didn't even like it. The worker helped him to accept that his drinking (up to a gallon of liquor a week) was an alcoholic pattern that needed to be stopped if he wanted really to be in recovery. He then attended AA as well as NA meetings and increased to "seven and seven"—daily Twelve-Step meetings. Two of these were gay meetings. The worker also weighed the pluses and minuses of HIV testing with Luke. There are compelling medical reasons to know if one is HIV positive. Luke weighed the information and decided to be tested. He was greatly relieved that the test was negative, which gave him further hope and energy for continuing recovery. Dealing with oppression and the tasks of managing a stigmatized identity seems to free individuals to focus on recovery.

Living and Coping with AIDS: Carmen Rivera and Her Family

In 1999 there were an estimated 5.6 million HIV-infected persons and 33.6 million living with AIDS (CBS News at 6:00, July 20, 2000). As we have noted earlier, women and adolescents constitute the fastest-growing categories of people with AIDS in the United States. Most HIV-infected women are poor, of color, and not well educated. In 1992 Hispanic women represented 20.5 percent of all cases of women with AIDS (Burgos-Ocasio 2000). AIDS goes undetected for longer periods and progresses more quickly in women, who contract it from heterosexual intercourse and, to a lesser extent, from direct intravenous drug abuse (Stuntzner-Gibson 1991; Getzel 1991). With the advent of drugs such as AZT and Bactrim (for PCP pneumonia), AIDS has become a chronic illness for many persons. While there is no cure as yet, persons with AIDS are living longer and continue to need ongoing support (Gabriel 1996).

Carmen Rivera is a twenty-nine-year-old Puerto Rican mother of four children (age five to thirteen) who was diagnosed with AIDS one year ago when she was hospitalized for PCP (pneumocystis carinii pneumonia). She was married to an IV drug user and had used drugs intravenously. In the past two years her husband, Felipe (age thirty-four), became increasingly violent toward her, beating her, forcing her to have sex, and injecting her with cocaine against her will. He did not submit to HIV testing.

At the point the social worker from the Visiting Nurses Association (VNA) picked up the case, Carmen was in a weakened condition and was requesting help to leave Felipe. Facing illness and mortality spurred her to open up to the worker. She quickly disclosed her life story, including the sexual abuse she sustained in childhood from her stepfather. Carmen was shifted from relative to relative until she became pregnant by Felipe at age fourteen. They married when she was sixteen. Felipe became involved with heroin and introduced Carmen to it after the birth of their son, Carlos, when Carmen was eighteen. She says she used it as "recreation" but that he was "hooked." He then experimented with cocaine and coerced her to use with him. The children missed much school, but no authoritative agency intervened. The family lost several apartments because of nonpayment of rent. They lived in motels until admission to a city housing project. Leaving Felipe would mean losing her housing. Her mother offered to let her double up in her small apartment, but she felt her mother was a stranger to her. She felt trapped.

The social worker was a thirty-two-year-old Latina woman with previous social work experience. She shared her feelings as she entered the situation:

I felt overwhelmed. Severe domestic violence, drug abuse, AIDS, and what about the children? The abuse Carmen suffered was difficult to hear. I was angry. I wanted to "save her" immediately, but I knew she had to save herself and make the move away from him. When she discussed having AIDS, I was deeply saddened. I had to be careful not to overidentify, as I was forced to confront my own mortality. I also had to help her mobilize her strengths and deal with all these realities. What is empowerment under these circumstances?

The social worker asks a good question. Ideally, Carmen might have met an empowering social worker somewhere else along the road before she contracted AIDS. But that is not always possible in the real world of practice. Tragic experiences like Carmen's can teach us, if we let them, to be fully human in our practice, to support the courage of the human spirit, to build on strengths without denying "pathology," and to trust people to empower themselves. We are overwhelmed when we lapse into thinking *we* are "to empower." When we learn to stand by the client's side and use our skills, clients will do the empowering work.

Basic skills of listening, extending empathy, partializing large problems into workable units, prioritizing the work, and building in support networks were needed here. Additional empowerment skills of helping the client to reflect and act on her oppressive situation, identifying internal and external obstacles to her freedom, and revising false beliefs were critical. Particular skills related to the ways in which people cope with and accept chronic illness and death are also needed. People are living longer with AIDS, but 90 percent have died within three years of its onset (Getzel 1991).

Social workers in agencies like the VNA routinely make home visits, sometimes in frightening situations. Often a nurse and social worker visit together. In this situation Felipe approved of the nurse visiting, but he forbade Carmen from seeing a social worker and from leaving the house. After Carmen disclosed Felipe's violence to the nurse, the social worker joined her on the next visit and posed as another nurse, with blood pressure apparatus and all. She worked with Carmen alone while the nurse examined the children in another room and engaged Felipe in conversation. The creativity and courage of two women (a nurse and a social worker) in reaching out to a third woman (called a client) is remarkable here. By the fourth session Carmen and the children left the house with her helpers, ostensibly to go to a clinic visit. Arrangements had been made for the Rivera family to return to Carmen's mother's home. Irma, the mother, was full of sadness and guilt about "Carmen's fate" and eager to help her daughter and grandchildren. Carmen refused a shelter for battered women, saying her time was short and she needed her family. She did not press charges against Felipe, to the worker's dismay. Restraining orders were obtained and Carmen began a new life under the family's protection. Carmen reflected that had the worker not helped her she might be dead from Felipe's abuse.

Once safe, Carmen and the worker continued to prioritize her needs. Carmen was referred to a local AIDS service and activist organization called Latinos/as Contra Sida (Latins Against AIDS). She was assigned an AIDS counselor and an AIDS buddy. Her counselor applied for a Section 8 subsidy to rehouse Carmen's and Irma's families together.

Carmen did not talk about her death in the abstract but referred to making plans for her children with her mother for "after she left." Once these plans were in place Carmen could focus more on herself. Kübler-Ross's

"stages of dying" are fluid conceptualizations that describe reactions of denial, anger, bargaining, and resignation or active acceptance (1969). However, AIDS has become more of a "limited-term" chronic illness, so the
person with AIDS is also challenged to live with AIDS. Carmen began by
bargaining for enough time to "set her life in order with her family." The
worker mediated between Irma and Carmen to facilitate a new kind of communication. She helped Carmen learn how to share with her mother as she
helped Irma understand Carmen's AIDS and addiction. Carmen attended
NA accompanied by an uncle. She continued her recovery, saying she "must
now attend to more important things." Both Irma and Carmen blamed
themselves for Carmen's past and present situation. In a very moving moment Carmen was able to disclose the early abuse and gain the loving supportive response she needed as a child. Carmen had never told anyone. The
two women reconciled. With Irma's expression of anger at the stepfather,
Carmen was able to share the anger she felt about Felipe's cruel treatment
of her and about having AIDS.

Daily life for eight persons in a two-bedroom apartment was difficult for
everyone. But Carmen and her children felt cared for and protected as her
mother and family came through for her.

A Focus on the Children

Intensive family work was done with Carmen and her thirteen-year-
old, Jenny. Carmen "saw herself in Jenny" and tried to discipline her too
harshly "to keep her from making my mistakes." The worker helped Jenny
and Carmen talk to each other about all they had been through together.
She helped them and helped Irma work out reasonable limits and rewards
for positive behaviors. She then helped Jenny and ten-year-old Carlos to
talk about their mother's illness and deal with the stigma that Jenny faced
when a friend told her classmates that Carmen had AIDS. Jenny had
handled it well, but she and Carlos were shaken by the experience. They
cried and confronted the unfairness of losing their mother to AIDS. The
worker focused on how they could be helpful to their mother since "only
God knows the time." It was Carmen who wanted this all handled "out
in the open." The worker's skills at identifying the obstacles to their sharing (like the fear that "the other person couldn't take it") enabled real
sharing and closeness.

A particularly effective idea the worker had was to encourage Carmen to write a journal. The journal had two purposes, a life review—to pull together her life's experiences both painful and joyful, oppressive and freeing—and to leave a legacy for the children. Carmen entered each child's life history as she recalled it in the journal and wrote messages to each child. Periodically, Carmen and her children met with the worker to share the journal. Little Maria and Tito (five and six years old) asked Carmen to read it to them in "story times." In this way knowledge of Carmen's illness was shared with them. The new family unit began to become a cohesive whole. The strengths of Puerto Rican families and the value placed on family ties and solidarity (*familismo*) enabled this to happen (Burgos-Ocasio 2000; Soriano 1994; Garcia-Preto 1982).

Carmen feels well and she continues to use the journal to "leave her legacy." She surprised herself at how many courageous and good things she had managed to do for herself and her children. All the children were developing well despite what they had been through. Carmen joined a group for women with AIDS and draws strength from this. Reflecting on her strengths helped her to raise consciousness about herself as a woman and to revise false negative beliefs. She is now optimistic that she may have some time to care about herself and others. She is involved with Latinos/as Contra Sida to educate others about AIDS and to advocate for the rights of persons with AIDS and their families. Carmen still awaits the promised housing. This is the political issue, along with funding for AIDS research and treatment, that she fights for. Carmen's story is one of strength and power. Empowerment is both the journey and the destination. The parting of Carmen and the worker was difficult, but the worker was able to end with Carmen knowing that Carmen had taken charge of her life, remained in recovery, and had good support networks in her family, her group, and Latinos/as Contra Sida. In addition, she no longer blamed herself for the violence and oppression she endured in her life. Despite AIDS, Carmen had a new lease on life.

We turn now to the empowerment group.

11 The Empowerment Group Approach

> Every human being is capable of looking critically at [the]
> world in dialogical encounters with others. . . . Each wins back [the] right to
> name the world. . . . No one can say a true word alone.
> — Paulo Freire

Chapters 11 and 12 will operationalize principle 4 of the empowerment approach: "People who share common ground need each other to attain empowerment." This chapter will focus on the empowering properties of groups, the empowerment group form, and making beginnings with empowerment groups. Chapter 12 will focus on the work (middle) and ending phases of empowerment group work.

The empowerment group is a particular type of group that exemplifies the empowerment approach to social work with groups. Many types of groups may empower people. The level of empowerment may differ according to the group's type, purpose, form, structure, processes, dynamics, and phase of development, and according to members' and workers' abilities. But to be an empowerment group the content and process must reflect empowerment principles and purposes. Issues of oppression must be dealt with explicitly, although this may be only one of the group's purposes. We turn first to the empowering properties of groups and to empowering group work skills.

The Empowering Properties of Groups

Groups may promote development and growth, collective problem solving, and social change. They have a major impact on identity and self-concept (Hartford 1971; Garvin 1987; McRoy and Shorkey 1985). Various groups, including the family and social work groups, have the power to influence socialization and members' capacities for change, choice, problem solving, and collective action (Hopps and Pinderhughes 1999; Toseland and Rivas 1998; Heap 1977). Although people are responsible for their own learning, a great deal of learning occurs in groups. Morale, affectional ties, exchange of views, and mutual identification of members in a group enhance learning. Groups also influence the formation or modification of values, beliefs, attitudes, and actual behavioral change (Hartford 1971). Groups that have the purpose of changing socioeconomic/political structures and institutions give life to local democracy (Lewis 1983). Groups may also help people attain new roles, reduce anomie (the state of normlessness or conflicting norms), attend to new tasks, and enhance role performance (Garvin 1987). Groups are the intervention of choice with overwhelmed and oppressed clients and persons living with the aftermath of trauma (Hopps and Pinderhughes 1999; Gabriel 1996).

Groups are therefore the optimum medium for empowerment on all levels. However, the empowering potentialities of groups are only realized by the worker's skills in defining empowerment as group purpose, challenging obstacles to the work, and enhancing the group processes that develop the group's power as a group. This relates to the worker's knowledge of group processes and to the particular group form or approach used.

Lang (1986) defines the *properties of groupness* that differentiate well-developed groups from aggregates and collectivities. A collectivity is midway on a continuum between an aggregate of people and a group. It lacks common group goals, autonomy, and cohesion. Limited time and space, abilities of members, stability of attendance, workers' skills in developing member-to-member interaction, too much worker control of process and content, and coleadership that creates a powerful subgroup may prevent the advancement of the entity beyond collectivity (Lang 1986).

Collectivities may be accidental or intended. They may also be inevitable in certain kinds of settings. For example, there is a weekly empowerment group in a shelter where homeless women may stay anywhere from one week to several months. When there are several members who have been there three weeks or more, the empowerment group can fulfill its potential as a group. When there is a high turnover of members, it is a collectivity. In a collectivity heightened learning and relational influences on behavior and attitudes take place but are more likely to be worker to member than member to member, an asymmetrical relationship. Group influence, power, autonomy, direction, and goals are limited in a collectivity (Lang 1986). Members do get experience in relating to new persons and in processing content and issues repeatedly. They may also get experience in handling conflict, for collectivities may be characterized by power and control issues. Reaping the fruits of membership in a close, cohesive small group is unlikely. By keeping the worker's role in the central position member to member, power or mutual aid is especially limited.

There are many *types of groups*. Groups are complex and therefore cannot be accurately categorized in dichotomous either/or categories such as "treatment" or "task" groups (Toseland and Rivas 1995). Groups for personal growth and individual change, psychotherapy, task-centered groups, mutual aid, self-help, support, educational, psychoeducational, structured, activity groups, self-directed and social action/social change groups are distinct forms (Garvin 1987; Weiner 1964; Goldberg Wood and Middleman 1989; Mullender and Ward 1989; Vinik and Levin 1991; Gabriel 1996). Mutual aid may be a component of all these group forms (Papell and Rothman 1980a; Papell 1997).

Group types may also be blended and utilized in a variety of group services and approaches. While personal growth or psychotherapy groups may strengthen coping abilities, unless they include wider focus on socioeconomic or political oppression they do not empower, according to our definitions of empowerment as personal and political. Empowerment implies a heightened critical consciousness and sense of peoplehood. All groups address some level of interpersonal empowerment as members learn relational skills. However, this is a limited form of empowerment, for power in relationships that helps people attain needed resources is desired, not just interpersonal comfort or skill.

Groups that seek change in the environment are empowering to the degree that their members have actually brought about and reflected upon the change (Heap 1977). Face-to-face "grassroots" groups in neighborhoods and communities (or "adult community groups") bridge an "interstitial area" between group work and community organization practice (Lewis 1983). Internationally such groups may be called community development or social development groups (Drysdale and Purcell 1999; Estes 1991). Political empowerment and social or economic change is the purpose, but personal satisfaction, growth, community or ethnic pride, and heightened self-esteem may be by-products of these experiences (Lewis 1983).

The Interactionist Approach and the Mutual Aid Group

The interactionist approach of William Schwartz (1974b) is a stepping-stone to an empowerment approach. The group is a microcosm of social interaction. The worker's role is to mediate the processes through which individuals and their systems reach out to each other, particularly when there are obstacles in these transactions — "when the ties are almost severed" (Schwartz 1974b). The group can serve therapeutic (personal) and/or socio-political goals. The key element of the approach is reciprocity, and the worker is seen as a mediator and enabler relative to the group's purpose. The knowledge base for the interactionist practitioner is ecological and systemic. The applicability of this approach to an empowerment approach lies in its appreciation of reciprocity and the strength of the group itself as a mutual aid and self-empowering system.

This approach makes use of formed or natural groups and can encompass a variety of empowerment purposes. The skills and tasks of the worker have been defined by Schwartz (1971, 1974a, b; Schwartz and Zalba 1971) and developed and refined by Shulman (1992), Gitterman (1991), Lee (1994a, b, 1987, 1989b, 1996), Berman-Rossi (1992), and others (Gitterman and Shulman 1994). The worker's tasks are to 1) tune-in, 2) arrive at a mutually agreeable contract and begin the work, 3) detect whether work invested with feeling is taking place and to challenge obstacles to the work and contribute ideas, facts, and values, 4) lend her own vision, and 5) help members use each other to deal with ending an empowering experience.

The elements of a "mainstream model" of social work with groups (Papell and Rothman 1980a; Papell 1997) draw heavily upon the interactionist approach: common goals, mutual aid, nonsynthetic experiences, a conception of group development that emanates from dynamic group processes, diversity of the types of groups and populations served, and flexibility of conception that is inclusive. Members are viewed as active and having the power to make a difference in the group, as social beings who need to belong and as social learners who help each other in learning. They establish bonds, empathy, and identification. Differences are supported and a balance is sought between the needs of the individual and the needs of the group. The worker has a repertoire of roles, but there is little professional mystique. The worker is authentic, forthright, and able to share her own feelings; she helps members to do the same.

Group psychotherapy that is intrapsychically focused and structured groups that are solely for learning purposes (e.g., training groups and classes) are outside the mainstream approach to social work with groups (Papell and Rothman 1980a). Modified structured groups may, however, incorporate mutual aid and be used by social workers for a variety of purposes, including empowerment work (Lee 1980). Didactic "jug and mug" teaching is not a social work approach. A blending of critical education and conscientization group methods with the interactionist and mainstream models (particularly the development of the group as a mutual aid system) form a foundation for the empowerment group approach.

Core Knowledge and Skills for Empowering Group Work

Building the Group

To promote "groupness" the worker begins by helping the group members gain a sense of each other and their groupness. She encourages the development of a mutual aid system by promoting member-to-member communication. Next, the worker respects and utilizes group process as the central change dynamic. Then the worker works to do herself out of a job, helping the group increase its autonomy. Finally, the worker helps the members reexperience and celebrate their groupness at the point of termination. The practitioner needs to be able to "think group": to understand group structure and dynamics and the skills of working with groups. Social work practice with groups must appreciate and utilize the whole group as the helping system (Goldberg Wood and Middleman 1989).

Communication

Goldberg Wood and Middleman (1989) distinguish types of communication in groups that may affect the development of the group as a mutual aid system: the "Maypole," where the worker talks to individuals one by one and dominates and controls the group; the "Round Robin," where each participant speaks in turn in relation to a given focus by a worker (the worker is still in control); the "Hot Seat," where the worker engages in an extended conversation with a member while the others are an audience and the worker maintains control; the "Agenda-Controlled" group, where new and old business and Robert's Rules dominate; and the "Free Form," where participants take responsibility to speak with any other person according to the dictates of the moment. Here the primary responsibility for the flow and form of the work rests with the participants, who observe matters of taking turns, consideration, and risk. This latter form of communication is the optimal pattern for empowering groups.

The worker must relinquish the role of expert as clinician or teacher and promote member-to-member transactions. This means not that the worker withholds her knowledge or expertise but that she shares it without taking center stage, recognizing that members are experts in their own realities. The worker must maximize the group members' potential for helping each other and for taking over their own leadership and direction (Lang 1986).

Group Forms

Lang (1986) examines some of the drawbacks in dyadic relationships, such as the worker/individual client constellation: a tendency to avoid conflict, a delicate balance of power with a strong tendency for asymmetrical roles to develop and no majority or appeal. Yet many practitioners preserve the dyadic relationship in the group by one-on-one communication patterns. Lang identifies four group forms:

1. The *individual-goals group*, where influence flows unilaterally from the worker or the group members to each individual toward individual goal accomplishment. In this form the group itself may not be fully developed.
2. The *collective-goals group*, which employs the fully developed group toward the realization of collectively held goals.
3. The *shared-goals group*, where there is a strong reciprocal influence capable of meeting the needs of its members.
4. The *mixed-goals group*, where some combination of these several goals operate together in a multiple-goals context with some sequencing of goals.

In such groups the source of influence is compounded, coming from both group and worker.

The Empowering Group

The empowering group includes provision for meeting individual and collective needs through group processes and can best be described as a *mixed-goals group* (Lang 1986) in which *a free-form style of communication* is used (Goldberg Wood and Middleman 1989). To empower, the group must attain its own power and cohesion as an entity. Group methods, techniques, and skills that develop the *group's power* while attending to the needs of individual members are empowering in both process and outcomes.

Issues of Group Composition

An old saying goes, "Well begun is half done." This applies to the pregroup phase of the group and to its beginnings. It includes issues of group purpose, composition, structure (including size, number of workers, open or closed, formal or informal), time frame, space, and some notions on the content of the work (Northen 1969, 1988; Hartford 1971; Garvin 1987; Brown 1991; Toseland and Rivas 1998). The purpose and content of an empowering group optimally includes empowerment and issues of oppression in explicit ways, although they may not be the sole purpose of the group. *Structures and composition* should be empowering. The size of a group relates to its purpose and to the interaction desired. Smaller groups provide opportunity for full involvement, intimacy, less anonymity, higher rates of participation, and greater influence on members. However, too small a group may disintegrate with attrition and will not provide adequate stimulation. An optimal number of participants in a small group is six to ten individuals (Northen 1988). A group composed for promotion of familylike structures can be four or five. For social action groups, or if greater anonymity is desirable based on assessment, larger groups are needed.

Groups may be composed in many ways. Self-selection and individual choice are usually the method in natural groups, self-help groups, self-directed groups (Mullender and Ward 1991), and some constructed groups. Referrals may be made by other social workers and helping professionals based on such criteria as suitability of group purpose, age, gender, ethclass commonalities, social experiences or assessment criteria, and individual goals. Members may also be recruited using such criteria. Groups may be based on commonalities, such as the needs or problems of people who are in the same place at a given time (e.g., a shelter, hospital, foster care agency, or neighborhood center). In these instances multiplying the commonalities

among members makes for a potentially stronger group. Redl's law of optimum distance applies: a group should have enough heterogeneity to provide
vitality and enough homogeneity to provide stability (Northen 1988; Gitterman 1986 and Shulman 1994).

Gender, Race, and Ethnicity

Although there is no science or magic to group composition, personal
characteristics (e.g., gender, race, ethclass background, sexual orientation,
and commonality of situation) are important to consider (Mistry and Brown
1997; Reed and Garvin 1983; Davis 1985; Chau 1990). Knowledge of the
interaction of race, gender, culture, and class are essential to the group
worker in composing empowering groups (Julia 2000; Gordon 1994). When
thinking about these factors, a "Noah's Ark" principle is helpful: there should
be more than one individual with similar important characteristics in the
group. To be the only "different one," or "token," is not helpful (Gitterman
and Shulman 1994).

This excerpt from a tenth group meeting of early adolescent girls in foster
care shows them struggling with issues of race and ethnicity. Issues such as
these exist in most groups, even when not spoken (Chau 1990; Mullender
1990). The members are five African American girls (one of whom, Henrietta, is very light complected), and two Puerto Rican girls, Lucy and Maria.
The worker is a Haitian-American woman in her late twenties. They are
dealing with who they are and who she is. The intimacy already established
permits this level of work, but the worker also has to hold them to the work.
Future work of this group included what it meant to be young women of
color and different cultures in this society. They also had a "celebration-of-
cultures" party where each brought ethnic food. The party develops ethnic
consciousness and multicultural understanding (Chau 1990). This openness
also frees group members to work on other important concerns.

Henrietta asked what we thought of her name. Shelly said that there was
nothing wrong with it, but Lucy said it sounded "colored." *I asked her if
she meant black.* [Picking up on taboo area.] Lucy said she didn't like the
terms *black* and *white*. *I said, "Why not?"* [Asking a critical question.]
She said, "Black is ugly." Stacey rolled her eyes at Lucy. Henrietta said
she liked Ray, a handsome, dark-skinned boy. Shelly and Stacey were very
serious. *I said, "Look at us. We have Lucy and Maria, who are Puerto*

Rican and different shades; Henrietta, who is very light skinned; and Shelly and Stacey and I, who are black. What do you think of that?" [Posing a critical question.] Henrietta and Lucy started a diversion to get off the subject, but I was so frustrated by this tactic that *I said that I didn't think it was fair. Here they were about to evade the subject again, because they didn't feel comfortable with it.* [Holding the focus.] That brought their attention back. Lucy, looking puzzled, said to me, "Are you black?" Shelly and Stacey said, "Sure! People from the West Indies are black!" *I said that I sure was, but that I am from a different culture.* [Personal sharing.] Maria and Lucy talked about Puerto Ricans and acceptance of all colors on the island. Lucy asked how Henrietta saw herself. Henrietta said, looking embarrassed, "As a person." *I said that it might be hard for Henrietta because she had said earlier that she considered herself black and yet she had a very fair complexion. It might be hard for her to fit with any one group.* [Conveying understanding.] *I said it was common enough for kids their age to go through all these questions about race, color. I asked them how they thought our group was working in spite of all the differences.* [Normalizing and asking for their work.] They said it was good. *I said that our differences didn't make life easy, but we'd give it a try.* [Lending a vision.] Shelly then brought up a painful concern about her foster father.

Homogeneity of gender, race, ethnicity, or sexual orientation is particularly helpful in consciousness-raising groups. In mixed-gender groups males tend to dominate group process (talk more and also devalue female members). It is helpful for the composition to be balanced in favor of females (Martin and Shanahan 1983; Gottleib et al. 1983). Similarly, minorities of color are more comfortable and able to participate in groups that are balanced in their direction or homogeneous on race (Davis 1985; Bilides 1990; Chau 1990; Hopps and Pinderhughes 1999). Ultimately, we are talking about issues of power and power deficit in group composition and maximizing composition to optimize the power of oppressed group members.

Assessment

Assessment may be done before and during a group's life. The assessment outline suggested in chapter 8 for work with individuals and families also applies to members of groups. Assessing manifestations of oppression in the members' lives and power blocks (internal or external), as well as power deficits and shortages, is pertinent in groups where members struggle with oppression. What strengths may group members share with each other? What obstacles to empowerment may exist? What cultural solutions and explanations are helpful or problematic? Does the member have any personal or mental health problems that may impede the work of the group? A group member's active substance abuse, for example, would block the group's work, as would a member's inability to listen to the other members or constant self-preoccupation. In addition, we assess where the group is in its stages of development (Henry 1992; Northen 1988; Toseland and Rivas 1998) and how it is accomplishing its purposes.

Generic Skills

Procedures and skills that are generic to all helping processes, such as the use of support and sustainment (including the instillation of hope), the use of structure (such as time, space, rituals, and so on), exploration for facts (getting the story) and feelings, education, advice (used sparingly), facilitation of decision making, confrontation (where appropriate), clarification, and promotion of reflective consideration of the person/environment transaction are pertinent in the group (Northen 1988). The worker's skill in engaging members with each other on common themes saves her from the mistake of "casework in the group," which renders the group powerless. An emerging arena for practice with homebound individuals and others unable to participate in fact-to-face groups are telephone- and computer-based (internet) groups. Such groups challenge the skills of the group worker but modifications in skill use can be made so that group members can develop positive support networks (Schopler, Galinsky, and Abell 1997).

Group-Focused Skills

To develop a group-centered mutual aid system the worker promotes clarity of communication through such behaviors as sending clear messages, listening sensitively, and checking out the understanding of messages sent. She encourages, attends, scans the group, and makes verbal and nonverbal gestures of support. She requests sharing and seeks responses from other members to the questions or comments of one. She encourages self-disclosure, modeling it as appropriate, and remains silent at times to stimulate members to contribute. She restates major ideas and reaches for integrative themes, using terms such as we and our to symbolize belonging (Northen 1988). Henry (1992) notes that the use of skills also relates to the positioning of the worker in the group (central, pivotal, or peripheral) and also to the stage of the group's development.

Empowerment Theory and Groups

Empowerment theory applied to group work was first introduced in 1983. Ruby Pernell heralded this new era in a rousing keynote speech at the Fifth Annual Symposium of the Association for the Advancement of Social Work with Groups (AASWG). She noted that group work is a natural vehicle for empowerment, as its historic goals include "growth toward social ends": "Empowerment as a goal addresses the problems of power insufficiency, where need satisfaction [and] growth potential . . . may be severely hampered by the inequities of power as experienced in interpersonal and environmental encounters" (1986:109).

Noting that black Americans have borne the lion's share of these inequities, Pernell emphasizes that empowerment practice cannot remain politically neutral.

> Empowerment as a goal is a political position, as it challenges the status quo and attempts to change existing power relationships. . . . It goes beyond "enabling." It requires of the worker the ability to analyze social processes and interpersonal behavior in terms of power and powerlessness . . . and . . . skills to enable group members to . . . influence themselves and others, and develop skills in using their influence effectively. (1986:111)

The skills of working with indigenous leadership, knowing resources (where the power lies and how to get it), and enabling the group members to do for themselves are important in attaining empowerment. Pernell ended with this definition of social group work: "a method with the potential for achieving power and empowerment" (1986:117).

At the same conference, Hirayama and Hirayama explored the process and goal of empowerment through group participation. They see coping as an expression of our power over the environment. This depends on the adequacy of personal resources that can be developed through groups. The roles of resource consultant, sensitizer, and teacher/trainer can help to empower groups (1986). Hirayama and Hirayama defined types of power and applied these concepts to a group of parents of hyperactive children. Also at this symposium, Coppola and Rivas discussed empowerment in a task-action group for the well elderly in a community residence (1986). At a plenary speech for the Sixth Annual Symposium of AASWG in Chicago in 1984 Lee discussed the personal and political empowerment of oppressed groups as central to group work function, using homeless women in a large urban shelter as an example (1987). Shapiro concludes that this thinking is ground-breaking:

> The recent work of Hirayama and Hirayama (1986), Pernell (1986), Lee (1986), Goldberg Wood and Middleman (1989), Lewis (1989), and Breton (1989) using the language of competence, consciousness-raising and empowerment is suggestive of theory which goes beyond the conceptualizations of the "social goals" model and its proponents. (1991:16)

Special editions of *Social Work with Groups* devoted to "Ethnicity in Social Work Practice" and "Ethnicity and Biculturalism" focused on group work with minorities of color and cultural differences (Davis 1984; Chau 1990). Race was acknowledged as a dynamic of oppression in American society, and culturally sensitive group work approaches were advocated. Mistry and Brown (1997) explore issues of race and group work in an international context. Lee et al. (1997) conceptualize and illustrate group work across racial and client-worker barriers in an agency serving homeless women in the United States. Schiller (1997) applied group stage development theory to women's groups in an article connecting recent theory on women's development to group work practice. Recent comprehensive works on social work with gay and lesbian clients and their families have noted the importance of groups for support, coming out, and empowerment (Woodman 1992; Appleby and Anastas 1998; Mallon 1998; Van Wormer, Wells, and Boes 2000). Peters (1997), Lenna (1992), and DeCrescenzo (1979) discuss group work with gay adolescents, and Getzel (1998) focuses on group work practice in the gay community, but there is relatively little in the group work journals regarding the empowerment of lesbians and gay men.

In the late 1980s and early 1990s there were several substantial efforts to apply empowerment concepts to social work with groups. Gutiérrez analyzed the effectiveness of empowerment-oriented group work, which includes ethnic consciousness and consciousness raising with Latinos. She emphasized the interrelatedness of personal, interpersonal, and political levels of empowerment (1989a, b, 1990). Garvin (1987) and Northen (1988) both included sections on oppressed groups in the second editions of their texts, as Shulman did in his third edition (1992). Goldberg Wood and Middleman (1989) used the words *empowerment group*, which they defined as action-oriented group work with people who define themselves as oppressed. Empowerment is built strongly into the second edition of Germain and Gitterman's life model approach, which includes practice with groups and communities as well as political practice (1996). Brown identified principles for working with oppressed persons in groups (1991). *Group Work with the Poor and Oppressed* (Lee 1989b) focused specifically on applying empowerment concepts to social work with groups in a variety of nontraditional settings. Chau (1990) addressed several different minority cultures, emphasizing biculturalism as adaptive and ethnic and ethclass sensitivity as imperative in empowering groups.

Relevant Group Approaches

Social action groups in North America

The legacy of Jane Addams and the settlement house movement is a legacy of social action (Addams 1910, 1930; see chapter 4). As Shapiro notes in his astute historical analysis:

> The pioneers in social work with groups shared a concern for the development of a democratic society within the United States and internationally. Their work can be traced in the association between Jane Addams and John Dewey in Chicago in the 1890s and in a more organized affiliation among Dewey, Mary Parker Follett, Eduard Lindeman, Grace Coyle and others in a group called The Inquiry in the 1920s and in the early 30s. (1991:8, 9)

The inquiry used political, social, and economic analysis as tools in building theory that emphasized harnessing group processes for social change goals. Grace Coyle (1979) translated much of this thinking for social group workers. She saw groups as tumultuous centers of potential change—the brewing social movements of the future (1930:227), as "tapping a great molten stream of social discontent and social injustice underlying present conditions" and providing direct education on social questions and social action (Shapiro 1991:11). This legacy of passion for democracy was quickly transmuted (by the 1940s) into a concern for "social responsibility" and the development of methodology, which displaced social action from the central concern of group work (Shapiro 1991). The 1960s saw a short-lived revival of social action groups (Weiner 1964). As groups are the key to community organizing as well, the dawn of the millennium is witnessing a renewed interest in activism-oriented community groups (Baptist, Bricker-Jenkins, and Dillon 1999).

The 1980s began a return to this earlier passion for social change and added other philosophical bases that would reunite group work and the personal and political levels of concern (Shapiro 1991; chapters 2 and 13). Vinik and Levin's edited work (1991) documents the revitalization of social action thinking in social work with groups.

Social Development and Social Work with Groups Internationally

Social development is a multidisciplinary integrative field of practice and an outcome in which group workers play an important part. Internationally, empowerment is a central objective of social development activity. It requires the active engagement of collectives working together toward shared objectives. Social development practitioners draw their theory base from sociology, political science, economics, education, and in some cases religion (liberation theology; Estes 1991). The reader is also referred to chapter 13 for expansion of ideas on international group work.

The word *liberation* (instead of *development*) more accurately encompasses the aspirations of poor people and avoids the antithesis of the term *underdevelopment*. *Developmentalism* has become associated with timid measures that often preserve the power of the wealthy, whereas the word *liberation* encompasses the radical change that is needed. *Liberation* means "to set free"—not only to set free the oppressed from injustice but to free the oppressor from the sin of oppressing. Liberation takes its practitioners to confrontation with power structures, whereas development may attempt to circumvent political change (Gutiérrez 1973).

Social development consists of six types of practice: personal empowerment, group empowerment, conflict resolution, institution building, nation building, and world building. For Estes (1991) conscientization is the road to personal and group empowerment as well as the destination of social transformation. His definitions are closer to what Gutiérrez defines as liberation.

Social Work with Groups in South America

Citing Lusk, Estes summarizes the central tenets of conscientization: the rejection of a neutral, scientific, and professional orientation to social reality, an awakening of consciousness in the work of the masses that recognizes the importance of perceiving power relationships in society, developing the capacity for critical analysis of causes of domination, an understanding of praxis, and acceptance of the responsibility to become what one should become through the sociology of liberation (Estes 1991). Conscientization is the dominant approach to social work practice throughout Latin America, where liberation theology and critical education are included in the knowledge base of the profession (Estes 1991). Critical education and liberation theology motivate and expand the knowledge base of modern group work practitioners.

The British Self-Directed Model

British group work has always bridged community practice. A particularly well-developed current British model is the self-directed model advanced by Mullender and Ward: "The essential features of self-directed groups include a dominant focus on empowering members to achieve external change, and open, voluntary and non-selected membership" (1989:5).

The premises of the model are the following: people's problems stem from structural factors, empowerment is a valid aim, group members have strengths, and workers must challenge oppressions, including those within themselves. The model focuses on external change and does not address internalized oppression, indirect blocks, or person/environment transactions as problematic. Workers start out with an overarching purpose in mind. The work may begin at the personal level of members' shared experiences and then move to the political level of broader social considerations. As in all good group work practice, the members define their issues and take responsibility for working on them. In a self-directed approach members freely elect to join, although the worker may make the group attractive and the members must have enough in common. The self-directed group has open membership, potentially unlimited size, open-ended length, and member-determined frequency, time, and location of meetings.

This autonomy and openness can be empowering for some groups but may be premature or too difficult for others and contribute to an early demise (Mondros and Berman-Rossi 1991). The empowerment group approach therefore is not prescriptive on these variables; instead it relates them to the specific group at hand. The values and several of the principles of the self-directed approach are quite compatible with this empowerment approach. Additionally, Drysdale and Purcell (1999) see group work as the primary method of the community development approach in Scotland that enables people to address issues of social exclusion and oppression.

A French Approach to Social Action Groups

Margot Breton of Canada describes a social action partnership approach to social work practice in France. Community partners include community politicians, entrepreneurs, social workers, and clients (in this case unemployed youth) who define and work on problems together. However, in the example given, the youths entered the partnership after the community partners planned a summer job program for them, which involves a somewhat unequal power situation. The youth groups provided feedback on the project. The partnership included conscientization about the problems, mobilization for action, and organization. The action that took place, the jobs program, was an important step forward in dealing with structural unemployment of youths. The young people experienced empowerment through social work groups as well as through the actual employment. Whether the personal struggles of the youths were dealt with is unclear. This model seems to use social development principles as well.

Breton makes a major contribution to empowerment theory. Her writings consistently identify issues of power in practice with groups. She emphasizes how difficult it is for social workers to give up power to group members and how much easier it is to nurture or assume a doctor/patient stance than it is to educate for critical consciousness (1989, 1991a, b). Breton stresses the community level of this work: "Consciousness raising on the nature and resolution of problems needs to take place not only within marginalized populations but also within the community" (1991b). This is consistent with the view that we should work with the oppressor (Solomon 1976; Gutiérrez 1973). Breton suggests that oppressed people and all social workers must come together to build both foci, the personal and the sociopolitical, into all social work practice (1991b). This means that the planning of social work interventions should never be of an "either/or" nature (Breton 1989). In recent years Breton wrestles with the turning of the new century as a possibly "post-empowerment" era, yet the type of group work she advocates remains consistent with empowerment principles (1998; Breton and Breton 1997).

In a panel discussion at the Fourteenth Annual AASWG Symposium in 1991, Northen described the kind of group in which the sociopolitical and personal interrelate as "clinical social work at its best." Breton countered that it was "social work at its best." Her concern was that the profession continues to dichotomize the personal and political. Most practitioners do not enact a dual focus, and most theoretical approaches do not prepare them to do this. The empowerment group approach builds on "clinical" knowledge as well as "social action groupwork" and seeks to join and infuse them with critical consciousness.

Critical Education and Conscientization

Paulo Freire developed his critical education approach in Brazil during the 1950s and 1960s. Brazil was a closed colonial society made up of the elite and the masses, both culturally alienated. To create a democratically open industrialized society, each citizen needs to develop a critical awareness of realities and to use that awareness to participate in and transform society. Alienated people, particularly poor people, often develop a culture of passive silence and apathy about their situations. For the Brazilian poor the problem of developing awareness was compounded by illiteracy. Freire used critical education to develop literacy and to develop critical thinkers who could transform their own societies (1973b).

Critical education means to confront, reflect on, and evaluate the problems and contradictions of society in order to change them. Critical awareness develops in a process of dialogue with others in groups. The development of critical awareness is called conscientization (Freire 1973b). The basic elements of Freire's method are:

- Participant observation of educators/workers who "tune-in" to the "vocabular" universe of people.
- An arduous search for words [and themes] rich in experiential involvement.
- A codification of these words into visual images—pictures, charts, skits that stimulate people submerged in the culture of silence to emerge as conscious makers of their own culture.
- The decodification by the culture circle and coordinator/worker in dialogue.
- A creative new codification explicitly critical and aimed at action.

The roles of the coordinator/worker are to "problematize" the situation, to pose critical questions about reality that group participants experience, to codify, decodify, reflect on, act on, reflect again (praxis), and develop their own awareness (Freire 1973b).

This critical education method has many parallels to social work with empowerment groups. Social movements in the United States such as the black liberation movement and the women's liberation movement have used similar critical education methods in the "freedom schools" of the 1960s and in consciousness-raising groups. Pence (1987) and others have used Freire's critical education method in working with battered women (see chapter 3).

Figure 11.1 illustrates the union of critical education and core group work knowledge and skills in an empowerment group approach.

The Empowerment Group Approach

The empowerment group utilizes the principles, knowledge base, and skills of the empowerment approach and explicitly defines empowerment as purpose, content, process, and outcome of the group's work (Lee 1991). It is not a support or mutual aid group, nor a "therapeutic group," a consciousness-raising or critical education group, or a political action group.

FIGURE 11.1
Critical Education and Empowerment Group Processes

The Beginning Phase of Work

1. As a major part of the "tuning-in" process:
   a) participant observation in the client's community/world
   b) Meeting with representative group to make an arduous search for their experiences, words, feelings, concerns and themes.

2. Formation of the empowerment group based on common ground and informed interest—"Try it and see" philosophy.

3. Mutually define the empowerment purpose, content, group structure, worker's role, and desired outcomes as part of the contracting process. To do this, experiences of oppression, discrimination, prejudice, and pride in peoplehood must be opened so that challenging direct and indirect power blocks may become a part of the empowerment contract.

4. Mutually choose a generative theme rich in experience and feeling to begin with.

The Work Phase

5. The worker uses the full range of generic and group oriented social work skills to develop the mutual aid system and develop the power of the group. This includes "thinking group" and "thinking empowerment" at the same time.

6. The worker must continually be a problem poser, asking critical questions to stimulate critical reflection. The "illusion of work" is challenged by worker and group members.

7. Group members are asked to analyze the problem on personal, institutional/systems, and cultural/political levels. This involves sharing experiences, feelings and thoughts.

8. Develop a code with the group that further stimulates a raised consciousness. A code is a program tool, a channel of communication which may include pictures, photos, music, poetry, drama, tapes, charts, or other mediums that present a situation which evokes emotion and is intimately familiar and complex enough to work on but not a puzzle or a game.

9. Decode the codification with the group, always encouraging their own words and the sharing of their own perceptions and experiences. Challenge the perceptions, continuing to ask critical questions. A new codification and raised consciousness may evolve in this process, one that is critical and aimed at action.

10. The group can now develop options for action on personal, institutional and cultural/political levels.

11. The group members take action.

12. The group reflects on its actions in an ongoing process of praxis: action-reflection-action invested with feeling and thought until they determine the work of the group and ending phase work is completed.

It is all the preceding and, by its unique combination of these, it is more. We will discuss and illustrate preparing for, forming, maintaining, and ending empowerment groups.

Beginning an Empowerment Group: Formation

Empowerment groups are appropriate for persons who face issues of pervasive external and internalized oppression in their lives. Children, youth, adults, and elders may all benefit from empowerment groups. The explicit purpose of the group is personal/political empowerment, including the building of a sense of pride in "peoplehood" and in shared common ground. Additional purposes may include building a sense of community, mutual support, and mutual aid, fostering age-appropriate socialization, and providing learning opportunities. By definition, such groups contain social action and social change goals as well as personal and interpersonal ones. These broad purposes are offered to group members who then determine what external power blocks, deficits, or shortages and areas of internalized oppression need to be addressed and how to address them. Sometimes people who experience pervasive oppression are so accustomed to living with it that they assume "that's just the way things are." An initial consciousness-raising effort is then needed to include oppression in the problem definition. To attain empowerment one has to name one's power problems and locate them in personal struggles and in the fabric of a society that seeks to marginate persons of difference. Then group members must work to change the power balance in their favor. The worker may initially need to name experiences of oppression for what they are, but will soon find that those who suffer are well able to develop the themes as they pursue empowerment.

Empowerment groups are composed on the basis of commonalities that include experiences of oppression. The greater the commonality, the greater the potential bond between group members. Within this commonality there is often a natural variety of strengths and enriching differences.

The style of group formation used relates to the agency setting as well as to the use of empowering principles. We have discussed a "commonalities" approach that can be used differentially in a variety of settings. Using this principle, people may be invited to join empowerment groups through publicity, outreach by workers and group members, signs strategically placed, and invitations. Individual outreach work may increase motivation for those overwhelmed by life's struggles. When an agency commonly sees individuals and families one by one, composing empowerment groups may involve a referral process in which workers open the possibilities for clients who may then self-refer. Workers may also refer individuals to the group and suggest that they give it a try a few times before deciding whether they want to belong. People may not be "joiners," may fear groups because of earlier life experiences, or may have a low level of trust of others like themselves because of internalized self-hatred. In some settings where groups are open-ended by necessity—as in shelters, hospitals, or substance abuse treatment facilities— there may be a requirement of group attendance so that new doors are opened. This requirement also establishes an ongoing nucleus of members working toward empowerment. If it is apparent that individuals cannot use the group, then exceptions are made.

Optimally, membership in an empowerment group is a matter of personal choice based on knowledge of the experience. In forming an empowerment group for women who had "graduated" from the services of a small inner-city shelter for homeless women and children, the worker began by inviting large groups to evening get-togethers. She used the format of a meal, informality, and then a formal period of group discussion when empowerment notions were introduced. After six meetings the worker noted that a self-selecting process was taking place. A strong nucleus of seven African American women between the ages of twenty-two and thirty-four who had children ranging from toddlerhood to early adolescence was most active in exploring issues of personal and political empowerment. The worker asked these seven women if they wanted to meet regularly to become a more focused empowerment group. The Successful Women's Group was formed and lasted for almost two years. Since there were regular empowerment groups in the shelter, those who seriously began empowerment work self-selected participation in the alumnae group.

The role of the worker changes as such groups become cohesive and more self-directing, although the degree of self-direction may vary with each empowerment group. In the Successful Women's Group the worker began as a more central figure in offering a beginning structure of weekly meetings to get momentum, contracting for and laying out the issues of empowerment, which they refined and developed, maintaining a work focus, and mediating where necessary. Within four months, however, the group developed its own structure, choosing meeting nights, time, frequency (biweekly), and content and reaching out to new members. They developed a club-style structure with a president, who called the meetings and maintained the work focus, and two other officers. The worker bolstered the leadership structure and continued to contribute information and to assist in guiding praxis and reflecting on feelings and facts to deepen the work focus. The worker also shared empowerment issues from her own experiences. In a sense she became advisory to the group, but in another sense she was a member of the group who had special roles related to safeguarding the group's empowerment focus.

Gathering Thematics: Tuning in to the "Shelter Alumnae" Empowerment Group

The worker used the six larger "get-together" meetings to have the women express the themes of their lives. Their work was invited on "personal struggles and triumphs" and on identifying forces "bigger than any one person's problems" that affected their lives. The themes that are offered for the empowerment work must be issues close to the core of their lives. Another way of obtaining these life themes is to ask new group members to "brainstorm" on the personal and "bigger" power issues in their lives. Asking people to brainstorm may evoke mostly intellectual responses. What we want are experiential themes that carry feelings.

Using her multifocal vision, knowledge, and empathy, the worker knew that young women of color face discrimination and external obstacles as they seek empowerment. She knew their complex ethclass and age-appropriate struggles and many of their life circumstances that made for internal power blocks as well. This tuning-in process made a bridge for beginning the work. But the young women themselves defined the work they needed to do to challenge and remove the roadblocks. The worker must listen, be there, witness, share if possible, deeply empathize, and identify the themes that members will choose to work on. As the themes emerge and are partialized for the work, the worker will help members codify and decode the themes in a new way, leading to praxis, raised consciousness, action, and reflection.

On the Personal Level   The following themes emerged: You have to fight to get what's coming to you; there is tremendous loneliness in living alone with small children; someone else, usually a man, is needed to protect you from violence and intrusion and from loneliness; sometimes, however, he brings the violence with him; but this is better than living alone, unless he "really hurts" you or the children; the nice extras he may provide are very important; your relatives helped you out, so you need to help them—besides it's better not to live alone, even if there's no room, because inside, "I don't feel ready or know how to be on my own. I'd really just like to turn back time to no kids and have a good time!" I want to better myself but I'm not sure I can do it. It's easier not to try. I am trying. I could sure use some support! But I also want to be totally independent of all rules and outer direction.

On the Wider Political Level   It's unfair. The housing is expensive, inadequate, and in disrepair, with rodents and bugs, no heat or hot water, other people using your electricity, and inadequate safety measures. The landlord takes advantage of our need for housing—charges too much and won't repair or provide services. Do white people have to live this way? We're trapped and stuck here; racism is everywhere—when you go for an apartment or job interview, when you go to pay your bills, even when you have a baby. Why is it that only the black and Latina women are required to go to a class on birth control? Why do they push tubal ligation on us? And why did the landlord ask me if my husband was around? Does he think that only men can pay rent? Why is it that only a few white women stay in shelters? How can they send our babies to the worst housing project in town? I know how to get on welfare and get my entitlements—but how do you get off when, if you work, they deduct your salary from your benefits and you make less working at McDonald's. Most workfare jobs are dead end. The day-care lists are so long—where can I leave my kids? The cards are stacked against us, the walls are too high to climb, and the support, if you try, is sorry. I like the political activities we did while in the shelter. On the other hand, I don't want to march openly and have people see me as a "welfare case."

Distilling the Themes

As we hear and feel the poignant struggles of these young women we may respond with outrage and sadness. There are many contradictions in the themes. It is important to distill the essence of the struggles and offer sharpened themes for empowerment work. First, there is the contradictory message to take care of yourself and your family with inadequate resources. What are the structural/external blocks to obtaining adequate resources? Which blocks are internal—from fears, feelings of inadequacy, and lack of knowledge? What human, financial, and material resources are needed, and how do we get them? What is a matter of resources, what is a matter of rights, what is a matter of readiness to gain access to these resources? The basic critical question inherent in the life themes is, "Why are the cards stacked against young women of color?" The daily experiences of living are the soil from which empowerment work springs.

The Contracting Process

Beginning an empowerment group requires explicit inclusion of empowerment as the primary purpose and an explanation of the dialogical process that will bring this about. In dialogical process there is horizontal relationship and intercommunication between equals, between worker and group members, and among group members. Each is an expert on the realities that must be known, equally capable of defining, symbolizing, and changing that reality (Freire 1973b). In all good group work practice, the worker must make the purpose of the group clear, must offer her stake and the agency stake in the contract offer, reach for the client's stake and purposes, and describe her own role in the process (Schwartz 1974b). This is also true in beginning an empowerment group: *the purpose* is multilevel empowerment; *the process* is dialogical encounter and mutual aid in the process of working on concerns, discussion, debate, action, and reflection; *the worker's role* is as a coequal teacher/learner/participant in dialogue who also has specific tasks in facilitating the work. Although this clarity needs to be offered in initial meetings, it may take much longer for the worker and group to comprehend and begin to deal with these purposes and processes as they emerge from life experiences. Empowerment group work is not usually a short-term endeavor.

From the Shelter Alumnae Empowerment Group (the Successful Women's Group)

The following are some examples in offering, clarifying, and negotiating group purpose and process. The alumnae group members initially met weekly at each other's homes. The worker reflects:

The first meeting was at Ebony's house. She prepared a meal and everyone contributed to it. Sitting around the kitchen table helped minimize
the distance between me and the members. In a sense it put the shoe on
the other foot. I am in their living space and the personal lives of all of
us are open to each other in a new way. It makes it easier to relinquish
the remnants of control and authority. It is harder to make a contract
offer, provide a focus, or mediate the process as I am used to doing. But
the nature of our work has to be clarified or we will be just another social
group.

The worker reflects on shifting traditionally comfortable roles to do this
work in dialogical encounter. Many mistakes will be made, so self-
monitoring is essential.

Contracting for Empowerment

When the meal was over and the sharing of the events of the week was
at a lull, the worker began to work on their purposes for gathering:
    *"Let's talk about why we are getting together and what you want to do
in these meetings. You agreed to become an empowerment group. We have
worked on issues of personal, interpersonal, and political empowerment in
our larger meetings, but what does empowerment mean to you? What are
we going to work on?* [The worker focuses the work and begins a contracting process, which includes and defines the empowerment goal.] Vesalie,
the oldest at thirty-four, smiled and looked around the room. She said,
"I usually stay to myself. I don't trust a lot of people. I usually don't tell
my business to anyone. But in coming to our meetings I realized how
much I kept in. You all are like sisters to me now. We have the same
struggles. . . . We can help each other because we've all been there."
Ebony replied, "Yes, I need this family; I can't count on mine. It's hard
out there with a baby." [They spoke of times they helped each other.]
Tanya said, "I'm thirty-two, right? But I'm having a hard time growing
up, even with three kids. What got in my way before was this man that
abused me. But he's history now. This group is helping me to face life. I
don't want to stay on welfare, but I'm scared to do anything else. I know
Amika is scared too, but we want to work too." *I asked, "Let me see if I*

hear you. To be empowered, to gain power, you need to feel you have people that care, people you trust, that are like family?" [Clarifying empowerment purposes; Checking out their meanings.] They heartily agreed. *I said, "Yes, that's what's gotten me through too."* [Personal sharing; Affirming the importance of mutual aid and caring.] Tracey said, "This group gives you the courage to face life."

I then asked what personal power was. [Asking for their definitions.] Tracey replied that we have what we need to get what we want! We were all pleased with her formulation. *I pressed, "What do you need?"* [Asking for their work.] Ves said, "Money!" Amika agreed and said, "Job training, and then a job." Ebony said, "We need what everyone needs, a nice place to live, money, love, and a chance to make it." *I said, "Yes, these should be basic human rights."* [Affirming; Empathizing.] *I asked, "Why don't you have it?"* [Asking again for the work.] Tracey said, "Well I didn't have the education or opportunity to get a good job until the shelter sent me to the training program." Ves agreed, adding that now she feels ready to go to college and her job pays for courses, so she has the opportunity. Shandra said that she was taught to believe she couldn't go to college, but she doesn't believe it anymore. Amika said, "But I feel I haven't had the opportunity. I came here with an eighth-grade education from Alabama. It's taking me forever to get my GED with three kids. I need a chance too." Tanya agreed, "The only opportunity I got was to work for the census, but that's every ten years. What kind of a career ladder is that?" "One fixed to keep you on the bottom," Tracey answered wisely. Everyone agreed.

I asked, "Why is it fixed that way?" [Posing a critical question.] Tracey replied, "So they can stay on top. Someone has to be on the bottom and do the work they don't want to do. It's still like slavery." *I nodded and asked how they felt about that.* [Reaching for the feelings connected to the awareness.] Ves said, "It's unfair and it makes me angry." Amika said, "But it's always been that way." Tanya said, "It ain't going to stay that way for my kids. It's got to stop." Each one agreed. *I said, "Now you are raising your consciousness and mine about the way things are."* [Validating their teaching role.] *"When we identify and act on specific things that are wrong, that is political empowerment."* [Naming the processes used to attain empowerment.] "Like when we all went to the Housing Now march in Washington," said Tanya. "Or when we testify at the legislature," said Tracey. *"Exactly,"* I agreed. *"And when you learn to think and see things as they are, as Shandra said."* [Affirming and broadening their understanding.] *"It's like the wall you spoke of in our earlier meetings—the wall that stands between you and power. We have to define it to tear it down."* [Suggesting a code.] They were nodding and verbally agreeing. *"I also think you are well on the road to empowerment."* [Giving credit for their hard work.] "It's a long road," said Tracey. "BUT WE CAN WALK IT, AND WE CAN CLIMB THAT WALL."

This group has done empowerment work without naming or conceptualizing it for themselves. Now that they have decided to meet regularly as an "empowerment group," the power of specific purpose is invoked by the worker's clarity and affirmation of their purposes. The specifics of the work, getting training and jobs, constitute the first personal/political offering defined by the group. Others are also named: abusive relationships, a history of blocked opportunities that necessitate opportunities for new learning and skill development, systemic abuse, poor education, and few real career opportunities, which demands systemic change. The importance of the group as a caring, mutual aid system is emphasized by the members. Connection makes empowerment possible.

Shelter Empowerment Groups Begin

In settings that involve a high degree of transience, group purpose must be defined in each meeting. Unlike the alumnae, newer members in this type of group do not usually know what the group is about. The following are examples of negotiating an empowerment contract in two shelters for homeless people.

In a Family Shelter Twelve people attended the meeting—one Pakistani couple, one Puerto Rican couple, six African American mothers, and two white (Italian-American and Franco-American) mothers. The worker is a white (Italian-American) woman in her late twenties.

"Welcome, several of you are new tonight. Perhaps the old members can tell why we're here." [Asking the members to share the group purpose.] Pam said, "Because we need each other's support in dealing with being here and finding housing." Daniel said, "So we can learn what is available, and how to get it." Raj said, "We have burned our bridges with relatives. That's why we are here, but it's so hard. I do not feel like a man." Tywanna said, "Raj, every day you and your wife go and buy fish and sell it. That's hard and smelly work, but you do it for your family." Raj replied, "But we don't make enough to get an apartment." "But," Dan said, "you are a man because you do your best and you will get it together." Maria said, "Both of the men here are real men because they are sticking with their families." Everyone agreed. *I said, "It is very hard for everyone here, and you can and do help each other to deal with it."* [Empathizing and crediting their work.] *"We are here to discuss your concerns, problems, solutions, and hopes and to share ideas. You want to get things together, save some money, get an apartment, and make it. This is a very tough job! I hear your feelings of frustration, sadness, and disappointment. But you have a lot of knowledge about the system and community resources and can identify and help change what's wrong with the system. Does anyone have a problem they'd like to start with?"* [Developing the contract, offering empathy, addressing them as pro-active people.]

Barbara said, "I have three kids with me and nowhere to go. I left my husband (in another state) because he beat me one time too many. But he used to do everything for me. I try so hard, but I'm even afraid of calling landlords. I get scared of answering machines and I leave dumb messages. When I get to talk to a landlord I forget his name." Pam said, "I was like that but I learned, and you can too." Several agreed. The group worked with Barbara, offering suggestions and role-playing until she felt comfortable about dealing with landlords. [Staying with the member's concern.] Barbara then told her story with much support from group members. She ended with her dismay at the lack of low-income housing options.

The work continued, turning to discussions of the "freeze" on Section 8 certificates.

I said, "It is awful. Is there anything we can do about it?" [Connecting feeling to action; Developing the political action part of the contract.] Pam said, "Well, all twenty-nine of us living here could go to Senator D's

office. I'm proud of my children, I want him to look at us and help us."
Barbara said, "That's scary." Raj agreed. Pam said, "But Section 8 is necessary. . . . Let's unite and explain homelessness to the big guys." *I said,*
"All right, Pam! You're correct. There's strength in numbers, and the big
guys do need to hear from you." [Encouraging their action.] Everyone
agreed, but some kept saying they couldn't go. Pam was saddened at this.
I said, "How about starting with a letter?" [Suggesting something they
may succeed at.] Everyone agreed, and Pam suggested that each write
their own stories and then put it all together to make sure it sounds OK.
Barbara said, "At the end of the letter we can invite him here to meet
us." They all agreed. *I asked, "Who would type it, proofread it, and so*
on?" [Naming the steps.] They divided the tasks and it seemed doable. *I*
said, "I think the letter is a great start. You're recognizing you have a voice.
Now let's use it. It's a hard fight, but the legislators need to hear about it
from you. I'm so proud of you for deciding to take a step to make your
voices heard. [Encouraging and emphasizing that they need to say their
own word, and act on it.]

In this example the worker develops the contract, moves back and forth
from the personal to the political, and helps them partialize the work into a
doable piece of action. She also encourages the use of their own voices. A
wonderful critical question would have been, "Why do we call officials 'the
big guys'? Who are the big guys, and who are the small guys?"

In a Men's Shelter   In a men's shelter seven men in their twenties and
thirties were present—six African Americans, one Puerto Rican. The worker
was a white (Irish-American) woman in her early thirties. The worker's approach was action oriented. She records in summary form:

After introductions we discussed their ideas of empowerment: homeless
individuals speaking for themselves, making themselves heard; not forgetting the experience of being homeless; being in control of one's life;
knowing how to make the most effective use of resources; and how to
work with various systems to make them responsive (especially political
systems). It was important to the men to dispute the "skidrow bum" image
of the homeless man. They thought education on who the "homeless"

are might counter this stereotype. Some thought they should establish a "speaker's bureau" to educate the public. Others thought they might volunteer their services to show they wanted to work and were useful. The worker *reached for and affirmed their ideas*. They agreed to work on these themes in their empowerment meetings.

The worker shared the "definition of empowerment" developed by the statewide Coalition for the Homeless for their input. They went over it, affirming and disagreeing, pleased that their input would be incorporated into the statement. They made the following statement:

> It is good to see people realizing that the common plight of homeless and poor people is really the common plight of all the human family . . . and that people who give care as part of their jobs are not above anyone . . . to act that way is against the good of the whole. We learn from each other as we walk along together, and united we can accomplish many things which we could not accomplish alone. . . . We are aiming for people to have personal and political power. A sense of power is essential to our well-being. . . . We need to grow in personal and political skills. . . . We discussed how we can be heard politically. An immediate concern was that a winter overflow shelter had not opened. We drafted a petition and decided how to get it circulated, and who should get it (i.e., the mayor, the finance committee, etc.). We also decided to develop a way to share job and apartment resources with all residents.

This group got off to a quick and active start. An ongoing nucleus remained together for eight months. This group had a political action focus and little focus on personal/political obstacles, like substance abuse or mental health issues. This sometimes hampered the political activities they attempted and the level of personal empowerment some would attain. But they attained collective empowerment through acting together. Requesting their input and definitions into the work of the statewide Coalition for the Homeless was empowering.

We have given four examples of making beginnings in a variety of empowerment groups. In each group the worker engages the members openly in a discussion of their empowerment needs, defines terms with the group members, and makes a mutual contract but leaves particular directions up to the members. The worker uses self-disclosure and promotes the sharing of vital concerns that the work proceeds from the real issues of members' lives.

Some groups may move to action in first meetings; others take the slower road of exploring, reflecting, and defining issues. Either approach is useful in developing a process of praxis in which those who explore must eventually act and those who act must continue to reflect and explore. It is a matter of assessment of the group to decide which should come first for a particular group. One caveat about action is that the group must be able to tolerate the frustration when results are not immediate. The worker should help the group successfully complete tasks as success breeds success. Reflection before, during, and after action yields a raised consciousness and increased effectiveness. Oppressed people must be thinkers as well as doers, and critical reflection is action: "A revolution is achieved with neither verbalism nor activism but, rather, with praxis" (Freire 1973a:120). The importance of good beginnings is in unearthing the themes to be worked on and establishing the understanding that working toward empowerment together can bring transformation.

12 Empowerment Groups: Working Together Toward Empowerment

The Work Phase

Once trust is established and agreement is reached on the empowerment purposes and themes of the group, the group is ready to do its work of sharing real concerns and helping each other to deal with the issues of life that brought them to the group, critical reflection, and praxis. In addition to *promoting mutual aid on common concerns*, we are working for *conscientization* (deepening of the attitude of awareness), which is characteristic of and leads to *emergence from being enmeshed in an intolerable situation* and *the ability to intervene* in historical reality as it is unveiled (Freire 1973a). Critical education methods, as discussed in chapter 3, are used to promote reflection and action in a continuous process of moving toward transformation of people and environments. Particularly in the work phase, the responsibility for the work and for the group is the group members' (Henry 1992). The worker may have a variable or peripheral role during this phase. At the ending of the empowerment group, the worker may at times return to a more central position to help members move on from the experience maintaining their gains in empowerment (Henry 1992).

Worker Role

The worker is a coinvestigator who stimulates dialogue. She poses critical questions, shares of herself, helps codify, and stimulates the decoding activities in which the members reflect and act in a process of praxis (Freire 1973a). Pence speaks of the worker's role in helping group members to become critical thinkers: "to give form to the process of probing deeper, looking wider, bringing together the personal and the political" (1987:10).

Henry (1992) notes that the worker's role taking must also relate to the *stage of development* the group is in. Stage development can vary depending on gender, age of members, and other variables (Schiller 1997).

Skills: the *group-oriented knowledge base and skills* discussed earlier differentiate this social work process from a critical education process. The worker uses social work skill to develop the mutual aid system that will do this empowerment work. He attends to the often profound and unfolding feeling levels of the work. This includes "clinical" skill in working toward the resolution of problems that arise in everyday life. It is artificial and virtually impossible to separate life's struggles from conscientization. People do not have to remain in unsolvable situations to raise consciousness. Rather, in working on the struggles and attaining some resolution, they are free to engage in reflection on the meaning and wider reasons for their struggles. This is an affective and cognitive process. Task-oriented and political skills aid the group in its action, and reflective and cognitive restructuring skills enhance the reflection process. This is a mutual aid group and it affords an opportunity to go to the next step in establishing critical understanding and praxis. In the process both worker and members are liberated from the power of oppression.

Using Codes to Stimulate Thinking, Feeling, and Acting

Group workers have long known that the use of program activities enhances the work of the group (Middleman 1968; Shulman 1991; Lee 1981; Northen 1988; Nisivoccia and Lynn 1992, 1999). The reader is referred to the explanations and example of using a code with a group in Guyana, South America in chapter 3 of this book. *Codifications* are also a program tool — one that stimulates feeling, thought, and action. Freire suggests principles to be used in choosing a picture, poem, play or enactment, photo, musical selection, or other consciousness-raising codification. First, codifications must represent situations familiar to the group members; the thematic nucleus should be neither overly explicit nor enigmatic (neither propaganda nor a puzzle or game); the codifications must objectively constitute a totality, and they must stimulate perception and knowledge; they should be inclusive of the contradictions of the area under study. Moreover, one can use simultaneous projection of different situations. The worker must listen to and challenge the perceptions and decoding with critical questions (Freire 1973a). The use of such codifications is an art and skill to develop in working with empowerment groups. Freire gives an example to show how rich this medium is and how complex. A group coordinator/worker wanted to focus on alcoholism with a group of tenement residents. He presented a scene showing a drunken man walking on the street and three young men conversing on the corner. The group participants commented that "the only one there who is productive and useful to his country is the souse who is returning home after working all day for low wages and who is worried about his family because he can't take care of their needs. He is the only worker. He is a decent worker and a souse like us." (1973a:111)

Freire analyzes the dialectics and consciousness-raising elements of the residents' responses. He concludes that the enactment disarmed denial and the residents identified themselves as alcoholic, with reasons. The meaning has to come from the group participants, and they also have to act to struggle against the obstacles to their humanization—in this case low wages, exploitation, and alcoholism (1973a).

Challenging the obstacles to the work of the group (Schwartz 1974b) could include this use of codification and consciousness raising, for it unblocks intellectualized illusions of work. The other tasks of the work phase that Schwartz describes—contributing facts and information and lending a vision—also apply to empowerment group work.

Codes are particularly helpful in middle-phase group life when the sharing of life themes has reached a certain plateau. The work may feel circular or "stuck" as group members hesitate to go to the depth below which painful experiences and feelings are hidden. Taboo thoughts and feelings are not easily shared, especially if the worker is from the dominant group. Posing critical questions as the codes are used helps to focus the work (Freire 1973a).

In the men's shelter group the worker used newspaper articles as codes. Debates and written rebuttals of the articles were used as vehicles for action and to aid the men in analyzing problems. Several of the articles depicted homeless men as lazy and "looking for a free ride"; some depicted all homeless men as addicts or mentally ill; others were analytical. In their empowerment group meetings the men joined a debate between two journalists on

what would solve the "problem of homelessness." They agreed with a complex analysis of the economy by Dennis Culhane (1990), "Single Room
Housing Won't End Homelessness," identifying with the unskilled laborers
who had little chance of good paying steady work. "Decoding" the articles
proved a powerful tool for analysis. It is unfortunate that the paper did not
publish any of their responses to the editor.

In the Successful Women's Group two themes were codified. One was
"barriers to success" and the other was "African American womanhood." On
the first theme the worker asked the group members to define success. It
was defined as personal achievement and "people-centered" accomplishments (giving back to the community). The Wall of Barriers was the code.

The members were asked to imagine and dramatically act out climbing
and pulling bricks down from a wall, which represented barriers. *The
worker posed the question, "What are the barriers to young African American women getting over the wall to success for themselves and their people?"* Amika was first to try to dramatize it. She said, "The wall is over
there. I'm going toward it. Oops," she said as she slipped and fell with a
great thud. "They greased the ground. I can't even get to the wall. Forget
it!" Everyone roared as Amika, a large, heavily built woman, dramatized
falling down in disarray. Tracey said, "It isn't really funny. Amika is right.
Some of us can't even get to the wall. The grease is prejudice and racism."
"And sexism," Ves added, "don't forget that." Shandra said, "Yeah, but
determination makes you try and you reach the wall. Like you finish high
school and you think you're somewhere, but you didn't take the right
courses to go to college, so you got to start all over again." Tracy said, "I
was angry too when I found out my diploma meant so little."

Shandra got up and started using a hammer and a chisel, saying, "And
this one you got to strike at. It's prejudice on the job. You get the job, but
they treat you like you're stupid just because you're black." She told of
how she was treated by a nurse she worked with. She unwedged the brick
and threw it down hard. Everyone applauded. Ves said, "OK Watch out!
I'm driving this bulldozer right into the wall. Later for brick by brick, or
climbing, the whole thing is coming down. Slam, crash." Everyone
cheered her on. "Wait," said Latoya, "a brick hit me, I'm hurt." She wiped
imagined blood from her head, "It's the brick of hating myself because I
believed if you're black stand back and I stood back and didn't go for

even what you all went for, a real job and all. But I survived and stand here to tell it. I'm going to get me some too!" Everyone encouraged her. Tracey got up and looked around, pretending to step over bricks as if they were dead bodies. She said, shaking her head, "We should pick up these bricks and throw them at all the racists we can find, but I guess we'd run out of bricks. Instead I'll just take one with me to remind me and my children how hard it was to get to the other side, so we don't forget where we came from or where we're going." She handed one to the worker, "Here's one for you to keep too because you didn't forget either." *The worker got up and hugged Tracey and Latoya, who were nearest.* All the women hugged each other.

The use of humor by African Americans is an adaptive mechanism. But no one should mistake the seriousness of the meanings in this dramatic enactment and decoding. Humor is also used to tell the truth. Once the group is at work, the worker can be less active, though always supportive. It was work like this that drew the group members into an in-depth understanding of their next codification on African American womanhood: the reading together of Ntozake Shange's choreopoem *For Colored Girls Who Have Considered Suicide When the Rainbow Is Enuf* (1977). After several readings of selected poems and their discussion, Tracey, who had committed some to memory, concluded:

"These are our lives. It could have gone either way for us, we too could have died, or chosen paths that lead to death of our spirits and our bodies. But we didn't because we found other women who was feeling what we were feeling and living what we was living. I will always see myself in Shandra. I will always be there for her. We found true shelter, and we found each other, and we found God in ourselves, like the poem says." "Yes," said Ves, "and we found the truth about our struggles too. And we are free—no turning back."

In this group the use of codes deepened the work. As the women identified with the characters in the poem, they explored the black women's experience together. They also began to discover African roots in the mythology and metaphors presented. They agreed to look further into African heritage and African American history.

A Children's Group: Worker and Children Learn Together

Empowerment work can be particularly effective with children and youth. Issues of competence, identity and self-esteem are intermingled with feelings about one's own community and ethnic group and other groups defined as outsiders. Violence plagues the lives of inner-city children, and they in turn may respond in many ways including fear, depression, apathy, and violence (Nisivoccia and Lynn 1999). They, like their economically advantaged counterparts are also taught a "pecking order" of subgroups in the community. Community stratification and values, both positive and negative, are reflected in children's groups. This group example takes place in a community center in a low-income, mostly African American community in southwest Florida. The children are members of a "peacemakers" group composed of ten fourth and fifth grade boys and girls who live in "rival" housing developments. Groups for girls and boys at this age are ideally not mixed gender (Northen 1988; Toseland and Rivas 1995), but same gender groups were impractical in the setting. There was a prolonged power and control (storming) stage and quite a bit of "baiting" between the boys and the girls. There were many fights before and after the tutoring session before the group was formed. The worker used activities selectively to help the group in its development.

The activity chosen for this meeting was to work together on drawing a community map on a large piece of paper . They were asked to draw what their present community looked like, who lived there, and what they hoped it might have that may not already exist. This was a *collective project in a middle-stage group meeting* intended to promote cohesion, belonging, and inclusive behavior, a norm in formation (Henry 1992; Nisivoccia and Lynn 1999)

A Meeting in the Work Phase of the Group

Anthony drew the church and a variety of people in attendance. Kenisha drew the school with a big playground. Nia drew a McDonald's and said,

"We need one here," and all agreed. James drew a food market with interesting fruits. He explained, "This is breadfruit. Jamaicans eat it. Sheena said it was good. Kenisha then said, "I hate Jamaicans. They don't talk right, they play all that soca music, they wear nappy braids, and they stink!" She moved away from the table and imitated "Jamaican dancing" mixing in lewd gestures. The other kids laughed and added to her litany except for Anthony and Sheena. Anthony said, "Y'all are acting stupid." Sheena looked down. The bedlam continued. The worker said, *"Wait, isn't Sammy Sosa from the Caribbean, and he's a baseball hero.* James said, "right and he's black and Spanish." Kenisha said she hates Spanish people too. James said his uncle was Spanish, but he didn't know from where. Kenisha was quiet. James began to draw a ball field, saying, "this is something else we need." Kenisha said baseball is stupid and so is soccer like the "Ja-boo-boos" play it. The group members laughed. She imitated seeing a cricket match. Sheena said that's not soccer, that's cricket, and explained the game. The worker said, *"Different cultures are beautiful, and we learn many new things from them. But it seems Kenisha has some strong feelings about Jamaicans, and she likes to make fun of them. Some of you may be Jamaican or have Jamaican relatives or friends. How does it feel when Kenisha does this?* Sheena said, strongly, my father is Jamaican and I am proud of him and my grandmother. You don't know how beautiful it is there, but I do. I have a book too. Kenisha laughed mockingly, but Anthony said he wanted to see the book and a cricket match. *The worker asked Sheena to bring the book next week and said she, too, would get some books and pictures to bring.* James said, "Good, Kenisha acts so dumb!" It was time to end and the children held hands in a circle and shouted, "Peacemakers," their ending ritual. *The worker said, "Today Anthony and James were peacemakers." She gave them stickers to their delight."*

In evaluating her interventions the worker, a middle-aged white student originally from Georgia, said she was exasperated at this meeting. She thought the activity chosen was a good one for their stage of group development. She was angry at Kenisha and she was sorry for Sheena's discomfort, and wanted to address prejudice and stereotypes but did not know how. She knew Sammy Sosa was Dominican, not Jamaican, but she didn't know enough about Jamaican culture to name another hero. She liked her attempt at reaching for feelings and she already had gone to the library and obtained books and pictures for the next meeting. She thought the activity was going well and that earlier in the group's life the whole meeting would have been lost if Kenisha did this. But now some group members, Anthony, James, and Sheena, were strong enough to handle it themselves and she stepped back and let them do it. In supervision the student was commended for a good try at handling a difficult moment in group life and for matching an activity with the stage of the group's development. She also assessed her strengths and weaknesses in intervening and the group's stage of development well. She was encouraged to help the group members to bring out their stereotypes and feelings about other groups, even if this was uncomfortable for members, so discussion and learning could take place. When asked what she would have rather said than the comment about Sosa, she said she wanted to say that stereotypes were wrong and define them with the group. When asked what held her back, she said fear of Kenisha's temper and of making it worse. The worker and supervisor role-played how she might do this. She realized she needed to reach for Kenisha's anger and then talk about stereotyping. She said she would help them define stereotypes and prejudice and use the picture books she found to dispel stereotypes. When asked if she has encountered her own stereotypes and prejudices, she smiled, remembering her own preconceptions and reflected on how different each of the children in the group was and how she had lumped them all together as "dysfunctional low-income African American kids" before getting to know them. She also recalled that she had been scared to go to the community at first. She realized that Kenisha and all the group members experience racism in Florida and that she also needs to open the work to include all their experiences of prejudice and discrimination. She noted that she would be careful not to "moralize" about stereotypes against any one group, including Jamaicans. She thought she also needed to promote difference in the group and cultural awareness. She decided to take the approach of "learning together" about prejudice, discrimination, and different cultures.

The Next Meeting

After Sheena and the worker shared their books and pictures with the group, Kenisha, calmly this time, said she wanted the worker to get a book on African Americans too. The worker said she would do that for next time.

She wondered if Kenisha felt African Americans were not getting enough credit here today and here in Florida. Kenisha looked directly at her and said yes. The worker agreed, and invited the children to share how prejudice felt to them. Each one poured out a story of hurt experienced personally or by a family member. Moved almost to tears, she said they were all excellent teachers and that she felt badly about the stereotypes she had of them and their community before knowing them. Anthony replied by giving her a sticker for "good work!" The group moved into a solid middle phase of work and intimacy after this hurdle was crossed. It is important as workers to encounter the obstacles of ethnocentrism, racism, and classism within ourselves even as we help group members to do this.

Saying Their Own Word—Raising Conscousness Together

Clients may be more courageous to say their own words in the group than in the one to one, particularly if they differ with the worker. The *power and authority* of the worker is equalized in the group by the strength in numbers (Northen 1988). Workers must welcome and encourage this *dialectical process.*

In a group at the shelter for women and children the clients teach the workers their own meanings of the word *ghetto*, and it is a powerful lesson. (This occurs in the context of discouragement over the freeze on Section 8 and other rental subsidy programs. The workers are J. and G. (who is also a religious sister). The shelter residents are angry at J., their social worker, because they think she is "dragging her feet." (G. records.)

J. said, "I know it is hard for you, living in the ghetto and . . ." She was cut off by Vanecia, who said, "What is that you said?" Delores also reacted. Vanecia said, "We are not in a GHETTO." *J. asked what Vanecia understood by the word.* She replied, "It's a place where everyone is alike and where people are low class. You can say [the name of the town] or a poor section, but this is not a ghetto." Delores said she too was offended by the word. We are all seen as the same and we're not. *I asked, "Is the word* ghetto *associated with being stereotyped?"* Vanecia said, "Exactly," and elaborated. She asked the other women what they thought. Betty said she did not mind the word, and the others spoke of its historic meaning and literal meaning. *J. said she had not meant it as an offense but to convey that she knew they were up against many obstacles. J. and I then said that it was good to hear their meanings."* [Backing up and welcoming views.]

This excerpt shows workers who are open to learning from group members. These are difficult practice moments. If workers are defensive and insist on their authority, the client is robbed of the chance to say her own word and define her own reality, and the worker is robbed of new meaning. A fruitless "battle of wills" may not only obscure the work but reinforce the view that clients who are members of oppressed groups should bow to "greater authority," when in fact it is their own authority that must be affirmed. Similarly, when workers are of the dominant groups (here, white), they must expect to be challenged and welcome the symbolic and actual challenge to the oppressor group. This too is hard for the worker, who is also a struggling human being who seeks positive response and acceptance.

Later in the same meeting:
    Delores said, "Lucy left the shelter because J. did not help her enough." J. said, "Together we may be able to speak to politicians and legislators about the freeze on Section 8, and she would love to be able to help them do that, but as a single person she can't help them get Section 8 while there is a freeze. She wishes she could." Delores said, "They ought to try living on this amount of money without subsidy." Vanecia turned to me and asked if I ever had it hard and faced discrimination. I said, "Sure I have! All women face discrimination." I shared examples from treatment by an auto mechanic and about the place of women in the church hierarchy. J. shared her treatment by the legal system when she was going through a divorce. Several were nodding in understanding, but some seemed in disbelief, so I asked if they thought white women had it easy. Donna said, "Not easy but not the same as us." I said, "African American women are up against racism, and that's on top of how women are treated." Vanecia said, "True, but you all can't know what it's like to be black. It's like people who drink. No one can understand unless they're alcoholic too." Delores said, "Lucy and I understood each other because we know what it is to want that drink. But we also cared and listened to each other. People who are different can understand

if they care and listen. You don't have to be the same." The others agreed with Delores. Betty said, "We know you both care." I said, "But we do need to listen better." Vanecia agreed and added, "J. and you have said that blacks have to overcome racism, but it's not us that need to deal with them; it's them that need to deal with us." I said, "Yes, and we need to learn to live, learn, and work with each other." (Nods in agreement.) J. said she thought Vanecia was right, that it is the oppressor that needs to change, but today she felt like they were expressing their anger toward all of white America toward her. Vanecia and Delores said she was right. J. said she was glad they expressed that anger, that it was a lot to have inside. Vanecia said it did feel good to get it out.

This was another difficult moment in the group. The theme returns to listening to people who struggle. They are the experts and the teachers. The workers listen and learn once again. They deal openly with racism and oppression. They stay close to the clients and abandon all easy formulations. In listening and learning, each one ("client" and worker) says her own word and is potentially transformed in the saying.

Developing Critical Thinking

Critical thinking is central to empowerment. In the following examples groups consider a critical question. They are asked to analyze on the personal, institutional/political, and cultural levels. The first skill was asking the critical question, *"What forces created your homelessness?"*

The Successful Women

In response to the critical question, Amika responded, "I had trouble classing myself as homeless. It wasn't me. I wasn't the poorest of the poor. I had a home, but the woman I was sharing it with didn't pay the landlord. I was houseless but not homeless." [Amika is defining her own terms.] "The problem was I couldn't afford a place by myself." Ves asked, "But why did you let the other woman manage the money?" Amika said, "Because it was her place legally. But I learned from that to manage your own money." Tracey said, "That's just it. I didn't know how to manage on my own. I shouldn't have been homeless either. I had family, but they had no room for three more when my marriage broke up." She told the story of how she went to an awful shelter where she was almost raped by a male resident before she found space at this shelter. *The worker and other women empathized deeply with her.* [Conveying empathy.] Tracey said, "That *was* horrible, but it was also frightening to be twenty-one years old and on your own with two children." Shandra said she felt exactly the same way.

I said, "That is hard." [Empathizing.] *"I hear two themes here. One has to do with the lack of preparation of young women for making it on their own and the other is that there is no affordable housing at this time. These are two hard problems to analyze. We have to analyze the personal part of it, the institutional/systems part, and the cultural part, what society dictates. Where shall we begin?"* [Clarifying the themes; Asking for analysis and for their direction.] Tracey said, "With ourselves. Why weren't we taught to make it on our own?" Ves said, "It's because we are women and other people own you. First your family, then your man. Then your boss," Tracey added. Shandra said she wound up paying her mother's bills for her. Ves said, "I once thought that girl children were born to be slaves—everyone says, 'Do this for me; do that.' Boys don't get used that way usually. Amika said she was raised by two aunts. One treated her like a slave, but the other treated her like a queen. Tracey said she was treated well too, but that didn't prepare her for life on her own because her family thought her husband would take care of her. "If somebody takes care of you, they own you," she said.

The worker asked, "What do you make of the thinking you've come up with?" [The worker asks for reflection on their critical thinking.] Amika said, "Until you can take care of yourself, you are not your own person. One of my aunts depended on her boyfriend. I started to fall into that too, it's easy, but it got me homeless." Ves said, "You must not let anyone own you. Black people were slaves to white people, but women are slaves to anyone who holds the money and takes care of financial matters. I definitely do that for myself. If you're on State, the state runs your life; if you let a man pay your way, he runs it." Amika said, "Men run your life even when they don't pay anything." They all laughed. Ves said, "It is true. We let men take us down. But that's up to us; we have to own ourselves, and the man has to own himself—then it's two equals, like I said to Trevor." "Yes," said Tracey, "but the black man has a hard time owning himself." Amika said, "My aunt can remember when they hung black men in Alabama for trying to own themselves." Shandra said, "Wasn't Martin Luther King Jr. about all of us owning ourselves?" The worker said, "So black men and women have had to fight against racism forever, and it's vicious. White domination is a common enemy of all people of color, regardless of sex." [Validating their perceptions of the experience of racism and clarifying the struggle.] "Yes," said Ves, "it's true, but, still, the black woman cannot be owned by the black man either!" "Right," said Tracey. "We know black men have it hard, but so do we, and we should not be punished for it. We have to work together with our men to advance our people—but not one above the other." "One next to the other," said Shandra, "Together." All agreed. Ves said," That's why I got a good job and I run my own life." Shandra said, "I work and I pay the bills, but other people still can control me." Ves said, "This is the summation—don't be anybody's slave!" *The worker said they had pretty thoroughly analyzed the personal level of homelessness and in fact they went way beyond that to the cultural level of a universal woman's struggle with being her own person, not in service to someone else.* "Now, why aren't there affordable apartments for people on modest incomes? Especially for poor people of color?" [The worker asked for institutional and cultural analyses.]

Tracey said, "There's no low-cost housing down here because of racism. If we don't have a decent place to live or good schools or jobs, we can't get up there where the white man is." Ves said, "If there was an equal start, if all people had decent housing, we just might beat them at their game. We're already good in sports—OK. They allow that. But we could be just as good at science or business or running the country." "No," Amika laughed. "They sure don't want that!" Ves said, "Sometimes I think it's too much to know. But if we all knew this, we'd have to change things." "Things will change," Tracey answered. "We do know!" Group members went on to specify issues at the local level that related to the Rental Assistance Program.

The worker experienced a pull in the work when the members talked about problems with men. Should she ask for particular stories and deepen the personal work? The risk is that the particulars might obscure the moment of analysis and raising consciousness, which moved into planning action. At this juncture she did not ask for the particulars, but she did in the next meeting.

In a moving and powerful way, Ves then shared that she had been in a physically abusive relationship that led to a brief psychiatric hospitalization and her move here from another part of the state. That's why she was so sure of how to set up the "ground rules" now. She gave intense and painful details. Latoya, who had been absent in the earlier meeting, then shared her history of two physically abusive relationships. The group members warned her about the man she was currently seeing, as he was a drug dealer known for his violence. Latoya and Amika both struggled with what they called their "need for a man" (sexually and emotionally) and what this did to their judgment. Shandra did not share her similar situation in the group, but she listened carefully.

Shandra's story is told in chapters 7, 8, and 9. Perhaps the worker needed to ask each woman whether she had ever been in a similar situation to help Shandra unlock this dangerous secret.

At the Shelter for Women and Children

Present for the meeting at the shelter for women and children are eight young women; five are African American and three are Puerto Rican. We have met the workers for the group earlier: J., the regular social worker for the shelter, and G., who records this meeting. The group members have invited the agency's executive director, J.B., to the meeting.

In response to the question about the *forces that created their home-lessness,* Michaela discusses her cocaine addiction. Although most studies of "the homeless" neglect substance abuse, experience in the field indicates that most homeless men and many homeless women struggle with substance abuse issues on either the personal or interpersonal level (Lee and Nisivoccia 1997; Lee 1997). Blau (1992) documents this but questions its cyclical nature: Which comes first, homelessness or substance abuse? In either event shelters must be responsive to the issue; otherwise they enable addiction. Moreover, it illuminates the need for adequate residential treatment facilities for women with children. This is Michaela's second time at the shelter, although she completed a drug treatment program and had good housing.

Michaela said, "I messed up again and here I am. I'm glad to be here and I'm glad for the curfew because sometimes I get the taste again." *I asked if she was saying that having a curfew helps her to stay away from drugs.* She said, "Yes, it does, and also the shelter policy that makes addicts go to Twelve-Step meetings helps." [Clarifying what helps.] Others nodded.

J. asked if anyone else had a similar problem with drugs. Ramona said that she "felt the pressure" where she was previously living but that since she came to the shelter she had not had any alcohol. *J. noted how peer pressure is a problem, and that there is another part of the disease, the physiological desire for drugs or alcohol, but that "no one outside of ourselves can make us drink."* [Providing information.] Michaela said that was right and talked about how she had gone to NA and AA meetings to help her. *I said, "This is what the group is about . . . talking about and helping each other with those things that brought them down . . . to the point that they became homeless."* [Contracting; Lending a vision.] The group members indicated that they have had to "do it alone." *I said, "It can be very difficult alone" and suggested that while they are here they might be able to help one another and possibly continue to help one another after they leave here.* [Encouraging mutual aid.]

Dora said, "Finding an apartment is the easy part. The difficult part is keeping it." *I said, "That is right and we have begun to hear from some group members that it was drugs or alcohol that brought them down.* [Offering the opportunity and demand for work.] Dora said she does pot [marijuana] but she has never done alcohol or other drugs like the other members. *J. said that pot is much more potent now than it was a few years back. I replied that whether it is pot, harder drugs like cocaine and crack, or alcohol, they are all drugs.* [Giving information.] Ramona and Michaela said that they all get you high, and the group members agreed. Ramona described how addicts often exchange food for drugs and how they will use food money for drugs and then say they do not have any money. *I nodded and asked if drugs were a problem for those who had been quiet up until now or if they had other things that brought them here.* [Reaching for silent members.] Elena said her situation was different. She told the group how she was with her husband since she was sixteen and that when she was pregnant with her second child he died. Everyone was moved by Elena's story. Dora told the group how her mother drank and let her down as a child and that she was raised by her grandmother.

They had to "do it" alone. (At this point they all had tears in their eyes.) *After a moment of quiet I asked how they picked themselves up from such difficult experiences in the past.* [Encouraging reflection and coping.] The women named faith in God and support from others (including fellow group members) as means of coping. Dora spoke of the racism of absentee landlords and of taking legal action against neglectful landlords. J.B. quietly entered the group during this time and was nodding and encouraging the members.

A very special and rare level of work follows as the workers, particularly J.B., the agency executive director, shared feelings about the women's struggles against racism and about being part of the oppressor group. Racism diminishes all of us. The bond of caring and suffering here is powerful.

Dora continued that at first she did not believe she could complete her nontraditional job training, but she did, and now she believed that she could do whatever she set out to do. *J. said she believed that.* [Encouraging her.] *I added that many might presume that first, as women, we are not as capable as men, and that, as women of color, they are not as capable as whites, especially in jobs white men have had. That is the nature of sexism and racism.* [Naming oppression; Moving from the personal to the political.] Dora said she almost believed it herself. She proved them wrong, but she shouldn't have to prove ignorance wrong. The others nodded, agreeing. *J. said, "It is awful. They are going to have a harder time than whites, but they are there to make a better life for themselves, and they can do it."* [Lending a vision.] Elena and Michaela were quietly crying. *J.B. said she was glad that J. had said this. Racism was very real. She had seen a movie the night before,* Heat Wave, *which was about the racial riots of the late 1960s. The group members had seen it too. J.B. began to get filled up. She said she knew that much of what they were going through was related to being young women of color in a world that has been cruel and unfair to blacks and Hispanics.* J.B. was crying at this point and Michaela held her hand. *She said that she was ashamed of being white because of this and because of what the police did to the blacks during the 1960s and sometimes now too, there had been a recent incident in the neighborhood.* [Owning being part of the oppressor group and how painful it is.] Dora said she knew the family where the young boy was killed by a policeman. Michaela, Dora, and Elena were also crying at this point. *After a moment of silence I said, "Maybe we can begin changing this by being together and talking like this. Hopefully, these times can help us to stand together rather than any one voice standing alone." J.B. said, "We are all sisters and we need to use that unity." She suggested that they might be able to begin to trust here, where it is safe.* [Lending a vision.] There was considerable nodding of heads and wiping of eyes.

I said I thought they had done a lot of hard work that day. I noted how the work of empowerment looks at the things that each person needs to do in order to take responsibility for her own situation as well as to look at bigger things, such as racism, that are outside of themselves. I suggested that they might be able to continue to help one another throughout the week in informal ways and that we would also continue next week. [Sessional ending skills.] *J. said she knew that a lot of hard work was done because of the real tears that were shared.* [Crediting the work.] Michaela, Elena, and Dora said they felt better after having cried. The group began to break up into a number of different conversations, and the meeting ended.

Empowerment groups emerge from empowering agencies. This agency worked at using an empowerment approach in all its programs and practices. The vision was one of "women helping women," which reached across eth-class and racial lines. Although the agency had grown to four programs under her leadership, Judy Beaumont, the executive director, sometimes still did "front-line practice." She attended groups when invited to maintain connections to the women and learn from them—to know and be known by them. The sharing that took place in this meeting is not an everyday occurrence, but it is a natural outflow of this philosophy of practice. Staff, consultants, and board members may be helped by the residents as much as they are there to help. This can happen when all levels of staff live a sisterhood/empowerment philosophy and practice authentic sharing of self across artificial divides (Lee et al. 1997). Residents also participated in the hiring practices of the agency and served on the board of directors.

Another example occurred in a board of directors meeting when G., who is also one of the program directors, presented the empowerment base of the work in all of the programs. Four residents of the transitional living facility also shared their experiences of empowerment. In return, the two alumnae on the board and several other board members shared similar experiences and words of encouragement. A young resident from Puerto Rico concluded:

I see here something I never saw in my life. Women are running this meeting, they are running this agency, and they do what I thought only men could do. But there is no difference among these women, or should I say among us. We are all human together, all helping each other. I have decided to go to college, because I know now I can do it. I want to become a social worker to be a woman helping women too.

Empowerment Group Work in a Psychosocial Rehabilitation Agency

Marshall Rubin, of Groups That Work, Inc., based in Tucson, Arizona, is an empowerment-oriented social worker and group work consultant who practices nationally and internationally in the area of psychosocial rehabilitation. He notes that the PSR (Psychosocial Rehabilitation) setting seeks to provide normative experiences usually including vocational and personal services geared toward prevention of unnecessary hospitalization and the enhancement of assuming productive roles in community life for people with a history of psychiatric hospitalization and/or developmental disabilities. Such settings are purposefully informal to reduce the psychological distance between staff and members as active participants in program planning. Rubin sees the worker's role in PSR settings as one of mediator (congruent with the definition of William Schwartz in Schwartz 1994) and empowerment coach (Lee 1996). He sees the empowerment approach as supportive of the principles of PSR including working from strengths, normalizing, developing and maintaining relationships, supporting attempts at growth, interacting with the larger community, providing a wide spectrum of involvement, and fostering interdependence (Rubin 1999). "Empowerment group principles are particularly applicable to the emphasis that PSR agencies place on involvement of members in governance functions of the agency. *Thinking empowerment* will help the group worker manage the quality of membership, sense of connectedness and common purpose throughout the PSR agency. This is equally important for staff groups" (Rubin 1999). In his consultation to PSR agencies Rubin advises regular house meetings and a resident advisory council as well as group meetings for all levels of staff, from kitchen staff on up, and a variety of group opportunities for members. For example, in one residence a debate club was a success. Menu planning and nutrition groups as well as social planning and residents relations committees are also important smaller group adjuncts to house meetings. He cautions against staff members using house meetings as reinforcement of authoritative control. He views house meetings as a "forum to promote opportunities for residents and staff to share authority and responsibility for decisions and the quality of relationships pertinent to the operation of the House."

A Freedom House Meeting

Freedom House is a group residence for men and women of various ages and ethnic groups who have formerly been institutionalized for chronic mental illness. Twelve Freedom House residents met on this occasion with Alberta, a staff member who is the group worker. Ray, another staff member, was also present. *Alberta began by asking the group members to help build the day's agenda.* Mary added three items, including van safety, chores not getting done, and messy bathrooms. She also announced a birthday party for herself. Alberta noted these items and asked for others. Dora mentioned the "stealing issue." Max agreed, adding that his cigarettes were stolen. Ray brought up the issue of "picking up cigarette butts." *Alberta then began, following the agenda agreed upon by group members.* When the agenda got to food planning and suggestions, the members were enthusiastic. They debated the merits of real crab meat versus imitation crab meat and shared recipes. Mary suggested group members learn how to cook themselves. Joe said he was not interested in cooking though others were. *Alberta summed up, some want to learn and some don't.* Jen complained of food on the weekend and *Alberta asked for sandwich ideas.* Several gave suggestions.

There then followed a heated discussion on cigarette butts. *Alberta decided those who smoke will pick up the butts, and those who don't can pick up papers.* Stealing also brought some lively responses. *Alberta suggested using a lock box,* but Dora replied that she would rather catch whoever is doing it. *Alberta suggested filing a police report.* Jen, who was robbed, had not reported it. *As the meeting drew to a close, Alberta asked members if there were some positive things to share.* Dora noted it was Jen's birthday, and the group congratulated her and Mary. Roy shared his happiness because his family was coming for a visit. Mary said proudly that the group did a lot of good work today, and the meeting ended on that note.

The house meeting was empowering to residents as they have a say in what goes on in the residence. Alberta did well in asking member input on the agenda. The consultant noted that sharing the agenda is a good way of sharing authority with the group, and soliciting this ahead of time and having a copy of the agenda for each member also shares power. Similarly, he suggested that minutes be made available to all members before the meeting. The group worker was effective in holding to the agenda but might have allowed group members to respond and problem solve more fully before deciding how the cigarette butt and stealing issues should be handled. The pull between "finishing an agenda" and promoting the group's ownership and work on their issues is a difficult balancing act. The consultant noted that feelings were overlooked in the rush to complete the agenda, particularly around the issue of stealing. Using a free form house meeting style may allow more latitude in helping residents to express feelings and work on the issues that concern them. There is also a middle ground in which an agenda is used for structure but tabled when charged issues are brought up. Indeed the group did do good work at this house meeting (Rubin 1999).

In a Feminist Agency: An Empowerment Group for Battered and Addicted Women

The Elizabeth Cady Stanton Agency was set up to meet the needs of battered women in a rural area. The staff was not trained in social work, but a second-year social work student initiated a group based on empowerment theory for women who struggled with both addiction to drugs and physical abuse. The members named the group the "Connections Group." Eight members joined the group, which was described as an empowerment group to aid in recovery from addiction and abusive relationships. They were asked also to reflect on their statuses as poor and working-class women and members of ethnic communities in the context of oppression. This contract offer was made clear in pregroup and early group meetings and was eagerly accepted. The women (in their thirties through fifties) represented Irish-American, Italian-American, Native American, and Puerto Rican ethnic groups. They all resided in a cluster of economically depressed towns where factories were closing, and most families were touched by alcoholism. Half of the women abused drugs as well as alcohol. The women were all in early to middle stages of recovery and were using AA and NA groups. The worker used an educational approach centered around women and addiction while promoting reflection and praxis on the areas of ethclass, gender, and battering.

The women worked hard. Only one woman chose to remain in her abusive relationship. They made the connections that being drunk or high made them more vulnerable to battering and that choosing recovery meant choosing life-giving relationships. Those who began new relationships chose nonabusive ones with men who were not addicted to substances. They made a connection between patterns of drinking or doing drugs that occurred after being beaten. They also connected the fact that, for the hard drug users, their male partners had introduced them to the drug "to keep me under his thumb forever." These connections helped them break into the circularity of battering and substance abuse.

Initially, the women used slogans from books on "codependency" or "women who love too much," which short-circuited their understanding of their complex situations. The worker observed that the women bought into the theories that conveniently blamed themselves for a disease and a man's violence. While encouraging members to take full responsibility for their own recovery, the worker insisted that the women use their own language to name their struggles and make their own connections. They used a good deal of role-play and enactment.

The worker reflected: "Handing women a framework like codependency on which to hang all their unhappiness is not honoring their desires and abilities to name their own problems and to solve them." She had them discuss areas like the depressed economy, job loss, ethnic heritage, and cultural and institutional supports for alcoholism and drug use and woman battering. The group members taught each other about their ethnic heritages.

In sixteen sessions they developed understanding of themselves, their families, and their communities in new ways that empower them. They have begun to understand their oppression in terms of their daily lives and to take responsibility for themselves in that context. In the last meeting a Native American group member, Martha RedCloud, expressed how she was empowered through the group, and others echoed similar kinds of awareness:

I grew up on a reservation. Almost everyone I knew there was drunk. The families had a lot of problems. I don't know what I felt most ashamed of, my people being drunks or my people being Indian. I was also ashamed to be a woman. Since that time I have learned that this was never the way my people set out to be; we have been killed, tortured, and maimed by the white man, for his purposes. I have found out that we have a whole culture, a Native American way of living that is completely different from the way that I grew up. My life on the reservation was us living like how the white man wanted us to be, a bunch of drunks too powerless to get up in the morning, let alone to raise our kids with pride in our culture. Then I got involved with men who hurt me; they hit me, insulted me; it was as if I let them hurt me the way white people treated Indians. I realized my people must no longer accept that exploitation and treatment and I must no longer accept it either. I realized that if I maintain my recovery, I can help my people, and that is what it really means to be an Indian woman—one who passes on a rich heritage.

Information/Knowledge Is Power

In this example we can see the importance of sharing knowledge in empowerment practice with groups. The workers shared information on battering and on the disease of alcoholism that helped members take control of their lives. As the women taught themselves and each other about their ethnic heritages, stereotypes were corrected and challenged. For Martha RedCloud learning and sharing her heritage freed her to make sense of her life in a new way. She was not an isolated alcoholic woman; she was part of a people who were politically controlled by alcohol throughout history. She did the research to discover this and shared it with the others.

In a Men's Shelter Empowerment Group: Adding Education to Support

Ricky tearfully spoke about losing a best friend to AIDS. Some of the other men offered consolation and to go to the funeral with him. Ricky accepted the offer and then admitted he was afraid of getting AIDS, as he had shared needles in the past. This brought out many questions on the transmission of the HIV virus. The worker and some of the men offered accurate information; others shared frightening mythology. The worker suggested that the men obtain information on AIDS and share it in the next meeting. Two men went to the library and brought back extensive materials. The worker also obtained flyers to hand out to all residents. The men's group then planned for a speaker from the Health Department so they could ask questions. The men from the group chaired and moderated this well-attended meeting. This was a potentially life-saving educational effort. A peer-led approach to AIDS education involved the residents in a dynamic and vital way.

A Residential Support Program for Formerly Homeless Women

In an empowerment group in a scattered-site residential support program for chronically mentally ill formerly homeless women the members work on dealing with demystifying and destigmatizing mental illness. The members are five African American women and a white (German-English) woman (Gina) between the ages of twenty-six and fifty-six. The worker is G., who is also the program director.

Gina said she wanted to bring a problem to the group for help. She described being upset because her new boyfriend did not call and she was thinking so fast that she couldn't slow her thoughts down. She began to think the TV was speaking to her, and then she knew she was freaking out. The other women validated that getting upset could get you sick. *I asked, "What helps when this happens?"* Brenda asked if she was taking her medication. She said she was but that she might need more now. Nelly said that when she has "man trouble," she sits down and writes and that that slows her down. Vicky said she could call one of them or another friend on the phone. Nelly said, "You could also tell yourself that the TV voices are not really talking to you. I say to myself, 'It's not real: I know it's not real.'" Gina said that that might help because she was too confused to write or call. Ida advised a walk or exercise. Gina said that she usually takes a walk but that it was too late. Brenda and Ida said that it was good thinking not to walk at night.

Then Nelly said angrily that no one knows what it's like to live with mental illness and they "blame you for it, call you crazy, and treat you with disrespect." All agreed. Nelly added, "It is really a chemical imbalance." Brenda said, "Yes." *I asked Nelly if she could say something about that.* She said, "Mental illness is from a chemical imbalance, and that is why we have to take medication." She went into a description of how unfair it is that they have to take medication that dopes them up but helps stop the voices. *I said, "I dislike the fact that their medications are the best way the doctors can treat their illnesses. Hopefully, in time they will have better ways of treating mental illness."* Vicky said, "It is unfair! They should do more to find a better way of dealing with illness." She added that she did not understand what happened to her. She wondered if it was the change of life or the drinking she did ten years ago that made her ill. Gina said she heard that people change every five years, and their medications need to be adjusted to those changes. *I agreed that "everyone changes as we . . ."* Gina said, "Mature." *I said, "Yes, and that can affect how they respond to medication and stress."* Vicky began to ask questions about her illness. *I said, "There is new information being learned about some types of mental illness." I explained how some bipolar studies are indicating that for some people with that illness there seems to be a problem with a chromosome. "Other studies are indicating that some other forms of mental illness involve a problem with the messages being sent from one brain cell to another." (I explained this more fully with analogies.)* Everyone was very interested in this information. *I said, "They are clearly not responsible for bringing mental illness on themselves."* Nelly said, "If this is so, people should treat them with greater understanding." "And we should be kinder to ourselves too," Brenda added.

Knowledge/information helps to free people from self-blame and self-depreciation. The coping mechanisms they use are very important to share. This group has invited speakers and participated in activities of self-help groups that educate about mental illness and advocate for the rights of people with mental illness. But as African Americans and poor women they also find solidarity and identity in political activity that benefits all poor women.

Taking Action and Reflecting on It: Guiding Praxis

Taking action and reflecting on it is central to empowerment group work. The action can be critical reflection, writing a letter or a creative work, or taking direct political action. The worker's role is to guide the group in this process of praxis and, where possible, to facilitate success in the action.

In this excerpt members of the group discuss an action taken and the worker contributes facts.

The group began by talking about the "Rebuild America" walk and rally group members attended last week. Ida proudly described how she shook Jesse Jackson's hand and that she walked in the front of the march near Jesse. Valerie and Ida described the purpose of the march, which was to bring attention to the problems that cities and towns are facing. *I added that it was also to request that more money be given to cities and towns to deal with problems that group members deal with, such as housing needs, drug activity, social services, and the general decay of our cities.* Ida quoted Jackson that it's not just minorities who are poor. She recalled how Jesse stated that there are more white people on welfare than minorities. Brenda said, "That is not the image that is shown on TV—that black folks are shown."

Vicky said, "All of us who are poor need to get together and talk to the decision makers so that we can be heard, like we did a few weeks ago. Ida told the group how the legislator we visited did not know much about state and city assistance and that our visit helped her to learn about who does and does not qualify for assistance. Ida added that the state representative told us it is important not to come too late for them to do anything about our requests. The group members said they were interested in meeting with legislators again this fall to "educate" the legislators and to listen to what the legislators plan to do in response to their meetings with us.

Ida said, "It is important not just to have hope but to act on it as we have done." She went on to say that she thought it was really smart how Jesse set up voter registration at the rally. It was so simple, but really important. She told the group how she could not complain about President Bush because she did not vote, but she registered at the rally. She said her one vote would probably not make a difference but that she would vote. *I added, "Legislators will listen to people more if they know that those talking are registered voters."* We went on to verify who is registered and who would take the others to register.

Ida said, "It is important for people who are talking to be knowledgeable about the issue." She told us that people do not have to have a master's degree and that just being able to talk is not enough. People have to have knowledge. She described how Rev. Jackson was so effective because he knew the information about this state and that we too need to get the information *necessary* to discuss something. She noted that Jesse said Hartford *is* the poorest city in the nation and Connecticut is the richest state in the country.

The women in this group were politically active during the elections and continue their legislative activity. Additional examples of political action will be given in chapter 13.

Empowerment Begins at Home

Agencies that utilize an empowerment approach to practice must be prepared to have group members react critically to the nearest environment, the agency itself. These efforts by group members signal that the process is working well and must be encouraged and welcomed. Yet it isn't easy to look at agency practices critically through the clients' eyes and revise accordingly. We turn to the efforts of members of an empowerment group in a men's shelter.

The group members were concerned with several issues at the shelter. They identified concerns and suggestions and circulated a petition to obtain wide support for their views. They then invited the assistant program director to their meeting to discuss the issues that were listed in the petition as follows:

1. Health concerns—we suggest that
    a) The "Protocol and Health Guidelines for Homeless Shelters" be reviewed by staff and that sections pertaining to lice and scabies be posted on the bulletin board.
    b) An elevated floor mat for the shower area be provided.
    c) The staff person ask offending guests to shower.
    d) The blankets be washed twice a week.
2. Disciplinary protocol concerns
3. We suggest considering alternative solutions when a resident is dismissed for a first-time minor offense.
4. Protocol for guests and staff relations
    a) Only a staff person will be allowed into closets.
    b) We request that staff persons begin directing new shelter guests to an empowerment group member for an informal orientation.

Mr. _____, we, as members of the Empowerment Group, feel that the preceding concerns are highly important to us and the general residency of the shelter. We appreciate your immediate serious attention to these matters and we look forward to your utmost conscientious reply.

Sincerely,
[Each group member and several residents signed.]

The "health concerns" and "protocol for guests and staff relations" ideas were well received and implemented after some discussion. However, their concerns for "disciplinary protocols" were not readily accepted. The men felt that temporary "disciplinary dismissals" were necessary when a guest was a danger to other guests but that "minor infractions" were handled arbitrarily. Hence they sought a revision of the existing grievance procedure to include guest/resident involvement in the process.

Charles noted that their city welfare benefits had been lowered so the shelter could receive payment for their stay, so they should have some rights to protect themselves against dismissal for minor infractions and to bring an unfair dismissal grievance within forty-eight hours. Harry felt that, payment or not, guests have human rights that have to be protected. Ricky noted the inconsistency of staff members and that guidelines would make for fairness.

Luis proposed organizing the guests to petition for the shelter to be opened twenty-four hours a day. Everyone agreed but decided to attend to the grievance process first and Luis's idea second.

The men drafted another petition that proposed a forty-eight-hour grievance procedure that included the aggrieved person and a trusted staff member and a guest review committee to act in an ombudsman role for aggrieved guests.

Although guest/resident participation in the grievance process was met with resistance, the group obtained the forty-eight-hour limit for the procedure, and a guest is now a mandated member of all review procedures. Through the involvement of the group members and their worker in the statewide Coalition for the Homeless (now called the Coalition to End Homelessness), this success was spread throughout all shelters in the state. The name change of the coalition is reflective of the raised consciousness of this group, which has adopted an empowerment approach. The efforts of the coalition have ensured that most shelters in the state are now open twenty-four hours a day and that services are provided.

Ending Empowerment Groups

The principles and skills related to ending any helping endeavor apply to the ending of empowerment groups. Henry (1992) notes that the termination stage of group life has its own distinctive dynamics: the worker returns to a primary role and central location and group-ending program media are used. Feelings about separation are a theme, and the worker needs to reach for these complex feelings in order to help group members let go and move on. In a sense members may have one foot in the past and the other in the future. Regressions may take place. In an especially poignant last group meeting, the *pre-teen girls* in Brooklyn Community Center locked the worker out of the room and uprooted the plants they had been growing, throwing them at one another. They were very angry that the group had to end and symbolically threatened to undo all the good that was done. As the worker regained entry and acknowledged the feelings, the girls returned to valuing what they had done, putting the little plants back in their pots with the worker's help.

In a last meeting *of developmentally disabled teens* one member pulled the blinds down, enclosing the room in darkness. He sang, "There's no sunshine when you're gone" as the others hummed along tearfully. The worker acknowledged the loss of the group and of her presence with them, for the group was scheduled to resume in the future with a new worker. She said she would miss them and everyone hugged. She then asked them to focus on what they had accomplished. Each one replied, looking back on individual and group achievements; then Paul said, "I learned I am as good as anyone in this world," and the members agreed that summed it up. The members then brought out a cake they had bought, which was inscribed to the worker, and the leaving turned into a celebration of friendships. Henry suggests that the work of separation is recapitulation and evaluation and stabilizing and generalizing the changes made. Program activities can help members in recapitulation. In *a substance abuse facility's multifamily group*, members sculpted how they started in the group and how they were as it ended to visualize the growth (Henry 1992). In a group of *middle school girls who had experienced violence*, the workers had the girls make each other cards, and the sentiments in the cards were developed into a group poem for each one to keep along with a group picture. One girl who had come to the U.S. from a wartorn country shared that she felt safe here now that she had made some friends. The others shared that they were learning to trust again too (Nisivoccia and Lynn 1999). Henry (1992) also notes that as the group ends members need to feel strong on their own, to individuate and own personal as well as group gains. In one group the members drew self-portraits to show the differences in beginning and ending the group. There are many ways we can help members own their gains and feel confident about moving on.

There are some variations depending on agency setting. Empowerment groups in settings involving transient populations continue while individual members leave. The leaving of individuals should be noted and celebrated. The feelings of the departing members regarding the meaning of the group and its loss, as well as work on what lies ahead for them, can also be grist for the mill. The members' achievements that enable them to leave the service may offer motivation to others. The feelings of those left behind are extremely important. In one *women's shelter group* a member who remained noted, "I'm happy for everyone who's going, but I don't know what I'm doing wrong." It is hard to remain behind when others leave. Additionally, it is important to note the accomplishments of the group as a whole. The use of "minutes" or a scrapbook can help in this. Some groups leave behind a legacy of action and achievement for the next cohort to build on. These precious gains must be counted, for they give foundation to the work ahead.

Some empowerment groups, like the Successful Women, come to a natural end as group members assess that personal and group goals have been accomplished and life moves on. After almost two years of meeting, the members began to change the frequency to monthly meetings or "reunions." They were pleased with the consciousness level they developed and the actions they had taken. They participated in several nationwide and statewide collective action events. They attended and participated in coalition functions, including testifying at the legislature. They had an impact on issues of policy and practice. They reached back to women currently in the shelter and had dialogues with current shelter empowerment groups. They spoke to outside groups. The president, Tracey, was on the board of directors of the agency. For a small group, they accomplished a great deal for themselves and others. They felt empowered. Slowly and with difficulty they gave up their monthly meeting and got on with their lives, remaining in contact in subgroups. Several years later, Tracey and Shandra are still helping each other through difficult times (see chapter 9). They have discovered that there is ongoing work to be done in the empowerment of themselves and other women like them.

13 Community and Political Empowerment Practice

Poor people do not want to manage poverty; they want to end it. While politicians, advocates, and service providers are the primary architects of institutional and policy responses to poverty, grassroots groups are challenging the assumptions about poverty and poor people upon which these policies and programs are constructed. Most especially they challenge the notion that poor people cannot define their own experience and lead a movement to end poverty.

—Willie Baptist, Mary Bricker-Jenkins, and Monica Dillon

"If you have come here to help me, you are wasting your time. But if you have come because your liberation is bound with mine, then let us work together" (Watson 1999). This sentiment of Australian Aboriginal activist Lilla Watson is quoted in an article about the New Freedom Bus campaign conceived of and led by a grassroots organization, the Kensington Welfare Rights Union (KWRU), a unit of the National Welfare Rights Union, by activists and authors Baptist, Bricker-Jenkins, and Dillon (1999). This chapter will feature grassroots efforts at community organizing in local, national, and international arenas. It is dedicated to Professor (and activist) Mary Bricker-Jenkins of Temple University School of Social Administration and her colleagues at KWRU, to Professor Stella Odie-Ali of the University of Guyana Department of Social Work in Georgetown, Guyana and her colleagues in community development and organizing, to Professor Carol Swenson of the Simmons College School of Social Work in Boston, Massachussets, and Greg Asbend and Lucas Benitez, dedicated and skillful leaders of the Coalition of Immokalee Workers in southwest Florida. These colleagues and members of my beloved community have shared their knowledge and practice for this chapter.

The words of Lilla Watson speak to the side-by-side stance of the empowerment approach and to the concept of *self-in-community* (Swenson 1995). Noting that an expanded view of the "mature" or "whole" self includes "a sense of overlapping boundaries with a complex array of "Others," Swenson emphasizes that the mature self recognizes its destiny is connected to all others in a deeply felt way—almost as a moral imperative. This recognition obviates the distance between workers and clients in the struggle for social and economic justice and in enacting the beloved community (Swenson 1998; hooks 1995).

The famous writer, Elie Wiesel, in speaking of the importance of community to the Jewish people, who have weathered centuries of anti-Semitism and human oppression, says that a Jew would be like a withered branch without his community. In connection to his people a Jew lives "more deeply and at a level where all threads are woven together" (Linzer 1978). This sense of self-in-community, peoplehood and the recognition of common bonds, both local and global, is needed for human transformation and liberation.

There is a universal ring to Wiesel's ideas. Yet community may be the vanishing element in a postmodern life full of transience, alienation, uncertainty, and competing values (Toffler 1977; Spergel 1987; hooks 1995). Ironically, social work practice often represents the value of self-contained individualism that further perpetuates alienation from community (Swenson 1994, 1995). Swenson notes, "There is a connection between an absence of constructive community relationships and the individual fragmentation, purposelessness, addiction, and violence which we . . . address" (1992:34). She suggests ways in which social workers can be community centered in their direct practice and challenges practitioners to explore clinical interventions that "empower the oppressed and challenge those who are privileged" (1992:34, 1994). Linzer compares the traditional Jewish values in Wiesel's words to contemporary American values: "The Jewish value system emphasizes *duty and responsibility* instead of rights; *community and individual* instead of individual; *other and self*, not just self; *giving* instead of taking; *doing* instead of being" (1978:181). Faith, community, and this value system have enabled Jews to survive generations of continuing discrimination and oppression, including the mass genocide of the Holocaust.

Like the Jewish people, most ethnic and other minorities deeply value peoplehood and community and adapt through a process of *biculturality*. For oppressed groups the community is a *critical mediating structure* between empowerment, liberation, and oppression. Community members can receive buffering and sustenance from community life; in turn, they are responsible for giving back: contributing to the strength, survival, and power of the community. As empowered people join together to address and act on community issues and wider political concerns, communities become empowered. In turn, empowered communities provide a growing place for empowering people and a critical mass for grassroots and other forms of community organizing.

Defining Community

Community is both subjectively and objectively defined. It signifies place and is both locality specific and nonplace specific (Germain 1991). When I grew up in Brooklyn, New York on the edge of the Bedford-Stuyvesant area, my community consisted initially of my "block," which housed four branches of our extended family. Until 1953, when white flight was completed, this was a multiethnic and multiracial community spanning an area of several blocks in which my school, church, friends, and neighborhood stores existed. The library, a favorite spot, was ten blocks away in neighboring Crown Heights, then a thriving Jewish community, now a community of remaining Orthodox Jews and African Americans and Afro-Caribbean-Americans beset with severe racial tensions. At fourteen I rode the subway or walked two miles to a nondistricted girls' high school, and my community widened. Going into Manhattan's wealthy Upper East Side to a branch of the City University rudely forced me to traverse vastly different worlds. I was intimidated by the opulence. I hated the towering buildings and the streets barren of trees and full of cold anonymity. Manhattan was not my community, although I lived and worked there, enjoying a supportive social network, for almost two decades. (See Rivera and Erlich 1992 for an appreciative view of community in Manhattan.) Leaving my last place community of fourteen years in the Hartford, Connecticut area to build new community ties in Fort Myers, Florida has made me gratefully aware that I have several nonplace communities: a faith community, a nationwide and international friendship network, a professional community, a gay community, and others. This is the nature of communities—subjectively defined and existing as "communities within a community, much like a nest of boxes, one within the other" (Germain 1991:39).

Lewis advocates social work's responsibility to the development of adult community groups that address societal injustice. She stresses that "a major commitment of social work resources should be to develop the knowledge and skill of citizens to interface with the formal organizations of our society, including the structures of public policymaking so as to maintain responsiveness and accountability, and to develop programs of action" (1983:7).

Making a distinction useful to social workers, Marins and Team (1983) discuss the difference between groups and community using the Basic Ecclesial Communities (the "bottom-up church") as an example. The group is transitory; it terminates when its reason for existing is no longer necessary, but community is an experience of permanent, constant, stable, social life. The group is specialized; whereas the community is a global response to the totality of life, the group is relatively homogeneous; whereas the community is pluralistic and heterogeneous, although it must be homogeneous with regard to goals and the exercise of social power; the group may be intimate, whereas the community extends friendship and communion and is inclusive.

Lewis notes that the idea of community has both spatial and spiritual dimensions. She identifies liberation theology and feminist theory as current and sophisticated frames for community social work practice that can integrate both personal becoming and community renewal as one practice (1991). Honkala, Bricker-Jenkins, and Baptist et al. (1999) emphasize that the manipulation of class distinctions have prevented the organization of "the kind of broad based movement to challenge a global economic arrangement that *requires* poverty as a core mechanism in its overall arrangement." All of the "isms," but especially the minimization of the contribution of people who are poor, prevent us from enacting the beloved community. The components of this community are: *capacity* (each member's ability to contribute), *collective effort* (shared work that requires many talents), *informality* (care, not service), *stories* (a reaching back to common histories for truth and future direction), *celebration* (the result of consensual association), *tragedy* (explicit common knowledge of tragedy, death, and suffering), and *activism toward social justice* (Lewis 1987).

Adult community groups are foundation structures in achieving social change. Such groups have their own autonomy and authority. They must deal with external threats, attempts at co-optation, delays, resistances, and the temptation to scapegoat each other if there are failures reaching goals. The worker needs group work skills to help the group define the problems it will tackle and to attain the level of a working group. The group needs to identify possible coalitions that would facilitate attaining the goal. The worker needs to help the group reject answers that don't remedy the problem, to tolerate conflict, and to resolve intragroup issues (Lewis 1987).

A Place of Connection

Community is "that combination of social unity and systems that perform the major functions having locality relevance" (Warren 1978:9). Community performs functions necessary for human survival (Netting, Kettner, and McMurtry 1998). A neighborhood is a component of a larger community that potentially provides people with life-sustaining social support and an action base. But not all neighborhoods are cohesive or effective in this (Germain and Gitterman 1996). In some locales people live in close proximity but lack a sense of shared interests and concerns. Communities—or a sense of solidarity based on similarity, intimacy, and reciprocity—make for a strong sense of identity (Germain 1991). Social workers may be catalytic in helping neighbors find their common ground and make common cause.

Communities can also be viewed as *shared institutions and values, as interaction of local people, as a distribution of power (needing a power structure analysis), and as a social system* (Warren 1978; Bricker-Jenkins 2000). They may consist of formal and informal organizations and relationships (Germain 1991). The community is important as the context, vehicle, and target of social work practice (Cox 1977). Communities, like people, can experience power deficits and can empower themselves. Bertha Reynolds said that communities are not often what they should be: "an organized body of people in some natural grouping, geographical or other, thinking and acting intelligently on matters that concern their welfare" (1934:21). Instead they can be *"pseudo-communities"* in which a ruling class whose interests are opposed to those of the individuals who become its clients dominate and retain power. Social change must occur and be safeguarded through the participation of all in political and economic power, free of all forces of exploitation. She saw the role of social work as mediating "between client and community" so individuals and their communities could attain this power (Reynolds 1934:126).

Communities in Poverty

All communities are sustaining of life to certain degrees, and each one has its strengths and weaknesses. A political power base is essential to community progress. People who are struggling to survive generally live in communities that are struggling for economic survival. Such communities often lack political power, and such key institutions as hospitals and schools often lack resources.

In many cities and rural areas racism relates directly to community struggle. Warren (1978) discusses the almost complete white flight phenomena characteristic of most urban centers by 1978. Institutional racism is a self-reinforcing basis to deny blacks and other minorities of color opportunity and representation within their communities. Warren poses a critical question: "Will a society that is not yet free of strong components of racism be as willing to focus effort and funds on improving living conditions in cities that are largely black as it would be if this were not the case?" (1978:346).

Warren describes the 1960s and 1970s "revolt of the poor" as poor people finding solutions, such as neighborhood and local control, participatory democracy (little city halls), and "alternative institutions" (e.g., "freedom schools"; 1978). Poor and working-class communities, no longer laboring under the illusion of inclusion, are also beginning to find their voices and power as the millennium dawns (Baptist, Bricker-Jenkins, and Dillon 1999). Communities may suffer crises, transitions, and intergroup conflict. To weather these, competence, self-direction, relatedness, and positive identity are essential attributes that communities as well as people can attain (Germain 1991). The example of Miriam Torres, a twenty-seven-year-old Puerto Rican woman who was empowered through consciousness-raising in a shelter, illustrates the circularity of personal and community empowerment and the *linking of individual and collective action* that addresses collectively created institutions and cultures (Bricker-Jenkins 2000).

Miriam was born in the same working-class and poor urban community she now lived in. She left high school to marry and become a mother at seventeen. She became homeless after her husband lost a succession of jobs and returned to Puerto Rico. She used the shelter stay to obtain subsidized housing, to learn to manage on her own, and to pursue further education. She was an enthusiastic empowerment group participant who returned to the alumnae group and shared how the empowerment group helped her to take her first steps at community and political action. Tired of living in a cold, unsafe building, she formed a *tenants' organization* to withhold rent in a legal way until the landlord made repairs and provided necessary services. She and two other women became spokespersons for the group and successfully negotiated their demands. When the demands were met she was instrumental in having the new tenants' group continue to meet on a monthly basis—"So we would be ready if the landlord slipped up again."

The tenants enjoyed their organization and went on to address other issues, such as safety in the building and drug sales in the vicinity. Miriam's personal/political empowerment helped her to risk leadership in the tenants' group and to succeed with the group as it attempted wider goals.

A Minority Community: The African American Urban Community

Using our multifocal lenses we will look at the African American urban community as a case in point to capture strengths and identify issues of struggle and concern to oppressed communities. Service delivery systems need to be responsive to the needs of minority communities. Community workers must be well versed in the history, problems, strengths and demographics of the community (Lum 2000). The worker should take a participant observer approach to the study of ethnosystems within the community, visiting churches, barber shops/beauty salons, restaurants and other community places (see chapter 6).

The distinctiveness of culture in African American communities is based on three perspectives: as one with a deep African heritage/roots, as an essentially American culture, and as a culture derived in relation to the collective experience in the American culture with some persistent African roots remaining. Black communities, although not always communities of choice, do have territorial boundaries and are marked by a high degree of personal intimacy and social cohesion. The extended kin family is a very strong example of the latter two qualities and is a primary structure in the black community. There is also great variation in cultural and linguistic characteristics and in views of community (Solomon 1976).

Blackwell defines the black community as a "highly diversified aggregate of people whose social organization and internal unity are a collective responsive to the external social forces unleashed by white racism, oppression, and systematic repression in the United States" (1975:295). In recognition of the diversity of black Americans, he sees unity without uniformity and the option to choose among several alternatives to empowerment as the rights of black individuals, groups, and communities. He stresses that the experiences of black Americans are united around their commonality. "These conditions have led blacks to organize for the attainment of group rights, individual choices, and the legitimization of the claim for institutional and psychological liberation" (1975:294). Devore and Schlesinger (1999) note that while the lines between social classes may at times be unclear in the African American community, there is a small upper class, a growing and aspiring middle class, a working class (both nonpoor and poor), and a group of persistent poor increasingly without hope. Blackwell sees the persistent poor as the "lower-lower" socioeconomic class/underclass (1975). The diverse lower socioeconomic community is the focus of our attention. Class position is determined by a person's relationship to the labor market and the economy. There is also an identifiable white underclass, though racism compounds the problem of entering the labor force (Devore and Schlesinger 1999; Friend 1994).

As noted in chapter 6 and well discussed by Devore and Schlesinger (1999), the term *underclass* is hotly debated because of concerns about "blaming the victim." Prosser defines the underclass in three ways: a geographic concentration of people living in poverty, common occurrence in a given locale of weak labor force attachment, dependency on welfare, teenage pregnancy, high school dropouts, and criminal activities, and the persistence of these behaviors across two or more generations (1991). Katz (1986) and others, this author included, see the term *underclass* as an unfortunate, demeaning term, a "catchall" that minimizes the key factor of poverty. The underclass is a small percentage of those living in poverty (Sawhill 1989). Wilson defines the underclass as those outside the labor force (1987). Blackwell, as well as Wilson, describes a portion of the underclass as members of the "world of shadies and the underworld," which exists in a parallel way to the legitimate black social structure, as it does in white society. These are people involved in vice and drug trafficking. The group that attains wealth in this way becomes models for lower-class minority youths who feel trapped by poverty and racism. For a stark and alarming literary description of this current phenomena see female rap star Sister Souljah's first novel (Souljah 1999). Middle-class and nonpoor working-class flight creates a diminishing number of positive role models for youth. Anderson (1990) describes a largely drug-connected underclass that values materialism and "the moment" in contrast to the values of the mainstream African American community. The working nonpoor, working poor, and most poor people have strong values on the family, church, community, education, and an atmosphere that keeps their children "out of trouble." This often makes for authoritative child-rearing practices. Many poor people are resigned to insufferable conditions, despair, hopelessness, and frustration. Some are so far removed from the mainstream that assimilation is unlikely. Religion, "making it" in the white man's world, sexual freedom and toleration of illegitimacy, trying to have a good time and communication through music all express a compelling effort to adapt to a world that has excluded them (Blackwell 1975; West 1993). Activism represents another essential level of adaptation (Baptist, Bricker-Jenkins, and Dillon 1999).

The church is and has been the primary community structure that often leads the way to social change activities. "Holding on" to youth lured by materialism and drugs is a critical struggle in churches and other community organizations. The challenge of empowerment practice in lower socioeconomic class communities is to promote access to resources and conscientization, including pride in peoplehood and heritage, that motivates people to collective activism for social change.

Approaches to Working with Communities

Community social work practice has a variety of names that describe difference in emphasis, nuance, purpose, conceptualization, and history. *Community organization* is the name most widely used, but *community work* is gaining momentum; other terms used are *social planning, community development,* and *social action.* Brager and Specht use *community work* and *community organizing* interchangeably (1973), whereas Germain and Gitterman (1995) define *community work* as a broader concept encompassing all levels of practice in the community. They see promoting informal community support systems, including natural helping networks and self-help and mutual aid groups, as an important means of empowering communities. Case management is important to the success of community-based care for physically and mentally challenged people. *Primary prevention* and *growth promotion* are legitimate foci of community-based work in addition to *community development* and *social action* (Germain and Gitterman 1995). Rothman (1992) sees case management as a critical component of community work.

Community organizing refers to efforts to mobilize people who are directly affected by a community condition, particularly the "victims," the unaffiliated, the unorganized, and the nonparticipating, into groups and organizations to enable them to take action on a social problem (Rivera and Erlich 1992). It is a "method of intervention whereby individuals, groups, and organizations engage in planned action to influence social problems."

Its two major related processes are planning (identifying problems, analyzing causes, and formulating solutions) and organizing (developing the constituencies and strategies necessary to effect action; Brager and Specht 1973:27). Social planning/community organization practice utilizes a problem-solving process as its major skill component. This entails problem identification and analysis, developing and implementing a plan of action, and evaluating its outcome. This process requires both analytical and interactional skills at all levels of practice. "Planners" rely heavily on conceptual and analytical skills, whereas "organizers" may utilize more interactional skills (Gilbert and Specht 1987). We focus here on organizational and social change efforts of people in community.

Rothman (1968) advanced a useful conceptualization of three types of community practice: *locality or community development, social planning, and social action*. He compared these three orientations on twelve variables and noted that the practitioner may use and blend the different forms of practice, which are both distinct and overlapping, at various stages in an effort or at different times for different purposes. Taylor and Roberts (1985) add program development and coordination and community liaison approaches to Rothman's typology. Weil and Gamble (1995) break down Rothman's broad categories into eight smaller categories including neighborhood and community organizing, organizing functional communities, community social and economic development, social planning, program development and community liaison, political and social action, coalition building, or multiorganizational power base building, and social movements. Social movements relate to organizing and political and social action, but movements may offer new paradigms, visions, and images for a particular populaton or issue (Weil and Gamble 1995).

Grassroots organizing also deserves its own category (Baptist and Bricker-Jenkins 1999; Rivera and Erlich 1992; Simmons 1994). Netting, Kettner, and McMurtry (1998) emphasize that Saleebey's strengths perspective (1997) is relevant in working with communities and that membership in a community carries civic and moral strength with it. It also carries responsibility. A sign above the reception desk in the Kensington Welfare Rights Union (KWRU) office in Philadelphia, Pennsylvania reads: "This is not a service agency. When we help you, we expect you to help someone else." The help can be outreach or organization building, but the concept of community responsibility member to member is thereby conveyed (Baptist, Bricker-Jenkins, and Dillon 1999).

We will now consider Rothman's three major types of community practice with local and global examples. We will also focus on organizing a poor people's movement, as Baptist and Bricker-Jenkins and others have been doing (1999).

Community development practice envisions the community as the client. In the United States locality or community development evolved from the settlement movement and the start of agricultural extension in the early 1900s (Jacobsen 1990). It involves a broad cross- section of people in determining and solving their own problems, including those with the least and those with the most power in a collaborative effort (Rothman 1968). How the power disparities are equalized is not always clear in this approach (Estes 1999). Because of conflicting interests, those in power may not acknowledge that a problem exists (Staples 1984). Cooperative and collaborative group strategies can be used when problems are acknowledged and there is mutual interest in finding solutions. A basic assumption is that the community is economically disadvantaged, oppressed, and underdeveloped in socioeconomic and political ways and that "grassroots" citizen participants working together in self-help and mutual aid, with the assistance of a community development worker and perhaps international organizations, can develop their abilities and bring about needed change (Spergel 1987; Jacobsen 1990; Estes 1999). See chapter 14 for a critique of the concept of community or social development practice.

Change occurs through working with *small task-oriented groups* (Rothman 1968). The face-to-face group based on felt needs and focused on issues that community people want to work on is the heart of community development practice (Lewis 1983; Spergel 1987). The community group experience may provide participants with desired changes and with extended knowledge and skill, heightened sense of self-image, personal capacity and power, and developed leadership capacity. The main purpose of the group, however, must be to change a condition that affects the community as a whole. It has social education, political development, and even therapeutic value (Spergel 1987).

The worker's roles in the community development process include enabler-catalyst, coordinator, teacher of problem-solving skills, planner, manager, negotiator, and promoter (Rothman 1968; Weil and Gamble 1995). The worker must also be a consultant, planner, and grant writer who may be an active leader or a laid-back adviser (Spergel 1987). The worker must attend to process goals that ensure the group's viability in functioning over time—group interaction and discussion, working on tasks, making decisions, reaching consensus, resolving conflict, problem solving, developing leadership, and attaining task goals. Action is sometimes less important than process in community development practice (Jacobsen 1990). Brager and Specht identify generic relational and group skills and particular organizational skills that build group identity and belonging and develop strong organizations (1973). This includes skill at coalition building and intergroup work that builds communication and alliances between community groups (Brager and Specht 1973; Rothman 1968, 1984). The community development worker requires the knowledge and skill of a political operative and community organizer, organizational developer, and group worker combined with the sensitivity of a caseworker (Spergel 1987).

Community development strives toward creating conditions of economic and social progress for the whole community through the community's own initiative. It addresses the acquisition and redistribution of resources and increases social and political awareness of the causes of the problems. It does not necessarily suggest an emerging critical consciousness or pose a threat to the sociopolitical structure, as it may also revitalize traditional political norms and values (Jacobsen 1990; Spergel 1987). But empowerment principles may be used and critical awareness heightened by empowerment oriented practitioners.

Community development has its *international counterpart in social development practice* that also operates on the grassroots community level. However, the goal of social development may include larger aspects, such as nation building and institution building, which go beyond the local community level. It depends on an alliance of many groups and organizations aimed at the creation of viable economic and social structures and a sense of shared political and social identity (Estes 1991, 1999).

Project COME: A Community Development and Organizing Effort in the Patwah Community of Greater Georgetown, Guyana

COME stands for *Community on the Move by Empowerment*. It is a community development and grassroots organizing project initially undertaken by the faculty and students in the Social Work Degree Program at the University of Guyana. The year 1996 was declared the year of the Eradication of Poverty by the government. An interdisciplinary group of faculty members decided to begin literally in their own backyard. The "Patwah" Squatter Community was located on idle university land adjacent to the Turkeyan Campus. (The community's name is disguised. *Patwah* is a Creole word that is the name of a local fish. The community members learned how to develop a business salting this fish.) Such squatters' communities come into being because of poverty and the lack of affordable housing. A section of this community was named Carplas by its illegal and impoverished residents, as the little makeshift shacks they lived in were made of cardboard and plastic. During the rainy season Patwah was a sea of mud that residents waded through to get to their homes. There were no roads or drainage systems or water or utilities. In a location full of health hazards there was no health center. Estimates of the population ranged from about twelve hundred to five thousand individuals. Many were female-headed single-parent families with more than half the residents under age thirty-five. Many were unemployed or underemployed. There were no schools or social service agencies located in the community. Children and youth were often left unsupervised as parents sought day labor on the docks or in the town. They banded together in roaming groups or gangs that were sometimes dangerous and hostile. One student described Patwah and other similar depressed areas as forgotten communities.

Determined that Patwah would not remain forgotten, UG faculty members and students, including social work professors Stella Odie-Ali and Neberne Scott, initiated dialogue with community members. Utilizing the empowerment approach, they saw the community as "made up of people with potentials that could be mobilized, people who have ideas about what their goals are and what they need to do to achieve them. In this perspective, the experience and skills that people in communities bring to a situation are as important as any that a program may contain for them" (Scott, David, Patterson, and Samuels 1997). The first steps in initiating dialogue are captured in this communication from Professor Odie-Ali:

> We walked from the campus to the Patwah Squatter Community. There were no roads so we walked through the bush until we reached where some people live. As we walked, people eyed us, and the suspicion was so thick it was almost a physical thing. They were probably afraid of losing their homes to the University. We knew this would not be the case, but why should they trust us? We began speaking to people one by one and in little groups. We asked them

about community needs. After a few such trips we identified some leaders and invited community members to come over to the campus and meet with us informally.

To our surprise over thirty community members came to the first meeting. The majority were women. We began with identifying the needs of children together. They were concerned about drugs and parenting skills, especially with teenagers. We asked them what services they needed to empower themselves. The first things they identified were water and utilities. We reflected with them on these needs as basic human needs and entitlements. By now they displayed trust and saw us as allies in their struggle to meet these needs. One woman stepped forth and recited a poem she had written on living in Patwah. Another group dramatized their needs in a skit. They shared a song they had composed. This was all spontaneous as we responded in dialogue to what they were saying and feeling. The theme was that they were all on the verge of becoming homeless. They responded to our critical question by saying: "We try to empower we self by building a roof over our heads." Obtaining proper building materials was then identified as the prime need. We pledged that we would help them find ways to meet their basic and legitimate needs. They then invited us to their homes and the exchange continued becoming friendlier and friendlier with each visit. They suggested questions for a needs assessment survey so we could determine where to begin."

The Community Needs Assessment

A sample of thirty-three heads of family responded to the needs assessment survey. An important question was about level of education. Almost 45.5 percent of the sample had not completed primary school while 42.4 percent did attend some years of secondary school. Four people had attended some vocational training and one person had no formal education. These percentages are much lower than in the nonsquatter society. Respondents were interested in training that would give them marketable skills. Another question asked from a strengths perspective was, What skills do you have? Twenty-seven percent had farming and livestock rearing skills while 21.2

percent did catering and cake decorating. Eighteen percent could type, do bookkeeping, hairdressing, and construction work. It was also asked if they would share their skill with the community, and most would do so. As noted earlier, water, utilities, drainage, and help with parenting skills were of greatest concern. Focus groups also reinforced these preliminary findings. All focus groups went beyond traditional research purposes in that residents were encouraged to analyze the problems critically as well. The research process itself in beginning and ending with community direction was also an empowering aspect of working with the community. Abu-Samah makes the point that research processes can include reflective and consciousness-raising aspects and help communities engage in praxis (1996).

Developing Project COME

Based on community input, Professor Neberne Scott and three students worked with indigenous community leaders to set up COME. Without any budget at all, they met in a small community building, staffed it three days a week with students and community leaders, and directed themselves to the tasks at hand. They formed three subgroups directing energies to problems of youth, women, and the environment. Each group discussed problems related to drug abuse, violence, including domestic violence, crime, teenage pregnancy, and lack of marketable skills. The environmental subgroup focused on the nonexistence of permanent public utilities, the need for building materials, and the declining ability of the government to provide adequate services of any sort. Community members determined that COME would focus on individual and group support for women, parents, and youth, offer skills and job training, and focus on getting public utilities set up and drainage and environmental health. Marketable craft and food preparation skills were taught such as fabric painting, chair repair, and making salted fish and pickled meat. This made for entrepreneurial growth as cottage industries developed. A reading corner (children's library) was set up and a new playing field is almost completed. They had movies about Caribbean issues on Sundays and utilized this for further consciousness-raising. Perhaps most important, the environment group took on the task of organizing the community to pressure the government for public utilities and services. A strong female and male leadership team emerged. While it did not happen all at once, they were successful in a serial way, and there is now potable water, drainage, electricity, access to public transportation and schools, a library, and roads. Many have earned enough to build wooden homes. They have also opened a day care center. They have regular cultural and community celebrations. Teenage crime and pregnancy is noticeably down, and community leaders and members continue to organize and advocate for themselves. The Patwah community continues to battle poverty and the lack of resources as people who are empowering themselves against the odds.

It is noteworthy that the Guyana Association of Professional Social Workers (GAPSW) has taken on the issue of child care in depressed communities. Under the leadership of Patrice La Fleur, Lieutenant Colonel Christine King and Mrs. Venus Wayne, successively, GAPSW developed a *Child-Care Management Project* along with the Women's Outreach Project and the Adult Education Association. This child-care project is open to all levels of people who work with children, including parents and teachers and day care providers. The demand for the course is overwhelming. The twelve-week experientially based course has attracted over one hundred women from diverse backgrounds, including women from Patwah who see better child care as a route to uplifting their community.

Social Planning

The social planning approach is based on a rational problem-solving process designed to have an impact on substantial social problems, such as housing and mental/physical health. Social planners are employed by large, often bureaucratic power structures and sponsors to gather and analyze facts about the pertinent social problem and plan and sometimes implement programs and policies that represent the most rational course of action. Clients are seen as consumers or recipients in this approach, but they rarely have more than a minor advisory role in the process (Rothman 1968). The approach assumes that change in a complex industrial environment requires experts who are highly trained and skilled, although they may have no direct experience with the problem at the community or personal level. Consumers may or may not play a role in the process. Technical roles are emphasized in social planning. The planner requires expertise in empirical research methodology and needs assessment tools. Most of the planner's work is done in formal organizations where the medium of change is the manipulation of data and of the formal organization itself (Jacobsen 1990; Rothman 1968).

Planners who genuinely involve community residents in the problem-solving process and who appreciate the ways in which their own agency might be oppressive may contribute to community empowerment. Planning that makes for changes that are clearly responsive to community needs contributes needed resources for empowerment as well, although the processes used may not have been empowering. Generally, planning is a process far removed from the community, although the social workers who helped design COME utilized planning and needs assessment as part of their organizing and development project.

Social Action

Social action in community organizing seeks a shift in power and resources so that those who suffer from socioeconomic disadvantage, social injustice, and inequity attain what is needed to "right the wrongs." This is necessary when there are scarce resources and conflicting interests that are not easily reconcilable. The change strategy is to work with people to crystallize the issues and organize to take action against powerful "enemy targets." The worker's roles include activist-advocate, agitator, broker, negotiator, and partisan (Rothman 1968). Baptist, Bricker-Jenkins, and Dillon (1999) also see "movement building" and its related skills and roles as the ultimate objective of social action. They dispute myth that poor people are incapable of organizing and movement building and the notion that a movement must be started or led by a single charismatic leader. Instead they see *indigenous leadership, rigorous analyses, disciplined tactical work, and skillful knitting together of relationships* among diverse groups of individuals as the ingredients of movement building. The poor in alliance with not currently poor and other people with raised consciousness are the essential leadership for the movement. The launching of a poor people's movement through their grassroots group, the Kensington Welfare Rights Union (KWRU), in alliance with groups all across the United States, Puerto Rico, and Canada will be discussed below.

Much of the knowledge used in community organizing comes from social activists who were not trained in schools of social work. The best known of these is Saul Alinsky, who began writing and sharing his wisdom about organizing people's movements in 1946 with *Reveille for Radicals*, which lays a foundation in both principles and skills of social action organizing.

Alinsky believed that a people's organization functioned to achieve power to realize the people's program—a set of principles, purposes, and practices commonly agreed upon by the people. This "program" must belong to the people, not to a few leaders or institutions (1969). People express themselves through indigenous leaders: "If a People's organization were to be thought of as a tree, the indigenous leaders would be the roots and the people themselves the soil" (1969). In 1969 Alinsky said that black communities need to organize and attain power through people's organizations; otherwise the "danger of black power is that there will be no black power" (213). He applied this to any group of urban inner-city dwellers who take what they are handed down and fail to organize in their own self-interest and make democracy a reality. Some community organizers feel that the Alinsky model is too "class focussed" and not appreciative enough of the struggles of people of color (Rivera and Erlich 1992). Rivera and Erlich (1992) suggest a twelve-step model-in-progress that focuses on cultural and ethnic sensitivity. They conceptualize three levels of intervention by the community organizer: *primary contact*, which can only be done by indigenous leaders or persons with "full ethnic solidarity "with the people," the *secondary* level, where language sameness is not mandatory but the practitioner can be of a similar group and act as liaison between the group and the outside, and the *tertiary level*, where cultural or race similarity is not a requirement but the role is limited to working with the outside infrastructure as an advocate or broker. While these divisions may or may not be ideal, this typology is in reality debated by thriving organizations in which ethnic bridges are crossed and confounded by the existence of diverse ethnic communities that struggle together for justice.

For example, the *Coalition of Immokalee Workers (CIW)* is a strong community-based grassroots multiethnic worker organization—mostly tomato and citrus pickers—that successfully mobilized in several campaigns to incrementally raise the wages of farm workers in Collier County, Florida. Department of Labor statistics for 1995 show that the median national personal income for farm workers is between $5000 and $7,500 and median household income is between $7,500 and $10,000, well below the poverty line for a family of three, and many families are much larger. Over three-fifths of farm worker households live in poverty, a level higher than 1990, when only half reported living in poverty. Hispanics born outside of the U.S. were at highest risk for the lowest wages. About 70 percent of the workers in Immokalee are of Mexican, Guatemalan, and other Latin groups. Haitians, African Americans, and whites make up the rest of the workforce. Yet, in Collier County, tomato crop profits were substantial during this same time period, 1990–1995 (Barry 1998; Navarro 1998). It is common knowledge that to keep profits up growers keep wages down, hence gaining any victory at all is momentous.

CIW states its purpose:

> We strive to build our strength as a community on the basis of reflection and analysis, constant attention to coalition building across age-old ethnic and linguistic divisions, and an ongoing investment in leadership development to help workers from the base continually develop their skills in community organization and education. From this basis we fight for . . . fair wages . . . more respect from our bosses . . . better and cheaper housing . . . stronger laws . . . against those who violate worker's rights . . . the right to organize without fear of retaliation and to end the abuse of undocumented workers. (Barry 1998)

This organization of over 750 workers had made important progress on all these fronts. They have also developed a thriving food cooperative and exposed situations of slavery and injustice in Immokalee. Two of the key leaders of this group are Lucas Benitez and Greg Asbend. Lucas is a dynamic young Mexican-American and Greg is a well-educated white activist who lives and works side by side with other farm workers year round. He is considered an insider by them. The group has used marches, hunger strikes, protests, civil disobedience, community education, and media events to make progress toward their cause. In the spring of 2000 Florida Gulf Coast University's social work and human services students and faculty joined with other students, faculty, and community organizations to support a fifteen-day CIW farm workers walk to dramatize low wages and brutal living conditions. Leaders and members of the KWRU mentioned earlier in this chapter, were also on this march in solidarity.

Alinsky's model has also been used effectively in African American and Hispanic communities. Alinsky saw popular education as an objective of a people's organization. His methods involved action but not praxis or conscientization. Basically, Alinsky saw the people's organization as a conflict group, even when this occasionally meant acting outside legal boundaries. Alinsky's list of guiding principles and tactics, *Rules for Radicals* (1972:127), continues to guide many of today's community organizers (Staples 1984).

An example of the use of Alinsky's basic principles with some important differences is the *"people power" approach to social action* organizing developed by Dean Brackley, S.J., Marjorie Tuite, O.P., and *South Bronx People for Change*. In response to the arson and abandonment that demolished South Bronx neighborhoods, organizers and local community residents focused on building the power of its people. The population of the South Bronx is uniformly poor and working poor Hispanic and African American residents. The author's community work in this neighborhood is described in the literature (Lee and Swenson 1978).

With a three-part philosophy of community organizing, reflection on faith, and power analysis, South Bronx People for Change worked for conscientization (eye-opening) with regard to power issues and building a strong multiissue neighborhood group. They taught resident members organizational and power theory using codes/comic books that represented the pyramidal structures the people depended on. They showed the way in which the people were divided, and at the bottom, whereas the power remained at the top. Their critical education and liberation theology approach intended that each resident member and leader had as much knowledge of power structures, groups, and organizing as the organizers did. Immersed in and sharing the "view from below," they developed excellent and inexpensive critical teaching materials that can be used in working with any oppressed groups (Brackley n.d.). Their vision statement reflected Judeo-Christian values:

> God . . . gives power and strength to his people" (Psalms 68:35). When people act together they have POWER! . . . Our communities and decide our future. . . . As we win battles on small issues we are a growing people's movement which will one day become a powerful people's organization. . . . For today we are fighting for more than just heat, street lights, hot water and jobs. . . . We are fighting to build a real community where we can live together with dignity and respect as real brothers and sisters of one another. . . . This is an old and powerful vision . . . called the Kingdom of God. . . . We [can make it happen] step by step and issue by issue [as we] have learned the nuts and bolts of organizing for social action: recruiting people, running meetings, defining issues, planning and executing actions and negotiating. . . . So let's get learning and let's get working! (Brackley n.d.:2)

This organization won victories and empowered its members through both process and outcome.

Lee Staples, a social work educator and veteran organizer, sees the development of a strong ongoing multi-issue, multitactic, multiconstituency, action-oriented, self-funded, democratically led *membership organization* as a necessary counterbalance to the powerlessness most low-income and moderate-income people experience (1984). Staples's excellent how-to book, *Roots to Power* (1984), describes a particular style of social action *grassroots organizing*, and the skills and strategies he discusses are based on years of actual practice and conceptualization. Staples believes that the "goal is to strengthen their collective capacities to bring about social change" (1984:1). For him the most potent source of power is strength in numbers that can be used in the economic arena, such as rent strikes, in the electoral arena, and, mainly, in direct actions.

Staples (1984) cautions that community organizations should go beyond being "issue oriented," although winning issues strengthens the organization, to building a strong long-term collective power base, which may develop into a national organization with local chapters. Contrasted to the Alinsky model where existing groups join as groups, this is a direct membership model. ACORN *(Association of Community Organizations for Reform Now)*, a national organization representing more than eighty thousand families, represents the type of people's organization that puts power into the hands of community members. Staples helped develop ACORN from the "roots to the tip," illustrating his approach to social action organizing. This organizing model relies heavily on door-to-door recruitment, power analysis, and development of an organizing committee that creates a constituency. Issues and strategies are then analyzed, and an action plan is chosen.

A strategy is a "stairway that takes us from our present condition to where we want to go," and tactics are the individual steps (Staples 1984). Brager and Specht (1973) and Brager and Holloway (1978) and Netting, Kettner, and McMurtry (1998) present a typology of change tactics, including collaborative, campaign, and contest tactics. Strategies and tactics may include the campaign strategy of negotiation, conflict strategies of direct action (protest or mass involvement campaigns, such as voter registration drives), noncooperation (e.g., strikes, boycotts, or absenteeism), and contest intervention (e.g., mass demonstrations and possible disruption) (Brager and Specht 1973). In the social action approach the worker "manipulates mass organizations and political processes" (Rothman 1968). People must make their choices, as they have in the 1992 riots in Los Angeles, but violence is not a choice for a social worker acting in role (Brager and Specht 1973). The confrontational quality of social action, though usually nonviolent, may have led to its decline in the 1980s. However, there is a new surge of interest in social action as people reach a limit to accepting the intolerable conditions of poverty and injustice perpetuated in the last decade (Baptist and Bricker-Jenkins 1999).

It is difficult to separate social action group work from social action community work. Recent work by Regan and Lee (1992) show their intimate and sometimes inseparable relationship. But the massiveness of the process, goals, and numbers of those involved is one difference. Social action community organizing can be on the level of a movement, whereas social action group work involves a much smaller unit of action and intervention. Although we have noted a wide repertoire of skills for community organizers, empowering group work skills are central (see chapter 10).

The following is an example of grassroots community organizing and movement building with a feminist perspective by poor people in alliance with professional social workers. The *KWRU, the Freedom Bus Ride, the Poor People's Summit, and the March of the Americas* are examples of poor people and social workers making common cause (Honkala, Bricker-Jenkins, and Baptist 1999).

Making a Movement: Riding the New Freedom Bus

The Organization: the Kensington Welfare Rights Union

The Kensington Welfare Rights Union was organized in the early 1990s by a small group of women on welfare who began meeting in a church basement in Kensington, the poorest district and the largest city in Pennsylvania. Kensington is a deindustrialized and impoverished multiethnic community of white, African American, and Latina populations in roughly equal proportions with a recent addition of Korean, Cambodian, and Vietnamese families living at the outskirts of the area. KWRU leaders note that "this mix provides KWRU a natural base for examining and confronting the ways in which racism and cultural conflicts are used to separate people and weaken a movement. KWRU's approach is not to ignore [racial conflict] but to contextualize [it] . . . there is constant reaffirmation of the condition that brings members and allies together-poverty" (Baptist, Bricker-Jenkins, and Dillon 1999). All of the destructive "isms" are discussed in dialogue and identified as threats to a movement which would challenge poverty at the core. KWRU believes that to end poverty power relations must shift. People must have enough of a power base to challenge the structures that keep them in poverty. People's organizations with indigenous leadership establish that base, and the coalition of such groups builds a movement. The initial catalytic event that galvanized KWRU was the 1991 threat of welfare cuts by Pennsylvania's Governor Casey. The group formed and continues to carry out three overarching goals:

1. to speak to the issues affecting their lives through testifying at hearings and lobbying and educating the public through a multimedia approach. They have websites at *http://www.kwru/ehrc/moa/ edl.html* and *http://www.libertynet.org/kwru*. They have put out three videos and published a number of articles toward this end.
2. To organize a broad-based movement to end poverty. To that end they have joined with several other groups in working for the needs of the poor in Kensington and world-wide. They spearheaded the organizing of the New Freedom Bus and coalesced with the Poor People's Economic Human Rights Campaign described below. They have taken over abandoned public properties and set up tent cities, marched and protested and engaged in civil disobedience. In August of 1996 they led a 140- mile March for Our Lives in protest of Clinton's signing of the welfare reform bill and the governor's enactment of these massive cuts. (See chapters 1 and 4.)
3. To help members and all poor people to get what is needed to survive. They assisted over four hundred families with housing and utilities and developed several human rights houses as bases for emergency housing and other types of help (Baptist, Bricker-Jenkins, and Dillon 1999).

Poor People's Movement

KWRU sought to realize at least four movement-building objectives: to develop clarity of analysis, to consolidate a core of leaders, to make intra-

and intergroup connections, and to build a culture of the movement (Baptist, Bricker-Jenkins, and Dillon 1999). They did this through several catalytic activities. These are some of the highlights of KWRU's leadership and activities in developing a Poor People's Movement:

The August 1996 *March for Our Lives* precipitated by welfare cuts involved organizing more than 50 homeless families to travel 140 miles to the State Capitol and camp out there to dramatize the effects of this travesty of human rights. The leadership developed to initiate and see this through became the core leadership of the organization. These leadership skills were consolidated in June of 1997, when 100 families marched from Philadelphia to the United Nations in another March for Our Lives, this time allying with Labor groups affirming the Universal Declaration of Human Rights and the International Bill of Human Rights for citizens of the United States who have been left out of the American market place and pushed aside by the global economy (see chapter 14).

The Poor Peoples Economic Human Rights Campaign (PPEHRC)

The PPEHRC is a national effort led by poor and homeless women, men, and children of all races to raise the issue of poverty as a human rights violation. The campaign is made up of over thirty-five poor people's organizations in the U.S. including mothers who have been cut off welfare and farm workers from Florida. The follow-up to the 1997 action was a scheduled Poor People's Summit to convene at the UN in October of 1998. To organize constituencies for this march, KWRU utilized the *New Freedom Bus Ride*.

The New Freedom Bus

In June of 1998 KWRU organized a bus ride to more than thirty towns and cities across the country. At each stop along the route local groups, many assisted by members of the Bertha C. Reynolds Society, organized rallies, demonstrations, speak-outs, and teach-ins focusing on the ways in which welfare reform policies violate the Economic Human Rights provisions of the UN Declaration of Human Rights. The culmination of the tour was on July 1, 1998, when the group marched with others across the George Washington Bridge to the United Nations and a tribunal at which representatives of America's poor people presented their case. Many of these groups reconvened at the summit in Philadelphia in October.

The Poor People's Summit (PPS)

The PPS was sponsored by the North-South Dialogue, a network of poor people's groups, allies, and advocates that came together at the Highlander Center for Research and Education in 1997. Participants from sixteen groups envisioned the summit as a means of advancing an emerging movement of the people. The KWRU and the Temple University School of Social Administration hosted this event. Ten other schools of social work helped mobilize groups to the event. This example of social workers and schools of social work cooperating with and supporting people's organizations is a model of mutual empowerment.

On October 9, 1998, over three hundred representatives of poor people's groups, along with fifty allies, convened in Philadelphia to share their political analyses and strategies in workshops and plenaries. A canvas graffiti wall was set up outside to graphically depict the analysis being explored inside: the relationship between global economic forces, advertising and media, crumbling infrastructures, children in poverty, and the rising tide of resistance to economic injustice (Baptist and Bricker-Jenkins 1999). This wall was a *code* that deepened the analysis. Another code was the song they sang, which was learned from a southern people's organization:

Goin' down to the rich man's house
Gonna take back what he stole from me
Gonna take back my dignity
Take back my humanity!

The 1999 follow-up, the March of the Americas, included groups from South, Central, and Latin America. In August 2000 about five thousand individuals dedicated to ending poverty: KWRU members, allies, and others protested and engaged in civil disobedience at the Republican presidential

convention in Philadelphia. In time, such a coalition may catalyze a countervailing force against the worldwide exploitation of the poor in this new
global economy.

Indeed, the KWRU and groups like it are part of a growing movement to
reestablish the dignity of poor people everywhere. Social work can not afford
to ignore this impetus.

Feminist Perspectives

The work of Mary Bricker-Jenkins, described above and elsewhere, exemplifies feminist consciousness in community organizing and practice.
The feminist vision of community consists of *common consciousness, deconstruction* of negative and disadvantaging definitions of reality, *naming* of new
realities through identifying the consequences of established structures and
patterns, trusting the *processes within the group to reconstruct* a new reality, a
belief in the *power of the group* and *action*, and a sense of community through
finding "same thinkers and doers" in the wider social context (Lewis 1983).

Brandwein claims Jane Addams and the women of the settlement movement as the earliest examples of female community organizers. She notes
that of Rothman's three models of community organization two fit male
gender stereotypes: social action in his descriptions was "tough, macho, and
conflict oriented" and social planning was "scientifically based, rational, and
logical." Only his third type, locality development, with its emphasis on
enabling and participation, could fit into a female gender stereotype (Brandwein 1987:115). Brandwein defines a feminist approach to working with
communities as *androgynous* (everyone can use all "organizing behaviors";
Brandwein 1982), *holistic* (*both* process *and* product oriented), and *syner-
gistic* (the participation and involvement of all in decision making means
better decisions will be made). Thus, through an interactive process, a better
product is achieved. It has a *win/win power orientation*—as an objective that
redefines in potential conflict situations; strategies are part of a chain or *web
of relationships* so outcomes can take place over time using a variety of tactics
and in the context of egalitarian relationships that lend themselves to conflict
resolution (1987).

A feminist framework for community organizing integrates methods and
strategies for action with feminist practice principles and has the empowerment of women as one of its goals. Community organizing is a "process

of pulling together to create a functional whole," whether this be by developing an organization or by orchestrating a strategy for achieving goals (Weil 1986:187).

Weil suggests using feminist ideology, values, and principles in a planning process where staff and clients are involved. She reminds us that rationality is not a sufficient basis for planning and that cultural and value issues should be kept in mind. She advises inclusion of women's issues (including health needs and economic needs) in socially and economically oriented community development work, and full involvement of women in community development processes. Supporting self-determination of community women in development, role equity, and role change is also advised. Full representation of women is also needed in social and political decision-making processes, with the goal of developing collective power. Promoting coalition building, alternative women-centered programs, and increased systems' responsibility to women is also important in feminist community practice. Consciousness-raising and praxis are critical in building collective strength from action (Weil 1986). In the feminist perspective power is facilitative, enabling, and shared within and among groups—as energy and initiative. Strategies for change address the congruence of means and ends and are provided in egalitarianism, consensus building, cooperation, collectivism, power sharing, self-help, and mutual responsibility.

An excellent example of feminist community practice is Osberger and Vaughn's feminist approach to community work with women who are homeless (Osberger and Vaughn n.d.). They have developed an approach that can be used in focusing action-oriented groups of homeless women on creating community and change in areas that benefit women: housing, child care, welfare, immigration, and formation of global connections. They use collected works of women who were homeless and newspaper articles and statistical analyses of problems as codes to involve women in discussion and action (Osberger and Vaughn n.d.).

All the approaches to community work described earlier may be empowering. Social planning must have real community involvement to meet this definition, whereas community development work and social action must be driven by the people themselves and not manipulated by outside (or inside) interests. Grassroots organizing can empower all who participate. But grassroots organizing can also disempower people if they are manipulated by the "good guys" (the community workers, organizers, or even indigenous leaders) who have their eyes on the "prize" of developing a strong organization, or on a particular action and not meeting the opened eyes of the people. Freire (1973a) considers any manipulation of the people antidialogical and antirevolutionary, noting that sometimes all that organizers can do is pursue unity and bear witness to the struggle. They cannot "make it happen."

Freire's Culture Circles as a Model of Community Work

Freire's critical education approach (discussed in earlier chapters) involves total community involvement. It represents social action, community development, and social change, so that people can "learn to read their own reality and write their own history." In large "culture circles" people developed their own programs for learning and for changing oppressive local conditions. The circles consisted of the teacher, a variety of professionals who represent the social sciences, students, and at least 10 percent of the population of the area. They coinvestigated the area and the contradictory themes that made for oppression, including illiteracy. This purpose is openly discussed with the community residents, and permission is sought for the coinvestigation to proceed. In an almost ecological approach the coinvestigators regard the area as a "totality in code"—a unique living code that must be decoded. In an attempt not to learn about the people but to come to know them and their reality, they observe and reflect on certain moments in the life of an area. They make note of the talk (how people construct their thought), the style of life, behavior at church and work, behavior in local meetings, the role played by women and youth, and home life. Written reports are shared in the community itself for the input of the inhabitants. The reports are discussed in a decoding process that gets closer and closer to the basic contradictions of their lives. Their fatalism may then be expressed and challenged as their potential consciousness is discovered. The coinvestigators then analyze themes across the social sciences— economically, politically, anthropologically, sociologically, and developmentally—and share this in the culture circle. After further reflection they prepare selected themes for codification and further consciousness-raising. Newspaper articles, taped debates, art, or music may be used as codes. "The thematics which have come from the people return to them, not as contents to be deposited, but as problems to be solved" (Freire 1973a:116). Community residents now become actors and thinkers, shapers of their own futures. Freire concludes that neither the outside organizer nor the people, while they are crushed by oppression, can construct a theory of liberating action, but they must do this in dialogue with each other. "Only ... in their communion, in their praxis, can this theory be built" (1973a:186) and empowerment attained.

Empowerment Principles and Skills and Community Work

Community work within an empowerment approach must utilize multifocal vision, embrace the values and principles of empowerment practice, and reflect the skills of this approach. As the practitioner tunes in to a particular community, the practitioner needs knowledge of the oppression (historic and current) experienced by the members of the community (including ethclass factors) and what social policies have maintained this, in addition to knowledge about the community gained through getting to know people, making studies, taking surveys and doing community and power analysis (Lamb 1977; Warren 1977; Staples 1984). The worker's reason for being there is the conviction that oppression as manifested in intolerable community conditions is destructive of life and should be challenged (principle 1). The worker needs the community members even as they need each other to establish and maintain a social change focus (principles 4 and 8).

Using an ecological view, the worker then observes and talks with people about how they cope with the existing conditions in the community and transact with the power structures that may loom larger than life. The worker may share her own experience of oppression as this relates to the resident's struggles. This may help establish equality and parity in communication that appreciates ethclass variables. Recognizing the strengths of the community will also help establish a reciprocal relationship with community residents (thereby enacting principle 5). This community has already solved a multitude of problems; it was not "born yesterday." Recognizing this helps the worker view community residents as victors, not victims (principle 7). It also makes for more accurate community assessment.

In appreciating the realities of class structure, racism, ethnocentrism, classism, sexism, and heterosexism as these play themselves out in the life of the community, the worker will take stock of how community residents may view his/her entry as well as how the community may be divided against itself or unified by common bonds. A feminist perspective recognizes that the personal is political and appreciates the struggles of the total being to attain empowerment. Therefore personal issues will be attended to even as their connection to the political issues at hand is drawn. Ultimately, from beginning to end community residents must say their own words, plan their own options, and act in ways that are their own (principles 3 and 6). Making conscientization and praxis an integral part of all community work and actions ensures that residents and worker alike develop and utilize a critical perspective in dealing with community problems. People in community then truly empower themselves. The worker may then assume other roles in the organization or be assured that the organization belongs to the people and will continue without the worker. The examples in this chapter exemplify empowerment oriented community organization and development.

A Nonplace Community Organization

Nationally and locally based groups for lesbian and gay civil rights represent a well-organized minority group interest. Though not readily visible, one out of ten individuals is likely to be gay (Moses and Hawkins 1982). The activities of these groups have won the passage of a gay rights bill in seven states and Washington, D.C. Using the range of collaborative, campaign and contest strategies, local groups have won each struggle against bigotry and discrimination after difficult and bitter battles. The gay rights bills grant gay people the basic rights to housing, employment, and use of public accommodations without discrimination. Such rights are denied in many states. In Connecticut the bill met defeat twice before gaining passage. The local Coalition for Lesbian and Gay Civil Rights used a combination of lobbying and contest strategies. An effective professional lobbyist spearheaded the final successful effort. A local ad hoc ACT UP group that included several prominent community leaders added to peaceful demonstration methods by lowering a banner from a balcony during legislative hearings. Their arrest further dramatized the cause and rallied support for the bill. Various state and national coalitions are also exploring the benefits of "domestic partnership" laws and the rights of domestic or life partners. The state of Massachusetts has passed a bill granting bereavement leave to gay and lesbian state workers and their partners. This bill also extends visiting rights at hospitals and prisons. The Connecticut Political Action Committee provided a list of candidates who were sympathetic to gay issues and were active in getting people to the polls. Candidates are sensitive to the fact that gay people vote. Local groups have found that constant awareness and vigilance are needed to maintain hard-won gains.

Although AIDS is not primarily a gay issue (the greatest spread of the HIV virus is in the heterosexual community, with adolescents and women being at high risk), the gay community has achieved most of the progress made in making the government responsive to AIDS as a health epidemic and a social issue of crisis proportions. Using the media, public education, lobbying, and demonstrations, gay groups continue to work for federal dollars for research, adequate health care coverage and treatment, and nondiscriminatory policies and programs that meet the needs of persons who live with AIDS and their caretakers. The Gay Men's Health Crisis in New York City is an example of a gay organization that has extended its services and political advocacy to all AIDS and HIV sufferers.

Political Empowerment

All empowerment work is political. This is especially true of community work. We have demonstrated that the actions of empowered community members can achieve desired change and tip the power balance in their favor. Throughout this book we have given illustrations of individuals and groups acting politically and reflecting on their actions. We turn here to a more in-depth discussion of the political knowledge and skills both workers and consumers of services may use in advocating social change.

Oppressed people need the power to "persuade the people with the power to make decisions to make the right decisions" (Richan 1991:3). Political power involves influencing government through a broad range of actions that may include research, analysis, letter writing and telephoning, organization of citizen participation, coalition building, drafting of a bill, support for or opposition to legislation, testimony, demonstration and rallying of public support, education on the issues, participation in electoral politics, or lobbying (Mahaffey 1987; Germain and Gitterman in press). Knowledge and skill in legislative advocacy are power for members of oppressed groups.

The legislative process is similar on local, state, and federal levels. The administrator (the president, governor, or mayor), a congressional committee, or an individual legislator (senator or representative) introduces a bill. Both the Senate and the House of Representatives must pass the bill, and the executive must sign it to make it law. If the executive vetoes the bill, a two-thirds override can make it a law. Then it is implemented by an agency within the executive branch that develops regulations and guidelines. At any point the policy's constitutionality may be challenged in the courts. If it is found wanting, the bill goes back to the drawing board (Richan 1991:254; Germain and Gitterman in press). The step-by-step process leaves many opportunities for citizens to influence the policymakers.

Richan (1991) offers an extensive conceptual and practical guide that makes the power of legislative advocacy available to all. It is based on two cardinal principles, "You have to do your homework and know what you are talking about, and you can take on the so-called experts on their own ground" (1991:2). "Doing your homework" requires obtaining facts on the chosen issue that are both verifiable and compelling and then building a well-organized case. Stating the facts and being clear on the bill in question is important in letter writing and petitioning as well as in the more powerful direct routes of interpersonal encounters with legislators. Presenting the case can be done in individual or group lobbying efforts. Richan notes that a group of three to five conveys a power base but that the speakers must agree. The legislator must be persuaded that your position will help her constituents. A well-prepared one-page summary of your position is also helpful to leave with the legislator. The approach is targeted to a specific individual. Brief written statements are also helpful at legislative hearings. When people who suffer with a problem lobby or testify, the sharing of pertinent personal experiences provides an authentic source of information that is a powerful means of influence.

People who live with the problem and social workers who assist them are experts on the problem. They usually don't possess large sums of money to get things done or large numbers of votes to sway the legislator, but there are assets that anyone can possess: commitment, time, allies, organization, and information. As people empower themselves with these assets, they can be formidable forces for change (Richan 1991).

An early step in "doing your homework" is getting to know your legislators. Zastrow suggests that agencies invite elected officials to meet with staff to share information and concerns when the legislature is not in session. He also suggests contacting legislators when you approve of what they have done, not simply when you want something, and he advocates not writing anyone off as "the enemy," for legislators may support a variety of issues (1992).

Examples from Practice

We will continue our political practice examples in the area of housing and homelessness. The statewide *Connecticut Coalition to End Homelessness* has a strong track record in legislative advocacy. They have fought successfully for the continuance of Section 8 subsidies, the rental assistance program, transitional and permanent housing programs with services, and security deposit programs, which we have discussed earlier in this book. The purpose of the Coalition is to do itself out of business as quickly as possible. The Executive Director is Mary McAtee, an activist and an experienced organizer. The Coalition sponsors training in legislative advocacy from nuts to bolts for consumers, staff, and administrators of shelters and related programs. They monitor legislative processes and set up opportunities for legislative testimony, lobbying, and mass demonstrations. They also have provided training in developing empowerment philosophy, practices, and groups in shelters led by this author and others.

In this politically aware community some political events are spontaneously planned by local groups; others are planned by the Coalition. Using the principle of getting to know your legislators, one local group planned a visit from a state representative during the election campaign period. Another local group saw involvement in electoral politics and voter registration as important leverage in advocacy. The Coalition also sponsors legislative breakfasts. Members of local groups spoke to legislators at these events and lobbied and testified at the legislature. They then reflected on participation in these events. Letter writing and media events are lower-risk activities that are also available to politically aware and empowered people

Preparation for Legislative Advocacy

People who advocate for legislative change must be prepared for the experience both cognitively and affectively. Whether the action is to demonstrate publicly, write a letter or draft a petition, or lobby or give legislative testimony, acting requires knowledge and confidence in one's knowledge and abilities to act and have an impact. Although such activities are empowering, they also flow from a raised consciousness and awareness of oppression and the determination to take some level of risk.

Information about the issues and sharing feelings about participation are requisites to empowerment. Many important events are poorly attended because people are uninformed. People may agree to participate in an event but fail to do so because of feelings of apprehension, fear, or inadequacy. The worker who uses the skills of sharing information and reaching for feelings about participation will help people succeed at their efforts and move significantly toward empowerment.

In one instance the women living in a transitional living facility were asked at the last minute to participate in a demonstration against proposed state welfare cuts on the steps of the capitol and to participate in lobbying on the issue. An enthusiastic worker and the program director, Robin Taylor, quickly arranged to bring the women to the rally and to lobby with them. The women dutifully complied; however, once there they were overwhelmed and anxious. Although a few energetically participated with the worker, most attempted to hide in the lobby to avoid the experience. Robin states:

When I asked about this, the women said that they were not sure what the issues were, why people were shouting and angry, or whether they wanted to be seen on T.V. with so many people who were "down and out." One said she didn't want to wear any signs that said she was a welfare mother. Another said it was just too chaotic for her. She couldn't think with all the noise, let alone talk to a legislator. I realized that we had not prepared the women enough ahead of time for why they were going, what the experience might be like, or what roles they might play. I recognized it was natural to be a little fearful and skeptical. I held them together in a group and explained what was going on. With the explanations, one woman said, "I think I will go outside and carry a sign—it *is* my fight." All except one agreed with her and entered the demonstration.

When the group members discussed it afterward and in their next meeting, most were excited about what they had done and what they had learned. They agreed that they needed to prepare beforehand in order to choose to participate with confidence and understanding. Although the program director "saved the day" beautifully, a major lesson in political action was learned: People are not "bodies" to be marshalled for a cause if their empowerment is the desired outcome. Thoroughly talking out the issues and the feelings before and after the experience (i.e., praxis that includes feelings) is an essential part of the empowerment process. Role-play, rehearsal, naming of feelings, problem solving, and other skills generic to all helping processes are also critical in political work.

In chapter 10 we introduced Brenda Gary and her testimony at an appropriations committee meeting on the Department of Mental Health budget. Brenda is a member of an empowerment group of formerly homeless mentally ill women in a scattered-site residential support program. Her group was vitally concerned with the proposed Department of Mental Health cutbacks. The worker and program director, Gail Bourdon, *prepared the group to understand the issues and the process of testifying before asking for their participation.* First, she shared specific details of the proposed cuts and elicited the group member's reactions. She proposed that they might want to learn how to testify at the hearings and speak up for themselves. Then, when interest was high, she took two volunteers (Brenda and Vicky) and the staff to a workshop on the legislative process. Two weeks later, during an empowerment meeting, a *summary of the legislative process was given to the group by the worker and the members who went to the workshop.*

I asked the members to make statements about their feelings on possible cuts in services They did this with much effort and insight. The group members were asked if anyone would be interested in writing down and presenting these comments or others at the hearing. Vicky stated that she would like to attend the hearing, but she did not feel she could say anything. Brenda said she would be able to do this for the group. The group members thanked and complimented her for her willingness. Brenda was given a copy of the comments made and it was arranged that Debbie, the assistant worker, would visit her early the following afternoon to assist. By 11:00 the following morning Brenda had composed her testimony. Early that evening *we went to testify.* Brenda patiently waited two hours in line and then an additional two and one-half hours before testifying. The testimony was presented in the hall of the House of Representatives. Brenda and I presented our testimony. It was a striking image to see Brenda, in her woolen hat, speaking so well from the seat of the "minority leader." One senator thanked Brenda for her testimony and shared how moved she was by Brenda's effort. Brenda, who has multiple problems, was clearly the group leader that night.

―――――――

The group then reflected on their actions in the next meeting. The worker invited praxis, the members' reflections on the process of testifying and going to the legislative hearing.

―――――――

The group began by discussing the picture of some group members in the *Hartford Courant* the day after Brenda testified. Group members read the entire article to each other. I asked what the women thought and felt about attending the hearings. Brenda smiled and proudly stated she felt good about having spoken.

I asked Vicky how she felt about attending the hearing. Vicky said, "I was happy. It was one of the happiest times in my life. I saw and heard things I never thought I'd even learn about." The entire group cheered. Vicky said she enjoyed hearing about people's situations and all the people talking about not wanting cuts. She stated, "It's terrible how Governor Wacker is cutting programs." I asked Brenda if she thought her message was heard. Brenda said she thought so because they did not ask her unfriendly questions. They accepted her word and even thanked her. I asked the group members who went how it was for them. Vicky replied, "It was wonderful, although I did not speak. Brenda spoke for all of us. She was a leader." Brenda added, "I combined information about my life with information from the group and said there shouldn't be cuts." I said maybe each person in the group could be a leader as she finds ways of speaking out for common concerns and sharing experiences. Vicky agreed that was possible and said, "I felt like I could do that sometime. I feel the strength." The entire group agreed, noting that they had a voice and were heard. Ida said that those who simply sat there also brought support and power in numbers, so they had a presence as well as a voice. Cocoa said that she got confused by the "sign-up sheet," so she couldn't talk, but she was glad she was there.

I asked Brenda to take the group through the experience with her. She described how she was nervous and did not feel that the experience was real until she began to read. She added, "It's good to know that I can accomplish things even with a mental illness. Sometimes people think you can't do things because you have a mental illness. I live with the illness, but this does not mean I am not able to take care of business." The other members thoughtfully agreed.

The careful preparation of the members paid off in the group members' confident action. The *skills of guiding praxis (reflection on the action) helped the members own their gains and expand their understanding as well as their self-esteem and self-direction.* This is now a group of activists for the concerns of the mentally ill and the homeless.

A Women's Shelter Empowerment Group Prepares for and Reflects on Legislative Action

In the following example an experienced social worker prepares her group to meet the legislators. She presents specific issues, asks for their responses, and works with them on how they might talk at legislative hearings. Legislative hearings or open committee meetings on a bill give consumer experts and social work experts the opportunity to testify or inform legislators on the issue at hand. The issue at hand may relate to the passage of a bill or to the regulatory processes of implementing a bill in accordance with the spirit and letter of the law. Hearings also draw the public's attention to the bill or to unfair regulatory processes. Hearings are associated with a bill's favorable committee consideration (Germain and Gitterman, 1996). Richan (1991) suggests that legislative hearings can be intimidating. It is healthy to admit you are afraid and to prepare to open with who you are and how your experiences pertain to the issue to establish credibility; to state the issue and make your points, illustrating them with experiences; and to welcome questions and take your time in answering them. He also suggests thinking out what unfriendly questions there may be and rehearsing responses.

In this example the worker helps the group members to connect their experiences to the regulatory issue of cutting an existing program. She discusses what lobbying and testifying at hearings entails, using role play and rehearsal. Afterward, the women reflect on their actions. Jean Konon is the social worker for this empowerment group and a member of the Advocacy Committee of the Connecticut Coalition to End Homelessness. Eight African American women twenty-two to thirty-six years old are present. Jean stated:

"I have to tell you something very important. The state's Security Deposit Program was canceled as of the 15th of January. I went to a legislative training session yesterday that was set up by the Coalition. They believe the best people to speak to the legislators would be the people who are living in the shelters. I want to hear what you think about this. There are expected to be further cuts in programs. The Security Deposit Program ended on January 15, 1992. The RAP (Rental Assistance Program), which most of you want, was only available for a few months. This *week there are legislative hearings where you can go and testify about your experiences and howthese cuts would affect you."* Johnette responded, "I think we should speak up. They only had a few shelters; now they have a lot. And it's going to keep on getting worse—because there are a lot of homeless people out there." The others elaborated with feelings of anger and sadness. I recognized their feelings and said, "Well, we can go talk to the legislators in their office. That's called lobbying. And we can go the legislature and give testimony at hearings that will be held on these cutbacks. The women were eager to go. *I suggested rehearsing.*

I asked, "How would it help you if these programs were now available?" Each one responded. "I recognized these are serious withdrawals of programs you need!" They agreed. I asked, "How would you say it's been for you being in a shelter if you were testifying? Let's play it out." Sandra said, "Well, I'd tell them that it hasn't been too great. It's crowded here. My children are so confused. Where do they live? Where's home? Where will they live? Will we have to go to Drug Village or Death Row [the nicknames for the nearby housing projects]? They'll have to change schools again! What if those programs are gone forever? Where is the hope?" Erna said, "I've been without my own place for eight months. My relatives got tired of us. Our only hope is a subsidy." Johnette said, "I'd tell them that I'd like some help. It hurts to be in a shelter. I just want to be given a chance for decent housing for my children."

I credited their fine rehearsal and explained who the legislators were and what visiting their offices and testifying publicly would be like. Marla said that she was too scared to talk but she would go for support. Johnette and Verlaine said they would talk. *I recognized that it is"nervous making" to talk in front of an audience but said that I thought they could do it. And they could also speak face to face with an elected official.* There was then more discussion of whether to bring the children to lobby. They thought that was a good idea. Johnette said, "Well I can say I've been helped a lot by different people in the shelter, but I need the security deposit to move on." I said, "That's very well said!" Johnette said, "I think they will listen. I think I can say it."

Taking Action

Testifying   The women testified at the legislative hearings and went with the worker to lobby an elected official. The Security Deposit Program was reinstated, but the Rent Assistance Program continued to be frozen. Although this made them angry, they experienced a sense of accomplishment in speaking for themselves to legislators and in the positive outcome on the Security Deposit Program. One woman, Johnette, also volunteered to represent the group at the legislative breakfast sponsored by the Coalition. The group helped her rehearse what "eating with important people" would be like. She felt able to handle the experience and brought it back to the group. Johnette describes the legislative breakfast experience (Jean records):

"They had a homeless breakfast, I call it. It was for the people who make the laws to meet with people who need the laws changed—that's us. I went to represent myself and our shelter. They had some people from other shelters get up and talk about the cuts they had in the programs. I spoke to a white man from the suburbs and to a Puerto Rican woman legislator. I have her name and phone number. I told them what my experiences were."

I asked, "How was that experience for you?" Johnette replied, "Well, it was all right. I was nervous first. I sat and waited a while because there were a lot of people there. They had wanted to put my son in the nursery but I kept him with me because he's homeless too. I talked to the legislators with my baby asleep in my arms. It was good for them to see me with my son because there are a lot of women and children who are homeless. I told them about how the Security Deposit Program helps us and how hard it is without it." Verlaine agreed and added, "Last week we also went up to the state capital and testified." Erna, Johnette, Shandra, and Tashika said they went too. Shandra said, "We sat before microphones. But I wasn't afraid because I was prepared. I told them we can't get out of shelters without RAPS." Each told what she said. Johnette concluded, "We did something important." Everyone agreed.

Lobbying   The two members of the group who went to lobby with the worker shared their firsthand experiences as examples to the points the worker had raised in arguing for the need for the Security Deposit Program. The elected official was very much interested in the issue and asked good questions. They left feeling that their visit made a difference. Richan sees lobbying as a "special pleading" and an exchange. The lobbyists want action on a bill and the representative wants reelection, and perhaps to be seen as a humanitarian. The legislator has the power to cast a vote for or against a proposed bill, and the lobbyists have the power of expertise, numbers, facts, and experiences. The most direct way of influencing the policy maker is to talk with him or her in person or to lobby (1991). Explanations of what lobbying is are important and avoid confusion. One group member thought lobbying meant standing in the lobby of the capitol shouting opposition to a bill as people entered. People must be prepared to talk and interact with a policymaker with the confidence that knowing the facts about the issue can bring. The experiences that only those who suffer can share give faces to facts and are ammunition to policymakers who favor a bill. Citing the arguments opponents might make and answering these are also helpful to the representative (Richan 1991). Richan's excellent guide on lobbying can help empower consumers of services.

Letters   The same worker prepared members of another shelter empowerment group to write letters to Congress regarding the Section 8 freeze and a proposed bill to release some Section 8 vouchers. The following letter was composed and sent by group members after their preparation. The opening lines should identify what the letter is about and who the writers are. Then an argument should be succinctly presented (in less than one page). Letters sent in a timely and thoughtful fashion can be powerful persuaders, especially when a great number of people write on the same subject (Richan 1991). They did receive a reply to their letter that affirmed the senator's action.

DEAR SENATOR DODD,

We are women who are living in a Shelter in Hartford and we are in desperate need of housing. We're requesting that more funds be added to the Section 8 Certificate and Voucher Programs; we support the FY93 House appropriation of 50,000 new vouchers and certificates. We need affordable housing now so we can afford to pay for rent and food for ourselves and our children. The food stamps we receive are not enough to cover the cost of food for our families for the whole month or to pay our other bills like electricity, heat and clothing. Now, we have to choose between the Hartford Housing Projects, which are unsafe for our children, or expensive market rate apartments. We want housing that is safe and affordable.

We all have applied for Section 8 Certificates, but we have been told that the wait for Section 8 housing is two to five years!

Would you please help us by supporting the FY93 House appropriation of 50,000 new vouchers and certificates? We know this is still not enough, but it is the best proposal presented this year.

Sincerely Yours,
Homeless and Concerned Mothers

Combining Advocacy Efforts

Often demonstrations are combined with testifying at the legislature or lobbying efforts to keep the pressure on legislators and to involve the public in the issue. Politically aware people and their allies in many states are rallying against TANF and the "welfare reform" as shown in the powerful the example given earlier in this chapter involving the KWRU, a branch of the National Welfare Rights Movement, and the Poor People's Summit (Baptist and Bricker-Jenkins 1999; Honkala, Bricker-Jenkins, and Baptist 1999). "Welfare reform" raises its ugly head in every electoral year, and legislators and the general public need education on how ineffective it is to seek to balance budgets on the backs of the poor, whether or not the proposal is couched in humanitarian "it's-good-for-them" terms. Katz aptly calls "welfare reform" a "war on welfare" (1986).

Newspaper and Media

The development of alternative presses and newspapers such as *Survival News* (source for information on the Massachusetts rally) and *Street News* (published by and for homeless people) is a powerful way to educate the public. Such publications are by and for the people who suffer with issues of oppression and their allies. They are free to no-income or low-income people, and they provide a vehicle for raising consciousness and "telling the story." *Survival News*, for example, pays $25 for articles written by low-income people. Such newspapers also provide extensive coverage on struggles for human rights and basic resources. Social workers can make sure their clients have subscriptions to such papers and assist them in preparing material for publication. They can also assist in letters to the editor in mainstream newspapers and in obtaining media coverage of actions. Richan (1991) advises that media exposure is a no-cost, highly effective way to reach the public with an issue. Once again the principle of thorough preparation applies and makes a difference in audience response.

Thus far in this chapter we have suggested that community members, consumers of services, and their allies can act together to change unjust and oppressive conditions in a variety of ways. These ways range from all forms of community-oriented practice to specific community development, social planning, and social action strategies to engaging in legislative advocacy using indirect and direct means to influence policymakers. All these activities are ultimately political activities, for they seek to disturb and change power relationships and balances that maintain oppression. Changing power relations and balances is very difficult. Actions toward empowerment are not earthshaking. They do not change the world order in a sweeping scourge. But empowered people continuing to act with confidence and strength can and do tip the balances toward the creation of a just society, as they cannot accept anything less for the human community.

The metaphor of "tipping or changing the balances" is an appropriate one to consider. On one level it describes the mythical scales of justice that are tipped heavily toward the wealthy and the politically powerful. On another it describes an unsteady balance of forces that maintain the status quo in dynamic tension (Lewin 1951; Brager and Holloway 1978; Germain and Gitterman 1996). To change things as they are to things as they should be (e.g., to make policies or programs/institutions that are free of oppression and exploitation), the unsteady and tense equilibrium that prevails must be disturbed. The forces must be analyzed and influenced in favor of desired change. Disequilibrium must be endured as forces are changed or realigned. When this happens, through the actions of empowered people, a new or different policy/law, program, service, or institution may come into being.

These ideas spring from Kurt Lewin's notion of force field analysis (1951). Lewin saw a unit of potential change as existing in a field of opposing (countervailing) forces that needed to be altered for change to occur. For community organizers Force Field Analysis can be used as a tool of power analysis and coalition building. Gil (1981) has applied Lewin's ideas to social policy analysis and the policymaking process, and Brager and Holloway (1978) have applied the concepts to bottom-up change initiated by frontline staff in human service organizations. Wax (1971) suggests that power may indeed tend to corrupt when it is highly concentrated, when those who use it are not held publicly accountable, and when it is not possible to develop countervailing power. He notes that social work is concerned with developing countervailing power among previously low-power groups in our society. We have illustrated this throughout this chapter. Lewin's notion of opposing, or countervailing, forces is important to understand. Empowerment of the people creates countervailing forces. Hence the tool of force field analysis is of central importance to the practitioner. It may be used to understand broad and pervasive problems of person/environment transactions in society—in communities, groups, families, and especially service organizations; to analyze policies that must be created or changed; to analyze organizations in need of change; and to strategize doable changes and to shift power arrangements.

It is a basic survival tool for social workers in agencies that have a variety of ideologies and practical considerations. Through listening to clients workers know best what clients are experiencing and what services are needed. They must involve clients directly in expressing their own needs and what would be most helpful to them. After receiving the clients' views, workers must know how to make change in their own organizations, where policies, programs, or lack of response is not hospitable to empowering clients. Wagner's recent study showed that workers struggled with losing their social change ideology when faced with practice realities (1990). Although some tried to blend ideals of a just society with social work practice and administration, many detached themselves from their ideals, and sometimes from the profession. This detachment came from negative job experiences and from mobility into powerful positions. An alternative to detachment is the slow, steady work of shaping social service agencies to realize the process and goal of empowerment. The force field analysis is useful in providing knowledge for analysis and action and for suggesting strategies that can help workers and clients/consumers of services realize this objective. The reader is referred to Brager and Holloway's extensive work (1978) and Germain and Gitterman (1996) for the how-to of force field analysis. In an empowerment approach, empowered clients must be part of the change process, acting on behalf of themselves and others like them.

The community work described in this chapter is reminiscent of the people's stirrings of an earlier time although with a greater degree of political so-phistication and a new global emphasis. In 1968, when people called clients demanded change in unjust institutions, Lloyd Setleis, a respected consul-tant, teacher, and dean at Yeshiva University, Wurzweiler School of Social Work, said that social workers and clients must participate in the transfor-mation of their institutions so that institutions can become just, relevant, and responsive to individual and social need. Agencies as well as social workers and clients must advocate for necessary institutional change. Social work agencies, he advised, must be organized more horizontally, so that clients, workers, and administrators who enact different functions and re-sponsibilities are "all on the same plane" with access to each other. Social work practice is political practice aimed at creating transformed social insti-tutions through the full energies of all segments of the human community (Setleis 1974). The right and the left hands are members of the same body. A caring and just society depends on the full empowerment of all, especially those who have been disenfranchised and oppressed. This empowerment approach will help the practitioner help people to empower themselves.

We have come full circle. While at a social work conference in Atlanta, Georgia, our group of social worker/activists walked the streets of the com-munity where Dr. Martin Luther King, Jr., was born and raised and from which his preaching, teaching, civil rights, and peace activism took hold. Someone said, "This is like the northeast end of Hartford." I said, "And this is like home." We visited Dr. King's birthplace and a few blocks away stood awed and moved to tears at his burial place. We knocked on the door of a small building on Auburn Street, where the sign said S.C.L.C. Headquar-ters. No one answered. We prayed at Ebeneezer Baptist Church, "where the dream began." We reverently picked up the hymnal, opened to "Marching to Zion," which lay on the organ where Dr. King's mother, Alberta Williams King, was assassinated as she played one Sunday in 1974. The church was empty, holy, full of resounding voices now silenced. On Sunday we returned to worship in a Catholic church across the street from Ebeneezer. The elderly African American deacon stood up and prayed for the five religious

Sisters who were killed in Liberia "for no reason at all," he said. "Just like King, and Malcolm X, and the Birmingham Five, and Schwerner and Goodman and Chaney, and Oscar Romero . . . and Sudeka," I said silently. The litany grows longer—James Byrd Jr., Matthew Shepard, Paul Laffin, a compassionate Hartford Homeless Shelter worker and activist murdered outside the shelter. . . . Hatred and oppression is "for no reason at all." For us the social work conference was on Auburn Street, not in a multimillion-dollar hotel. We realized that when we knocked there had been an answer. The answer is that people who are empowered can transform the world, and build the beloved community together, and that we must.

The dispossessed of this nation . . . live in a cruelly unjust society. They must organize a revolution against that injustice, not against the lives of persons who are their fellow citizens, but against the structures through which society is refusing to take means which have been called for, and which are at hand to lift the load of poverty.

—Martin Luther King Jr., *The Trumpet of Conscience*

14 Empowerment in Global Perspective: Social And Economic Justice For All

Our solidarity with the people of all countries causes us to seek to expand the community of interests and values needed to manage problems that respect no borders. . . . All people are made less secure by the poverty and misery that exist in the world.
—IDC, "Shaping the Twenty-First Century"

There is a new world dawning at the break of the twenty-first century. It is characterized by economic interdependence, cross cultural communication through technological advances, and, potentially, mutually beneficial exchange and interconnection. The globalization of the economy may benefit economically poor countries but it may also add to exploitation of the world's resources, its workers, and its poorest citizens (Blau 1998). It may reflect the cultural and economic imperialism of dominant and powerful countries. For example, Australians traditionally value egalitarianism, collectivism, and "mateship," while market realities of the new global economy stress efficiency and growth, presenting a conflict of political ideologies shaped by globalization (Capling, Considine, and Crozier 1998; Owens 1998). The global economy is also largely unregulated by national or international bodies, which creates fertile ground for human oppression. Hence it is imperative to work toward a global vision of the beloved community where there is social and economic justice for all people. This is the vision of the empowerment approach to social work practice.

It's a Small World After All

Distinctions are blurring between the global "North" and "South," "East" and "West" (IDC 1996). Macedo and Araujo-Freire (1998) note that many countries of the industrialized North have significant pockets of poverty and despair, violence and attendant social problems similar to countries of the global South. Hence social development is needed in fully industrialized and less industrialized countries alike. Conversely, there are areas of economic advancement and wealth throughout the global South. The widening gap between rich and poor is a worldwide phenomena. Issues are no longer "domestic" or "international." Risks of social disintegration and social and economic exclusion (Elliot and Mayadas 1999; chapters 2 and 4) affect all countries, as do the opportunities and risks of participating in a rapidly growing global economic system (IDC 1996). The difficulties in protecting worker's hardwon rights for a basic living wage and minimally acceptable working conditions when labor is interchangeable across the globe is the "downside" of greatly enhanced opportunities for global South and worldwide economic advancement.

It is necessary to reflect on the meanings of the concept *empowerment* in the context of *economic globalization*. The use of the word *empowerment* in discourse (or meaning making) about economic globalization is at odds with definitions of empowerment as part of the *anti-oppressive discourse* related to human rights for all. In anti-oppressive discourse value is placed on the person and human dignity. As it is used in the context of economics the words *consumer empowerment* are just buzzwords; the value is on the market (Owens 1998). Attaining economic resources continues to be an essential goal in empowerment-oriented anti-oppressive practice as it is used in global social work and social development (Midgely 1999). Yet there is more to becoming an empowered individual, family, group, community, or nation than economic prosperity. We continue to define empowerment broadly as a personal/political phenomena with the ends of human dignity and social and economic justice for all (see chapter 1). Global perspective and international collaboration, and the monitoring of situations of great economic disparity and those where worker's rights and human dignity are at issue, could contribute to a win-win scenario for all the world's people (Blau 1998).

Having a *global perspective* and approach to social work practice enables us to appreciate the universals in human experience. Recognition of commonalities and increased respect for differences helps to dissipate fear and mistrust and to promote world peace, international cooperation, and global justice. A global perspective offers new ways and multiple dimensions of analysis from a multicultural and pluralistic viewpoint (Elliot and Mayadas 1999). While there has been a retreat in international spending by the government of the United States since the Vietnam War, the profession of social work has identified many mutual benefits of international social work practice and the utilization of a global perspective in viewing all social work practice. There are both barriers to and opportunities in developing and enacting such a perspective. Ethnocentrism and a lack of knowledge or curiosity about other cultures is an initial barrier. Differences in salaries, professional qualifications, training, and preferred theoretical and regional approaches including favoring theories of the global North, license requirements, language, and communication may all present barriers. Yet global efforts to include international curricula and international learning opportunities, exchanges, and partnerships are underway in many schools of social work. International content is mandated curricula by accrediting bodies, but sharing learning with others globally is a basic task that needs further implementation in social work curriculum. Further, the exchange of learning must be equally bidirectional between the global South and the global North (Elliot and Mayadas 1999; Ramanathan and Link 1999).

Social workers have a unique role to play in the establishment of the global beloved community as we assist localities in empowering themselves to meet the needs of all citizens, particularly the most vulnerable and disenfranchised. In this sense, a *social development* approach or *social investment* approach to social welfare and social work practice (Estes 1993, 1999; Midgley 1999) is congruous with an empowerment approach. Such an approach emphasizes community development and prevention over remedial measures, although in some cases both prevention and remediation are needed simultaneously. "Development" does not mean that people should "pick themselves up by their own bootstraps," when they do not have boots, or, simplistically, "get a job." It does mean that communities are helped to develop and sustain economic and social resources through the participation of all citizens including the most marginalized or socially excluded. This "requires substantial resource allocations by governments to invest in those who need to acquire the skills that will insure their integration into the economy. They also require supports to ensure that they are able to use the opportunities available to them" (Midgley 1999:198).

Estes suggests that there are seven levels of international social development-oriented practice. *Individual and group empowerment* are achieved through conscientization and praxis—reflection, action, and reflection in a spiraling manner. *Conflict resolution* development practice is concerned with efforts directed at reducing grievances between persons and groups, especially when there are asymmetrical power relationships. *Com-*

munity building is achieved through increased participation and the enlivening of people to respond more equitably to the needs of all members of
the community. *Institution building* refers to the process of humanizing
existing social institutions and developing new ones to meet basic human
needs. *Nation building* works toward the integration of a nation's social,
economic, and cultural institutions, while *region building* does this on a
wider regional level. *World building* is the process of working toward the
establishment of a new system of international social, political, economic,
and ecological relationships guided by the quest for world peace and social
and economic justice and preservation of the world's environmental resources (Estes 1999, 1993, 1991). All of these levels of development/libera-
tion practice contribute toward building the global beloved community.

World population trends indicate that more young people than ever are
entering their childbearing and working years while the number and proportion of people over age sixty-five are rapidly increasing (UNFPA 1998).
Basic life supports, such as food, shelter, education, employment, and health
care as well as vehicles to develop and maintain personal and cultural meaning in life are therefore the purview of empowering social work practice. For
example, social work students in Guyana, South America, in a course on
aging, worked on ways to improve intergenerational dialogue and sharing as
well as to preserve cultural heritage by combining children's groups with
groups of elders who were acting as crafts teachers. This addressed economic
issues, as the crafts were marketable. It was also aimed at the current social
issues of elders' growing isolation, related to being left alone all day by working adult children, and the widening gap between generations as youth are
exposed TV and other media. This creative, preventive, and empowering
communitywide strategy was supported and further developed by the Guyana Association of Professional Social Workers. The world's future will depend on how well families and societies meet the basic needs of the young
and the old (UNFPA 1998).

Basic Services for All

In 1995 the United Nations established a *Task Force on Basic Social
Services For All* to achieve the goals and commitments of all of its divisions.
The goal is to provide assistance to countries for a concerted attack on pov-
erty and to strengthen the follow-up mechanisms of each UN conference

for the delivery of coordinated assistance at country and regional levels (UNDP 1997). Incorporating critical education (conscientization), social development, and individual and community empowerment methods, social workers are the professionals best suited to assist localities in developing basic social services for all.

Basic social services as defined by the UN include universal availability of preventive and curative health care with access for all, especially vulnerable and disadvantaged groups—in particular women and children, universal access to safe and reliable family-planning methods, access to safe water and sanitation, and adequate shelter for all. Early in the twenty-first century the following intolerable phenomena should be greatly reduced: underweight prevalence among preschool children and maternal, infant, and under-five mortality rates. The following should be increased: life expectancy at birth, school enrollment ratio, and adult literacy (UNDP 1997). The development of nations is measured by the achievement of these goals. Almost all nations, except those in sub-Saharan Africa where recent natural and man-made disasters have wreaked havoc, have made recent dramatic progress in these basic goals (UNDP 1997). Social workers can be strategically located to help empower people and their communities to attain these universally basic entitlements.

The goals of empowerment coincide with the goals of sustainable human development in that a higher quality of life for all people means that people will attain increased power. To achieve this the unfinished tasks include overcoming extreme poverty, achieving food security, increasing effectiveness of economies and government, fostering regional cooperation, enhancing participation of all people—notably women, and reducing the dependency of the poorest people and countries by increasing their capacities for self-reliance. There needs to be substantial progress in primary education, gender equality, and the empowerment of women and the end of discrimination against women and girls. Ensuring the rights and empowerment of women and children and the economic well-being of families with opportunities for all family members are primary goals of international development work. Sustaining environmental resources is a key to realizing all other goals as are international cooperation, assistance, and partnership efforts (IDC 1996).

More often than not in world history international economic interests have meant the exploitation of a less developed area's richest resources for the gain of the few and the loss of the many. In his poem "Sugarcane" Aaron

Blackman, a Guyanese poet and social work student at the University of Guyana, characterizes the loss of environmental resources and exploitation under colonialism and in the current time:

Once the world's pride
Now crumbling with the world's worst market price
Under pressure with the best rice
While the oppressors keep throwing their dice
Having filled their pockets with sugar money. . . .
Kings they brought from Africa lands
To work as slaves in their backlands
Producing sugar under their plans. . . .
While Missi and Massa enjoyed their destruction.
Indentured servants coming from India
Suffer the same fate as Africa. . . .
Working sugarcane and filling the slave master's coffer. . . .
Together we must work to stop this sugar unrest
If we are to survive in this land of the oppressor's mess.

While ending economic and other types of exploitation are goals of crucial importance in considering empowerment, they are much bigger than the purview of any one profession. Yet social workers are finding mutual benefit and enriched learning in their partnership efforts with their counterparts in other countries (Ramanathan and Link 1999). Later in this chapter I will discuss the mutually beneficial five-year collaboration of two social work educators and their institutions from the global North and South that includes faculty exchange, the visiting of social work students and faculty, and the participation of local agencies in both countries.

Empowerment is not an ethnocentric or Eurocentric concept. It is universal. We have demonstrated throughout the book that empowerment practice has roots in many countries and takes place all over the globe. In this chapter we will discuss cross-national empowerment-oriented social work and empowerment practice in a variety of countries. Such practice will relate to the goals discussed in the preceding section of this chapter and to the values, knowledge base, and methods of the empowerment approach to social work practice.

The empowerment approach relates directly to individual, sociopolitical, and economic development/liberation in the face of human oppression. The empowerment approach draws on social development/liberation theory, although it emphasizes that highly industrialized countries have areas that are desperately in need of social development just as less industrialized countries do. Homelessness and the poverty of children are global phenomena that will be presented as cases in point.

In chapter 1 we noted the importance of language in social work practice. Ramanathan and Link (1999) note that this is especially true in international practice: "It is critical that we rethink our tendency to categorize nations in value-laden terms that devalue whole groups of people" (222). They note the words *underdeveloped* and *third world* are particularly problematic. They are based on certain indicators, like the GNP that fails to take into account such things as per capita deaths from domestic violence or by handguns, for example. Brown (1984) notes his aversion to the construct "Third World." The term *third world* became popular during the cold war in the mid 1950s when nations not wanting to align with either the United States ("First World") or the Soviet Union ("Second World") identified themselves as "Third World." The construct, however, sounds demeaning (third world third rate?) and lumps into one category all kinds of diverse peoples. Brown calls the third world the two-thirds world as "the number of those who suffer deprivation and oppression at the hands of the rest of us is at least two thirds, if not more, of the human family (1984:13). In terms of the history of civilization, the so-called third world can actually be considered the first world. Estes (1991) notes that while social and economic development and their associated methods are desirable, the word *developmentalism* has become associated with timid measures that often preserve the power of the wealthy, whereas the word *liberation* more often encompasses the radical changes that are needed to ensure social and economic justice. This text will therefore use the words *not fully industrialized* instead of *un-* or *underdeveloped* or *third world* to describe impoverished areas of the world and *development/ liberation* practice where the word *development* is usually used.

The Empowerment Approach as Paradigm

The empowerment approach is a paradigm for international social work practice as its conceptual framework (chapter 1 and 2) specifies the ingredients needed to practice with poor and oppressed groups beyond national boundaries and throughout the world. The approach relates to individual as well as sociopolitical and economic development and liberation in the face of human oppression. Additional to a range of social work skills, consciousness-raising, empowering group process, and the process of praxis—action-reflection-action—are the core processes of the empowerment approach *and* of conscientization and social development practice (Estes 1991; Lee 1996b). Conscientization is the dominant approach to social work practice throughout Latin America.

Sociopolitical conflict, economic hardship, and the uneven distribution of resources are a problem all over the world (Staub-Bernasconi 1992). Homelessness in the United States is prototypic of poverty in the midst of affluence (Lee 1991, 1999a; Lee, Odie-Ali, and Botsko 2000; Lee and Odie-Ali 2000; Alston 1999). While counting the homeless poses many problems, Link and his colleagues note that 13.5 million—7.4 percent—of adult Americans have experienced literal homelessness during their lives (Rosenheck 1996). Yet, homelessness is a global phenomenon (Glasser 1994). I have been working with social workers in Georgetown, Guyana to address the issue of homelessness there. Many aspects of homelessness are similar, although the resources to meet the needs depend mostly on the creativity of people in less industrialized countries (Lee, Odie-Ali, and Botsko 2000).

A theme in this book has been the poverty of children. This is a tragic phenomena in fully industrialized as well as less industrialized countries. In Brazil more than twelve million children live on the streets. This reflects, in part, rapid urbanization and the breakdown of family structures, another global problem. In 1990 54 percent of Brazilian children lived in families whose per capita income was less than half the minimum wage of $65 a month. The distribution of wealth in Brazil is one of the most unjust in the world (Sandoval 1994). Yet the gap between rich and poor children in the United States is the greatest in the world (NCH 1998; Alston 1999). Over two million children per year live on the streets in the U.S., despite this country's resources (NCH 1998). In Guyana, formerly British Guiana, located in South America, at least 50 percent of the population live in abject poverty (USDS 1999). The minimum wage of civil service workers is about $63 a month and private sector wages are not regulated (USDS 1999). Even the most experienced social workers earn less than $200 a month, 70 percent of which is usually spent on housing and another portion often going to helping clients for whom there are few resources.

The process and findings of a *collaborative study on street children in Georgetown, Guyana* will be discussed in this chapter.

The empowerment approach addresses social work's role and function in the midst of worldwide human rights violations and lack of provision for basic human needs. In addition to severe poverty, victimization of many types, especially violence against women and children, is a worldwide problem that occurs in every strata of society (Hokenstad and Midgley 1997). Battered women constitute 40 percent of homeless families in New York. World Watch Institute found the number one problem shared by women in villages around the world to be "my husband beats me" (EWAR Project 1992). In Guyana, four out of five women in a study by Danns and Parsad (1989) were beaten by their male partners. The group is the "treatment of choice" for both victims and perpetrators of violence, for the oppressed and those who oppress or permit oppression.

At the base of the *empowerment approach* is the belief that people can join together to affirm life and promote social justice and equal opportunity. Empowerment practice asserts that it is unethical to "treat" victims clinically or interpersonally without offering to help them raise consciousness, throw the oppressor(s) off their backs, and become victors. Forrest Harris, a leading African American theologian, notes that oppressed people who have not raised their consciousness "have been victimized by their powerlessness and fear and their translation of these into internal appropriation of subservient and menial roles. [They] turn their frustration inward, destroying themselves and each other" (1993:000). In turn, they face further retribution by the dominant society. Gang violence, drug abuse, family disintegration, and many other forms of violence appear globally and have root in internalized oppression and blocked opportunities. This is also a cause of the high rate of suicide among minority of color youths in the U.S. (West 1993). Harris concludes that helping professionals in a time of social crisis must address themselves to *both* the inner *and* outer liberation of persons. The empowerment approach seeks to channel personal/clinical/interpersonal practice and political/social change/activism practice into one mighty flow.

As defined in chapters 1 and 2, *critical education* means to confront, reflect on, and evaluate the problems and contradictions of society in order to change them. Critical awareness develops in a process of dialogue with others in groups. It must be done on a personal, cultural/societal, and political level. The development of critical awareness is called *conscientization* (Freire 1973a, b). The basic elements of Freire's method are described in chapters 1, 2, and 10. Critical education approaches have been developed and utilized in many countries. They have been used in Western Africa for many years. A particularly helpful and practical set of guides for critical education and community development/liberation practice based on community work started in Kenya in 1974 is a three-volume set of workbooks entitled *Training for Transformation* by Anne Hope and Sally Timmel (1984, 1995). These books are based on Friere's work and concepts from liberation theology and the general anti-oppressive discourse. Hope and Timmel call the facilitator of culture circles and community groups the *animator*. They note that the role of the animator is to help people unveil their situations by providing a framework for thinking, creative, active participants to consider a common problem and find solutions. The animator does not "give solutions" but asks *why*, *how*, and *who* and helps participants to describe, analyze, suggest, decide, and plan. In that way people are actively involved in the social construction of knowledge. They stress that it is important to accept people's problem definitions and solutions, as those who live with a problem know it best. Reflecting on an actual experience in Uganda, they note that in one community where health issues seemed paramount to outsiders, community members wanted most of all to put up a football field. When this was done the community gained self-confidence, a structure for communication, and a sense of the power to change things. Later they attacked health problems with a confidence that they could achieve their goals. They advise that when the animator helps the group reflect on and survey generative themes (essential community problems) they list what they expect to hear on one side of the survey and what community members actually say on the other side to make sure the animator(s) hear the group members accurately.

The critical education approach was used in my work as a *teacher-learner and consultant-collaborator* in Guyana, South America. Consultation and collaboration began when Professor Odie-Ali, coordinator of the University of Guyana Department of Social Work, approached me, as she thought that the empowerment approach belonged to developing/transforming nations such as Guyana. I agreed to pursue the possibility of its relevance. We found that she was right, since the approach, without the formal name, is already well developed and utilized in Guyana as in other areas of the Caribbean and in many industrializing countries. I have been working with her and the Guyana Association of Professional Social Workers and other helping persons in Guyana in mutually empowering dialogue and collaboration since 1995. The work in Guyana has focused on consultation, teaching, practice, and research in the areas of the empowerment of women, especially battered and abused women and children, the needs of the mentally ill homeless, and the needs of other homeless populations including street children.

Developing *cultural competence* is essential in working cross-nationally. Immersing oneself in the host culture, experiencing it in as many ways as possible without judgment, is the first step in the process. While reading and viewing videos as well as talking with persons raised in the culture is a good start at immersion, going to the community itself and meeting with community representatives in a "culture circle" is an excellent follow-up process. Some writers suggest that there is a continuum of cultural competence. This continuum ranges from negative and destructive attitudes and actions stemming from the heritage of colonialism, or insular attitudes toward the rest of the world, to neutral ideas based on geocentricism, to a precompetence as learning starts, to competence and advanced competence in cultural interaction, including reaching to participate in globally oriented work (Ramanathan and Link 1999). Exposure to other cultures, particularly in dialogic interchange, mitigates against the dangers of ethnocentrism. Empowerment practice develops strengths in indigenous leaders, people, theories, and approaches to social problems. The use of "culture circles" (broad-based groups of community representatives gathered to define and analyze local problems) is necessary before any theory can be blindly applied to problem solving (Ramanathan and Link 1999).

In *Race and Group Work* (Mistry and Brown 1997) Paul Taylor reflects on the barriers to cross-cultural work created by the way people think, behave, and speak. He notes that "cross-national group work demands that we confront each other . . . honestly and authentically, otherwise there will be no group or group life" (Taylor 1997:44). He suggests that the preconditions of cross-national group work are that we should not be seduced by the attractiveness of different cultures, should not export our own moral judgments, and should not import a "confining tolerance." He suggests that outsiders can develop accurate views of a culture if they have an accurate view of themselves and their own cultures. Yet there are five barriers a cross-national group must confront before it can work effectively together: language, hierarchy (the continuum of power in relationships), individualism, gender, and uncertainty. Truly understanding the use of language is the primary factor in cross-cultural relations and, beyond that, the boundaries we build around ourselves in attempting cross-national work (Taylor 1997; Lee 1999b).

In the cross-cultural Guyana-U.S. collaboration it was tremendously help-ful that Guyanese social workers saw the empowerment of themselves and their people, especially women, as their own goal and experienced the em-powerment approach in written and spoken word as congruous with their values. This helped to establish a common language and a beginning trust. Indeed, English is spoken in Guyana, but there is also Creolese, Hindi, and other Indian dialects, all of which change the meaning of English as I know it as a Northern American. I did work hard at understanding the Creole with fair to good success, although the acquisition of East Indian culture and meanings is slower. In Guyana there is cultural respect for a "professor," and this helps initially, although I have to work harder at promoting parity in communication and equity in dialogue. Guyana is a traditional male-dominant culture, yet, as an industrializing country, women who work to improve the good of all are valued. And there, as in most countries, more women than men are social workers and clients. Hence to some degree gender has been a factor, as has culture and, for some, color, but these have not impeded effective communication because of the efforts made on both sides to cross these potential barriers. But I am ever aware of the need to keep Taylor's principles in mind as I quite literally cross bridges. Some of the ways I have done this is in the authentic presentation of self and the utilization of empowering skills in developing and working with culture circles and community groups, as in the following examples.

Beginnings in Guyana-Forming Culture Circles

My first steps in addressing the needs of battered women and homeless populations in Guyana were to meet with educators, media representatives, medical personnel, social workers, the police commissioner and his head officers, and groups of nonprofessionally trained service providers and in-terested citizens. These dialogue experiences were types of *culture circles* that helped me to understand the concerns of the people regarding the empowerment of women and homeless people living on the streets in Guyana.

In one such culture circle dialogue with the police around how to enforce the new (1996) domestic violence law was remarkable. The commissioner of police for all Guyana, Mr. Laurie Lewis, firmly stated his belief in the importance of the law and had all of his head officers at the meeting. A wise and experienced man with unusual insight and compassion, he asked the consultants and social work leaders to give a brief talk on the dynamics of domestic violence. When this was met with polite silence, he encouraged his chiefs to respond with their experiences. Regional police chiefs shared stories of how when police were called on the physical abuse of a woman, the abused woman would often say nothing had happened even though she stood there bleeding. Female social workers present responded by sharing stories about how fearful the woman might be of reprisals or loss of economic support and income. The police chiefs (two were women) pressed for how they might respond, then, to help the victimized woman make the charge. The head of the GAPSW, also the nation's highest ranking female army officer, Lieutenant Colonel Christine King, along with Professor Odie-Ali and the consultants, then role-played responses with volunteer chiefs. My intervention was to ask that the role-playing be based on actual police cases. The work was filled with energy and excitement as strategies were developed. When the commissioner asked how he could help, Sr. Jacinta Sukhraj, the administrator of the new rural battered women's shelter spoke of the need for security and police surveillance. The commissioner directed the police chief in charge of that area to develop a plan for surveillance and assistance. Male and female police officers were eventually assigned to the task. Everyone present learned from the dialogue. Other follow-up meetings were planned on the separate but not unrelated issues of domestic violence and homeless street dwellers.

In the rural community where the battered women's shelter, Genesis Home and Complex, is located the administrator formed a culture circle of community leaders and women interested in helping battered women. She invited a wide range of people from this and another similar community to meet with the consultants, myself, and Judith Beaumont, the executive director of a program serving a similar population in the U.S. We were asked to facilitate the dialogue about the new shelter, teach about domestic violence, discuss the 1996 Domestic Violence Law, Guyana's first, and share how similar programs in the United States are structured and how they help physically and/or sexually abused women and girls. Thirty to forty people attended the all-day meeting. The following is an excerpt from the morning's culture circle experience (The worker's skills in facilitating the meeting are in italics):

Sister Jacinta, the administrator of the new shelter for abused women, shared the hopes and plans for Genesis House with the group. She noted that women are welcome from anywhere in Guyana. The program was planned to be economically self-sustaining as a farm, and an educational/ vocational building were also to be parts of the complex. Community members would be invited to participate in these employment and learning opportunities, although they are located separately from the shelter. . . . Her opening statements were greeted with much enthusiasm although I noted that a young Indian (Indo-Guyanese) man sat silently and registered confusion nonverbally. Sister then introduced us to the group. We were greeted warmly, especially by the social workers and the women we met with the night before. (See the group meeting in chapter 3).

After going around the circle and having each one tell who she or he was and why they came today, *I gave global perspective* , explaining that domestic violence was a big problem everywhere in the world including the United States. I gave some brief U.S. examples and prevalence statistics. *I then emphasized that they were the experts* here and their views were essential in informing anything we would have to say on domestic violence. I said we wanted to understand how they experienced domestic violence and what their analysis of the problem was—*suggesting critical analysis. I explained* analysis of such a problem could be on the personal, cultural/societal, and political levels of living. *I asked a group member* to read aloud a newspaper article from a local paper about a man who beat his wife, children, and mother-in-law and passed the article and the picture around—suggesting a familiar code. The situation was well known and drew much commentary. As they analyzed, they told stories from their lives—"My sister's husband beats her and the kids—." *I empathized and interjected knowledge* about perpetrators, the need for a protocol, including a safety plan, and so on. *From this I highlighted* their personal responses—knowing similar stories or having family members in similar situations, cultural issues, including religious issues, and wider political issues—the struggle it took to enact the law. *They taught* about the three different religions represented (Hindu, Christian, and Muslim) and compared Indo-Guyanese and Afro-Guyanese cultures regarding the roles of men and women and children.

I now invited their reflections on the three levels of analysis we had begun. Several people said how much the shelter was needed, citing personal stories. *I then reached for the negatives*—did anyone feel a little uneasy about this agency and its service? After a silence the young Indo-Guyanese man spoke up. He said he was an associate pundit (Hindu religious leader) from a nearby village. He said, "The Village is very skeptical about the program, but I have heard some things here today that make me think the older pundits might not understand what the shelter is about." He explained that Hindu religious leaders, especially the older ones, have no understanding of worldly issues, no training in pastoral counseling, and no wish to be involved in the personal lives of their people. "They see the job as totally spiritual," he said. Yet, he continued, the religion is against the violence described here today. "I see my role as counseling couples and helping the other leaders to see that they can help, not remain neutral or silent, in situations of domestic violence. I have received education and I would like to share it in my village. I do not think we need to be against this thing." The group members heartily applauded him and his resolve. This brought forth dialogue on how all religions, though based on values of love and caring, may play a part in keeping women in powerless positions. The religious leader shared that he was part of a younger group of clergy. He would bring what he has learned this day back to his group and ask for their support regarding the issues of women and children. This part of the day ended with *a summary from group members on the personal, cultural, and political meanings of abusing women and children.* I let the community members *know how much I learned* about their world and their experiences. They, in turn, thanked me for sharing experiences and knowledge that helped them see the problem as universal.

The use of *codes* for consciousness-raising in the empowerment process is discussed and illustrated in chapters 1, 2, 3, and 12. In chapter 3 the use of women's names became a code related to the meaning of patriarchy in situations of abuse with some members of this same group of helpers. The use of another code takes place later in that same group meeting.

The Meaning of Hands: Another Code

"I asked if the women could form pairs and draw each other's left hands on the same sheet of paper. They talked quietly to each other as they did this and it was a special time. I asked how it felt to do this exercise. Mary said, 'Women's hands are so soft and gentle.' Shirley, who was my partner, added, 'To draw the hand, you had to touch the other person's hand, and it was so nice to get closer.' I said, as we looked at the drawing, that it was very hard to tell Shirley's hand from mine, as they were almost the same size. Wilma said Faria's hand was strong like her mother's hand. Faria said Wilma's hand was large and yet gentle. She could imagine it cradling a baby. Trisha said women's hands are nurturing hands and sister's hands are especially beautiful as they help so many. Sister said Trisha's touch was soft and soothing. Zeila said, 'There is strength in women joining hands together as we are doing tonight.' And Portia added, 'and comfort.' She said she too had experienced abuse, but continued, 'It was a long time ago and he is long dead.' Gentle laughter.

I said, 'You said, women's hands nurture, comfort, and soothe, but you are saying now that men's hands hit, beat, and hurt.' They added, 'kill, murder, cut, rape, and take advantage of women and children' to the litany. The impact of violence on children was discussed. Mary said she had a gentle husband and she was thankful, but she had a cousin who was beaten regularly. Zeila added, 'Even when they caress they can hurt, as it is getting to be the custom to have more than one woman among so-called Christians now as well as the Hindu and Muslim. This is a custom for men's needs, not women's. It can hurt women deeply.' All agreed. Bibi told the story of her sister whose husband beat her mercilessly. Then the son learned to do the same while the daughter hides in corners. She does not know how to help. Gently and hesitatingly, advice was given. I introduced the notion of a safety plan. Gene said Bibi was the safety valve and just having her sister try to help her was important. Bibi said her sister knew she could come to her house and be protected as Bibi's husband would help her sister too. The work continued with more definitions of abuse and examples from their lives."

Drawing to a Close

"Mary then said there was a song they sang in working with children in her church, but she thinks it should be for women too. She began to sing softly, 'Oh Lord, educate these children, Oh Lord, teach them to be strong.' Others joined in. When Wilma caught on, it became a booming chant of 'Oh Lord, educate these women. Oh Lord, teach them to be strong.' We sang it several times, and I suggested we stand, hold hands again and sing it one last time. It was beautiful, one of the most remarkable moments in my group work practice experience" (Lee 1999b).

The empowerment approach *blends the personal and political* and emphasizes seeing people of different, often oppressed, ethnic, cultural, and class backgrounds with new eyes/lenses. Eyes that see and appreciate the history of a people and the structural relationships of people in the social and political realities of a country and in relationships to global realities bring light to the process of dialogue. Some problems are global, such as behavior toward women in a still patriarchal world, and the oppression of the poorest and most vulnerable in most societies, yet they are also unique in how they are manifested and dealt with in each locality. Stepping into another culture, even when invited to assist in an empowerment process, is a humbling experience. Yet it is never trite to discover that sisterhood is real across national and cultural boundaries and that we receive much more than we can ever give in such encounters (Lee 1999b).

Other Examples of Empowerment-Oriented International Work

In many countries empowerment practice is part of an "anti-oppressive discourse," an attempt to define practice with marginalized and disenfranchised groups in the context of relieving oppression (Mullender and Ward 1991; Chorcora, Jennings, and Lordan 1994; Breton 1998; Shera and Wells 1999; Owens 1998). Because such practice is sometimes difficult to carry out in traditional agencies, and it is difficult to achieve in oppressive societies, some have questioned its operability (Chorcora, Jennings, and Lordan 1994; Breton 1998). Yet even while questioning it (a healthy activity), the practice is taking place and examples of exciting empowerment practice abound on the international scene. A few such examples are presented here and others are in chapters 2, 8, 10, and 13. The example of liberating community organizing by members of the Patwah Project of the University of Guyana Department of Social Work in chapter 13 is a comprehensive example of such empowerment practice. Examples from Ireland, a Caribbean country, and Australia will be given here to illustrate the method and effectiveness of empowerment practice with agencies, groups, and individuals in other than North American countries.

Ireland: Persons with Disabilities

Chorcora, Jennings, and Lordan (1994) describe the process of moving from the personal to the political in a group of disabled people in Cork, Ireland. Noting that people with disabilities are a marginalized group in Irish society, they say that social agencies tend to approve of clients' individual or group problem solving on personal matters but do not encourage groups that may make changes in the agency's service or in the community. In that way, agencies and the powers that exist retain control of their turf. In the absence of local or nationwide policies and legislation about the rights of the disabled and services beyond "sheltered workshops" to assist people who have disabilities in financial, educational, vocational, or emotional ways (by providing access to support groups, for example), people are dependent on a philanthropy or charity model of help that is uneven at best and not empowering at worst. People with disabilities are hardly represented in decision-making processes that affect their lives. For example, the allocation of European funding is done in Brussels by an organization of nondisabled people. In Ireland there is a forum of disabled people, but groups are fighting with each other for scarce resources.

The group of persons with disabilities who reside in Cork began with six people who came together to seek mutual support in getting the issue of disability on the political agenda as a rights issue and to develop strategies to combat ignorance and discrimination. They were also aware of the need for emotional support in dealing with both their disabilities and the societal reaction to them. As all people with disabilities of any kind were welcome, the group members initially worked on learning about each other's disabilities. Nuala Lordon, a social worker and faculty member of University College Cork assisted the group. The group grew to twenty members who meet regularly. The Adult Education Department of University College Cork, in partnership with this group, launched a training program for twelve disabled persons to become *disability equality trainers*. This subgroup learned empowerment principles and skills in helping people deal with discrimination and attain rights as well as positive self-regard. Some of the empowering principles and skills they used were the acceptance of difference, a positive focus on abilities, skills to deal with structural problems, negotiating different ways of being and recognizing oppression for what it is, and learning through action, experience/action, and reflection, or a praxis approach. In this way, an accompanying drawing by S. O'Shaughnessy shows, a tiny seed of acceptance of difference grows into a tall and beautiful tree embellished by activism and self-acceptance. Through the group experience group members "recognize that they have abilities to make things happen and to move from dependence to taking control of their lives." The group and worker sustain each other in facing much adversity and many obstacles by celebrating small steps and valuing each other's support. As one group member, Eddie, traced his struggle in adjusting to multiple sclerosis, a degenerative and unpredictable disease of the central nervous system, he said that the loss of his job after confiding that he had MS to his employer pushed him into depression. Only when he was trained as a youth community worker and became a founding member of the Disability Equality Group did he regain meaning and hope in his life. He noted:

> People just do not hear disabled people or do not give them a chance. Group members have a sense of possible power to change their own situation and circumstances. . . . This programme is about training people with disabilities to be able to speak for themselves. It is a unique group. . . . It added a definite focus and direction to my life for which I had been looking. (Chorcora, Jennings, and Lordan 1994)

Living with AIDS in a Caribbean Country

In my travels throughout the Caribbean I have made contact with agencies and individuals who are dedicated to providing service, support, information, resources, advocacy, and activism for and with persons who are living with the HIV+ virus and AIDS. The twofold problem of inadequate medical and financial resources for PWA's and the extent of the stigma and discrimination associated with the disease in Caribbean countries, particularly if the sufferer is a gay man, makes living with AIDS an extraordinarily challenging existence. Mrs. Fermine Wright (name disguised), a social worker volunteering for the AIDS Network, an agency set up to assist those living with HIV+ and/or AIDS, shared her struggles with me. She was particularly moved by a letter from one of her clients. Both she and her client eagerly consented to share the letter in this book "to teach the world about living with AIDS in the Caribbean." She asked that the material be completely disguised as she feared reprisals for her client, whom we will call Keith.

Mrs. Wright reports that the most difficult part of her job was knowing that medications were available in the United States and elsewhere that were not available in her country. People were dying so quickly and so much suffering was now preventable—"but not here," she said sadly. She noted that basic T cell counts that showed how vulnerable an individual was to infection and other blood tests can not be done routinely. Her client, an HIV+ twenty-nine-year-old gay man, recently was hospitalized with pneumonia. They did not have the testing or diagnostic capability available to know whether it was PCP pneumonia, a symptom of full-blown AIDS, or not. No AZT, certainly no mixed drugs, "cocktails," no Bactrim and no megavitamin supplements were available. One of the islands has some good treatment available, but most of her clients did not have the money, or the strength left, to travel there. International organizations were helping, but the help did not make a dent in the problem.

Yet, she said, "I love my work. I work with individuals and caretakers, when they are available. I try to become the family that has rejected them. Sometimes I can get a group together. Then we are all like a family. I also love the advocacy the group engages in. I love the dedication of my clients. We have done so much AIDS education and we know it is helping the youth. My job is very satisfying—but it is also deeply and profoundly sad. It is so unfair that medicine is not free and available for people who need it throughout the world. Maybe it is because, unlike malaria, the victims are blamed for getting the virus. Maybe wealthy nations and people of means are just callous and greedy. Maybe it's because we are people of color. Whatever it is, we in the network are going to make the need known, for that is what we can do. Our power comes from our love and caring for each other, as Keith says. Maybe the rest of the world just doesn't know that we have so few medical resources here."

The following are excerpts from Keith's letter:

Dear Mrs. Wright,

I am glad you told me I could put my thoughts down on paper because sometimes I just can not speak about having AIDS. I realize now that miracles come every day, but there is one I did not recognize until recently.

It was six years ago that I received my HIV test results. I remember walking into your office praying, "Oh Lord, please let I be all right. Of course my interpretation of "all right" was not what the Lord had in mind. You told me what my results were, that I was HIV positive. I was shocked, and I thought it was the end of my life. I remember saying, "Oh Lord, why me?" I remember you put your arms around me as I cried and told you I could not tell my family or my lover. My family does not accept me, or my being gay—now they will really throw me away. You said we would take it one day at a time and that I was in shock and it would take time to deal with it.

We agreed I had to tell my companion, Tom, so he could be tested too. I was so glad I told him and that he did not have it. But then I wondered if he would leave me and I'd have no one. He did leave me for over a year as you know. But he came back. Just when I thought God did not answer my prayers, I realized the answer had come in the love of Tom and people like your self. For a while I was dehydrating fast. All through the night Tom would bring me water through a straw and touch water to my lips and forehead. I have never experienced love before. It is a most unexpected blessing.

Ever since I discovered my status I've realised how true it is to say "if you want something badly enough, it happens." Most of all, I did not want to be alone in this. I wanted to experience love. I wanted to work for the cause of all people with AIDS. I wanted the time for love and for AIDS activism. My life has been blessed by the touch of many beautiful people. As I walk on the path of life accompanied by my infection there have been a number of "Simon's of Cyrene" who have made my cross lighter. God has always sent caregivers, supporters, and props when I least expected them. My infection has helped me to see myself in a more humble light. The term friendship has become so important. My friends are fewer, true— and much more valued. Among the greatest of my blessings is Tom, my companion. Although he is HIV negative, his love and support has been my greatest source of strength.

In a country such as mine where antiviral drugs are inaccessible, emotional support becomes the major source of sustenance. This emotional support is what has given me the strength to go on. Even as I write this, my very existence is because of the empathy and support of my friends and Tom, my life's companion. My most unexpected gift.

To my brothers and sisters living with HIV/AIDS I say, Do not despair. God always sends a caregiver. As a gay man living with HIV/AIDS it is even more difficult since society does not allow you to enjoy the love you deserve as a human being. My relationship is condemned. My biggest fear is not of dying but of Tom's going on alone. Who will Tom be able to turn to for support when I am gone? There will be no family to embrace him and share the grief. No one will thank him for being there for me. He will be so alone in his grief. The thought is unbearable. I know, at least, you will be there for him—we are not totally alone, though we are shunned and cast aside. Yet Tom stands by my side. For him and all the other friends, social workers and blessings I say, Thank you, Lord! I bless God, for the miracle of love, hope, and care continues. And as it does, I now recognise it. Thank you Lord!

Love, from Keith

Keith's letter and Mrs. Wright's work speaks for itself and for the empowerment that comes through love and the use of professional skills in advocacy and in working with individuals and families to meet the basic needs of persons with AIDS. Despite United Nations declarations about basic services for all, including health-related services, basic needs for medication and treatment go unmet in many less industrialized countries. The flames of activism for all HIV + /AIDS sufferers burn brightly here in social worker and client alike. Indeed, Keith is a living example of the power of caring. The activism that both enact makes an urgent appeal for global response.

Catherine House, Adelaide, Australia

We turn now to another group of people who are despised and ignored in most countries, the mentally ill homeless. In Australia, as elsewhere, empowerment-oriented social workers are grappling with the contradictory demands to make services to the most vulnerable populations consumer oriented, cost effective and efficient and implementing programs based on a moral and ethical value system. Such value systems provide the conditions for empowerment. The values of human dignity, community, caring, participatory democracy, and equalizing the power of people with low psychological and material resources by providing outside support are seen as part of empowerment-oriented agency programs. Empowering helping agencies can ally with vulnerable clients in their struggle to attain power, providing the outside force needed to allow the most vulnerable learn the skills and gain the confidence to approach bureaucratic and powerful systems and successfully champion for their rights as citizens (Owens 1998; Owens and Gregory 1999).

Catherine House is an agency that provides a continuum of care for single homeless women, many of whom suffer from mental illness and/or substance abuse problems, including a shelter, a transitional living facility (Salem House), and permanent housing with services. The agency actively seeks "to create an environment where a sense of belonging to a supportive structure is fostered." They seek the development of community more than the attaining goals and outcomes. Based on the value that "all life has beauty and value," residents are valued as people worthy of respect. Residents are encouraged to set and monitor goals for themselves in dialogue with their workers and to settle disputes based on mutual respect more than authoritative dictum. Weekly house meetings are held where openness of communication, "realness," and honesty are encouraged. This type of dialogue is also encouraged in regular staff meetings in which community building and empowerment are part of the process and goals of the work. Owens and Gregory note that the support of the helping agency as a power equalizer helps the most vulnerable of women take steps toward empowerment and affirming their self-worth and dignity (1998). The conceptualization of the empowerment-oriented agency as power equalizer is a very important piece of the empowerment paradigm for international practice.

Research: A Tool for Empowerment

Research skill and technology is value neutral. It may be used to procrastinate or avoid action on social issues (as in endless counts of the homeless in fully industrialized countries) or it may be used to empower social workers, advocates, and clients in their struggles for a just society. Research may be used as a tool in empowerment practice in the following ways: it may help localities discover the nature and scope of yet unknown or unmet human needs, it may give a voice to the most vulnerable as they tell their

own stories and define their own needs, it may give support and documentation to social workers and others in their advocacy of the needs of the most
vulnerable in a society and their attempts to make systems more responsive,
and, finally, it may empower the most vulnerable with the common concerns
(beyond individual concerns) and the data they need to advocate for themselves. Both quantitative and qualitative data may help with documentation,
but only qualitative data gives the voiceless a voice that all can hear. An
example of using qualitative study to amplify voices is a recent study on the
subjective experience of homelessness of eighty mothers with children in
Buffalo, New York by Choi and Snyder (1999). The combination of quantitative and qualitative data is optimal in utilizing research toward the ends
of empowering those who usually do not speak for themselves. This is especially true in domestic or international situations where few resources are
directed toward the needs of the poor. The following is an example of research that potentially empowers by its process and its findings. It is excerpted from an article published by this author and Stella Odie-Ali (2000)
in *Journal of Social Work Research and Evaluation: An International Publication* where the reader can find a fuller description of the study, including
tables. The findings are also in the process of publication by UNICEF in
Guyana as part of their advocacy for street children in Guyana and everywhere.

A Collaborative Study of Street Children in Georgetown, Guyana

Alfred stood behind the tree watching me as I interviewed Bibi, an older
street woman. He drew closer as I gave her a small meal and a jersey
(T-shirt). He was maybe twelve years old. He was dirty and he had no
shirt on. He eyed the jersey shyly. I pulled the last one out of my bag and
held it out to him. He smiled broadly. As he put it on he said that he
often helped Bibi at night. He carried her cardboard and things for her.
In return she shared her cardboard and onion bags with him. Sometimes
the evil men did not see him under the bags next to Bibi. And if they did
come, Bibi is so mad (psychotic) that she scream and wave her stick and
curse. If they come too close her foul odor drive them away. He felt safe

with her. When I asked him how long he was on the streets he said four-five months. I asked why and he said his auntie die and his alcoholic uncle try to kill him. He concluded, "I have no one, only Bibi." I asked him if he wanted me to find him a home, and he said yes, he is very afraid of the men. He felt very bad leaving Bibi alone. I said I would try to help Bibi too. In about a month I found him a place (through church connections). There is still no night shelter for Bibi.

This anecdote was reported by one of the interviewers conducting a 1998 study on homeless people living on the streets of Georgetown, Guyana (Lee, Odie-Ali, and Botsko 2000). This study was the precursor of a 1999 study of women, children, and elders living on the streets. The study of street children in Georgetown, a crowded capital city (population two hundred thousand) on the northern coast of Guyana is the focus here. It was the story of Alfred and other poignant observations of the interviewers that motivated the study of street children. Is Alfred typical of other children who live on the streets? Who are the street children in Georgetown? Why are they there? What do they say about their experience? What services do they need to end their homelessness?

The *United Nations Habitat Agenda* places street children as a priority for action (UNDP 1997). A 1991 estimate by World Vision International supported by UNICEF is one hundred million street children. Of these, twenty-three million are estimated to actually live and sleep on the streets and an additional seven million are abandoned children living on the streets (Glasser 1994). The phenomenon of street children, like homelessness itself, exists in industrialized as well as "developing" countries (Alston 1999; Agnelli 1986). For example, estimates of the total number of homeless youth in the United States of America ranges between one hundred thousand on any given night to two million per year. According to the U.S. Conference of Mayors, unaccompanied youth account for 4 percent of the urban homeless population (NCH 1998). Worldwide structural inequities, poverty, rural-urban migration, family breakdown, unemployment, chronic alcoholism, mental illness, other individual vulnerabilities, and community breakdown interact with the lack of affordable housing in urban areas to "redefine" housing as a luxury instead of a basic human need (Lee 1994a, 1999a, b; Glasser 1994; Agnelli 1986). Homelessness due to chronic poverty and structural inequities here differentiated from homelessness precipitated by wars and natural disasters, such as the homelessness of one million people in Mozambique in 2000 due to prolonged torrential rains and flooding. The international beloved community must address itself to homelessness regardless of its cause.

History of the Study

Early in 1998, with the assistance of local Guyanese psychiatrists and other helping professionals and others, a study of the homeless and mentally ill living on the streets of Georgetown was conducted. Four local research interviewers were trained on site by the collaborators (the author and Stella Odie-Ali). Obtaining a sample of 104 adults (36 women and 78 men ranging in age from eighteen to eighty-three), it was determined that 64 percent of homeless persons in the sample carried coexisting mental disorders (mental illness and substance abuse disorders). Shelter, health, and victimization were critical issues for those living on the streets. They found that women were faring far worse than men on all mental health indicators, including an attempted suicide rate of 35 percent (Odie-Ali 1998a; Lee, Odie-Ali, and Botsko 2000). The study findings were presented in an open public forum and conducted in the style of the culture circle, to disseminate information and catalyze problem solving and action on behalf of the homeless and mentally ill. Several suggestions were made, including a recommendation for further research.

Prior to mounting the second study, a count of the homeless in Georgetown was undertaken. In November of 1998 the entire social work class at the University of Guyana (UG) conducted a one-night count of the homeless. The students were divided into teams at various locations. Four hundred and forty-eight individuals ranging in age from infancy to old age were observed sleeping on the streets of Georgetown (Odie-Ali 1998b). Many had observable health problems. Of the total number, 69 were female and 22 were children. In the process of doing the one-night count it was learned that many children sleep in abandoned buildings and therefore could not be easily counted.

The collaborators then planned and implemented a follow-up study of women, children, and elders living on the streets that was conducted early in 1999. Ninety-six individuals, including 25 children, were interviewed. This is the report on the street children (N 25 males ranging in age from 9 to 17) who participated in this study.

Definitions

A helpful typology of street children was developed by UNICEF (1986). The typology suggests two major categories of street children: children *on* the street, who work on the streets during the day and return home most nights, and children *of* the streets, who work and sleep on the streets, often having little contact with families. A third category, used by the street child advocacy agency CHILDHOPE, is the truly abandoned or orphaned child whose life revolves entirely around peers on the street. CHILDHOPE estimates that 75 percent of the world's street children are those "on" the street, 20 percent are those "of" the street, and 5 percent are truly abandoned (Rocky 1989). The number of girls living on the streets tend to be significantly underestimated as those prostituting or working in the market are usually not counted (Ward 1987).

This study was directed toward children "of" the street. It utilized the first part of the definition of street children put forth by the Inter-NGO (Non Governmental Organization) Programme on Street Children: "Any girl or boy who has not reached adulthood, for whom the street—in the widest sense of the word, including unoccupied dwellings . . . has become his/her habitual abode" (1983:24).

Study Design

A mixed study design was used. It consisted of ten qualitative questions designed to help the child tell his/her story and perceptions of the experience of street dwelling in his/her own words, and a survey instrument. The survey was designed to gather demographic data and determine emotional/mental problems and health problems, including substance abuse, and to reveal coping strategies, educational level, and family ties and/or support systems. The HSC (Hopelessness Scale for Children, a seventeen-item scale standardized to measure depression in children) (Kazdin 1983; in Corcoran and Fisher 1987) was included in the survey. The approach was to learn through ethnographic study, or in-depth interviewing in the child's natural environment, who the children of the streets are, how they cope, and what they think will help them. The ethnographic approach utilizes a convenience sample and is useful in illuminating strengths (Thrasher and Mowbray 1995).

Methodology   The interviewer for the street children was a remarkable young woman, Sharmin Prince, a UG social work graduate who also participated in the 1998 study and the November count. Her special interest and expertise was engaging street children. Her own life experiences included working in the market as a child and youth outreach work through her church. Her stance was that of a participant observer and a researcher activist. She spent time in making relationships with the children, offering food and clothing and referral and advocacy as well as the interviewee fee of 500 Guyana dollars (currently about $3.00 U.S.).

Once trust was established, the boys took her to an abandoned building where, she discovered, thirty-six boys live. They explained that they had to hide their dwelling place as older male predators physically and sexually abused them and stole their money when they slept in the open. To enter the building Ms. Prince had to climb up on pallets and enter a hidden entrance with the boys, literally swinging on the rafters. Over a month's time she was able to conduct in-depth interviews with seventeen boys at that site and eight others at sites near the markets for a total of twenty-five interviews. She counted forty-five boys who were sleeping on the streets. The response rate of twenty-five boys can be considered substantial in the observed population. It is expected that there are more boys "in hiding."

The interviewer began with the open-ended (qualitative) questions and then moved to the survey instrument. The interview could take from one to two hours to complete. The HSC was then administered (Kazdin 1983, cited in Corcoran and Fischer 1987). The HSC is a seventeen-item instrument that measures hopelessness, a construct pertinent to depression and suicidal ideation. It has a second-grade reading comprehension level, though the questions were read to the participants. Scores on the HSC have been associated with the severity of depression and self-esteem. The HSC was normed on a population of children both white and of color, male and female, though most were white males, mean age 10.5, in an inpatient psychiatric facility. The mean score on the HSC was 5.2, with a standard deviation of

3.2. Higher scores indicate a greater degree of hopelessness. After administering the HSC, the final qualitative question was asked: What would you like next year to be like for you?

Data Analysis and Findings

The quantitative data was analyzed using multivariate analysis (SPSS 1998). Frequencies and correlations were determined. Scores on the HSC were correlated with age, time on the street, substance abuse, and victimization. The qualitative data was analyzed using a grounded theory approach to glean categories and frequencies (Glaser and Strauss 1967).

Demographic Picture   The boys ranged in age from nine to seventeen. Thirty-two percent were age twelve and under. Guyana is a multicultural, multiracial society. The majority (50 percent) is of Indian heritage, the descendants of indentured servants; next is African heritage (38 percent) and indigenous Amerindian (7 percent). Sixty-eight percent of the boys were Afro-Guyanese, 16 percent were Indo-Guyanese, 8 percent were Amerindian, and 8 percent were of mixed parentage. Seventy-six percent of the boys came from depressed areas in and around Georgetown. It is noteworthy that 56 percent of the boys lived on the streets less than one year and 36 percent lived on the streets for less than one month. Yet 60 percent of the boys complained of physical health problems. Many boys were unable to write their first names to indicate they had received the interviewee payment.

Reasons for Homelessness   Causes of homelessness among youth fall into three interrelated categories: family problems, including abuse, economic problems/family poverty, and residential instability/migration (NCH 1998). In the Guyana study it is important to note that 52 percent of the boys were not raised by either of their parents. Most were raised by their impoverished grandmothers. One boy said, "I lived with my grandmother and there was no money to pay the rent and we had to leave the home so I started living on the streets." Three boys reported abuse by stepparents. One boy noted, "I lived with my stepmother, who physically abused me. One day it was more than I could take and I ran away (to the streets)." Regarding reasons for living on the streets 36 percent of the boys said they left home to escape physical abuse. Twelve percent said they had no one after the death of their parents or grandparents. One boy said simply, "I don't know what it means to have a mother." Another said, "I lived with my uncle and grandmother. My uncle died and my grandmother began worrying and died. Then I have no one to take care of me and I left the home." One boy was abandoned by an uncle who brought him to Georgetown from the interior. One followed his mentally ill mother into the streets, and one described living with an abusive alcoholic father. Forty percent noted the lack of money (family poverty or financial need) as a reason for living on the streets. Two mentioned hunger as a reason for leaving home. One ten-year-old said, "I became hungry and decided to beg on the streets. Then I started living on the streets." Only one boy mentioned rebelliousness, or doing what he felt like without heed to parental wishes, as a reason for his homelessness.

Coping and Surviving

The boys described begging and/or working on the streets to survive and, in some cases, to contribute to their families. Forty-eight percent survived through begging and 60 percent survived through working. The work included selling plastic bags, catching and selling fish, and doing odd jobs. Sixty-four percent of the boys described sharing food, cardboard, and clothing with "my fellow street boys." Sixty-four percent also described help from caring strangers who gave food or money or intervened protectively on their behalf. Sixteen percent said they were helped by professionals: a social worker, a probation officer, and a police officer. Fifty-six percent of the boys said their family helped them in some way. Two boys described help from older men who would also give them "whatever they wanted." This seemed to be a way of discussing survival sex. Sleeping in abandoned buildings instead of places visible to predators was described as the best way to deal with physical and sexual abuse at the mercy of older and stronger men. Some younger boys noted that they were attacked by older boys while sleeping in a group so that they had to be very careful about where they slept and who they trusted. One said, "Other street boys burn your feet while you're sleeping and the older ones take advantage of you."

Victimization   Ninety-two percent of the boys said that they were physically or sexually abused while living on the streets. Sixty percent said they were beaten and/or otherwise physically abused. Thirty-two percent said they had been sexually abused, including, for some, sodomization. The perpetrators described were street men, older street boys, and men who were not street dwellers.

Substance Abuse   Fifty-six percent of the boys admitted to abusing alcohol, namely, drinking Banko, a cheap local wine. Two older boys described smoking marijuana. None reported use of other street drugs.

Hopelessness and Depression   The mean score of the Guyana street children on the HSC was 5.760 with a standard deviation of 2.521. The study sample had a higher mean score and a smaller standard deviation than the normal population of children in a psychiatric hospital, indicating a higher degree of hopelessness. The HSC was negatively associated with age and time children were on the street, indicating that older children and children on the street longer felt less hopeless than their younger counterparts perhaps because of acculturation to street life and somewhat less vulnerability due to age and size. The relationship was not statistically significant probably because of the small sample. Children who drank had a higher HSC (mean 6.5) than children who didn't drink. The amount of alcohol drunk was also positively correlated with HSC (P 42) but the relationships were not significant because of the small number (25). As alcohol is a depressant, the higher scores are expectable.

Children who were sexually molested had a higher HSC (mean 6.6) than children who were not (mean 5.4). This is an expectable finding as sexual abuse is positively correlated with depression and other mental health problems.

What Living on the Streets Is Like   Ninety-two percent of the boys used strongly negative words to describe living on the streets. Seventy-six percent used the words *rough, hard,* and *bad.* The words *not easy, not nice,* and *not good* were also used. Sixteen percent spoke of hunger, but almost all included the search for food as a major preoccupation of their daily life. Forty-eight percent spoke of "insults and advantage" (being bullied) as main problems in daily living.

A Day on the Streets   When asked to describe a typical day on the streets (like yesterday), the boys described the following activities as usual and important to them (in rank order of those named most frequently): bathing (60 percent), working (60 percent), eating and begging (each 48 percent), playing (23 percent), smoking cigarettes and sleeping (each 12 percent). The forms of recreation mentioned were football, cards, gambling, games, and swimming. One was able to watch television. One boy said that he prayed.

What It Would Take to Get Off the Streets

When the boys were asked what help they needed to get off the streets or to make life easier for them now, the resounding answer was said in two words: 84 percent said, "A HOME." Their words were "Carry me home," "Take me home," "Take me home to my mother," "Talk to my mother," "Put me in a home," "Find me a home," "Get me adopted and send me to school," "Find me a home where I can be comfortable and get me a job." Thirty-two percent wanted to return to relatives while 36 percent said they would live with "anyone." Sixteen percent requested that the researcher mediate between them and their family. All of those who wanted "a home" spoke of a family—a biological family or a familylike atmosphere—a foster or adoptive family or other small group familylike set-up. There was a yearning for caring and attachment to people who cared. There was a belief that a social worker could do something to "get them a home." Boys' institutions, were considered to be a "jail," not a home.

Hopes   When asked what they hoped next year would be like, only some of the boys were optimistic enough to dream. Thirty-two percent hoped they would have a home. Twenty-four percent thought they would be off the streets. Thirty-six percent hoped they would have a job; 8 percent wanted job training; 16 percent thought they would be with family; 8 percent thought they would be in school; and one boy wanted to join a church and change his life. One boy concluded, "I must not be on the road anymore."

Discussion

The children of the streets in Georgetown, Guyana have spoken here for themselves. They have expressed the same needs for attachment and security, food and shelter, recreation, earnings, education, and protection as children throughout the world. An important fact illuminated by this study is that over half these children do not have a mother or a father. Forty-four percent report no family contact. This is a high percentage of virtually orphaned and abandoned children. Perhaps this explains the longing for a home expressed by the majority of the boys.

A typical road into living on the streets for children throughout the world is severe poverty combined with family crisis and disintegration, including abusive parenting (Agnelli 1986; Glasser, 1994). It is no wonder that some of those who are abused in turn abuse others. Glasser (1994) notes that homeless children are extremely vulnerable to violence by adults as well, including rape, beatings, torture, and murder. Tragically, such victimization is a reality for the children in this study. Mental health problems such as depression and its correlation to suicide are ominous outcomes of the losses and levels of victimization experienced by the boys in this study. The mean of almost 6 on the Hopelessness Score for Children (Corcoran and Fischer 1987) when a normed score is 5.2, and more than 6.5 for those who drank or were sexually abused, documents the effects of living on the streets in the lives of these children. The fact that more than half the boys are abusing alcohol is also a foreboding sign. Serious health problems are also typical of street children, another fact borne out in this study.

Some Comparisons

United Nations studies indicate that less industrialized countries tend to have a higher rate of children under twelve on the streets (Agnelli 1986) while more industrialized countries have a higher rate of adolescent street youths. The 32 percent of children under twelve in this study may tend to bear this out. Homeless children throughout the world report physical abuse and neglect (Agnelli 1986). One-fifth of the youth in shelters in the United States in 1995 reported physical abuse as compared to over one-third of the children in this study (U.S. Department of Health and Human Services 1996). Disruptive family conditions may be the principal reason that young people in the United States leave home (U.S. Department of Health and Human Services 1996). As noted above, family disruption in Guyana includes losing both parents for 52 percent of the boys and having no one at all for 12 percent of the boys. This may be the result of the emigration of the parents without the children or loss to drugs, alcohol, mental illness, physical illness, or death. This far exceeds the 5 percent (CHILDHOPE estimate) reported by Rocky (1989). In the United States, children who lived in foster care have a higher chance of becoming homeless than children with their own families (NCH 1998).

Economic instability and family poverty causes families to become homeless in both industrialized and developing countries. Victimization, including sexual exploitation, as dramatically shown in this study, is a worldwide occurrence effecting street youth (Agnelli 1986; Glasser 1994). Homeless youth in the United States are at greater risk than youths with homes of contacting AIDS or HIV+ related illnesses because of the prevalence of survival sex and sexual exploitation (Robertson 1996). While the level of sexual exploitation is 36 percent by self-report, there are as yet no statistics in Guyana about children of the street and HIV/AIDS. Street youth are also at high risk for drug and alcohol abuse, a fact borne out by more that half the Guyanese study sample (Agnelli 1986).

Homeless children and youth often suffer from severe anxiety and depression (NCH 1998). The high rate of depression among the Guyanese children as evidenced by the HSC (Kazdin 1983, cited in Corcoran and Fisher 1987) is a predictable finding as is its exacerbation by substance abuse and victimization.

While there are some differences in the Guyanese sample, notably in the high rate of children having no parents, the sample compares well to both worldwide and United States patterns of homeless youth. While the lack of a child welfare system is an operative factor in the Guyanese sample, the failures of the child welfare system are operative in the U.S. sample. Clearly, developing and maintaining adequate preventive and protective child welfare systems could be helpful in both cases. Mitigating the causes and effects of poverty is essential. Affordable housing and a living wage are basic global issues to be addressed (NCH 1998).

The phenomenon of street children in Georgetown exists on a small scale where remediation, intervention, and prevention are still feasible. The relatively short time on the streets for over half the boys, for example, may bode well for early intervention. A concerted and timely effort may have a significant impact on the lives of these endangered children.

Intervention must be particular to a locality, but there is a growing body of international literature to inform problem solving. One effective approach is to deploy outreach workers to connect with and engage the children and help them attain needed resources. Such workers may be called street educators or field workers or social workers. They may be deployed by a variety of government or, typically, nongovernmental agencies or international organizations. The approach must not be judicial or punitive and the legal system is not usually to be involved in this type of outreach (Glasser 1994; Agnelli 1986). Well-trained outreach workers may also be effective in reuniting some families and helping them improve their lot.

Street children and other homeless adolescents respond to programs that meet immediate needs first and then address other aspects of their lives. Programs that minimize institutional demands and offer a range of services including educational and vocational training, transitional living facilities, and health care have been effective in helping homeless youth to get back on their feet (Robertson 1996). In terms of the basic need for "a home" for children of the street, it is widely recognized that closed residential institutions are not the answer. They may tend to "brutalize and deform, rather than reform the characters of children" (Agnelli 1986). Many children's institutions in Latin America are being closed, and familylike group homes are being developed in their place. Foster care and adoption are also feasible solutions where numbers are not so large. For children of the street who do not have meaningful family contact it is not enough to offer education or jobs or even a night shelter without making provision for a caring substitute family of some sort. If a child is not given the opportunity for attachment and connection in an appropriate way he will create his own out of street peers or youth gangs (Agnelli 1986).

The twenty-one comprehensive recommendations of the Independent Commission on International Humanitarian Issues focused on street children (Agnelli 1986) are guides to action. Both preventive and remedial intervention must be focused on local communities whose resources can be strengthened by government and international support. This includes the services of community social workers and organizers who will help depressed (and "squatter") communities meet basic needs for children and adults more fully. The resources of universities should be brought to bear in the analysis and remediation of the problem (Agnelli 1986:114). Guyanese professional social workers are an excellent and highly trained human resource that can be marshaled for preventive and remedial community work and as outreach workers for street children (LaFleur 1998). However, Agnelli's point on this is well taken: such outreach workers, or street educators, "should be accorded full professional status with an appropriate career structure to facilitate recruitment" (1986:114). Next steps would include further analysis of the problem and the mobilization and collaboration of community, government, UNICEF, NGOs, and international organizations. But children can not wait until all this takes place. A Drop-In-Centre opened by UNICEF and Guyana's Ministry of Human Services on April 25, 1999, is a positive and noteworthy first step. Industrialized countries might learn from this educationally oriented outreach model. For the street children of Guyana, and all children in the global village outreach and compassionate shelter must be offered now.

Building the Beloved Community Community: The Conclusion

Social workers practicing the empowerment approach are uniquely prepared and situated to assist people in empowering themselves to live the fullest of life and to respond to social problems with action, equity, and justice. They are able to build bridges across racial, class, age, gender, religious, and other deep and wide divides set in place by hatred and discrimination. They stand on the solid ground of trust and relationship with people of difference and poverty as they reach with them for the dream of a new world where everyone has enough. They raise consciousness with people and use the tools of individual, family, group, and community work and research and policy making to give a voice to the silenced toward the ends of justice for all. In the global village as well as in our localities, empowerment-oriented social workers are using practice with individuals, families, groups, communities, and political systems to build the beloved community. In the lives of Niki and Mrs. Ciano, Sra. Luz, and Anthony and James, Lorna Rabinowitz, Luke Amato, Carmen Rivera and her children, and Tracey and Shandra, Tomika and Selina, and Lisa, Kevin and Greg,

Mr. Hom, Miss Lettie, Mrs. Riley, Brenda Gary, Tyrone, Alma, and Keith, and Alfred and Bibi, and all of the world's Alfreds and Bibis, the foundations of the building are laid. The beloved community is a work in progress.

> *We're marching,*
>> *Marching on to*
>>> *Zion,*
>>>> *That beautiful*
>>>>> *City*
>>>>>> *of*
>>>>>>> *God.*

References

Abadinsky, Howard. 1989. *Drug Abuse: An Introduction*. Chicago: Nelson Hall.

Abramovitz, Mimi. 1998. "Social Work and Social Reform: An Area of Struggle." *Social Work* 43(6):512–525.

—— 1989a. *Regulating the Lives of Women*. Boston: South End.

—— 1989b. "Everyone Is on Welfare: The Role of Redistribution in Social Policy Revisited." In Ira C. Colby, ed., *Social Welfare Policy: Perspectives, Patterns, Insights*, pp. 34–36. Chicago: Dorsey.

Abu-Samah, Asnarulkhadi. 1996. "Empowering Research Process: Using Groups in Research to Empower the People." *Groupwork* 9(2):221–252.

Ackenbaum, W. Andrew. 1989. "Social Security: The Early Years." In Donald T. Critchlow and Ellis W. Hawley, eds., *Poverty and Public Policy in Modern America*, pp. 110–114. Chicago: Dorsey.

Adam, Barry D. 1978. "Interiorization and Self-Esteem." *Social Psychology Quarterly* 41:47–53.

Addams, Jane. 1910. *Twenty Years at Hull House*. Rpt. New York: Macmillan, 1961.

—— 1922. *Peace and Bread in Time of War*. New York: Macmillan.

—— 1930. *The Second Twenty Years at Hull House*. New York: Macmillan.

Agnelli, Susanna. 1986. *Street Children: A Growing Urban Tragedy*. London: Wiedenfeld and Nicolson.

Alinsky, Saul. 1969. *Reveille for Radicals*. New York: Vintage.

—— 1972. *Rules for Radicals*. New York: Vintage.

Allport, Gordon. 1958. *The Nature of Prejudice*. Garden City, N.Y.: Doubleday/Anchor.

Alston, Philip. 1999. "Industrialized Countries: Commentary-Hardship in the Midst of Plenty." [Online.] The Progress of Nations 1998. Available: http://www.unicef.org/pon98/indust1.htm (May 3, 1999).

Alter, Jonathan, Karen Bradford, and Karen Springer. 1988. "Why We Can't Wait Any Longer." *Newsweek* (March 7):42–43.

Anderson, Elijah. 1990. *Steetwise: Race, Class and Change in an Urban Community.* Chicago: University of Chicago Press.

Anderson, Margaret L. 1988. *Thinking About Women.* New York: Macmillan.

Anderson, Margaret L., and Patricia Hill Collins, eds. 1998. *Race, Class, and Gender: An American Anthology.* California: Wadsworth.

Angelou, Maya. 1981. "I Rise." In Maya Angelou, *Poems*, pp. 154–155. New York: Bantam.

Annuziata, Frank. 1989. "The Revolt Against the Welfare State: Goldwater Conservatism and the Election of 1964." In Donald T. Critchlow and Ellis W. Hawley, eds., *Poverty and Public Policy in Modern America*, pp. 260–268. Chicago: Dorsey.

Ansbro, John J. 1982. *Martin Luther King, Jr.: The Making of a Mind.* Maryknoll, N.Y.: Orbis.

APA (American Psychiatric Association). 1994. *Diagnostic and Statistical Manual of Disorders—Revised (DSM IV).* 4th ed. Washington, D.C.: American Psychiatric Association.

Appleby, George Alan, and Jean W. Anastas, eds. 1998. *Not Just a Passing Phase: Social Work with Gay, Lesbian, and Bisexual People.* New York: Columbia University Press.

Argeriou, Milton, and Dennis McCarty, eds. 1990. *Treating Alcoholism and Drug Abuse Among Homeless Men and Women.* New York: Haworth.

Atteneave, Carolyn. 1982. "American Indians and Alaskan Native Families: Emigrants in Their Own Homeland." In Monica McGoldrick, John K. Pearce, and Joseph Giordano, eds., *Ethnicity and Family Therapy*, pp. 55–83. New York: Guilford.

Austrian, Sonia G. 1995. *Mental Disorders, Medications, and Clinical Social Work.* New York: Columbia University Press.

Babbie, Earl. 1989. *The Practice of Social Research*, 5th ed. Belmont, Cal.: Wadsworth.

Baptist, Willie, and Mary Bricker-Jenkins. 1999. "Gonna Take Back What He Stole from Me–": A Report on the Poor Peoples' Summit." *Bertha C. Reynolds Newsletter.*

Baptist, Willie, Mary Bricker-Jenkins, and Monica Dillon. 1999. "Taking the Struggle on the Road: The New Freedom Bus—Freedom from Unemployment, Hunger, and Homelessness." *Journal of Progressive Human Services* 10(2):7–29.

Barlett, Donald L., and James B. Steele. 1998. "The Empire of Pigs: A Little-Known Company Is a Master at Milking Governments for Welfare." *Time*, November 30, 1998, pp. 52–64.

Barry, D. Marshall. 1998. "Tomato Harvester Economic Report." Miami: Labor Research Center of Boston and Miami, Inc., with the Coalition of Immokalee Workers. Unpublished. (941)657–8311.

Bartlett, Harriet M. 1958. "Toward Clarification and Improvement of Social Work Practice." *Social Work* 3(April):5–9.

Beasley, Lou M., Anne Fields-Ford, and Verline Dotson. 1992. *1991–1992 Annual Report of the Saturday Academy*. Atlanta: Atlanta University School of Social Work.

Beaumont, Judith A. 1987. "Prison Witness: Exposing the Injustice." In Arthur J. Laffin and Anne Montgomery, eds., *Swords Into Plowshares: Nonviolent Direct Action for Disarmament*, pp. 80–85. New York: Harper and Row.

Beck, Bertram M. 1959. "Shaping America's Social Welfare Policy." In Alfred J. Kahn, ed., *Issues in American Social Work*, pp. 191–218. New York: Columbia University Press.

———— 1983. "Empowerment: A Future Goal for Social Work." Paper presented at National Association of Social Work Conference.

Bein, Andrew, and Kate Allen. 1999. "Hand in Glove? It Fits Better Than You Think." *Social Work* 44(3):274–277.

Bellak, Leopold, Marvin Hurvich, and Helen Gediman, eds. 1973. *Ego Functions in Schizophrenics, Neurotics, and Normals*. New York: Wiley.

Berger, Diane, and Lisa Berger. 1991. *We Heard the Angels of Madness: A Family Guide to Coping with Manic Depression*. New York: Quill, William Morrow.

Berkowitz, Edward, and Kim McQuaid. 1989. "Welfare Reform in the 1950s." In Donald T. Critchlow and Ellis W. Hawley, eds., *Poverty and Public Policy in Modern America*, pp. 200–210. Chicago: Dorsey.

Berlin, Sharon. 1983. "Cognitive Behavioral Approaches." In Allan Rosenblatt and Dana Waldfogel, eds., *The Handbook of Clinical Social Work*, pp. 1095–1119. San Francisco: Jossey-Bass.

Berman-Rossi, Toby. 1992. "Empowering Groups Through Understanding Stages of Group Development." In James A. Garland, ed., *Group Work Reaching Out: People, Places, and Power*, pp. 239–256. New York: Haworth.

Berman-Rossi, Toby, ed. 1994. *Social Work: The Collected Writings of William Schwartz*. Itasca, Ill.: Peacock.

Berman-Rossi, Toby, and Marcia B. Cohen. 1989. "Group Development and Shared Decision Making: Working with Homeless Mentally Ill Women." In Judith A. B. Lee, ed., *Group Work with the Poor and Oppressed*, pp. 63–78. New York: Haworth.

Berman-Rossi, Toby, and Irving Miller. 1992. "Racism and the Settlement Movement." Paper presented at the Fourteenth Annual Symposium for the Advancement of Social Work with Groups, Atlanta.

Berzon, E. 1979. *Positively Gay*. Berkeley: Celestial Arts.

Betson, David M., and Robert T. Michael. 1997. "Why So Many Children Are Poor." *Future of Children* 7(2)(Summer/Fall):25–39.

Biegel, David E., and Arthur Blum. 1999. *Innovations in Practice and Service Delivery Across the Lifespan*. New York: Oxford University Press.

Biestek, Felix P., Fr. 1957. *The Casework Relationship*. Chicago: Loyola University Press.

Bilides, David G. 1990. "Race, Color, Ethnicity, and Class: Issues of Biculturalism in School-Based Adolescent Counseling Groups." *Social Work with Groups* 13(4):43–58.

Billingsley, Andrew. 1968. *Black Families in White America*. Englewood Cliffs, N.J.: Prentice-Hall.

—— 1987. "Black Families in a Changing Society." In J. Dewart, ed., *The State of Black America*, pp. 97–111. New York: National Urban League.

Blackwell, James E. 1975. *The Black Community: Diversity and Unity*. New York: Harper and Row.

Blanchard, Evelyn L. 1987. "American Indians and Alaska Natives." *Encyclopedia of Social Work*, pp. 142–150. 18th ed. Silver Spring, Md.: National Association of Social Workers.

Blau, Joel. 1992. *The Visible Poor: Homelessness in the United States*. New York: Oxford University Press.

—— 1998. "Globalization of the Economy: A Whole New World." *BCR Reports* 10(1)(Spring):1.

Bloom, Martin, and Joel Fischer. 1997. *Evaluating Practice: Guidelines for the Accountable Professional*. Englewood Cliffs, N.J.: Prentice-Hall.

Blume, Sue E. 1985. "Substance Abuse: Of Being Queer, Magic Pills, and Social Lubricants." In Hilda Hidalgo, Travis L. Peterson, and Natalie Jane Goodman, eds., *Lesbian and Gay Issues: A Resource Manual for Social Workers*, pp. 79–87. Silver Spring, Md.: National Association of Social Workers.

Boulding, Kenneth E. 1990. *Three Faces of Power*. Newbury Park, Cal.: Sage.

Bourdon, Gail M. 1999. "Reclaiming and Constructing Identities: The Journey Out of Homelessness for Persons with Mental Illness." Dissertation for the Degree of Doctor of Philosophy at Simmons College of Social Work.

Bowker, Joan, and Laura Davis. 1988. "Living with Mental Illness: Examining Personal Experience." In Joan Bowker, ed., *Chronically Mentally Ill: New Approaches for Mental Health Professionals*, 1:1–17. Washington, D.C.: Council on Social Work Education.

Bowlby, John. 1969. *Attachment and Loss*. Vol 1: *Attachment*. New York: Basic.

—— 1973. "Affectional Bonds: Their Nature and Origin." In Robert S. Weiss, ed., *Loneliness: The Experience of Emotional and Social Isolation*, pp. 38–52. Cambridge: MIT Press.

———— 1991. "Postscript." In Colin Murray Parkes, Joan Stevenson-Hinde, and Peter Marris, eds., *Attachment Across the Life Cycle*, pp. 293–297. London: Routledge.

Boxhill, Nancy A. 1990. *Homeless Children: The Watchers and the Waiters*. New York: Haworth.

Brackley, Dean, S.J. N.d. *People Power*. Mahwah, N.J.: Paulist.

Brager, George, and Stephen Holloway. 1978. *Changing Human Service Organizations: Politics and Practice*. New York: Free Press.

Brager, George, and Harry Specht. 1973. *Community Organizing*. New York: Columbia University Press.

Brager, George, Harry Specht, and J. L. Torczyner. 1987. *Community Organizing* 2d ed. New York: Columbia University Press.

Brandwein, Ruth A. 1982. "Toward Androgyny in Community and Organizational Practice." In Anne Weick and Susan Vandiver, eds., *Women, Power, and Change*, pp. 158–172. Silver Spring, Md.: National Association of Social Workers.

———— 1986. Women, Community, and Organizing." In Nan Van Den Bergh and Lynn B. Cooper, eds., *Feminist Vision for Social Work*, pp. 187–210. Silver Spring, Md.: National Association of Social Workers.

———— 1987. "Women and Community Organizing." In Dianne S. Burden and Naomi Gottleib, eds., *The Woman Client*, pp. 111–126. New York: Tavistock.

Bratter, Thomas E., and Gary G. Forrest. 1985. *Alcoholism and Substance Abuse: Strategies for Clinical Intervention*. New York: Free Press.

Brauer, Carl M. 1989. "Kennedy, Johnson, and the War on Poverty." In Donald T. Critchlow and Ellis W. Hawley, eds., *Poverty and Public Policy in Modern America*, pp. 223–237. Chicago: Dorsey.

Brazelton, T. Berry. 1990. "Is America Failing Its Children?" *New York Times Magazine*, September 9, pp. 40–43, 50–51, 90.

Bremner, Robert H. 1967. *From the Depths*. New York: New York University Press.

———— 1989. "The New Deal and Social Welfare." In Donald T. Critchlow and Ellis W. Hawley, eds., *Poverty and Public Policy in Modern America*, pp. 132–150. Chicago: Dorsey.

Breton, Albert, and Margot Breton. 1997. "Democracy and Empowerment." In Albert Breton, G. Galeotti, P. Salmon, and R. Wintrobe, eds., *Understanding Democracy: Economic and Political Perspectives*, pp. 176–195. New York: Cambridge University Press.

Breton, Margot. 1985. "Reaching and Engaging People: Issues and Practice Principles." *Social Work with Groups* 8(3):7–21.

———— 1989. "The Need for Mutual Aid Groups in a Drop-in for Homeless Women: The Sistering Case." In Judith A. B. Lee, ed., *Group Work with the Poor and Oppressed*, pp. 47–59. New York: Haworth.

——— 1991a. "Reflections on Social Action Practice in France." *Social Work with Groups* 15:3.

——— 1991b. "Toward a Model of Social Groupwork Practice with Marginalized Populations." *Groupwork* 4(1):31–47.

——— 1992. "Liberation Theology, Group Work, and the Right of the Poor and Oppressed to Participate in the Life of the Community." In James A. Garland, ed., *Group Work Reaching Out: People, Places, and Power*, pp. 257–270. New York: Haworth.

——— 1998. "Empowerment Practice in a Post-Empowerment Era." In Wes Shera and Lilian M. Wells, eds., *Empowerment Practice in Social Work: Developing Richer Conceptual Foundations*, pp. 201–229. Toronto: Canadian Scholars' Press.

Briar, Scott. 1971. "Social Casework and Social Group Work: Historical Foundations." *Encyclopedia of Social Work*, pp. 1237–1245. 16th ed. Silver Spring, Md.: National Association of Social Workers.

Bricker-Jenkins, Mary. 2000. "No Expectations, No Disappointments." Review of Marcia Hill, ed., *Feminist Therapy as a Political Act.. Affilia: Journal of Women in Social Work.*

Bricker-Jenkins, Mary, and Nancy R. Hooyman. 1986. *Not for Women Only: Social Work Practice for a Feminist Future*. Silver Spring, Md.: National Association of Social Workers.

Bricker-Jenkins, Mary, Nancy R. Hooyman, and Naomi Gottlieb, eds. 1991. *Feminist Social Work Practice in Clinical Settings*. Newbury Park: SAGE.

Brieland, Donald. 1987. "History and Evolution of Social Work Practice." *Encyclopedia of Social Work*, pp. 739–754. 18th ed. Silver Spring, Md.: National Association of Social Workers.

Brisbane, Frances L. 1989. "Alcohol Problems and Black Youth." *Adolescent Counselor*, April/May.

Brisbane, Frances L., and Reginald C. Wells. 1989. "Treatment and Prevention of Alcoholism Among Blacks." In T. D. Watts and Roosevelt Wright Jr., *Alcoholism in Minority Populations*, pp. 33–51. Springfield, Ill.: Thomas.

Brisbane, Frances L., and Maxine Womble. 1985. *The Treatment of Black Alcoholics*. New York: Haworth.

Brody, Claire M., ed. 1987. *Women's Therapy Groups: Paradigms of Feminist Treatment*. New York: Springer.

Bronfenbrenner, Urie. 1979. *The Ecology of Human Development: Experiments by Nature and Design*. Cambridge, Mass.: Harvard University Press.

Brown, Leonard N. 1991. *Groups for Growth and Change*. New York: Longman.

Brown, Robert McAfee. 1984. *Unexpected News: Reading the Bible with Third World Eyes*. Philadelphia: Westminster.

Buber, Martin. 1971. *I and Thou*. New York: Scribner.

——— 1972. *Knowledge of Man*. New York: Harper and Row.

Budman, Simon H., and Alan S. Gurman. 1988. *Theory and Practice of Brief Therapy*. New York: Guilford.

Burden, Diane, and Naomi Gottleib, eds. 1987. *The Woman Client: Providing Human Services in a Changing World.* New York: Tavistock.

Burghardt, Steve. 1996. "A Materialist Framework for Social Work Theory and Practice" In Francis J. Turner, ed., *Social Work Treatment: Interlocking Theoretical Approaches,* pp. 389–408. New York: Free Press.

Burgos-Ocasio, Hilda. 2000. "Hispanic Women." In Maria Julia, ed., *Constructing Gender: Multicultural Perspectives in Working with Women,* pp. 109–138. Belmont, Cal.: Brooks/Cole.

Burman, Sandra, and Paula Allen-Meares. 1991. "Criteria for Selecting Practice Theories: Working with Alcoholic Women." *Families in Society* 72(7):387–393.

Cain, Roy. 1991. "Stigma Management and Gay Identity Development." *Social Work* 36(1):67–73.

Canino, Ian A., and Jeanne Spurlock. 1994. *Culturally Diverse Children and Adolescents: Assessment, Diagnosis and Treatment.* New York: Guilford.

Capling, M., M. Considine, and M. Crozier. 1998. *Australian Politics in the Global Era.* Australia: Addison Wesley and Longman.

Carlton-LaMay, Iris. 1999. "African/American Social Work, Pioneers' Response to Need." *Social Work* 44(4):311–321.

Carmichael, Stokely, and Charles V. Hamilton. 1967. *Black Power: The Politics of Liberation in America.* New York: Vintage.

Carpenter, Donald. 1996. "Constructivism and Social Work Treatment." In Francis J. Turner, ed., *Social Work Treatment: Interlocking Theoretical Approaches,* pp. 146–167. New York: Free Press.

Carson, Clayborne, ed. 1998. *The Autobiography of Martin Luther King, Jr.* New York: Warner.

Cass, Vivien. 1979. "Homosexual Identity Formation: A Theoretical Model." *Journal of Homosexuality* 4:211–219.

CDFBCCC, Children's Defense Fund. "The Black Community Crusade for Children." [Online.] Available: http://www.childrensdefense.org/bccc.html

Chafetz, Janet Saltzman. 1988. *Feminist Sociology: An Overview of Contemporary Theories.* Itasca, Ill.: Peacock.

Chau, Kenneth, ed. 1990. *Ethnicity and Biculturalism: Emerging Perspectives of Social Group Work.* New York: Haworth.

Chenitz, Carole, and Janice M. Swanson. 1986. *From Practice to Grounded Theory: Qualitative Research in Nursing.* Reading, Mass.: Addison-Wesley.

Chestang, Leon. 1972. "Character Development in a Hostile Environment." School of Social Service Administration, University of Chicago, Occasional Paper no. 3 (November); also published in Martin Bloom, ed., *Life Span Development.* New York: Macmillan, 1980.

——— 1976. "Environmental Influences on Social Functioning: The Black Experience." In P. San Juan Cafferty and Leon Chestang, eds., *The Diverse Society:*

Implications for Social Policy, pp. 59–74. Washington, D.C.: National Association of Social Workers.

—— 1979. "Competence and Knowledge in Clinical Social Work: A Dual Perspective." In Patricia L. Ewalt, ed., *Towards a Definition of Clinical Social Work*, pp. 8–16. Washington, D.C.: National Association of Social Workers.

—— 1988. *Raising Children Who Will Run the World: The Eleventh Annual Konopka Lecture*. St. Paul: Center for Youth Development and Research, University of Minnesota.

Choi, Namkee G., and Lidia J. Snyder. 1999. *Homeless Families with Children: A Subjective Experience of Homelessness*. New York: Springer.

Chorcora, Marie M., Eddie Jennings, and Nuala Lordan. 1994. "Issues of Empowerment: Anti-Oppressive Groupwork by Disabled People in Ireland." *Groupwork* 7(1):63–78.

Clark, Kenneth B., and Mamie P. Clark. 1939. "The Development of Consciousness of Self and the Emergence of Racial Identification in Negro Pre-School Children." *Journal of Social Psychology* 10:591–599.

Cohen, Nathan, E. 1958. *Social Work in the American Tradition*. New York: Holt, Rinehart and Winston.

Colby, Ira C. 1989. *Social Welfare Policy: Perspectives, Patterns, and Insights*. Chicago: Dorsey.

Cole, Johnetta. 1998. "Commonalities and Differences." In Margaret L. Anderson and Patricia Hill Collins, eds., *Race, Class, and Gender*, pp. 175–180. Belmont, Cal.: Wadsworth.

Combahee River Collective. 1982. "A Black Feminist Statement." In Gloria T. Hall, Patricia Bell Scott, and Barbara Smith, eds., *All the Women Are White, All the Blacks Are Men, but Some of Us Are Brave: Black Women's Studies*, p. 14. New York: Feminist Press of the City University.

Congress, Elaine P. 1997. "Using the Culturagram or Assess and Empower Culturally Diverse Families." In Elaine P. Congress, Ed. *Multicultural Perspectives in Working with Families*. New York: Springer.

Connell, Sarah. 1987. "Homelessness." *Encyclopedia of Social Work*, pp. 789–794. 18th ed. Silver Spring, Md.: National Association of Social Workers.

Cooper, Shirley. 1977. "Social Work: A Dissenting Profession." *Social Work* 22(5):360–367.

Coppola, Mary, and Robert Rivas. 1986. "The Task-Action Group Technique: A Case Study of Empowering the Elderly," in Marvin Parnes, ed., *Innovations in Social Group Work*, pp. 133–148. New York: Haworth.

Corcoran, Kevin, and Joel Fischer. 1987. *Measures for Clinical Practice: A Sourcebook*. New York: Free Press.

Corcoran, Kevin and Vikki Vandiver. 1996. *Maneuvering the Maze of Managed Care: Skills for Mental Health Practitioners*. New York: Free Press.

Corcoran, Mary E. and Ajay Chaudry. 1997. "The Dynamics of Childhood Poverty." *Future of Children* 7(2)(Summer/Fall)):40–54.

Coyle, Grace L. 1979 [1930]. *Social Process in Organized Groups*. Hebron, Conn.: Practitioner's.

Cox, Enid Opal. 1989. "Empowerment of the Low Income Elderly Through Group Work." In Judith A. B. Lee, ed., *Group Work with the Poor and Oppressed*, pp. 111–125. New York: Haworth.

Cox, Fred M. 1977. "Alternative Conceptions of Community." In Fred M. Cox, John L. Erlich, Jack Rothman, and John E. Tropman, eds., *Tactics and Techniques of Community Practice*, pp. 224–234. Itasca, Ill.: Peacock.

Cox, Fred M., John L. Erlich, Jack Rothman, and John Tropman, eds. 1977. *Tactics and Techniques of Community Practice*. Itasca, Ill.: Peacock.

Critchlow, Donald T., and Ellis W. Hawley, eds. 1989. *Poverty and Public Policy in Modern America*. Chicago: Dorsey.

Culbert, Samuel A. 1976. "Consciousness-Raising: A Five Stage Model for Social and Organizational Change." In Warren G. Bennis, Kenneth D. Benne, and Robert Chin, eds., *The Planning of Change*, pp. 231–245. 3d ed. New York: Holt, Rinehart and Winston.

Culhane, Dennis. 1990. "Single Room Housing Won't End Homelessness." Letter to the Editor. *New Haven Register*, March 1.

Currents of the New York City Chapter, NASW. "Watchdog on Managed Care." *Currents of the New York City Chapter, NASW* 41:5.

Daly, Mary. 1978. *Gyn/Ecology: The Metaethics of Radical Feminism*. Boston: Beacon.

Danns, G.K., and B. Shiw Parsad. 1989. *Domestic Violence and Marital Relationships in the Caribbean: A Guyana Case Study*. Georgetown: Women's Studies Unit, University of Guyana.

Danziger, Sheldon H. 1987. "Poverty." *Encyclopedia of Social Work*, pp. 294–302. 18th ed. Silver Spring, Md.: National Association of Social Workers.

Danziger, Sheldon H., and Daniel H. Weinberg, eds. 1986. *Fighting Poverty: What Works and What Doesn't*. Cambridge: Harvard University Press.

Davis, Allen F. 1973. *American Heroine: The Life and Legend of Jane Addams*. New York: Oxford University Press.

Davis, Angela Y. 1981. *Women, Race, and Class*. New York: Random House.

Davis, Larry, E. 1984. *Ethnicity in Social Group Work Practice*. New York: Haworth.
—— 1985. "Group Work Practice with Ethnic Minorities of Color." In Martin Sundel, Paul Glasser, Rosemary Sarri, and Robert Vinter, eds., *Individual Change Through Small Groups*, pp. 324–345. New York: Free Press.

Davis, Larry, E., and Enola K. Proctor. 1989. *Race, Gender, and Class: Guidelines for Working with Individuals, Families, and Groups*. Englewood Cliffs, N.J.: Prentice-Hall.

Davis, Liane V. 1985. "Female and Male Voices in Social Work." *Social Work* 30:106–113.

Dean, Ruth G. 1993. "Constructivism: An Approach to Clinical Practice." *Smith College Studies in Social Work* 63(2)(March):127–146.

Dean, Walter R. Jr. 1977. "Back to Activism." *Social Work* 22(5):369–373.

DeCrescenzo, Theresa. 1979. "Group Work with Gay Adolescents." *Social Work with Groups* 2(1):35–44.

Devaney, Barbara L., Marilyn Elwood, and John M. Love. 1997. "Programs That Mitigate the Effects of Poverty on Children." *Future of Poverty* 7(2)(Summer/Fall 1997):88–112.

Devore, Wynetta, and Elfriede Schlesinger. 1999. *Ethnic Sensitive Social Work Practice.* 5th ed. Boston: Allyn and Bacon.

Dobzhansky, Theodosius. 1976. "The Myths of Genetic Predestination and Tabula Rasa." *Perspectives in Biology and Medicine* 19(January):156–170.

Doolittle, Fred C. 1987. "Social Welfare Financing." *Encyclopedia of Social Work*, pp. 660–664. 18th ed. Silver Spring, Md.: National Association of Social Workers.

Douglass, Frederick. 1968. *Narrative of the Life of Frederick Douglass An American Slave Written by Himself.* New York: Signet.

Draper, Barbara. 1979. "Black Language as an Adaptive Response to a Hostile Environment." In Carel B. Germain, ed., *Social Work Practice: People and Environments—An Ecological Perspective*, pp. 267–281. New York: Columbia University Press.

Drysdale, Jacky, and Rod Purcell. 1999. "Breaking the Culture of Silence: Groupwork and Community Development." *Groupwork* 11(3):70–87.

Du Bois, W. E. B. 1964. *Black Reconstruction in America.* New York: Meridian.

Dunkel, Joan, and S. Hatfield. 1986. "Countertransference Issues in Working with Persons with AIDS." *Social Work* (March/April):114–117.

Dunst, Carl, Carol Trivelle and Angela Deal. Eds. 1994. *Supporting and Strengthening Families.* Cambridge: Brookline.

Echols, Ivor J., and Ruth Martin. 1989. "Recapturing the Purpose of Settlements Through the Oral Histories of Pioneers." Paper presented at the Council on Social Work Education Conference, Chicago.

Ehrlich, Elizabeth. 1988. "Homelessness: The Policy Failure Haunting America." *Business Week* (April 25):132–135.

Elliot, Doreen, and Nazneen Mayadas. 1999. "Infusing Global Perspectives into Social Work Practice." In Chathapuram S. Ramanathan and Rosemary J. Link, eds., *All Our Futures: Principles and Resources for Social Work Practice in a Global Era*, pp. 52–65. Pacific Grove, Cal.: Brooks/Cole.

Elmer-Dewitt, Philip. 1992. "Depression: The Growing Role of Drug Therapies." *Time* (July 6):57–60.

Encyclopedia of Social Work. 1987. "Appendix 1. Code of Ethics of the National Association of Social Workers," pp. 951–956. Silver Spring, Md.: National Association of Social Workers.

Erikson, Erik H. 1959. "Growth and Crises of the Healthy Personality." In Erik H. Erikson, *Identity and the Life Cycle: Selected Papers by Erik H. Erikson*, pp. 50–100. New York: International Universities Press.

—— 1969. *Childhood and Society*. New York: Norton.

Erlich, John L., J. Tropman, and J. Rothman. 1995. Techniques and Tactics of Community Intervention. Itasca, Ill.: Peacock.

Estes, Richard. 1991. "Social Development and Social Work with Groups." Plenary speech presented at the Thirteenth Annual Symposium of the Association for the Advancement of Social Work with Groups, Akron, Ohio.

—— 1993. "Toward Sustainable Development: From Theory to Praxis." *Social Development Issues* 15(3):1–29.

—— 1999. "Informational Tools for Social Workers: Research in the Global Age." In Chathapuram S. Ramanathan and Rosemary J. Link. 1999. *All Our Futures: Principles and Resources For Social Work Practice in a Global Era*, pp. 121–137. Pacific Grove, Cal.: Brooks/Cole.

Estrada, Leobardo F. 1987. "Hispanics." *Encyclopedia of Social Work*, pp. 732–739. 18th ed. Silver Spring, Md.: National Association of Social Workers.

Evans, Estella N. 1992. "Liberation Theology, Empowerment Theory and Social Work Practice with the Oppressed." *International Social Work* 35:3–15.

Falck, Hans. 1988. *Social Work: The Membership Perspective*. New York: Springer.

Finkelhor, David. 1979. *Sexually Victimized Children*. New York: Free Press.

—— 1987. *Child Sexual Abuse: New Theory and Research*. New York: Free Press.

Fox, Raymond. 1993. *Elements of the Helping Processs: A Guide for Clinicians*. New York: Haworth.

Franklin, Anderson J. 1992. "Therapy with African American Men." *Families and Society* 73(6):350–355.

Franklin, John Hope, and Alfred A. Moss Jr. 1988. *From Slavery to Freedom: A History of Negro Americans*. 6th ed. New York: Knopf.

Freeman, Edith M. 1990. "The Black Family's Life Cycle: Operationalizing a Strengths Perspective." In Sadye Logan, Edith Freeman, and Ruth McRoy, eds., *Social Work Practice with Black Families*, pp. 55–72. New York: Longman.

Freire, Paulo. 1973a. *Pedagogy of the Oppressed*. New York: Seabury.

—— 1973b. *Education for Critical Consciousness*. New York: Continuum.

—— 1990. "A Critical Understanding of Social Work." *Journal of Progressive Human Services* 1(1):3–9.

—— 1997. *Pedagogy of the Heart*. New York: Continuum.

—— 1998. *Teachers as Cultural Workers: Letters to Those Who Dare to Teach*. Boulder, Col.: Westview.

Freud, Anna. 1936. *The Ego and the Mechanisms of Defense*. New York: International Universities Press.

Freud, Sigmund. 1961. "The Ego and the Id." In James Strachey, ed., *The Standard Edition of the Complete Psychological Works of Sigmund Freud*, vol. 19. London: Hogarth.

Friedman, Thomas. 1992. "Aides Say Clinton Will Swiftly Void G.O.P. Initiatives." *New York Times*, November 6, pp. A1, A18.

Friend, T. 1994. "The White Trashing of America." *New York* 27(33):22–31.

Gabriel, Martha A. 1996. *AIDS Trauma and Support Group Therapy*. New York: Free Press.

Galper, Jeffry H. 1978. *The Politics of Social Services*. Englewood Cliffs, N.J.: Prentice-Hall.

—— 1980. *Social Work Practice: A Radical Perspective*. Englewood Cliffs, N.J.: Prentice-Hall.

Gambrill, Eileen D. 1987. "Behavioral Approach." *Encyclopedia of Social Work*, pp. 184–194. 18th ed. Silver Spring, Md.: National Association of Social Workers.

Garcia, Betty, and Carol R. Swenson. 1992. "Writing the Stories of White Racism." *Journal of Teaching for Social Work* 6(2):3–17.

Garcia-Preto, Nydia. 1982. "Puerto Rican Families." In Monica McGoldrick, John K. Pearce, and Joseph Giordano, eds., *Ethnicity and Family Therapy*, pp. 164–186. New York: Guilford.

Garrow, David J. 1988. *Bearing the Cross: Martin Luther King, Jr., and the Southern Christian Leadership Conference*. New York: Vintage.

Garvin, Charles D. 1985. "Work with Disadvantaged and Oppressed Groups." In Martin Sundel, Paul Glasser, Rosemary Sarri, and Robert Vinter, eds., *Individual Change Through Small Groups*, pp. 461–472. 2d ed. New York: Free Press.

—— 1987. *Contemporary Group Work*. 2d ed. Englewood Cliffs, N.J.: Prentice-Hall.

Gary, Lawrence E., and Robenia B. Gary. 1985. "Treatment Needs of Black Alcoholic Women." *Alcoholism Treatment Quarterly* 2(3–4):97–114.

Gary, Robenia B., and Lawrence E. Gary. 1975. "Profile of Black Female Social Welfare Leaders During the 1920's." National Institute of Mental Health Grant no. MH–25551–02, pp. 9–13.

Germain, Carel B. 1974. "Casework and Science: A Historical Encounter." In Robert W. Robert and Robert H. Nee, eds., *Theories of Social Casework*, pp. 3–32. Chicago: University of Chicago Press.

—— 1979. *Social Work Practice: People and Environments*, pp. 1–22. New York: Columbia University Press.

—— 1984. *Social Work Practice in Health Care*. New York: Free Press.

—— 1987. "Ecological Perspective." *Encyclopedia of Social Work*, pp. 488–499. 18th ed. Silver Spring, Md.: National Association of Social Workers.

—— 1990. "Life Forces and the Anatomy of Practice." *Smith College Studies in Social Work* 60(March 2):138–152.

—— 1991. *Human Behavior in the Social Environment.* New York: Columbia University Press.

Germain, Carel B., and Alex Gitterman. 1980. *The Life Model of Social Work Practice.* New York: Columbia University Press.

—— 1996. *The Life Model of Social Work Practice: Advances in Theory and Practice.* 2d ed. New York: Columbia University Press.

Getzel, George. 1991. "AIDS." In Alex Gitterman, ed., *Handbook of Social Work Practice with Vulnerable Populations,* pp. 35–64. New York: Columbia University Press.

—— 1998. "Group Work Practice with Gay Men and Lesbians." in Gerald P. Mallon, ed., *Foundations of Social Work Practice with Lesbian and Gay Persons,* pp. 131–144. New York: Harrington Park.

Ghali, Sonia Badillo. 1977. "Culture Sensitivity and the Puerto Rican Client." In Armando Morales and Bradford W. Sheafor, eds., *Social Work: A Profession of Many Faces,* pp. 349–364. Boston: Allyn and Bacon.

Gibbs, Jewelle Taylor. 1984. "Black Adolescents and Youth: An Endangered Species." *American Journal of Orthopsychiatry* 54(January):6–21.

Gil, David G. 1981. *Unraveling Social Policy: Theory, Analysis, and Political Action Towards Social Equality.* 3d ed. Cambridge, Mass.: Schenkman.

Gilbert, Neil, and Harry Specht. 1987. "Social Planning and Community Organization." *Encyclopedia of Social Work,* pp. 602–619. 18th ed. Silver Spring, Md.: National Association of Social Workers.

Gilder, George. 1989. "The Nature of Poverty." In Ira C. Colby, ed., *Social Welfare Policy: Perspectives, Patterns, Insights,* pp. 47–57. Chicago: Dorsey.

Gilligan, Carol. 1982. *In a Different Voice: Psychological Theory and Women's Development.* Cambridge: Harvard University Press.

Gitterman, Alex. 1989. "Building Mutual Support in Groups." *Social Work with Groups* 12(2):5–21.

Gitterman, Alex, ed. 1991. *Handbook of Social Work Practice with Vulnerable Populations,* pp. 1–32. New York: Columbia University Press.

Gitterman, Alex, and Lawrence Shulman. 1986. *Mutual Aid and the Life Cycle.* Itasca, Ill.: Peacock.

Glaser, B. and Anselun Strauss. 1967. *The Discovery of Grounded Theory.* Chicago: Aldine.

Glasser, Irene. 1994. *Homelessness in Global Perspective.* New York: G. K. Hall.

Glassman, Urania, and Len Kates. 1990. *Group Work: A Humanistic Approach.* Newbury Park, Cal.: Sage.

Goffman, Erving. 1959. *The Presentation of Self in Everyday Life.* Englewood Cliffs, N.J.: Prentice-Hall.

—— 1963. *Stigma: Notes on the Management of Spoiled Identity.* Englewood Cliffs, N.J.: Prentice-Hall.

Golan, Naomi. 1978. *Treatment in Crisis Situations.* New York: Free Press.

Goldberg Wood, Gale, and Ruth R. Middleman. 1989. *The Structural Approach to Direct Practice in Social Work.* New York: Columbia University Press.

Goldstein, Eda. 1984. *Ego Psychology and Social Work Practice.* 2d ed. New York: Free Press.

——— 1995. *Ego Psychology and Social Work Practice.* New York: Free Press.

Goldstein, Howard. 1991. "Qualitative Research and Social Work Practice: Partners in Discovery." *Journal of Sociology and Social Welfare* 18(4):101–119.

Goleman, Daniel. 1987. "Feeling of Inferiority Reportedly Common in Black Children." *New York Times*, August 31, pp. 1, 13.

Goodman, Bernice. 1980. "Some Mothers Are Lesbians." In Elaine Norman and Arlene Mancuso, eds., *Women's Issues and Social Work Practice*, pp. 153–180. Itasca, Ill.: Peacock.

Gordon, Jacob U., ed. 1994a. *Managing Multiculturalism in Substance Abuse Services.* Thousand Oaks, Cal.: Sage.

——— 1994b. "African American Perspective." In Jacob U. Gordon, ed., *Managing Multiculturalism in Substance Abuse Services*, pp. 45–71. Thousand Oaks, Cal.: Sage.

Gordon, Milton M. 1978. *Human Nature, Class and Ethnicity.* New York: Oxford University Press.

Gordon, William E. 1962. "A Critique of the Working Definition." *Social Work* 7(October):3–13.

——— 1969. "Basic Constructs from an Integrative and Generative Conception of Social Work." In Gordon Hearn, ed., *The General Systems Approach: Contributions to an Holistic Conception of Social Work*, p. 6. New York: Council on Social Work Education.

Goroff, Norman N. 1981. "Humanism and Social Work: Praxis, Problems, and Promises." *Journal of Sociology and Social Welfare* 8:1.

Gottleib, Naomi, Dianne Burden, Ruth McCormick, and Ginny NiCarthy. 1983. "The Distinctive Attributes of Feminist Groups." *Social Work with Groups* 6(3–4):81–94.

Grace, John. 1985. "Coming Out in Social Work: Worker Survival, Support and Success." In Hilda Hidalgo, Travis L. Peterson, and Natalie Jane Goodman, eds., *Lesbian and Gay Issues: A Resource Manual for Social Workers.* Silver Spring, Md.: National Association of Social Workers.

Graham, Renee. 1990. "Alcoholism Found High Among Gays." *Boston Globe* (October 8):1.

Green, James W. 1999. *Cultural Awareness in the Human Services: A Multiethnic Approach.* 3d. ed. Boston: Allyn and Bacon.

Green, Sidney L. 1972. "Evaluation of Ego Adequacy." Unpublished. New York University School of Social Work.

Grier, William H., and Price M. Cobbs. 1969. *Black Rage.* New York: Bantam.

Gutiérrez, Gustavo. 1973. *A Theology of Liberation*. Maryknoll, N.Y.: Orbis.

Gutiérrez, Lorraine M. 1989a. "Empowerment in Social Work Practice: Considerations for Practice and Education." Paper presented at the Annual Meeting of the Council on Social Work Education, Chicago.

—— 1989b. "Using Group Work to Empower Latinos: A Preliminary Analysis." *Proceedings of the Eleventh Annual Symposium of the Association for the Advancement of Social Work with Groups*, Montreal.

—— 1990. "Working with Women of Color: An Empowerment Perspective." *Social Work* 35:149–155.

Gutiérrez, Lorraine M., and Edith A. Lewis. 1990. "Feminist Organizing with Women of Color." In J. Erhlich and F. Rivera, eds., *Community Organizing with People of Color*. Beverly Hills: Sage.

Gutiérrez, Lorraine M., Ruth J. Parsons, and Enid Opal Cox, eds. 1998. *Empowerment in Social Work Practice: A Sourcebook*. Pacific Grove, Cal.: Brooks/Cole.

Hanrahan, Virginia D. 1991. "Two Paradigms of Housing: Homeless Families Need More Than a Home." Master's thesis, Yale University School of Public Health, Department of Epidemiology.

Hamilton, Dona C. and Charles V. Hamilton. 1997. *The Dual Agenda: Race and Social Welfare Policies of Civil Rights Organizations*. New York: Columbia University Press.

Hamilton, Charles V., and Dona C. Hamilton. 1986. "Social Policies, Civil Rights, and Poverty." In Sheldon Danziger and Daniel Weinberg, eds., *Fighting Poverty: What Works and What Doesn't*, pp. 287–311. Cambridge: Harvard University Press.

Hanson, Meridith. 1991. "Alcoholism and Other Drug Addictions." In Alex Gitterman, ed., *Handbook of Social Work Practice with Vulnerable Populations*, pp. 65–100. New York: Columbia University Press.

Hardy, Kenneth, and Tracy A. Laszloffy, 1992. "Training Racially Sensitive Geriatric Family Therapists: Context, Content, and Contact." *Families in Society* 73(6):364–370.

Harley, Sharon. 1978. "The Northern Black Female Workers: Jacksonian Era." In Sharon Harley and Rosalyn Terborg-Penn, eds., *The Afro-American Woman: Struggles and Images*, pp. 7–8. Port Washington, N.Y.: Kennicat.

Harrington, Michael. 1965. *The Accidental Century*. Baltimore: Penguin.

Harris, Forrest E. 1993. *Ministry for Social Crisis: Theology and Praxis in the Black Church Tradition*. Macon, Ga.: Mercer University Press.

Hartford, Margaret. 1971. *Groups in Social Work: Application of Small Group Theory and Research to Social Work Practice*. New York: Columbia University Press.

Hartman, Ann, and Joan Laird. 1983. *Family-Centered Social Work Practice*. New York: Free Press.

Hartmann, Heinz. 1958. *Ego Psychology and the Problem of Adaptation*. New York: International Universities Press.

Hasenfeld, Yeshehekel. 1987. "Power in Social Work Practice." *Service Review* 61(3):469–483.

Hatfield, Agnes, and Harriet Lefley. 1987. *Families of the Mentally Ill.* New York: Guilford.

Haveman, Jon D., Sheldon Danziger, and Robert D. Plotnick. 1991. "State Poverty Rates for Whites, Blacks, and Hispanics in the Late 1980s." *Focus* 13(Spring):1–7.

Hayakawa, S. I. 1962. *The Use and Misuse of Language.* Greenwich, Conn.: Fawcett.

Heap, Ken. 1977. *Group Theory for Social Workers.* New York: Pergamon.

Heclo, Hugh. 1986. "The Political Foundations of Antipoverty Policy." In Sheldon Danziger and Daniel Weinberg, eds., *Fighting Poverty: What Works and What Doesn't,* pp. 312–340. Cambridge: Harvard University Press.

Heineman Pieper, Martha, and Katherine Tyson. 1999. "Response to Padgett's 'Does the Glove Really Fit?' " *Social Work* 44(3):278–279.

Henry, P. B. 1989. *Practical Approaches in Treating Adolescent Chemical Dependency: A Guide to Clinical Assessment and Intervention.* Binghamton, N.Y.: Haworth.

Henry, Sue. 1992. *Group Skills in Social Work: A Four Dimensional Approach.* 2d ed. Pacific Grove, Cal.: Brooks/Cole.

Hepworth, Dean H., and JoAnn Larsen. 1986. *Direct Social Work Practice: Theory and Skill,* pp. 116–118. Chicago: Dorsey.

Herd, D. 1989. "The Epidemology of Drinking Patterns and Alcohol Related Problems Among U.S. Blacks." In *Alcohol Use Among Ethnic Minorities,* pp. 3–50. Rockville, Md.: National Institute on Alcohol Abuse and Alcoholism (DHHS Publication No. ADM 89–1435).

Hershberg, Theodore. 1989. "Free Blacks in Antebellum Philadelphia: A Study of Ex-Slaves, Freeborn, and Socioeconomic Decline." In Ira C. Colby, ed., *Social Welfare Policy: Perspectices, Pattern, Insights.* Chicago: Dorsey.

Hines, Paulette Moore, Nydia Garcia-Preto, Monica McGoldrick, Rhea Almeida, and Susan Weltman. 1992. "Intergenerational Relationships Across Cultures." *Families in Society* 73(6):323–338.

Hill, Robert B. 1972. *The Strengths of Black Families.* New York: Emerson Hall.

Hirayama, Hisashi, and Kasumi Hirayama. 1986. "Empowerment Through Group Participation: Process and Goal." In Marvin Parnes, ed., *Innovations in Social Group Work: Feedback from Practice to Theory,* pp. 119–181. New York: Haworth.

Ho, Man Keung. 1994. "Asian American Perspective." In Jacob U. Gordon, ed., *Managing Multiculturalism in Substance Abuse Services,* pp. 72–98. Thousand Oaks, Cal.: Sage.

Hokenstad, M. C., and James Midgley. 1997. "Realities of Global Interdependence: Challenges for Social Work in a New Century. In M. C. Hokenstad and James Midgley, eds., *Issues in International Social Work: Global Challenges For a New Century,* pp. 1–10. Washington, D.C.: NASW Press.

Hollis, Florence, and Mary E. Woods. 1981. *Casework: A Psychosocial Therapy.* 3d ed. New York: Random House.

Holt, Thomas C. 1982. "The Lonely Warrior: Ida B. Wells-Barnett and the Struggle for Black Leadership." In John Hope Franklin and August Meier, eds., *Black Leaders of the Twentieth Century.* Urbana: University of Illinois Press.

Hong-Kingston, Maxine. 1980. *China Men.* New York: Knopf.

Honkala, Cheri, Mary Bricker-Jenkins, and Willie Baptist. 1999. "Making Connection/Making a Movement." Unpublished. Kensington, Pa.: KWRU.

hooks, bell. 1990. *Yearning: Race, Gender, and Cultural Politics.* Boston: South End.

—— 1995. *Killing Rage: Ending Racism.* New York: Holt.

Hope, Anne and Sally Timmel. 1995. *Training for Transformation: A Handbook for Community Workers.* Rev. ed. Vol. 1. Zimbabwe: Mambo Press.

Hopps, June G. 1982. "Oppression Based on Color." *Social Casework* 27(January):3–6.

Hopps, June G., Elaine Pinderhughes and Richard Shankar. 1995. *The Power to Care: Clinical Practice Effectiveness with Overwhelmed Clients.* New York: Free Press.

—— 1987. "Minorities of Color." *Encyclopedia of Social Work*, pp. 161–170. 18th ed. Silver Spring, Md.: National Association of Social Workers.

Hopps, June G. and Elaine Pinderhughes. 1999. *Groupwork with Overwhelmed Clients.* New York: Free Press.

Hraba, Joseph, and Geoffrey Grant. 1970. "Black Is Beautiful: A Reexamination of Racial Preference and Identification." *Journal of Personality and Social Psychology* 16:399–402.

IDC. 1996. "Shaping the Twenty-First Century: The Contribution of Development Co-Operation, Development Assistance Committee, May 1996: Introduction and Summary." [Online.] Available: http://www.idc.org/coop.htm (September 30, 1998).

Inglehart, Alfreda P. and Rosina M. Becerra. 1995. *Social Services and the Ethnic Community.* Needham Heights, Mass.: Allyn and Bacon.

Ivanoff, Andr,, Betty J. Blythe, and Scott Briar. 1987. "The Empirical Clinical Practice Debate." *Social Work* 68(5):290–298.

IWPR. 1998. *Statistics on Women's Earnings.* [Online.] Available: http://www.iwpr.org/release98.htm

Jacobsen, Michael. 1990. "Working with Communities." In H. Wayne Johnson, ed., *The Social Services: An Introduction*, pp. 385–403. 3d ed. Itasca, Ill.: Peacock.

James, Beverly. 1994. *Handbook for Treatment of Attachment-Trauma Problems in Children.* New York: Lexington.

Jansson, Bruce S. 1988. *The Reluctant Welfare State: A History of American Social Welfare Policies.* Belmont, Cal.: Wadsworth.

—— 1993. *The Reluctant Welfare State.* 2d ed. Calif. Brooks/Cole.

Johnson, Alice K. 1999. Globalization from Below: Using the Internet to Internationalize Social Work Education. *Journal of Social Work Education* 35(3)377–393.

Johnson, Alice K., and Judith A. B. Lee. 1994. "Empowerment Work with Homeless Women." In Marsha M. Pravder, ed., *Women in Context: Toward a Feminist Reconstruction of Psychotherapy*, pp. 408–432. New York: Guilford.

Johnson, Paul. 1983. *Modern Times: The World from the Twenties to the Eighties*. New York: Harper and Row.

Jones, Arthur. 1999. "America's Invisible Poor: Welfare Reform Makes Children Prime Victims." *National Catholic Reporter*. April 30, pp. 14–16.

Jones, Jacqueline. 1985. *Labor of Love, Labor of Sorrow: Black Women, Work and Family, from Slavery to the Present*. New York: Vintage.

Jordon, Winthrop. 1974. *The White Man's Burden: Historical Origins of Racism in the United States*. New York: Oxford University Press.

Joseph, Barbara. 1980. "Ain't I a Woman." In Elaine Norman and Arlene Mancuso, eds., *Women's Issues and Social Work Practice*, pp. 91–112. Itasca, Ill.: Peacock.

Julia, Maria. 2000. *Constructing Gender: Multicultural Perspectives in Working with Women*. Belmont, Cal.: Brooks/Cole.

Kantrowitz, Barbara and Karen Springer. 1998. "A Tenuous Bond From 9 to 5". *Newsweek* (March 7): 24–25.

Kaplan, Harold I., Benjamin J. Sadock, and Jacka Grebb. 1998. *Comprehensive Textbook of Psychiatry*. 8th ed. Baltimore: Williams and Wilkins.

—— 1991. *Synopsis of Psychiatry*. Baltimore: Williams and Wilkins.

Karls, James M., and Karin E. Wandrei. 1991. *PIE: Person in Environment Assessment*. Silver Spring, Md.: National Association of Social Workers.

—— 1992. "PIE: A New Language for Social Work." *Social Work* 37(1):80–85.

Katz, Michael B. 1986. *In the Shadow of the Poorhouse: A Social History of Welfare in America*. New York: Basic.

—— 1989a. "Origins of the Institutional State." In Donald T. Critchlow and Ellis W. Hawley, eds., *Poverty and Public Policy in Modern America*, pp. 5–17. Chicago: Dorsey.

—— 1989b. *The Undeserving Poor: From the War on Poverty to the War on Welfare*. New York: Pantheon.

Kelley, Patricia. 1996. "Narrative Theory and Social Work Treatment: Interlocking Theoretical Approaches," pp. 434–460. New York: Free Press.

Kelly, R. 1997. "Gotham City." New York: Zomba Songs/Zomba Recording/Kelly.

Kernberg, Otto. 1975. *Borderline Conditions and Pathological Narcissism*. New York: Jason Aronson.

Khinduka, S. K. 1987. "Social Work and the Human Services." *Encyclopedia of Social Work*, pp. 681–695. 18th ed. Silver Spring, Md.: National Association of Social Workers.

King, Martin Luther, Jr. 1963. *Why We Can't Wait*. New York: Harper and Row.

—— 1967. *The Trumpet of Conscience*. New York: Harper and Row.

Kitano, Harry H. L. 1987. "Asian Americans." *Encyclopedia of Social Work*, pp. 156–171. 18th ed. Silver Spring, Md.: National Association of Social Workers.

Kohut, Heinz. 1981. *The Analysis of the Self.* New York: International Universities Press.

Kominars, Sheppard B. 1989. *Accepting Ourselves: The Twelve-Step Journey of Recovery from Addiction for Gay Men and Lesbians.* New York: Harper and Row.

Konopka, Gisela. 1972. *Social Group Work: A Helping Process.* 2d ed. Englewood Cliffs, N.J.: Prentice-Hall.

——— 1978. "The Significance of Social Group Work Based on Ethical Values." *Social Work with Groups* 1(2):123–131.

——— 1988. *Courage and Love.* Edina, Minn.: Burgess.

——— 1991. "All Lives Are Connected to Other Lives: The Meaning of Social Group Work." In Marie Weil, Kenneth Chau, and Dannia Southerland, eds., *Theory and Practice in Social Group Work: Creative Connections*, pp. 29–38. New York: Haworth.

Kratochwill, Thomas R., and Richard J. Morris. 1991. *The Practice of Child Therapy.* 2d ed. Boston: Allyn and Bacon.

Kübler-Ross, Elisabeth. 1969. *On Death and Dying.* New York: Macmillan.

Kuenstler, Peter, ed. 1965. *Social Group Work in Great Britain.* London: Faber and Faber.

Kutchins, Herbert, and Stuart A. Kirk. 1987. "DSM-III and Social Work Malpractice." *Social Work* (May–June):206–211.

Ladner, Joyce A. 1972. *Tomorrow's Tomorrow.* New York: Anchor.

La Fleur, Patrice D. A. 1998. *Steps for Organising and Community Development: At the Grassroots Level.* Georgetown, Guyana: Andaiye.

Lamb, Robert K. 1977. "Suggestions for a Study of Your Home Town." In Fred M. Cox, John L. Erlich, Jack Rothman, and John E. Tropman, eds., *Tactics and Techniques of Community Practice*, pp. 17–23. Itasca, Ill.: Peacock.

Lang, Norma. 1986. "Social Work Practice in Small Social Forms: Identifying Collectivity." In Norma Lang and Joanne Sulman, eds., *Collectivity in Social Group Work: Concept and Practice.* New York: Haworth; also in *Social Work with Groups* 9(4):7–32.

Lang, Norma, and Sulman, Joanne, eds. 1986. *Collectivity in Social Group Work: Concept and Practice.* New York: Haworth.

Langellier, Regis. 1982. "French Candian Families." In Monica McGoldrick, John K. Pearce, and Joseph Giordano, eds., *Ethnicity and Family Therapy*, pp. 229–246. New York: Guilford.

Lantz, Jim. 1996. "Cognitive Theory and Social Work Treatment." In Francis J. Turner, ed. *Social Work Treatment: Interlocking Theoretical Approaches*, pp. 69–93. New York: Free Press.

Lawson, Gary W., D. C. Ellis, and P. Clayton Rivers. 1984. *Essentials of Chemical Dependency Counseling.* Rockville, Md.: Aspen.

Lawson, Gary W. and Ann W. Lawson, eds. 1989. *Alcoholism and Substance Abuse in Special Populations.* Rockville, Md.: Aspen.

Lawson, Gary, James S. Peterson, and Ann Lawson. 1983. *Alcoholism and the Family: A Guide to Treatment and Prevention.* Rockville, Md.: Aspen.

Lebow, L. 1973. "Pseudosenility: Acute and Reversible Organic Brain Syndromes." *Journal of the American Geriatric Society* 21:112–120.

Lee, Janine M. 1994. "Historical and Theoretical Considerations: Implications for Multiculturalism in Substance Abuse Services." In Jacob U. Gordon, ed., *Managing Multiculturalism in Substance Abuse Services*, pp. 3–21. Thousand Oaks, Cal.: Sage.

Lee, Judith A. B. 1979. "The Foster Parents Workshop: A Social Work Approach to Learning for New Foster Parents." *Social Work with Groups* 2(2):129–144.

——— 1980. "The Helping Professional's Use of Language in Describing the Poor." *American Journal of Orthopsychiatry* 50(October):580–584.

——— 1981. "Human Relatedness and the Mentally Impaired Older Person." *Journal of Gerontological Social Work* 4(Winter):5–15.

——— 1987. "Social Work with Oppressed Populations: Jane Addams, Won't You Please Come Home?" In Joseph Lassner, Kathleen Powell, and Elaine Finnegan, eds., *Social Group Work: Competence and Values in Practice*, pp. 1–16. New York: Haworth.

——— 1989a. "An Ecological View of Aging: Luisa's Plight." *Journal of Gerontological Social Work* 14(1–2):175–190.

——— 1990. "When I Was Well, I Was a Sister: Social Work with Homeless Women." *Jewish Social Work Forum* 26(Spring):22–30.

——— 1991. "Empowerment Through Mutual Aid Groups: A Practice-Grounded Conceptual Framework." *Groupwork* 4(1):5–21.

——— 1992a. "Jane Addams in Boston: Intersecting Time and Space." In James A. Garland, ed., *Group Work Reaching Out: People, Places, and Power*, pp. 7–22. New York: Haworth.

——— 1992b. "Teaching Content Related to Lesbian and Gay Identity Formation." In Natalie J. Woodman, ed., *Lesbian and Gay Lifestyles: A Guide for Counseling and Education.* New York: Irvington.

——— 1994a. "No Place to Go: Homeless Women." In Alex Gitterman and Lawrence Shulman, eds., *Mutual Aid Groups, Vulnerable Populations, and the Life Cycle*, pp. 297–314. Itasca, Ill.: Peacock.

——— 1994b. "The Concept of Mutual Aid." In Alex Gitterman and Lawrence Shulman, eds., *Mutual Aid Groups, Vulnerable Populations, and the Life Cycle*, pp. 413–430. 2d ed. Itasca, Ill.: Peacock.

——— 1996a. "The Empowerment Approach to Social Work Practice." In Francis J. Turner, ed., *Social Work Practice: Interlocking Theoretical Approaches.* Pp. 218–249. New York: Free Press.

——— 1999a. "Innovation in Practice with Homeless Populations: Partnership in the Struggle for Empowerment." In David E. Biegel and Arthur Blum, eds., *Innovations in Practice and Service Delivery Across the Lifespan*, pp. 221–248. New York: Oxford University Press.

——— 1999b. Crossing Bridges: Groupwork in Guyana. *Groupwork* 11(1):6–23.

Lee, Judith A. B., ed. 1989b. *Group Work with the Poor and Oppressed*. New York: Haworth.

—— 1996b. "The Empowerment Group Approach: An International Paradigm." In Joan K. Parry, ed., *From Prevention to Wellness*. New York: Haworth.

Lee, Judith A. B., Group Members, and Ruth R. Martin. 1997. "The Empowerment Group in Action." In Albert S. Alissi and Catherine G. Corto Mergins, eds., *Voices from the Field: Groupwork Responds*, pp. 23–42. New York: Haworth.

Lee, Judith A. B., and Ruth Martin, Judith A. Beaumont, Rosalind Moore-Beckham, Gail Bourdon, Christy King, Jean Konon, and Evelyn Thorpe. 1997. "Reflections on Empowerment Groupwork Across Racial Lines." In Tara Mistry and Allen Brown, eds., *Race and Groupwork*, pp. 66–98. London: Whiting and Birch.

Lee, Judith A. B., and Danielle Nisivoccia. 1989. *Walk a Mile in My Shoes: A Book About Biological Parents for Foster Parents and Social Workers*. Washington, D.C.: Child Welfare League of America.

—— 1997. "Substance Abuse and Homeless Mothers: Multiple Oppression and Empowerment." In Elaine P. Congress, ed., *Multicultural Perspectives in Working with Families*, pp. 288–310. New York: Springer.

Lee, Judith A. B., and Stella Odie-Ali. 2000. "Carry Me Home. A Collaborative Study of Street Children in Guyana, South America. *Journal of Social Work Research and Evaluation: An International Publication* 1(2).

Lee, Judith A. B., Stella Odie-Ali, and Michael Botsko. 2000. "The Invisible Visibles: A Study of the Needs of the Homeless and Mentally Ill in Guyana." *Journal of International Social Work* (43)2:163–178..

Lee, Judith A. B., and Danielle N. Park. 1978. "A Group Approach to the Depressed Adolescent Girl in Foster Care." *American Journal of Orthopsychiatry* 48(3):516–517.

—— 1983. "A Group Approach to Depressed Girl in Foster Care." In Ester S. Buchholz and Judith M. Mishne, eds., *Ego and Self Psychology: Group Interventions with Children, Adolescents, and Parents*, pp. 185–206. New York: Jason Aronson.

Lee, Judith A. B., and Carol R. Swenson. 1978. "A Community Social Service Agency: Theory in Action." *Social Casework* 59 (June):359–369.

Legislative Alert. 1991. Silver Spring, Md.: National Association of Social Workers, March 5.

Legislative Update. 1991. Silver Spring, Md.: National Association of Social Workers, April 5.

Leigh, J. W., and J. W. Green. 1982. "The Structure of the Black Community: The Knowledge Base for Social Services." In J. W. Green, ed., *Cultural Awareness in the Human Services*. Englewood Cliffs, N.J.: Prentice-Hall.

Leiken, Celia. 1986. "Identifying and Treating the Alcoholic Client." *Social Casework* 67(1):67–73.

Lemann, Nicholas. 1991. *The Promised Land: The Great Black Migration and How It Changed America*. New York: Random House.

Lenna, Harry R. 1992. "The Outsiders: Group Work with Young Homosexuals." In Natalie Jane Woodman, ed., *Lesbian and Gay Life Styles: A Guide for Counseling and Education*, pp. 67–86. New York: Irvington.

Levine, Eric. 1990. "The Ethical-Ritual in Judaism: A Review of Sources in Torah Study and Social Action." *Jewish Social Work Forum* 26 (Spring):44–50.

Levy, Charles. 1976. *Social Work Ethics*. New York: Human Sciences.

Lewin, Kurt. 1951. *Field Theory in Social Science*. New York: Harper and Row.

Lewis, Dillona. 1999. "School's Out for Welfare Recipients: College Students Forced to Abandon Studies by Welfare Reform." *Currents of the New York City Chapter NASW* (September):3,9.

Lewis, Elizabeth. 1983. "Social Group Work in Community Life: Group Characteristics and Worker Role." *Social Work with Groups* 6(2):3–18.

——— 1987. "Regaining Promise: Feminist Perspectives for Social Group Work Practice." Speech at 9th Annual Symposium of Association for the Advancement of Social Work with Groups, Boston, October 29–November 1; also published in James Garland, ed., *Group Work Reaching Out: People, Places, and Power*, pp. 271–284. New York: Haworth, 1992.

——— 1991. "Social Change and Citizen Action: A Philosophical Explanation for Modern Social Group Work." In Abe Vinik and Morris Levin, eds., *Social Action in Group Work*, pp. 23–34. New York: Haworth.

Lewis, Harold. 1972. "Developing a Program Responsive to New Knowledge and Values." In Edward J. Mullen, James R. Dumpson, and associates, eds., *Evaluation of Social Intervention*, pp. 71–89. San Francisco: Jossey-Bass.

Lewis, J. A., R. Q. Dana, and G. A. Blevens. 1988. *Substance Abuse Counseling: An Individualized Approach*. Pacific Grove, Cal.: Brooks/Cole.

Lewis, LouAnn. 1984. "The Coming Out Process for Lesbians: Integrating a Stable Identity." *Social Work* 29(5):464–469.

Lewit, Eugene M. Donna L. Terman and Richard E. Behrman. 1997. "Children and Poverty: Analysis and Recommendations." *Future of Children.* 7(2)(Summer/Fall):4–24.

Libassi, Mary Frances. 1988. "The Chronically Mentally Ill: A Practice Approach." *Social Casework* 69(2):88–96.

Lieberman, Florence. 1979. *Social Work with Children*. New York: Human Sciences.

——— 1982. "Work with Children." In D. Waldfogel and A. Rosenblatt, eds., *Handbook of Clinical Social Work*, pp. 441–465. San Francisco: Jossey-Bass.

Lindemann, Erich. 1965. "Symptomatology and Management of Acute Grief." In Howard J. Parad, ed., *Crisis Intervention*, pp. 7–21. New York: Family Service Association of America.

Link, Rosemary, Chathapuram S. Ramanathan, and Yvonne Asamoah. 1999. "Understanding the Human Condition and Human Behavior in a Global Era." In Chathapuram S. Ramanathan and Rosemary J. Link, eds., *All Our Futures*, pp. 30–46. Boston: Allyn and Bacon.

Linzer, Norman. 1978. *The Nature of Man in Judaism and Social Work*. New York: Federation of Jewish Philanthropies.

Lloyd, Gary. 1987. "Social Work Education." *Encyclopedia of Social Work*, pp. 695–705. 18th ed. Silver Spring, Md.: National Association of Social Workers.

Loewenberg, Frank M. 1988. *Religion and Social Work Practice in Contemporary Society*. New York: Columbia University Press.

Logan, Sadye M. L. 1990. "Diversity Among Black Families: Assessing Structure and Function." In Sadye M. Logan, Edith M. Freeman, and Ruth G. McRoy, eds., *Social Work Practice with Black Families*, pp. 73–96. New York: Longman.

Logan, Sadye M. L., Edith M. Freeman, and Ruth G. McRoy. 1990. *Social Work Practice with Black Families: A Culturally Specific Perspective*. New York: Longman.

Longres, John F. 1982. "Minority Groups: An Interest Group Perspective." *Social Casework* 27(January):7–14.

—— 1987. "Biography of Beatriz Lassalle." *Encyclopedia of Social Work*, p. 931. 18th ed. Silver Spring, Md.: National Association of Social Workers.

—— 1990. *Human Behavior in the Social Environment*. Itasca, Ill.: Peacock.

—— 1995. *Human Behavior in the Social Environment*. 2d ed. Itasca, Ill.: Peacock.

Lucco, Alfred A. 1991. "Assessment of the School Age Child." *Families in Society* 72(7):394–407.

Lum, Doman. 1986. *Social Work Practice and People of Color: A Process Stage Approach*. Monterey, Cal.: Brooks/Cole.

—— 2000. *Social Work Practice and People of Color: A Process Stage Approach*. 4th ed. Monterey, Cal.: Brooks/Cole.

McAdoo, Harriette P. 1987. "Blacks." *Encyclopedia of Social Work*, pp. 194–206. 18th ed. Silver Spring, Md.: National Association of Social Workers.

Macedo, Donaldo, an Ana Maria Araújo Freire. 1998. "Foreword." In Paulo Freire, *Teachers as Cultural Workers*, pp. ix–xix. Boulder: Westview.

McGoldrick, Monica. 1982. "Irish Families." In Monica McGoldrick, John K. Pearce, and Joseph Giordano, eds., *Ethnicity and Family Therapy*, pp. 310–339. New York: Guilford.

McGoldrick, Monica, John K. Pearce, and Joseph Giordano, eds. 1982. *Ethnicity and Family Therapy*. New York: Guilford.

MacGowan, Mark J. 1990. "A Group Intervention with African-American Substance Abusing Youths: Clinical and Research Findings." Paper presented at the Twelfth Annual Symposium of the Association for the Advancement of Social Work with Groups, Miami.

McIntosh, Peggy. 1998. "White Privilege and Male Privilege: A Personal Account." In Margaret L. Anderson and and Patricia Hill Collins, eds., *Race, Class and Gender: An American Anthology*, pp. 94–105. Cal.: Wadsworth.

Mack, John E., and Holly Hickler. 1981. *Vivienne*. Boston: Mentor.

McRoy, Ruth G., and C. T. Shorkey. 1985. "Alcohol Use and Abuse Among Blacks." In Edith M. Freeman, ed., *Social Work Practice with Clients Who Have Alcohol Problems*, pp. 202–213. Springfield, Ill.: Thomas.

McSettin, Joan M., and Dana Bramel. 1981. "Intersecting Class and Gender in Biasing Clinical Judgment." *American Journal of Orthopsychiatry* 51(3):510–520.

McSteen, Martha A. 1989. "Fifty Years of Social Security." In Ira C. Colby, ed., *Social Welfare Policy: Perspectives, Patterns, and Insights*, pp. 166–180. Chicago: Dorsey.

Mahaffey, Maryann. 1987. "Political Action in Social Work." *Encyclopedia of Social Work*, pp. 283–293. 18th ed. Silver Spring, Md.: National Association of Social Workers.

Mahler, Margaret S., Fred Pine, and Anni Bergman. 1975. *The Psychological Birth of the Human Infant*. New York: Basic.

Malcolm X. 1965. *The Autobiography of Malcolm X*. New York: Grove.

Mallon, Gerald P. 1998. *Foundations of Social Work Practice with Gay and Lesbian Persons*. New York: Harrington Park.

Maluccio, Anthony N. 1979. *Learning from Clients*. New York: Free Press.

Maluccio, Anthony N., ed. 1981. *Promoting Competence in Clients: A New/Old Approach to Social Work Practice*. New York: Free Press.

Mancoske, Ronald J., and Jeanne M. Hunzeker. 1989. *Empowerment Based Generalist Practice: Direct Services with Individuals*. New York: Cummings and Hathaway.

Mancusco, Arlene. 1980. "No Drums, No Trumpets: Working Class Women." In Elaine Norman and Arlene Mancusco, eds., *Women's Issues and Social Work Practice*, pp. 41–55. Itasca, Ill: Peacock.

Mann, Bonnie. 1987. "Working with Battered Women: Radical Education or Therapy." In Ellen Pence, ed., *In Our Best Interest: A Process for Personal and Social Change*, pp. 104–116. Duluth: Minnesota Program Development.

Marins, Jose, and Team. 1983. *Basic Ecclesial Communities: The Church from the Roots*. Quezon City, Philippines: Claretian.

Martin, Patricia Y., and Kristin A. Shanahan. 1983. "Transcending the Effects of Sex Composition in Small Groups." *Social Work with Groups* 6(3–4):35–42.

Martin, Ruth R. 1987. "Oral History in Social Work Education: The Black Experience." *Journal of Social Work Education* 23(3):5–10.

—— 1989. "Black Family Adaptation, Survival, and Growth Strategies: An Oral History Research Project." In A. Rodgers, ed., *The Black Family at the Crossroads of Development*, pp. 80–113. Columbia: University of South Carolina Press.

—— 1992. "An Oral History Research Project: Pliny Street Block Association." *Community Social Services Series*, vol. 1. West Hartford: University of Connecticut School of Social Work.

—— 1995. *Oral History in Social Work: Research, Assessment and Intervention*. Thousand Oaks, Cal.: Sage.

Matorin, Susan. 1991. "Schizophrenia." In Alex Gitterman, ed., *Handbook of Social Work Practice with Vulnerable Populations*, pp. 286–316. New York: Columbia University Press.

Mayeroff, Milton. 1971. *On Caring*. New York: Harper and Row.

Mead, George H. 1934. *Mind, Self, and Society*. Chicago: University of Chicago Press.

Mechanic, David. 1974. "Social Structure and Personal Adaptation." In George V. Coelho, David A. Hamburg, and John E. Adams, eds., *Coping and Adaptation*, pp. 32–46. New York: Basic.

Middleman, Ruth R. 1968. *The Non-Verbal Method in Working with Groups*. New York: Association Press.

————— 1999. "Social Development in Social Work: Learning From Global Dialogue. In Chathapuram S. Ramanathan and Rosemary J. Link, eds., *All Our Futures: Principles and Resources for Social Work Practice in a Global Era*.pp. 193–204. California: Wadsworth.

Middleman, Ruth R., and Gale Goldberg. 1974. *Social Service Delivery: A Structural Approach to Social Work Practice*. New York: Columbia University Press.

Middleman, Ruth R., and Gale Goldberg Wood. 1990. *Skills for Direct Practice Social Work*. New York: Columbia University Press.

Midgley, James. 1991. "Social Development and Multicultural Social Work." In *Multicultural Social Work* 1(1):85–100.

————— 1997. "Toward a Developmental Model of Social Policy: Relevance of Third World Competence." *Journal of Sociology and Social Welfare* 23(1):59–74.

————— 1999. "Social Development in Social Work: Learning from Global Dialogue." In Chathapuram S. Ramanathan and Rosemary J. Link, eds., *All Our Futures: Social Work Practice in a Global Era*, pp. 193–205. Belmont, Cal.: Wadsworth.

Miley, Karla K. 1999. "Empowerment Articles." Personal communication.

Miley, Karla K., and Brenda Du Bois. 1998. "Empowerment-Based Social Work Practice: An Annotated Bibliography." Unpublished. Black Hawk College, Moline, Illinois.

Miley, Karla K., Michael O'Melia, and Brenda L. DuBois. 1998. *Generalist Social Work Practice*. Boston: Allyn and Bacon.

Minahan, Anne, and Pincas, Alan. 1977. "Conceptual Frameworks for Social Work Practice." *Social Work* 22(5):347–352.

Minkler, Meredith, ed. 1998. *Community Organizing and Community Building for Health*. New Brunswick, N.J.: Rutgers University Press.

Minority Trendsletter. 1990–1991. Center for Third World Organizing, Oakland, Cal. (Winter).

Mischler, E. 1986. *The Research Interview: Context and Narrative*, pp. 116–144. Cambridge: Harvard University Press.

Mistry, Tara, and Allan Brown, eds. 1997. *Race and Groupwork*. London: Whiting and Birch.

Mondros, Jacqueline, and Toby Berman-Rossi. 1991. "The Relevance of Stages of Group Development Theory to Community Organization Practice." *Social Work with Groups* 14(3–4):125–140.

Moore, Joan W. 1985. "Isolation and Stigmatization in the Development of an Underclass: The Case of Chicano Gangs in East Los Angeles." *Social Problems* 23:1–12.

Moore-Hines, Paulette, and Nancy Boyd-Franklin. 1982. "Black Families." In Monica McGoldrick, John K. Pearce, and Joseph Giordano, eds., *Ethnicity and Family Therapy*, pp. 84–108. New York: Guilford.

Morales, Armando. 1977. "Beyond Traditional Conceptual Frameworks." *Social Work* 22(5):387–393.

Morales, Armando, and Bradford W. Sheafor. 1983. *Social Work: A Profession of Many Faces*. 3d ed. Boston: Allyn and Bacon.

Morales, Julio. 1986. *Puerto Rican Poverty and Migration: We Just Had to Try Elsewhere*. New York: Praeger.

Morgan, Edmond S. 1972. "Slavery and Freedom: The American Paradox." *Journal of American History* 59(June):14–29.

Morris, Robert. 1989. "A Welfare Agenda for the End of the Century: Recasting the Future on Foundations." In Ira C. Colby, ed., *Social Welfare Policy: Perspectives, Patterns, and Insights*, pp. 455–494. Chicago: Dorsey.

Moses, Alice Elfin. 1978. *Identity Management in Lesbian Women*. New York: Praeger.

Moses, Alice Elfin, and Robert O. Hawkins Jr. 1982. *Counseling Lesbian Women and Gay Men: A Life-Issues Approach*. St. Louis: Mosby.

Mullaly, Robert P., and Eric F. Keating. 1991. "Similarities, Differences and Dialectics of Radical Social Work." *Journal of Progressive Human Services* 2(2):49–78.

Mullender, Audrey. 1990. "The Ebony Project–Bicultural Group Work with Transracial Foster Parents." *Social Work with Groups* 13(4):23–42.

———— 1991. "Empowerment Through Social Action Group Work: The –Self-Directed' Approach." *Social Work with Groups* 14(3–4):125–139.

Mullender, Audrey, and David Ward. 1989. "Challenging Familiar Assumptions: Preparing for and Initiating a Self-Directed Group." *Groupwork* 2(1):5–26.

———— 1991. *Self-Directed Groupwork: Users Take Action for Empowerment*. London: Whiting and Birch.

National Association of Social Workers. 1980. *The National Association of Social Workers Code of Ethics*. Silver Spring, Md.: National Association of Social Workers.

National Council on Alcoholism and Drug Dependence. 1990 "Fact Sheet." New York: National Council on Alcoholism and Drug Dependence.

New York Times. 1992 "Poverty in America." September 4, pp. A1, A14.

Navarro, Mireya. 1998. "Florida Tomato Pickers Take on Growers." *New York Times*. February 1, p. 14.

NCAPP/ASAM Joint Committee (National Council on Alcoholism and Drug Dependence and American Society of Addiction Medicine). 1992. "The Definition of Alcoholism." *JAMA* 268:1012–1014.

NCCP. 1997. "Status of African-American Children Under Three Living in Poverty." [Online.] *Child Poverty News and Issues* 2(3)(Fall 1992). Available: http://cpmcnet.columbia.edu/dept/nccp/news/newi00067.htm (February 4, 1999).

NCCP. 1998. "Early Childhood Poverty Research, Brief 1." National Center for Children in Poverty. New York: Columbia University.

NCH. 1998. "Homeless Youth." Factsheet #11. [Online.] The National Coalition for the Homeless. May 1998. Available: http://nch.ari.net/youth.html [1999, May 18].

Netting, F. Ellen, Peter M. Kettner, and Steven L. McMurtry. 1998. 2d ed. *Social Work Macro Practice*. New York: Addison Wesley Longman.

News-Press. 1998. "Poorest Children Getting Poorer in Nation's Most Populous States." *News-Press* (Lee County, Florida). July 10, 1998, p. 5A.

Nisivoccia, Danielle, and Maxine Lynn. 1992. "The Use of Program with Special Populations." Paper presented at the Fourteenth Annual Symposium of the Association for the Advancement of Social Work with Groups, Atlanta.

——— 1999. "Helping Forgotton Victims: Using Activity Groups with Children in Crisis." In Nancy Webb, ed., *Social Work with Children*, pp. 176–198. 2d ed. New York: Guilford.

Northen, Helen. 1969. *Social Work with Groups*. New York: Columbia University Press.

——— 1995. *Clinical Social Work: Knowledge and Skills*, 2d ed. New York: Columbia University Press.

——— 1988. *Social Work with Groups*. 2d ed. New York: Columbia University Press.

Nunez, Ralph D. 1994. *Hopes, Dreams and Promises. The Future of Homeless Children in America*. New York: Institute for Children and Poverty. Homes for the Homeless, Inc.

O'Connell, Brian. 1978. "From Science to Advocacy to Empowerment." *Social Casework* 59(4):195–202.

O'Malley, P. 1989. *The AIDS Epidemic*. Boston: Beacon.

Osberger, Kathy, and Judy Vaughn. N.d. *Homeless Women: Creating Community, Creating Change*. Chicago: National Association of Religious Women.

Owens, Helen. 1998. "Empowerment: Globalization and Anti-Oppression—Uneasy Bedfellows." Unpublished. Adelaide, Australia.

Owens, Helen, and Anne Gregory. 1999. "Empowerment as Both a Right and Left Wing Activity: Catherine House—Holding It All Together." Unpublished. Adelaide, Australia.

Ozawa, Martha N. 1989. "Nonwhites and the Demographic Imperative in Social Welfare Spending." In Ira C. Colby, *Social Welfare Policy*, pp. 437–454. Chicago: Dorsey.

Padgett, D. K. 1998a. *Qualitative Methods in Social Work Research: Challenges and Rewards*. Thousand Oaks, Cal.: Sage.

——— 1998b. "Does the Glove Really Fit? Qualitative Research and Clinical Social Work Practice." *Social Work* 43, 373–381.

Papell, Catherine P. 1997. "Thinking About Thinking About Group Work: Thirty Years Later." Social Work with Groups 20(4):5–17.

Papell, Catherine P., and Beulah Rothman. 1980a. "Relating the Mainstream Model of Social Work with Groups to Group Psychotherapy and the Structural Group Approach." *Social Work with Groups* 3(Summer):5–22.

———— 1980b. "Social Group Work Models: Possession and Heritage." In Albert S. Alissi, ed., *Perspectives on Social Group Work Practice*. New York: Free Press.

Parkes, Colin Murray, Joan Stevenson-Hinde, and Peter Marris, eds. 1991. *Attachment Across the Life-cycle*. London: Routledge.

Parkes, Jennifer L. 1981. "Social Work Is a Lesbian Heritage." Paper presented at National Association of Social Workers Conference, November.

Parsons, Ruth J. 1989. "Empowerment for Role Alternatives for Low Income Minority Girls: A Group Work Approach." In Judith A. B. Lee, ed., *Group Work with the Poor and Oppressed*, pp. 27–46. New York: Haworth.

———— 1991. "Empowerment: Purpose and Practice Principles in Social Work." *Social Work with Groups* 14(2):7–21.

———— 1998. *Empowerment in Social Work Practice: A Sourcebook*. Pacific Grove, Cal.: Brooks/Cole.

Parsons, Ruth J., James D. Jorgensen and Santos H. Hernandez. 1994. *The Integration of Social Work Practice*. California: Brooks/Cole.

Patti, Rino J., and Herman Resnick. 1975. "Changing the Agency from Within." In Beulah R. Compton and Burt Galaway, eds., *Social Work Processes*, pp. 499–551. Homewood, Ill.: Dorsey.

Pearce, Roy H. 1966. "Introduction." In Walt Whitman, *Leaves of Grass*, pp. vii–li. Facsimile ed. New York: Cornell University Press.

Peebles-Wilkins, Wilma. 1987. Biographies of "Janie Porter Barrett," p. 914; "William Edward Burghardt Du Bois," p. 921; "Edward Franklin Frazier," p. 924; "Mary Eliza Church Terell," p. 942; and "Ida B. Wells-Barnett," p. 945. *Encyclopedia of Social Work*. 18th ed. Silver Spring, Md.: National Association of Social Workers.

Peiper, Martha H. 1994. "Science Not Scientism: The Robustness of Naturalistic and Clinical Research." In E. Sherman and William J. Reed, eds., *Qualitative Research in Social Work*. New York: Columbia University Press.

Pelton, Leroy H. 1978. "Child Abuse and Neglect: The Myth of Classlessness." *American Journal of Orthopsychiatry* 48(October 4):608–617.

Pence, Ellen. 1987. *In Our Best Interests: A Process for Personal and Social Change*. Duluth: Minnesota Program Development.

Perlman, Helen H. 1957a. "Social Casework: A Problem Solving Approach." *Encyclopedia of Social Work*, pp. 1206–1216. 16th ed. Silver Spring, Md.: National Association of Social Workers.

———— 1957b. *Social Casework: A Problem Solving Process*. Chicago: University of Chicago Press.

———— 1974a. "Confessions, Concerns, and Commitment of an Ex-Clinical Social Worker." *Clinical Social Work Journal* 2(3):1–11.

———— 1974b. "The Problem-Solving Model in Social Casework." In Robert W. Roberts and Robert Nee, eds., *Theories of Social Casework*, pp. 129–180. Chicago: University of Chicago Press.

——— 1979. *Relationship: The Heart of Helping People.* Chicago: University of Chicago Press.

——— 1986. "The Problem Solving Model." In Francis J. Turner, ed., *Social Work Treatment: Interlocking Theoretical Approaches*, pp. 245–266. 3d ed. New York: Free Press.

Pernell, Ruby B. 1986. "Empowerment and Social Group Work." In Marvin Parnes, ed., *Innovations in Social Group Work: Feedback from Practice to Theory*, pp. 107–118. New York: Haworth.

Peters, Andrew J. 1997. "Themes in Group Work with Lesbian and Gay Adolescents." *Social Work with Groups* 20(2):51–70.

Phillips, Helen U. 1957. *Essentials of Social Group Work Skill.* New York: Association.

Phillips, Michael H., and Marilyn A. Markowitz. 1989. *The Mutual Aid Model of Group Services: Experiences of New York Archdiocese Drug Abuse Prevention Program.* New York: Fordham University Graduate School of Social Service.

Piaget, Jean, and Barbel Inhelder. 1969. *The Psychology of the Child.* New York: Basic.

Pincus, Allen, and Anne Minahan. 1973. *Social Work Practice: Model and Method.* Itasca, Ill.: Peacock.

Pinderhughes, Elaine. 1979. "Teaching Empathy in Cross-Cultural Social Work." *Social Work* 24(4):312–316.

——— 1982a. "Afro-American Families and the Victim System." In M. McGoldrick, J. K. Pearce, and J. Giordano, eds., *Ethnicity and Family Therapy*, pp. 108–122. New York: Guilford.

——— 1982b. "Family Functioning of African Americans." *Social Work* 27:91–96.

——— 1984. "Teaching Empathy: Ethnicity, Race, and Power at the Cross-Cultural Treatment Interface." *American Journal of Social Psychiatry* 4(Winter):5–12.

Piven, Frances Fox, and Richard Cloward. 1971. *Regulating the Poor.* New York: Vintage.

——— 1977. *Poor People's Movements: How They Succeed, Why They Fail.* New York: Pantheon.

Plotnick, Robert D. 1997. "Child Poverty Can Be Reduced." *Future of Children* 7(2)(Summer/Fall):72–87.

Potok, Chaim. 1975. *In the Beginning.* Greenwich, Conn.: Fawcett.

Pottick, Kathleen. 1989. "Jane Addams Revisited: Practice Theory and Social Economics." In Judith A. B. Lee, ed., *Group Work with the Poor and Oppressed*, pp. 11–26. New York: Haworth.

Pound, Ezra. 1957. *The Selected Poems of Ezra Pound.* New York: New Directions.

"Presidential Commission Report, 1981." 1989. In Ira C. Colby, ed., *Social Welfare Policy.* Chicago: Dorsey.

Prosser, William R. 1991. "The Underclass: Assessing What We Have Learned." *Focus* 13(2):1–5, 9–18.

Pumphrey, Ralph E., and Muriel W. Pumphrey, eds. 1961. *The Heritage of American Social Work: Readings in Its Philosophical and Institutional Development*. New York: Columbia University Press.

Quinn, Patricia O. 1997. *Attention Deficit Disorder: Diagnosis and Treatment from Infancy to Adulthood*. New York: Brunner/Mazel.

Rainwater, Lee and Timothy M. Smeeding. 1996. "U.S. Doint Poorly—Compared to Others—Policy Point of View." [Online.] National Center for Children in Poverty—Child Poverty News and Issues. (5)3(Fall 1995). Available: http://cpmcnet.columbia.edu/news/childpov/newi0008.html

Ramanathan, Chathapuram S. and Rosemary J. Link. 1999. *All Our Futures: Principles and Resources For Social Work Practice in a Global Era*. Pacific Grove, Cal.: Brooks/Cole.

Rampersad, Arnold. 1994. *The Collected Poems of Langston Hughes*. New York: Knopf.

Rank, Mark R., and Thomas Hirschl. 1999. "The Likelihood of Poverty Across the American Adult Life Span." *Social Work*. 44(3)(May 8):217–227.

Rapoport, Judith L., and Deborah R. Ismond. 1996. *DSM-IV Training Guide for Diagnosis of Childhood Disorders*. New York: Brunner/Mazel.

Rappaport, J., C. Smith, and R. Hess, eds. 1988. *Shades in Empowerment: Toward Understanding and Action*. New York: Haworth.

Raskin, Miriam S. and Dennis C. Daley. 1991. "Assessment of Addiction Problems." In Dennis C. Daley and Miriam S. Raskin, eds., *Treating the Chemically Dependent and Their Families*, pp. 22–50. Newbury Park, Cal.: Sage.

Raymond, Jan. 1986. *A Passion for Friends: Toward a Philosophy of Female Affection*. Boston: Beacon.

Reed, Beth G., and Charles D. Garvin, eds. 1983. "Groupwork with Women/Groupwork with Men: An Overview of Gender Issues in Social Groupwork Practice." *Social Work with Groups* 6(3–4)(Special issue).

Regan, Sandra, and Glenn Lee. 1992. "The Interplay Among Social Group Work, Community, and Social Action." *Social Work with Groups* 15(1):35–50.

Reid, William, and Audrey D. Smith. 1989. *Research in Social Work*. 2d ed. New York: Columbia University Press.

Reid-Mandell, Betty. 1991. "Work Houses Without Walls Proposed for Massachusetts." *Survival News* 5(2):1, 4, 6.

Reischauer, Robert D., Henry G. Cisneros, Stephen B. Heintz, Nancy A. Humphreys, and Roxanne H. Jones. 1987. "America's Underclass." *Public Welfare* 45(4):26–31.

Renz-Beaulaurier, Richard 1998. "Empowering People with Disabilities: The Role of Choice." In Lorraine M. Guttíerez, Ruth Parsons, and Enid Opal Cox, eds., *Empowerment in Social Work Practice*, pp. 73–83. Pacific Grove, Cal.: Brooks/Cole.

Reynolds, Bertha C. 1934. *Between Client and Community: A Study in Responsibility in Social Casework*. New York: Oriole.

———— 1942. *Learning and Teaching in the Practice of Social Work*. New York: Russell and Russell.

———— 1951. *Social Work and Social Living: Explorations in Philosophy and Practice*. Silver Spring, Md.: National Association of Social Workers.

———— 1953. "Fear in Our Culture." Paper presented at meeting of the Cleveland Council of Arts, Sciences, and Professions, June 4; also in *Catalyst: A Socialist Journal of the Social Services* 6(1):67–74, 1987.

———— 1964. *An Uncharted Journey: Fifty Years of Growth in Social Work*. Hebron, Conn.: Practitioner's.

Richan, Willard C. 1991. *Lobbying for Social Change*. New York: Haworth.

Rivera, Felix G., and John L. Erlich. 1992. "The African American Community in the 1990's: The Search for a Practice Method." *In Community Organizing in a Diverse Society*. Needham Heights, Mass.: Allyn and Bacon.

Robbins, Susan P., Pranab Chatterjee, and Edward R. Canda. 1998. *Human Behavior Theory: A Critical Perspective for Social Work*. Boston: Allyn and Bacon.

Robertson, Marjorie. 1996. "Homeless Youth on Their Own." Berkeley: Alcohol Research Group.

Rocky, M. 1989. Testimony before the Senate Committee on Appropriations, Subcommittee on Foreign Operations. CHILDHOPE. New York.

Rosenheck, Robert. 1996. "Homelessness Is a Serious Problem." In Tamara L. Roleff, ed., *The Homeless: Opposing Viewpoints*, pp. 17–21. San Diego, Ca: Greenhaven Press.

Rothman, Jack. 1968. "Three Models of Community Organization Practice." *Social Work Practice*, pp. 16–47.

———— 1984. "Models of Community Organization and Macro Practice Perspectives: Their Mixing and Phasing." In Fred M. Cox, John L. Erlich, Jack Rothman, and John E. Tropman, eds., *Strategies of Community Organization*. 4th ed. Itasca, Ill.: Peacock.

———— 1992. *Guide for Case Management: Putting Research to Professional Use*. Itasca, Ill.: Peacock.

Rothman, Jack, J. Erlich, and J. Tropman. 1995. *Strategies of Community Intervention*. Itasca, Ill.: Peacock.

Royce, James E., and David Scratchley. 1996. *Alcoholism and Other Drug Problems*. New York: Free Press.

Rubin, Lillian B. 1976. *Worlds of Pain: Life in the Working Class Community*. New York: Basic Books.

Rubin, Marshall. 1999. "Liberty House Meeting and Analysis: Group Example." Unpublished. Tucson, Arizona: Marshall Rubin.

Rudwick, Elliot. 1982. "W. E. B. Du Bois: Protagonist of the Afro-American Protest." In John Hope Franklin and August Meier, eds., *Black Leaders of the Twentieth Century*, p. 65. Urbana: University of Illinois Press.

Ryan, William. 1971. *Blaming the Victim*. New York: Vintage.

Saleebey, Dennis, ed. 1997. *The Strengths Perspective in Social Work Practice*. 2d ed. New York: Longman.

Sandoval, Moises. 1994. *Tragedy in the Streets. Mary Knoll* 88(6): 50–52.

Sands, Roberta G., and Kathleen Nuccio. 1992. "Postmodern Feminist Theory and Social Work." *Social Work* 37(6):489–494.

Sancier, Betty. 1984. "A Challenge to the Profession." In *Practice Digest: Working with Gay and Lesbian Clients*. Silver Spring, Md.: National Association of Social Workers.

Sarri, Rosemary C. 1989. "Federal Policy Changes and the Feminization of Poverty." In Ira C. Colby, ed., *Social Welfare Policy*, pp. 248–260. Chicago: Dorsey.

Saulnier, Christine F. 1997. "Alcohol Problems and Marginalization: Group Social Work with Lesbians." *Social Work with Groups* 20(3):37–59.

Sawhill, Isabel. 1988. "Poverty and the Underclass." In Isabel V. Sawhill, ed., *The Urban Challenge to Leadership: Economic and Social Issues for the Next Decade*, pp. 215–252. Washington, D.C.: Institute Press.

—— 1989. "The Underclass: An Overview." *Public Interest* 97(43):3–15.

Schecter, S. 1987. *Guidelines for Mental Health Practitioners in Domestic Violence Cases*. Washington, D.C.: National Coalition Against Domestic Violence.

Scherz, Frances. 1974. "Theory and Practice of Family Therapy." In Robert W. Roberts and Robert H. Nee, eds., *Theories of Social Casework*, pp. 219–264. Chicago: University of Chicago Press.

Schiller, Linda Yael. 1997. "Rethinking Stages of Development in Women's Groups: Implications for Practice." *Social Work with Groups* 20(3):3–19.

Schopler, Janice H., Maeda Galinsky, and Melissa Abell. 1997. "Creating Community Through Telephone and Computer Groups: Theoretical and Practice Perspectives." *Social Work with Groups* 20(4):19–34.

Schon, D. A. 1995. *Reflective Inquiry in Social Work Practice*. In Peg M. Hess and Edward J. Mullen, eds., *Practitioner-Researcher Partnerships: Building Knowledge from, in, and for Practice*, pp. 31–55. Washington, D.C.: NASW.

Schorr, Lisbeth B. 1997. *Common Purpose: Strengthening Families and Neighborhoods to Rebuild America*. New York: Anchor Doubleday.

Schwartz, Arthur. 1983. "Behavioral Principles and Approaches." In A. Rosenblatt and D. Waldfogel, eds., *The Handbook of Clinical Social Work*, pp. 202–228. San Francisco: Jossey-Bass.

Schwartz, William. 1959. "Group Work and the Social Scene." In Alfred J. Kahn, ed., *Issues in American Social Work*, pp. 110–137. New York: Columbia University Press.

—— 1971. "Social Group Work: The Interactionist Approach." *Encyclopedia of Social Work*, pp. 1252–1263. 16th ed. Silver Spring, Md.: National Association of Social Workers.

—— 1974a. "Private Troubles and Public Issues: One Social Work Job or Two?" In Robert W. Klenk and Robert W. Ryan, eds., *The Practice of Social Work*, pp. 62–81. 2d ed. Belmont, Cal.: Wadsworth.

——— 1974b. "The Social Worker in the Group." In Robert W. Klenk and Robert W. Ryan, eds., *The Practice of Social Work*, pp. 208–228. 2d ed. Belmont, Cal.: Wadsworth.

——— 1976. "Between Client and System: The Mediating Function." In Robert W. Roberts and Helen Northen, eds., *Theories of Social Work with Groups*, pp. 171–197. New York: Columbia University Press.

——— 1986. "The Group Work Tradition and Social Work Practice." In Alex Gitterman and Lawrence Shulman, eds., *The Legacy of William Schwartz: Group Practice as Shared Interaction*, pp. 7–28. New York: Haworth.

——— 1994. *Social Work: The Collected Writings of William Schwartz*. Ed. Toby Berman-Rossi. Itasca, Ill.: Peacock.

Schwartz, William, and Serapio Zalba. 1971. *The Practice of Group Work*. New York: Columbia University Press.

Scott, Neberne, C. B. David, C. Samuels, and W. Patterson. 1997. "Community Empowerment: Project COME." Unpublished. University of Guyana. Georgetown, Guyana.

Seccombe, Karen. 1999. "So You Think I Drive a Cadillac? Welfare Recipients Perspectives on the System and Its Reform." Boston: Allyn and Bacon.

Segall, Marshall H., Pierre R. Dasen, John W. Berry, and Ype H. Poortinga. 1990. *Human Behavior in Global Perspective*. New York: Pergamon.

Sennett, R. 1998. *The Corrosion of Character—The Personal Consequences of Work in the New Capitalism*. London and New York: Norton.

Setleis, Lloyd. 1974. "Social Work Practice as Political Activity." In Robert W. Klenk and Robert M. Ryan, eds., *The Practice of Social Work*, pp. 311–318. 2d ed. Belmont, Cal.: Wadsworth.

Shange, Ntozake. 1977. *For Colored Girls Who Have Considered Suicide When the Rainbow Is Enuf*. New York: Macmillan.

Shapiro, Ben-Zion. 1991. "Social Action, the Group, and Society." *Social Work with Groups* 14(3–4):7–22.

Shapiro, Joan. 1984. "Commitment to Disenfranchised Clients." In A. Rosenblatt and D. Waldfogel, eds., *Handbook of Clinical Social Work*. San Francisco: Jossey-Bass.

Shera, Wes, and Lilian M. Wells, eds. 1999. *Empowerment Practice in Social Work: Developing Richer Conceptual Foundations*. Toronto: Canadian Scholars' Press.

Sherman, Arloc. 1997. "Poverty Matters: The Cost of Child Poverty in America. [Online.] The Childrens Defense Fund. Available: http://www.childrensdefense.org/

Sherman, E., and William J. Reid, eds. *Qualitative Research in Social Work*. New York: Columbia University Press.

Shulman, Lawrence. 1991. *Interactional Social Work Practice: Toward an Empirical Theory*. Itasca, Ill: Peacock.

——— 1992. *The Skills of Helping Individuals, Families, and Groups*. Itasca, Ill.: Peacock.

———— 1996. *The Skills of Helping Individuals, Families, Groups and Communities.* 4th ed. Itasca, Ill.: Peacock.

Silverman, Beth, Barbara Simon, and Richard Woodrow. 1991. "Workers in Job Jeopardy." In Alex Gitterman, ed., *Handbook of Social Work Practice with Vulnerable Populations*, pp. 710–748. New York: Columbia University Press.

Simmons, Louise B. 1994. *Organizing in Hard Times: Labor and Neighborhoods in Hartford.* Philadelphia: Temple University Press.

Simmons, Roberta G. 1978. "Blacks and High Self-Esteem: A Puzzle." *Social Psychology Quarterly* 41:54–57.

Simon, Barbara L. 1990. "Rethinking Empowerment." *Journal of Progressive Human Services* 1(1):27–39.

Smalley, Ruth E. 1967. *Theory for Social Work Practice.* New York: Columbia University Press.

———— 1971. "Social Casework: The Functional Approach." *Encyclopedia of Social Work*, pp. 1195–1206. 16th ed. Silver Spring, Md.: National Association of Social Workers.

———— 1974. "The Functional Approach to Casework Practice." In Robert W. Roberts and Robert H. Nee, eds., *Theories of Social Casework*. Chicago: University of Chicago Press.

Smedley, Agnes. 1976. *Daughter of Earth.* New York: Feminist Press.

Smith, Barbara. 1986. "Some Home Truths on the Contemporary Black Feminist Movement." In Nan Van Den Bergh and Lynn B. Cooper, eds., *Feminist Visions for Social Work*, pp. 45–60. Silver Spring, Md.: NASW.

Social Work. 1981. "Special Issue on Conceptual Frameworks II." *Social Work* 26(1).

Solomon, Alison. 1992. "Clinical Diagnosis Among Diverse Populations: A Multicultural Perspective." *Families in Society* 73(6):371–377.

Solomon, Barbara B. 1976. *Black Empowerment: Social Work in Oppressed Communities.* New York: Columbia University Press.

———— 1986. "Social Work with Afro-Americans." In Armando Morales and Bradford Sheafor, eds., *Social Work: A Profession of Many Faces*, pp. 501–521. Boston: Allyn and Bacon.

Soriano, Fernando I. 1994. "The Latino Perspective: A Sociocultural Portrait." In Jacob U. Gordon, ed., *Managing Multiculturalism in Substance Abuse Services*, pp. 117–147. Thousand Oaks, Cal.: Sage.

Souflee, Federico, Jr. 1977. "Social Work: The Acquiescing Profession." *Social Work* 22(5):419–421.

Souljah, Sister. 1999. *The Coldest Winter Ever.* New York: First Pocket/Simon and Schuster.

Spergel, Irving A. 1987. "Community Development" *Encyclopedia of Social Work*, pp. 299–308. Silver Spring, Md.: National Association of Social Workers.

Spoto, Donald. 1999. *The Hidden Jesus: A New Life.* New York: St. Martin's.

Staples, Lee. 1984. *Roots to Power*. New York: Praeger.

——— 1990. "Powerful Ideas About Empowerment." *Social Work* 17:29–41.

Staub-Bernasconi, Silvia. 1992. "Social Action, Empowerment, and Social Work: An Integrative Theoretical Framework for Social Work and Social Work with Groups." *Social Work with Groups* 14(3/4):35–52.

Stern, Daniel. 1985. *The Interpersonal World of the Infant*. New York: Basic.

Stevens, Wallace. 1967. *The Collected Poems of Wallace Stevens*. New York: Knopf.

Storey, James R. 1989. "Income Security." In Ira C. Colby, ed., *Social Welfare Policy*, pp. 370–403. Chicago: Dorsey.

Strickland, William. 1990. "The Black Male." *Essence Magazine* (February).

Stuntzver-Gibson, Denise. 1991. "Women and HIV Disease: An Emerging Social Crisis." *Social Work* 36(1):22–28.

Survival News. 1991. West Roxbury, Mass. (Winter/Spring).

Swenson, Carol R. 1992. "Clinical Practice and the Decline of Community." Paper presented at the Council on Social Work Education Annual Program Meeting, March, Kansas City, Missouri.

——— 1994. "Clinical Practice and the Decline of Community." *Journal of Teaching in Social Work*. 10(1/2) 1994: 195–212.

——— 1995. "Professional Understandings of Community: At a Loss for Words." In P. Adams and K. Nelson, eds., *Reinventing Human Services: Community and Family Oriented Practice*, pp. 223–243. Hawthorne, N.Y.: de Gruyter.

——— 1997. "Clinical Social Work." *Encyclopedia of Social Work*, pp. 502–512. 19th ed. Silver Spring, Md. National Association of Social Workers.

——— 1998. "Clinical Social Works' Contribution to a Social Justice Perspective." *Social Work*.43(6) Nov. 1998: 527–537.

Szasz, Thomas S. 1970. "The Myth of Mental Illness." In T. S. Szasz, *Ideology and Insanity: Essays on the Psychiatric Dehumanization of Man*. Garden City, N.Y.: Doubleday/Anchor.

Tamez, Elsa. 1982. *Bible of the Oppressed*. Maryknoll, N.Y.: Orbis.

Taylor, Paul. 1997. "The Linguistic and Cultura Barriers to Cross-National Group-work." In Tara Mistry and Allan Brown, eds., *Race and Groupwork*, pp. 43–57. London. Whiting and Birch.

Taylor, Samuel H., and Robert W. Roberts, eds. 1985. *Theory and Practice of Community Social Work*. New York: Columbia University Press.

Thomas, Ianthe. 1978. "Death of a Young Poet." *Village Voice*, March 20, pp. 2, 26–27.

Thomlison, Ray J. 1986. "Behavior Therapy in Social Work Practice." In Francis J. Turner, ed., *Social Work Treatment: Interlocking Theoretical Approaches*, pp. 131–153. 3d ed. New York: Free Press.

Thrasher, S. P., and C. T. Mowbray. 1995. "A Strength's Perspective: An Ethnographic Study of Homeless Women with children." *Social Work* 2(May):95–101.

Titmus, Richard M. 1958. *Essay on the Welfare State*. London: Routledge and Kegan Paul.

Toffler, Alvin. 1977. *Future Shock*. New York: Random House.

Tolman, Richard M., Donald D. Mowry, Linda E. Jones, and John Brekke. 1986. "Developing a Profeminist Commitment Among Men in Social Work." In Nan Van Den Bergh and Lynn B. Cooper, eds., *Feminist Visions for Social Work*, pp. 61–79. Silver Spring, Md.: National Association of Social Workers.

Toner, Robin. 1992. "Watershed Is Seen." *New York Times*, November 4, pp. A1, B3.

Toseland, Ronald W., and Robert F. Rivas. 1998. *An Introduction to Group Work Practice*. 3d ed. Boston: Allyn and Bacon.

Tropp, Emanuel. 1971. "Social Group Work: The Developmental Approach." *Encyclopedia of Social Work*, pp. 1246–1252. 16th ed. Silver Spring, Md.: National Association of Social Workers.

———— 1980. "A Humanistic View of Social Work–Worker and Member on a Common Human Level." In Albert S. Alissi, ed., *Perspectives in Social Group Work Practice*. New York: Free Press.

Trotman, Frances K., and Abisola H. Gallagher. 1987. "Group Therapy with Black Women." In Claire M. Brody, ed., *Women's Therapy Groups*. New York: Springer.

Turner, Francis J, ed. 1996. *Social Work Treatment: Interlocking Theoretical Approaches*. 4th ed. New York: Free Press.

Tyson, Katherine. 1995. *New Foundations for Scientific Social Behavioral Research: The Heuristic Paradigm*. Needham Heights, Mass.: Allyn and Bacon.

UNDP. N.d. "The Habitat Agenda. United Nations Development Program. Section IVB: Adequate Shelter for All." [Online.] Available: http://www.undr.org/un/habitat/agenda/ch-4b-1.html

UNDP. 1997. "Basic Social Service For All, 1997: Goals Agreed Upon at the United Nations Conferences for Selected BSSA Indicators. [Online.] Available: http://www.undp.org/popin/wdtrends/bss/bssgoal.htm (September 30, 1998).

UNFPA. 1998 "The State of World Population." [Online.] Available: http://www.unfpa.org/swp/1998/thestate.htm (November 19, 1999).

USDHHS. 1996. "Report to the Congress on the Runaway and Homeless Youth Program of the Family and Youth Services Bureau for Fiscal Year 1995–1996." Silver Spring, Md.: National Clearinghouse on Families and Youth.

USDS. 1999. Guyana country report on human rights practices for 1998. Released by the Bureau of Democracy, Human Rights and Labor, February 26, 1999. http://www.state.gov./www/global/human-rights/1998-hrp-report/(6/22/99).

Vaillant, George. 1983. *The Natural History of Alcoholism*. Cambridge: Harvard University Press.

Valentich, Mary. 1996. "Feminist Theory and Social Work Practice." In Francis J. Turner, ed., *Social Work Treatment: Interlocking Theoretical Approaches*, pp. 250–281. New York: Free Press.

Van Den Bergh, Nan, ed. 1995. *Feminist Practice in the Twenty-First Century*. Washington, D.C.: NASW.

Van Den Bergh, Nan, and Lynne B. Cooper, eds. 1986. *Feminist Visions for Social Work*. Silver Spring, Md.: National Association of Social Workers.

Van Wormer, Katherine, Joel W. Wells, and Mary Boes. 2000. *Social Work with Lesbians, Gays and Bisexuals: A Strengths Perspective*. Boston. Allyn and Bacon.

Vinik, Abe, and Morris Levin, eds. 1991. *Social Action in Group Work*. New York: Haworth.

Wagner, David. 1989. "Fate of Idealism in Social Work: Alternative Experiences of Professional Careers." *Social Work* 34(5):385–480.

—— 1990. *The Quest for a Radical Profession: Social Service Careers and Political Ideology*. New York: University Press of America.

Wallis, Claudia, and James Willwerth, 1992. "Schizophrenia: A New Drug Brings Patients Back to Life." *Time*, July 6, pp. 53–57.

Walz, T. and Groze. V. 1991. "The Mission of Social Work Revisited: An Agenda for the 1990s." *Social Work* 36, 500–504.

Ward, V. 1987. "Street Girls: The Most Vulnerable of Street Kids." *Our Child, Our Hope: Journal of the International Movement on Behalf of Street Children*. CHILDHOPE (12):1, 10.

Warren, Roland. 1977. "Organizing a County Survey." In Fred M. Cox, John L. Erlich, Jack Rothman, and John Tropman, eds., *Tactics and Techniques of Community Practice*, pp. 23–35. Itasca, Ill.: Peacock.

—— 1978. *The Community in America*. 3d ed. Chicago: Rand McNally.

Wasserman, Sidney L. 1979. "Ego Psychology." In Francis Turner, ed., *Social Work Treatment: Interlocking Theoretical Approaches*, pp. 33–66. 2d ed. New York: Free Press.

Watson, Lilla. 1999. [Online.] "Liberation Australia: Aboriginal (January 2000)."

Watts, T. D., and Roosevelt Wright, Jr. 1989. *Alcoholism in Minority Populations*. Springfield, Ill.: Thomas.

Webb, Nancy Boyd. 1999. *Play Therapy with Children in Crisis*. 2d ed. New York: Guilford.

Wax, John. 1971. "Power Theory and Institutional Change." *Social Services Review* 45(3):274–288.

Weick, Ann. 1982. "Issues of Power in Social Work Practice." In Ann Weick and Susan T. Vandiver, eds., *Women, Power, and Change*, pp. 173–185. Silver Spring, Md.: National Association of Social Workers.

Weick, Ann, and Susan T. Vandiver, eds., 1982. *Women, Power, and Change*. Silver Spring, Md.: National Association of Social Workers.

Weil, Marie. 1986. "Women, Community and Organizing." In Nan Van Den Bergh and Lynn B. Cooper, eds., *Feminist Visions for Social Work*, pp. 187–210. Silver Spring, Md.: National Association of Social Workers.

Weil, Marie, and D. N. Gamble. 1995. "Community Practice Models." In *The Encyclopedia of Social Work*, pp. 577–593. 19th ed. Washington, D.C.: NASW.

Weiner, Hyman J. 1964. "Social Change and Group Work Practice." *Social Work* 9(3):106–112.

Weisen-Cook, Blanche. 1986. "Urged to Deny the Secrets." In Mary Bricker-Jenkins and Nancy Hooyman, eds., *Not for Women Only*, p. 1. Silver Spring, Md.: National Association of Social Workers.

Weiss, Roger D., and Steven M. Mirin. 1987. *Cocaine: The Human Danger, the Social Costs, the Treatment Alternatives*. New York: Ballantine.

Werner, Harold D. 1986. "Cognitive Theory." In Francis J. Turner, ed., *Social Work Treatment: Interlocking Theoretical Approaches*, pp. 91–129. 3d ed. New York: Free Press.

West, Cornel. 1993. *Race Matters*. Boston: Beacon Press.

White, Robert W. 1959. "Motivation Reconsidered: The Concept of Competence." *Psychology Review* 66(September):297–333.

——— 1974. "Strategies of Adaptation: An Attempt at Systematic Description." In George Coelho, David A. Hamburg, and John E. Adams, eds., *Coping and Adaptation*, pp. 47–68. New York: Basic.

White, Robert. 1984. *The Psychology of Blacks: An Afro-American Perspective*. Englewood Cliffs, N.J.: Prentice-Hall.

Wilensky, Harold, and Charles Lebeaux. 1965. *Industrial Society and Social Welfare*. New York: Russell Sage.

Williams, Howell V. 1989. "Benjamin Franklin and the Poor Laws." In Ira C. Colby, ed., *Social Welfare Policy*, pp. 68–88. Chicago: Dorsey.

Wilson, William Julius. 1987. *The Truly Disadvantaged: The Inner City, the Under Class, and Public Policy*. Chicago: University of Chicago Press.

Woodman, Natalie J., ed. 1992. *Lesbian and Gay Lifestyles: A Guide for Counseling and Education*. New York: Irvington.

Woodroofe, Kathleen. 1966. *From Charity to Social Work in England and the United States*. London: Routledge and Kegan Paul.

Woods, Mary E. and Florence Hollis. 1990. *Casework: A Psychcosocial Therapy*. 4th ed. New York: McGraw Hill.

Wright, Roosevelt, Jr., Barbara Lynn Kail, and Robert F. Creecy. 1990. "Culturally Sensitive Social Work Practice with Black Alcoholics and Their Families." In Sadye M. L. Logan, Edith M. Freeman, and Ruth G. McRoy, eds., *Social Work Practice with Black Families*, pp. 102–222. New York: Longman.

Wright, Roosevelt Jr., and T. D. Watts, eds. 1985. *Prevention of Black Alcoholism: Issues and Strategies*. Springfield, Ill.: Thomas.

Wylie, Ruth C. 1979. *The Self-Concept*. Lincoln: University of Nebraska Press.

Zastrow, Charles. 1992. *The Practice of Social Work*. 4th ed. Belmont, Cal.: Wadsworth.

Zipple, Anthony M., and LeRoy Spaniol. 1987. "Current Educational and Supportive Models of Family Intervention." In Agnes B. Hatfield and Harriet P. Lefley, eds., *Families of the Mentally Ill: Coping and Adaptation*, pp. 261–277. New York: Guilford.

Some Suggested Web Resources

Children

Children's Defense Fund. http://www.childrensdefense.org/
http://www.childrensdefense.org/fairstart_status.html
http://www.futureofchildren.org/
http://www.childrensdefense.org/bccc.html
NCCP. 1997. "Status of African American Children Under Three Living in Poverty."
[Online.] National Center for Children Living in Poverty. *Child Poverty News and Issues* 2(3)(Fall 1992). Available: http://cpmcnet.columbia.edu/dept/nccp/news/newi0067.html (February 4, 1999).
UNICEF http://www.unicef.org/
NCH Factsheet no. 11. 1998. "Homeless Youth." [Online.] National Coalition for the Homeless. May 1998. Available: http://nch.ari.net/youth.html (May 18, 1999).

Government

National Center for Policy Analysis—Idea House. Http://ncpa.org/pa/govern/pd022499h.html
U.S. Department of State. http://www.state.gov./www/global/human-rights/1998-hrp-report/.

Homeless

Fact Sheet—The Rights of Homeless Children. http://www.nlchp.org/rights.htm
Homeless Assistance Act: U.S. Code Title 42 Chapter 119. http://www4.law.cornell.edu/uscode/42/ch119.html

Institute for Research on Poverty. http://www.ssc.wisc.edu/irp/
International HOMELESS Discussion List and Archives. http://csf.colorado.edu/
    homelessness/index.html
National Coalition for Homeless Veterans. http://www.nchv.org/
National Law Center on Homelessness and Poverty. http://www.nlchp.org/
North American Street Newspaper Association. http://www.speakeasy.org/nasna/

International

PRAXIS — http://www.ssw.upenn.edu/

Mentally Ill

http://www.nami.org/

United Nations

World   Population: http://www.unfpa.org/swp/swp98/pdf.files.htm.   http://
    www.un.org/ecosocdev/geninfo/population/icpd.htm
IDC. 1996. "Shaping the Twenty-First Century: The Contribution of Development
    Cooperation, Development Assistance Committee, May 1996: Introduction
    and Summary." [Online.] Available: http://www.idc.org/coop.htm (September
    30, 1998).
UNDP. 1997. "Basic Social Service for All, 1997: Goals Agreed Upon at the United
    Nations Conferences for Selected BSSA Indicators." [Online.] Available: http:/
    /www.undp.org/popin/wdtrends/bss/bssgoal.htm (September 30, 1998).
UNDP. N.d. [Online.] "The Habitat Agenda. United Nations Development Pro-
    gram. Section IVB: Adequate Shelter for All." Available: http://www.undp.org/
    un/habitat/agenda/ch-4b-1.html. See also ch-1a.html.
UNFPA. 1998. "The State of World Population." 1998. [Online.] Available: http://
    www.unfpa.org/swp/1998/thestate.htm (November 19, 1999).

Women

IWPR. 1998. [Online.] "Statistics on Women's Earnings." Available: http://
    www.iwpr.org/release98.htm

Name Index

Subject Index

HV91 .L355 2001
Lee, Judith A. B.
The empowerment approach to
social work practice :
building the beloved
community

SIMMONS COLLEGE LIBRARY
SSW COLLECTION

DATE DUE

Demco, Inc. 38-293